THE EXULTET IN SOUTHERN ITALY

The Exultet in Southern Italy

Thomas Forrest Kelly

New York   Oxford
OXFORD UNIVERSITY PRESS
1996

Oxford University Press

Oxford   New York
Athens   Auckland   Bangkok   Bogota   Bombay
Buenos Aires   Calcutta   Cape Town   Dar es Salaam
Delhi   Florence   Hong Kong   Istanbul   Karachi
Kuala Lumpur   Madras   Madrid   Melbourne
Mexico City   Nairobi   Paris   Singapore
Taipei   Tokyo   Toronto

and associated companies in
Berlin   Ibadan

Copyright © 1996 by Oxford University Press, Inc.

Published by Oxford University Press, Inc.,
198 Madison Avenue, New York, New York 10016

Oxford is a registered trademark of Oxford University Press

Library of Congress Cataloging-in-Publication Data
Kelly, Thomas Forrest.
The exultet in Southern Italy / Thomas Forrest Kelly.
p.   cm.
Includes bibliographical references and index.
ISBN 0-19-509527-8
1. Exultets (Liturgy)—History.   2. Exultet rolls—Italy,
Southern—History.   3. Catholic Church—Italy, Southern—Liturgy—
History.   4. Italy, Southern—Church history.   I. Title.
BX2045.E89K45   1996
264'.0201—dc20   95-10960

1 3 5 7 9 8 6 4 2

Printed in the United States of America
on acid-free paper

To Barbara Gray Henderson Kelly

PREFACE

"He who writes," says Saint Jerome, "takes on many judges" (Qui scribit multos sumit iudices). Jerome was not setting out to write a scholarly book: he was talking about the Exultet. His friend Praesidius of Piacenza had written to ask the father's help in the composition of a "benedictio cerei" for the following Easter, and Jerome refused to help in writing, though he suggested that an off-the-record verbal assistance might be possible.

In the case of this book, he who writes takes on many subjects, in most of which he is no expert. And yet he has taken on many friends and learned much.

This book owes its existence not to the Exultet and its marvelous ceremony but to the presence in southern Italy of the remarkable Exultet rolls. These have fascinated scholars, particularly historians of art, for a long time. Toward the end of the last century, Dom Latil made efforts to reproduce many illustrations of the then-known Exultets in a series of elegantly produced color lithographic plates. The most systematic approach to the illustrations was carried out by Myrtilla Avery, whose volume of facsimiles with brief commentary was published in 1936. This volume contained reproductions of the illustrations in all the known Exultet rolls of southern Italy; it is regrettable that the promised additional volume, which was to have contained much further scholarly information and study, was never achieved.

Although a few rolls were published in complete facsimile (Vat. lat. 9820; later Barberini, Salerno), much of the scholarly study of Exultets has dealt with art-historical matters: sources of iconography; relative dating of rolls based largely on stylistic grounds; studies of individual cycles of illustrations; Byzantine and monastic matters; symbology; representations of secular and religious authority; and much of what can be learned about furniture, vesture, crowns, tiaras, and the like.

The importance of the illustrations in the history of art means that these rolls have been used as a source of all sorts of material, and they are mentioned almost without fail in general histories of medieval art, often with a picture or two; the result is that a complete bibliography of the Exultet rolls would be vast, repetitive, and mostly derivative or worse.

The important 1973 monographic study of Guglielmo Cavallo, *Rotoli di Exultet dell'Italia meridionale,* reproduced the illustrated rolls of Bari and Troia and included significant studies of them, as well as of the Exultet in southern Italy. In a number of important articles, Cavallo had already studied the origin and development of the Exultet roll. Cavallo's book reproduces the entire written surfaces of the rolls of Bari and Troia, not just the pictures; thus it is possible to study the texts and the music (though the choice of reproducing the pictures right-side-up makes readers of the text turn the volume upside down).

Little study has actually been given to the texts, the music, or the support of the Exultet rolls; little, again, to the ceremonies and the liturgy in which these documents were used. In this context, not much attention has been focused on the other documents from southern Italy, about as many as the Exultet rolls, that also contain the Exultet.

In recent years, scholars in other disciplines have given increasing attention to liturgical, cultural, musical, and paleographical matters in the area of southern Italy where the Beneventan script was written. These have contributed much to providing a richer view of the context in which the Exultet rolls were used. Virginia Brown, the eminent paleographer, has continued the pioneering paleographical work of Elias Avery Lowe and in 1980 produced a revised and enlarged second edition of his magisterial *The Beneventan Script* (1914); she regularly publishes new lists of discoveries in Beneventan script and has widened our perception of the important place of liturgical manuscripts in the Beneventan zone. Brown, along with Roger Reynolds and Richard Gyug, directs the Monumenta Liturgica Beneventana, an ambitious project of research and publication that has launched a substantial series of liturgical editions. My own research in the old Beneventan liturgy and its music, including my *The Beneventan Chant* (1989), has summarized much of what can be recovered about the old liturgy of the southern Lombards (in which the Exultet played an important part), and the publications entitled *Beneventanum troporum corpus,* edited by Alejandro Planchart and John Boe, are presenting another very important regional repertory. A series of conferences at Montecassino on the age of Abbot Desiderius, the proceedings of which are now in the process of publication, adds much to our understanding of this cultural high point. Thus in the last twenty years there has been a considerable revival in studies of the cultural context of the south Italian liturgy.

Now in 1994 comes a millenary event that completes in many ways the work undertaken by so many historians and artists: an exhibition of all the known Exultet rolls at the abbey of Montecassino, along with a catalogue (*Exultet: Rotoli liturgici del medioevo meridionale*) that provides mostly complete and accurate color reproductions of them all. This is a remarkable accomplishment, requiring the efforts of the highest levels of the Italian government, the Vatican Library, the abbey of Montecassino, the University of Cassino, and the coordinating efforts of Guglielmo Cavallo and of many others. The catalogue provides clear descriptions of the rolls, and introductory essays place much of the cultural and artistic contexts before us.

Why then this book, if such a marvelous compendium exists? For two reasons: first, because the catalogue tells us that we are at a stage when we can summarize our knowledge about these documents and their significance, and this book has this as its intention; second, because there is still no satisfactory treatment of matters not generally considered by art historians: liturgy, ceremonial, text, music, the other aspects of the Exultet, and the real reasons these documents existed at all. An Exultet is a text performed to music at a specific moment in the liturgy: if it is sung from a scroll, and if that scroll is elaborately decorated, so much the better—but those are not the essential elements. What is essential is the setting, the words, and the music. It is to those aspects that this book will give considerable attention, in the hope that this may contribute significantly to our understanding of these remarkable documents and their special place in the liturgy and in the lives of those who used them.

A particular interest of this book is how the rolls were made, for this tells us much about how they were meant to be used. It gives a chance to see medieval artisans at work and to estimate the relative importance given to picture, decoration, text, and music. What is more, the question of planning, of preparing membranes, of ruling lines for receiving text, and leaving space blank for pictures; of planning where a picture ought to go in relation to the text it illustrates; the care (or lack of it) that goes into the planning of joints between membranes; and the planning of ample and harmonious spacing for contents put in at different times—all these give us a good means of estimating the best available workmanship, of making useful comparisons among various working methods, of assessing kinship among documents, and of providing a view into the fascinating world of the medieval scriptorium.

Many previous works on Exultet rolls have dealt with individual items or with a few of them; and much scholarship has been given to careful descriptions of individual works or individual iconographical topoi. I do not intend to repeat these descriptions (very ample ones are given in the recent Exultet catalogue), but to use the often-fascinating work of others, and some observations of my own, to consider the phenomenon of the Exultet roll in its entirety, and from an ensemble point of view.

Many readers will not be interested in everything in this book; some will be interested in music, others in liturgy, some in codicology, some in the history of art. I have tried to make those relevant portions relatively accessible by using topical chapters and many subheadings; the table of contents will help orient casual and specialist readers. Nevertheless, the book as a whole intends to underline the composite nature of the Exultet, as an example of a complex cultural phenomenon understood best in its larger context, and nothing should be construed as suggesting that individual topics are best studied alone.

Earlier versions of portions of this material have appeared in *Exultet: Rotoli liturgici* and in *Essays on Medieval Music in Honor of David G. Hughes.*

Fellowships from the National Endowment for the Arts and from Oberlin College have provided substantial support for this research, and I hereby express my sincere thanks.

I have profited much from discussions, sometimes enthusiastic, with colleagues in a variety of disciplines. From them I have learned much and refined my thinking in many ways. I therefore express sincere and collegial thanks to Faustino Avagliano, Peggy Badenhausen, Bonifacio Baroffio, John Boe, Virginia Brown, Guglielmo Cavallo, Julian Gardner, Dorothy Glass, Richard Gyug, Charles Hilken, Jean Mallet, James McKinnon, Francis Newton, Valentino Pace, Roger Reynolds, Lucinia Speciale, André Thibaut. Malcolm Bothwell wrote the elegant Beneventan neumes in chapter 4. The index was prepared by Christina Huemer.

I am grateful to the authorities of the libraries that own the manuscript sources of the Exultet. They have been unfailingly courteous and helpful.

In prefaces of this kind one often reads that portions of the manuscripts were read by colleagues, that their suggestions have improved the book, though the author assumes responsibility for all remaining errors. Such a statement, in such small type, seems an inappropriate expression of the debt I owe to John Boe, Francis Newton, Jeffrey Hamburger, Richard Gyug, and Roger Reynolds. That such experts should take time to give detailed attention to early versions of this study is a tribute to their unselfish dedication to scholarship, and they have made this book, from its larger organization to its smallest detail, far better than I could have managed. I have incorporated suggestions, information, and language from these colleagues, making this book really as much a collaboration as the work of a single author. Their attention has been a source of anguish at first, of learning in the middle, and of a deep sense of friendship and gratitude all along.

Cambridge, Massachusetts   T.F.K.
October 1995

CONTENTS

PLATES

ABBREVIATIONS

Dates are indicated in a shorthand as follows: s11in, s11med, s11ex (beginning, middle, end of eleventh century); s12¾ (third quarter of the twelfth century); s8/9 (eighth or ninth century).

Titles of pictures in Exultet rolls have been given largely as they are used in the art-historical literature to date: namely, by reference to the nearby text that the picture is presumed to illustrate. My use of these labels is for ease of reference and for the convenience of the reader and is not intended to convey my own judgment as to the subject of the picture. Both text and picture titles are in quotation marks.

Bibliographical references in the text and in the notes are made by author and short title, allowing for consultation of the full reference in the bibliography.

The following bibliographical abbreviations are used.

Aggiornamento = Adriano Prandi, ed. *L'art dans l'Italie méridionale: Aggiornamento dell'opera di Émile Bertaux.* 4 vols. (numbered 4–6 plus Indici): Rome: École Française de Rome, Palais Farnèse, 1978.

Analecta hymnica = *Analecta hymnica medii aevi,* ed. Guido Maria Dreves, Clemens Blume, and Henry Marriott Bannister. 55 vols. Leipzig: O. R. Reisland, 1886–1922.

Avitabile, Censimento 1 = Lidia Avitabile, Maria Clara Di Franco, Viviana Jemolo, and Armando Petrucci. "Censimento dei codici dei secoli 10–12," *Studi medievali,* ser. 3, 9/2 (1968): 1,115–94.

Avitabile, Censimento 2 = Lidia Avitabile, Franca De Marco, Maria Clara Di Franco, and Viviana Jemolo. "Censimento dei codici dei secoli 10–12," *Studi medievali,* ser. 3, 11/2 (1970): 1,013–133.

DACL = *Dictionnaire d'archéologie chrétienne et de liturgie,* ed. Fernand Cabrol, Henri Leclercq, and Henri Marrou. 15 vols. Paris: Letouzey et Ané, 1903–53.

Exultet = Guglielmo Cavallo, Giulia Orofino, and Oronzo Pecere, eds. *Exultet: Rotoli liturgici del medioevo meridionale.* Rome: Istituto Poligrafico e Zecca dello Stato, 1994.

Gamber, *CLLA* = Klaus Gamber. *Codices liturgici latini antiquiores.* 2 vols. in 3 parts. Spicilegii Friburgensis subsidia no. 1. Fribourg: University Press, 1963. Vols. 1, pt. 1 and 1, pt. 2, 2d ed. 1968; vol. 1A (supplement), 1988.

Kehr, *IP* = Paul Fridolin Kehr. *Regesta pontificum Romanorum: Italia pontificia.* 10 vols. Berlin: Weidmann, 1906–77.

Kelly, *TBC* = Thomas Forrest Kelly. *The Beneventan Chant.* Cambridge: Cambridge University Press, 1989.

Lowe, *TBS* = Elias Avery Lowe. *The Beneventan Script: A History of the South Italian Miniscule.* 2 vols. 2d ed. prep. and enl. by Virginia Brown. Sussidi eruditi nos. 33–34. Rome: Edizioni di Storia e Letteratura, 1980.

MGH = *Monumenta germaniae historica.*

MGH Epistolae 1 = *MGH Epistolarum tomus 1: Gregorii I papae registrum epistolarum Tomus 1*, ed. Paul Ewald and Ludwig M. Hartmann. Berlin: Weidmann, 1887–91.

MGH Epistolae 2 = *MGH Epistolarum tomus 2: Gregorii papae registrum epistolarum Tomus 2*, ed. Ludwig M. Hartmann. Berlin: Weidmann, 1893–99.

MGH Epistolae 3 = *MGH Epistolarum tomus 3. Epistolae merowingici et karolini aevi, 1.* Berlin: Weidmann, 1892.

MGH Scriptores 7 = *MGH Scriptorum tomus 7.* Hannover: Hahn, 1986.

MGH SS Lang. = *MGH Scriptores rerum Langobardicarum et Italicarum saec. 6–9.* Hannover: Hahn, 1878; repr. 1964.

MMA = Herbert Bloch. *Monte Cassino in the Middle Ages.* 3 vols. Cambridge: Harvard University Press, 1986.

PL = Jacques-Paul Migne. *Patrologiae cursus completus: Series latina.* 221 vols. Paris: Migne, 1878–90.

PM = *Paléographie musicale: Les principaux manuscrits de chant grégorien, ambrosien, mozarabe, gallican, publiés en fac-similés phototypiques par les moines de Solesmes.* Successively edited by André Mocquereau, Joseph Gajard, and Jean Claire. Solesmes and elsewhere: 1899– .

THE EXULTET IN SOUTHERN ITALY

1

INTRODUCTION

The Exultet and the Roll

The illuminated Exultet rolls of southern Italy were extraordinary objects when they were made, and even now they fascinate us on account of their beautiful miniatures, sometimes painted upside down with respect to the liturgical text with its musical notation.

These southern Italian Exultets are documents of almost unparalleled luxury, and they take a rare form. Rolls are uncommon in the tenth and eleventh centuries; parchment membranes, attached end to end, and written in a single long column, were unusual in the manufacture of written documents. Why was the Exultet written on a scroll? Not because the Exultet was sung from the pulpit, nor because it was sung by the deacon. The purpose was to lend importance, solemnity, and magnificence to the occasion. The fact that something is in scroll form gives it a special significance, and the use of a scroll in the liturgy of the Easter vigil is particularly suitable. Even more ingenious is the subsequent idea of reversing the pictures.

The south Italian Exultet rolls are generally quite large, using parchment limited only by the size of a single animal (larger membranes can be some 30 by 80 centimeters), and ranging in length up to 9 meters. The pictures painted on these rolls are as generous in size as any Western manuscript paintings up to their time.

The Exultet in the Liturgy

Despite their size and their remarkable beauty, the Exultet rolls are functional documents, designed for a specific place in liturgical ceremony.

Their purpose is to provide the text used by the deacon for the blessing of the Paschal candle on the vigil of Easter. The portion of the roll indispensable to the ceremony is not the pictures: it is the words and the music used by the deacon as he performs his function.

The importance of the Exultet in the ceremonies of the Easter vigil can be judged from the value of the manuscripts prepared especially for this one moment in the year, much as the luxury of many gospel books is a measure, at least in part, of the importance of the Gospel reading in the ceremonies of the Mass. The vigil services of Holy Saturday are of great antiquity and descend from the ancient custom of keeping watch through the night until the dawn of the day of Resurrection; thus in all the Western liturgies the vigil consists of a series of lections and prayers, recounting the history of God's relation to man, from the creation, through the history of the people of Israel, to the prophecies of the redemption of humankind. As a moment of renewal, Holy Saturday has traditionally been a time for the admission of new members by baptism, and this rite, with the blessing of baptismal water, is a feature of the vigil in most churches (though usually not in monasteries). In this context, the Exultet is a solemn and picturesque moment, though its use and placement vary. The blessing of new fire, the lighting of a special candle that is blessed with a prayer of particular solemnity, and sometimes a procession with the announcement *Lumen Christi* are found in many liturgies.

Illustration in Exultet Rolls

In some medieval scrolls, illustrative material of unusual shape dictates the use of a roll; in other cases, illustration combines with the form of the roll itself to make a particularly formal and solemn document. In addition to the famous Exultet rolls, illustrated medieval rolls range from the Joshua Roll in the Vatican Library to later illuminated rolls including those given by Brother Henry to Stift Gottweig in the twelfth century: rolls painted with the liberal arts, the Trojan War, and other scenes;[1] the thirteenth-century English band of pictures now at Velletri;[2] and such items of luxury as Charles of Orléans's "Vie de Nostre Dame, toute historiée, en un roule de parchemin, couvert de drap d'or, en françois"[3] or Jean de Berry's "bible abréviée en un grand role, richement historiée et enluminée" with his two parchment *mappemondes* rolled in cases.[4]

---

1. See p. 19 and n. 43.
2. See Amato, *Tesori*, 238–39; some would see the Velletri roll as a French work: cf. Morgan, *Early Gothic Manuscripts*, vol. 1, reviewed by A. Stones in *Speculum*, January 1993, 213.
3. Le Roux de Lincy, "La bibliothèque," 76.
4. Wattenbach, *Schriftwesen*, 167, citing Hiver de Beauvoir, *La librarie de Jean duc de Berry* (Paris, 1870), 17 and 57.

Connected series of pictures in a strip are known in a variety of decorative uses and media: the Bayeux tapestry, the fourteenth-century Florentine embroidered band in silk with gold and silver containing scenes from the life of the Virgin in the Toledo (Ohio) Museum of Art, the pictures found sometimes in the orphreys of medieval liturgical vestments, and so on. Such series, though closely related to the problems of illustration in scrolls, differ from them in medium and purpose and deserve a study of their own.

A vertical roll presents a single stream to the eye when pictures and text are oriented in the same direction, as they always are except in some Exultet rolls with inverted pictures.[5] In such cases, the illustrator interrupts the column of text to insert a picture, choosing a place where illustration and its related text will be visible at the same time. More normal in antiquity, however, is the horizontal roll, organized in a series of short columns from left to right along the length of the document; this represents a single column stream cut into shorter segments—essentially the same process as when a vertical-column roll is transferred to a codex. These shorter segments—pages, as we call them when they are in a codex—increase the illustrator's problems, for when a picture is related to nearby text, the planner of a codex (or, indeed, of a horizontal scroll) must not only place the illustration at a place near the text, but must choose a place where both text and picture will fit within the frame of the page (or the portion of column).

Since codices allow easy reference from one page to another, pictures can be readily recalled to view when they are not on the page at hand. But in a scroll, unless for some reason the entire length is displayed at once, a picture must be very near or in the middle of its related text in order to be visible at the same time. In Exultet rolls where the pictures are reversed, the problem may be somewhat different, for the pictures in such cases are putatively not for the reader but for the hearer and viewer. They should therefore appear over the top of the pulpit at the same time the deacon sings the related text; and this means that they must be painted onto the roll at a place well in advance of the text they illustrate. This is how it ought to work, assuming that the simultaneity of word and picture is the goal; but the structure of the actual documents will cause us to reexamine this assumption.

Exultet rolls sometimes reproduce illustrative features of the more common codex. In a codex, easy access to all pages makes it possible to separate picture from text, by the use of backgrounds and frames, or by placing pictures in a separate place; illustrations can also be used to illustrate—or decorate—a codex as a whole, rather than a specific place in

---

5. Morrison, *History as a Visual Art,* 109, makes this point by distinguishing between a "scroll" (*volumen*) and a "roll" (*rotula*). I see no evidence that the difference between vertical and horizontal orientation of the script was generally a distinction between these two Latin terms.

the text.[6] What Kurt Weitzmann has called the emancipation of the miniature from the text[7] is particularly relevant to the frontispieces of some
Exultets: these are prologues, series of scenes related to the ceremony at
hand, or to the phenomenon of Easter as a whole, independent of a specific
place in the text to follow.

A significant portion of this book is devoted to an appreciation of
the physical structure of the Exultet rolls, with particular attention to their
manufacture. The tasks of preparation, writing, notation, drawing, and
illustration—not to speak of the planning that must go into the preparation
of each membrane and of the document as a whole—provide a fascinating
window onto the practices of medieval scribes and allow us to make some
observations about the purpose and destination of the illustrated Exultet
rolls.

The Exultet as a Mirror of Change

In southern Italy from the tenth to the twelfth century the Exultet un-
derwent many changes. Each new version, each alternative, owes its existence to a choice that reflects something of local history and of cultural
and even political traditions.

Exultet rolls contain one of two texts, which we will call the Beneventan and the Franco-Roman versions. The Beneventan text is a survival
of the old Beneventan liturgy; this is the ancient liturgical rite of the area,
associated with the Lombard duchy of Benevento at least as far back as
the eighth century and almost completely suppressed in the course of the
eleventh century under the joint forces of papal reform and Norman invasion. The Franco-Roman text reflects the rites of the church of Rome
as received in the south, whose authority only gradually asserted itself in
southern Italy during the ninth and tenth centuries. Hence when we see,
as we do in many of the Exultet rolls, the old Beneventan text erased and
the imported Franco-Roman text substituted in the course of the eleventh
and twelfth centuries, we see also the decline of Lombard power in the
south and the increased importance of the Roman church and the so-called
Reform Papacy.

The beauty of the Exultet rolls makes them objects of special value,
and the result is that they are not discarded, like so many other liturgical
manuscripts, when needs change. As a result, these are particularly interesting historical documents; they are altered or rearranged when the
need is felt for a new text, or a new melody, or a new style of musical
notation. They provide a historical palimpsest and, together with other

6. The classic study of these phenomena is Weitzmann, *Illustration in Roll and Codex;*
Weitzmann's method has been doubted, however, and is now under sustained attack: cf.
Lowden, *The Octateuchs,* chap. 8. On the survival of the orientation to scrolls, see also
Morrison, *History as a Visual Art,* 104–20.

7. Weitzmann, *Illustration in Roll and Codex,* 89.

sources to be mentioned in a moment, can outline a picture of changing influences and attitudes. In later chapters we will see a variety of changes: from the Beneventan to the Franco-Roman text; from the local to an imported melody; various revisions at the end of the text; and others as well. Taken together these provide a panorama of political and cultural influences: the waning of Lombard power; the rising influence of the centralized church of Rome; the external influence of the conquering Normans.

Introduction to the Sources

The surviving Exultet rolls, with two exceptions, are from southern Italy and date from the tenth through the fourteenth centuries. Exultet rolls were evidently in use for a longer time still: two tenth-century references to Exultet rolls, neither of which seems to be describing a novelty, suggest that a number of earlier rolls may be lost to us.[8] And the continued use of the existing rolls, far beyond the time of their manufacture, is shown by the many names of secular and ecclesiastical authorities added in later centuries. Indeed, at Pisa and Salerno, the rolls continued to be used in some fashion into the eighteenth and nineteenth centuries.[9] These rolls are central to the study of the Exultet and are among the chief wonders of southern medieval art. It is small wonder that they continued to be used, valued, and treasured. But the rolls are not the only source of the Exultet.

The Exultet is a text with its music, sung for a particular ceremony. As such, it is found in numbers of ecclesiastical books as part of the repertory of music and ceremony of the liturgical year. The Exultet in southern Italy is found about as often in other books as in scroll form. Table 1 summarizes the appearance of the Exultet in manuscript sources related to southern Italy, and Appendix 1 gives detailed descriptions of these sources.

Each book says something about how the Exultet is viewed. A document containing only the Exultet particularizes a ceremonial moment; made in the form of a roll, and enriched with illustrations, with gold and colors, it is very precious indeed. But when the Exultet is not recorded separately, the choice of repository is not always self-evident. Should it be included in music books? in books of readings? in books of special ceremonies?

Sometimes, especially in Dalmatian sources, the Exultet is included in liturgical gospel books or *evangelistaries*. This is in a way an obvious choice, since the gospel book is used by the deacon when he sings the

---

8. For these texts, see Appendix 3.

9. Antonia d'Aniello, in *Exultet*, 393, says that the Salerno Exultet was displayed hanging from the ambo annually on Holy Saturday until the early years of the twentieth century. In the eighteenth century, the Pisa roll from southern Italy was displayed on the anniversary of the dedication of the cathedral (Giuseppe Martini, *Appendix ad Theatrum*, cited in Masetti, "L'Exultet duecentesco," 217–18n1).

	Date	Deposit	Text	Type	Provenance
1.	10ex	Vat. lat. 9820 (LS)	Ben	Exultet roll	Benevento
2.	10/11	Benevento 33	Ben	missal	unknown
3.	10/11	Vat. lat. 10673	Ben	gradual	unknown
4.	10/11	Manchester, Rylands 2	Ben	Exultet roll	unknown
5.	11½	Bari, Exultet 1	Ben	Exultet roll	Bari
6.	11	Farfa-Trento A	Ben	gradual	Veroli?
7.	11	Farfa-Trento B	F-R	gradual	Veroli?
8.	11	Mirabella Eclano Exultet 1	Ben	Exultet roll	Benevento?
9.	11	Gaeta, Exultet 1 (LS)	Ben	Exultet roll	Gaeta?
10.	11	Montecassino 1	Ben	Exultet roll	Amalfi (?)
11.	11med	Avezzano, Curia vescovile	F-R	Exultet roll	Montecassino
12.	11med	Vat. lat. 4770	F-R	missal	Abruzzo
13.	11½	Capua, Bibl. Arcivescovile	F-R	Exultet roll	Capua? Montecassino?
14.	11	Gaeta, Exultet 2	F-R	Exultet roll	Gaeta?
15.	11	Pisa, Exultet 2	F-R	Exultet roll	Montecassino
16.	11⅔	Vat. lat. 3784	Ben	Exultet roll	Montecassino
17.	11⅔	Troia, Exultet 1	Ben	Exultet roll	Troia
18.	11⅔	Rome, Vall. C 32	F-R	ritual	Montecassino?
19.	11⅔	Vat. Barb. lat. 560	F-R	missal	Subiaco?
20.	11ex	Bari, Exultet 2 (LS)	Ben	Exultet roll	Bari
21.	11ex	Velletri, Museo Capitolare	F-R	Exultet roll	Montecassino
22.	11ex	London, BL add. 30337	F-R	Exultet roll	Montecassino
23.	11ex	Oxford, Can. Bibl. lat. 61	F-R	evangeliary	Zadar
24.	11ex	Vat. Barb. lat. 592	F-R	Exultet roll	Montecassino
25.	11ex?	Montecassino 451	F-R	pontifical	Montecassino
26.	11ex?	Rome, Vall. D 5	F-R	pontifical	Montecassino
27.	1082	Vat. Borg. lat. 339	F-R	evangelistary	Osor
28.	11/12	New York, Morgan M 379	F-R	missal	Foligno
29.	12in	Gaeta, Exultet 3	F-R	Exultet roll	Gaeta
30.	12½	Paris, B. N., n.a. lat. 710	F-R	Exultet roll	Fondi
31.	12in	Rome, Vall. F 29	F-R	ritual	Farfa
32.	12½	Mirabella Eclano, Exultet 2	F-R	Exultet roll	Mirabella? Benevento?
33.	12½	Troia, Exultet 2	Ben	Exultet roll	Troia
34.	1106–20	Montecassino 2	F-R	Exultet roll	Sorrento
35.	12	Rome, Vall B 23	F-R	missal	Norcia
36.	12	Berlin, Staatsb. Lat fol. 920	F-R	missal	Kotor
37.	12	London, BL Eg 3511	F-R	missal	Benevento
38.	12	Troia, Exultet 3 (LS)	F-R	Exultet roll	Troia
39.	12	Rome, Casanat. 724	F-R	Exultet roll	Benevento
40.	12	Vat. lat. 6082	F-R	missal	Montecassino?
41.	12ex	Rome, Vall. B 43	F-R	missal	central Italy
42.	12ex	Vat. lat. 9820 (US)	F-R	Exultet roll	Benevento
43.	12ex	Naples VI G 34	F-R	processional	Troia
44.	12ex	Vat. Barb. lat. 699	F-R	missal	Veroli? Sulmona?

45.	12/13	Salerno, Exultet	F-R	Exultet roll	Salerno
46.	12/13	Vat. Ottob. lat. 576	F-R	missal	Montecassino
47.	12/13	Vat. Barb. lat. 603	F-R	missal	Caiazzo?
48.	13	Bari, Exultet 3	F-R	Exultet roll	Bari
49.	13	Subiaco XVIII	F-R	missal	Subiaco
50.	13	Oxford, Bod. Can. liturg. 342	F-R	missal	Dubrovnik
51.	13	Bari 2 (US melody 1)	F-R	Exultet roll	Bari
52.	13½	Bari 2 (US melody 2)	F-R	Exultet roll	Bari
53.	13?	Naples VI G 38	F-R	missal	Franciscan
54.	14	Gaeta, Exultet 1 (US)	F-R	Exultet roll	Gaeta
55.	14	Vat. lat. 3784A	F-R	Exultet roll	Naples
56.	15	Salerno 3	Ben	missal	Salerno
57.	15	Salerno 4	Ben	missal	Salerno
58.	15	Rome, Casanat. 1103	F-R	missal	Montevergine

Note: Some sources are included more than once, when they contain two texts (as in the fragments of Farfa and Trento), or when they were substantially revised from an earlier form to provide a later text (as Vat. lat. 9820, Bari 2, and others). Abbreviations: LS = lower script; US = upper script; Ben = Beneventan text; F-R = Franco-Roman text.

Gospel from the ambo; and the deacon will sing the Exultet from the same place, even though the Exultet itself is not biblical. The Dalmatian custom, however, was not that of southern Italy, whose many surviving gospel books do not include the Exultet. *Pontificals,* books of ceremonies performed by the bishop, often contain the special rites of Holy Week in which the bishop participates, including those of Holy Saturday. However, the only south Italian pontificals in which the Exultet is written are the twin copies of the Roman-German Pontifical made at Montecassino in the late eleventh century.[10] These are copies of an imported document, perhaps used more as books of reference than as material for the performance of the liturgy. The absence of the Exultet in most native southern Italian pontificals may result from the practice of separating the Exultet on a roll. *Processionals,* which record occasional chants for use on special days (including many sung in procession), sometimes contain the Exultet. Such volumes are often something of a general compendium, and the inclusion of the Exultet in such an occasional anthology is no surprise, given the Exultet's uniqueness. *Missals,* which contain all the necessary materials for the celebration of the Mass, often also include materials for the special rites of Holy Week; thus eighteen missals related to the Beneventan area contain the Exultet. Although elsewhere the Exultet is not normally a part of *rituals* (which include rites performed by priests), two south Italian rituals contain the Exultet, either as part of the priest's ritual of Holy Saturday or as a separate element.

10. See pp. 64–65 and Appendix 1.

Music books are not the place to look for the Exultet: it is not a chant for specialist singers. Only two south Italian *graduals* contain the Exultet: the early Vat. lat. 10673, and the Farfa-Trento fragments. This latter is a very unusual document; it is the only place in which the Beneventan and the Franco-Roman texts appear together, and it may have been an exceptional book in other ways as well.

These manuscript sources provide a larger context for the study of the Exultet, and they cannot be overlooked when considering the text and the music of this important moment of the liturgical year. They will have an important role to play in the further consideration of the text, the melody, and the ceremonial of the Exultet.

Special Character of the South Italian Exultet

The Exultet in southern Italy has unusual features worth underscoring at the outset. The roll itself, and its illustration, is the principal interest of many observers. And yet these rolls are part of a phenomenon that is broader, culturally and chronologically, than what we can determine from the rolls alone. These particular features are:

1. A text, for the blessing of the candle at the Easter vigil, that is different from the texts used elsewhere for the same function. This "Beneventan" blessing is related to the old Beneventan liturgy of southern Italy and gradually disappears in the course of the centuries that produced the Exultet rolls. As a result, the Beneventan text and the history of its transmission and disappearance have much to tell us about the changing cultural influences.

2. A melody that is of south Italian origin. This melody arises from the larger context of the Beneventan liturgy, where it was used for lections, recitations, and prayers. We can see in the case of the Exultet that the melody survives longer than its associated text. When rejecting the Beneventan text in favor of the Franco-Roman, scribes often retained the Beneventan melody, keeping a portion of the older liturgy while rejecting the rest (here the musician can assist the art historian in detecting Lombard conservatism).

   Musical aspects of the Exultet teach us also about how manuscripts were made and about how they were used; indeed, it is not possible to make a good Exultet roll without knowing how to sing the Exultet. Often it is clear that a scribe is reinventing the melody as he writes, singing to himself a formula that he knows, applying it to a text, and writing the result. The surviving Exultets also give us a look at medieval embellishment, for some of the surviving Exultets give ornamented versions of th⌐

Beneventan melody and provide a window on the practice of musical elaboration—a practice that may have been part of the deacon's challenge as he performed.

3. The unusual placement of the Exultet ceremony in the course of the Holy Saturday ritual. Except in southern Italy, the blessing of the candle is the first public event of a long vigil, followed by a series of lections and canticles, blessing of water, baptisms, and Mass. In the Beneventan liturgy, however, at least in the earliest stages known to us, the candle is blessed in the course of the vigil, after the lections. This is unparalleled anywhere else. As a result, when we learn that as late as the fourteenth and fifteenth centuries some southern Italian churches still blessed the candle after the lessons, we have a good indication that such places once practiced the Beneventan liturgy in its entirety, including the pure Beneventan Exultet. We can thus expand our view of the history and chronology of the Beneventan Exultet, and of the Beneventan liturgy, in cases where more direct sources do not survive.

4. A particular ceremonial for the blessing of the candle. This varies with time and place, but its elements include a very large candlestick, the singing of *Lumen christi,* and the lighting of the candle.

These elements, along with the unfurling of the rotulus, contribute to the ceremony of the Exultet and make of it a moment of high importance in the Beneventan vigil. The beautiful illustrated roll is only a part of an impressive ceremony, performed at the center of the liturgical year. Words, music, sight, sound, all contribute to an impressive ritual. It is the ensemble of these aspects that this book seeks to address, considering them carefully and separately; it will also give a perspective on the southern Italian practices that gave rise to the physical phenomenon of the Exultet roll; and it will trace its geography and chronology in ways that allow this one moment in liturgical time to reflect much of the changing culture of medieval southern Italy.

2

THE ROTULUS

A *rotulus,* or roll, or scroll, is a length of papyrus, leather, or parchment, on which writing is preserved, and which is stored in a rolled form. These are most often made by fastening together, with glue, thread, or thongs, several separate pieces to make a scroll of some length. Rolls are often, but not always, written on one side only, for reasons of convenience and concern for the text being written. An *opisthographic* roll is one written on both sides, either originally or in the process of reusing the blank outer side of an older scroll.

Rolls are usually wound around a central baton, the *umbilicus.* The papyrus, leather, or parchment nearest the center, although it might bear the weight of the length of the scroll, generally receives far less wear than the outer portions, since the outer membranes must be handled at every use in reaching the center. In order to be read, a roll must be unrolled (*explicitus*), and thus the *explicit* of medieval books and the explication of their texts derive from the process of unrolling such a document.

Scrolls are oriented either horizontally or vertically. The writing is sometimes arranged in columns written from top to bottom of the width, with the document held sideways for reading and writing; this is the most common layout, almost universal in antiquity. (It is of course very rare for a horizontal scroll to be written in long lines across the entire long dimension, because this entails the full-length rolling of the scroll for each line of text.) Other rolls are oriented vertically, usually with a single continuous column of text (unless interrupted by diagrams or illustrations) from top to bottom; this is the arrangement for all the medieval Exultet rolls.

Early History

Most of the terms generally used for books were at first applied to rolls exclusively, since the roll was for many centuries the standard format for the preservation of writing. The Greek terms χάρτης (Latin *charta,* which becomes both paper and charter), like βύβλος or βίβλος, refers both to writing materials and also to its rolled form. More specific terms are Greek κύλινδρος and Latin *uolumen,* referring to the shape of the roll. A *tomus* (τομός) in its original sense is a cutting from a *uolumen,* hence a portion of a larger roll; later the term came to mean a part of a larger work and ultimately a book in itself.[1] The term *rotulus* is a later Latin coinage for a rolled document and is used in many other languages (rotolo, roule, rouleau, rodillo, rodel, roll); it is the term most often used in the period of the Beneventan Exultet rolls, and we will generally prefer it here to *uolumen.*

The rotulus is the standard way of preserving a text in antiquity. Among the Egyptians, the Greeks, the Romans, and other ancient civilizations, rolls are depicted, described, and occasionally preserved, showing that they are the standard form of book. The papyrus roll was known four thousand years before Christ, though the oldest surviving roll is from the third millenium B.C.E.[2] The use of the roll came to the Greeks at the latest by the sixth century B.C.E. and from them passed to the Romans.[3]

The oldest surviving rolls are all of papyrus; such rolls are usually from 6 to 10 meters long, but sometimes as long as 20 to 40 meters, and range from 5 to 40 centimenters wide, averaging somewhere around 30 centimeters.[4] Papyrus continued to be used until the sixth century. Indeed, the Easter letters of the patriarchs of Alexandria were written on papyrus in the eighth century,[5] and papyrus rolls continued to be used for archival documents until the eleventh century: the last such papyrus, according to Leo Santifaller, is a document of Pope Victor II of 1057.[6] The earliest scroll to contain what may be a liturgical text is a fourth-century

1. The discussion to follow of the early history of the rotulus and the codex is drawn from materials presented in the following works, to which the reader is referred for detailed information: Altsalos, *La terminologie;* Arns, *La technique du livre;* Birt, *Die Buchrolle;* Bischoff, *Paläographie;* Bömer, "Die Schrift"; Hunger, "Antikes und mittelalterliches"; Leclercq, "Livre," in *DACL* 9.2, cols. 1,754–1,772; Maunde Thompson, *An Introduction,* 44–51; Colin H. Roberts, "The Codex"; Roberts and Skeat, *The Birth of the Codex;* Santifaller, *Beiträge;* Santifaller, "Über Papierrollen"; Santifaller, "Über späte Papyrusrollen"; Wattenbach, *Das Schriftwesen.*

2. Santifaller, *Beiträge,* 27–28, 153–54.

3. On papyrus rolls in classical antiquity, see Lewis, *Papyrus.*

4. Exultet rolls vary in width from about 200 mm to 475 mm; most are between 270 and 330 mm wide; see Table 13 (p. 175).

5. Cf. Berlin papyrus 10677: see Schubart, *Papyri,* pl. 50 and commentary, pp. XXXII–XXXIII.

6. Kehr, *IP* 2:27. Santifaller, "Über späte Papyrusrollen," 126 (no. 57).

papyrus of Oxyrhynchus, whose allusions to, or reminiscences of, the
Greek of the Old Testament suggest a possible liturgical use.[7] Parchment
rolls survive from as early as the second century B.C.E., and parchment
eventually becomes the medium of choice for writing, whether rolled or
folded.

By the fourth century C.E., the codex became the most usual way of
preserving a text.[8] Early codices are not luxury products: in its early form
the codex is descended from the simple folded pocket-book used by the
Romans. There are obvious advantages to the codex: easy reference to any
part of the text; relatively uniform wear (the outer parts of a rotulus always
wear out first); the ability to include much text in a smaller space[9] (Gregory the Great noted that within the space of six codices he had compressed
a work that had occupied thirty-five rolls).[10] But there may have been
more than practicality involved in the transition.

Early Christian texts are written as codices much more frequently
than as rolls.[11] The growth of Christianity, and of its literature, had a great
deal to do with the increasingly frequent use of the codex. The portability
of the codex, indeed its ability to be easily hidden and passed along seems
to have encouraged the use of codices among Christians and, later, in
Christian society.[12] Saint Jerome use the words *liber* and *uolumen* seemingly interchangeably, although he apparently uses *liber* when he is thinking of the work transmitted and *uolumen* when he thinks of the material:
thus several *libri* can be contained in one *uolumen*. Jerome does, apparently, mean a scroll when he says *uolumen*, and he refers especially to
Hebrew scriptures as being *uolumina*.[13]

Already by the end of the fourth century, then, the roll has taken on
the function of offical or solemn use. According to Optatus of Miletus,
writing in the 370s and 380s, the *uolumen* is used for official documents

7. Cf. Hunt, *The Oxyrhynchus Papyri*, 17:5 (no. 2,068).
8. The oldest fragmentary evidence of codices comes from the first or second century
C.E.; in the third century it seems clear that codex and rotulus are about equally common,
and in the fourth century the codex begins to prevail (Santifaller, "Über späte Papyrusrollen," 117). In his classic article "The Codex," Colin H. Roberts (p. 184) calculates the
increasing percentages of codices in the total of Greek literary and scientific writing, excluding Christian literature. The percentage of codices increases from 2.31 percent in the
second century to 73.95 percent in the fourth century.
9. Rolls can contain a great deal, however, if we credit the report of the Byzantine
historian Zonaras, who reports that the great library of 120,000 books at Constantinople
included a roll 120 feet long, made from the intestine of a serpent, which contained the *Iliad*
and the *Odyssey* written in letters of gold (IV. 2, in Büttner-Wobst, *Ioannis Zonarae*, 3:131).
10. "Opus hoc per triginta et quinque volumina extensum in sex codicibus explevi";
Gregory, Registrum epistolarum. 5.53a, *MGH Epistolae 2*, 355. The letter is not in Norberg's edition.
11. Roberts, "The Codex," 186. Note that Roberts nowhere else speaks of the early
history of the liturgical use of the codex or of the survival of the roll in the liturgy.
12. Roberts and Skeat, *The Birth of the Codex*.
13. Arns, *La technique*, 118–21.

and for Jewish law and scriptures; otherwise *membranae* are used.[14] This archaizing function is to remain the roll's principal province from then on.

The Medieval Rotulus: Ceremonial, Practical, and Decorative

In the Middle Ages, the rotulus ceases to be the chief vehicle for writing; instead, it serves practical or ceremonial purposes. Rolls of special ceremonial or liturgical character, and rolls whose contents dictated the shape, continue to be made and used throughout the Middle Ages. Indeed, these are the reasons for making rolls today: practical reasons dictate the manufacture of microfilm, motion picture film, paper for printing and facsimile machines, and scrolling computer screens; and ceremonial considerations lead to the production of Torah scrolls, citations, and academic diplomas. A review of the kinds of scroll made in the Middle Ages, and of the reasons for their manufacture, will provide a context in which to consider the scrolls from which the Exultet was performed.

Charters and Diplomas

Most parchment archival documents in Italy and southern France, and many elsewhere, are stored rolled up. Royal decrees in England are promulgated on parchment charters (looked after by a Master of the Rolls); many other formal documents have such a presentation. Indeed, the word for charter (*carta*) is often taken in the Middle Ages to mean a roll, as in the illustrated Exultet roll ("carta benedictionis cerei .i. isturiata") mentioned by brother Ludovicus in 1372.[15] Many rotuli record such notarial matters as legal disputes, inventories, and the like;[16] rolls of accounts, names, and other records are often the standard way of keeping records; to "enroll" is to place a name in the rolls. In England during the Middle Ages, there are Fine, Close, Patent, Liberate, Charter, Gaol Delivery, Pipe, and other rolls (though not all of them are actually rolls).[17] Such rolls, interesting and numerous as they are, do not form part of the body of rolls containing literary matter and are not discussed further in this context.

---

14. Roberts, "The Codex," 199.
15. Inguanez, *Catalogi codicum*, 63; see Appendix 3.
16. See Santifaller, "Über Papierrollen," 367–71, for examples on paper; Wattenbach, *Das Buchwesen*, 170–71. Some specific examples of rolls containing charters include Paris, Bibl. nat. lat. 8989, a thirteenth-century roll of Cluny; Paris, Bib. nat. lat. 10085, a collection of fragments of fourteenth- and fifteenth-century rent and inventory rolls from abbeys of Normandy.
17. There is some material on these in Galbraith, *Studies in the Public Records;* more recently, see Clanchy, *From Memory to Written Record*, 135–44.

Council Reports

While at least two rolls record the actions of church councils,[18] the many depictions of councils in medieval art indicate that conciliar acts were normally recorded on rolls (or perhaps they were so depicted because of the importance of conciliar authority).[19]

Obituary Rolls

Mortuary rolls announce the death of an important personage, and they can be lengthened at will; the bearer (called the *roliger, rotulifer, bajulus rotoli, breuiger, gerulus,* etc.) carried the roll from place to place, and individual establishments added their own acknowledgments, often in poetic form, sometimes with requests of their own for intercessions.[20] Such rolls grew as they traveled and attained sometimes quite remarkable lengths.[21] Obituary rolls are known in the literature from the eighth century, but the earliest surviving fragments date from the second half of the tenth century;[22] rolls survive from as late as the beginning of the sixteenth century, notably the series of rolls from the Saint Lambrecht monastery at Steier-

18. Colmar, Archives départementales, "Murbach statutes," Gorze, eleventh century, a report on the Aachen synod of 816 (Bischoff, *Latin Palaeography*, 32n105); Munich Clm 29555/3, council report, ca. 813; see Mordek, "Karolingische Kapitularien," 33.

19. On the iconography of councils, see Sieben, *Konzilsdarstellungen.* In the Utrecht psalter, scribes are shown recording the action of a council on rolls, and the decisions of the council of Toledo are similarly recorded on rolls in illustrations in two codices in the Escorial (Utrecht, Universiteitsbibliotheek MS 32; El Escorial, Real Biblioteca de San Lorenzo MSS D I 1 and D I 2); relevant facsimiles and discussion in Walker, *L'iconographie;* see also Reynolds, "Rites and Signs."

20. Léopold Delisle, in a classic study (Delisle, *Rouleaux;* see also Huyghebaert, *Les documents nécrologiques*) lists over a hundred obituary rolls, and Jean Dufour has evidently identified 160 ("Les rouleaux," 98, but no list is provided). The actual survival of documents created in roll form is smaller, however, although there are many records of individual *tituli* added to rolls, transcriptions of lost rolls, extracts in other documents, and the like. Some important rolls have been destroyed or lost (such as the roll of Oliva, bishop of Vich, destroyed by fire at Ripoll in 1835; see Junyent, "Le rouleau funéraire"), but there are also references to obituary "rolls" where it is not established that the original document was in roll form (see, e.g., Stiennon, "Routes et courants"; Morin, "Un rouleau mortuaire"; Leclercq, "Un nouveau manuscrit"). Most of the early survivals are small pieces of mortuary announcements now found as flyleaves in codices, and it is thus not always easy to tell whether the document traveled originally in rolled form.

21. The roll of Matilda, daughter of William the Conqueror and abbess of La Trinité of Caen, was over 20 meters long. The roll was unfortunately destroyed in the French Revolution. See Delisle, *Rouleaux,* 177–279.

22. The oldest fragment surviving dates from 968 to 977 and announces the death of Gauzebert, monk of Saint Martial, Limoges (Paris, BN lat. 2262, f. 2); the earliest roll with substantial survivals is the roll of Hugh, abbot of Saint-Amand (d. 1107); see Dufour, "Les rouleaux," 100n31.

mark.[23] Until the eleventh century, most obituary rolls are from central and northern France or from Catalonia; their use spread later to include England, Belgium, Germany, and Austria. It is worth noting in this context that obituary rolls seem not to have been much in use in Italy (nor in Spain or Portugal).

Maps, Genealogies, Chronicles

Certain documents, because of their illustrative material, or because of the linearity of their contents,[24] suggest roll form as the best way of presentation. Illustrated chronicles, of universal history or of a smaller portion of it—usually of a ruling house—survive in roll form, owing to the importance of the subject and the need to show chronology in a line.[25] Pilgrim's maps of the Holy Land or of the marvels of Rome are sometimes presented on rolls, whose shape facilitates the illustrated presentation.[26] Likewise, genealogical charts, whose tree shape invites a longways presentation, survive in roll form. These include charts of the genealogy of Christ, in the version of Peter of Poitiers and others, and genealogies of royal and noble houses, of which several splendid illustrated examples survive. Most of the surviving examples of these types are from later centuries,[27] where the roll surely takes on a ceremonial and archaizing significance, particularly in the case of noble genealogies and chronicles.

Drama, Poetry, Music

Rolls can have a practical use when they are small, easily held in the hand, and of easy reference. It seems that actors often used rolls, to judge by the survival of individual dramatic parts on separate rolls.[28] Poets and singers

23. On these, see Bünger, *Admonter Totenroteln;* Wichner, "Eine Admonter Totenrotel"; Schmid, "Die St. Lambrechter Todtenrotel."

24. The latter consideration may have influenced the form of the chronicle of Novalesa, a roll whose surviving twenty-eight membranes give it a length of more than 11 meters (edited, with facsimiles, in Cipolla, *Monumenta*, vol. 2; another edition is Bethmann, *Chronicon*). The roll is now in the Archivio di Stato of Turin.

25. For some examples, see Bühler, "Prayers"; Mather and Robinson, "Two Manuscript Rolls"; Monroe, "A Roll Manuscript"; on the various forms of the fifteenth-century rolls illustrating the descent of the English crown, see de la Mare, *Catalogue*, 80–85.

26. On the famous Tabula Peutingeriana, showing pilgrim routes to Rome, see Bosio, *La tabula;* on rolls showing the *mirabilia Romae*, see Bischoff, *Latin Palaeography*, 33n111.

27. But not all: consider Vat. lat. 3783, a genealogy of Christ from the twelfth century.

28. Including a single part (fourth guardian of the sepulcher) of a fourteenth-century Easter play (Sulmona, Archivio Capitolare di San Panfilo, Fasc. 47 n. 9: see Young, *The Drama*, 501, 701–8; Inguanez, *Un dramma* is the text of the whole play) and an older Assize roll with a role from an early fifteenth-century English play copied onto the dorse (Oxford, Bodleian Library MS Eng. Poet. f. 2 (R) (SC 30516) s13 (Rouse, "Roll and Codex," 121 and n. 38) or s14in (Davis, *Non-Cycle Plays*, c–cxi). Other rolls include indications for the

are frequently depicted holding long strips, or little rolls, from which they evidently recite or sing.[29] There are a great many references to poetry being recited or sung from rolls,[30] but, as Richard Rouse says, the rolls do not often survive, being simple and ephemeral.[31] Nevertheless, there are survivals of poetry written on rolls, some of which may be of the sort used by poets themselves.[32]

Musical compositions recorded on and performed from rolls are also well documented. Notker of Saint Gall's story of how he came to compose his sequences is recorded in the preface to his *Liber hymnorum,* addressed in 884 to Liutward, bishop of Vercelli. Notker describes his early efforts as being written on pieces of paper or parchment and at a second stage being gathered together into rotuli by his master Marcellus ("in rotulas eos congessit").[33] The assembly of the rolls may have been the act of attaching successive single-sheet libelli: if Notker's first versions were written in a single column on one side of a strip of paper or parchment—like those held by other poets—a rotulus would result from their attachment end-to-end.

Polyphonic music survives in fragments of thirteenth-century rolls[34] and in a fourteenth-century roll from Picardy (Brussels, Bibl. Royale 19606); a little strip with Guillaume de Machaut's "Lay mortel" was discovered in 1927.[35] Pictures of medieval musicians singing from rolls are not numerous,[36] with the exception, of course, of the liturgical scenes in Exultet rolls.

Prayer Rolls, Amulets, Charms

Rolls have many private uses. "Have written on a scroll whatever you do not know," says the English rule for anchorites;[37] this simplest use of a roll may be a simple shopping list, or a prayer, or a talisman of some sort. Private prayers may be on scrolls, evidently for personal (rather than li-

director (Frankfurt am Main, Stadt- und Universitätsbibliothek, Barth. 178, s14in) or whole plays (Easter Play of Muri, s13, facs. *Das Osterspiel;* Périgueux roll, Wattenbach, *Das Schriftwesen,* 168).

29. Rouse, "Roll and Codex," discusses pictures relating to medieval German poetry and gives reproductions of illustrations; he points out that in the great Manesse and Weingarten anthologies a substantial majority of the author portraits showing written material show a long parchment strip.

30. Some are in Wattenbach, *Das Schriftwesen,* 169–70.

31. Rouse, "Roll and Codex," 110.

32. The strip at Harvard College Library (Ms Lat 198) that records the medieval "Ganymede and Helena" is such a document, and the thirteenth-century fragments in Los Angeles (University of California Research Library MS A1T 36s) record another such survival. See, respectively, Schröbler, "Zur Überlieferung," and Rouse, "Roll and Codex."

33. See Steinen, *Notker,* 2:10; Huglo, "Codicologie," 72–73.

34. Paris, Bibl. nat. Coll. de Picardie 67; Cambridge, Trinity College O.3.58; Oxford, Bodl. 652; cited in Huglo, "Codicologie."

35. See Huglo, "Codicologie," 73.

36. Some are listed in Huglo, "Codicologie."

37. "On an scrouwe"; Ackerman and Dahood, *Ancrene riwle,* 74–75.

turgical) devotion.[38] Saints' lives are sometimes in roll form; particularly famous is a roll (ca. 1210) illustrating the life of Saint Guthlac of Crowland.[39] A particular talismanic importance was given to the life of Saint Margaret, of which several versions survive in French; they seem to have had special importance for pregnant women.[40]

Some scrolls serve a meditative and apotropaic purpose. In particular, a group of surviving scrolls, designed to be worn, are the precise length of Christ's body.[41] The "Arma Christi" rolls, containing meditations in English on the instruments of the Crucifixion, also have the function of amulets.[42]

Lists of Rolls in Catalogues

Medieval catalogues of books often place rolls at the end of a long list, undoubtedly because of their format, which tends to group them together for storage. Moreover, since many of these rolls are illustrated or otherwise rather uncommon, their separate consideration is probably warranted in some cases at least by their special contents. At the very end of Brother Henry's donations to Stift Gottweig in the twelfth century comes a group of illustrated documents, evidently rolls.[43] An eleventh-century list of the books of the abbey of Gorze lists at the end a group of items called "rotula" and "pagina," which are probably both rolled, the latter, however, being only a single membrane. One of these may be a liturgical rotulus — "rotula officii sancti baptiste * * grece compositi" — but its content is

38. For example, the fifteenth-century illustrated roll of prayers now in Utrecht, Catharijneconvent (MS ABM h4a). On prayers from the hours, see Wüstefeld, *Middeleeuwse Boeken*, 176–77; London Br. Lib. Eg. 3044, s14 Flemish; hours, with illuminations. "The daily handling of this roll must have added greatly to the discipline of private devotion": see A. J. C., "A Book of Hours."

39. London, British Library Harley Roll Y. 6. See the edition by Warner, *The Guthlac Roll;* see also Jane Roberts, "An Inventory," 208; Morgan, *Early Gothic Manuscripts* 1:67–68 (illus. 72–75).

40. Examples include London, Wellcome Historical Medical Library MS 50834 and 58035, both of the early fifteenth century (see Ker, *Medieval manuscripts*, 400–401) and New York, Morgan Library MS M 779 (see Bühler, "Prayers," 270n7; *Pierpont Morgan Library, Review*, 93–94).

41. Examples include London, Br. Lib. Harley Rolls 43 A 14; Harley Rot. T 11; London, Wellcome Historical Medical Library MS 632, all of the fifteenth century; on the last, see Moorat, *Catalogue*, 1:491–93; on these scrolls in general, see Bühler, "Prayers," 272n23 and passim.

42. Examples include Oxford, Bodleian Lib. 2975 and 29110 (a); London, British Library Add. 22029 and 32006; Stonyhurst College LXIV; Esopus, N.Y., Mount Saint Alphonsus Seminary; on these, see Brown and Robbins, *Index*, 405 (no. 2,577).

43. "Isti sunt libri, quos frater HEINRICH huic contulit ecclesie: . . . Rodale, in quo VII liberales artes depicte. Item rodale, in quo Troianum bellum depictum. Item rodale, in quo varia pictura. Item quaternio depictus" (from Stift Gottweig MS 33, cited in Gottlieb, *Mittelalterliche Bibliothekskataloge*, 12).

enigmatic.[44] The fifteenth-century inventory of books at the cathedral of Benevento lists a large number of rolls, most of which are liturgical. Several of these rolls survive, and they are considered below in the context of liturgical rolls.

The Rotulus in the Liturgy

The Byzantine Rotulus

Most surviving Greek rolls are liturgical. However, rolls were also used for certain types of documents: registers, chrysobulls, and sometimes "typica" and inventories.[45] Santifaller[46] lists forty-nine Greek parchment rolls from the third through the fifteenth centuries; one has scientific content (third century), twenty-three are ecclesiastical (sixth to sixteenth centuries), and twenty-five are charters (971–1439). As late as the eighth century, the Easter letters of the patriarchs of Alexandria were written on papyrus rolls.[47] Perhaps the most famous of illustrated rolls, at least of Greek rolls, is the Joshua Roll (Vatican Pal. graec. 431), an idiosyncratic illustrated roll of the book of Joshua in Greek; the roll is written horizontally in columns and is highly illustrated. It has been much discussed, and art historians are not agreed as to its date (seventh century? tenth?) or its nature as copy or creation.[48]

Liturgical rolls are frequent in the Byzantine world. A great many of them survive, the oldest from the eighth and ninth centuries (from about the time, that is—or a little earlier—of the oldest evidence of Exultet rolls). Such rolls are called κοντάκια, but also εἰλητά, εἰλητάρια. The liturgical compositions called κοντάκια may be named for the rolled form that originally recorded them, the κόντος, κοντάξ being the umbilicus around which the roll is wrapped.[49] Guglielmo Cavallo has suggested an unbroken tradition in the Byzantine world of the use of the rotulus since earliest times in Christian worship, and this is a key point in Cavallo's argument for the Byzantine-inspired origin of the Beneventan Exultet

44. "Rotula capitulorum sparsim collectorum ab Adriano papa et Angelranno Mediomatricae episcopo missorum. Glosarius super nouum et uetus testamentum. Item Glossae de ueteri ac nouo testamento, usque Danielis prophetae librum. Pagina Ingmari metrice composita et Karolo regi missa. Pagina terrae repromissionis. Rotula officii sancti baptiste * * grece compositi. et Capitulare nouarum consuetudinum monachorum. . . . Rotula uetustissima ex arithmetica Boecii. Pagina de situ orbis. mappa scilicet mundi. Pagina quomodo ex philosophia diversae diffinitiones—quasi quidam fontes emanent. Rotula grecorum nominum. Pagina scutil. ludi. Bede presbyteri. Pagina figurarum de arte musica" (Morin, "Le catalogue des manuscrits," 9–10).
45. See Altsalos, *La terminologie*, 148–76.
46. "Über späte Papyrusrollen."
47. An example is Berlin papyrus 10677; see note 5.
48. A classic monograph on the roll, with which others have disagreed, is Weitzmann, *The Joshua Roll*. Complete facsimile in *Josua-Rolle*.
49. Altsalos, *La terminologie*, 165–70.

roll.[50] However, the dates of the surviving rolls, together with a significant change in the manner of depicting liturgical figures in church paintings, suggests that the regular use of rolls in the Byzantine liturgy began only in the eleventh and twelfth centuries, thus too late to inspire the Exultet rolls of southern Italy.[51]

The earliest surviving example of a Byzantine liturgical roll dates from as early as the late eighth century.[52] From the eleventh century onward, there is a substantial survival of liturgical rolls.[53] Farmakovskii's famous list of ninety-five liturgical rolls,[54] though it was made many years ago and needs to be updated, is a clear witness of the richness of the Byzantine rotulus. From modern catalogues and from library visits, I have compiled a list of 206 surviving Byzantine liturgical rolls; the great majority of these are from the religious centers at Athos, Patmos, Meteora, Sinai, and Jerusalem and in principal libraries. The list is far from complete, but it makes clear that the rotulus is an important and continuing feature of the Byzantine liturgy. The use of rolls in the Byzantine liturgy is not demonstrably older than the Italian practice of using a roll for the Exultet; most Byzantine rolls date from the eleventh century and later, and although there are Byzantine liturgical scrolls known to have been produced and used in southern Italy,[55] they do not antedate the Exultet scrolls of the region. But in one late case at least the Greek precedence is clear: a Byzantine liturgical scroll, erased and turned, provides the writing material for a thirteenth-century Exultet roll at Bari.

Byzantine liturgical rolls, like the Western Exultet scrolls, are oriented vertically in a single long column. They usually contain one (or both) of the two most frequently used eucharistic liturgies, those of Saint John Chrysostom and of St. Basil the Great; they are thus intended to be read by the celebrant at the altar. Occasionally, other texts are written on rolls: prayers for ordinations, the liturgy of the presanctified, the greater blessing of water at the Epiphany. There are no Byzantine rolls corresponding to the Western Exultet, since this ceremony is not used in the Orthodox liturgy.

Byzantine rolls sometimes include illumination. Most often this consists only of an opening picture of the author of the liturgy to follow—thus

50. See Cavallo, "La genesi," esp. 223.

51. See Gerstel, "Liturgical Scrolls."

52. This is the meneon Sinai, Saint Catherine 591, s 8/9 (see Gardthausen, *Catalogus*, 140; Santifaller, "Über späte Papyrusrollen," 129, no. 3); earlier documents that ought perhaps to be considered liturgical include Berlin, Papyrus 9794 (s3, prayers, papyrus fragment: see Santifaller, "Über späte Papyrusrollen," 125, no. 43); the Oxyrhynchus papyrus no. 2068 (s4, three fragments, papyrus, liturgical?; see Hunt, *Oxyrhynchus Papyri*, 17:125, no. 43; Santifaller, "Über späte Papyrusrollen," 125, no. 51); a Vienna roll in a private collection (s6, contains Psalm 26; see Wessely, "Eine Pergamentrolle").

53. A convenient listing of early Byzantine liturgical rolls is in Cavallo, "La genesi," 221–22.

54. Farmakovskii, "Vizantijskii," 257–63.

55. A convenient list is in Cavallo, "La genesi," 223–25.

usually Saint Basil the Great or Saint John Chrysostom—but there are also a few more extensively illuminated rolls.[56]

The Liturgical Rotulus in the Medieval West

The solemnity of a document is one of the reasons for writing it in the form of a roll. In the same way that ecclesiastical vesture is based on earlier modes of dress, that liturgical language tends toward the archaic, the conservatism of the liturgy suggests the archaic form of the roll for the most solemn uses. Although Western liturgy, like Western culture, adopted the codex as the usual form of written record, the rotulus continued in liturgical use for certain specific and solemn occasions.

The oldest roll containing texts for use in the liturgy comes probably from the seventh century,[57] but there are literary references to the use of rolls in Western liturgy from earlier dates. According to Gennadius of Marseille, in his fifth-century *Liber de viris inlustribus*, Museus of Marseille (d. 460)

> conposuit Sacramentorum egregium et non parvum volumen, per membra quidem pro opportunitate officiorum et temporum, pro lectionum textu psalmorumque serie et cantatione discretum.[58]

And of Voconius, bishop of Mauretania, Gennadius notes that he too "conposuit etiam Sacramentorum egregium volumen."[59] The word "uolumen" here most likely refers to a roll, though by the fifth century the word was also used generally to mean a book.[60]

In the ninth century, Agnellus of Ravenna, in his *Liber pontificalis*, says that his mid-sixth-century predecessor Maximinianus

> edidit nanque misales per totum circulum anni et sanctorum omnium, cotidianis nanque et quadragesimalibus temporis, vel quicquid ad ećlesia ritum pertinet, omnia ibi sine dubio invenietis; grande volumen mire exaratum.[61]

---

56. Two such rolls have been known for some time. The roll from the Greek patriarchate of Jerusalem described by Grabar ("Un rouleau"), who also provides a general discussion of illumination in Byzantine liturgical rolls, is from late eleventh-century Constantinople and contains the liturgy of Saint John Chrysostom (a piece was added to the 8.5-meter roll in the twelfth century to give additional space for the liturgy of Saint Basil on the back); the roll, in addition to decorative borders, contains illustrations at the top and a series of miniatures in the margins, sometimes serving as initials. The early fourteenth-century roll Lavra 2, containing the liturgy of Saint Basil on both sides, includes illuminations, within the sequence of the text, occupying the full writing width of the roll (see Bréhier, "Les peintures").

57. This is the rotulus of Ravenna; see n. 69.

58. Gennadius, *Liber de viris*, 88.

59. Ibid.

60. Both these texts are cited both by Benz (*Der Rotulus*, 217), who is convinced that they refer to rolls, and by Cavallo ("La genesi," 217), who is not so sure.

61. Testi Rasponi, *Codex pontificalis*, 208–9; another edition, Holder-Egger, "Agnelli," 332.

This is a great deal to put in one rotulus; a sacramentary, in the sense of the prayers of the Mass said by the celebrant, could well fit on a roll. A missal, if it includes also the lections and the chants of all Masses, would be enormous when rolled up. Agnellus may well mean here a codex; this is the usual sense of *uolumen* in his day and indeed was already being used in this sense in Maximianus'.[62]

A roll containing the canon of the Mass is mentioned by Pope Zacharias (741–52) in a letter to Saint Boniface:

> nam et hoc flagitasti a nobis, sanctissime frater, in sacri canonis celebratione quot in locis cruces fieri debeant, ut tuae significemus sanctitati. Votis autem tuis clementer inclinati, in rotulo dato Lul religioso presbytero tuo, per loca signa sanctae crucis quanta fieri debeant infiximus.[63]

It seems entirely possible that the canon of the Latin Mass was written on scrolls more often than once; it is a common occurrence in the Eastern church, and the text is of suitable length for a manageable, even a luxurious, rotulus. But if such documents were used at the time of Pope Zacharias, or indeed even later, they seem not to have survived. Probably the earliest sacramentaries were assembled from individual libelli with separate Masses: perhaps some of these libelli were rotuli. In any case it is clear, from the ninth century onward, that the canon is regularly written in codices, so that rolls, if they existed at all, were exceptional.[64] Indeed, from the early fifth century the codex is the usual form of writing in the Latin church;[65] this is as true for liturgical books as it is for biblical and patristic texts.

Early Christian art does not give any evidence of a special place given to the rotulus in worship. Guglielmo Cavallo, who conducted a preliminary survey of Roman church paintings and mosaics of the fourth through the thirteenth centuries, found that the rotulus almost entirely disappears from the fifth century onward in favor of the codex.[66] A number of appearances of the rotulus in early Christian art are derived from pagan archetypes, as Roberts suggests: "Since Christian art necessarily employs pagan technique and some pagan motifs, the figures of readers on Christian monuments scarcely differ from those on contemporary pagan monuments, and when it became the fashion to represent Christianity as the *vera philosophia*, the Christian sage is portrayed holding a roll, as does his pagan counterpart."[67]

62. On the change of meaning of *uolumen*, see Santifaller, "Beiträge zur Geschichte," 156–58; Cavallo, "La genesi," 218 and nn. 14–15.

63. *PL* 89: col. 953; *MGH Epistolae 1*, 372.

64. On the idea of the canon of the Mass in rotulus form, see Rule, *The Missal*, clxiii f.

65. Santifaller, "Beiträge zur Geschichte," 181; Roberts, "The Codex," 186; Cavallo, "La genesi," 219.

66. Cavallo, "La genesi," 219–20. For further information on the rotulus in early Western art, see Birt, *Die Buchrolle*.

67. Roberts, "The Codex," 193.

In later medieval art, however, the roll tends to take on the same function in pictures as in reality: it stands as symbol or expression of speech or oral performance, and usually of important speech—the words of angels, evangelists, and prophets. Rolls continue commonplace in pictures even after they were largely defunct in practice.[68]

The roll remains, then, a powerful idea in medieval book culture: the scroll as containing important words, and words that are spoken, not read. This special function contributes much to an understanding of how the scroll comes to be used in the liturgy in the Middle Ages.

Lost and Surviving Liturgical Rolls

The oldest Western liturgical roll is the seventh-century rotulus of Ravenna,[69] which contains prayers for use in Advent. It is not clear how the roll was used or whether it had any ceremonial function. A roll of obviously special importance is the litanies or *laudes* of Lorsch from the mid-ninth century, arranged on a roll in three columns and written in gold and silver.[70]

The rite of exorcism was sometimes performed from a roll, if we can judge from an illustration on the late tenth-century pontifical roll Rome Casanatense 724 (i), where a scroll (referred to on the page as a "libellus") is being handed to an exorcist.[71]

Liturgical Rolls in South Italy: Pontifical

The solemn functions exercised by the bishop were performed from rolls at least on occasion in the Middle Ages. Such pontifical rolls, often of great luxury, survive in the greatest number in southern Italy, where they are closely connected with the practice of writing the Exultet on scrolls.

Two tenth-century rolls of Benevento preserve pontifical offices and are illustrated with pictures of liturgical ceremonies being performed. Rome Casanatense 724 (i), just mentioned, contains a series of pontifical

---

68. On rolls as visible representations of speech and expression, see Flett, "The Significance of Text Scrolls"; Camille, "Seeing and Reading"; Cahn, "Représentations de la parole"; Clausberg, "Spruchbandaussagen."

69. Milan, Biblioteca Ambrosiana S. P. cassaf. 1; edition in Benz, *Der Rotulus.*

70. Frankfurt am Main, Stadt- und Universitätsbibliothek MS Barth. 179; for facsimiles and commentary, see *Der Lorscher Rotulus;* Bischoff, *Lorsch im Spiegel,* 45; facsimile in Powitz, *Die datierten Handschriften,* taf. 1.

71. Commentary by Beat Brenk and facsimile in *Exultet,* 75–85; partial facsimile in Avery, *The Exultet Rolls,* pl. 106; on this very important roll, see Lowe, *TBS,* 2:122, and the literature cited there; particularly important is the study in Belting, *Studien,* 144–52. As Richard Gyug points out ("A Fragment," 270n9), the Roman-German Pontifical prescribes a "libellus" for the exorcist; Professor Roger Reynolds communicates that in the illustrations of the *traditio instrumentorum* to exorcists in many late medieval pontificals, it is a roll, not a codex, that is presented.

blessings: of doorkeepers, lectors, exorcists, acolytes, subdeacons, deacons, and priests.[72] In one of the illustrations, the bishop reads a blessing of doorkeepers from a scroll held by an assistant;[73] the scroll in the illustration is written horizontally, an unusual orientation, especially since the scroll on which the illustration appears—written vertically—is in some sense the scroll in the illustration.

A similar illustration of a scroll being held by an assistant is found in the second pontifical scroll in the Casanatense,[74] which includes the blessing of water for baptism. Here an assistant holds a roll while the officiant lowers a candle into the water: this time the scroll is vertical, and on it can be read the prayer to be said at that point. One is only a step away from a series of endless mirrors: if the roll in the picture were to be illustrated like the roll on which it is painted . . .

In an eleventh-century roll of Bari for the blessing of baptismal water, a similar illustration shows a bishop blessing the water, an assistant holding the candle, and an assistant (standing in a group of assistants) holding a codex that is closed.[75]

A fragment survives of a later twelfth-century roll at Montecassino with portions of the solemn prayers for Good Friday.[76] There is now no trace, however, of the roll that was among the possessions of the monastery of Santa Maria de Fontanella, Amalfi, in 1007; it contained penitential material, the blessing of water, and the blessing either of wax or of the Paschal candle—perhaps the Exultet?[77] Another such roll, now lost, was given by Duke Gregory of Gaeta to the church of Saint Michael in Planciano, described in 964 as "unum rotulum ad benedicendum cereum et fontes."[78]

Pontifical Rolls Elsewhere in Europe

There are other witnesses to pontifical offices in Europe being performed from rolls. Hincmar of Reims, writing about 850 to Adventius of Metz about the ordination of bishops, indicates the use of a roll that contains

72. On this roll, see the previous note.

73. See the illustration in Avery, *The Exultet Rolls*, pl. 106, and in *Exultet*, 79.

74. Rome, Biblioteca Casanatense MS 724 (ii); see Lowe, *TBS*, 2:122–23; commentary by Beat Brenk and facsimile in *Exultet*, 87–100; the illustration is reproduced in Avery, *The Exultet Rolls*, pl. 116; *Exultet*, 97.

75. Bari, Archivio del Duomo, Benedictional roll, s11½; commentary by Magistrale and facsmile in *Exultet*, 143–50; Lowe, *TBS*, 2:15; the illustration is found in Cavallo, *Rotoli di Exultet*, tav. 15; Avery, *The Exultet Rolls*, pl. 14; *Exultet*, 148.

76. Montecassino, Archivio della Badia, Compactiones XVI; see Gyug, "A Fragment"; Magistrale in *Exultet*, 477–79, with facsimile.

77. "Rotulum unum de penitentia cum benedictione da fonti et alia benedictione de ipse cirio." From a list of donations of 1007; Camera, *Memorie*, 1:221–22. Most of the possessions of the monastery were destroyed by fire in 1383. For the history of Santa Maria de Fontanella, see Salvati and Pilone, *Gli archivi*, introduction.

78. See Appendix 3.

at least the prayers necessary for the ordination: "Et post *Gloria in excelsis Deo,* dicat hanc orationem, que prima est in rotula consecrationis."[79]

According to an ordo of the eleventh or twelfth century, an archdeacon reads the great admonition for the reconciliation of penitents from a roll:

> Postea [sc. the epistle of Maundy Thursday] sedeat episcopus in sede iuxta altare. et non dicat *dominus vobiscum.* sed archidiaconus legat coram eo et populo rotulam in qua continentur quedam indicia de penitentum reconciliacione.[80]

A fragment of an eleventh-century roll containing rites of ordination from northern Italy survives as Asti, Biblioteca Capitolare MS XIII.[81] Pontifical rolls seem not to survive north of the Alps from before the thirteenth century, but there are several English rolls of later date. A thirteenth-century roll now in the British Library contains pontifical offices and blessings;[82] an early fourteenth-century roll at Emmanuel College, Cambridge, containing pontifical offices is written on both sides and from both ends;[83] and a fifteenth-century roll at Keble College, Oxford, containing pontifical blessings, is headed by a miniature showing the bishop reading from a roll held by an attendant.[84] The order for coronations is also sometimes found on rolls, as in the roll in the Public Record Office in London.[85]

The Liturgical Rotulus at Milan

Rolls were regularly used in the Ambrosian liturgy of Milan, and surviving sources give a clear view of their employment in worship. The twelfth-century ordinal of Beroldus, the contemporaneous Codex Metropolitanus, and the thirteenth-century "Beroldus nouus" all describe the use of the rotulus in the Milanese liturgy. The rotulus contained collects, which the archbishop or his vice-presbyter said at the Office hours and at suppli-

79. *PL* 126: col. 187. See Andrieu, "Le sacre," 36n3, for Hincmar's other uses of the word *rotula,* for a sermon, and for a "rotula prolixissima" of recriminations made by Hincmar's nephew Hincmar of Laon.

80. This ordo for Maundy Thursday is from an addition made at Évreux to the pontifical of Egbert, Paris, Bibl. nat. MS lat. 10575, fol. 181v; edition in Banting, *Two Anglo-Saxon Pontificals;* see also Rasmussen, "Unité et diversité," 399–401.

81. See Dell'Oro, "Frammento di rotolo."

82. British Library, Cotton Charter Roll XIII.4; see Brückmann, "Latin Manuscript Pontificals," 438.

83. Cambridge, Emmanuel College MS III.2.24 (James 230); see Brückmann, "Latin Manuscript Pontificals," 408.

84. Oxford, Keble College Roll I; see Parkes, *Medieval Manuscripts,* 332; Brückmann, "Latin Manuscript Pontificals," 456.

85. Coronation Roll I (C. 57–1), early fourteenth century, evidently made after the fact and not used in the coronation itself; see Brückmann, "Latin Manuscript Pontificals," 443.

cations called *litaniae*. At Vespers, for instance, a *rotulus orationum* is placed on the altar by the *minor custodum*, and the priest takes it up to say the prayer; the same *custos* takes it back from the priest later.[86] When the archbishop himself is present, his *rotularius* holds the roll for him while he says the prayer. There are references also to a *rotulus letaniarum*, which is perhaps a different document from the *rotulus orationum*.[87] Indeed, according to one passage there seem to be at least three separate litany rolls, for use in three separate weeks.[88] A rotulus is also used for the Exultet at the Easter vigil, as is made clear both in Beroldus and Beroldus nouus:

> et unus subdiaconus ebdomadarius debet portare rotulum similiter indutus alba, et debet tenere ipsum rotulum ante diaconum, donec legerit, et bene-dixerit ceram et ignem [here Beroldus nouus clarifies by adding] dicendo sic: *Exultet iam*, etc.[89]

Because of the close connection of the Milanese liturgy with the Beneventan liturgy of south Italy, we shall return to the question of their relationship as regards the rotulus and the Exultet when we come to consider matters of origins in chapter 7. The Milanese liturgist Marco Magistretti justly found it particularly regrettable that no trace of any one of these Milanese rotuli seemed to have survived.[90]

In fact, however, Ambrosian liturgical rolls do survive. A Milanese roll of about 1300 has recently been acquired by the Beinecke Rare Book and Manuscript Library of Yale University. It contains antiphons and responsories, with music, for the three major litany days in the week before Pentecost; it has now been separated into three rolls, one for each of three days.[91] MS Z 256 sup. in the Biblioteca Ambrosiana consists of two rolls, attached end-to-end, containing antiphons and psallendae for use in in the procession of the minor litanies on Tuesday and Wednesday. They contain only music, for use in procession, and for singing psallendae in honor of the various saints to which churches on the processional route

86. Magistretti, *Beroldus*, 55–56.
87. This is not easy to determine, since the *rotulus orationum* is specifically referred to as lying on the altar at Vespers (Magistretti, *Beroldus*, 55), while the *rotulus letaniarum* (ibid., 57, 89, 91) is also referred to as a *rotulus letaniarum et vespertinum* both in the Beroldus ordinal (ibid., 59) and in the Codex Metropolitanus (ibid., 84); this rotulus might be the same document, then, containing prayers and the necessary materials for the litanies.
88. Ibid., 89.
89. Ibid., 110; the passage from "Beroldus nouus" is cited in Magistretti, *Manuale*, 2:198n1.
90. "Dolendum quod nullum exemplar huiusmodi *rotuli* ambrosiani ad nos perveniret"; Magistretti, *Manuale*, 2:7; however, a libellus of litanies (London, British Library MS Egerton 3762, of the early eleventh century) may be a descendant of the separate rotulus: see Gamber, *CLLA*, 281–82 (no. 577).
91. The roll bears the shelf number 810; before being separated it measured some 675 centimeters in length and is about 16 centimeters wide; I am preparing a study of this roll. Dr. Robert Babcock of the Beinecke Library generously called this roll to my attention.

were dedicated.[92] The rolls do not include prayers or any material for use by the bishop. Dating only from the thirteenth through the fifteenth century, they nevertheless suggest a continuing connection of rolls with litanies and perhaps are witnesses to an unbroken tradition of many centuries.[93]

There may be other surviving Ambrosian rolls as well. Neils Krogh Rasmussen indicates that the inventory of the Biblioteca Capitolare mentions several rolls for the use of celebrants in the cathedral.[94] Meanwhile, we can surmise that the antiquity of the Ambrosian rite of Milan, despite the relatively recent documentation of the ordinals and the surviving rolls, indicates the use of rotuli there for a long time before the eleventh century; the litanies of Pentecost can be traced back to the time of Bishop Lazarus (438–49),[95] and perhaps the litany rolls were used continuously ever since.

The Liturgical Rotulus at Benevento

Benevento, source of the earliest surviving Exultet roll, preserves a number of later medieval scrolls used for liturgical purposes. The Exultets in the Vatican and the Casanatense, along with the Casanantense pontifical rolls, are among the chief glories of Beneventan production. But the Biblioteca Capitolare preserves also five small rotuli, of the thirteenth through the fifteenth centuries, evidently used for specific places in the liturgy: one has the *Stabat mater* (for use on Good Friday?), a second has a series of collects for feasts of saints, and three others contain hymns with musical notation, perhaps for use in procession.

---

92. Attached to the rolls is a typewritten description signed by Ernesto Moneta Caglio and dated 31 January 1953. His description is as follows: "1) Rotulus Letaniarum diei secundi in Letaniis minoribus Ambrosianis. Rotolo di cm. 280 × 20 contenente antifone e sallende da cantarsi nella processione delle Litanie minori ambrosiane il martedì. Il rotolo era certamente ad uso del mestro di coro della Metropolitana perchè a) continene tutte e sole le antifone da cantarsi nel tragitto da una chiesa all'altra; non contiene le invocazioni letaniche da cantarsi nell'interno di ciascuna chiesa stazionale: ogni singola chiesa doveva avere il suo elenco in loco. b) contiene però la sallenda santorale appropriata al santo titulare di ciascuna chiesa a cui la processione si dirigeva, di volta in volta, seguita dalle antifone penitenziali delle litanie vere e proprie. La presenza delle antifone santorali e l'indicazione delle chiese stazionali comprova che questo rotolo non era usato da chiese del contado, ma dagli organizzatori della processione cittadina. Non può trattarsi che della metropolitana. La scrittura è del sec. xiv–xv. 2) Rotulus Letaniarum diei tertii in Letaniis minoribus Ambrosianis. Rotolo di cm. 420 × 20 contenente antifone e sallende da cantarsi nella processione delle Litanie minori il mercoledì. (Per la descrizione, vedi sopra, come il rotolo precedente.)" The roll is mentioned in Huglo et al., *Fonti*, 77 (no. 141bis).

93. I am grateful to my colleague Professor Robert Kendrick for obtaining information about these rolls from the Ambrosiana Project at Notre Dame University.

94. Rasmussen, "Les pontificaux," 425n32. Mercati thought that perhaps the Ambrosian dedication ordo appended to Lucca, Bibl. capitolare MS 605 (edited in *Antiche reliquie*, 5–27) might be the transcription of a roll (p. 15). Alberto Turco has kindly informed me that the Biblioteca capitolare now contains no rolls.

95. Gamber, *CLLA*, 281.

These later rolls are only a small part of the rolls once kept at the Chapter Library. The inventory of 1430–35, reviewed by the librarian Theuli in 1447, enumerates what seem to be at least twelve rolls (if we can assume that a *carta* in this context is a roll). They include:

Item carta una cum notis pro processione sancti Bartholomei.
Item liber constitutionum antiquarum capitularium dicto [*sic*] ecclesie.
Item Rotus unus cum orationibus pro letaniis
Item Rotus unus cum letania.
Item Rotus unus cum orationibus adorande crucis in parasceue.
Item Roti duo cum ympnis pro processionibus
Item alius Rotus magnus cum ympnis pro processionibus
Item alius Rotus cum letania
Item quaternus consitutionum quondam Gasparis archiepiscopi beneventani
Item sacca una . . .
Bulla una . . .
Item carta processionis crismatis que incipit *o redemptor*
Item carta lectionis palmarum que incipit *lectio libri exodi*
Item carta ubi est *exultet iam angelica.*
Item carta una ubi est rotus cum lectione *noueritis fratres charissimi.*
Item instrumentum unum . . .[96]

This collection of rolls, some of which surely survive among those now in the library (is the Exultet mentioned here one of the surviving Exultets from Benevento?), indicates that the roll was extensively used in the liturgy. Noteworthy is the presence of three rolls for use with litanies, as well as a number of other processional rolls. This is an arrangement that reminds us of the practice of Milan, to which the rite of Benevento is closely related.[97]

The chief glory of liturgical rolls, however, is the group of south Italian Exultets. These, along with other south Italian witnesses of the text and its music, are the subject of this book.

---

96. Zazo, "L'inventario," 10, but with errors. The list above is transcribed as corrected by Theuli. That the then librarian of Benevento was named Theuli and not Feoli, as Zazo and others record, see Mallet and Thibaut, *Les manuscrits*, 10n1.
97. See Kelly, *TBC*, 181–203; Bailey, "Ambrosian Chant in Southern Italy."

3

THE TEXTS

The Exultet in southern Italy, whether written in roll or codex, is always one of two texts, which we shall call the Beneventan and the Franco-Roman versions. The Beneventan text, used in the pre-Gregorian liturgical rite of the southern Lombards, is present in the oldest sources. In the course of the eleventh century, older rolls are replaced by new documents (or rewritten) with the Franco-Roman text of the Exultet, an importation from the north; this text represents the efforts of Carolingian reform corrupted by Gallican obstinacy and its adoption as part of a growing tendency toward unification in the church, acknowledging at the same time the primacy of the liturgy of Rome. Although this "Roman" text is not Roman in origin, it came to be universally adopted and reflects the rites of the church of Rome as they were understood in the south. It is essentially the text used in the Roman liturgy to this day.[1]

One version of the text, then, originates with the Beneventan liturgy and is used only in southern Italy, while the other, though not strictly Roman, arrived in the south along with the Roman liturgy, which ultimately supplanted the Beneventan. The Beneventan text (sometimes also called the Bari text, since it was first noticed in the Bari Exultets) may or may not be as old as the Franco-Roman Exultet, but it was surely present in southern Italy before the arrival of the Franco-Roman text. The Franco-Roman text is also called the "Vulgate" by Bannister, to match his coining

---

1. On the Franco-Roman and Beneventan liturgies in the history of southern Italy, see Kelly, *TBC*, 6–40; a classic article that deals with the changing role of the church at Benevento is Belting, "Studien zum beneventanischen Hof."

of the term "Vetus Itala" for the Beneventan text.[2] The analogy with biblical texts, the Vetus Itala being supplanted by the Vulgate, is perhaps useful in one sense, but it must be remembered that neither text has the authority of scripture.

The Exultet, in its Beneventan and Franco-Roman forms, is given in Table 2. Appendix 2 reports variants in these texts from all the south Italian sources. In these two and other versions, the text consists of two parts: an opening section, the prologue ("Exultet iam angelica turba celorum"), and a further section, the preface, usually sung to a preface tone and beginning like the preface of the Mass ("Sursum corda . . . Vere quia dignum et iustum est"). The prologue—the opening *Exultet* up to the preface—is shared by both texts. It was perhaps created in the fourth or fifth century, and it entered a variety of liturgies—Franco-Roman, Ambrosian, Beneventan—at a date before these liturgies fixed their various versions of the preface. This common prologue may actually be an early elaboration of the deacon's request that those present pray with him: in the Exultet, he says "astantibus uobis, fratres karissimi, . . . una mecum quaeso Dei omnipotentis misericordiam inuocate." Various ordines Romani from the late eighth century onward note that the deacon shall ask to be prayed for, and then he immediately begins the *second* portion of the Exultet, with the preface *Dominus uobiscum*. He has not skipped part of the Exultet: the request to pray for him was itself the first portion of the Exultet.[3]

Early History of the Exultet

Both texts that will concern us are a sort of liturgical prose that is not typical of Roman liturgical texts. Rhapsodic, oratorical, and florid, they are perhaps among the best examples of a much earlier tradition in which the Exultet was improvised anew by the deacon each year.

The use of a special candle for the Easter vigil, with its own blessing, may have originated in the lucernarium of the East, the simple lighting of a lamp and blessing of light at evening;[4] by the fifth century at Jerusalem, and doubtless before, a candle was lit at the Church of the Anastasis on

2. Bannister, "The *Vetus Itala*," edits the Beneventan text, but incompletely and with errors. The Beneventan text is conveniently available in *PM* 14:385–86, Cavallo, *Rotoli,* 26; *Exultet,* 485–86.

3. Andrieu, *Les ordines,* 3:190, ordo 17.103–4 (s8ex): "ille qui cereum benedici debet, stans in medio, postulans eos pro se orare et faciens crucem super cereum et accipiens a subdiacono lumen, quod in parasceven absconsum fuerit, et accenso cyreo dicit: *Dominus vobiscum.* Resp[ondent] omnes: *Et cum spiritu tuo.* . . . Iterum dicit: *Sursum corda.* Resp[ondent]: *Habemus a domino.* Et iterum dicit: *Gratias agamus domino Deo nostro.* Resp[ondent]: *Dignum et iustum est,* vel omnia sicut in Sacramentorum commemorat. Benedicto autem cereo, revertuntur in sacrario." The same process is described in ordo 28 (ca. 900), Andrieu, *Les ordines,* 3:403–4, and in ordo 32 (s10), ibid., 3:531.

4. See Gamber, *Sacrificium vespertinum;* Pinell, "Vestigis del lucernari."

TABLE 2.   Text of the Exultet

Prologue (Beneventan, Milanese, Franco-Roman Liturgies)

Exultet iam angelica turba celorum,	Rejoice now, angelic choir of the heavens,
exultent diuina misteria,	let the divine mysteries rejoice
et pro tanti regis uictoria	and for the victory of such a king
tuba intonet salutaris.	let the trumpet of salvation sound.
Gaudeat se tantis tellus irradiata fulgoribus	Let the earth rejoice, enlightened with such brightness,
et eterni regis splendore lustrata	and shining with the splendor of the eternal king,
totius orbis se sentiat amisisse caliginem.	feel the darkness of the whole world dispelled.
Letetur et mater ecclesia tanti luminis adornata fulgore	Let mother church, too, be glad, adorned with the brightness of such splendor;
et magnis populorum uocibus hec aula resultet.	and let this hall resound with the great voices of the people.
Quapropter astantibus uobis fratres karissimi	Wherefore, dearest brethren, standing here
ad tam miram sancti huius luminis claritatem	in the presence of the wonderful splendor of this holy light,
una mecum queso dei omnipotentis misericordiam inuocate.	invoke with me, I pray you, the mercy of God the omnipotent.
Vt qui me non meis meritis	So that he who not through my
in leuitarum numero dignatus est aggregare	merits has deigned to number me among the priests,
luminis sui gratiam infundens	pouring the grace of his light, may
cerei huius laudem implere precipiat.	direct me to accomplish the praise of this candle.
Per dominum nostrum Iesum Christum filium suum	Through his son our lord Jesus Christ,
uiuentem secum atque regnantem	living and reigning with him
in unitate spiritus sancti Deum	in the unity of the Holy Spirit, God
Per omnia secula seculorum.	for all the ages of ages.
Amen.	Amen.

Preface (Beneventan Version)

Dominus uobiscum.	The Lord be with you.
Et cum spiritu tuo.	And with your spirit.
Sursum corda.	Lift up your hearts.
Habemus ad dominum.	We have [lifted them] to the Lord.
Gratias agamus domino deo nostro.	Let us give thanks to the Lord our God.
Dignum et iustum est.	It is fitting and just.

Vere quia dignum et iustum est
per christum dominum nostrum,

Qui nos ad noctem istam,

non tenebrarum sed luminis matrem
perducere dignatus est,
in qua exorta est ab inferis in eterna
die resurrectio mortuorum.

Solutis quippe nexibus et calcato
mortis aculeo

resurrexit a mortuis qui fuerat inter
mortuos liber.

Unde et nox ipsa sidereo pro ecclesiarum ornatu

cereorum splendore tamquam dies
illuminata collucet,
quia in eius matutino, resurgente
christo,
mors occidit redemptorum, et emersit uita credentium.

Vere tu pretiosus es opifex, formator es omnium,

cui qualitas in agendi non fuit officio, sed in sermonis imperio.

Qui ornatum atque habitum mundo,

nec ad ampliandum quasi inops potentie
nec ad ditandum quasi egenus glorie
condidisti.

Totus ac plenus in te es,

qui dum per uirginea uiscera mundo
illaberis,
uirginitatem etiam creature commendas.

Apes siquidem dum ore concipiunt
ore parturiunt,

casto corpore non fedo desiderio
copulantur.

Truly it is fitting and just
through Christ our Lord,

Who has deigned to lead us to this
night
not of shadows, but the mother of
light,
in which there has arisen from the
underworld into eternal day the
resurrection of the dead.

And surely having broken the bonds
and trodden down the sting of
death,
he arose from the dead who among
the dead had been free.

Wherefore also the same night by
the starry ornament of the
churches,
the splendor of candles, shines as
clear as the day,
for in his morning, with Christ arising,
the death of the redeemer is un-
done, and the life of believers
emerges.

Truly you are the precious maker,
you are the former of all
things,
whose nature was not in carrying
out a function, but in the
power of the word.

Who established the furnishing and
character for the world,
not as though without power to en-
large
nor to enrich as though lacking the
glory to enrich.

You are all and complete in your-
self,
who while you slip into the world
through a virgin womb,
yet you value the virginity of your
creature.

If indeed the bees, while they con-
ceive by mouth, so they give
birth by mouth;
it is with a chaste body, not from
foul desire, that they copulate.

TABLE 2. *Continued*

Denique uirginitatem seruantes, posteritatem generant;	Finally, preserving their virginity, they generate offspring;
sobole gaudent; matres dicuntur; intacte perdurant;	they are glad with progeny; they are called mothers; they remain untouched;
filios generant; et uiros non norunt.	they generate sons, and they do not know husbands.
Flore utuntur coniuge; flore funguntur genere;	They use the flower as a husband; with the flower they furnish offspring;
flore domos instruunt;	with the flower they build their houses;
flore diuitias conuehunt; flore ceram conficiunt.	with the flower they gather riches; with the flower they fashion wax.
O admirandus apium feruor! ad commune opus pacifica turba concurrunt et operantibus plurimis una augetur substantia.	O admirable ardor of the bees! For their common task they gather as a peaceful throng, and though many are working a single substance is increased.
O inuisibile artificium! primo culmina pro fundamentis edificant et tam ponderosam mellis sarcinam pendentibus domiciliis, imponere non uerentur.	O invisible skill! At first they build the summit to serve as foundations and then they do not fear to impose upon their hanging dwellings such a weighty load of honey.
O uirginitatis insignia que non possessori damna, sed sibi lucra conuectant;	O splendid examples of virginity who convey not harm to the possessor, but riches to themselves;
auferunt quidem predam, et cum preda minime tollunt peccatum.	they do indeed bear away the prize, and with the prize they take on no sin.
Spoliant quidem florum cutem et morsuum non annotant cicatricem.	They do indeed rob the surface of the flower, and impose no scar of the bites.
Sed inter hec que credimus huius cerei gratiam predicemus.	But among the things in which we believe, let us proclaim the favor of this candle.
Cuius odor suauis est et flamma hilaris;	Whose odor is sweet, and whose flame cheerful;
non tetro odore aruina desudat, sed iocundissima suauitate;	its fat does not exude a foul odor, but a most joyful sweetness.
qui peregrinis non inficitur pigmentis, sed illuminatur Spiritu Sancto.	which is not tainted by foreign colorings, but is illuminated by the Holy Spirit.

Qui ut accensus, proprias corporis
  compages depascit;
ita coagolatas lacrimas in riuulos
  fundit guttarum.

Quique semiusta membra ambroseo
  sanguine, flauea uena distollit

habitum bibit ignis humorem.

In huius autem cerei luminis corpore te omnipotens postulamus

ut superne benedictionis munus accommodes.

Ut si quis hunc sumpserit aduersus
  flabra uentorum,

aduersus spiritus procellarum,
sit ei domine singulare perfugium,

sit murus ab hoste fidelibus.

Saluum fac populum tuum Domine
  et benedic hereditatem tuam
ut redeuntes ad festiuitatem pasche,
per hec uisibilibus et inuisibilibus
  tuis inhiantes,
dum presentium usufruuntur

futurorum desideria accendantur.

Una cum beatissimo papa nostro il.

et famulo tuo pontifice nostro il.
sed et omnibus presbiteris diaconibus subdiaconibus
cunctoque clero uel plebe.

Memorare Domine famulum tuum
imperatorem nostrum il.
et principem nostrum il.
et eorum exercitum uniuersum,

Qui uiuis cum Patre et Spiritu
  Sancto
et regnas Deus in secula seculorum.
                                    Amen.

Which when it is lit feeds on the
  fabric of its own body,
thus weeps tears bound together in
  rivulets of drops.

And which disperses as a yellow
  vein the half-consumed portions
  as a divine blood,
as the flame absorbs the received
  fluid.

We pray you, however, almighty
  God, in the body of this candle-
  light
that you will grant the gift of supernal blessing.

That if anyone should take up this
  candle against the blasts of the
  winds,
against the breath of the hurricane,
let it be for him, Lord, a special
  refuge,
let it be a wall for the faithful
  against the enemy.

Save your people, Lord, and bless
  your heritage
that returning to the Paschal feast,
aspiring by these rites to your
  things visible and invisible,
while they benefit from things
  present
they may be inflamed with the desire of things to come.

Together with our most blessed
  pope *N*
and your servant our pontiff *N*
and with all priests, deacons, subdeacons,
and all the clergy and people.

Remember Lord your servant
our emperor *N*,
and our prince *N*,
and the whole of their armies,

you who live with the Father and
  the Holy Spirit
and reign, God for ages of ages.
                                    Amen.

TABLE 2. *Continued*

Preface (Franco-Roman Version)

Dominus uobiscum.	The Lord be with you.
Et cum spiritu tuo.	And with your spirit.
Sursum corda.	Lift up your hearts.
Habemus ad dominum.	We have [lifted them] to the Lord.
Gratias agamus domino Deo nostro.	Let us give thanks to the Lord our God.
Dignum est iustum est.	It is fitting and just.
Vere quia dignum et iustum est equum et salutare	It is truly fitting and just, right and wholesome,
Te inuisibilem deum patrem omnipotentem	to sing your praise, invisible God, father omnipotent,
filiumque tuum unigenitum	and your only-begotten Son,
dominum nostrum Iesum Christum	our Lord Jesus Christ,
toto cordis ac mentis affectu	with all the effort of heart and mind
et uocis ministerio personare.	and with the help of the voice.
Qui pro nobis tibi eterno patri Ade debitum soluit	Who for us repaid the debt of Adam to you, eternal father,
et ueteris piaculi cautionem pio cruore detersit.	and with his holy blood washed away the debt of old sin.
Hec sunt enim festa paschalia	For this is the Paschal feast
in quibus uerus ille agnus occiditur	in which he the true lamb is slain
eiusque sanguis postibus consecratur.	and whose blood is dedicated on the doorposts.
Hec nox est in qua primum patres nostros	This is the night on which first you caused our fathers,
filios Israhel eductos ex Egypto	the children of Israel being led out of Egypt,
rubrum mare sicco uestigio transire fecisti.	to cross the Red Sea with dry feet.
Hec igitur nox est que peccatorum tenebras	This therefore is the night which purged the shadows of sin
columne illuminatione purgauit.	with a column of light.
Hec nox est que hodie per uniuersum mundum in Christo credentes	This is the night which through all the world for those who believe in Christ,
a uitiis seculi segregatos et caligine peccatorum	who are separated from the vices of the world and the darkness of sin,
reddit gratie sociat sanctitati.	restores them today to grace and unites them to holiness.
Hec nox est in qua destructis uinculis mortis	This is the night in which, after destroying the bonds of death,
Christus ab inferis uictor ascendit.	Christ ascends a victor from the underworld.

Nichil enim nobis nasci profuit nisi redimi profuisset.	For it profits us nothing to be born unless we have benefited by being redeemed.
O mira circa nos tue pietatis digna- tio, o inestimabilis dilectio caritatis, ut seruum redimeres filium tradi- disti.	O wondrous honor of your tender- ness to us! O inestimable favor of charity that to redeem a servant you sacri- ficed a son!
O certe necessarium Ade peccatum quod Christi morte deletum est O felix culpa que talem ac tantum meruit habere redemptorem.	O certainly necessary sin of Adam's which is canceled by Christ's death! O happy blame which merited such and so much a redeemer!
O beata nox que sola meruit scire tempus et horam	O blessed night which alone was worthy to know the time and the hour
in qua Christus ab inferis resurrexit.	in which Christ arose from the under- world.
Hec nox est de qua scriptum est	This is the night of which it was written
"et nox ut dies illuminabitur," et "nox illuminatio mea in deliciis meis."	"and night shall be as bright as day" and "night shall be my light in my gladness."
Huius igitur sanctificatio noctis fu- gat scelera culpas lauat reddit innocentiam lap- sis mestis letitiam fugat odia	Therefore the blessedness of this night banishes misfortunes, washes away sins, restores innocence to the fallen, gladness to the sorrowful, puts ha- tred to flight,
concordiam parat et curuat imperia.	procures concord and subdues pow- ers.
In huius igitur noctis gratia suscipe sancte Pater incensi huius sacrificium uespertinum quod tibi in hac cerei oblatione sol- lemni per ministrorum manus	In the grace of this night, then, accept, Holy Father, the evening sacrifice of this flame, which, by the hands of its ministers in this solemn offering of the candle
de operibus apum sacrosancta reddit ecclesia.	from the work of the bees, your holy church offers up to you.
Sed iam columne huius preconia nouimus quam in honore Dei rutilans ignis accendit.	But we already know the praises of this column which the vivid flame ignites in honor of God.
Qui licet sit diuisus in partes	The flame which though it may be divided into parts,
mutuati tamen luminis detrimenta non nouit.	yet knows no diminution of the di- vided flame.

TABLE 2. *Continued*

Alitur liquantibus ceris quam in substantiam pretiose huius lampadis apes mater eduxit.	It is nourished by the melting waxes which mother bee fashioned into the substance of this precious lamp.
Apis ceteris que subiecta sunt hom- ini animantibus antecellit.	The bee surpasses all the other liv- ing things that are subject to man.
Cum sit enim minima corporis paruitate ingentes animos angusto uersat in pectore uiribus imbecillis sed fortis ingenio.	Though she be tiny in the smallness of her body, she revolves prodigious knowledge in her tiny breast, weak in force but forceful in abili- ties.
Hec explorata temporum uices cum canitiem pruisosam hiberna posuerint et glaciale senium uerni temporis moderata deterserint statim prodeundi ad laborem cura succedit.	She, having determined the change of season, when winter has deposited the hoary frost and then the moderating climate of springtime has swept away the glacial feebleness, she immediately feels the need to come forth to her work.
Disperseque per agros libratis pau- lulum pennis cruribus suspensis insidunt.	And scattered through the fields stretching their wings a little, they settle on their balanced legs.
Partim ore legentes flosculos onerate uictualibus suis ad castra remeant.	Part of them gather blossoms with their mouth and burdened with their provisions return to the hive.
Ibique alie inestimabili arte cellulas tenaci glutino instruunt; alie liquantia mella stipant; alie uertunt flores in ceram; alie ore natos fingunt; alie collectum e foliis nectar inclu- dunt.	And there others with inestimable skill construct cells with clinging glue; others press together the flowing honey; others turn flowers into wax; others mold the newborn with the mouth; others seal up the nectar collected from flowers.
O uere mirabilis apis cuius nec sexum masculi uiolant, fetus non quassat nec filii destruunt castitatem.	O truly marvelous bee, whose sex is not violated by the male, nor shattered by childbearing, nei- ther do children destroy her chastity.

Sicut sancta concepit uirgo Maria

uirgo peperit et uirgo permansit.

O uere beata nox que expoliauit
Egyptios ditauit Hebreos

nox in qua terrenis celestia iunguntur.

Oramus te Domine ut cereus iste
in honorem nominis tui consecratus

ad noctis huius caliginem destruendam indeficiens perseueret,

et in odorem suauitatis acceptus

supernis luminaribus misceatur.

Flammas eius lucifer matutinus
inueniat
ille inquam lucifer qui nescit occasum
ille qui regressus ab inferis

humano generi serenus illuxit.

Precamur ergo te Domine ut nos
famulos tuos
omnem clerum et deuotissimum
populum
una cum beatissimo papa nostro ill

et antistite nostro ill
et patre nostro ill
cum cuncta congregatione sibi commissa
presentis uite quiete concessa
in his paschalibus gaudiis conseruare
digneris.

Memento etiam domine famuli tui
imperatoris nostri ill
necnon et famuli tui principis nostri
ill
et celestem eis concede uictoriam
cum omni exercitu eorum.

Et his qui tibi offerunt hoc sacrificium laudis
premia eterna largiatis.

Just as holy Mary conceived as a
virgin,
gave birth as a virgin and remained
a virgin.

O truly blessed night, which de-
spoiled the Egyptians and enriched the Hebrews;
night in which celestial things are
joined to the earthly.

We pray you, Lord, that this candle
consecrated to the honor of your
name
may unfailingly persevere in the de-
struction of the gloom of this
night,
and received into the odor of sweet-
ness
may it be mixed with the lights of
heaven.

May the morning star find its flames
burning;
may that morning star, I say, that
knows no setting,
that serene star who, returned from
the underworld,
enlighten humankind.

We pray you therefore, Lord, for
us your servants,
all the clergy and the very devout
people
together with our most blessed pope
N
and our bishop N
and our father N
with all the congregation in his
charge
that granted peace in this life
you will deign to keep us in these
Paschal joys.

Remember also, Lord, your servant
our emperor N,
as well as your servant our prince N,

and grant them celestial victory
with all their army.

And on those who offer you this
sacrifice of praise
may you bestow eternal rewards.

TABLE 2. *Continued*

Per dominum nostrum Ieesum
    Christum filium tuum
qui tecum et cum Spiritu Sancto
    uiuit et regnat
Deus per omnia secula seculorum.
                                 Amen.
	Through our Lord Jesus Christ,
	    your son,
	who with you and with the Holy
	    Spirit lives and reigns,
	God for all the ages of ages.
	                                 Amen.

Translated by the author.

the vigil of Easter.[5] The seventh-century canonarium of Jerusalem cites a more developed (or perhaps better described) ceremonial, in which a triple candelabrum is lit in the Anastasis by the bishop, carried into the basilica, and then carried three times around the church in procession.[6] The imitation of Jerusalem custom is a likely source for bringing a lit candle into the principal church from elsewhere: it is known in most Latin liturgies: Old Spanish, Milanese, and Beneventan. Whereas the blessing of the Paschal candle may well be related at its origin to the more general and widespread practice, it is the particular Easter practice in the West that concerns us here.[7]

It is clear that the text for the blessing of the Paschal candle originated in two stages. In a first stage, the officiant (usually a deacon) blessed the candle following a general pattern of thanksgiving and praise of the night of Resurrection, of the candle itself, of the bees who made it, and so on. These blessings were developed in a variety of ways, of which several versions survive; they represent a period of individual composition or of improvisation. Only at a second stage were various versions of the text stabilized and fixed in writing so as to be repeated year after year.

In the fourth century, the practice of blessing the Paschal candle was known in northern Italy, in Spain, and presumably widely elsewhere as well, but not at Rome, where the practice, at least in the papal liturgy, was introduced substantially later.[8]

Saint Jerome himself had strong opinions about the Easter candle. In a letter written in 384, he replies to the deacon Praesidius of Piacenza, who had requested from Jerome a *praeconium paschale* for his own use.[9]

5. Conybeare, *Rituale Armenorum*, 522; see also Capelle, "La procession," 105.

6. These Jerusalem texts, from indirect Armenian and Georgian sources, are cited in Capelle, "La procession," 105–6.

7. The best summaries of the early history of the blessing of the Paschal candle remain Franz, *Die kirchlichen Benediktionen*, 1:519–53, and Benoît-Castelli, "Le praeconium paschale." Pinell, "La benediccio," provides almost all the early texts.

8. The practice of the Exultet at Rome is the subject of my forthcoming study "The Exultet at Rome."

9. The letter is attributed to Jerome by Morin in "Un écrit méconnu"; and, despite doubts going back as far as Erasmus, and voiced anew by Duchesne (*Le liber pontificalis*, 3:84), Morin continued to champion Jerome's authorship: see his *Études, textes, découvertes,*

Praesidius was evidently expected to produce a prayer every Easter; the text of the prayer was not fixed, and he was no doubt seeking the highest quality in appealing to Jerome. He probably did not expect such a strong and caustic reply.

Jerome did not like this kind of composition at all: it did not have the authority of scripture. Indeed, he did not approve of the use of candles: a Paschal candle was not blessed with a freely invented praeconium at Rome; moreover, there was no candle at all to bless. Composers of such prayers, says Jerome, borrow from pagan authors and adopt their rhetorical style: he particularly singles out with vehemence the praise of the bees, whose language is borrowed from Virgil. Jerome says that the praeconium paschale is a difficult matter and that no one has done it well so far; he has evidently heard (or seen) several unsuccessful versions. He refuses Praesidius' request for a written praeconium but agrees to help him orally.

In Ravenna, it was the bishop who sang the praeconium, to judge from a letter of 601, in which Pope Gregory the Great encourages the ailing Bishop Marinianus to avoid the exertions of the approaching Easter season, which for him would include the "prayers which are to be said over the candle in the church of Ravenna."[10]

In 633, the Council of Toledo noted that the Paschal candle was used in some churches and not in others and judged that it was a practice to be commended.[11]

21–22, and "La lettre"; on the history of the attribution of the letter, see Leclercq, "Pâques," cols. 1,569–70. Dekkers, *Clavis patrum*, at no. 621, p. 141, says "Valde dubium uidetur"; but at no. 633, p. 145, "omnino genuina." Lambert, *Bibliotheca Hieronymiana*, 1:1,074–77, no. 155, gives the manuscript tradition, the earliest witnesses being of the ninth century; he cites it also in 3:317, no. 318, and says (echoing Dekkers?) "omnino genuina." Rebenich, *Hieronymus und sein Kreis*, 170n182: "Die Authentizität des Briefes darf aber nunmehr als gesichert gelten." J. N. D. Kelly, *Jerome*, 111n24, sees the letter as authentic: "The whole tone, the underlying ideas, and the satiric cuts are all typical of Jerome, as is the style; many expressions found in it recur in acknowledged writings of this time." Most recently, de Vogüé, *Histoire littéraire*, discusses this letter in 1:216–33 and supports the authenticity. The letter itself is printed, among other places, in Schmidt, *Hebdomada sancta*, 2:629–33; Morin, "Pour l'authenticité," 54–58; *PL* 30: cols. 188–94. I am grateful to Paul Meyvaert for his assistance with this question.

10. "A vigiliis quoque temperandum est, sed et preces illae quae super cereum in Rauennati ciuitate dici solent uel expositiones evangelii, quae circa paschalem sollemnitatem a sacerdotibus fiunt, per alium dicantur" (Norberg, *S. Gregorii Magni registrum*, 2:892; also *MGH Epistolae 2*, 282–83).

11. "Lucerna & cereus in praevigiliis paschae apud quasquam ecclesias non benedicuntur & cur a nobis benedicantur, inquirunt. Propter gloriosum enim noctis ipsius sacramentum solenniter haec benedicimus. . . . Et quia haec observatis per multarum loca terrarum, regionesque Hispaniae, in ecclesiis commendatur, dignum est, ut propter unitatem pacis, in Gallicanis ecclesiis conservetur." Mansi, *Sacrorum conciliorum*, 10: col. 620; I have been unable to consult the more recent edition in Vives, *Concilios*.

First Stage: Individual Texts for the Blessing
of the Paschal Candle

Surviving texts for the blessing of the candle come from as early as the fifth century. Texts related to the blessing of the candle are listed below; they are mostly not directly related to the texts of southern Italy, but they demonstrate that the practice was widespread, with a freedom of invention that resulted in many surviving versions. The known early texts are the following:

1. Saint Augustine (354–430) quotes, in *De civitate Dei* (413–26), a passage from his own *laus cerei*, in hexameters.[12]
2. Ennodius, bishop of Pavia (d. 521), has left two lengthy formulas for blessing the candle; his emphatic, oratorical style shows the themes that recur throughout the history of the form, and he shows also, perhaps, the qualities that Jerome deplored in his letter ("oratorum clamor, florum pratorum descriptio").[13]
3. The hymn of Prudentius, *Inventor rutili*, which is called "de nouo lumine paschalis sabbati," a Vespers hymn that parallels the themes of the annual dedication of the Paschal candle, makes it clear that the praeconium was practiced in Spain as well in the fourth and fifth centuries.[14]
4. A text, preserved as a sermon attributed to Saint Augustine, is likely, as Pierre-Patrick Verbraken has argued, to be a north African blessing of the Paschal candle from around the time of Bishop Fulgentius of Ruspe (d. 533).[15]
5. A unique blessing (*contestata*) is found in a seventh-century Escorial manuscript (*Quam mirabilis sit ecclesiae catholicae pulcritudo*).[16]
6. The prayer *Deus mundi conditor*, perhaps of Roman origin, is used in the Gelasian sacramentary.[17]
7. The hymn *Ignis creator igneus*, found in the seventh-century antiphonary of Bangor (Milan, Bibl. Ambrosiana, MS C.5. inf, there labeled *Hymnus quando coeria* [usually printed as *cereum*] *benedicitur*) and in a tenth-century Bobbio manuscript (Turin, Bib. naz. MS G. v. 38, there labeled

12. "Quod in laude quadam Cerei breviter versibus dixi: Haec tua sunt, bona sunt, quia tu bona ista creasti. / Nil nostrum est in eis, nisi quo peccamus amantes / ordine neglecto pro te, quod conditor abs te." The text is widely reproduced: Augustinus, *De civitate*, ed. Hoffmann, 2:108; Schmidt, *Hebdomada sancta*, 2:627; Pinell, "La benediccio," 100.

13. Ennodius' two formulas for blessing the candle begin with the preface, presumably because the Exultet that preceded was already fixed. His texts are printed in Schmidt, *Hebdomada sancta*, 2:633–37, and Pinell, "La benediccio," 92–95, both based on Hartel, *Magni Felicis Ennodii opera omnia*, 415–22; also edited in Fredericus Vogel, *Magni Felicis Ennodii opera*, 18–20, 109–10. A praeconium skipping the Exultet and beginning with the preface is to be found also in a fragmentary leaf dating from about 800 (see n.79).

14. Franz, *Die kirchlichen Benediktionen*, 531; Pinell, "La benediccio," 4n3; the text is printed in Bergman, *Aurelii Prudentii Clementis carmina*, 25–31; also in *PL* 59: cols. 813–831.

15. Verbraken, "Une 'laus cerei' "; the text is printed there, 303–6; also in *PL* 46: cols. 817–21.

16. Edited in Pinell, "La benediccio," 97–100; Mercati, *Un frammento*, 40–43.

17. See pp. 60–61.

as *Ymnus in Sabato sanctum ad cereum benedicere*),[18] is a blessing of the Paschal candle, influenced in its language by the Gelasian *Deus mundi conditor* and likely composed at Bobbio, where the Gelasian blessing was surely in circulation by the early seventh century.[19]

8. A *carmen de cereo paschale* by the ninth-century Drepanius (Florus of Lyons)[20] is modeled on older texts and gives evidence of the pervasive influence of the ceremonies and the language of the Easter vigil, but it is a later reflection of the earlier texts.[21]

9. Guillaume Durand, bishop of Mende, refers to a composition by a certain Peter, a deacon of Montecassino, no longer in use.[22] This text apparently does not survive, unless, of course, it refers to the Beneventan Exultet.

10. A twelfth-century text was used in Reims and Besançon for the blessing of a candle at Pentecost on the analogy of the Paschal candle. This is an adaptation of the Franco-Roman text of the Exultet and need not concern us here.[23]

Second Stage: Single Texts in Western Liturgies

The various Western liturgies have preserved single texts for the blessing of the Paschal candle. The later practice of using a fixed text seems to date from the seventh or eighth century, when Old Spanish, Milanese, Beneventan, and Gallican liturgies developed individual ways of blessing the Paschal candle.

OLD SPANISH

The Old Spanish liturgy sets itself apart from the others in that it does not use the opening text "Exultet iam angelica," which is shared alike by the Beneventan, Gallican ("Roman"), and Milanese blessings. Old Spanish sources provide a blessing of fire and a blessing of the candle itself,

18. Printed, from Bangor, in Warren, *The Antiphonary of Bangor*, 2:11; *Analecta hymnica*, 51:296; Mercati, *Un frammento*, 25–27; Pinell, "La benediccià," 101–2; from both MSS, in Walpole, *Early Latin Hymns*, 346–49.

19. Chavasse, *Le sacramentaire gélasien*, 687–89; for a discussion of the hymn and its sources, see Curran, *The Antiphonary of Bangor*, 59–65, and notes, pp. 216–19.

20. Dreves (in *Analecta hymnica* 50:210) suggests that Drepanius is the mid-ninth-century Florus, a deacon of the church of Lyons; the hymn is printed in *Analecta hymnica* 50:217–18, *PL* 61: cols. 1,087–88.

21. For a significant collection of texts relating to the blessing of fire and of candles, and in some cases to the Easter vigil, see Pinell, "Vestigis del lucernari," and the supplementary texts in his "La benediccià," 101–7.

22. "Subsequenter benedicitur cereus ex institutione Zozimi, et Theodiro primi Papae: sed beatus Ambros. benedictionem dictavit; quanquam Augu. et Petrus diaconus Cassinensis monachus, alias benedictiones dictaverunt, quae in usu non sunt" (Durandus, *Rationale*, bk. 6, chap. 80; Schmidt, *Hebdomada sancta*, 2:628). Durand might be referring to the eminent twelfth-century librarian of Montecassino Peter the Deacon, author and falsifier. On Peter the Deacon, see Bloch, "Der Autor," 61–66; Meyvaert, "The Autographs"; Caspar, *Petrus diaconus*, esp. 19–21; and the introduction to Rodgers, *Petri diaconi ortus*.

23. On this interesting phenomenon, see Strittmatter, "The Pentecost Exultet," where the text is edited.

each in the prolix style of the Old Spanish liturgy; in the tenth-century antiphoner of Léon the two portions are labeled *Benedictio lucerne ante altare* and *Benedictio cerei*.[24] Both Pinell and Bernal have shown these two prayers to be a single unit.[25] The language is unique, but many usual points are touched on: the unworthiness of the deacon who sings; the special character of this night; the fabrication of the candle from wax made by bees whose virginity is lauded; the citation of ecclesiastical and secular authorities. The author of the Old Spanish texts—who may even have been Saint Isidore—seems to have been inspired both by the Milanese text and by those of Ennodius.[26]

MILANESE

The praeconium that survives in the Milanese liturgy shares the *Exultet* prologue with the Beneventan and Franco-Roman texts. The Milanese version is attested only from the tenth century, in the sacramentary of Bergamo.[27] However, it must not be much more recent than the fifth or sixth century, since it observes the rules of the metrical cursus.[28] It was in use by the beginning of the seventh, if Cardinal Mercati is right in thinking that Ennodius was inspired by the Ambrosian formula.[29] The Milanese version, perhaps not as successful a literary composition as the Franco-Roman Exultet, contributes information to the question of the author of the Exultet. The Franco-Roman Exultet must not be the work of Saint Ambrose (as is sometimes suggested), for, as Huglo asks, why would Milan, the zealous guardian of Ambrose's hymns, preserve another, arguably inferior, product if Ambrose himself had composed the text we now call Roman?[30]

Two other liturgical traditions also employ the *Exultet*, each appending a different second section, or "preface." These are the Beneventan and the Franco-Roman versions, and each will deserve special attention here. But first we should consider a stylistic feature of both texts—a feature that is important to both the time of its origin and the understanding of its musical settings.

24. Bernal, "La 'laus cerei,' " 317n1.
25. Pinell, "La benediccò," 108–19 gives a careful edition of relevant Old Spanish texts for the Easter vigil; the texts are also presented and discussed in Bernal, "La 'laus cerei.' " Schmidt, *Hebdomada sancta*, 2:648–50, has only two selected texts from the larger Old Spanish complex.
26. Bernal, "La 'laus cerei,' " 339–45.
27. Cagin, *Codex sacramentorum*, 65.
28. On the metrical cursus, see pp. 45–50. The Milanese Exultet is printed in Pinell, "La benediccò," 90–92, from Magistretti, *Manuale* 2:199–202; in Schmidt, *Hebdomada sancta*, 2:645–47, from Pamelius' 1571 edition; in Heiming, *Corpus Ambrosianus*, 110–12; and in Cagin, *Codex sacramentorum*, 65, from the tenth-century sacramentary of Bergamo; a critical edition is Suñol, "Versione critica."
29. Mercati, *Un frammento*, 6.
30. Huglo, "L'auteur," 86.

The Cursus in the Texts of the Beneventan and Franco-Roman Exultet

The texts of the Roman and the Beneventan Exultet are written in a prose that uses euphonious cadences at the ends of textual periods.[31] The term *cursus* applied to these endings is usually used to describe medieval Latin texts (most often of the twelfth century and later) in which sentences and clauses end in one of a small group of accentual rhythmic patterns. The term *cursus* came into regular use with the rhetoricians of the twelfth century, who in reviving the use of rhythmic prose summarized the many metrical quantitative endings into three basic cursus, which they called *planus, tardus,* and *uelox.*

After scholars had discovered the cursus, they realized that such rhythmical clauses had been employed already in late antiquity and that they had originated in metrical patterns (*clausulae*) that had been in use in classical prose both Greek and Latin. In reference to the Middle Ages the terms *metrical* and *rhythmical* are usually kept distinct, the former referring to accentual and the latter to quantitative forms. The Exultet, coming at a time when quantitative forms were giving way to accentual, has aspects of both.

From prose stylists such as Cicero and Quintilian we know that from classical times writers and speakers of elevated prose sought to end periods with a suitably dignified close (*clausula*). For this they employed cadences carefully constructed to provide suitable closing metrical patterns, using the principles also important in metrical poetry.

These cadences were based on principles of quantity. Each syllable has a quantity, either long or short, and thus a succession of syllables provided a specific pattern of lengths according to the quantities of the constituent syllables. Put very simply, syllables may be long by nature when their vowel is a long vowel; they may be long by position when their vowel is followed by two consonants; in other cases they are short. Cadences conclude with a word of three or four syllables preceded by a word of two or more syllables. The relation of the accents of these words to the quantities of their syllables produces the variety of rhythms of the classical cursus. The features most readily noticeable in the cursus are the closure on a word of three or four syllables[32] and the regular placement of a long syllable before the final accent in many versions of the cursus.

---

31. The summary that follows is based on the following sources among others. The reader is referred to them and to their bibliographies for further and more detailed studies of the cursus. Janson, *Prose Rhythm;* Nicolau, *L'origine du 'cursus' rhythmique;* Mocquereau, "Le cursus"; Leclercq, "Cursus"; Ferretti, *Il cursus;* di Capua, "Il ritmo nella prosa liturgica"; I am also indebted to Professor Jan Ziolkowsky for his advice, and to Professor John Boe for making available to me a preliminary version of his summary of the use of the cursus in the preface, forthcoming in *Beneventanum troporum corpus* (Madison, Wisc.).

32. Or its equivalent; a three-syllable word with a closely related monosyllable may be used in the place of a word of four syllables.

The rhythms of the metrical cursus were used in liturgical and ec-clesiastical Latin from the fourth century until some time in the seventh; thus many of the prayers and prefaces found in the Leonine and Gelasian sacramentaries, along with contemporaneous composition in rhythmical prose such as the Exultet, display the cadenced rhythms that came to be called the cursus.

During these same centuries, Latin usage made the gradual but very important shift from metrical to accentual usage. Words had always borne accents, but the use of quantity in pronunciation and composition gave way to the emphasis on accent to provide patterned structures in verse and prose. In liturgical pieces of rhythmic prose composed after the early sev-enth century, metrical matters are often disregarded and the accentual pattern alone is retained.

The three cadences of the medieval theorists (planus, tardus, and uelox) are all accentual, but they arise from patterns originally quantita-tive. A fourth cadence, used less frequently than the others, was called *trispondaïque* by André Mocquereau, a term adopted also by Leclercq.

Table 3 gives a selection of the principal forms of the rhythmic cur-sus as found in the liturgical language of the earlier Middle Ages. These are arranged to show their rhythmic patterns; the accentual patterns of the same endings are also shown, and these accentual patterns are labeled with the names assigned them by the twelfth-century theorists. Many theorists of the cursus arrange patterns based on the many possible combinations of metrical feet: an arrangement suitable for study of classical language but highly complex and requiring a command of metrics that is beyond our purpose here. There are of course many more possible combinations than are shown here, but these patterns account for a large proportion of the cadential patterns in metrical cursus of liturgical medieval Latin, and in particular of the Exultet.

Planus, tardus, and uelox describe practically all the final cadences in the Roman and Beneventan texts of the Exultet. These final cadences are given in Tables 4 and 5, which tabulate all the cadences of these texts of the Exultet. The accentual patterns are those later identified as cursus planus, uelox, or tardus. Moreover, the frequent use of the same quan-tities, especially for the cursus planus, suggests that both Exultets were composed in places and times in which quantitative metrical prose was regularly composed. If both were composed before 700 and probably be-fore 650, when this kind of writing with quantitative elements disap-peared, then it is unlikely that the "Beneventan" Exultet is a composition of the southern Lombards after their conversion to Catholicism. It may have been imported from Milan or from an area, perhaps related to Rome, where such texts may have been in use for a long time.

There appears to be a fondness in the Beneventan Exultet for an unusual form of the cursus planus, using exclusively long syllables; further study of south Italian texts might indicate that this is a regional charac-teristic. A cadence ending in a two-syllable word is used twice in the Beneventan Exultet; it was known to Cicero but was generally avoided by

TABLE 3. Principal metrical forms of the cursus

Syllables	Accentual pattern	Medieval name of pattern
Final word of three syllables accented on penult		
- ˘ | - - ˘ turba ce- lo- rum	/ . | . / .	cursus planus
Final word of four syllables		
Accented on penult		
- ˘ ˘ | - ˘ - ˘ secula seculorum	/ . . | . . / .	cursus uelox
- ˘ - | - ˘ - ˘ sociat sanctitate	/ . . | . . / .	cursus uelox
˘ ˘ - | - ˘ - ˘ [precibus consequamur]	/ . . | . . / .	cursus uelox; this form is not found in the Exultet
- ˘ | ˘ ˘ - ˘ [nostra cumulentur]	/ . | . . / .	cursus trispondaicus; this form is not found in the Exultet
- - | - ˘ - ˘ redimi profuisset	/ . | . . / .	cursus trispondaicus
- ˘ | ˘ - - ˘ habere redemptorem	/ . | . . / .	cursus trispondaicus
Accented on antepenult		
- ˘ | - ˘ ˘ ˘ implere pre-ci-pi-at	/ . | . / . .	cursus tardus
- ˘ | - - ˘ ˘ di-vi-na mi-ste-ri-a	/ . | . / . .	cursus tardus

Note: This table arranges verbal cadences according to the patterns most frequently found in the rhythmic prose of the Middle Ages. Metrical patterns indicate long and short syllables (ˉ ˘) and at the ends of the cadences indicate the presence of a *syllaba anceps* (˘), a syllable that may be indifferently long or short. Breaks between words are indicated with a vertical line. Beside each cadence is its accentual pattern, showing accented (/) and unaccented (.) syllables, and the medieval name of this accentual pattern.

medieval writers of elevated prose. This cadence, which has the same rhythm as the cursus planus, may have been acceptable or desirable at Benevento.

Many interior cadences of both Exultets are made according to the cursus; in particular, the prologue of the Exultet uses the cursus in essentially each of its smaller members. The tables here are presented only to indicate the regular presence of the metrical forms of the cursus, not to

TABLE 4. Cadences in the Franco-Roman Exultet

Cursus planus / . | . / .

¯ ˘ | ¯ ¯ ˘

cruore detersit
transire fecisti
illuminatione purgauit
uictor ascendit
morte deletum est [elision of
    final two syllables]
ignis accendit
detrimenta non nouit
mater eduxit
cura succedit

nectar includunt
uirgo permansit ["uirgo" by
    permission]
serenus illuxit
conseruare digneris

¯ ¯ | ¯ ¯ ˘

suspensis insidunt

¯ ˘ | ˘ ¯ ˘

aula resultet

Cursus tardus / . | . / . .

¯ ˘ | ¯ ¯ ˘ ˘

reddit ecclesia
fortis ingenio
amisisse caliginem

¯ ˘ | ¯ ˘ ˘ ˘

curuat imperia
implere precipiat

Cursus uelox / . . | . . / .

¯ ˘ ˘ | ¯ ˘ ¯ ˘

misericordiam inuocate
animantibus antecellit
secula seculorum

¯ ˘ ¯ | ˘ ¯ ¯ ˘

intonet salutaris
inferis resurrexit

¯ ˘ ¯ | ¯ ˘ ˘ ˘

sociat sanctitate
filium tradidisti
destruunt castitatem
redimi profuisset
luminaribus misceatur
postibus consecratur

˘ ˘ ¯ | ¯ ˘ ˘ ˘

ministerio personare

Cursus trispondaicus / . | . . / .

¯ ˘ | ˘ ¯ ¯ ˘

habere redemptorem

Exceptional Cadences

¯ ˘ ˘ ¯ | ¯ ˘

deliciis meis [biblical quotation]

¯ ˘ | ˘ ˘ ˘

castra remeant

¯ ˘ ˘ | ¯ ¯ ˘

celestia iunguntur [trisponda-
    icus except for word break]

Note: This table lists all the main *clausulae* of the Franco-Roman text of the Exultet. The clausulae are arranged according to their accentual patterns (planus, tardus, uelox, trispondaicus) and within these groupings according to their quantitative patterns. Symbols: ¯ = long; ˘ = short; = *syllaba anceps* (long or short); / = accented; . = unaccented.

48

TABLE 5. Cadences in the Beneventan Exultet

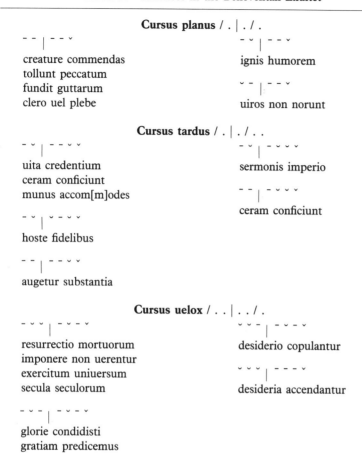

Cursus planus / . | . / .

creature commendas
tollunt peccatum
fundit guttarum
clero uel plebe

ignis humorem

uiros non norunt

Cursus tardus / . | . / . .

uita credentium
ceram conficiunt
munus accom[m]odes

sermonis imperio

ceram conficiunt

hoste fidelibus

augetur substantia

Cursus uelox / . . | . . / .

resurrectio mortuorum
imponere non uerentur
exercitum uniuersum
secula seculorum

desiderio copulantur

desideria accendantur

glorie condidisti
gratiam predicemus

Exceptional Cadence

Same rhythm as planus, and known to Cicero and Quintilian, but usually avoided in liturgical language; a two-syllable final word is not really part of the medieval cursus.

mortuos liber
spiritu sancto

Note: This table lists all the main *clausulae* in the second portion (preface) of the Beneventan version of the Exultet. (The prologue of the Beneventan Exultet is identical with that of the Franco-Roman version, and its cadences are included in Table 4.) The clausulae are arranged according to their accentual patterns (planus, tardus, uelox, trispondaicus) and within these groupings according to their quantitative patterns. Symbols: ‾ = long; ˘ = short; ˅ = *syllaba anceps* (long or short); / = accented; . = unaccented.

provide an exhaustive study of the rhythms of these texts. As we shall see in chapter 4, the musical settings of these texts do not follow the quantities, or all the accentual patterns, of the cursus, suggesting that the extant musical settings date from a time when quantity was no longer observed and accent was the governing feature of musical declamation.

Origin and Author of the Exultet

Medieval tradition ascribes the Exultet variously to Augustine of Hippo, Ambrose of Milan, Jerome, and others, but the composite nature of the Exultet suggests a more complex origin. Klaus Gamber, noting that the eucharistic prayer in the Missale Gothicum seemed to him very early and perhaps from Africa, was led to wonder whether the Mass books of this type (which include the earliest examples of the Exultet) might be, at least in part, of African origin.[33] This might give new significance to the rubrics found in these books (Gothicum, Gallicanum vetus, Bobbio) attributing the Exultet to Saint Augustine: "Incipit benedictio caerae beati augustini episcopi quam adhuc diaconus cum esset edidit et cecinnit feliciter."[34]

It may be this attribution to Saint Augustine, or the fact that Saint Augustine was known to have composed a *laus cerei,* that gave impetus to a tradition, going back at least to the late ninth century, that asserts his authorship of the version which, revised by Saint Jerome (who saw to the removal of the pagan Virgilian bees), was then sung throughout the church. As the author of the so-called pontifical of Poitiers puts it:

> Vsum benedicendi cereum a beato Augustino repertum tradit eclesia. Qui benedictionem illius perficiens a sancto Hieronimo reprehensus est, cur virgiliaca verba inseruerit. Sed sicut ab eodem beato Hieronimo emendata tunc fuit, ita nunc per eclesias canitur.[35]

Another tradition, as we have seen, attributes the authorship of the Exultet to Ambrose of Milan. Both Honorius[36] in the twelfth century and Durandus[37] in the thirteenth ascribe it to Ambrose. More recently,

---

33. Gamber, *Sacramentartypen,* 13.

34. Mohlberg, Eizenhöfer, and Siffrin, *Missale Gallicanum vetus,* 35; slightly different readings in Lowe, *The Bobbio Missal,* 69, and Mohlberg, *Missale Gothicum,* 59. See Appendix 2.

35. Paris, Bibl. de l'Arsenal 227, s9ex; Aldo Martini, *Il cosiddetto pontificale,* 218–19; See Schmidt, *Hebdomada sancta,* 2:628, and Franz, *Die kirchlichen Benediktionen,* 1:533–54.

36. "Cereum benedici Sozimus papa constituit, sed Ambrosius episcopus benedictionem composuit" (Honorius, *Gemma animae,* bk. 3, chap. 102; *PL* 17: col. 668; see also Schmidt, *Hebdomada sancta,* 2:628).

37. See n. 22.

Bernard Capelle too argued for Saint Ambrose as the author,[38] on the basis
of the language used; but others, notably Bonifatius Fischer and Michel
Huglo, have argued convincingly against this. Fischer argues that the author of the Roman Exultet is a rhetorically trained and oriented ecclesi-
astic, writing not much after 600.[39] The clausulae—the cadences at the
ends of phrases and sentences—are carefully controlled, but they are
quantitative in the opening portion and increasingly accentual as the text
proceeds.[40] In addition, the author (unlike Ambrose) uses exclusively the
cursus planus, tardus, and velox, about equally mixed at the beginning but
later increasingly oriented toward the cursus tardus.

The Franco-Roman preface draws on a variety of sources. The praise
of the bees and of their virginity generally borrows ideas from Virgil's
Georgics and in some cases borrows Virgil's language and vocabulary.[41]
Some examples:

VIRGIL: ingentis animos angusto in pectore uersant (*Georgics* IV.83)
EXULTET: ingentes animos angusto uersat in pectore

VIRGIL: aliae, spem gentis, adultos educunt fetus; aliae purissima mella stipant, et liquido distendunt nectare cellas. (*Georgics,* IV.162–64)
EXULTET: alie inestimabile arte cellulas tenaci glutino instruunt, alie liquantia mella stipant, alie ore natos fingunt.

The special praise of the Easter night is not unique to the Exultet and
can be found widely in sermons. But perhaps the words of Asterios the
Sophist, writing in the third or fourth century, gives a clear indication of
the spirit in which the Exultet was composed: his praise of the Easter night
gives special emphasis to the newly baptized, it uses many vivid images,
and, like the Exultet, it repeats the invocation "O night" (ὦ νύξ).[42]

The second portion—the preface—of the Franco-Roman Exultet
quotes the book of Psalms, in versions that convince Huglo the author was
Frankish, not Italian.[43] Further evidence for a Gallican origin includes the

38. Capelle, "L'Exultet pascal"; in addition to many stylistic traits, he points out
(p. 230) the passage in Ambrose's *Expositio in Lucam* ("non prodesset nasci nisi redimi
profuisset") closely paralleled in the Exultet ("nihil enim nobis nasci profuit nisi redemi
profuisset").

39. Fischer, "Ambrosius der Verfasser," esp. 73–74.

40. Fischer, 64; on the cursus in the Franco-Roman Exultet, see *PM* 4:171–85; di
Capua, "Il ritmo nella prosa liturgica"; Ferretti, *Il cursus metrico,* esp. 195–200.

41. A convenient comparison is available in Capelle, "L'Exultet pascal," 233–35.

42. Auf der Maur, "Eine Vorform."

43. These quotations, from Psalm 138, verses 12 and 11, use versions of the psalm
text that are revealing. The passage "et nox illuminatio" (omitting "mea," as the Missale
Gothicum and Angoulême do) is as in Greek and is maintained in African and some Gallican
psalters. (The "mea" might well have been put back in by later sources to harmonize with
Psalm 26:1). The passage "et nox ut dies" might have been "sicut dies," as in the Roman
psalter, or "tamquam dies," as in African psalters. Apparently the quoter of this psalm is
a Frank; see Huglo, "L'auteur," 84–85.

considerable use in the Exultet of liturgical language commonly found in the Gallican liturgy. Huglo points out that the opening of the preface portion in the oldest sources presents the Gallican form "Dignum est iustum est" (the Roman form always begins "Vere dignum est iustum").[44] In the Missale Gothicum of the early eighth century, and the Missale Gallicanum vetus of the second half of the eighth century, the form is "Dignum et iustum est, vere quia dignum et iustum est"; the Bobbio missal, also of the eighth century, uses "Dignum et iustum est," as does the Ambrosian preface. The two texts of Ennodius also begin "Dignum et iustum est, vere dignum et iustum est."[45]

The longer original opening ("Dignum et iustum est, uere quia dignum et iustum est") is shortened in some Gelasian sacramentaries of the eighth century by skipping the first four words;[46] others precede the abbreviated form "Vere quia dignum et iustum est" with the abbreviation sign VD;[47] in later sources, to accommodate the Exultet to the more usual Roman form, the unusual "quia" is dropped as well, resulting finally in a normal-looking (for the Roman liturgy) "Vere dignum et iustum est." The Roman text as it is received in southern Italy, however, begins this portion with "Vere quia dignum et iustum est," indicating that it arrived at a date later than the eighth-century changes just discussed.[48]

The composition of the Exultet has two stages: the prologue is much older than the preface. The prologue—the opening *Exultet* up to the preface—was perhaps created in the fourth or fifth century. It may well have been known to Ennodius in the sixth century (his texts begin with the preface, presumably because the *Exultet* that preceded was already fixed),[49] and it entered a variety of liturgies—Franco-Roman, Ambrosian, Beneventan—at a date before these composed their various versions of the preface.

44. On the authentic Gallican quality of this text, and for this argument in general, see Huglo, "L'auteur," 80–81; Huglo points out that the Masses of Mone always start their *Contestatio* with "Dignum et iustum est," as does the Old Spanish *Inlatio;* and that forty-four of sixty-nine prefaces in the Missale Gothicum begin in the same way.

45. Mohlberg, *Missale Gothicum,* 60; Mohlberg, *Missale Gallicanum vetus,* 35; Lowe, *The Bobbio Missal,* 69; the Ambrosian preface can be found in Pinell, "La benediccciò," 92–94.

46. St. Gall 348 (Mohlberg, *Das fränkische,* 81); Fulda (Richter and Schönfelder, *Sacramentarium Fuldense,* 84).

47. Berlin, Deutsche Staatsbibliothek MS lat. 105, *olim* Phillipps 1667 (Heiming, *Liber sacramentorum,* 62); the Rheinau sacramentary (Hänggi and Schönherr, *Sacramentarium Rheinaugense,* 131); and Ordo Romanus 25, from Wolfenbüttel, Herzog August Bibliothek MS 4175 (Andrieu, *Les ordines,* 3:305).

48. Ernst Kantorowicz has pointed out that Petrus de Vinea and members of the Capuan school of epistolary style (s11–12) often borrowed from the language of the Exultet in letters that have such beginnings as "Exultet universa turba fidelium" and "Exultet iam Romanum imperium" (Kantorowicz, "A Norman Finale," 134n18). These borrowings, of course, do not imply the presence of the Franco-Roman Exultet text at the time, since the prologue of the Beneventan Exultet uses the same opening.

49. A praeconium skipping the Exultet and beginning with the preface is to be found also in a fragmentary leaf from about 800 (see n. 79).

As for the preface portion, the evidence of some quotations suggests that it was composed before the end of the sixth century. The preface of the Exultet is quoted in a sermon sometimes attributed to Saint Augustine (although perhaps dating from the sixth century); this sermon helps to date the Exultet itself (presuming that the quotation is not in the other direction), which must thus not be much later than 600.[50] The Exultet's preface is also quoted in two Gallican Masses, for Friday in Easter Week and for Holy Saturday;[51] if these passages quote the Exultet, and not the other way around, then the preface may well have had its text fixed at least by 585, when the second Council of Mâcon prescribed attendance at Masses of Easter Week. The council does not specify Mass texts, but there must have been specific Masses if the council wanted them attended. These Gallican Masses seem likely to be the texts said at least from 585; quoting a fixed Exultet from the previous week, they provide echoes of the Easter vigil during the week that follows.[52]

The Beneventan Text of the Exultet

The Beneventan text of the Exultet, like the Milanese, is known only from the tenth century. It is the oldest surviving text from southern Italy for blessing the Paschal candle, though it was replaced by the gradual adoption of the Franco-Roman text. This liturgical change may have begun as early as the eighth century, but no Franco-Roman Exultet survived from before the eleventh. The Beneventan text is preserved in relatively few documents,[53] probably because of the suppression of the Beneventan liturgy in the course of the eleventh century and the replacement of the Beneventan text with the Roman. A number of undoubtedly Beneventan

50. The sermon includes "Ipse est etiam vitulus qui pro nobis in ara crucis deo patri oblatus, humani generis debitum solvit, et antiqui facinoris cautionem pio cruore delevit" (quoted in Fischer, "Ambrosius der Verfasser," 73); compare the Exultet: "Qui pro nobis eterno patri ade debitum soluit, et ueteris piaculi cautionem pio cruore detersit."

51. The *Contestatio* for Friday of Easter contains this passage: "[in missa quinta feria] O mira circa nos pietatis tuae dignacio. O ineffabilis dilectio caritatis: ut servos redimeres, filium tradidisti. O certe necessarium Adae peccatum, quod Christi morte[m] deletum est. O fidelem culpam, que talem ac tantum meruit habere redemptorem" (Mohlberg, *Missale Gallicanum vetus*, 49); the same passage with variants is in the Missale gothicum (Mohlberg, *Missale Gothicum*, 77, sexta feria); compare the Exultet: "O mira circa nos tue pietatis dignatio; O inestimabilis dilectio caritatis, ut seruum redimeres filium tradidisti. O certe necessarium ade peccatum quod christi morte deletum est. O felix culpa que talem ac tantum meruit habere redemptorem." The *Contestatio* for Holy Saturday includes this: "O vere beata nox, quae sola meruit scire tempus et hora[m], qua Christus resurrexit, de qua iam in psalmo fuerat prophetatum: Quia nox ut dies inluminabitur" (Mohlberg, *Missale Gothicum*, 69); compare the Exultet: "O beata nox que sola meruit scire tempus et horam in qua christus ab inferis resurrexit. Hec nox est de qua scriptum est, Et nox ut dies illumunabitur."

52. Clercq, *Concilia*, 240; Mansi, *Sacrorum conciliorum*, 9: cols. 950–51; see Huglo, "L'auteur," 83; note that Gamber, "Älteste Eucharistiegebete," feels that the borrowing may have been in the other direction.

53. See the edition in Appendix 2.

Exultets now preserve only the opening portion, the *Exultet* prologue, replacing the rest with the Franco-Roman continuation. The opening is still useful, but the Beneventan part of the text is discarded.[54]

Sources and Origin of the Beneventan Text

The age of the Beneventan Exultet is not entirely easy to determine. The Beneventan liturgy, as an independent and organized rite, is itself probably no older than the seventh century. The Lombards of the south, like their kinsmen in the north, were Arians before the seventh century, and indeed Lombard paganism still survived at Benevento at the time of Bishop Saint Barbatus in the 670s.[55] The Exultet in its Beneventan version might date only from the seventh or eighth century, and yet the text of the Beneventan Exultet must be older. Not only does it employ the cursus in both portions of its text, suggesting that it was composed probably by about 650, but also it has relationships with two other texts that bear on its date.

1. The Beneventan Exultet shares textual material with one of the blessings of Ennodius of Pavia (d. 521);[56] there may be a Lombard connection here, Pavia being the capital of the Lombard kingdom in Italy until its fall to Charlemagne in 774.
2. Dom C. Coebergh has pointed out that the Beneventan Exultet shares some passages with the Old Spanish sacramentary and shares another passage both with the Old Spanish sacramentary and with the Verona sacramentary (known as the "Leonine" sacramentary) written in the seventh century.[57] The many Roman

54. This is true, for example, of the Exultet rolls Mirabella Eclano 1, Vat. lat. 3784, and the lower script of Bari 2.

55. See Kelly, *TBC*, 7–9.

56. Ennodius' first *Benedictio cerei* includes this passage: "in huius autem cerei luminis corpore te, domine, postulamus, ut supernae benedictionis munus adcomodes et, si quis hinc sumpserit adversus flabra ventorum, adversus spiritus procellarum tua iussa faciens, sit illi singulare perfugium, sit murus ab hoste fidelibus" (Schmidt, *Hebdomada sancta*, 2:635); the Beneventan text cites this passage almost exactly: "In huius autem cerei luminis corpore te omnipotens postulamus ut superne benedictionis munus accommodes; ut si quis hinc sumpserit aduersus flabra uentorum aduersus spiritus procellarum sit ei domine singulare perfugium, sit murus ab hoste fidelibus" (see Appendix 2).

57. Coebergh, "Sacramentaire léonien," 301–4. The following passage of the Beneventan Exultet ("quia in eius matutino resurgente Christo mors occidit redemptorum et emersit uita credentium") is similar to the Holy Saturday *Inlatio* of the ninth-century Mozarabic sacramentary Toledo 35.3: "In cuius matutinis resurgente Christo mors occidit delictorum et exorta est uita credentium" (edition in Férotin, *Le liber mozarabicus sacramentorum*, col. 250); a version of this passage is found in the "Leonine" sacramentary (Verona, Bibl. capitolare LXXXV [80]) in a preface for the month of October: "Uere dignum: in cuius resurrectione mirabili mors occidit redemptorum, et orta est uita credentium. Et ideo cum angelis . . ." (Mohlberg, Eizenhöfer, and Siffrin, *Sacramentarium Veronense*, 143). Another passage is shared by the Beneventan Exultet ("qui nos ad noctem istam non tene-

borrowings in the Old Spanish liturgy must have their origins in individual Roman Mass libelli that survive only in part among Masses gathered in the Verona sacramentary. The maker of the Beneventan Exultet must have borrowed from similar sources, at a period when these prefaces were still in use and in circulation; if they traveled to Spain via southern Gaul to be received and adapted in Spain in the sixth and seventh centuries,[58] one might posit a similar age for the Beneventan Exultet, borrowing from the same Roman sources.

Is the Beneventan Exultet itself originally a Roman text? The Verona sacramentary is fragmentary, a somewhat haphazard collection of Mass texts. Now incomplete, it starts only in mid-April, and so it does not contain texts for Holy Saturday. The Beneventan Exultet might itself be one of the many texts once in use in Rome but not preserved in the incomplete Verona sacramentary and otherwise fallen into disuse. This idea is to be rejected, however, for at least two reasons. First, the blessing of the candle is an importation to Rome, adopted only gradually in the course of the seventh century and at first using the prayer *Deus mundi conditor*.[59] Such a prayer would be an unlikely element in the seventh-century Verona sacramentary. Second, even if some earlier form of the Verona sacramentary—or the rites it represents—had included a blessing of the Paschal candle that was borrowed by the Beneventan rite, then this text would hardly be quoted elsewhere in the same sacramentary, and the Spanish liturgy would not have needed to assemble its Holy Saturday *Inlatio* from a variety of other Roman sources if this complete version were already available for adoption or adaptation. The Beneventan Exultet, though it draws on Roman sources, is not itself a Roman product.

The Roman source for these shared passages, though not a blessing of the Paschal candle, may have been a preface or some other text for Easter or its vigil, now lost. It is an extraordinary coincidence that both the Old Spanish and Beneventan blessings should have borrowed Easter texts from a Roman feast for October. If Rome provided the common text, that text is more likely to have originated at Easter, the same feast as the Spanish and Beneventan compilers were assembling. How is one to account, moreover, for the second Old Spanish–Beneventan parallel, whose text is not in the Verona sacramentary? The connection is either directly between Spain and southern Italy (the Verona text having traveled from Rome via Spain) or via some lost Roman text for Holy Saturday.

---

brarum sed luminis matrem perducere dignatus est, in qua exorta est ab inferis in eterna die resurrectio mortuorum") and the Mozarabic *Inlatio* of Holy Saturday ("Nox enim ista non tenebrarum sed luminis mater est, in qua exortus est in eternum dies resurrectio nostra Dominus Jesus Christus" Férotin, *Le liber mozarabicus sacramentorum*, col. 249).

58. Coebergh, "Sacramentaire léonien," 303–4.
59. See Kelly, "The Exultet in Rome," and pp. 59–61.

The Beneventan text may be the adoption or adaptation of a Holy Saturday text that was known in the area around Rome for a long time and that survives because of its use in the south, adopted there by the Lombard liturgy. The quotation from Ennodius, however, might suggest a more northern origin, the southern Lombards looking to Pavian or Milanese sources when compiling an Easter ceremonial. At any rate, the age of the Beneventan Exultet suggests that it was in existence before the formation of the Beneventan liturgy as it now survives.

The Beneventan Paschal vigil is an amalgam of practices. The ancient rites of the area were combined with those imported by the Lombards to produce the indigenous Beneventan liturgy, and that rite's Exultet shows its ancestry. There had been, of course, Christian worship in southern Italy before the Lombard invasion of the sixth century, and the liturgy that developed on southern soil undoubtedly adopted many elements already used in the south.[60] Among these is certainly a Paschal vigil, though perhaps without a candle. The Lombard liturgy as it developed in the south, however, is closely related to the Lombard liturgy of the north: the Ambrosian liturgy of Milan. Beneventan and Milanese practices share so many elements that a common Lombard ancestor is easy to postulate,[61] and the blessing of a Paschal candle, practiced at Milan from a relatively early date, must have been adopted by the Lombards of the south in the process of formulating a liturgy of their own.

It appears that the Exultet is not an original part of the Beneventan liturgy. As at Rome,[62] the earlier forms of the Beneventan liturgy probably used no Paschal candle. This is suggested by the placement of the Exultet in the Beneventan ceremony, not at the beginning, as in all other rites that use the Exultet, nor after the lections as a fulfilment of the foregoing prophecies, but interrupting the course of the lections with which the vigil begins. The Exultet appears before the last lection, *Hec est hereditas*, which in turn precedes the procession to the font.[63]

The use of the Paschal candle must have begun at a time when the prologue was fixed but the preface remained variable, since the Beneventan Exultet has its own preface. It must have occurred after Ennodius composed his texts in the sixth century (assuming always that the borrowing was in that direction). If the borrowing took place in the seventh

60. For some other liturgical features that may be remnants of ancient practice in southern Italy, see Kelly, *TBC*, 63–65.

61. See Kelly, *TBC*, 181–203.

62. Ordo Romanus 23 (ca. 700–750; edition in Andrieu, *Les ordines*, 3:272–73) and others (ordo 24, s8$\frac{2}{2}$, ibid., 295; ordo 30B, s8ex, ibid., 471–72, etc.) make clear that the practice at the Lateran basilica does not include the blessing of a candle. Other churches of the vicinity of Rome did bless a candle (with the prayer *Deus mundi conditor*, as is evident from the Gelasian sacramentary (edition in Mohlberg, Eizenhöfer, and Siffrin, *Liber sacramentorum*, 68–70). The earliest reference to the Paschal candle at the Lateran is from the *Liber politicus* of Canon Benedict, ca. 1140: edition in Fabre and Duchesne, *Le liber censuum*, 2:151. See Kelly, "The Exultet at Rome."

63. For details on the ceremonial, see chapter 6.

century (the likely period for the formation of the Beneventan liturgy), then we are provided with a date before which the Exultet retained its flexibility. Beneventan and Ambrosian, two branches of Lombard liturgy, then develop and fix in writing their separate versions of the preface.

Persistence of the Beneventan Text

Even when the Beneventan text is replaced by the Franco-Roman, the scribes of some of the later Exultets include parts of the older Beneventan text. Elements of the Beneventan Exultet survive in the following documents with Franco-Roman text:

> Bari 2 and Bari 3, the two later Exultets of the city, both contain the passage with which the Beneventan text commemorates those present and the authorities:
>> Saluum fac populum tuum domine et benedic hereditati tue ut redeuntes ad festiuitatem pasche per hec uisibilibus et inuisibilibus tuis inhians dum presentium usufruuntur futurorum desiderio accendantur.
>
> Reminiscent of the *Te Deum* (and of the psalm it quotes), this passage is inserted at different places in the two rolls: in Bari 2 it appears where the Franco-Roman commemoration ("Precamur ergo te domine ut nos famulos tuos") ought to begin (the continuation of the roll is unfortunately lost). In Bari 3, however, the passage is inserted after the Franco-Roman commemoration. These are not two copies of the same recension, but it is clear that the Beneventan text was still known, at least in part, in thirteenth-century Bari.
>
> Gaeta 2 and the Dalmatian missal Oxford, Bodl. Canon. liturg. 342 preserve (along with Bari 2, Bari 3, and Montecassino 2) a Beneventan version of the opening of the preface: "Vere quia dignum et iustum est *per Christum dominum nostrum.*" These last four words appear in all witnesses of the Beneventan text, but not normally in the Franco-Roman: its use in these cases is a further echo of the Beneventan version.[64]
>
> Pisa 2, a roll made at Montecassino, retains excerpts from the Beneventan Exultet and the Gelasian *Deus mundi conditor* in the course of its Franco-Roman Exultet. Two passages cite the Beneventan Exultet: (1) the repetitive text beginning "Flore utuntur coniuge," inserted immediately after the similarly repetitive passage in the Roman text ("Alie liquantia mella stipant," etc.); (2) the passage beginning "Cuius odor suauis et flamma hilaris," which may have been brought to mind by the "suauitas" in the Roman text preceding the insertion ("in odorem suauitatis acceptus, supernis luminaribus misceatur"). However, this was not a sudden inspiration: the insertion was intended before copying, to judge from the fact that this Beneventan excerpt was at first inserted earlier in the text (after "fetus non quassant nec

---

64. Gaeta 1 also retained the words "per christum dominum nostrum" from its earlier Beneventan text when the roll was rewritten; however, this portion of the text was also rewritten elsewhere, omitting these words. In the Casanatense roll, the words "per christum dominum nostrum" are written very small in a later hand after two intervening illustrations.

filii destruunt castitatem") where it is entirely inappropriate and eradicated by the next membrane, which is pasted over this portion of the text. The manuscript may also have contained the Beneventan "Vere quia dignum et iustum est *per Christum dominum nostrum,*" but the last four words are now replaced with the Roman "equum et salutare." This Pisan text recalls also the old Gelasian prayer *Deus mundi conditor,* from which it repeats a thought about the bees: the passage "legunt pedibus flores, et nullum damnum in floribus invenitur" is prefixed immediately before the Roman text "partim ore legere flosculos."

Montecassino 2 uses essentially the same additions from the Beneventan text as does Pisa 2. It adds the text beginning "flore utuntur coniuge," but it is a shorter excerpt than is used in Pisa, and it is inserted at a different place. The passage "cuius odor suauis" is also used here, but the excerpt is longer than at Pisa and inserted at a different place, where the common reference may be to the lighting of the candle.[65] This manuscript also has "per Christum Dominum nostrum," a Beneventan symptom.

Oxford, Bodl. Canon. bibl. lat. 61, a gospel book of Zadar, preserves the favored passage, used also in Pisa 2 and Montecassino 2, beginning "flore utuntur coniuge." But here it comes near the end of the praise of the bees, after "nectar includunt," yet a third place for the insertion of the same passage.

Vat. lat. 3784A, the fourteenth-century Franco-Roman text appended to the remains of a handsome Montecassino roll, contains a brief quotation of the Beneventan Exultet. This text, which omits the same portion of the praise of the bees as do the manuscripts of Benevento and Troia, substitutes for the omission a passage from the Beneventan text: "Apes siquidem dum ore concipiunt ore parturiunt, casto corpore non fetido desiderio copulantur." This is a very late echo of the Beneventan Exultet.

The fragments of Farfa and Trento, two bifolia from a single eleventh-century gradual, show a particularly interesting transitional stage; this manuscript contained two versions of the Exultet—the one Beneventan with its usual melody, and the other Roman with a unique melody. The Beneventan Exultet begins at the preface, presumably because the Roman version used the same text, which thus need not be written out twice (unfortunately, the beginning of the Roman text is lost, so we cannot see its melody).

There were moments when a choice for the Franco-Roman text was made cleanly, in a straightforward way, by making a new roll or adopting an old one. And yet the memory of the older text persists, and its favorite moments are inserted into the new text (by a scribe working from memory or compiling a deliberately heterodox text from such a reference work as the Farfa-Trento fragments?).

---

65. Coming just after the Roman words "ignis accendit," the inserted Beneventan text reads "cuius odor suauis est, et flama hilaris, non tetro odore aruina desudat, sed iocondissima suauitate; qui peregrinus non inficitur pigmentis sed illuminetur spiritu sancto."

One wonders how often a choice might have been involved. There is no known injunction that specifically forbids the singing of the Beneventan text,[66] and there may have been many Easters when a deacon might choose either version of the Exultet. The Farfa-Trento fragments seem to suggest this when they provide both forms of the text; and the fact that Montecassino copied both versions of the text, including a relatively late version of the Beneventan text, suggests that both versions retained their validity.[67] If Salerno's Exultet roll illustrates the Roman text, the Beneventan text has not necessarily been supplanted there, since it reappears in two fifteenth-century missals. And at Bari, Gaeta, Mirabella, and Troia, how can we be sure that the older Beneventan rolls were retired after the creation of a Franco-Roman text? Perhaps they were retained as alternatives.

The Franco-Roman Text of the Exultet

What we here call the Franco-Roman text of the Exultet, that "admirable masterpiece of Christian lyric," as the eminent philologist Christine Mohrmann called it,[68] may or may not be exactly the text so strongly deplored by Saint Jerome. It is probably of Gallican origin; it was known in northern Italy and southeast Gaul from the sixth century,[69] and its earliest sources are the famous Gallican sacramentaries—Mass books, without musical notation, that preserve the earliest surviving versions of the liturgy practiced in northern Italy and in Gaul. Though the books themselves date from the eighth century, their liturgical material is undoubtedly older.[70] There were, however, two blessings of the candle circulating in the Gallican books (and presumably in the region) at the time of our early written records, and only gradually did the Exultet take the dominant position.

Early Manuscript Sources

We can trace three separate threads in what was to become the Franco-Roman version of the Exultet: (1) the Gallican sacramentaries, which all provide the Exultet for the blessing of the candle;[71] (2) the Gelasian

66. On Pope Stephen IX's forbidding of Ambrosianus cantus at Montecassino, see pp. 62–63.

67. Vat. lat. 3784, which may have contained the Beneventan text, is now mutilated; and later Montecassino rolls are Roman (British Library, Barberini); and yet the Velletri roll returns to the Beneventan text.

68. Mohrmann, "Exultent divina mysteria," 274.

69. See p. 53.

70. On the Gallican liturgy and its books in general, see Cyrille Vogel, *Medieval Liturgy*, 107–9, 275–77, and the literature cited there.

71. The three pure Gallican sacramentaries are (1) the Missale Gallicanum vetus, early eighth century (Vatican, Biblioteca Apostolica Vaticana, MS Pal. lat. 493; edition in

sacramentary (a copy, ca. 750, of a seventh-century Roman presbyteral book), whose tradition provides the prayer *Deus mundi conditor* but not the Exultet[72] (this prayer may have originated at Rome, in the context of the liturgies of the churches of the city, where the Paschal candle was in use earlier than in the papal liturgy);[73] (3) the papal tradition of Rome, represented by the Gregorian sacramentary, which provides for no candle and no blessing.[74]

At a later stage, the two Gallican blessings are combined in various ways in the mixed Gelasian sacramentaries of the eighth century. Three of these, the Saint Gall, Rheinau, and Prague sacramentaries, continue the Gallican practice of the Exultet;[75] the others (Gellone, Angoulême, Phillipps) combine the two practices, giving first the *Deus mundi conditor* and then the Exultet (Phillipps reverses this order).[76]

When a Roman Mass book was sent north to Charlemagne by Pope Hadrian I, the papal liturgy contained in the so-called Gregorian sacramentary of Hadrian (or Hadrianum) naturally made no reference to the blessing of a candle.[77] Benedict of Aniane added a supplement to the

Mohlberg, Eizenhöfer, and Siffrin, *Missale Gallicanum vetus;* the Exultet, nos. 132–35, pp. 35–37); (2) the Bobbio missal, eighth century (Paris, Bib. nat. MS lat. 13246; edition in Lowe, *The Bobbio Missal;* the Exultet, no. 227, pp. 69–70); (3) the Missale Gothicum, Autun, eighth century (Vatican, Biblioteca Apostolica Vaticana, MS Reg. lat. 317; edition in Mohlberg, *Missale Gothicum;* the Exultet, no. 225, pp. 59–61).

72. Vatican, Bibl. Ap. Vaticana MS Reg. lat. 316 + Paris, Bibl. nat. lat. 7193; edition in Mohlberg, Eizenhöfer, and Siffrin, *Liber sacramentorum;* an ordo Romanus of about 800 follows this tradition, providing only the prayer *Deus mundi conditor* for the blessing of the candle; see Ordo 30A in Andrieu, *Les ordines,* 3:457.

73. On the Roman origin of *Deus mundi conditor,* see Chavasse, *Le sacramentaire gélasien,* 102–6; Pinell, "La benediccìò," 9–10, 51–52, 67–79, 80–81. An interesting visual argument for the Italian origin of the prayer is made in Klauser, "Eine rätselhafte Exultetillustration." Schmidt, however (*Hebdomada sancta,* 2:638), sees the matter differently: *Deus mundi* is of northern Italian or southern Gallican origin, whence it was added at a later stage to the Gelasian sacramentaries.

74. The many witnesses are edited in Deshusses, *Le sacramentaire grégorien,* vol. 1.

75. Unless of course they represent a subsequent purification of the double transmission of the other eighth-century Gelasians.

76. The Saint Gall sacramentary, Saint Gall, eighth century (Sankt Gallen, Stiftsbibliothek, MS 348, edition in Mohlberg, *Das fränkische:* the Exultet, nos. 538–39, pp. 81–83); the Rheinau sacramentary, eighth or ninth century, Chur (Zürich, Zentralbibliothek, MS Rh 30, edition in Hänggi, *Sacramentarium rheinaugiense:* the Exultet, nos. 424–45, pp. 130–32); the Prague sacramentary, late eighth century, Regensburg (Prague, Knihovna Metropolitní Kapituli, MS O. 83, edition in Dold and Eizenhöfer, *Das prager Sacramentar:* the Exultet, no. 95, pp. 55*–57*); the sacramentary of Gellone, eighth century (Paris, Bib. nat. MS lat. 12048, edition in Dumas and Deshusses, *Liber sacramentorum Gellonensis:* the Exultet, nos. 677–78, pp. 93–95); the sacramentary of Angoulême, eighth century (Paris, Bib. nat. MS lat. 816), edition in Saint-Roch, *Liber sacramentorum Engolismensis:* the Exultet, nos. 733–34, pp. 108–10; the "Phillipps" sacramentary, eighth century (Berlin, Deutsche Staatsbibliothek, MS lat. 105, *olim* Phillipps 1667), edition in Heiming, *Liber sacramentorum Augustodunensis:* the Exultet, nos. 520–21, pp. 61–63.

77. The Exultet is also lacking in many mixed Gregorian sacramentaries, such as Paris, Bibl. nat. MS lat. 12051, of the second half of the ninth century; see Gamber, *CLLA,* 255, and no. 901, pp. 409–10.

Hadrianum to bring it into line with prevailing Frankish practice of the early ninth century; he began the supplement with additions for the rites of Holy Saturday, and he included from the eighth-century Gelasians both the *Deus mundi conditor* and the Exultet.[78] The two blessings are also presented as alternatives in a few early fragmentary sources,[79] and in the Roman-German Pontifical, a compilation of the early tenth century made in Mainz for use by east-Frankish bishops.[80]

Gradually, however, the Exultet gained the upper hand, and the tradition of *Deus mundi conditor* fades.[81] Sometimes the received Roman liturgy is supplemented using only the Exultet and not the double tradition of Benedict of Aniane: a sacramentary of Salzburg of the early ninth century, which is otherwise identical to the Gregorian sacramentary of Padua, inserts the Exultet before the prayers for the lections of the Holy Saturday vigil.[82]

By the time the Roman liturgy began to be adopted in substitution for the Beneventan, the Exultet in its "Roman" form, whatever its origin, was in widespread use in Rome and throughout the West.

---

78. Autun, Bibliothèque municipale MS 19bis; edition with other witnesses in Deshusses, *Le sacramentaire grégorien*, vol. 1 part 2; the Exultet, nos. 1,021–22, 1:160–63).

79. The *Deus mundi conditor* precedes the Exultet in a fragment of a Gelasian sacramentary of the eighth/ninth century from southeast Germany: Vienna, Österreichische Nationalbibliothek, Cod. Ser. n. 13706 (see Gamber, "Eine ältere Schwesterhandschrift," 160–61); and in a fragmentary leaf from about 800, the *Deus mundi conditor* is followed by the rubric "item benedictio cerei" and then only the second portion of the Exultet, from the preface onward: see Gamber, *CLLA*, no. 633, pp. 310–11, and Gamber, "Eine ältere Schwesterhandschrift," 159–60).

80. See Vogel and Elze, *Le pontifical*, 95–99.

81. The *Deus mundi conditor* has, however, a little more history. In the pontifical of the late ninth or early tenth century cited by Martène as being from Poitiers, and now recognized as Paris, Bibl. de l'Arsenal 227, the prayer survives as a blessing of three candles used to ward off lightning, thunder, tempest, pestilence and other evils: "Finita laetania, completur a tribus praesbiteris benedictio trium cereorum ante altare fontium statutorum, contra fulgura, tonitrua, temptestates, pestilentias et caetera mala hominibus infesta. Cuius benedictio initium est: *Deus mundi conditor*" (edition in Martini, *Il cosiddetto pontificale*, 216). The final portion of the prayer, which begins "Veniat ergo super hunc incensum," gradually was separated and, through a misunderstanding of the word *incensum* (which originally referred to the lit candle), survived as a blessing of incense or of the grains of incense inserted into the Paschal candle. The *Veniat* is an integral part of *Deus mundi conditor* in the Gellone, Angoulême, and Phillipps sacramentaries. In the Gelasian Sacramentary the *Veniat* is separated from the main prayer and labeled *Benedictio super incensum*, still presumably referring to the candle (Mohlberg, Eizenhöfer, and Siffrin, *Liber sacramentorum*, no. 429, pp. 69–70). The *Veniat* is lacking at the end of the version of *Deus mundi conditor* transmitted in the tenth-century Roman-German pontifical (see Vogel and Elze, *Le pontifical*, 95–96). In later Roman pontificals, however, the *Veniat* survives as a blessing of incense (see Andrieu, *Le pontifical*, 3:471. See also Franz, *Die kirchlichen Benediktionen*, 1:530–31; Schmidt, *Hebdomada sancta*, 2:638).

82. The sacramentary (Deshusses' siglum Z5) survives as fragments in Salzburg, Munich, and Vienna. See Deshusses, *Le sacramentaire grégorien*, 1:715.

The Arrival of the Franco-Roman Exultet in Southern Italy

The Roman Exultet did not arrive in southern Italy at the time the text first found its way into Frankish liturgical books. The Gregorian sacramentary and its supplement containing the Exultet did not circulate as early in central and southern Italy as elsewhere. Klaus Gamber has posited that the Roman liturgy in the south, so far as can be determined, was based on older Gelasian sacramentaries now lost;[83] it is a characteristic of the Gelasian sacramentary, at least in the form that survives, that it provides not the Exultet, but the prayer *Deus mundi conditor*, for the blessing of the Paschal candle. Likewise, the Roman-German Pontifical is not the conduit for the Franco-Roman Exultet, because it omits portions of the Exultet that are nevertheless present in southern Italy.[84]

The Franco-Roman Exultet, already in widespread use, replaced the Beneventan text only in the course of the eleventh and twelfth centuries. Whether the Beneventan text itself is older than the Frankish may be doubted, but it held a primary place in those areas of southern Italy where the Beneventan liturgy was practiced, and the gradual replacement of the Beneventan liturgy by the Roman, mostly in the course of the eleventh century, was the occasion for the adoption of the Frankish Exultet, now become universal, or "Roman."

Beat Brenk[85] and others have suggested that the visit of Pope Stephen IX to Montecassino in 1058, in which he is reported to have forbidden the use of "Ambrosianus cantus,"[86] is the moment when Montecassino, and perhaps much of the rest of the south, changed from the Beneventan to the Franco-Roman text of the Exultet. Stephen IX, the former Frederick of Lorraine, had been elected abbot of Montecassino shortly before his elevation to the papacy; long a leader in the papal reform movement of the eleventh century, he was doubtless no friend of deviant local practices with which, as a foreigner, he was unfamiliar.[87]

"Ambrosian," at Montecassino and elsewhere, was the local name for the local chant; Beneventan chant is labeled only when it is found alongside Gregorian chant, and then it is always called "Ambrosian."[88]

---

83. Gamber, *Sacramentartypen*, 64–65. An exception is Montecassino 271, which is a mixed sacramentary now palimpsest and datable perhaps to 700; see Gamber, *CLLA*, no. 701 and Supplement. See also Gyug, *Missale ragusinum*, 17–20.

84. See pp. 64–69.

85. In *Exultet*, 212.

86. "Tunc etiam et Ambrosianum cantum in ecclesia ista cantari penitus interdixit" (*Chron. mon. Cas.*, 2:94).

87. On Frederick's career as related to Montecassino, see Bloch, *Monte Cassino*, 1:32–40; Gay, *L'Italie meridionale*, 509–11. Frederick had opportunities to hear the "Ambrosian" chant not only at Montecassino, but also at Benevento and Tremiti. See Kelly, "Montecassino," 80–82; Kelly, "Beneventan and Milanese."

88. For the many places where Beneventan scribes call their local chant "Ambrosian," see Kelly, "Beneventan and Milanese." A leaf of genuine Ambrosian music, but in

Possibly the scribes believed that the Beneventan chant was the same as the Ambrosian chant of Milan; there are important connections between the Beneventan rite and that of Milan, but the chants are not identical.[89] This "Ambrosian" name, however, recognizes an important historical and cultural connection with the Lombards of the north. Moreover, it opposes the authority of Saint Ambrose to that of the chant associated with Saint Gregory, perhaps as part of an effort to protect an endangered local repertory. What Pope Stephen forbids is the singing of the local Ambrosian chant: the music we now call Beneventan.

It is not at all clear, however, that the Beneventan text of the Exultet is intended to be included in Pope Stephen's ban. The melody of the Exultet, the south Italian melody closely associated with the Beneventan liturgy, continued to be used for centuries after Pope Stephen's order, and the text that was sung to it only gradually gave way to the text used in the Roman liturgy.

Although the Beneventan chant was almost completely eradicated from Montecassino in the course of the eleventh century,[90] the Beneventan text of the Exultet was not; of rolls made at Montecassino, probably Vat. lat. 3784 (whose Beneventan text may have caused its present mutilation), and certainly the roll of Velletri, contained the Beneventan text; both were made well after Pope Stephen's visit, and it appears that the Beneventan text, along with the Franco-Roman, continued to be used at Montecassino.

Pope Stephen's interdiction of "ambrosianus cantus" is not the watershed moment when the old text was abandoned. The change was more gradual, leading to the adoption of the Roman text over the course of many decades. The Beneventan text does not seem to have been associated with the distinction between "Ambrosian" and "Roman," between universal liturgy and local practice, between reform and tradition.

The Franco-Roman Text of the Exultet in Southern Italy

The edition of the Franco-Roman text that appears in Appendix 2 allows us to make observations about the south Italian sources of the Franco-Roman text of the Exultet. Not surprisingly, the texts often group themselves geographically, and we shall see that melodic factors often confirm

---

a Beneventan hand, survives from Montecassino (as the front flyleaf in the Cassinese martyrology Vatican Ottob. lat. 3). Whether it is part of a larger manuscript is not known: but there was evidently access to the Milanese liturgy, and interest in it, at Montecassino in the eleventh century. The leaf is printed in facsimile in *PM* 14: pl. XXXII, XXXIII, and in Bannister, *Monumenti*, 2: pl. 72 (see also 1:124, no. 354).

89. See Kelly, "Beneventan and Milanese Chant"; Kelly, *TBC*, chap. 5; on the connection between the Ambrosian and the Beneventan rites as regards the Exultet, see pp. 208–11.

90. See Kelly, "Montecassino."

these groupings. However, the situation is not so clear that it allows us to assign every surviving witness to a place in a stemmatic organization that would describe for us the reception and adaptation of the Franco-Roman text in southern Italy. A number of significant sources, such as the fragments of Farfa and Trento, remain difficult to assign. Nevertheless, a few observations based on textual situations are possible. First, however, we need to review those passages in the text that are of particular interest for the southern Italian sources.

Special Passages in the Textual Transmission of the Exultet

The text of the Franco-Roman Exultet in southern Italy is essentially the text used widely in the Latin west. It does not have a special version of its own that sets it apart or provides special information about transmission. Nevertheless, there are aspects of the text that can help to explain the relationship of manuscripts and others that are useful in sketching the arrival and dissemination of the text in southern Italy.

The earliest texts of the Exultet, we have seen, are in the Gallican sacramentaries and the eighth-century Gelasian sacramentaries, Frankish books representing the practices of the eighth century—hence well after the composition of the Exultet. Fairly early on, certain alterations were practiced on the original text, for theological or aesthetic reasons. Two passages are particularly noteworthy in this respect. One is the omission of a reference to the necessity—and desirability—of Adam's sin ("O certe necessarium Adae peccatum, quod Christi morte deletum est; O felix culpa quae talem ac tantum meruit habere redemptorem"); this passage is lacking in manuscripts from as early as the ninth century. Likewise, the extensive praise of the bees, considered to be of questionable taste by Saint Jerome, is removed from the version of the Exultet transmitted in the Roman-German Pontifical of the tenth century and in many later manuscripts. The absence of these two passages in a witness indicates that the Exultet was adopted relatively late, or altered under Frankish influence.[91]

We will consider briefly these and other passages of the text that are of special interest.

"O CERTE NECESSARIUM"

The passage about the necessity of Adam's sin, challenged early on theological grounds, is lacking in manuscripts from the ninth century and in the witnesses of Andrieu's Ordo Romanus 50,[92] adopted into the Roman-

91. On these passages in other manuscripts, see Kelly, "The Exultet at Rome"; Ebner, "Handschriftliche Studien"; Roberts, "The Exultet Hymn."

92. Andrieu, *Les ordines*, 5:269–70. These include the eleventh-century south Italian manuscripts Montecassino 451 and Rome, Vallicelliana D 5, which are in fact the base texts for Andrieu's Ordo 50.

German Pontifical of about 960, which also omits it.[93] It is missing in many German manuscripts,[94] and some French ones,[95] though it is normally present in Italy. Ulrich of Cluny reports that Abbot Hugo (d. 1109) had it removed from books at the abbey (in which it presumably was present until that time): "In cuius [sc. the Exultet] quodam loco cum aliquando non bene haberetur *O felix culpa, et quod peccatum Adae necessarium esset,* ante hos annos domnus abbas optime fecit, quod fecit abradi et ne amplius legeretur interdixit."[96]

The passage is only rarely absent in sources from southern Italy, but occasionally it is removed at a later stage.[97]

THE PRAISE OF THE BEES

The long praise of the bees, a feature of the Exultet in all its forms from earliest times, has been criticized from Saint Jerome onward. Critics have wondered whether the elaborate description of the bees and their activities was a worthy subject for the Easter vigil. The modern version of the Exultet, beginning with the missal of Pius V, omits the offending passage entirely; this version arises from the Roman-Franciscan missal of the thirteenth century, coming from the reforms of Innocent III (1198–1216). But the situation in the Middle Ages was far from stable, and although as early as the tenth century the Roman-German Pontifical removed the passage praising the bees (while retaining brief references to the bees as the source of wax), manuscripts not affected by this tradition continued to preserve all or a part of this passage.

The south Italian manuscripts make clear that the praise of the bees is a part of the Franco-Roman Exultet as received. However, a variety of abridgements is also effected in the region. Table 6 indicates the various omissions made in the manuscripts considered here. Generally speaking, the full praise of the bees is present in the versions of the Franco-Roman text used in southern Italy. It is present in all the Exultet rolls that use the Franco-Roman text, except for Troia 3 and Bari 3, and the later upper scripts of Vat. lat. 9820 (which omits much of the passage) and Bari 2.It is present at Montecassino in the considerable series of rolls produced

93. Vogel and Elze, *Le pontifical,* 2:98.

94. In German sources, the passage is present in the Rheinau and Saint Gall sacramentaries and in Saint Gall MS 251; but it is already absent in the supplement to the Hadrianum as presented in Cologne 88 and 137 (ninth/tenth century; Deshusses, *Le sacramentaire grégorien,* siglum V), and in later manuscripts of Saint Gall (338, 339, 341, 342). The passage is also lacking in the "pontifical of Poitiers" (Paris, Arsenal 227, s9ex) and in the Bobbio missal (which, however, has other more unusual abridgements as well).

95. Franz, *Die kirchlichen Benediktionen,* 1:540–41.

96. *PL* 149: col. 663.

97. The text is present, but the notation omitted, in the Caiazzo missal Vatican Barb. lat. 603, and the passage is marked for omission in Vat. Barb. lat. 699 (Veroli?); it is also absent in a group of central Italian manuscripts that adopt the Beneventan melody: New York, Morgan M 379; Rome, Vall. F 29; Rome, Vall. B 23.

In huius igitur noctis gratia
suscipe sancte pater incensi huius sacrificium uespertinum
quod tibi in hac cerei
oblatione sollemni per ministrorum manus
de operibus apum sacrosancta reddit ecclesia

A --

Sed iam columne huius preconia nouimus
quam in honore dei rutilans ignis accendit

Qui licet sit diuisus in partes
mutuati tamen luminis detrimenta non nouit

B --

Alitur liquantibus ceris
quam in substantiam pretiose huius lampadis
apis mater eduxit

C ------------------------------

D ----------------------------

E ----------------------------

Apis ceteris que subiecta sunt homini
animantibus antecellit
Cum sit enim minima corporis paruitate
ingentes animos angusto uersat in pectore
uiribus imbecillis sed fortis ingenio

Hec explorata temporum uices
cum canitiem pruisosam hiberna posuerint
et glaciale senium
uerni temporis moderata deterserint
statim prodeundi ad laborem cura succedit

Disperseque per agros libratis paululum pennis
cruribus suspensis insidunt

Partim ore legentes flosculos
onerate uictualibus suis ad castra remeant

Ibique alie inestimabili arte
cellulas tenaci glutino instruunt

E ----------------------------

alie liquantia mella stipant
alie uertunt flores in ceram
alie ore natos fingunt
alie collectum e foliis nectar includunt

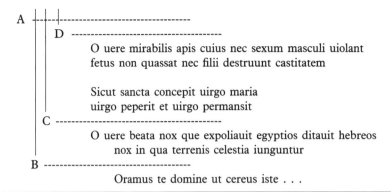

A

    D

O uere mirabilis apis cuius nec sexum masculi uiolant
fetus non quassat nec filii destruunt castitatem

Sicut sancta concepit uirgo maria
uirgo peperit et uirgo permansit

    C

O uere beata nox que expoliauit egyptios ditauit hebreos
nox in qua terrenis celestia iunguntur

  B

Oramus te domine ut cereus iste . . .

Note: Brackets show the text *omitted* in the manuscripts indicated. These manuscripts are summarized in chapter 1 and described in more detail in Appendix 1.

A: Vat. lat. 6082
B: Rome, Vall. B 43 (central Italy)
C: (= PRG) *Exultet rolls:* Bari 2; Bari 3; Casanatense Exultet (*marked for omission in a later hand*); Gaeta 3 (*marked for omission in a later hand*); Gaeta 1, upper script; [*also* the Pisan rolls Pisa 2, Pisa 3]. *Codices:* Barb. lat. 699; Naples VI G 38, *corrected in a later hand to* D *by the addition of the missing text;* (*also* the central Italian manuscripts Vat. lat. 4770; Vall. B 8; Vall. B 23 [*the text is present, but without notation, marked* "hic mutat sensum quasi legens"])
D: *Exultet rolls:* Casanatense Exultet (*marked for omission in a later hand*); Troia 3; *Codices:* London, BL Eg. 3511 (*altered to* version C *in a later hand by marking text to be eliminated*); Vat. lat. 9820, upper script; Vat. lat. 3784A, *with addition from Beneventan text; marked for omission in a later hand in* Oxford, Can. bibl. lat. 61, includes Beneventan additions; Naples VI G 34 (Troia); Vat. Barb. lat. 603; (*also* the central Italian Subiaco XVIII and Rome, Vall. F 29)
E: New York, Morgan M 379 (central Italy)

there (Vat. lat. 6082, in many textual details similar to Montecassino texts, is unusual in its partial omission of the bees and unique in the portion it omits). Later practice is shown in some older rolls where the passage, present in the text, is marked for omission (Casanatense Exultet, Gaeta 3).

At Benevento, the Franco-Roman Exultet uses omission D (see Table 6): London, BL Eg. 3511 (after correction) and the upper script of Vat. lat. 9820 are both from Benevento, as is the Casanatense roll, which was later adjusted to this version.[98] This is the tradition adopted at Troia also, judging from Troia 3 and Naples VI G 34. The Franciscan manuscript Naples VI G 38 is adapted also to this tradition: the longer omission C

---

98. The scribe of the Casanatense roll, however, apparently worked from a text that used version B, but provided the text for the bees from elsewhere. The scribe writes "Apis mater eduxit. O uere beata nox que expoliauit egyptios ditauit hebreos." This last sentence is canceled with "ua- -cat," followed by an illustration of bees and the full text of the bees; the previous sentence is repeated at its place. Only at a later stage is the omission marked in the margins.

is corrected by the addition of the missing text, for use in a place that followed this practice.

The Bari tradition (Bari 2, upper script, and Bari 3) adopted a text with omission C, but it is not a straightforward version of the Roman-German Pontifical, since the "O certe necessarium" passage is retained. Gaeta adopted the same omission, but at a later stage, since the full text is written in the Gaeta rolls 2 and 3, the omission indicated by later intervention; only the much later upper script of Gaeta 1 incorporates the omission.

The praise of the bees is omitted in some peripheral and later sources. In Vat. Barb. lat. 699 (s12ex Sulmona?), Vat. Barb. lat. 603 (Caiazzo s12/13, where the melody is partially Roman), and a number of the manuscripts from the monastic area around Rome that adopted the Beneventan melody,[99] various of these abridgements have been adopted, sometimes by omitting the text, and sometimes by leaving out its notation. Two of these central Italian manuscripts (Morgan and Vall. B 43) have unique omissions, and others use version B or C; evidently, this area received its Franco-Roman text, probably with the Beneventan melody, at a time before the arrival of the tenth-century Roman-German Pontifical. Under later influence, each monastery devised a way to eliminate the apiary excess, but each devised a local solution.

Sometimes a later decision caused revisions in the text. At Gaeta it was decided to omit the passage already present in the rolls: it is marked for omission in Gaeta 2 (beginning "Apis ceteris"), but the place where the omission would stop is mutilated; it was undoubtedly the same omission as is marked in Gaeta 3 ("Apis ceteris . . . permansit"). In the Dalmatian gospel book Oxford Can. Bibl. lat. 61 (Zadar, s11ex), a later, non-Beneventan hand excludes the bees but leaves at the end a portion beginning "O vere mirabilis"; other corrections in the manuscript suggest that the text is being revised according to a newer model.

In some cases the omission caused problems. The Casanatense scribe copied from a text that omitted the bees. After copying part of the text that follows the omission, he crossed out the portion that followed the omission, wrote out the full praise of the bees, and wrote the subsequent text again; but the passage was canceled in a still later hand. In Naples VI G 38, a portion of the praise of the bees, most of which is omitted in the main text, is added in a bottom margin, from "O uere [beata et] mirabilis . . . virgo permansit."

An odd sort of compromise seems to have been adopted in the central Italian missal Rome, Vall. B 23, s12in: the rubric "Hic mutat sensum

---

99. The manuscripts include Subiaco XVIII (19), a missal of the thirteenth century, which, among other things, contains the complete Good Friday Vespers of the old Beneventan liturgy; Vallicelliana F 29 (s12in) from Farfa; Vall. B 43 (of undetermined provenance, but not from Subiaco [Supino Martini, *Roma*, 334]; it was used at Santa Maria de Ninfa, Rome[?]); Vall. B 23 (from Norcia, s12 [Supino Martini, *Roma*, 224]); New York, Morgan M 379 (Foligno s 11/12 [Supino Martini, *Roma*, 225–26 n. 66]).

quasi legens" introduces the praise of the bees, which is written without notation; the deacon stops singing, *speaks* the praise of the bees (audibly?), and sings again where the Exultet continues with musical notation.

The Franco-Roman text was received in southern Italy in its full form, before the Roman-German Pontifical influenced many churches to abbreviate this section.[100] The pontifical was copied in southern Italy, but in a second wave of influence.[101] The Exultet was present already, and already in use; local practice abbreviated the praise of the bees, sometimes as in the Roman-German Pontifical, but often otherwise.[102] It is worth remembering that the Beneventan text—the text replaced by the Franco-Roman Exultet—itself contained a lengthy praise of the bees, though using different language.

THE ENDING: BLESSINGS OF AUTHORITIES

The earliest versions of the Franco-Roman Exultet contain a closing formula, *Precamur,* which invokes God's blessing on the clergy and people, on the pope, and sometimes also on the local ecclesiastical authority, bishop or abbot. To this paragraph were eventually added the names of secular rulers as well, sometimes including wives and children. This is a flexible and evidently later part of the text; it does not obey the principles of the metrical cursus.

The textual development of this closing passage may be sketched as follows in the earliest surviving sources (further detail is to be found in Appendix 2 and the editions named there):

1. Simplest form:
   Precamur ergo domine ut nos famulos tuos omnem (et famulas tuas omnemque: Gothicum) clerum et deuotissimum \populum\ quiete temporum concessa in his {pascalibus} conseruare | digneris | . (Bobbio; Missale Gallicanum uetus; Missale Gothicum)

---

100. The only musical text in Beneventan script that might depend on the PRG is Vat. Barb. lat. 699; others that omit both the reference to Adam's sin and the praise of the bees are Vat. lat. 4770 and Vallicelliana B 8 (S. Eutizio, Norcia, s11) and B 23; Vallicelliana F 29 and New York Morgan M 379 omit most of the praise of the bees, but in the wrong amounts to match the PRG.

101. The twin pontificals Rome, Vall. D 5 and Montecassino 451 are eleventh-century Montecassino copies of the PRG.

102. A similar situation obtains in Rome in the period between the regular adoption of the Exultet and the standardization of its text in the thirteenth century. Version C (or, PRG) is present in Rome (in Bibl. Alessandrina 173, a s12 copy of the PRG) and in Vatican, Santa Maria Maggiore 40 (s13); Vatican San Pietro F 12 (s12); San Pietro B 78 (s13); San Pietro F 14 (s12in); but it is far from uniformly adopted. Exultets with the complete praise of the bees are Rome, Vallicelliana E 15 (San Lorenzo in Damaso, s11in) and Vatican San Pietro F 15 (s12); a shorter omission (D) is found in Florence, Bibl. Riccardiana 299 (late eleventh century); and a longer omission (different from all those here, beginning like B with the omission of "Alitur liquantibus," but concluding like C with "uirgo permansit") is in Vat. lat. 12989 (from the Lateran, ca. 1200), and Bibl. Angelica 1606 (s18 copy of a lost original s13).

2. Addition of a blessing of the pope:
   supplement to Gregorian sacramentary of Hadrian
   \populum una cum patre nostro papa illo\
   {pascalibus gaudiis}
   Missale Gothicum
   \populum una cum patre nostro beatissimo viro illo\
   St. Gall sacramentary
   \populum una cum patre nostro beatissimo uiro papa illo\
3. Addition of secular rulers:
   Rheinau sacramentary
   \populum una cum patre nostro beatissimo uiro illo necnon et cle-
   mentissimo rege nostro illo coniugeque eius ac filiis cunctuque exercitu francorum\
   | dignetur |
   Roman-German Pontifical
   \populum una cum beatissimo papa nostro N., et antistite nostro N.,
   et gloriosissimo imperatore nostro N., eiusque nobilissima prole\
   {paschalibus festis}
4. At another stage, or in a separate development, the secular powers were
   separated from the ecclesiastical, and a second invocation, beginning
   usually either with "Memento" or "Respice," was added later in the text
   to invoke a separate blessing on the secular powers.

   Memento etiam Domine famuli tui imperatoris nostri ( ) necnon et
   famuli tui comitis nostri ( ) cum omni exercitu eorum et celestem
   eis concede uictoriam. (Vat. Barb. lat. 592)

   Respice etiam domine et deuotissimum famulum tuum imperatorem
   nostrum .ill. cuius tu deus desiderii uota pronoscens ineffabili pietate et misericordie tue munere tranquillum perpetue pacis accommoda et celestem illi de throno tuo concede uictoriam cum omni
   populo suo. (Rome, Vallicelliana MS B 43)[103]

   Or, sometimes, the two paragraphs are combined:
   Memento   etiam   Domine   famulorum   tuorum   imperatorum
   nostrorum .ill. et celestem illis de tuo throno concede uictoriam
   cum omni exercitu eorum. Respice quesumus domine super
   deuotissimos famulos tuos duces nostros, quorum tu deus desiderii
   uota prenoscens, ineffabilis pietatis et misericordie tue munere,
   tranquillos perpetue pacis accommoda. Vt in his pascalibus gaudiis,
   assidua protectione regere, gubernare, et conseruare digneris. (Pisa,
   Exultet 2)

---

103. This is essentially the version adopted in Franciscan versions of the Exultet and
continued in manuscripts and printed books up to the twentieth century. Although the text
was omitted after 1806 at the end of the Holy Roman Empire, the Sacred Congregation of
Rites decreed as late as 1860 that it was still to be printed as part of the Exultet. (*Decreta
authentica*, 2:428, no. 3103, Dubium iii.) The decree of 9 February 1951, restoring the
nocturnal Paschal vigil, altered this passage to read: "Respice etiam ad eos, qui nos in
potestate regunt, et ineffabili pietatis et misericordiae tuae munere, dirige cogitationes eorum
ad iustitiam et pacem, ut de terrena operositate ad caelestem patriam perveniant cum omni
populo tuo." See Strittmatter, "The Pentecost Exultet," 389 and n.23.

The Franco-Roman Exultets of southern Italy use a variety of these commemorations and others. (The Beneventan text has its own commemoration: see below). The versions accompanying the Franco-Roman text are presented in Table 7 (for descriptions of manuscripts see Appendix 1; for full texts see Appendix 2):

The Beneventan Exultet has its own commemorations, including a separate "Memorare" for secular rulers:

> Vna cum beatissimo papa nostro il. et famulo tuo pontifice nostro il. omnibus presbiteris diaconibus cunctoque clero uel plebe. Memorare domine famulum tuum imperatorem nostrum il. et principem nostrum il. et eorum exercitum uniuersum.

Only the fifteenth-century Exultets of Salerno substitute the "Respice quesumus" of the Roman Exultet for the Beneventan "Memorare." Versions of the Beneventan commemoration can be seen inserted in the Franco-Roman texts of Bari 3 and Casanatense 1103, the latter from fifteenth-century Montevergine.[104]

As we shall see in viewing individual documents, this variety of conclusions means that the close of the Exultet is highly interesting for the later history of the text. The long use of many of the Exultet rolls means that these portions have been repeatedly altered, and they provide a fascinating window onto history and changing usages.[105]

BLESSING OF DONORS

South Italian manuscripts often add, after the commemoration of religious and secular authorities, and before the concluding doxology, a memorial of the donors of the candle itself: "Et his qui tibi offerunt hoc sacrificium laudis, premia eterna largiaris" (Avezzano Exultet).

This text is present in the substantial series of manuscripts deriving from Montecassino, and at Gaeta and Mirabella and in the Dalmatian manuscripts. It is lacking, however, in the Benevento-Troia series of manuscripts that practice the D-version of the omission of the praise of the bees.[106] It is missing also in the Bari texts (Bari 2, upper script; Bari 3); the Capua Exultet, in Vat. Barb. lat. 699 and Vat. Barb. lat. 603, and in all the Roman-monastic group of manuscripts.[107]

104. For details of these texts, see the editions in the appendices. Ladner, "The 'Portraits,' " 191–92n1, suggests that the "Memento" and "Memorare" commemorations of secular rulers continue the tradition of the commemoration of the living or of the dead in the *Memento* of the Roman mass.

105. Notable examples are the first Exultet of Bari, to which a long series of names has been added over many years; and the third Exultet of Gaeta, whose ending has been altered many times. For details of these, see Appendix 1.

106. Vatican Vat. lat. 9820, upper script; Casanatense Exultet; London, BL Eg. 3511; Troia Exultet 3; Naples VI G 34.

107. For further details, see the edition in Appendix 2.

A. MEMENTO etiam domine famuli[a] tui imperatoris nostri[b] il. (*or* N. *or* blank space)[c] et[d] celestem illi concede uictoriam cum omni exercitu suo.

> **Exultets:** Avezzano; Capua, part 1 of commemoration; Gaeta 3; London BL add. 30337; Mirabella 2, part 1 of commemoration; Paris, B.N. lat. 710; Pisa 2; Vat. Barb. lat. 592.

> **Codices:** Berlin 920; Farfa; Oxford, Bodl. Canon. bibl. lit. 61, part 1 of commemoration; Rome, Casanat. 1103; Rome, Vall. C 32; Vat. Borg. lat. 339; Vat. Ottob. lat. 576; Vat. lat. 6082.

> [a]Avezzano: famulorum tuorum imperatorum nostrorum il., et exercitus eorum uniuersi, atque barbaras nationes illorum dicioni potenter substerne.
> [b]Oxf. 361, part 1: *omits from* nostri, *adds* necnon et famuli tui prioris nostri ill. et universi populi huius ciuitatis qui tibi offerunt hoc sacrificium laudis. ut his omnibus premia eterna largiaris.
> [c]Paris 710, London 30337, Vat. Barb. lat. 592, Farfa, Vat. lat. 6082, Rome, Vall. C 32: *adds* necnon et famuli tui (Farfa: famulorum tuorum) consulis (London, Barberini: comitis Farfa: principum Vat. 6082, Vall. C 32: principis) nostri (Farfa: nostrorum) LEONI (London, Barberini: *space* Farfa: il. et il. Vat. 6082, Vall. C 32: il.); Oxford 61, part 1, Vat. Borg. lat 339: *omit to end.*
> [d]Vat. Barb. 592: cum omni exercitu eorum et celestem eis concede uictoriam; Casanat. 1103 Part 2: cum universo exercitu suo, ut celestem eis concedas uictoriam; Mirabella Exultet 2 part 1: cum omni exercitu eius nobis ipsum redde placatum.

B. RESPICE quesumus domine ad deuotissimum famulum tuum imperatorem nostrum[a] il. (*or* N.) cuius tu deus desiderii uota prenoscens ineffabilis pietatis et misericordie tue munere tranquillum perpetue pacis accomoda; ut[b] in his pascalibus gaudiis assidua protectione regere gubernare et conseruare digneris.

> **Exultets:** Gaeta 1; Mirabella 2, part 2 of commemoration; Pisa 2, part 2 of commemoration; Vat. lat. 3784A.

> **Codices:** Oxford, Bodl. Canon. Bibl. lat. 61, part 2 of commemoration; Salerno missals 3 and 4; [Rome, Vall. B 43: central Italy].

> [a]Oxford 61, part 2: ad devotionem famule tue abbatisse nostre n. totiusque congregationis sancte marie sibi commisse.
> [b]Vall. B 43, Vat. 3784A: *from this point use the ending of "Memento":* et celestem illi de throno tuo concede uictoriam cum omni populo suo (3784A: eius); Oxford 61, pt. 2: et eas per hec pascalia festa assidua. . . .

C. MEMORARE domine famuli tui regis nostri N. et eius exercitus uniuersi.

> Rome, Casanat. 1103, part 1 of commemoration

MEMORARE domine famulum tuum regem nostrum il. et cunctum eius exercitum et omnium circumstantium. Saluum fac populum tuum domine et benedic hereditati tue ut redeuntes ad festiuitatem pasce per hec uisibilibus et inuisibilibus tuis inians dum presentium usufruuntur futurorum desiderio accendantur.

> Bari 3. The continuation of the text is borrowed from the Beneventan text: see Appendix 2).

D. PROTEGE quoque domine piisimos [*corr. to* piisimus] principes nostros ill. et ill. cum omni exercitu eorum [*corr. to* eius] et concede eis [*corr. to* ei] ubique uictoriam ad laudem nominis tui et ad nostram qui tibi sacris famulamur officiis prope tuam defensionem.

> Capua Exultet, part 2 of commemoration.

E. MEMENTO domine famulum tuum imperatorem nostrum et consules et duces nostros, ut per hec pascalia gaudia excellentiores eos facias, et semper uictoriam de celo conceda, gloria multiplices, letitia muneres, honor(e) exaltes, et eorum exercitum uniuersum.

> Montecassino, Exultet 2.

Combinations:
Memento/Respice: Pisa 2, Mirabella 2, Oxford 61
Memento/special: Capua
Memorare/Saluum: Bari 3
Respice/Memento: Vat. 3784A.

Note: This table presents special commemorations of rulers from south Italian versions of the Franco-Roman Exultet. It reproduces only the original text, and not the variety of additions made when rulers changed. For details on the manuscripts and their texts, see Appendices 1 and 2.

ENDING DOXOLOGIES

The Exultet may end in a number of ways. Most simply, its written text ends with the invocation of authorities. Early sources indicate some sort of doxological ending, sometimes abbreviated. These abbreviated forms may indicate only that the endings are familiar from their use within the tradition of prayer recorded in sacramentaries, which need not be as full as a deluxe, stand-alone work like an Exultet roll.

The endings in the early Franco-Roman sources may be summarized as follows (details in Appendix 2):

1. Simplest form: no conclusion given. (Bobbio missal; supplement to the Gregorian sacramentary of Hadrian)
2. Per. (Missale Gallicanum vetus)
3. per dominum. (Rheinau sacramentary)
4. per dominum nostrum. (Gellone, Angoulême, Phillipps, St. Gall sacramentaries)
5. per resurgentem a mortuis dominum nostrum filium tuum. (Missale Gothicum)
6. Per eumdem dominum nostrum Iesum Christum filium tuum qui tecum uiuit et regnat Deus, in unitate eiusdem spiritus sancti, per omnia secula seculorum. (Roman-German Pontifical)

A variety of endings is found in the south Italian Exultet. The most frequent is "Per dominum nostrum Iesum Christum filium tuum qui tecum et cum spiritu sancto uiuit et regnat Deus per omnia secula seculorum." But other endings are found as well:

> Qui uenturus est iudicare uiuos et mortuos et omne seculum per ignem, uiuens et regnans Deus per omnia secula seculorum. (Pisa 2; Mirabella 2; Vat. Barb. lat. 603)

> Qui tecum uiuit et regnat in unitate spiritus sancti Deus per omnia secula seculorum. (Montecassino, Exultet 2; Capua; Casanatense, later hand; Vat. Ottob. 576 with variants)

THE "NORMAN FINALE"

An ending of the Exultet, first called the "Norman finale" by Ernst Kantorowicz,[108] borrows from the Frankish *Laudes regiae* ("Christus uincit, Christus regnat, Christus imperat") and from the conclusion of the *Gloria in excelsis* for a final doxology different from those generally used to close the Exultet: "Qui semper uiuis regnas imperas necnon et gloriaris solus Deus, solus altissimus, Iesu Christe, cum sancto spiritu in gloria Dei patris." Kantorowicz thought this Norman finale originated in Norman Sicily and passed from there to Normandy and to the rite of Sarum; but more recently David Hiley has found it in many manuscripts of Normandy and has suggested that the transmission is likely to have been from north to south.[109]

This Norman finale is found also in southern Italy: in the processional Naples VI G 34 and in Troia, Exultet 3 (both from Troia, a Norman foundation). It was added in the fourteenth century to the third Exultet of Gaeta. More often, however, it comes from the periphery of the Beneventan zone, where the many traditions meet. An example is manuscript M. 379 in the Pierpont Morgan Library—a central Italian monastic missal in ordinary minuscule. The Exultet has the Roman text, but the melody is the old Beneventan one—at least at the beginning: it switches to the Roman preface tone in the middle, at just the place where the two texts diverge. At the end comes the Norman finale; the rubric that follows demonstrates the foreign origin of what has preceded: "benedictione cerei finita, secundum teutonicum ordinem." It is not clear what is Teutonic about the foregoing. Is it the Norman finale? The Morgan missal, and those like it (Subiaco XVIII and Rome, Vall. B 23), may well reproduce an earlier source that physically substituted the Franco-Roman melody for the Beneventan.

    108. See Kantorowicz, "A Norman Finale," and idem, *Laudes regiae*, 231–33.
    109. Hiley, "The Liturgical Music of Norman Sicily," 31; on the Norman finale in Sicilian manuscripts in particular, see Roberts, "The Exultet Hymn."

Groups of South Italian Exultets Related by Their Texts

Textual details in the south Italian traditions of the Exultet lead to observations about relations among manuscripts. A number of related groups can be described, most of them, not surprisingly, consisting of sources from the same place or area. These groups are useful in what they tell about textual transmission, but they also contribute to a larger observation, namely that the transmission of text, music, and pictures can and often do follow separate paths.

A GROUP OF FRANCO-ROMAN TEXTS FROM BENEVENTO

Two manuscripts of Benevento have virtually identical texts. These are the upper script of Vat. lat. 9820, from the monastery of Saint Peter's *extra muros*, and London, BL Eg. 3511, for the other monastery of Saint Peter, within the walls. They suggest the presence of a written liturgical tradition and a regular scriptorium—though not necessarily at either monastery. Related to these textually is the Casanatense roll, also from Benevento. This is not quite so close textually: it includes the bees, but it has corrections in a later hand that bring it closer still. The Sorrento roll Montecassino 2 has many things that set it apart from Montecassino texts and relate it to the Beneventan group, especially to Casanatense. But it is not very close, and it uniquely quotes the old Beneventan text.

A TROIA GROUP OF TEXTS

The two early Exultets of Troia have the Beneventan text, but the third Exultet roll of Troia (s12) and Naples VI G 34, a processional of Troia (s12ex), are closely related, including the "Norman finale."[110] Troia 3 is the first Franco-Roman Exultet at Norman-influenced Troia, and Naples VI G 34 is the oldest source of the "Roman" melody of the Exultet in southern Italy.[111] The same Roman melody is added in a later hand to Troia 3. It is possible that the strong Norman influence at Troia gradually brought the use of the Norman text of the Exultet, with a melody that was at first rejected though it may well have arrived with its text, only later being accepted at Troia and universally as the "Roman" melody of the Exultet.

---

110. There are a few variants in addition to the Norman finale unique to this pair of manuscripts: "qui cum eo uiuit et regnat"; "sed sicut"; "O [uere] beata nox." The few disagreements are mostly matters of orthography, except for: alitur/alitur enim; christum/christo; luminibus/luminaribus.

111. Indeed it is older than Roman sources for the same melody; see Kelly, "The Exultet in Rome."

A MONTECASSINO GROUP OF TEXTS

A number of rolls manufactured at Montecassino share many textual similarities. These include the rolls of Avezzano, London, Pisa, the Barberini roll at the Vatican, and the manuscript Rome, Vall. C 32, whose text is very close to the Montecassino tradition.[112] To these may be added, from a textual point of view, the roll now in Paris, executed for the cathedral of Fondi, but whose textual tradition is that of the Montecassino rolls.[113] Certain other sources often associated with Montecassino do not seem by their texts to be closely related to this tradition. These include the Capua Exultet, the Exultet now Montecassino 2, the missals Vat. lat. 6082 and Vat. Ottob. lat. 576. A regular feature of the text of Montecassino Exultets, not used at Benevento or in some other places, is the invocation of a blessing on the donors of the candle: "et his qui tibi offerunt hoc sacrificium laudis premia eterna largiaris."

As will be seen in chapter 4, the music of these rolls is not copied from one roll to another, or from a lost model (with the possible exception of the London and Barberini rolls, which seem to have some aspect of a written tradition behind them). Likewise, the texts here are not uniform, but they have a great many details in common, and they suggest that a textual tradition of sorts was understood as the practice of Montecassino.[114]

THE FRANCO-ROMAN TEXT IN BARI

In chapter 4 we will see that the melodic tradition of Bari is one of gradual and continual development from one source to another. For the text, however, there is a certain degree of independence from one stage to the next.

The earliest Franco-Roman text in Bari is the upper script of the second Exultet roll (s11¾, rewritten s13), written over the erased Beneventan text; it shares a number of variants with Troia 3, which might suggest a Norman influence (no more surprising at Bari than at Troia), but few of the common variants are unique to these two sources. Bari 2 adopts an ending ("Saluum fac populum") from the Beneventan text, a tradition

112. Odermatt, *Ein Rituale,* 96, is hesitant to assign the manuscript to Montecassino.
113. There are other rolls evidently manufactured at Montecassino: Vat. lat. 3784, and the Velletri roll; but both rolls are now fragmentary. At least one of them (the Velletri roll), and probably both, contained the Beneventan text.
114. These details can be ferreted out of Appendix 2, where south Italian Roman texts are edited; there are a few details that are shared by most Montecassino Exultets and that set them apart from most of the other sources. They include the variants "filiumque tuum" (for "filiumque eius"); "senium" (for "senio"); "partim" (for "parte"); "legentes" (for "legere"); "onerate" (for "oneratis"); "collectum" (for "collectis"), perhaps "quassat" (for "quassant") though this is shared by many other manuscripts. Additionally, in the conclusion, the phrase "presentis uite quiete concessa gaudiis facias perfrui sempiternis" is unique in the south to Paris, London, Vall. C 32, and Vat. lat. 6082.

it passes along to Bari 3. This latter roll is close to Bari 2 in some things such as spellings, and it adopts the "Saluum fac" ending from the Beneventan text but uses it at a different place and with other elements not found in Bari 2. Unlike Bari 2, Bari 3 does not seem to bear much relation to Troia 3.

A CENTRAL ITALIAN GROUP OF TEXTS

There is a connection between southern traditions and those of the important monasteries of the Roman region, as seen in sources from Farfa, Subiaco, and some related manuscripts. These are missals for the most part, written in ordinary minuscule; they show a relation with the south when they give the first part of the Exultet with the Beneventan melody and the second part (after the *Sursum corda*) with the Franco-Roman preface tone.[115] Perhaps Farfa and Subiaco once used the Beneventan text of the Exultet; this would explain the presence of a double melody.

In this same group of manuscripts, the *Lumen Christi* is present, with a progressively elaborated melody for each of the three announcements.[116] The same elaborate music is found in Vat. lat. 4770, whose connection with southern Italy is made not through the Exultet (which is not notated here), but through many details of the Beneventan liturgy preserved in this manuscript of the early eleventh century from central Italy (Abruzzo?).[117]

These central Italian manuscripts share many textual characteristics, several of them indicating a relationship to the Roman-German Pontifical. Closest to the pontifical in this respect is Vat. lat. 4770, and related also to this group through their texts are the peripheral manuscripts Vat. Barb. lat. 699 (Veroli, s12ex; the Exultet is without notation) and Vat. Barb. lat. 603 (Caiazzo, s12/13),[118] both in Beneventan script.

A form of the Franco-Roman Exultet was used in the region around Rome before the arrival of the Roman-German Pontifical and subsequently affected by it. The varying amounts of text omitted for the praise of the bees (Table 6) indicates that the full text was originally present. Certain other textual details shared by these manuscripts are used in the Pontifical but not in the south.[119] The use of the word "sociatque" instead

---

115. See n. 99 and Appendix 1. The manuscripts include Subiaco XVIII; Rome, Vallicelliana F 29; Vall. B 43 (s12 ex); Vall. B 23; New York, Morgan M 379.

116. This elaborated version is not present in Vallicelliana B 43, which has only a single notation for *Lumen Christi*, with an indication that it is to be repeated.

117. On the MS, see Supino Martini, *Roma*, 153–59; on the south Italian connection, see Kelly, *TBC*, 45, 315–16.

118. Like the central Italian monastic manuscripts, this Caiazzo missal begins the Exultet with the Beneventan melody and switches to the Roman; unlike them, however, it returns to the Beneventan melody at the end.

119. They include the variants "tellus tantis," "infundendo," "quos postea," "liquentibus," and others.

of "sociat" is particularly interesting: it is the version of the Roman-German Pontifical, and it is used in this central-Italian group, and also at Benevento, but not at Montecassino, which keeps "sociat."

THE DALMATIAN SOURCES

Four Dalmatian manuscripts preserve versions of the Exultet with melodic and textual ties to southern Italy (Oxford, Bodl. Canon. Bibl. lat. 61; Canon. liturg. 342; Vat. Borg. lat. 339; Berlin 920). One might expect them to reveal regional groupings of textual variants, with some indication of their dependence on a particular place in southern Italy—Bari, perhaps, or Montecassino—as the source of their version of the text. However, the manuscripts are different enough among themselves as to suggest that there was not a single conduit through which liturgical and musical information passed to the churches and monasteries of the Dalmatian shore.

4

THE MUSIC

The south Italian Exultet has one of the simplest melodies ever written down; it uses only three adjacent pitches. A complete performance of the Exultet might last twenty minutes; the effect of the seemingly endless repetitions of the same few musical phrases is potentially stupefying or mesmerizing. And yet this melody is so intimately bound up with the text, so closely associated with the phraseology, the rhetorical structure of the words sung, that even the unfamiliar listener, soon made aware that the melody serves to heighten and underscore the larger and smaller phraseology of the text, is eventually drawn into an understanding of the performance as a sort of heightened speech or formal recitation, where the importance is on the shape of the poetical text being presented. The opening of the Exultet as sung in southern Italy is given in Example 1.

This southern Italian melody is not used for the Exultet anywhere else in Europe; it is a melody from the old Beneventan liturgy. The uniform adoption of the melody sung in the Roman rite of the twentieth century is essentially the result of the reforms of plainsong practice instituted by Pope Pius X and undertaken by the monks of Solesmes. The present text of the Exultet was adopted into the Roman missal of Pius V (1570), but there was still considerable melodic variety from place to place.[1] What we now recognize as the Roman melody of the Exultet, beautiful as it is, was not the first melody used in southern Italy, although it reached there by the twelfth century.

So far as we know, there is no musical notation for the Exultet anywhere before the tenth century; thus the oldest Beneventan sources are as

---

1. In 1826, there was still printed at Paris a missal for use in Spain that had a special melody as a result of a permission given by Pius V himself on 12 December 1570 (Benoît-Castelli, "Le praeconium paschale," 310).

EXAMPLE 1. The Beneventan melody of the Exultet

Vatican, Vat. lat. 6082, fol. 120v–121.

Ex-ul- tet iam an-ge- li-ca tur- ba ce-lo-   rum,

ex- ul- tent di- ui- na mi- ste- ri-   a,

et pro tan-ti re- gis uic-to- ri- a tu- ba in-to- net   sa- lu-   ta- ris.

Gau-de- at se tan-tis tel- lus ir-ra-di- a- ta ful-go- ri- bus

et e- ter-ni re- gis splen-do- re il- lu-stra-   ta,

to-ti- us or-bis se sen-ti- at a-mi-sis-   se ca- li-gi- nem.

Le- te- tur et ma- ter ec-cle- si- a tan-ti lu- mi- nis ad- or-na ta   ful-go ri- bus,

et mag-nis po-pu- lo-rum uo- ci- bus hec au-   la re-   sul-tet.

Qua- prop- ter a-stan- ti- bus uo- bis fra- tres ka- ris- si- mi,

ad tam mi- ram sanc-ti hu- ius lu-mi- nis cla- ri- ta-   tem,

80

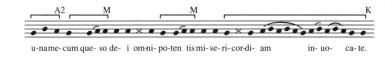

u-na-me-cum que- so de- i om-ni- po-ten tis mi-se-ri-cor-di- am   in- uo-   ca- te.

Vt qui me non me- is me- ri- tis in-tra le- ui- ta-rum nu- me- rum dig-na-tus est ag-gre-ga-   re,

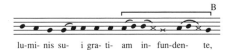

lu-mi- nis su-   i gra- ti- am   in- fun-den-   te,

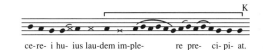

ce-re- i hu- ius lau-dem im-ple-   re pre- ci-pi- at.

Per do- mi- num nos-trum ie- sum chris- tum fi- li-   um su-   um,

ui- uen-tem se-cum at-que reg-nan- tem in u- ni- ta   te spi- ri- tus sanc- ti de-   us,

per om-ni- a se-cu- la   se- cu-   lo- rum.

old as any surviving melodies. The earliest melodic information about the Exultet is in Ordo Romanus 28, a Frankish document of about 800. The deacon, having completed the first part of the blessing of the candle (the Exultet text is not named), continues, after *Sursum corda,* with the second part, "inde uero accedit in consecrationem cerei, decantando quasi canonem."[2] That is, the deacon sings the melody used for the canon of the Mass (beginning with the preface). Evidently, what went before was sung to a different melody—perhaps it was that now used for the Roman Exultet.[3]

2. Andrieu, *Les ordines* 3:403–4.
3. The origins of the Roman melody of the Exultet are beyond the scope of this discussion, though we will return to its melody in southern Italy. Benoît-Castelli, "Le praeconium paschale," gives the best treatment, the result of comparing some 160 manuscripts and forty printed versions. There is no witness to the Roman Exultet melody before the

This practice of about 800 is followed in most liturgies for the Exultet: a special melody for the prologue and the local preface tone for what follows. The south Italian Exultet is unique among Western liturgies in singing both to the melody of the prologue and not shifting to a preface tone for the second part.

The Context of the Beneventan Melody

We shall presently turn to the melody itself, and how it is made; understanding the melody's structure will allow us to consider its transmission, its copying and composition, and will permit some observations about the relations of the surviving documents to each other. But first it might be well to be aware of some aspects of the context in which the melody is found. A few basic observations will help focus the discussion to follow.

1. *The melody is closely allied with the old Beneventan chant and its liturgy.* The Beneventan Exultet melody, whether it appears in the context of the old Beneventan liturgy or not, is nevertheless a product of that liturgy: it did not come from elsewhere, nor was it created in a liturgical context related to the imported Roman liturgy.

How do we know this? For one thing, all the earliest sources using this melody use it for the Beneventan text, and this text, appearing only in the south, is associated with the melody in the two sources (Benevento 33, Vat. lat. 10673) where the surrounding rubrics make it clear that the liturgical context is Beneventan, not Roman.[4] For another, the melody used for the Exultet is used also for singing other texts, all in the context of the old Beneventan liturgy: it is a regular musical feature of that liturgy and is not limited to the Exultet.

2. *The melody is not unique to the Exultet.* The Exultet melody is used for other rites of Holy Week as practiced in the Beneventan liturgy. Closely related is a tone used for prayers when they are part of a sung reading, a special tone to which the lector turns within a normal lection when the text quotes a prayer (or, as the manuscripts call it, a canticle): the prayer of Jonah, the prayer of Jeremiah, the prayer of the three children in the fiery furnace. The Exultet is not in itself a lection, and it is

---

twelfth century; the melody itself may be the development of either a German or a French tone; the modern tone is found in many Norman and English manuscripts, but not before the twelfth century. The "Norman" tone, found often in Franciscan and Dominican missals, passed from there to the missal of the Roman curia of the fourteenth and fifteenth centuries. Benoît-Castelli (p. 334) cites the Franciscan missal Naples VI G 38, of 1230–50, in Beneventan script, whose presumably Beneventan melody was erased and replaced by the "Norman" version of the melody, in square notation. We should note also the very simple, and possibly related, melodies of Brussels, Bibliothèque Royale II 3824 and Provins, Bibl. mun. 12, whose melodies resemble in some ways the inflections of the Beneventan melody. See Hiley, "The Liturgical Music of Norman Sicily," 35.

4. See Appendix 3.

not a quotation of a biblical prayer, like those of Jonah, Jeremiah, or the three children; but it is, of course, itself a prayer, at least in its second part, and is perhaps the source of inspiration for the singing of the biblical prayers to the same solemn tone in the following contexts (Example 2 compares these melodies with that of the Exultet):[5]

1. The reading of the book of Jonah, found in three manuscripts (Benevento 33, Vat. lat. 10673, Lucca, Biblioteca Capitolare 606) for Maundy Thursday, and in many others among the lessons for the Paschal vigil; this includes Jonah's prayer beginning "Clamaui de tribulatione," sung to the tone of the Exultet.[6]
2. A reading from the book of Daniel, including the canticle of Azarias and that of the three children, used in Beneventan manuscripts (Benevento 33, 39, 40, Vat . lat. 10673) for Good Friday, and at Montecassino and elsewhere for Holy Saturday.[7]
3. The prayer of Jeremiah preserved as a lection for Matins of Holy Saturday in Rome, Vall. R 32, fol. 22v and in Naples, Bib. Naz. VI AA 3.[8]

This melody is used, then, in the central events of the Beneventan liturgy. We do not have a complete understanding of the Beneventan liturgy, owing to a lack of documents, but it is clear that in its various formulations the melody was familiar to regular worshipers in Beneventan southern Italy. The Exultet was the final time this tone was heard during Holy Week. At Benevento it was heard on three days—Thursday (Jonah), Friday (Canticle of the Three Children), and probably, although no manuscript of Benevento preserves it, also Saturday Matins (prayer of Jeremiah) —before being performed at the Paschal vigil to announce the solemnity of the Resurrection. In the Montecassino tradition as it survives from the late eleventh century, these events are all compressed into the Easter vigil itself. The canticle of Jonah and that of the three children are sung as part of the twelve lections of the Easter vigil, followed by the Exultet after the lections; but when the blessing of the candle is moved to the beginning of the vigil, as in later Montecassino practice, the effect is reversed: the

5. For more detail on these lections and their music, see Kelly, *TBC*, 131–33, 158–60; *PM* 14:271–73, 318–21, 417n1.

6. The prophet Jonah is widely represented on south Italian ambos, often in two panels, Jonah being swallowed on one side and reappearing on the other. This is usually seen as a prefiguration of the Resurrection and as such has much to do with the symbolism of Easter. Such panels are represented on the ambo painted in the Pisa Exultet roll. On Jonah pulpits, see Glass, *Romanesque Sculpture*, 203–13.

7. A study on the wider use of this canticle in a variety of liturgies and with a variety of melodies is found in Bernard, "Le cantique."

8. Facsimile of the Naples source in *PM* 2: pl. 24. The prayer is also found to the same melody in manuscripts not in Beneventan script: Rome, Biblioteca nazionale, MS Farfense 32, and in Vatican City, Biblioteca Apostolica Vaticana San Pietro C 92, according to information generously supplied by John Boe.

EXAMPLE 2. The Beneventan Exultet and related recitation tones

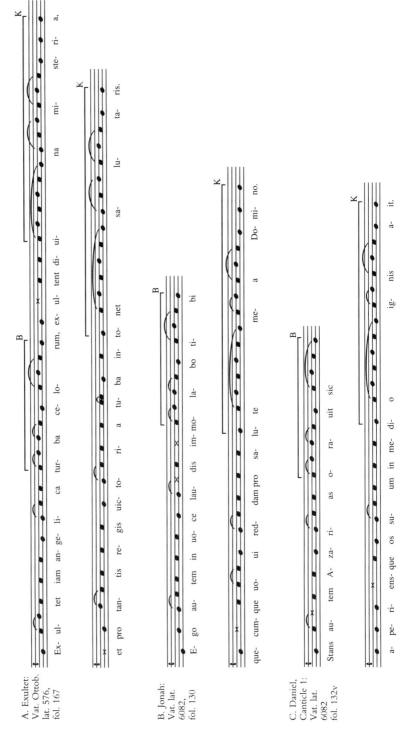

A. Exultet:
Vat. Ottob.
lat. 576,
fol. 167

Ex- ul- tet iam an- ge- li- ca tur- ba ce- lo- rum, ex- ul- tent di- ui- na mi- ste- ri- a,

et pro tan- tis re- gis uic- to- ri- a tu- ba in- to- net sa- lu- ta- ris.

B. Jonah:
Vat. lat.
6082,
fol. 130

E- go au- tem in uo- ce lau- dis im- mo- la- bo ti- bi

que- cum- que uo- ui red- dam pro sa- lu- te me- a Do- mi- no.

C. Daniel,
Canticle 1:
Vat. lat.
6082
fol. 132v

Stans au- tem A- za- ri- as o- ra- uit sic

a- pe- ri- ens- que os su- um in me- di- o ig- nis a- it.

84

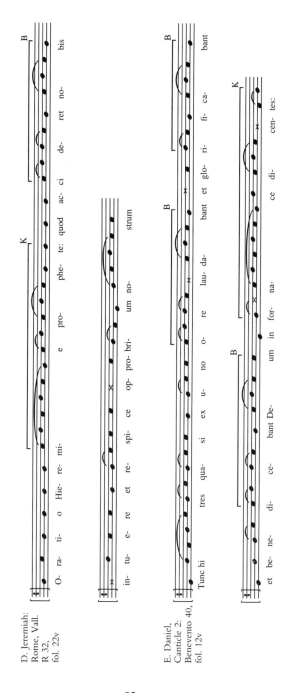

D. Jeremiah:
Rome, Vall.
R 32,
fol. 22v

O- ra- ti- o Hie- re- mi- e pro- phe- te: quod ac- ci de- ret no- bis

in- tu- e- re et re- spi- ce op- pro- bri- um no- strum

E. Daniel,
Canticle 2:
Benevento 40,
fol. 12v

Tunc hi tres qua- si u- no o- re lau- da- bant et glo- ri- fi- ca- bant

et be- ne- di- ce- bant De- um in for- na- ce di- cen- tes:

85

Exultet is no longer a culmination, but a prefiguring of the history of redemption to be narrated in the lections.

This tone is surprisingly widespread, being found also in Roman and central Italian manuscripts, as we shall see: it may represent a very old layer of Italian chant.

3. *This is the only Exultet that uses the same melody for the prologue and the preface.* The Beneventan Exultet is remarkable not only for its simplicity but also for its coherence: it is used for the opening portion of the blessing, the *Exultet iam angelica turba,* a text that is shared by the Beneventan, Roman, and Milanese rites and of considerable antiquity; but it is also sung for the continuation, beginning *Vere quia dignum,* whose text continues differently in the various rites. Here all other European practices change melody, beginning the *Vere* with the tone of the preface used in the Mass (which varies from place to place). The Beneventan Exultet is the only one that uses the same melody throughout.

Is the Beneventan Exultet melody also the melody of the preface in the old Beneventan Mass? This seems unlikely, if the preface tone found in the course of the old Beneventan Easter Mass in the eleventh-century gradual Benevento 40 is the usual old Beneventan preface. It resembles the Roman preface and is very close to the melody used in the older Benevento 33, though added slightly later to that text, and not there in an old Beneventan context. This Easter Mass may represent an amalgam of practices, but it is the only evidence we have about singing the preface in the old Beneventan liturgy.[9]

4. *The melody is not limited to the Beneventan text of the Exultet: it persists long after the Beneventan text has disappeared.* We have seen that this melody is highly adaptable. It is used for several texts in the Holy Week liturgy of Benevento, and it is made in such a way that it is easily adjusted to a variety of texts. Thus it is no surprise to find that it can be sung without difficulty to the Franco-Roman text of the Exultet, even though its original destination was Beneventan.

The Franco-Roman text was imported to the Beneventan zone well after the establishment of the Beneventan liturgy, as we have seen in chapter 3. The adoption of this text reflects a desire to adhere to the practices of the Roman church. But even when the Franco-Roman text was adopted, its melody—if it had a special melody on arrival—was discarded, and the deacons of southern Italy continued for a long time to sing the Exultet to the tone that they knew and evidently preferred. There is perhaps also an element of Lombard conservatism here, for elsewhere also there were efforts to preserve parts of the Beneventan liturgy in the face

---

9. We do know a little about recitation tones at Benevento: the pontifical roll (Rome, Bib. Casanatense 724 [i]) refers to three kinds of tones: "in sono lectionis," "in sono orationis," "in sono precis" (these last two seem to be the same tone, judging from a few elements of musical notation, and are not the Exultet tone); the Casanatense baptismal roll (MS 724 [ii]) refers to "in sono precis prephatio" for the *Sursum corda* introduction to the blessing of water: the notation is like that of the orationis-precis tone of the Casanatense pontifical and resembles the "Roman" preface tone.

of the increasingly prevalent Roman rite. Such efforts at conservation might well include the preservation of ancient solemn song for the central events of the liturgical year.

5. *The melody traveled widely and gives our best view of the extent of the Beneventan liturgy.* The Beneventan liturgy was practiced almost exclusively in the area dominated by the Lombards of southern Italy—the same area, that is, where the characteristic Beneventan script was written. Because of the special quality and beauty of the Exultet rolls, these have survived where many manuscripts have perished, and thus these rolls, along with the other sources of the Beneventan melody, can give a fuller view of Beneventan practice than might otherwise be possible. Wherever we find the Beneventan text of the Exultet, or the Beneventan melody of the Exultet, we hear echoes from a place that once employed the Beneventan liturgy.[10]

The influence of the Beneventan melody of the Exultet, and presumably of other aspects of the Beneventan liturgy, extended on occasion even beyond the Beneventan zone, to include Rome and the important monasteries in the Roman area. Two Roman churches preserve documents that use the Beneventan prayer tone: a lectionary of Santa Cecilia in Trastevere[11] indicates special singing for the prayer of Jonah and for the Canticle of the Three Children in the lections of Holy Saturday; and a similar practice is preserved in an epistle lectionary of the monastery of San Saba on the Aventine.[12] Interestingly, both churches have connections with Montecassino; Desiderius of Montecassino was cardinal priest of Santa Cecilia, and San Saba is sometimes said to have been populated by Cassinese monks.[13] The ritual of San Saba as regards the Exultet, however, is not that of Montecassino; the rubrics match none of the surviving Cassinese texts.[14]

In the important monasteries of central Italy near Rome, the Beneventan melody of the Exultet was sung from at least the late eleventh

---

10. A map outlining locations for the Beneventan liturgy is in Kelly, *TBC*, xvi. A similar map for the Beneventan script is in Lowe, *TBS*, 1: facing p. 48.

11. Kew (London), S. B. Cron collection S.N., formerly the property of Sir Sidney Cockerell.

12. Rome, Biblioteca Angelica 1383, s11.

13. Desiderius, abbot of Montecassino, cardinal priest of Santa Cecilia since 1058, was elevated to the papacy as Victor III in 1086. Desiderius is Montecassino's greatest abbot; he presided over the renewal of the buildings, the books, and the liturgy of his monastery. That Desiderius should have had some influence on the important activities of eleventh-century Santa Cecilia has often been supposed, but remains to be demonstrated in detail. See the discussion in Connolly, "The Graduale of S. Cecilia in Trastevere," especially 436–38; Levy, "Lux de luce," 44. On San Saba, see Supino Martini, *Roma*, 140–42; Jounel, *Le culte des saints*, 33, 65–66. The entry of San Saba in *Monasticon Italiae* 1:75–76 makes no mention of Cassinese influence.

14. The deacon sings *Lumen Christi* in procession, for example, which is not done at Montecassino. The rubrics of Rome, Angelica 1383, are provided in my study "The Exultet at Rome."

century until the fourteenth.[15] A significant group of monastic manuscripts, all of which provide the Roman text of the Exultet, use the Beneventan melody. These manuscripts are New York, Morgan M. 379
(s11/12, Foligno); Rome,Vall. B 23 (s12½, Norcia); Rome, Vall. F 29
(s12in, Farfa); Rome, Vall. B 43 (s12ex, used at Rome); Subiaco, S. Scolastica XVIII (s13, Subiaco). In two of these cases (Morgan and Vall. B
23), the Beneventan melody is sung for the first portion of the text, up to
the *Sursum corda;* afterward, the Roman preface tone is used. Such a practice makes it appear that here, when the new Roman text was adopted, the
portion that was old retained its old melody, while the new text carried its
(Roman) melody with it.[16]

The Beneventan Melody of the Exultet

Musical Notation

The melodic notation of the Exultet is that used for all music, Beneventan,
Roman, or otherwise, in Latin south Italy. Indeed, the earliest practical
sources of music notation in the south are Exultets or sources that include
the Exultet. They include the Benevento roll Vat. lat. 9820, the first rolls
of Gaeta and Troia, the first roll of Bari, the missals Benevento 33 and Vat.
lat. 10673, and others.[17]

    Beneventan musical notation, like most other music in this period,
uses a series of signs, called neumes, written in the space above the syllables to which they are to be sung. Each neume represents one or more
notes, and the neumes are generally arranged higher and lower in the
available space to represent higher and lower pitch; in later stages of the
notation this aspect takes on increasing importance.

---

15. The practice is probably still older. In addition to the manuscripts that include
the Beneventan melody of the Exultet, the Abruzzese (?) missal Vat. lat. 4770, s10/11, which
has many details of the Beneventan liturgy, has an Exultet text that probably was sung to
the Beneventan tone; but the only notation is that of the elaborate *Lumen Christi*, which
matches exactly that provided in all the other central Italian manuscripts except Vall. B 43
and seems to be as characteristic of the manuscripts of this area as does the Beneventan tone
for the Exultet. The central Italian missal Vat. Barb. lat. 560 (s11½, without notation, from
the area around Rome, perhaps Subiaco, according to Supino Martini [*Roma*]) is probably
also a member of this group, owing to its many liturgical similarities to Vat lat. 4770: unfortunately, it does not provide any musical notation at this point.
    16. For further information on the Exultet in these manuscripts, and their impor-
tance for the practices of Rome, see my forthcoming study, "The Exultet at Rome"; see also
pp. 77–78.
    17. Musical notation is also added to the two early rolls of Benevento now in the
Biblioteca Casanatense, Rome, kept together with the Exultet roll and all using the same
shelf mark: a pontifical roll, 969–82, and a roll for the baptismal rite (before 969). These are
not documents prepared for musical notation, however, and it is difficult to establish that
the notation is contemporaneous with the script; however, the notation includes all the
feaures of the earliest Beneventan notational style. See also n. 9.

The signs used in Beneventan notation, as elsewhere, are few, though they may be combined in a variety of ways. Single notes are written either as *virga* [ꜩ], a climactic note higher than the preceding, or as *punctum*, whose shape depends on whether it is higher [ꞏ], lower [ꞏ], or at the same pitch [-] as the preceding note. Neumes of more than one note, like the rising *podatus* [ꜩ] and the descending *clivis* [ꜩ], may have slightly different shapes depending on whether they begin higher [ꜩ] or lower [ꜩ] than the preceding note. Three-note neumes include the rising *scandicus* [ꜩ], the descending *climacus* [ꜩ], the *torculus* [ꜩ] and *porrectus* [ꜩ], and the ornamental *quilisma* [ꜩ], whose meaning is not well understood. Longer neumes [ꜩ, ꜩ] are made from combinations of these signs.

Any neume may be altered in its last note to become *liquescent*, that is, to represent the singing of a semivowel, a diphthong, or the end of a syllable ending with a consonant. Some liquescences add to the length of their neume, and others seem to decrease it. Some examples:

```
virga      ꜩ   ꜩ
punctum    ꜩ   ꜩ
clivis     ꜩ   ꜩ
podatus    ꜩ   ꜩ
```

A few other expressive signs are used by Beneventan scribes. They include the lengthening of notes by doubling them or by overlapping two neumes in a *pressus* [ꜩ + ꜩ = ꜩ]; the *oriscus* [ꜩ], used at high points, at the unison with the note preceding or one note lower; and the tiny *episema*, a barely visible stroke or line, usually below a note, with which scribes sometimes indicate a lengthening or separation. At the end of a line, and occasionally elsewhere, a *custos*, in the form of a little check mark, indicates the first pitch on the next line or the pitch of the note to follow on the same line when an adjustment in the height of the notation is required.

The chronological development of Beneventan notation can be divided very roughly into four stages, and these can be useful in the relative dating of musical manuscripts.[18]

Type 1, or early Beneventan notation (tenth to early eleventh century). In the earliest surviving specimens of Beneventan notation, the neumes are written *in campo aperto*—with no line to guide the height of the neumes. They are finely drawn, thinner than text written by the same scribe, and only roughly diastematic: that is, the signs are arranged higher and lower in the available space to indicate pitch, but not in a regularly measurable fashion. Ascending and descending single notes are often drawn as slanting lines rather than as points, and there are a number of details that will ultimately disappear from the notational system: neumes with loops, episemata, the quilisma. Not all these details are visible in the relatively simple music of the Exultet.

18. Facsimiles of Beneventan notations of all types can be readily examined in *PM* 21.

Type 2 (early to late eleventh century). The thin, spidery early Beneventan notation gave way in the early eleventh century to a style that is more vertically oriented and which matches the Beneventan script in many particulars: it includes many more strictly vertical strokes; it uses the contrasting thin and thick lines typical of the script; and it is written with a pen of generally the same breadth as that used for the text. It still lacks horizontal lines for orientation of the heightening—the lines that will become the musical staff—but the neumes are arranged so as to display pitches by the relative heights of the signs. The increasing thickness of the lines causes the disappearance of certain notational details used in type 1 notation: episemata, neumes with internal loops.

Type 3 (late eleventh to twelfth century). This is the classic Beneventan notation, matching in its calligraphic precision the high point of the Beneventan script seen in the late eleventh and the twelfth century at Montecassino and elsewhere. Here musical pitch is of primary importance: horizontal dry-point lines orient the music vertically, and in musical manuscripts they are colored, red and yellow, to show the notes C and F. Letters sometimes identify these lines. The neumes assume a regularity, an uprightness, and an elegance that match the maturity of the script. It is at this stage that certain further refinements of the old notation fall into disuse: notable among these is the quilisma, which drops out of use after the eleventh century.

The distinction between type 2 and type 3 notation is not easily made in the case of manuscripts that contain only the Exultet, since the simplicity of the Exultet's melody makes it impossible to observe the presence or absence of certain notational details. Moreover, the standard Beneventan Exultet uses only three pitches for most of the melody, and the relative heights of the notes is usually clear in such a situation, so that the intention of providing absolutely clear pitch indications—a clear sign of type 3 notation—is not easy to identify. It should be noted further that peripheral areas are slower to change than centers such as Montecassino and Benevento; signs such as the quilisma persist well into the twelfth century along the Dalmatian coast and in certain other peripheral sources.

Type 4 (thirteenth century–). A fourth stage, datable mostly from the thirteenth century and found often in peripheral areas, sees a decline in the regularity of the musical writing and an increasing fussiness in some unimportant details. A clear sign of this dissolution is the disregard of the "punctum rule" of Beneventan notation. This rule, part of the canon of classic Beneventan notation, holds that a punctum's shape depends on its position: rising stroke ascending, lozenge descending, square at the unison; this is abandoned in later notations in favor of a uniform shape everywhere.

The earliest notations (types 1 and 2) reproduce the contours of a melody, so that it reminds without prescribing: singers cannot read from them a melody they do not already know. Such documents are not intended for use in performance but to provide reference material for the memory and to provide records of what has been sung in the past and what is to be sung in the future.

Notations of types 3 and 4 are specific with regard to the pitch of the notes; they are legible in such a way that they can be read from during the performance, even by a deacon not skilled in adapting the melody to this text. This is, of course, a reason for making new Exultet rolls in cities where an older roll provided the older style of notation. Later generations might wish to discard their older Exultet rolls in favor of newer ones meeting newer notational requirements. This may be among the reasons for producing subsequent Exultet rolls in Bari, Benevento, Troia, Mirabella, Gaeta, and doubtless elsewhere also.

The transition from memory to writing, however, is not so easy to define as these categories might suggest. In particular, the simplicity of the melody of the Beneventan Exultet means that almost any one of these documents, even type 1 notation, would be all that is needed for even an inexperienced deacon. However, the general and perhaps gradual transition from dependence on memory (with previous reference to notation as a guide) to dependence on notation (with memories of past performances) is typified by the developments in notation characterized here, a development seen in many other places besides southern Italy.

Table 8 divides the surviving south Italian Exultets by notational type. The earliest Exultets, both in roll and codex, have type 1 notation. This is true of all the cities that have multiple rolls: the first roll has type 1 notation, and there soon follows a second roll in a more up-to-date notation. Note also that Troia seems to be a bit late getting started: this is owing perhaps to other factors as well, but Troia is in some sense a peripheral center as regards the development of notation.

The beautiful rolls of Montecassino are mostly of type 3 notation, with one example (Vat. lat. 3784) of type 2. Remember that the distinction between type 2 and type 3 is difficult in cases such as the Exultet, where the range is limited and the small number of signs is small. I have assigned most of the Montecassino rolls to type 3, even though most of them do not have clefs or staff lines, because of the care with which the heightening is indicated and the absence of the quilisma and certain other type 2 signs. This preponderance of later notational styles does not mean that Montecassino did not also use type 1 notation. Fragments of such notation do survive there,[19] but the renewal of liturgical books under Abbot Desiderius at the end of the eleventh century was so thorough that no complete musical documents from pre-Desiderian Montecassino seem to have survived.[20]

The square notation on colored lines known all over Europe from the thirteenth century is used in southern Italy from that date also, but not because the Beneventan notation was no longer considered appropriate.

---

19. Indeed, what may be the oldest surviving example of Beneventan notation—the colophon of Montecassino 269—was written by a Montecassino scribe; see Kelly, "The Oldest Musical Notation," which lists a number of type 1 survivals from the abbey.

20. See Kelly, *TBC*, 39–40.

TABLE 8. Types of musical notation in south Italian Exultets

Beneventan Notation

Type 1 notation

Exultet rolls: Bari 1 (s11½), Gaeta 1 (probably; s11in); Manchester (ca. 1100); Mirabella 1 (s11in); Montecassino 1 (s11[in?]); Troia 1 (s11 med or s11²⁄₂); Vat. lat. 9820 (981–87)

Codices: Benevento 33 (s10ex?); Vat. lat. 10673 (s10ex?)

Type 2 notation

Exultet rolls: Capua (s11½), or late type 1?; Bari 2 lower script (s11ex)?; Montecassino 2 (s12in); Pisa 2 (s11); Rome, Casanatense (s12); Vat. lat. 3784, hand 1 (ca. 1070); Velletri (s11ex?): an example of older style notation?

Codices: Farfa-Trento, s11; Oxford Can. Bibl. lit. 61 (s11ex); Vat. Borg. lat. 339 (s11ex)

Type 3 notation

Exultet rolls: Mirabella 2 (s12½); Gaeta 2 (s11); Gaeta 3 (s12½); Paris 710 (s12½); Troia 2 (s12½); Troia 3 (s12); London, BL add. 30337 (ca. 1080); Barberini (s11ex); Vat. lat. 3784, hand 2 (ca. 1070); Vat. lat. 9820 upper script (s12)

Codices: London, BL Eg. 3511 (s 12); Rome Vall. C 32 (s11²⁄₂); Berlin 920 (s12½); Naples VI G 34 (s12ex); Oxford Can. lit. 342 (s13); Vat. Barb. lat. 603 (s12/13); Vat. Ottob. lat. 576 (s12) Vat. lat. 6082 (s12)

Type 4 notation

Exultet roll: Troia 3, revised prologue (s13)

Other Notations

Italian notation

Exultet rolls: Pisa 1 (central Italian, s11); Pisa 3 (Italian, s13)

Beneventan-related central Italian notation[a]

Codices: Vat. lat 4770 (s11med); New York, Morgan M 379 (s11/12); Rome Vall. B 23 (s12½); Rome Vall. B 43 (s12ex); Rome Vall. F 29 (s12in); Subiaco XVIII (s13)

Square notation

Exultet rolls: upper script of Bari 2 (s13¾); Bari 3 (s13); Gaeta 1, upper script (s14); Vat. lat. 3784A (s14)

Codices: Naples VI G 38 (s13); Salerno 3 (s15); Salerno 4 (s15)

---

[a]Sometimes called "notation de transition" because of its combination of Beneventan-related notation with non-Beneventan text.

Square notation is used only when making new documents (Vat. lat. 3784A, the missals of Salerno, and so on) or when making a melodic change in an older roll. Older Exultets continued to be used well into the fourteenth century, and possibly much longer, evidently without there being any need to update their notation.[21]

How the Melody Functions

The Beneventan melody of the Exultet is a recitation using three adjacent notes. It can be adapted to essentially any text, though very short phrases can cause difficulty. Applying the melody to the text requires an understanding of the grammatical and rhetorical shape of the language, and of the variables in the melody, so that adjustments can be made at the appropriate places in the course of the Exultet. This process is the same whether carried out by a deacon in performance or a scribe in producing a new manuscript, and the process is the same regardless of the text to be sung.

The opening of the Exultet is given in Example 1. The text is divided into periods, and each period is usually divided into three subdivisions (or two, or four, depending on the length and structure); we can call each subdivision a *colon,* as medieval rhetoricians would have done.

A special musical formula marks the beginning of each period: this affects the first syllable of the period, which receives a special two-note accent (A1). The only exception is the opening word "Exultet," which receives the neume on its second syllable.[22]

Likewise, a special formula (K) marks the end of each period. This formula is anchored to the last accented syllable and applied to the five syllables that precede it: the formula is adjustable, therefore, for oxytone and proparoxytone endings, but it is not inflected otherwise to reflect the accentual or quantitative values of the final syllables. The little melisma of six notes may appear anywhere in the structure of a word: this is not a formula to enhance these particular words, but to show the close of a long section. A singing deacon, or a writing scribe (unless he is simply copying), must identify the last accent (the second or third syllable from the end), then count backward five syllables (while singing forward!) and begin the formula when he arrives at that syllable. It seems that

21. On the prolonged use of the Exultet rolls, see chapter 7.
22. In several later manuscripts, the accentual emphasis used for the word "Exultet" is borrowed for other paragraph openings where an accent clearly falls on the second or third syllable ("O felix," "Oramus te," "Ut si quis," "Solutis," etc.), and the neume is transferred to the accented syllable rather than left on the first syllable. This phenomenon appears, for example, in the Casanatense roll, in the Beneventan melody of the Farfa-Trento fragments, and in several Dalmatian sources. Later sources that have elaborated melodies also often use ornamental figures for certain period openings, particularly those beginning with the word "O."

musical notation is a matter of considerable convenience, even in such a formulaic music.

Within each larger period, subdivisions are made in the same way. A normal period may be subdivided into two or three cola, and each colon is identified by a special formula at its beginning and at its end. It must be remembered, though, that the opening and closing formulas for the period take precedence over those for the colon. Thus a period having three cola with beginning and ending formulas A2 and B:

A2 . . . B

A2 . . . B

A2 . . . B

will actually be performed with the period formulas superimposed, thus:

A1 . . . B

A2 . . . B

A2 . . . K

These interior cola, the real center of the recitation, are made like the periods. An opening formula (A2) is sung on the basis of accentuation, rising to the top note on the first accent ("EXUL-tent divina mysteria"; "ET PRO TAN-ti regis"). The closing formula (B) is melodically similar to the larger closing K. Here in B, the cadence is adjusted, as in K, for oxytone and proparoxytone cadences: the three-note neume (ce-LO-rum) of the oxytone-accented syllable is divided into two two-note neumes (mi-STE-RI-a) to accommodate the additional syllable of proparoxytones; the three syllables before the accent have special music.

With these formulas, the Exultet is complete, or almost. Everything not occupied by one of these formulas is sung, one note to a syllable, on the central note. However, this recitation may be articulated by inserting pauses: where the recitation might be too long for the singer, or too tedious for the listener, an intermediate pause, as it were a musical comma in punctuation, is used. This medial pause (M) is made by identifying the last syllables of the sense-unit after which the pause is to be made, applying a two-note neume to the last accent, and singing the preceding note to the pitch below the recitation (regis VICTORIA).[23]

Writing the Melody

The singing formula just described is used for the Exultet in most of the surviving Exultet rolls and in many other documents besides. It could be

---

23. More detailed discussions of this melody may be seen in *PM* 14:375–90; *PM* 4:171–85.

used to sing any text at all by simply studying the words and applying the rules as described.

However, the rules might be applied differently by different singers or scribes; one might divide a period into three cola, another into two; a medial pause (M) might be inserted by one singer and not another. Finally, there are a few places in both the Beneventan text and the Roman where exceptional language—usually short repetitive or exclamatory phrases—make it necessary to inflect the rules by overlapping one formula with another, by skipping out parts of melodies, and the like.

Such a passage appears in the Roman text:

> Huius igitur sanctificatio noctis
> fugat scelera
> culpas lauat
> et reddit innocentiam lapsis,
> mestis letitiam,
> fugat odia,
> concordiam parat
> et curuat imperia.

Or a similar passage in the Beneventan text:

> Flore utuntur coniuge
> flore funguntur genere
> flore domos instruunt
> flore divitias conuehunt
> Flore ceram conficiunt.

Examples of Scribes Applying the Melody to the Text

A few Exultets seem clearly to be made by copying a model. Such is the case with the Montecassino rolls now in the British Library and in the Barberini collection at the Vatican: where they might have proceeded differently (and where other Exultets of Montecassino do proceed differently), these two follow exactly the same procedure. This is of course entirely in keeping with the textual identity of the two rolls and the close similarity of their pictures.

In other cases, scribes solve the same problem in different ways. Example 3 shows a variety of ways of adjusting the melody to the short Roman text just discussed: various scribes choose to divide the text differently and to abridge and adapt the melody for this short-winded passage. Such passages suggest that transmission involves re-creation: that singers, or scribes, make a new application of the melodic rules to the shape of the text when a new document is needed. The London and Barberini rolls are the *only* Exultets whose text and music might have been copied from a single exemplar.

EXAMPLE 3. Varying applications of Exultet melodic formulas

Some further examples can make it clear that the process of creating an Exultet requires the ability to apply the music to the text as the process of notation proceeds. In the Capua Exultet roll, the scribe notated the beginning of "O felix culpa" in the normal way for beginning a period, with formula A1—and then erased the beginning in order to fit in all of formula B on "O felix culpa" (see Example 4 and Plate 5). This is the second thought of a scribe applying the formula as he writes; we see the process only in difficult places such as this.

In the Casanatense Exultet, the scribe apparently worked from a text that omitted the praise of the bees: he writes "Apis mater eduxit," skips the long praise of the bees, and continues with "O uere beata nox que expoliauit Egyptios ditauit Hebreos." But this last sentence is canceled with "ua- -cat," followed by an illustration of bees and the full text of the omission; only after all this is the previously canceled sentence repeated at its place after the praise of the bees. But the sentence has different music the second time, because in this new position it no longer ends the period (see Example 5). The notator, at least, is not copying but is adjusting the music to the text as he sees it laid out in context.

Such examples suggest that an Exultet, or any other musical text made in this way, is not a record of a remembered performance; it is more aptly thought of as a new performance, a new application of the rules of singing to a given text. This procedure draws, of course, on aural memory and on many other kinds of knowledge and experience, but it is created on the spot, in a situation somewhat more tolerant than the moment of ecclesiastical performance.

It should be evident that the text scribe, like the notator, must know the music. Whereas it might be possible to lay out much of the text in periods, to divide it into cola with punctuation and in some cases (Avezzano, Paris) with subsidiary colored capitals, there are many places where it becomes difficult to write this text properly if you cannot sing it. The text scribe and the music scribe are probably the same person, even where, as is usual, the text is written first.

EXAMPLE 4. *O felix culpa* in the Capua Exultet

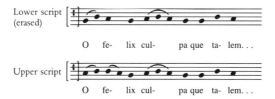

EXAMPLE 5. *O uere beata nox* as written twice in the Casanatense
Exultet

Variants in Formulas: Benevento and Montecassino

The systematic formula in each surviving source of the "standard" Beneventan melody shows variants that group sources into melodic families.
These families may have arisen from a unique single melody, but they can
best be studied in their later groupings before considering their origins.

The manuscripts of Montecassino show certain traits that suggest a
melodic tradition familiar at the abbey. Example 6 shows characteristic
places in the recitation. The opening formula A does not leap, but provides a two-note figure that fills the third; likewise the first neume of
formula K uses the same two-note figure (note that Pisa does not share this
version), which is used again at the beginning of formula A2. It might be
noted that the Avezzano Exultet uses an opening formula (both A1 and
A2) with a leap of a third, unlike other Montecassino manuscripts.

Manuscripts of Benevento have characteristics of their own. Example 7 shows manuscripts from Benevento, with two others (Ottoboni 576
and Montecassino 2) that share certain characteristics. Most notable is the
three-note figure at K; equally characteristic is the skip of a third, both
at the beginning (A1) and in A2, where an intervening note (on "et PRO
tantis") is not used.[24] The melodies of Ottoboni 576 and Montecassino 2,
like that of the Casanatense roll, use the characteristic three-note figure at
K but at A resemble the melody of Montecassino.

Example 8 shows a melody (melody Y) that appears in some early
sources and is the version used in most Dalmatian manuscripts. Here also
the third is not filled in, not even in formula K, where a single virga is used

24. In these leaps, the melody is similar to that of Avezzano.

EXAMPLE 6. The Exultet melody of Montecassino (Each passage shows the normal form of this formula in the melody of its manuscript. The texts of adjacent columns are often not contiguous in the Exultet's text. The columns are labeled with formulas used in Example 1 and elsewhere.)

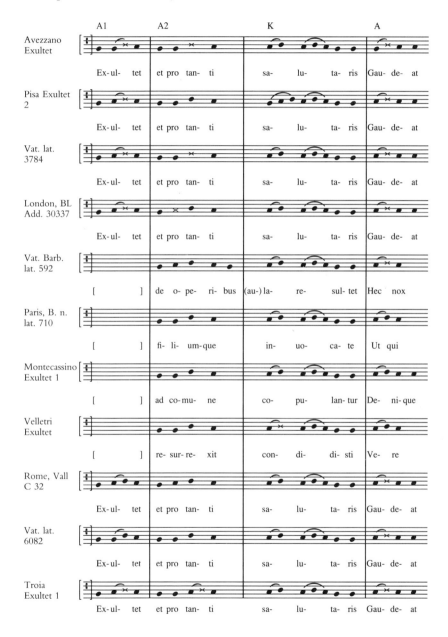

EXAMPLE 7.   The Exultet melody of Benevento (Each passage shows
the normal form of this formula in the melody of its manuscript. The
texts of adjacent columns are often not contiguous in the Exultet's
text. The columns are labeled with formulas used in Example 1 and
elsewhere.)

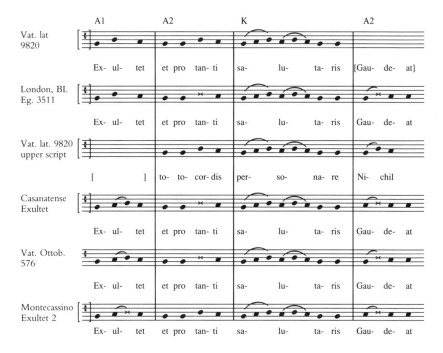

where other melodies use a two- or three-note figure. Exceptional is Oxford 342, which is a somewhat elaborated melody, and which fills in the
third at K in what might be called Beneventan fashion. The manuscripts
of central Italy are included in this example, but really only one of them,
Vallicelliana B 43, matches melody Y; the others are all closely related and
have a somewhat more developed melody that has a mixture of the characteristics we have seen.

One last melody (melody Z), including some of the oldest surviving
sources, suggests the original from which the other melodies may have
developed. In this version (shown in Example 9), it is difficult to be certain
of the melody because of the fragmentary nature of Vat. lat. 10673 and the
uncertainty of the intervals in Benevento 33. Nevertheless, the quilisma
at K (and, at Bari at least, also at A) suggests that this particular place,
and sound, caused difficulties when later notators tried to provide it with
unequivocal pitches.

The quilisma is an ornamental neume whose significance is not completely understood. It appears to require a special performance of the

EXAMPLE 8. Melody Y

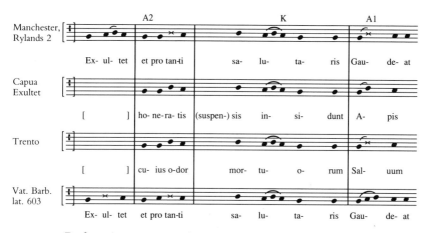

| | A2 | K | A1 |

Manchester, Rylands 2
Ex- ul- tet / et pro tan-ti / sa- lu- ta- ris / Gau- de- at

Capua Exultet
[ ] / ho- ne-ra- tis / (suspen-) sis in- si- dunt / A- pis

Trento
[ ] / cu- ius o-dor / mor- tu- o- rum / Sal- uum

Vat. Barb. lat. 603
Ex- ul- tet / et pro tan-ti / sa- lu- ta- ris / Gau- de- at

Dalmatian manuscripts

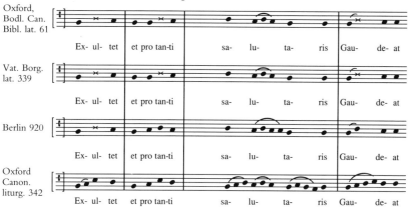

Oxford, Bodl. Can. Bibl. lat. 61
Ex- ul- tet / et pro tan-ti / sa- lu- ta- ris / Gau- de- at

Vat. Borg. lat. 339
Ex- ul- tet / et pro tan-ti / sa- lu- ta- ris / Gau- de- at

Berlin 920
Ex- ul- tet / et pro tan-ti / sa- lu- ta- ris / Gau- de- at

Oxford Canon. liturg. 342
Ex- ul- tet / et pro tan-ti / sa- lu- ta- ris / Gau- de- at

Central Italian manuscripts

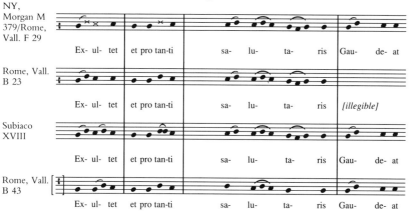

NY, Morgan M 379/Rome, Vall. F 29
Ex- ul- tet / et pro tan-ti / sa- lu- ta- ris / Gau- de- at

Rome, Vall. B 23
Ex- ul- tet / et pro tan-ti / sa- lu- ta- ris / [illegible]

Subiaco XVIII
Ex- ul- tet / et pro tan-ti / sa- lu- ta- ris / Gau- de- at

Rome, Vall. B 43
Ex- ul- tet / et pro tan-ti / sa- lu- ta- ris / Gau- de- at

EXAMPLE 9.   Melody Z

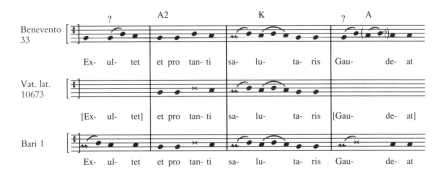

central pitch in a rising series of three; perhaps some wavering, rolling, or trembling is required, as is suggested by the wavy line with which the sign is written. In any event, this central pitch is to some degree unstable, since in later manuscripts it is sometimes written as the central note, sometimes as the top note.[25] The quilisma is written in a special way in southern Italy as apparently a two-note group covering the space of a third (elsewhere it appears most often as a three-note group with the wavy sign in the center); when it drops out of use toward the end of the eleventh century, it is the duty of scribes to resolve the ornamental sign into specific constituent notes. Such a process, no matter how conscientious, inevitably requires interpretation and choices on the part of scribes, and it is possible that the transcriptions of the quilisma—by one scribe as three notes, by another as the outer two of these, and by a third as the upper two—may represent a summary of how a quilisma might sound, and could also result in separate scribal traditions leading to the melodies of Benevento (three notes), melody Y (gapped notes), and Montecassino (the upper two notes).

At all events, it appears that separate scribal traditions exist. Though they may stem from a more unified performing tradition of the tenth century and earlier, they undoubtedly also represent families of melodies that indicate the distribution and influence of written transmission.

Not every melody fits perfectly into one of these groups, though. The surviving Beneventan melodies of Gaeta show characteristics of the Montecassino style at K but preserves the gapped third of Benevento and of melody Y at A.

In all these manuscripts, the melody is applied to the text in a formulaic and regular way. There are, however, the occasional small variants that we find in almost all chant transmission; these often occur at difficult or important places in the text. Example 10 shows the beginning of nine

---

25. For an introduction to the quilisma, see Hiley, *Western Plainchant,* 358 and index, p. 656.

EXAMPLE 10.   Openings of selected Exultets

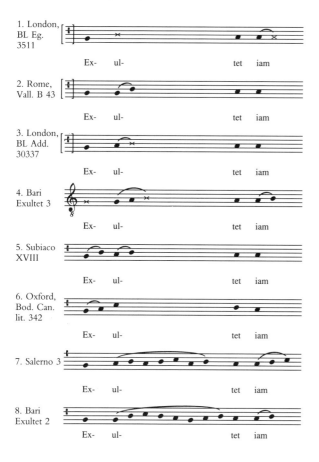

Exultets: all different, but all designed to emphasize the first accent of the text.

The first four are from the "standard" groups that present the original melody, but they are chosen to show a variety of openings related to the melodic families we have already examined. The leap of number 1 is in fact the only leap in this manuscript's otherwise entirely stepwise melody. The melody leaps a third, emphasizing the opening accent, before settling to the tenor on the central pitch. Number 2 compresses this leap to a single syllable, giving the further weight of length to the accented syllable. Number 3 keeps the weight but avoids the leap by filling in the third. Number 4 can be viewed as filling in the leap as presented in number 2; and number 5, perhaps related to number 3, creates a new leap on the first syllable, anticipating the high note of the second syllable.

The last three beginnings are from later, consciously embellished Exultets. Number 6 leaps beyond the range of the traditional Exultet on its first accented syllable, and numbers 7 and 8 use this high note as part of an extended flourish.

Melodic Decoration in Performance and Writing

The examples just considered lead into the realm of conscious variation from an established norm, a process that might be called elaboration, variation, or decoration; but they evidently point toward an aesthetic of performance that owes more to extemporization than to the faithful reproduction of an unvarying tradition. The Exultet provides us with a valuable view of how scribes and performers viewed their tasks and shows us some later medieval musicians at work on the music they inherited.

A comparative look at the elaborated Exultets will show many basic principles at work. Example 11 shows typical cadences from eight Exultets. The two versions of the intermediate cadence appear in columns B1 through B9, and the final cadences in columns K1 through K8. I have selected a Montecassino Exultet of the late eleventh century, British Library Additional MS 30337, as representative of the "standard" version of the melody, and its cadences are transcribed at the top.

In arranging the versions in order of ascending complexity, it is important to avoid the temptation to view them as a single development. Each version is a single way of singing the Exultet on a given occasion and is not necessarily based on one or another slightly less decorated melody in another source. A better approach, in most cases, is to consider each version in comparison with the "standard" melody, whose widespread familiarity is certain.

The Dalmatian missal Berlin 920 is quite close to the standard melody. It does, however, alter the typical torculus in column B5 to provide an anticipation of the final, and in column K3 it sometimes, but not always, extends the range to the upper fourth.

Subiaco XVIII, also a peripheral manuscript, uses in column B5 the same anticipation seen in Berlin 920 and extends the range, not upward, but below the final at the end—in columns K6 and K7.

The second Exultet of Troia extends the range in both directions. In the medial cadence at column B3, it precedes the standard clivis with another providing upper and lower auxiliaries and reaching the upper fourth; and in the final cadence the subfinal is reached by continuing downward at K3, and the subfinal is repeated, at K7, in proparoxytone endings.

The Melodies of Bari

With the three Exultet rolls of Bari, we are fortunate to be able to study the changes to the Exultet melody in the same place. The three melodies of Bari are clearly related to one another but show increasing elaboration in successive copies.

The first Exultet of Bari is one of the oldest extant witnesses of the traditional melody and the Beneventan text. Later in the eleventh century, a second Beneventan Exultet was made at Bari with a clearer musical notation. This second roll, however, was altered at a later date—somewhere around the turn of the thirteenth century; the Beneventan portions of its text were erased to provide for the Franco-Roman text in Gothic script, and its Beneventan melody was replaced throughout with a more elaborate version in an awkward square notation (Plate 3).

Bari also preserves a third Exultet roll, usually dated earlier than the revision of Bari 2 but whose melodic version clearly is a later development. This third roll has been little studied because it has no pictures; it is made, not too carefully, from an older scroll that once contained a Greek liturgical text (see Plate 4).

Example 12 compares these three Bari melodies. It is important to remember that, although Bari 2 and Bari 3 present embellished forms of the melody, they still follow the standard formal procedures for the Exultet: the formulas are regular and consistently applied.

Bari 1 presents a version of the "standard" melody. Noteworthy here is the quilisma in column K4, which is not typical of most later versions (see melody Y in Example 8).

Bari 2, after its revision, shows a development of this basic melody. The intermediate cadence B reaches beyond the third at column B2, continuing the upward motion. On the word "celorum" (columns B4–B5), the typical torculus is divided, its first note given to the first syllable. This produces, by analogy, the podatus at the corresponding place in the proparoxytone cadence ("MIsteria"), even though this version of the cadence lacks the original torculus, and the extra syllable allows a move to the upper fourth on the second syllable of "misteria"; this upper fourth is reached only on the three-syllable proparoxytone cadence.

Bari 2 never reaches this upper fourth in the closing formula K. Instead, there is an elaboration of the figure at K3 with an opening torculus and a final scalewise continuation down to the subfinal.

Bari 2's arch at K4, replacing the quilisma of Bari 1, is followed by what seems like its inversion at K5. The subfinal returns at the final cadence, but only where there is an extra syllable, as on "caliginem," column K7.

As for the melody of Bari 3, a glance will confirm that it is a development of the revised Bari 2, not an independent branch from the original melody of Bari 1. One of the most striking developments is the feminine ending of the medial cadence (columns B6, B9), achieved by a reallocation of the last three pitches, giving two of them to the final syllable. The elaborated figure in column B5 surrounds the two-note figure of Bari 2 with two rising three-note scandicus. The result is, in fact, that the last two syllables (ce-LORUM) are a reprise of the whole phrase: or more exactly, of the precise notes of "turba celorum" in Bari 2. The similar figure in column B8 (on "fulgoRIbus") is simpler because the phrase has already risen to the upper fourth on the previous syllable.

EXAMPLE 11. Cadential formulae of selected Exultets (*continues on pages 108–109*)

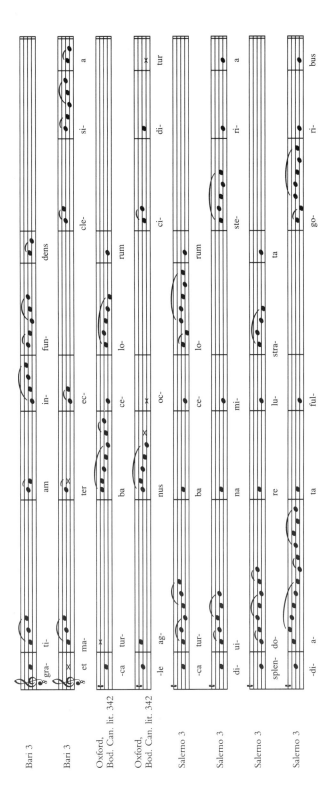

EXAMPLE 11 (*Continued*)

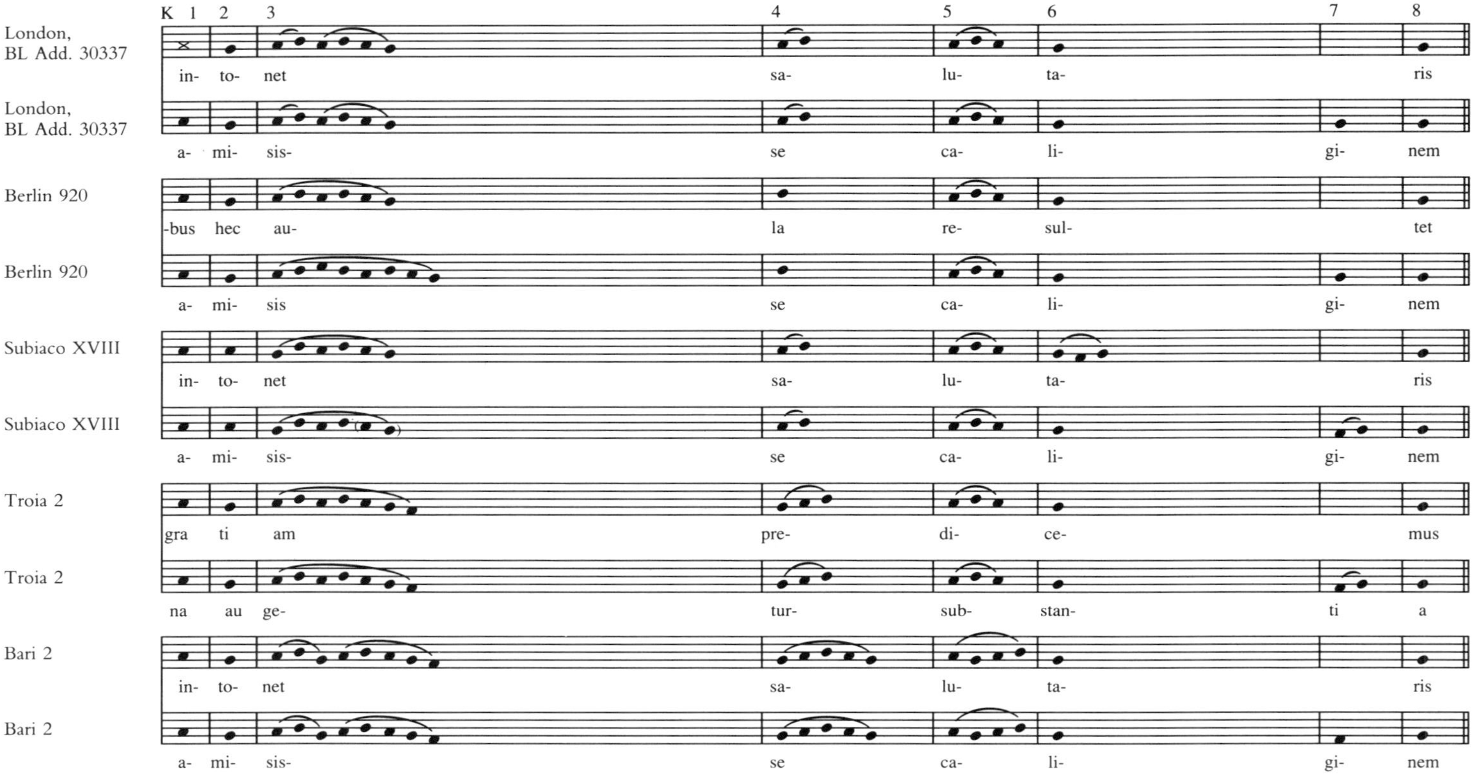

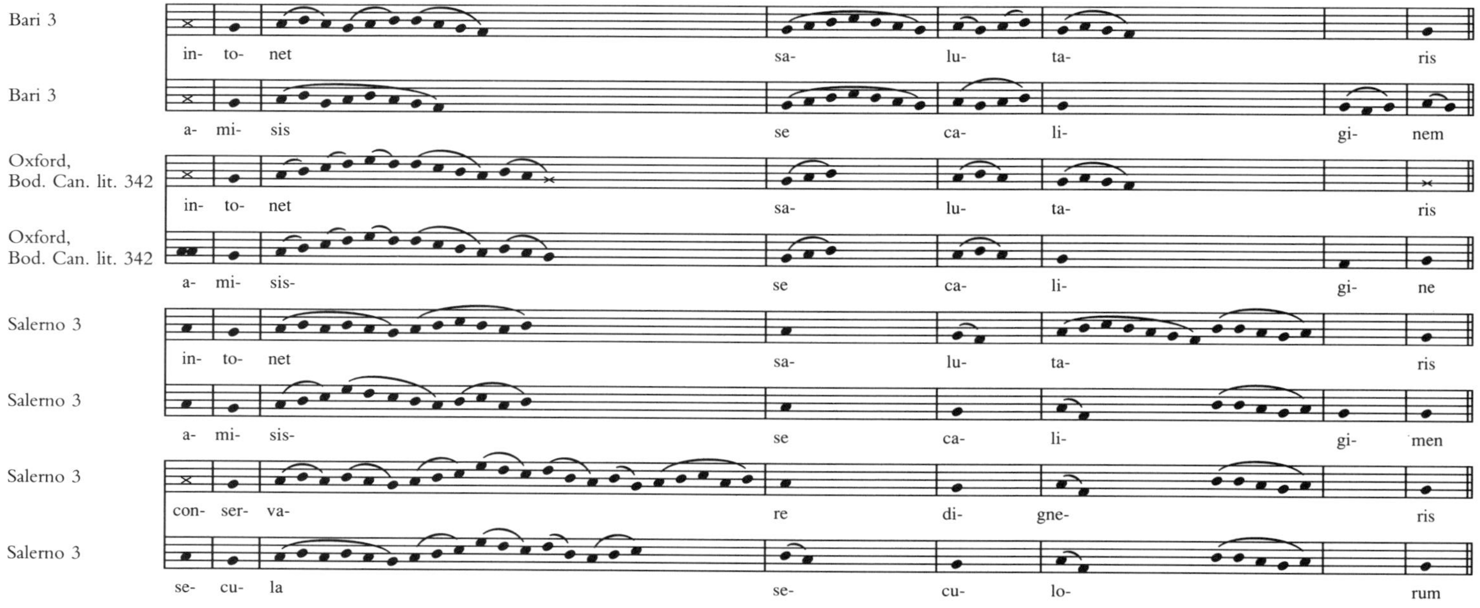

Bari 3
in- to- net sa- lu- ta- ris
Bari 3
a- mi- sis se ca- li- gi- nem
Oxford, Bod. Can. lit. 342
in- to- net sa- lu- ta- ris
Oxford, Bod. Can. lit. 342
a- mi- sis- se ca- li- gi- ne
Salerno 3
in- to- net sa- lu- ta- ris
Salerno 3
a- mi- sis- se ca- li- gi- men
Salerno 3
con- ser- va- re di- gne- ris
Salerno 3
se- cu- la se- cu- lo- rum

EXAMPLE 12. Cadences from Exultets of Bari

The final cadences of Bari 3 show some typical developments from Bari 2. On "intonet" (column K3), Bari 3 fills in a gap in the version of Bari 2. The arched figure at K4 is taken one step higher in Bari 3, to the upper fourth. And the final cadence, in both its accentuations, reaches the subfinal, which in Bari 2 was used only in the three-syllable cadence.

The Melody of Salerno

Two highly ornamented versions of the Beneventan Exultet remain to be considered. The thirteenth-century Dalmatian missal now in the Bodleian Library, Canonici liturg. 342, uses an elaborate melody (see Example 11), characterized by a loosening of the formulaic constraints of the original system. This Dalmatian melody was studied in some detail by Dom Hesbert in volume 14 of the *Paléographie musicale,* and we refer the reader there for an analysis of a melody that is ultimately derived from the simpler Beneventan melody as found in other Dalmatian manuscripts.[26]

The Exultet preserved in two fifteenth-century missals of Salerno differs from the versions considered so far in that it shows a loosening of the formulaic understanding of the melody and presents extravagant and florid melodies.[27] These twin missals, though they are written in Gothic script with occasional square notation, seem to be retrospective books, representing the liturgy of the twelfth century at Salerno, probably the liturgy as reorganized by Archbishop Romualdo Guarna. They contain many elements of the old Beneventan rite for Holy Week—including, as it happens, one antiphon whose melody is known nowhere else.[28] The Exultet has the Beneventan text—extremely unusual for the fifteenth century, but not so rare for the twelfth—and the Exultet is placed, in Beneventan fashion, after the lections. The Beneventan antiphons and tracts transcribed in these missals are remarkably close to versions preserved in eleventh- and twelfth-century manuscripts—except for the Exultet, whose exuberance probably represents not so much the development of several centuries as it does a Salerno practice of great virtuosity on the part of the deacon.

Some typical cadences are transcribed at the end of Example 11. Despite the melodic prolixity, and the fact that the cadences are not identically formulaic, we can see elements of the basic Beneventan melody. The decoration in column B5 and the elaborations in K3 occur at places where the Beneventan melody has its longest figures. Indeed, in column K3 we can recognize the original Beneventan melody in the first six notes of three of the cadences.

But the Salerno melody is more attentive to accented syllables than is the standard melody. The original Beneventan final cadence is entirely

26. *PM* 14:399–417.

27. This melody was first discussed in Latil, "Un 'Exultet' inedito."

28. Facsimiles of the complete Exultet, and of other Beneventan elements, are in *PM* 21:279–99; see the commentary, pp. 388–90.

oriented to the single accent in column K6, though the syllable itself is normally sung to a single note; the Salerno singers emphasize the accented syllable with an extended figure. They do the same in column B2 for a syllable that is often, but not always, accented, and when the emphatic musical formula is sung to an unaccented syllable in the text the result is awkward.

The Salerno Exultet follows the outline, and the general shape, of the Beneventan melody, but it does not limit itself to repeating the same formula when the same situation recurs. Indeed, it seems a part of the singer's duty to vary these inflections as his virtuosity makes possible. Some clear examples of this process of immediate variation and development are transcribed in Example 13, the Salerno versions of the threefold *Lumen Christi* and the passage in the Beneventan text beginning "Flore utuntur," whose short repetitive phrases surely seem to cry out for virtuosity, at least to a singer in the Salerno style.

The Dalmatian Sources

Melodies from the Dalmatian coast, as we have seen, belong to a melodic family as regards their standard version of the melody; and later Dalmatian sources include evidence of melodic elaboration. Berlin 920 gives a somewhat decorated version of the Beneventan Exultet, and Oxford 342 gives one of the most elaborate surviving melodies. There is, however, no evidence from the melodies themselves that there is a single tradition of progressive elaboration as at Bari. Perhaps if there were more intervening sources we could see the ornate melody of Oxford 342 as the product of progressive regional development. But these Dalmatian manuscripts also have individual and independent versions of the text; the Dalmatian coast, continually in contact with southern Italy, was not a single isolated cultural area.

Virtuoso Singers or Creative Scribes?

Even the standard Beneventan melody of the Exultet is no easy matter to perform. The singer must be an expert, and it is easy to imagine a temptation to embroider the melody at hand. One wonders how many of the "standard" Exultets were sung precisely as written; perhaps in the hands of an adventurous and capable deacon the Beneventan melody served as a framework for extempore embellishment. Perhaps it is a change of writing habit, not of performance style, that gives us our few decorated melodies. They are perhaps records of a singer's performance, rather than the foundation on which he builds.

An example of this change of style, or change of habit, may be seen in the Casanatense Exultet. The roll has the standard melody, and the text ends with an abbreviation "Per dnm," the rest of the doxology being so well known as not to require writing out. A later hand, however, has

EXAMPLE 13. Decorated phrases in the Salerno Exultet (Salerno, Archivio del Museo del Duomo, manuscript without shelf-number [Capone 3])

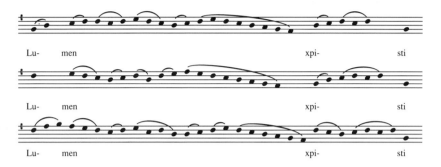

Lu- men   xpi-   sti

Lu- men   xpi-   sti

Lu- men   xpi-   sti

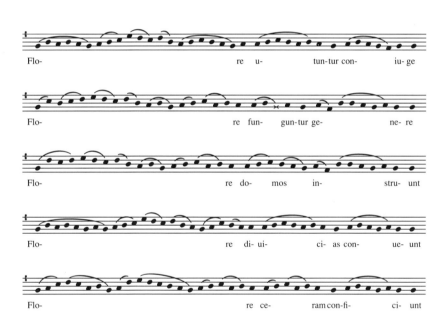

Flo-   re u-   tun-tur con-   iu- ge

Flo-   re fun-   gun-tur ge-   ne- re

Flo-   re do-   mos   in-   stru- unt

Flo-   re di- ui-   ci- as con-   ue- unt

Flo-   re ce-   ram con-fi-   ci- unt

EXAMPLE 14. Phrase openings in the upper script of Vat. lat. 9820

Sed   iam . . . A-   li-   tur . . . Hec   nox   est . . .

written out the full ending, and the notation provides a melodic flourish not seen in the original text (see Plate 6). Is this a decoration to mark the end, or is it possible that this melodic elaboration was applied to the whole Exultet when it was sung from the Casanatense roll at the later date when the ending was entered?

Perhaps, too, the alterations in the melody of the upper script of the Beneventan Exultet roll Vat. lat. 9820 show a tendency to extempore embellishment preserved in writing. Here the little embellishments come on the opening syllables of periods, not at their ends; but they describe what may be a widespread unwritten practice (Example 14).

At some point in the later history of the Barberini roll, a more elaborate melody was sung from the roll; a second hand has added tiny neumes above certain portions of the text, usually the beginnings of periods (Example 15 and Plate 7). Where they can be read, they represent a more elaborate melody than that provided by the original notator. Whether this was a decorated version of the Beneventan melody or another melody altogether cannot be determined from the few legible additions that survive. It is clear, though, that at least one deacon needed to add something to the roll and that the melody written by the original notator was not then sung exactly as written.

Evidently the practice of ornamentation, of elaboration, was more widespread than our surviving documents indicate. But some of these ornamented melodies do survive, and they permit us to study at close range the nature of medieval musical elaboration. It is remarkable how often musicologists speak of a decorated melody, of a melodic embellishment—and how seldom we actually can compare framework and ornamentation. This melody gives us such an opportunity, and it is a rare one. With further study, we may come closer to a medieval, rather than a modern, appreciation of this and other music; and the music of the Exultet rolls of southern Italy may once again take its rightful place, with the illustrations, in our esteem for the beauties of these extraordinary documents.

Other Melodies: The "Roman Melody" in Southern Italy

Sources of the Exultet from southern Italy use the Beneventan melody, with few exceptions, which are generally late or peripheral. The exceptions are (1) a unique melody in the Farfa-Trento fragments; (2) the missal

EXAMPLE 15.   Musical alterations in the Barberini Exultet

Hec   nox est . . .   reddit   Hec . . .

Vat. Barb. lat. 603, perhaps of Caiazzo, which begins with the Beneventan tone, switches to the "Roman" preface tone, and returns to the Beneventan melody for the ending; and (3) five witnesses to the "Roman" melody of the Exultet (Naples VI G 34; Naples VI G 38; Vat. lat. 3784A; Gaeta 1; Troia 3).

The two bifolia from a Beneventan missal, now divided between libraries at Farfa and Trento, have the distinction of presenting two versions of the Exultet: the Beneventan text with the Beneventan melody, and the Franco-Roman text with a melody unique to this remarkable fragment. This second melody, a decorated recitation, must be derived from one of many *toni sollemniores* for prayers.[29] The beginning of the surviving portion is given in Example 16.

The melody has characteristics now familiar: an opening formula (A), here applied to either two or three syllables and used alike for beginnings of periods and of interior cola. The closing formula K is based on two accents (shown in capital letters) and is adjustable in both accents by adding or omitting the notes in parentheses. An intermediate cadence B is based on a single accent, preceded by two two-note neumes; the last syllables are adjustable for oxytone and proparoxytone endings. An intermediate pause (M) is similar to that in the Beneventan melody.[30]

Unfortunately, the lacunary state of the fragment deprives us of all of the prologue: we cannot tell whether it was sung to this same recitation. But it is possible to surmise that it was not. The Beneventan Exultet that follows immediately begins, not with the prologue, but directly with the preface; rewriting the prologue, which is the same in both texts, is unnecessary, especially if it is sung to the same melody both times. It seems unlikely that the local traditional text—the Beneventan Exultet—was sung in this south Italian manuscript with any other melody for its preface than that which accompanies the Beneventan continuation; in both versions transmitted in this fragment, the prologue was sung to the melody usual in the south, and the continuation was sung to a new melody that arrived with, or was invented to accompany, the newly received text.

This is not an isolated phenomenon: there is physical evidence of such a change, in the Exultet roll Vat. lat. 3784, in which a Cassinese prologue with Beneventan melody is paired with a Neapolitan roll made much later, with Franco-Roman text and melody (one laments the loss of

29. I am grateful to John Boe for his expertise on south Italian recitation tones.
30. This melody has been studied in much detail in *PM* 14:390–98.

EXAMPLE 16.   From the first of two melodies of the Exultet contained in Farfa, Biblioteca dell'Abbazia, Ms. AF. 338 Musica XI

the original continuation!). The same combination of melodies is seen in the central Italian manuscripts that combine the Beneventan prologue with a Franco-Roman continuation using the Roman preface tone.[31] These manuscripts represent in a single writing the same process so brutally exemplified in the amputation of Vat. lat. 3784. In the missal Vat. Barb. lat. 603, the Exultet begins with the Beneventan melody and switches to the Roman preface tone; but here the melody returns to the Beneventan for the final commemorations, "Precamur ergo te domine": a process that looks like the substitution of a Roman portion in the middle of a formerly Beneventan Exultet. However, the return to the Beneventan tone does not return to the Beneventan text. The Beneventan commemoration "Saluum fac" is not used here; it might be that the Beneventan Exultet at Caiazzo once used the Franco-Roman "Precamur" ending, even for the Beneventan text,[32] and that this memory switched the melody back to Beneventan in Barb. lat. 603 despite the textual difference.

The "Roman" melody of the prologue is rare in southern Italy even in the thirteenth century. It is found in the Franciscan missal Naples VI G 38, of the thirteenth century. Here the Exultet is notated in a different

31. Subiaco XVIII; New York, Morgan M 379; Rome, Vall. B 23; Vall. F 29 (we presume this from the fact that the prologue with Beneventan melody is followed by the Roman text without notation, but with the indication "p[re]ph[atio]."

32. This would not be the only case; the "precamur" ending is written as an alternative ending for the Beneventan text in the Farfa-Trento fragments; see the edition in Appendix 2.

and later hand from that which wrote the rest of the musical notation in the manuscript.[33] The presence of the Roman melody in the fourteenth-century upper script of Gaeta 1 should be no surprise: not only did Gaeta have Franciscan bishops,[34] but also the Roman liturgy, in its uniform Franciscan guise, had been adopted almost universally. The beginning of the Roman melody is given in Example 17.

Elsewhere, the "Roman" melody of the prologue is found with Franco-Roman texts that also include the "Norman finale."[35] One might be tempted to think that the Norman influence in southern Italy, bringing with it imported liturgical practices, was the impetus for the change to the Roman melody. The processional Naples VI G 34 (s12ex), from Norman-influenced Troia, is the only south Italian source that provides the Roman melody in the original hand (except for the very late Vat. lat. 3784A).

However, the Norman finale is found also in Troia 3, an Exultet roll of the second half of the twelfth century, whose music is Beneventan; it was altered at a later date (probably in the thirteenth century) to the Roman melody.[36] The Norman finale was added in the fourteenth century to Gaeta 3, without any attempt to change the roll's Beneventan melody. So the Norman finale arrives, but the Beneventan melody remains. The Norman conquest of southern Italy, of which the Norman finale of the Exultet is a very small side effect, was not also the impetus for the change to the Roman melody.[37] The cause for this change must be sought elsewhere: perhaps in the thirteenth-century standardization of Roman books, or in the spread of the reformed liturgy of Montecassino in its regional adaptation of the Roman-German Pontifical.

What is surprising, on the other hand, is the survival of the Beneventan melody at all. Doubtless it continued to be sung, here and there, in places where there are Exultet rolls; and indeed it is written anew, though in an ornamented form almost unrecognizable, in two missals of fifteenth-century Salerno.

---

33. But it is not palimpsest, as is suggested by Huglo, "Exultet," 336.

34. See the description of Gaeta Exultet 1 in Appendix 1.

35. Three related missals from central Italy (Subiaco XVIII, Morgan M 379, and Rome, Vallicelliana B 23) all have the Norman finale, and all use the Beneventan melody. These are sources peripheral to the Beneventan zone, written in ordinary minuscule; but they use the Beneventan melody for the first part of the Exultet and the Roman preface tone thereafter. In the Morgan missal, the rubric that follows the Exultet demonstrates the foreign origin of what has preceded: "benedictione cerei finita, secundum teutonicum ordinem." But what is Teutonic about the foregoing: is it the Roman melody? the Norman finale?

36. The Roman melody is not found in Rome before the thirteenth century, and it may be through the adoption of Franciscan books that the melody of the prologue arrived in Rome (the preface tone, of course, was already in use); thus Naples VI G 38 may be among the earliest witnesses of the Roman melody in this Franciscan context. See my "The Exultet at Rome."

37. On the Normans in southern Italy, including a salutary debunking of the importance given to their influence, see Davis, *The Normans and Their Myth,* 77–101.

EXAMPLE 17. The "Roman" melody of the Exultet, from Naples VI G 34

5

THE PICTURES

Almost all the Exultet rolls of southern Italy are adorned with series of illuminations placed in the course of the text and the music. These pictures, among the largest manuscript illuminations made up to their time in the Middle Ages, have been the chief source of interest in the Exultet rolls. Much has been written about them by historians of art, and much has been learned. In this chapter we will consider the pictures, but our interest here is not in the pictures as individual compositions or in the sources, the models, the imagery, or the artistry of the individual pictures. These matters have been treated in detail by others, and all the pictures can be seen both in the recent catalogue entitled *Exultet* (where almost the full length of every roll is reproduced in color) and in Myrtilla Avery's pioneering *The Exultet Rolls of South Italy*. Both publications provide substantial commentary on the pictures, and the bibliography at the end of this book provides many references to further art-historical studies.

In almost every case, the pictures that appear on Exultet rolls occupy the full width of the roll,[1] and since Exultet rolls are written vertically, with a single column of text, it follows that any picture that is not at the head of the roll before the words begin, or at the end of the roll after the words finish, must interrupt the column of text, which will resume after the picture. As it happens, most pictures do appear in the course of the text, and so the interruption they cause in the process of reading has to be chosen. This choice might be made purely on a visual basis: placing the pictures evenly throughout the roll, making certain to avoid placing them where they will not fit on a single membrane. Even so, placement might

---

1. Exceptions are rare; in the Pisa roll, a column ("Sed iam columne huius preconia nouimus") runs alongside its text for six lines; in the Manchester roll, two illustrations of bees fill the spaces at the ends of short lines.

take into account the requirements of a reader, inserting pictures where it is convenient for a reader to pause for breath, at the end of some larger grouping of the text. Or if a picture illustrates some passage in the text, an effort might be made to insert it as near as possible to that passage.

In fact, all these considerations go into the placement of pictures in Exultets. Some pictures do appear in groups at the head of a roll before the text begins (Pisa, Gaeta 3, Vat. lat. 9820, and others). Although it is unusual to save pictures for placement after the text has finished, there are pictures of the presentation of the roll to Saint Peter in Vat. lat. 9820, and to Christ in Montecassino 2, final pictures that are about the roll itself, at least in part, and that stand outside the text.[2] Some illustrations do seem to appear at convenient places in the course of a membrane or of a roll, even when they are thus displaced from the text to which they refer. The portraits of ecclesiastical and secular authorities, whose texts come too close together for convenience, are sometimes placed in this way: in Bari 1, for instance, the two pictures are arranged in the penultimate membrane without much regard to their texts. And it is also true that pictures are often—indeed, usually—inserted with at least some regard to the larger structure of the text. The two large divisions of the text are articulated usually by two illuminated letters: the E of "Exultet" and the V of "Vere dignum"; these letters cannot, of course, really come anywhere else, since they are actually part of the text; but they are often as large as any of the other pictures, and just as decorative, so that they do serve to articulate the text, visually, at the same time that they need to be counted among the pictures. Further, makers of Exultet rolls usually take care to insert a picture at a relatively convenient place in the text: lines do not generally stop partway across the page to accommodate a picture (one might be tempted to stop right away at the word "tellus," for example, or "ecclesia"), and generally pictures are inserted between the end of one poetic-musical period and the beginning of another. This is significant, it seems to me, in what it tells us about the collaboration of musician, scribe, and painter.

The pictures are one among several elements that work together to make an Exultet. We have considered the text and its changes, the music and its varying possibilities, and here we will consider the pictures in the same way, with a view to discussing the varieties of transmission of these elements in a later chapter.

What Is in the Pictures?

The pictures on Exultet rolls can be divided into categories based on their subject matter. Pictures of every type appear in virtually every one of the illustrated rolls.

---

2. The mounted knight at the end of Troia 2 is such a final picture, but it is a later addition.

1. *Decorated letters.* The initial letters E(xultet) and V(ere quia dignum), of which the latter often contains a figure of Christ, mark the beginnings of the two principal portions of the text and are usually very large, of a size similar to the figural illustrations. There are often many smaller decorated letters as well, but these are not of a scale to be considered among the illustrations.

2. *Pictures of allegorical or biblical subjects named in the text.* This is a category easy to define in itself but difficult to distinguish from the two that follow. Here I mean the representation of such nouns as "tellus," "ecclesia," "angelica turba celorum," "apis": things not present but being sung about. Historical pictures include the passage of the Red Sea ("Hec est nox in qua primum patres nostros filios Israhel eductos de Egypto rubrum mare sicco uestigio transire fecisti") and the Harrowing of Hell ("Hec nox est in qua destructis uinculis mortis Christus ab inferis uictor ascendit"), to name the two most frequent. But the text is highly poetic and evocative, and there are many other passages that suggest pictures, at least to some illustrators: the virginity of Mary ("Sicut sancta concepit uirgo Maria"), the sin of Adam ("O certe necessarium Ade peccatum"), and others. The category, then, extends from the very particular noun to the rather more general concept. Finally, in fact, there are some pictures whose very religious nature makes them appropriate subjects in a liturgical document (the Lamb of God surrounded by symbols of the Evangelists; the Crucifixion) but whose specific relationship to this text is not nearly so clear as is that of most of the pictures.

3. *Representations of ecclesiastical and secular authorities.* These figures, referred to in the commemorations near the end of the text, are different from the previous group in that they are pictures of living persons: pope, bishop, emperor, king—or at least of existing orders of authority. They are for the most part not portraits in the sense of attempting a likeness,[3] but praying for the (living) pope and seeing a picture of a pope on a throne connects the two.

4. *Pictures of the liturgical ceremony of the Paschal candle.* At the beginning of the text, and at places in the text that refer to the singer ("Quapropter astantibus uobis fratres karissimi . . . una mecum queso dei omnipotentis") or to the candle ("sed iam columne huius preconia nouimus quam in honore dei rutilans ignis accendit"), there are often pictures that show the elements of the ceremony: the deacon, the ambo, the Paschal candle, the Exultet roll itself. These are in some sense representations of the ceremony during which the document on which they are painted is used.

5. *Frontispiece paintings.* In some rolls, one or more paintings precede the text itself, and these often have only an indirect connection with the illustration of the text. The subjects may range from a single Lamb of God, or Christ enthroned, to a long series of paintings of the life of Christ. These series will be given further consideration shortly.

3. Ladner, "The 'Portraits.' "

How Are the Pictures Arranged?

The pictures in the illustrated Exultet rolls generally interrupt the column of text and occupy the full width of the roll. The two portions of the text are articulated by the two large initial letters. Preceding the letter E of "Exultet," one or more pictures may serve as a frontispiece. Occasionally a picture may come after the text is finished, as a sort of colophon. The remaining pictures usually are found as individual illuminations in the course of the text and are placed near the passage in the text they illustrate.

Table 9 shows in a schematic form the illustrative content of four Exultet rolls: it is a shame to represent such beautiful objects by such a pedestrian list, and the reader is urged to see these as pictures, not descriptions. Yet the table may help to see certain general patterns of illustration and will be a useful reference in further discussions.

These four rolls do not present the only arrangements of pictures in Exultet rolls, but they are in some ways important representatives.

1. Bari 1 is not the oldest Exultet, but of the old rolls preserving the Beneventan text it is the only one that is complete; its pictures are reversed with respect to the writing.
2. Vat. lat. 9820 is the oldest surviving Exultet roll, but it has been mutilated and reordered. The picture series summarized here is that of the original Beneventan text, so far as it can be reconstructed; a lacuna in the roll might have contained further pictures. The pictures were originally oriented in the same direction as the script, but the erased and reordered roll has turned them upside down.
3. The Casanatense roll is from Benevento and is based on the illustration cycle used also in Vat. lat. 9820: most of its common pictures are the same pictures, not just the same subject. But the Casanatense roll uses the Franco-Roman text and thus needs to adjust some pictures to new places and adds certain scenes not suitable in the Beneventan text.
4. The London Exultet (British Library Add. 30337) is a beautiful roll of Montecassino, one of the artistic high points of this genre, and presents another solution to the problem of illustrating the Franco-Roman text.

Much is not represented here: the passage in the text that each picture illustrates is not given, nor is the placement of the picture with relationship to that text. This is a matter of some importance, but it is a complex question and will be dealt with separately in chapter 7, where there is a discussion of the problems of manufacture and layout in Exultet rolls.

The table does show some basic facts. Many subjects are common to all four rolls and to many others. This is sometimes because the text is so colorful, or the word so suggestive (earth, church, bees), that the subject seems inevitable. Other subjects, however, may be part of a larger tradition of illustrated Exultets.

TABLE 9. Arrangement of pictures in four Exultet rolls

Bari 1	Vat. lat. 9820	Casanatense Exultet	London Exultet
	1. Bishop on throne	1. Bishop on throne	
1. Christ in glory	2. Lamb of God	2. Lamb of God	1. Christ enthroned
2. Angelica turba	3. Angelica turba (with seraphs)	3. Angelica turba	
		4. Seraphs	
	4. Harrowing of Hell	5. Harrowing of Hell	
	5. Lighting of candle	6. Lighting of candle	
3. E(xultet)	6. E(xultet)	7. E(xultet)	2. E(xultet)
....	....	....	....
			3. Angelica turba celorum
			....
			4. Ecclesia
			....
4. Tellus	7. Tellus	8. Tellus	5. Tellus
....	....	....	
	8. Ecclesia	9. Ecclesia	5. Ecclesia
	....	10. Populus	....
	9. Populus	....	
	....		
5. Deacon ("fratres": or Ecclesia?)	10. Deacon ("Fratres karissimi")	11. Deacon ("Fratres karissimi")	6. Deacon ("Fratres karissimi")
....	....	....	....
6. V(ere)	11. V(ere)	12. V(ere)	7. V(ere)
....	....	....	
		13. Crucifixion	8. Crucifixion
			....
		14. Red Sea	9. Red Sea
		....	....
7. Harrowing of Hell	12. Harrowing of Hell	15. Harrowing of Hell	10. Harrowing of Hell
....	....	....	....
			11. Adam and Eve ("O certe necessarium Ade peccatum)
			....
8. Rose of winds			12. Noli me tangere.
			....
			13. Candle censed ("Sacrificium uespertinum")
			....

123

TABLE 9.   *Continued*

Bari 1	Vat. lat. 9820	Casanatense Exultet	London Exultet
9. Bees	13. Bees	16. Bees	14. Bees
	....	....	....
		17. Virgin enthroned	15. Virgin enthroned
		....	....
	14. "Superne benedictionis" (Consecration of candle)	18. "Cereus iste" (Consecration of candle)	16. "Cereus iste" (Consecration of candle)
		....	....
	....		
	15. Archbishop with saints ("Saluum fac")		
	....		
10. Ecclesiastical authorities	16. Ecclesiastical authorities	(*note the absence of ecclesiastical authorities*)	(*note the absence of ecclesiastical authorities*)
....	....		
		....	
11. Temporal authorities	17. Temporal authorities	19. Temporal authorities	(*note the absence of temporal authorities*)
....	18. Armies	....	
	....		
....	19. St. Peter and donor		

Note: Lines of dots indicate the presence of portions of the text of the Exultet before or after pictures. Where there is no such indication, the pictures succeed each other with no text between.

   The Bari roll has what might be considered a basic series of pictures. Except for its unique pictures of the Rose of the Winds (a compass-drawn circle with Christ at the center and the various winds, each labeled), all its subjects appear in each of the other three rolls. An opening picture of Christ in Glory (in the Bari roll, Christ is in a mandorla supported by angels) corresponds to other Christological scenes, though the composition may be different (Vat. lat. 9820 and Casanatense have the Agnus Dei in a circle surrounded by symbols of the Evangelists; the London Exultet shows Christ enthroned with angels). The Bari roll does not have a separate picture of the "Mater ecclesia" (which appears in almost every illustrated roll at "Letetur et mater ecclesia"), but its picture number 5, a liturgical scene in a church, is placed in the text where the ecclesia picture would normally be found; there is a sort of elision here where one picture serves for two.

Vat. lat. 9820 has a much longer frontispiece series. In addition, it has an extraordinary emphasis on the archbishop, who appears in two special pictures (nos. 1 and 15), as well as in several more usual scenes. This roll adds unique pictures (no. 9, "Magnis populorum uocibus"; no. 18, armies; and the dedicatory scene, no. 19 at the end).

The Casanatense Exultet follows the pattern of Vat. lat. 9820, except that it adjusts the series to the Franco-Roman text, adding a number of scenes that are specific to that text: the Crucifixion, the Red Sea, the Virgin Enthroned.

The London Exultet, a Montecassino roll, also illustrates the Franco-Roman text and includes the same "Roman-text" subjects (Crucifixion, Red Sea, Virgin enthroned) as the Casanatense roll, adding also a scene of Adam and Eve ("O certe necessarium Ade peccatum") and a further liturgical scene for "Sacrificium uespertinum." Note too that the "Angelica turba celorum" does not appear in the frontispiece, but within the text. This roll with its pictures is related to other Montecassino rolls, especially that in the Barberini collection; the rolls of Montecassino will be discussed later.

There are many other patterns of illustration to be observed in other Exultet rolls and many details to be discussed about these. The reader should not think that these are the standard patterns for Exultets or that the artist of Vat. lat. 9820 had the Bari series under his eyes. Although we will see that there are certain patterns of transmission for pictures, there is much variety, and the choice, placement, composition, and execution of pictures are subjects vastly more complex than this introductory diagram might suggest. Each roll is described in some detail in Appendix 1.

Transmission of Illustrative Cycles

The groups of illustrations, and individual arrangements of illustrations, in Exultet rolls make it clear that visual material has its own routes of transmission in these documents. Illustrations do not necessarily travel as part of a textual, or a musical, package. Our focus here is on how one roll influences another, how pictures are selected and arranged. I propose the "Benevento" and the "Montecassino" models of transmission of pictures, distinguishing between rolls that are versions of older rolls (the Benevento process) and those that result from a more varied selection from a wide range of possible visual material (the Montecassino process). Not every roll can conveniently be assigned to one or the other model, and I do not mean to suggest that working procedures in these two places were always carried out in just one fashion, or that these procedures happened in only one place, or that only one sort of transmission happened with each roll. However, the characteristic aspects of the transmission of visual materials indicate these two models as poles in a range of artistic procedures.

Rolls of the Same City

Bari 2 reproduces, in a less imaginative way, the layout, borders, and certain illustrations of Bari 1. But the artist is not very skilled, and his purpose is different; he included a headpiece with scenes from the life of Christ, which was not like Bari 1; he skipped most of the elaborate paintings in Bari 1 (Tellus; Harrowing of Hell; spiritual and temporal authorities); he changed the arrangement of the liturgical scenes; and he produced a document with much less illustrative content and much less luxurious quality. He knew and followed the existing models but did not reproduce them exactly.

At Troia, the somewhat maladroit maker of Troia 2 borrows iconographical schemes from Troia 1 where convenient ("Saluum fac"; commemoration of rulers), but he does not copy the document. He turns his illustrations the other way, his text is slightly different, and his musical version is a little more elaborate.

Frontispiece Paintings

Some rolls have a sort of frontispiece, a picture or series of pictures coming before the text itself. A frontispiece displaying Christ in majesty, an evangelist, or the author of the liturgy or other text to follow is a frequent feature of Byzantine liturgical rolls, even when, as is usual, the roll itself will have no further illustrations.

Just such a headpiece is found in the Bari Benedictional roll,[4] where the donor Silvester kneels before the figure of Christ between Saint Mary and a haloed figure, probably Saint John the Evangelist. This may be inspired directly from Byzantine manuscripts or rolls or from the slightly earlier Exultet 1, where a Christ in majesty is surrounded by angels, including two trumpeter angels who serve as a transition to the subject of the Exultet itself and to the decorative letter that opens its text.

Troia 1 has a picture of Christ enthroned that precedes the text. Here Christ is flanked by angels with trumpets, a subject that links the frontispiece to the opening of the Exultet's text. It is, however, a headpiece and not an illustration of a particular point in the text.

Montecassino used frontispieces in at least some of its rolls. The London roll has a Christ enthroned with angels reversed like the other pictures in the roll; the frontispiece is preceded by the triple "Lumen Christi" oriented opposite to the main text to follow. The same elements appeared at the beginning of the later Barberini roll, but they survive only in Gerbert's eighteenth-century engraving;[5] there, the elements are rearranged in a way that makes it unclear which way is the beginning of the

---

4. Facsimile in Cavallo, *Rotoli;* and in *Exultet,* 147.
5. Reproduced in various places, including Speciale, *Montecassino e la riforma,* fig. 1.

roll, but in any orientation the Christ in majesty is not at the beginning. There is confusion, either on the scribe's part, or on Gerbert's.

The second Exultet of Montecassino has a frontispiece that now consists of a scene of the deacon on the ambo (similar to that of the Pisa roll) and a Christ in majesty surrounded by angels (including trumpeters) before the text begins; these are inverted, as are the rest of the pictures on this roll. Perhaps there was something more: the beginning is mutilated, but the opening membrane is approximately full length, so any additional scenes in this frontispiece series would have been on a further membrane, which is unlikely given the state of the present opening membrane.

Several Exultets may have had headpieces now lost. The Avezzano roll has a first membrane, now incomplete, that might have had a frontispiece. What might have preceded the Exultet? A picture of Bishop Pandolf? The *Lumen Christi?* A Christ in majesty, like other Montecassino Exultets? We cannot be so sure that Avezzano had no pictures (except for the one small head preserved in an initial); perhaps its original frontispiece now is displayed as a painting. It is possible that the first Exultet of Bari contained an illustration at its head that is now lost. The opening membrane would surely not be other than standard size; and if so, there was room for one or two more pictures: at the corresponding place in Vat. lat. 9820 comes first a picture of the bishop and then the Lamb of God with the four Evangelists.

THE BENEVENTO FRONTISPIECE SERIES

Where many other rolls have a frontispiece with Christ, the series of Exultets stemming from Benevento places the archbishop in this position. Vat. lat. 9820, the oldest of this series (but not the original), begins with a picture of the bishop handing the roll to the deacon; there follows a series of scenes related increasingly to the Exultet itself: (1) a frontispiece painting of the Agnus Dei amid Evangelist symbols; (2) the "Angelica turba celorum"; (3) a Harrowing of Hell (not much related to the Exultet as a whole, or to any nearby text, but suitable in general to the period between Good Friday and Easter); (4) the Lighting of the Candle; and (5) the initial E, which begins the text. The Casanatense Exultet has the same series, beginning with the bishop.

It must be remembered, however, that the pictures in the Casanatense roll are inverted; turning the pictures the other way makes for a considerable difference in the appearance of a frontispiece, especially when a series of pictures is involved. Though the pictures may come in the same order, inverting each picture at its place means that the bottom, for example, of each picture is not adjacent to the same picture as in a series not inverted. Inverting this series of pictures, perhaps tried for the first time in the Casanatense roll, is a work requiring planning and skill, particularly since it involves the addition of new pictures for the Roman text.

The frontispiece paintings in the Salerno Exultet follow essentially the same order, but there are difficulties: it appears to begin with the letter E (which is followed by only a little text, the rest of the roll having no words); the other pictures follow in order, but the candle-lighting scene is omitted here and appears only later in the roll.[6]

CHRISTOLOGICAL CYCLES

Three surviving Exultets present a series of scenes from the life of Christ as a frontispiece to the Exultet itself. They are not versions of the same recension, however, as each is presented in a different way. The idea of such a series of scenes, not directly illustrating the text at hand, is unusual in a book (but not so unusual on a wall) but might be a natural idea arising from a frontispiece; such a series is a preface to the document as a whole, unlike the interior pictures, which illustrate specific elements of the text.

The second Exultet of Bari, instead of using a single-scene frontispiece as in Bari 1, begins with a series of scenes from the life of Christ: Baptism, Transfiguration, Pentecost, all precede the initial letter. Several scenes—five or six—are lost from the opening membrane. This was an extensive cycle, not directly related to the text of the Exultet. The frontispiece, like the other illustrations, is reversed with respect to the text. Thus when the scroll is unrolled downward, the series of Bari 2 is read from the bottom up, the earliest historical scene appearing below later ones.

Troia 3 has several Resurrection scenes before the text begins.[7] The series is incomplete at its beginning. It might have had a whole life of Christ. More likely is that only a little (15 cm) is lacking, unless a whole lost membrane was used, unlikely given the wear on the present first membrane. These pictures, like the rest of those on the roll, are not reversed, and thus they read from top (outside end) to bottom, oriented with the script: they would appear upside down if unrolled from the ambo. There are really two frontispieces in Troia 3, for after the series of six (or more) Resurrection scenes there follows a group of three frontispiece paintings (Lighting the Candle; Christ in Majesty; "Angelica turba") related to the Exultet itself, preceding the initial E; these are on a larger scale than the first set of frontispiece pictures, and they begin on the second membrane.

6. The letter E, on a separate membrane, cannot have come where it does in the other rolls, since the lighting of the candle and the Tellus picture are painted on the same membrane with no separation: between these comes the E in the other two rolls. The membranes are now separated, but the state of the roll before its restoration, shown in a 1917 photograph on display in the Museo Diocesano, Salerno (reproduced in Cavallo and d'Aniello, *L'Exultet di Salerno*), shows the letter E coming first, followed by the other scenes in order, but without the candle lighting. Mayo says inversion was rejected in the Salerno roll ("Borders in Bari," 35n11); on this matter, see Appendix 2.

7. The Marys at the tomb (fragmentary); Noli me tangere; Apparition at Emmaus (three scenes); Appearance to the disciples; Incredulity of Thomas. Cavallo (*Rotoli*, 231–32) points out similarities with Peregrinus plays.

PLATE 1. Montecassino, Biblioteca dell'Abbazia, Exultet 2, rolled on a replacement umbilicus and restored with new parchment.

PLATE 2. Avezzano, Archivio Diocesano, Exultet SN (detail). The entire second membrane is visible here, attached to the preceding and following membranes with thongs. Each period of the text begins with one or more decorated initials centered in the membrane and followed with a gold band in which the first few words of text are written. These opening words have been transcribed by a later non-Beneventan hand.

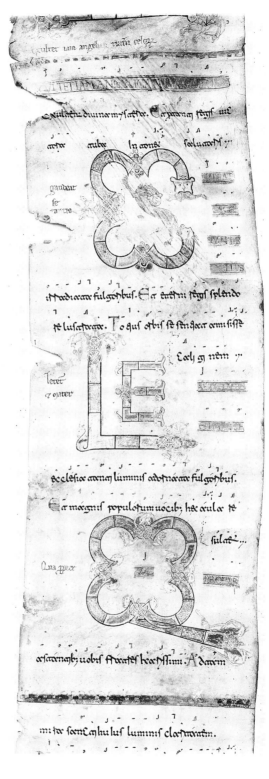

PLATE 3. Bari, Archivio del Duomo, Exultet roll 2 (detail). Note the awkward state of the joint between membranes. The original Beneventan script is visible for the first portion of the preface but is erased beginning with *invisibilem deum*. The original notation has been erased throughout and replaced with square staff notation. The initial letters of the Beneventan text are preserved on the left, even though they no longer correspond to the substituted text.

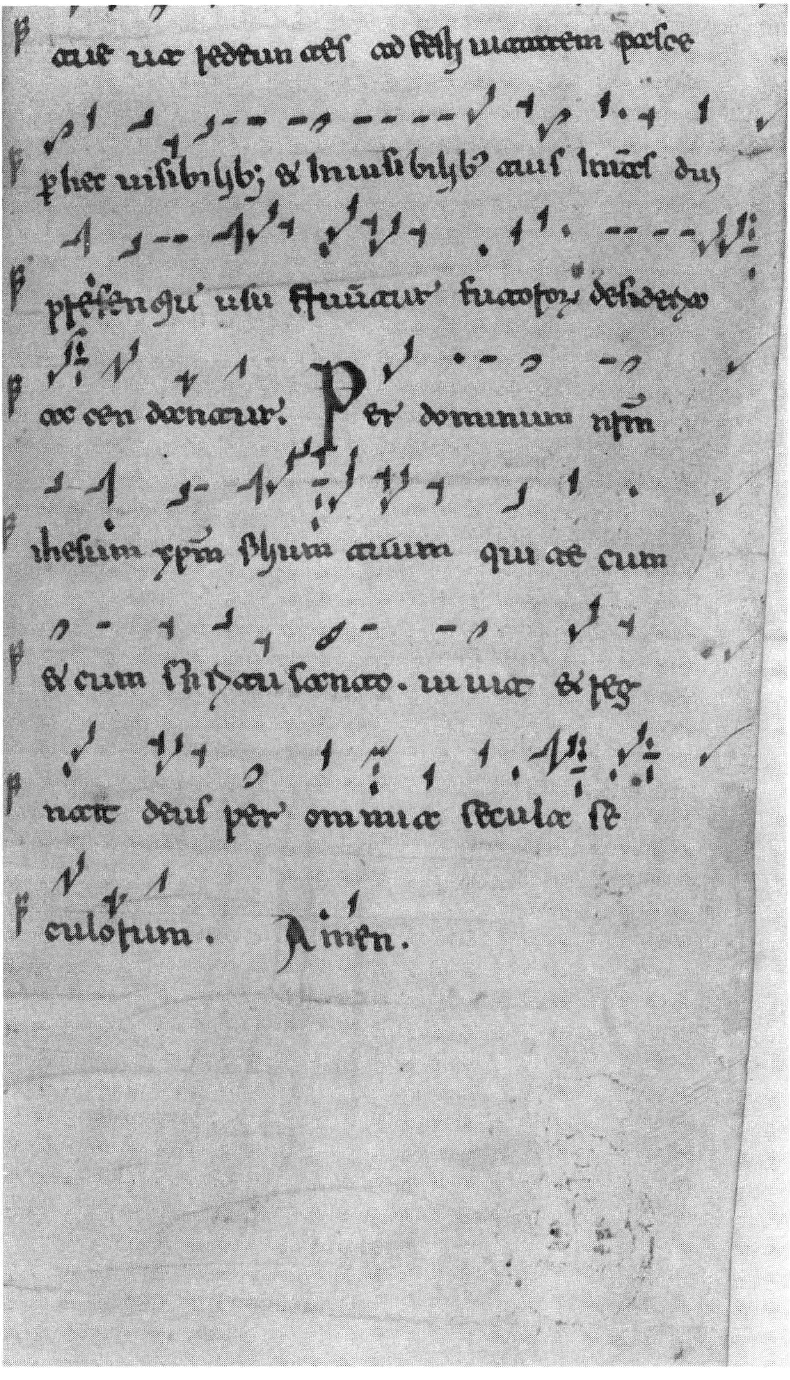

... aut uia pedtun ad ... cæli uia ... parce

phec uisibilib; & inuisibilib' aut ... du;

presentem gui usu ... tua ... deuocio

... cen denætur. Per dominum nrm

ihesum xpm filium tuum qui æ cum

& cum spiritu sancto. in uia & per

... deus per omnia secula se-

culorum. Amen.

Plate 4. Bari, Archivio del Duomo, Exultet roll 3 (detail). The end of the Exultet's text leaves blank parchment from the original roll, now erased. Portions of the Greek original, and a drawing of a bust, can be seen reversed in the blank area.

PLATE 5. Capua, Tesoro della Cattedrale, Exultet roll (detail). The unusual illustration of the Marys at the sepulcher is placed after the text period "O felix culpa," whose musical notation shows a correction at the beginning that indicates the scribe's reliance on an understanding of the application of musical formulas. See chapter 4.

PLATE 6.   Rome, Biblioteca Casanatense MS 724 (B I 13) III
(detail). The end of this roll shows later alterations: *Et preposito
nostro* has been substituted; *presentis uite quiete* has been substituted for earlier text; the ending, originally written as *per
dominum* (the remainder presumably to be supplied from
memory) has been finished in a later hand and with a more
elaborate melody than that of the main text of the roll.

PLATE 7.   Vatican City, Biblioteca Apostolica Vaticana MS Barb. lat. 592 (detail). This detail from membrane 3 shows the tiny neumes added by a later hand to this late eleventh-century roll, evidently to assist in an embellished performance. Above the gold band carrying the concluding letters of "Hec nox est," a fine hand has written two neumes to the left of the original first neume of the line. Another added neume can be seen on the line above, to the right of the first neume of the original notation.

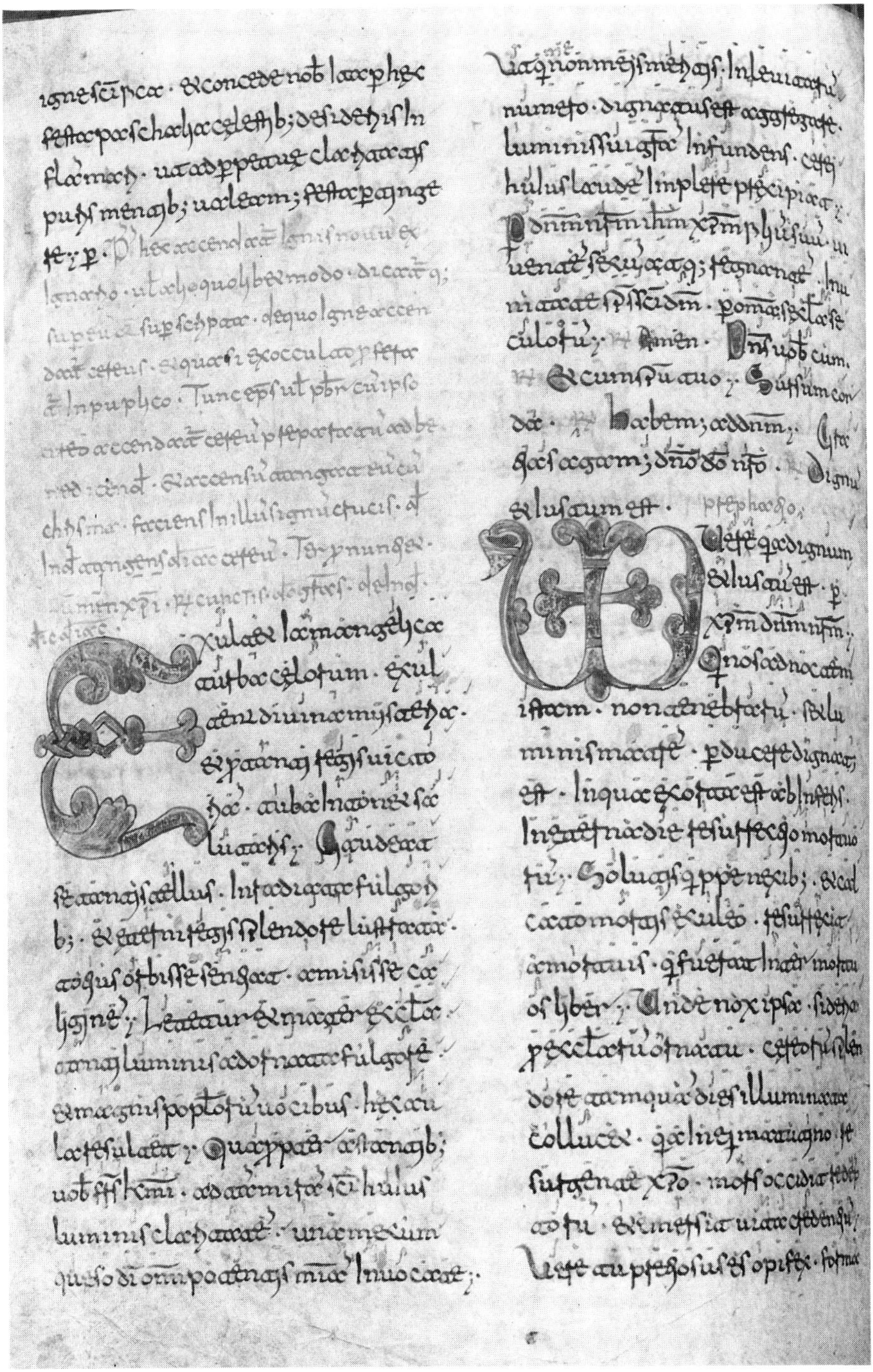

PLATE 8.   Benevento, Biblioteca Capitolare MS 33, fol. 76v. The beginning of the Beneventan text of the Exultet is accompanied by notation in another ink. The preceding rubric, describing the Beneventan ceremony, is transcribed in Appendix 3 and discussed in chapter 6.

PLATE 9.   Vatican City, Biblioteca Apostolica Vaticana MS Vat. lat.
10673, fol. 35v. This is the final surviving page of this incomplete tenth-
century gradual of unknown south Italian provenance. The illustration
shows the deacon singing from a roll on which is written the beginning
of the Exultet; an assistant, drawn smaller, keeps the roll open. The
Paschal candle, placed at the same level as the deacon, is touched by
another assistant (probably not the bishop, given his small size and lack
of obvious episcopal insignia). There is no evidence of an ambo. At the
bottom of the page, the text of the Exulet is incomplete after four lines;
the continuation was probably the Beneventan version. The top of the
page contains the end of a rubric describing the Beneventan version of
the Exultet ceremony (compare plate 3); this rubric is transcribed in
Appendix 3 and discussed in chapter 6.

PLATE 10.   Vatican City, Biblioteca Apostolica Vaticana MS 9820 (detail). This illumination decorated the original state of this tenth-century roll of Benevento. Slits for attaching this membrane to its neighbor appear at the top of the photograph. The picture shows the bishop lighting the Paschal candle, while the deacon touches the candle and sings. An assistant stands by holding the vessel of chrism, which the bishop will use to touch the lit candle. These details of the Beneventan ceremony are discussed in chapter 6.

PLATE II.   Vatican City, Biblioteca Apostolica Vaticana MS Vat. lat. 9820
(detail). This illumination decorated the original state of this tenth-century roll
of Benevento. The archbishop of Benevento, wearing the pallium and seated
on a throne, hands the scroll to the deacon on his right. This trapezoidal headpiece was probably in the possession of Cardinal Borgia when it passed to the
Museo Borgiano of the Propaganda Fidei, and thence to the Borgia collection
at the Vatican, where it was recognized in 1927 by Myrtilla Avery as belonging
to this roll and reunited with it.

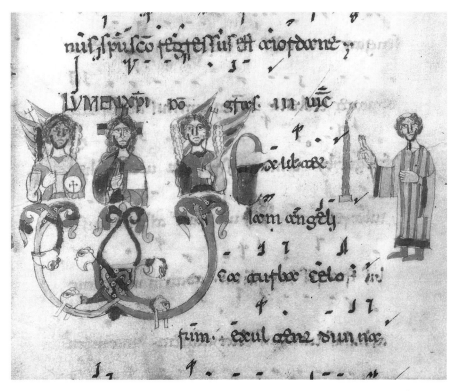

PLATE 12.   Vatican City, Biblioteca Apostolica Vaticana MS Borg. lat. 339, fol.
53 (detail). A decorated evangelistary, 1081–82, from San Nicola, Osor
(Dalmatia). The Exultet, with Franco-Roman text and Beneventan melody, is
decorated at its beginning with a deacon standing in a void, blessing a small
Paschal candle, and with an initial letter V decorated with half-length figures
of Christ and angels; this letter bears no relationship to the text at hand.

PLATE 13.   Gaeta, Tesoro della Cattedrale, Exultet 2 (detail). A complete membrane from this roll, showing the inverted pictures (which are only partially colored, the remaining colors never having been applied). The illustration at one end shows the deacon on the ambo, with the bishop seated nearby. The illustration is drawn between the writing of one period and the next; the picture uses the space left free by the incomplete line written before ("curbat imperia"), but then extends a little too far into the text (or at least notation) area. Note that the drawing of bees is oriented with the text and thus upside down with respect to the other two pictures.

PLATE 14. Troia, Archivio Capitolare, Exultet 3 (detail). This highly inventive roll has illustrations turned the same way as the text and evidently drawn in after, or in the course of, the writing. The illustration of the deacon on the ambo shows an assistant holding the bottom of the scroll. The Paschal candle extends upward into the area left free by an incomplete line of text ("celestia iunguntur") and uses as its base the line scored for the musical notation of the following line.

PLATE 15.   London, British Library, Additional MS 30337 (detail). The increasing height of the opening neume at each repetition of "Lumen Christi" indicates some sort of raising of the voice.

PLATE 16. London, British Library, Additional MS 30337 (detail). The deacon on the ambo sings from the scroll as an acolyte lights the Paschal candle; the description of the Montecassino ceremony is found in Appendix 3 and discussed in chapter 6. The ambo here may be a representation of the wooden ambo that stood in the abbey church of Montecassino before it was replaced by Abbot Desiderius.

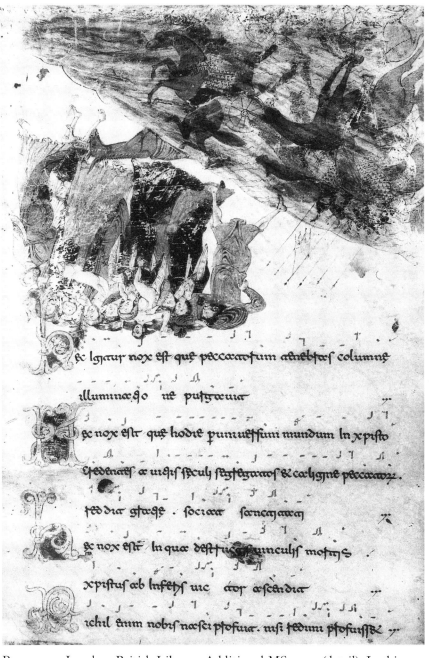

he Igitur nox est que peccatorum tenebras columne

illuminae. Io ut putgaeuia

he nox est que hodie puniuefisimi mundum In xpisto

Credentes et unesis seculi fastransgaos & caligine peccator.

Redia gtaese . socieca soneajaca

he nox est In qua destruens uinculis mortis

xpistus ab Infesis uie ceor ascendia

Ichil enim nobis naesei ptofuit. nisi redimi ptofuisse

PLATE 17.   London, British Library, Additional MS 30337 (detail). In this
roll, the pictures were painted in a separate campaign before the initial letters, to judge from the initial H which obscures faces crossing the Red Sea.
Although the text may have been present when the picture was painted, the
neumes, written in red, were added after the painting, and, since their placement gives them much of their meaning, they must occasionally overlap the
painting.

Perhaps the first membrane is a sort of prelude to the frontispiece; it has received much more wear than the rest of the roll (this is usual, of course, but the difference between the first and second membrane is noticeable) and perhaps had a separate purpose, being displayed with the roll open only this far (opened this way for viewing, the roll must be unrolled *upward*, the umbilicus on the bottom).

The only complete Christological frontispiece cycle is in the Pisa roll, where a long series of scenes from the life of Christ precedes a headpiece of the Montecassino type (Christ in Majesty, followed by a picture of the deacon on the ambo with *Lumen Christi*, and then the letter E). These scenes are meant to be read away from the headpiece—that is, in the reverse order from which the scroll itself is read. They are intended to be viewed with the scroll open: unrolling the scroll a little at a time will show these pictures in reverse order but rightside up. If, instead, the scroll is hanging somewhere, it can be read downward (like a book or a scroll!) in chronological order. The remaining pictures, in the text, are read in the opposite order and the opposite direction but are not meant to be seen outside their textual context.

The Benevento Cycle of Illustrations

One of the most famous groups of illustrations is known in essentially three versions: the series of illustrations from Vat. lat. 9820 (itself modeled on an earlier witness)[8] is repeated, with variations, in the Casanatense Exultet, which, however, needed to be arranged so as to accommodate pictures originally conceived with the Beneventan text and used now with the Franco-Roman; and they reappear in the Salerno Exultet, with changes for the new circumstances. The first Exultet of Mirabella Eclano, now very incomplete, seems also to have been based on this iconographical series[9] and is perhaps the first of the rolls in the series to have inverted the pictures. Likewise, the Velletri Exultet, now very incomplete, seems to be based on this Beneventan series.

Characteristic of this series—in addition, of course, to the specific pictures included—are certain approaches to manufacture. This series of rolls has decorative borders that run along both sides of the membranes and horizontal borders that serve to frame the pictures. The pictures themselves are generally painted on colored grounds, with the result that a picture fills its decorative frame with color, looking like a full-page miniature from a codex transferred onto a roll.[10]

8. On this subject, see Belting, *Studien*, 178f., and Brenk, "Bischöfliche und monastiche 'Commitenza,' 287–88.

9. This has been suggested by Bertaux (*L'art*, 224), Wettstein ("Les Exultet"), and Orofino (in *Exultet*, 305). While the opening illustration of Mirabella is indeed similar to the candle-lighting scene of 9820, there does not seem to be the same intention at Mirabella to follow what is essentially a whole decorative program.

10. Mirabella 1, however, has neither decorative borders nor painted grounds.

The Casanatense pictures are essentially the series of Vat. lat. 9820, but their differences are interesting in what they suggest about the adherence to tradition.[11] Two subjects that appear in all three rolls have different compositions in each: (1) the liturgical subject involving the deacon that appears at "Oramus te domine ut cereus iste" (for the Franco-Roman text) or "Ut superne benedictione," and (2) the commemoration of secular rulers. The artist tends to split into two pictures scenes that were a single composition in 9820: thus the seraphs forming part of 9820's "Angelica turba" are given a separate frame by the Casanatense artist; and the remarkable "Mater ecclesia" (a figure seated on a church building with a row of candelabra) is reinterpreted in the Casanatense roll as two scenes, the space formerly occupied by the church now filled with people ("magnis populorum uocibus").

The Casanatense roll, like Salerno, includes three further pictures (Crucifixion, Red Sea, and Virgin enthroned) that are not in Vat. lat. 9820. The Virgin and child is appropriate for the Roman text ("sicut sancta concepit"), but not for the Beneventan, and the Red Sea is a natural addition, since only the Roman text mentions the passage of the Red Sea. The Crucifixion, too, might be an almost automatic response from an artist used to decorating Mass books, for having done a V for the preface, he would be accustomed to painting a Crucifixion immediately afterward for the "Te igitur" of the canon of the Mass. The Casanatense roll lacks any pictorial commemoration of the clergy, whereas 9820 and Salerno have portraits of the bishop enthroned.

The arrangement of the letter V of "Vere dignum" and the orientation of the figure of Christ within it are matters of some interest in these rolls. In 9820's original state, the figure of Christ is oriented toward the reader, as are all the illustrations; in Mirabella 1, the whole design has been inverted, so that the figure of Christ reads with the rest of the pictures, but the letter itself is upside down for the reader. In the Casanatense roll, the letter V is oriented with the script, but the figure of Christ is turned to be oriented with the pictures (all the illustrations are there reversed), so that the letter is read from one way, the figure from another. In Salerno (as in 9820), the figure is also oriented for the reader, so that the figure does not match the orientation of the other illustrations.

The model for the Salerno "Vere" could not have been 9820 in its first state, since 9820's V originally had the same orientation as the

11. The Mater ecclesia in Casanatense is a different composition from that found in 9820 and Salerno. Skubiszewski, "Ecclesia," 170–71, makes a convincing argument for the Cassiopea of Montecassino 3 (a Benevento MS of ca. 878) as the model for the Vat. lat. 9820 Ecclesia. Such images show the church's concern in the tenth and eleventh centuries to regain her sovereignty. Vat. lat. 9820, the most "Lombard" of the sources, is at the beginning of this "Roman" movement; one might even suggest that the whole phenomenon of the Exultet roll, and not just those of Montecassino, or those having the Roman text, is an aspect of ecclesiastical reform, were it not for the fact that such concerns are so general as to be applicable to many times and places.

illustrations. A roll like Casanatense is not quite the model either: in Casanatense the figure of Christ is reversed to be seen the other way from the letter V. The only surviving model for this particular orientation of the letter is the mutilated version of 9820, where the original V, with its figure oriented with the letter, is left in its original orientation while the rest of the pictures are reversed. This seems an odd thing to copy, but it must be remembered that the Salerno roll is a puzzling document, in that it includes initial letters but virtually no text; if there ever was a pure transmission of a pictorial cycle, the Salerno roll may be it.

The Benevento series seems to have been known also at Montecassino, to judge from the surviving pictures in the Velletri roll. This is a relatively late roll, made after the rolls now in London and the Barberini collection. Yet it has the decorative borders and filled-in grounds of the Benevento series, and its illustration of a figure seated on a church building is highly characteristic.

Other rolls influenced by this series of illustrations are Gaeta 2 (which adapts its versions of the Harrowing of Hell from the Benevento series) and Gaeta 3 (which derives from Gaeta 2). In these rolls, however, the whole cycle is not present, nor are the characteristics of a full ground and framing borders present.

Montecassino Illustrations

The illustrative series of Montecassino is not so clearly followed in all the rolls of the Cassinese orbit as is the Benevento picture series by its adherents. Nevertheless, there are characteristics of the decoration of Montecassino rolls that contrast with the Benevento series: they do not have decorative borders, and the pictures are drawn onto empty parchment, with color added to figures and objects, so that the pictures sometimes seem to float in space; there is seldom an attempt to frame them.[12]

Copying, or at least careful modeling, relates the illustrations in the Barberini and London Exultet rolls from Montecassino. These two documents are the most closely related of all Exultets and show a great deal of copying, of text, music, and pictures. Many have argued the priority of one manuscript over the other, and others have posited a common model at least for the illustrative material; at the same time, it is worth remembering that in the scriptorium in which these "twin" manuscripts were made, that of Montecassino, other Exultets were fabricated that do not derive so directly from a single recognizable model: Vat. lat. 3784, the Velletri Exultet, the Pisa and Avezzano Exultets—all were produced at the

---

12. There are exceptions; the Pisa and Velletri rolls both have decorated borders, the Velletri border especially being a reference to the Beneventan style of decoration in an arguably conservative roll.

same place as the Barberini and London Exultets.[13] There was evidently a variety of ways in which to assemble and to transmit visual information.

At Montecassino, there seems to be a repertory of pictures that are employed with more or less freedom. London and Barberini, the two closest rolls, essentially following the same iconographic model, still have substantial differences. The Fondi roll in Paris, whose text is very close to the Cassinese tradition, likewise uses some, but not all, of the Cassinese pictures: the initial V, the Crucifixion, the Red Sea, all provide non-Cassinese versions of the subjects. But many other pictures in the Fondi roll are related to the London-Barberini set. The Pisa Exultet, also made at Montecassino, has its own illustrative cycle, as does Vat. lat. 3784, to judge from what remains of it.[14] The Montecassino roll now at Velletri is based on the Beneventan picture series.

At Montecassino, as probably everywhere, making an Exultet roll brought together a variety of transmissions—text, music, illustration—and new documents combined transcription and copying with invention and performance. Each new roll presented a new challenge to be solved in a new way; the solution depended on tradition, but probably even more on the individual requirements and preferences of scribe and possessor. We will return to questions of fabrication and of purpose in later chapters and to a more detailed discussion of the rolls of Montecassino.

There is a great variety of visual arrangements in Exultet rolls, some of them highly elegant, others quite rough. Each roll is described as to its manufacture in Appendix 1; here we will summarize a few characteristics of the process of selecting and arranging the pictures in the Exultet rolls.

First, visual material, when it is based on earlier models, may have more than one source; the planning and layout and execution that go into a frontispiece may not be based on the same ideas and models as the further illustrations in the same roll.

Second, we have examined briefly two possible ways of working: the Benevento model and the Montecassino model. By the Benevento model is meant the adaptation of a complete series of pictures to a new context; this is true for the rolls that share the Benevento picture series, but the procedure can be seen also in derivative rolls such as Bari 2 and Gaeta 2. The process here is to borrow as much as is convenient, making such adjustments as are suggested by new circumstances or by artistic abilities (or ineptitude).

13. I can offer no proof that these manuscripts of Cassinese aspect were all made in a single scriptorium (though not at the same time). Montecassino had many nearby dependent monasteries, which might well have had scriptoria of their own. However, the care and refinement of these rolls, and the fact that many are destined for distant users, suggests their manufacture at the center of the Cassinese orbit.

14. Vat. lat. 3784 does, however, have close connections with other activities at Montecassino, in particular the illustration of the famous lectionary Vat. lat. 1202. See Brenk, *Das Lektionar.*

The Montecassino model, on the other hand, involves a fabrication that draws from a repertory of visual imagery, assembling for each roll (always with the exception of the London-Barberini pair) such material as is judged suitable. This is a working procedure that is appropriate for a large scriptorium providing easy access to other artists, to many other pictures, and to a long tradition of the making of books. Moreover, it helps to explain apparent stylistic discontinuities at Montecassino, for if each roll is specifically new and represents a seeking for distinction and distinctiveness, if it represents to some extent the preferences of a single person, then tradition plays only a modest part in the process. A new roll is not a "version" of an older one, though it may share some ideas and indeed some compositions and will be based on the broad Exultet tradition.

6

THE LITURGY

$\mathbf{T}$he importance of the Exultet in the ceremonies of the Easter vigil can be judged from the value of the manuscripts prepared especially for this one moment in the year, much as the luxury of many gospel books is a measure, at least in part, of the importance of the Gospel in the ceremonies of the Mass. The vigil services of Holy Saturday consist of a series of lections and prayers.[1] The rite of Baptism, with the accompanying blessing of baptismal water, is a feature of the vigil in most churches, though often not in monasteries, where there was often no font and no one to baptize. The vigil concludes with the first Mass of Easter.

In this context, the Exultet has a solemn and picturesque place. The blessing of new fire, the lighting of a great candle that is blessed with a prayer of particular solemnity, and sometimes a procession with the announcement *Lumen Christi* are found in many but not all liturgies; the ceremony is not used in the papal liturgy at all, for example, until relatively late. The blessing of a candle, but with other texts, is found in the Old Spanish rite and the Gelasian sacramentary; and the Exultet itself has a variety of texts: Roman, Beneventan, Milanese. These facts have been sketched in chapter 3.

Where the Exultet is present in liturgical documents, it is generally found as the first public event of the many actions of the vigil. Only in the old Beneventan liturgy is the Exultet placed elsewhere, and this sets the Beneventan practice apart from all other Western liturgies. Likewise it is only in southern Italy, in the area that practiced the Beneventan

---

1. The number of lections varies from place to place and is the subject of much scholarly discussion. See, for example, Chavasse, *Le sacramentaire gélasian,* 107–26; on the situation in Beneventan manuscripts, see Hesbert, "L' 'antiphonale missarum,' " 155–71; *PM* 14:342–60.

liturgy, that elaborately illustrated Exultet rolls were used. Thus the area has unique practices that connect the Exultet rolls with the particular characteristics of the Beneventan liturgy; this chapter will explore those practices.

The Exultet in the Beneventan Liturgy

The surviving Exultet rolls do not tell us the position they took in the liturgy. Their text is that of a single event in the context of many. For information on liturgical and ceremonial practices, we must turn to other documents: missals and other books where the Exultet may be seen in context.

General Shape of the Beneventan Vigil

The Beneventan vigil of Easter begins, in the earliest sources, with a litany; it continues with lections, followed by the blessing of the candle; this in turn is followed by a final lection from Isaiah, *Hec est hereditas;* then follow the procession to the font, the baptisms, and the Mass. In summary:

> [litanies]
> lections (5? 11?), with canticles and prayers
> Exultet (preceded by *Lumen Christi*)
> final lection *Hec est hereditas*
> procession to font (antiphon *Omnes sitientes*)
> baptisms
> Mass

Sources Describing the Beneventan Order

Benevento, ancient Lombard capital and liturgical center for the old Beneventan rite, preserves a number of documents that give information about the Exultet in that city. Unfortunately, none of them is complete or pure:[2] they are mixed, in varying degrees, with material from the Roman rite, and as a result it is difficult to reconstruct the context in which the Exultet was sung. The practice as described in surviving documents is not uniform, although there are Beneventan characteristics that are easily recognizable survivals of the older liturgy.

---

2. One possible exception is the music for Holy Saturday in the gradual Benevento 40; however, this provides only the choral chant pieces and gives little information about ceremony. Another document, the Bari benedictional roll, may well represent the pure Beneventan liturgy, but it covers only a small portion of the rites of Holy Saturday: the blessing of new fire, the procession to the font, and the blessing of baptismal water. Complete facsimile in Cavallo, *Rotoli*, pls. 12–17.

THE OLDEST ORDO OF THE BENEVENTAN RITE

The Beneventan order for Holy Saturday must be reconstructed from a variety of sources. These include the two oldest codices, both unfortunately of uncertain provenance, but probably not from the cathedral of Benevento. Their rubrics are transcribed in Appendix 3: it is evident that they derive from a single textual and liturgical tradition that must be closely related to the rites of the city of Benevento. Indeed, their language is quoted in a later document of Benevento.[3] They are the gradual Vat. lat. 10673 and the missal Benevento 33, both of the late tenth or early eleventh century.

Both these manuscripts include the Exultet and give our clearest and most detailed view of the Holy Saturday rites. But neither is both complete and accurate: Vat. lat. 10673 (Plate 9) breaks off in the first portion of the Exultet; and Benevento 33 (Plate 8), very clear and complete otherwise, omits the collect *Deus qui tribus pueris*, which should follow the lesson from Daniel with its Canticle of the Three Children, *Benedictus es.*

Nevertheless, the rubrics they provide are derived from the same textual tradition and give us certain details about the Beneventan rite that we cannot find elsewhere. The translation below is from Vat. lat. 10673:

> After this [the lections and their canticles] new fire is to be lit from a lighter [*ex ignario*] or by any other means, and over it is to be said this prayer: "Deus qui per filium tuum angularem scilicet lapidem" . . . from which fire a candle is to be lit, and as though from a hidden place it is to be brought forth in public [10673: & quasi ex occulto proferatur in puplico; Benevento 33: & quasi ex occulto proferatur in puplicum: or, into the pulpit?]. Then let the bishop or the priest with that same candle light the candle prepared to be blessed. And when it is lit let him touch it with chrism, making on it the sign of the holy cross. Then let the deacon, taking the candle, three times pronounce "Lumen Christi"; in chorus the response "Deo gratias," and he begins to bless [with the] blessing which is here notated. Then he begins the blessing of the candle, "Exultet . . . [incomplete, owing to a lacuna]."

> Post hec accendatur ignis nouus ex ignario uel alio quoliuet modo dicaturque super eum oratio hec. Deus qui per filium tuum angularem . . . de quo igne benedicto accendatur cereus & quasi ex occulto proferatur in puplicum. Tunc episcopus aut prebyter cum eodem cereo accendat cerei preparatum ad benedicendum. Et accensum tangat cum crisma faciendo in illum signaculum sancte crucis. Deinde diaconus sumens cereum ter pronuntiet. "Lumen Xpisti." Respondit in choro "Deo gratias." et incipit benedicere benedictio que hic notata est. Deinde incipit benedictionem cerei. "Exultet. . . ." (Vatican, Vat. lat. 10673, fols. 35–35v)

---

3. The twelfth-century Benevento pontifical now at Macerata repeats these words from Benevento 33: "Tunc episcopus aut presbyter cum eodem cereo accendat cerei preparatum ad benedicendum," but without mentioning the taper (?) used to light the Paschal candle. Macerata: "Tunc episcopus aut presbyter accendat cereum preparatum ad benedicendum." On the manuscript, see pp. 144–145, and the texts in Appendix 3.

The scribe here has added to a normal gradual a set of directions for the ceremony: this passage is taken entire from another source and inserted into a manuscript that normally would not include such rubrics.[4] The insertion concludes with the indication of the Exultet: "and he begins to bless with the blessing which is here notated." And then the gradual itself resumes with a repetition of this instruction: "Then he begins the blessing of the candle, *Exultet.* . . ." The description he inserts, however, is not of his own invention, but part of a written tradition, since it appears essentially unchanged in Benevento 33.[5]

BARI, ELEVENTH CENTURY

The well-known Bari benedictional roll of the eleventh century (Bari, Archivio della Cattedrale, Benedictional s. n.) gives a confirmation of the ordo described in Benevento 33 and Vat. lat. 10673. This roll, evidently for use by the bishop of Bari, contains the prayers and blessings he is to say on Holy Saturday, as well as a number of liturgical chants, all of which come from the Beneventan liturgy. (This may, in fact, be the only surviving complete document of the Beneventan liturgy except for the few Exultet rolls with Beneventan text.) It begins with the blessing of fire and continues with the Exultet; there is procession to the font, and only then is the last lection *Hec est hereditas* read, with the tract *Sicut cervus*, before proceeding to the blessing of the baptismal water. Clearly, the roll begins after the lections and indicates the placement of the Exultet before the last lection. The rubrics in question are these:

> The blessing of new fire on Holy Saturday. When the deacon wishes to go to bless the candle. [Or.] "Deus qui per filium tuum angularem scilicet lapidem. . . ." After the completed blessing of the candle [the first processional candle? or the large candle?] this prayer is to be said: "Domine Deus pater omnipotens exaudi nos lumen indeficiens. . . ." When this prayer has been said, let the bishop dip his thumb in chrism and make a cross on the same candle. Then the pontiff proceeds to the font, the clergy singing this antiphon: *Omnes sitientes.* . . . Arriving at the font, the bishop begins the litanies: "Christe audi nos. . . ." Then is read the lection *Hec est hereditas.* Tract *Sicut cervus.*

> Benedictio ignis nouo in sancto sabbato. Quando uult diaconus ire ad cereum benedicere. [Or.] "Deus qui per filium tuum angularem scilicet

---

4. This is what textual critics call contamination, a practice that the scribes of Exultets would have known in all manner of manuscripts. On contamination, see, e.g., West, *Textual Criticism*, 12–14.

5. The same sort of descriptive insertion is practiced by the scribe of Vat. lat. 10673 for Good Friday. After presenting a hybrid version of Beneventan and Roman practices, the scribe inserts a long description of the pure Beneventan rite of Good Friday, beginning "Item qualiter peragatur officium sexta feria in Parasceben secundum ambrosianum." See Kelly, *TBC*, 88; *PM* 14:296–97. Benevento 33, while it does not duplicate the detailed language of Vat. lat. 10673 for Good Friday, preserves the same order of liturgical items. See the table in *PM* 14:296–97.

lapidem. . . ." Post completa[m] benedictionem cerei dicatur hec oratio: "Domine deus pater omnipotens exaudi nos lumen indeficiens. . . ." Hac oratione data, intingat pollicem episcopus in chrisma, et faciat crucem in ipso cereo. Tunc procedit pontifex ad fontem cantante clero antiphonam hanc: *Omnes sitientes.* . . . Venientes ad fontem, incipit episcopus letanias: "Christe audi nos. . . ." Deinde legitur lectio *Hec est hereditas.* Tractus *Sicut ceruus.* (Bari, Archivio della Cattedrale, Benedictional)

There is some question here as to whether the bishop touches the candle with chrism after the Exultet; in the ordo of Vat. lat. 10673, this is done just after the large candle is lit and before the deacon sings *Lumen Christi.* Here, however, the fact that the rubrics give only the information required by the bishop leaves us in some doubt. Even though the rubric specifies the prayer after the "blessing of the candle" ("Post completa[m] benedictionem cerei dicatur hec oratio"), the prayer that follows is a bless-ing of fire and is usually found in the ceremonies preceding the Exultet.[6] It is possible, then, that the candle mentioned here ("after the blessing of the candle") refers to the little candle that, according to the ordo of Vat. lat. 10673, is lit by the bishop from the new fire and brought into the church: this candle is more relevant to the activities of the bishop, and it is for the bishop that this Bari roll is made. Thus if the prayer *Domine Deus pater omnipotens* is said before bringing the little candle into the church, the Bari ordo as described here matches and complements that of the Vatican and Benevento ordines.

Other Manuscripts Giving Some Detail of the Beneventan Order

Some other musical manuscripts give supporting evidence of this order of events, but they do not all agree in every detail, and most have no rubrics giving specifics of the ceremonial.[7] They include:

Benevento 38, an eleventh-century Gregorian gradual of Benevento that con-tains a significant amount of Beneventan chant. Here the blessing of the Paschal candle is placed after the eleventh lection with its Canticle of the Three Children, but before the collect *Deus qui tribus pueris,* thus separating the lection and canticle from the collect that belongs with it and that refers to the three children in the fiery furnace.[8]

6. It is found most often as the second prayer for the blessing of new fire, as in the twelfth-century Benevento pontifical Macerata 378. For further examples, see Kelly, "The Exultet at Rome," appendix 1.

7. Useful comparative tables of the contents of these and other manuscripts for the Paschal vigil are found in the tables in *PM* 14:340–41, 344–45, 348–49, and 351.

8. See the facsimiles in *PM* 21: pl. 128; the Exultet is mentioned only in a rubric: "Hoc peractis ben[edicatur] cerei. Qua finita dicatur oratio *Deus qui tribus pueris.* Expleta oratione legatur lectio Esaye prophete, *Hec est hereditas.*" See the table in *PM* 14:341. Of four

The Farfa-Trento fragments, fragments of an eleventh-century gradual of un-known provenance. This document uniquely provides both Roman and Beneventan versions of the Exultet. At the end of the Beneventan text of the Exultet, a rubric indicates "Lectio *Hec est hereditas,*" followed by the tract *Sicut cervus* in its Gregorian version, and other elements of the Beneventan Holy Saturday rite.

Vat. Barb. lat. 560. As far north as the orbit of monasteries around Rome, the Beneventan rite seems to have been practiced at least in part. The eleventh-century missal Vat. Barb. lat. 560, perhaps from Subiaco, pre-serves the Beneventan order of events, though the Exultet has the Roman text; unfortunately, the extensive rubrics detailing the rite have been erased and substituted with newer directions for adapting the materials into Roman practice. But the fact that the lections are presented before the Exultet and a few other hints of Beneventan practice (the indication of the *Sicut cervus* after the lection *Hec est hereditas;* the singing of the Jonah and Daniel can-ticles,[9] for example) make us hope for a technological advance that will allow the deciphering of the original rubrics.

The pontifical of Benevento (now Macerata, Biblioteca Comunale Ms. 378).[10] This manuscript of the early twelfth century gives a clear presentation of the overall order of the Beneventan liturgy for Holy Saturday. It preserves many details of the older ordo (and indeed quotes its language),[11] though it retains almost nothing of the old Beneventan chant. Although the Holy Saturday liturgy here has only six lections, and although there are some changes in ceremonial, the ordo presented has several Beneventan details: the vigil be-gins with a litany;[12] tracts are provided after each lection;[13] it has the ab-breviated Daniel lection characteristic of Benevento, with its canticle and collect;[14] and it places the lesson *Hec est hereditas* at the end, preceded by the blessing of fire, *Lumen Christi,* and *Exultet.*

The Beneventan Order in Other Churches

When other sources present the Exultet after the lections, even where nothing else remains of the old Beneventan liturgy, we can presume that

other graduals of Benevento from the eleventh and twelfth centuries (Benevento 34, 35, 39, 40), none gives any indication of the Exultet.

9. See pp. 82–86.

10. On this manuscript, see Gyug, "A Pontifical of Benevento."

11. See n. 3.

12. "Incipiatur a cleris in choro hec letania" (fol. 125); cf. "In primis faciant leta-nias" (Benevento 38); "In primis letanias faciat" (Benevento 40); "In primis letania" (Bene-vento 33).

13. The tracts here seem to be Gregorian, judging from the cue "Vinea," whose Beneventan version begins with "Cantabo." On the very complex matter of tracts and lessons at Benevento and in the Beneventan rite, see Hesbert, "L' 'antiphonale missarum,' " 155–71; *PM* 14:342–60. Cf. Kelly, *TBC*, 90, for an estimate of the number or lections in the Beneventan rite (probably five).

14. Cf. *PM* 14:343, 353 n. 1.

the church in question once practiced the old Beneventan rite and has preserved parts of it. This placement of the Exultet in its Beneventan position can be detected in rubrics that otherwise give us little information, from churches that have in most respects adopted the Franco-Roman liturgy. These sources continue through the fifteenth century and add information to that preserved in the Exultets themselves about the distribution and chronology of the Beneventan use of the Exultet (full texts of the following extracts can be found in Appendix 3).

The thirteenth-century ordinal of Salerno is a copy of a twelfth-century ordinal and describes the Exultet being sung after the lections:

> Let it be known that in the church of Salerno, according to antique custom, twelve lections are read, eight in Latin and four in Greek, and if there are no Greeks, they are read in Latin. And after the twelfth lection, after the tract and the prayer, the candle is blessed. [Then the lections and prayers are named.]
>
> This [the blessings of fire and of incense] being finished, the candle is to be sprinkled with holy water and incensed, and let the candle be lit from new fire, and likewise let the seven lamps and the candles which are in the candelabra be lit. Then let the bishop press five grains of incense into the candle in the shape of a cross. Then let the deacon ask a blessing and having received it go to bless the candle.
>
> And after he ascends the pulpit, first in a medium voice let him sing "Lumen Christi," a second time higher, and a third in his highest voice, the clergy and people each time responding "Deo gratias."

> Sciendum est quod in in ecclesia Salernitana de antiquo more leguntur duodecim lectiones, octo latine et quattuor grece; et si greci non fuerint, leguntur latine. et post duodecimam lectionem dicto tractu et dicta oratione, benedicitur cereus. . . . [lections and prayers named; blessing of new fire]
>
> Qua [the blessing of fire after the lections] finita aspergatur aqua benedicta et adoleatur incenso. Dehinc accendatur cereus de nouo igne similiter septem lampada et cerei qui sunt in candelabris illuminentur. Post hec episcopus infigat in cereo in modum crucis quinque frusta incensi benedicti. Deinde diaconus postulet benedictionem, qua recepta uadat ad benedicendum cereum. Postque uero ascenderit pulpitum, primo media uoce dicat cum notis "Lumen Xpisti," secundo alciori, tercio excelsa uoce clero et populo uice qualibet respondente "Deo gratias." (thirteenth-century copy of twelfth-century ordinal, Salerno, Archivio Capitolare, MS; Capone, *Il duomo* 2: no. 7)

In 1337, Archbishop Giovanni Orsini drew up constitutions for the church of Naples, including customs "which from ancient times have been, and ought to be, observed." The description of the Holy Saturday rite places the Exultet in the Beneventan position:

> On Holy Saturday the lord archbishop was accustomed to vest in the chapel of his palace, to which the deacons and cardinal priests should come to put on their copes. The count also, dressed in a cope, and four deacon acolytes in tunics, with the cross, candles, candelabra, thurible, and everything else necessary, should assemble in the same chapel.
>
> The said archbishop with all these mentioned goes in procession to the church, using the manner and order as at Christmas, with the addition that at the beginning of the office the lord archbishop, dressed in a purple cope, proceeds to the blessing of new fire by the cimilarch in front of the basilica, and he lights the candle and carries it in his hand to the altar, which he then used to give to the sacristan of the church of Naples; and thus vested, the lord archbishop was accustomed to sit in the seat near the altar, and while he is seated there twelve lections are to be read; when they are finished, immediately the deacon who reads the gospel comes and blesses the candle, dressed in a white alb.
>
> The said lord archbishop used to give to the deacon who blesses the candle the rest of the chrism, which he reserved in a vessel on Maundy Thursday. When the candle has been blessed, the said lord archbishop with the whole chapter goes in procession to bless the font, and going and returning the master of the scholars of the choir of Primicerii sings the litany with one colleague, and he used to receive from the lord archbishop one tarenus from Amalfi.

> In die Sabbati sancti Dominus Archiepiscopus induere se consuevit in cappella palatii sui, ad quam convenire debent et se pluvialibus induere Diaconi et presbyteri Cardinales. Comitus autem pluviali indutus et quattuor diaconi acoliti camisis, cum Cruce cannulis candelabris thuribulo aliisque necessariis, ad eandam cappellam convenire debent. Dictus Archiepiscopus cum omnibus supradictis processionaliter ad ecclesiam pergit, modo et ordine servatis ut in festo Nativitatis Domini, addito quod in principio Officii Dominus Archiepiscopus, indutus pluviali de colore violato, accedit ad ignem benedictum per Cimilarcha ante fores ecclesiae, et accendit cereum et portat in manu usque ad altare, quem dare cumsuevit Sacristae ecclesiae Neapolitanae; et sic indutus Dominus Archiepiscopus stare consuevit in sede iuxta altare, et eo sedente legi debent duodecim lectiones, quibus lectis, statim Diaconus qui legit evangelium accedit et benedicit cereum, indutus dalmatica alba. Dominus Archiepiscopus supradictus Diacono qui cereum benedicit dare consuevit residuum balsami, quod reservavit in ampulla die Iovis sancto. Cereo vero benedicto, dictus Dominus Archiepiscopus cum toto Capitulo cum processione accedit ad benedicendum fontem, et in eundo et redeundo magister scholarum chori Primicerii vadit cantando litanias cum uno socio, et habere consuevit a Domino Archiepiscopo tarenum unum de Amalphia. (From the constitutions drawn up in 1337 by Archbishop Giovanni Orsini, "cum in hac nostra Neapolitana ecclesia certi ritus modi et consuetudines ab antiquo fuerint et debeant observari," transcribed from the now-lost original in the seventeenth century by Camillo Tutini [Naples, Bibl. Naz., Bibl. Brancacciana I.F.2], as transcribed in Mallardo, "La Pasqua," 33)

CAPUA, ELEVENTH TO FOURTEENTH CENTURIES

The Beneventan ordo was known at Capua in the eleventh century, according to Francescantonio Natale's 1776 report of a fragment of a missal containing the end of the Beneventan Exultet, followed by a prayer (mentioning the three children in the fiery furnace who were the subject of the eleventh lection), the lection *Hec est hereditas,* and the baptisms.[15]

A lost ordinal of Capua probably of the thirteenth century, also known only through Natale's citation of the "antico Breviario Capuano," gives a description of the Holy Saturday rites (Appendix 3, text N). During the eleventh lection the archbishop in procession goes to the door of the church and blesses new fire, incense, and a small candle; from this, three candles are lit, and, placed in a triple candelabrum, they are brought into the church to light the great candle, which is blessed before the twelfth lection *Hec est hereditas;* then follow tract, prayer, litany, and baptisms.[16] There is no indication of which text of the Exultet is used (but it was probably the Franco-Roman text, which was known from the eleventh-century Exultet roll).

The Beneventan placement of the Exultet is still acknowledged in a fourteenth-century missal of Capua. Two rubrics in the course of a "standard Roman" Holy Saturday rite describe an alternative (Roman) practice in use in some places, though the Beneventan order is the norm here:

> [A] Then are read the lections; but in some places first the candle is blessed and then the lections are read.
> [B] When the baptism is completed, in some churches is read the lection *Hec est hereditas.*
>
> Deinde leguntur lectiones. Sed in aliquibus locis primo benedicitur cereus et postea leguntur lectiones. (fol. 28)
> Completo baptismo, in aliquibis ecclesiis legitur lectio *Hec est hereditas.* (fol. 31) (Paris, Bibl. Nat. lat. 829)

The Exultet is not given in this manuscript, and its placement would be unclear were it not for the rubrics. Evidently the missal was meant to be used where the Exultet comes after the lections, in Beneventan fashion, although the rubric acknowledges the possibility of the ("Roman") practice of placing the Exultet before the lections.

---

15. Natale, *Lettera,* 65–66.

16. The date of the original is uncertain; the presence of the triple candlestick and of incense suggests a date in the thirteenth century; though these features are found elsewhere in the twelfth century, their adoption in the south seems generally to have taken place later. There is an unusual practice of singing the hymn *Veni creator spiritus* and lighting the great candle at the words "Accende lumen sensibus."

MONTEVERGINE, FIFTEENTH CENTURY

A fifteenth-century missal of the abbey of Montevergine describes the blessing of the candle after the lections, and it borrows language from the earlier customs of Montecassino when it speaks of the *benedictio cerei* lying on the altar:[17]

> These [lections and collects] being finished, let the priest and ministers return to the sacristy. Then he is to accept the candlestick from the hand of the sacristan with a small candle lit, and let them pass through the middle to the ambo, with the ministers preceding in the solemn rite, namely candlebearers with extinguished candlesticks, and two deacons, and a subdeacon with a burning thurible. Let the deacon who is to bless the candle take the *benedictio cerei* from off the altar and make his prayer before the abbot and turn to the community and say "Pray for me, brothers," at which all should rise, and let them [*sic*] go up to the ambo. The priest is to light the candle; and let the deacon, having incensed the *testa evangelii*, say three times in festive way "Lumen Christi"; let all respond "Deo gratias"; and let him say, in prayer tone, "Exultet." When the candle is lit all the candles and lamps are to be lit, and all stand erect.

> Quibus expletis [lections and collects], Sacerdos cum ministris redeant in sacrario. Tunc accipiat arundinem de manu sacriste cum cereo paruulo accenso, antecedentibus ministris ritu sollempni uidelicet ceroferarii cum candelabris extinctis et duobus diaconibus et subdiaconus cum thuribulo fumigante, medius pergant ad ammonem. diaconus qui benedicendus est cereum tollat benedictionem cerei desuper altare faciatque suam orationem ante abbatem cedat et uersus ad conuentus dicat: "Orate pro me fratres." Cui omnes assurgant et ascendant [*sic*] ad ammonem. Sacerdos accendat cereum; et diaconus incensato testa euangelii dicat festiue .iiij. uicibus "Lumen Xpisti." Respondeant omnes "Deo gratias." et dicat in modo precis. "Exultet." Accenso cereo accendantur candele et omnes lampades. et stent omnes erecti. (From the missal Rome, Biblioteca Casanatense MS 1103, fol. 118v)

The Adoption of Franco-Roman Practice: Benevento and Montecassino

Most of the southern Italian sources of the Exultet provide the Franco-Roman text, and for a great many of these we do not know how the Exultet fits into the ceremonies of the church for which they were made. We must not assume, though, that a change to the Roman text automatically entails a change to the Roman ceremonial, placing the Exultet at the beginning of the ceremony. The Montevergine ordo of the fifteenth century has the Roman text but retains the Beneventan placement. Nor can we assume

17. For the Montecassino text, see pp. 148–49, and Appendix 3, text 14.

that changes happened everywhere at about the same time. The Beneventan text survives in fifteenth-century missals of Salerno, much later than anywhere else.

A full description of these changes over time requires many more documents than survive. But we can sketch some changes in ceremonial in two important places: Benevento, the ancient center of the old Beneventan rite, and Montecassino, advocate, after the mid-eleventh century, of all things Roman and source of a steady stream of Exultet rolls from that point on.

BENEVENTO REMAINS CONSERVATIVE

Even in conservative Benevento in the tenth century, both rites may have existed side by side and resulted in some confusion. The scribe of Vat. lat. 10673 acknowledges the impossibility of reconciling the two rites when he adds the rubric "The lection *Hec est hereditas,* which is placed fifth according to the Roman rite, should be read here; according to the Ambrosian [that is, the Beneventan rite] it should be read after the blessing of the candle."[18]

Even with these few sources two important if obvious points can be made. First, ceremonial varies from church to church. The practices of the cathedral, described in the old ordo and in the Macerata pontifical, are different from those of Santa Sofia, which by the twelfth century had adopted almost entirely the practices of Montecassino, to which it had always been related.[19] This Santa Sofia practice will be considered in a moment when we examine the practice of Montecassino. Second, ceremonial changes over time. Between the tenth-century ordo and that of the Macerata pontifical, several changes had taken place. Both documents refer to the cathedral, given that they speak of actions performed by the bishop. But things may have changed: the ambo is specified for blessing the candle, and the candle itself has become very large. Table 10 compares these two texts.

Many elements are held in common, though they are expressed differently. The new fire is blessed after the lections (§ 1), though by the twelfth century there has been added a blessing of incense and a large collection of prayers.[20] The fire is brought into the church, and the bishop (or the priest) lights the Paschal candle (§ 3). The deacon, touching the lit candle, proclaims "Lumen Christi," and then begins the Exultet (§ 5).

18. The text of the rubric is in Appendix 3. The lection *Hec est hereditas,* as we have seen, in the Beneventan rite precedes the procession to the font and includes the text of the processional antiphon *Omnes sitientes;* it is found in that position in Benevento 33, 38, 39. See *PM* 14:346; Hesbert, "L' 'antiphonale missarum,' " 157–58.

19. On the relation of Santa Sofia of Benevento to Montecassino, see Kelly, *TBC,* 30–37; Bloch, *MMA,* 1:264–72.

20. On the sources of these prayers, two of which appear to be unique, see Gyug, "A Pontifical," 396–97.

TABLE 10.   Texts of Benevento 33 and Macerata 378 compared

Benevento 33, fols. 76v–77	Macerata 378, fols. 127v–131
1. Post hec [lections and canticles] accendatur ignis nouum ex ignario uel alio quolibet modo. dicaturque super eum oratio superscripta.	1. Dum hoc [the *Benedictus es, Domine* after the preceding lection] canitur, interim episcopus benedicat ignem incenden[dum]. Benedictio. Deus qui per filium tuum angularem scilicet lapidem. . . . Alia. Domine deus pater omnipotens exaudi nos lumen indeficiens. . . . Benedictio incensi noui. Omnipotens sempiterne deus mundi conditor. . . . Alia. Domine deus noster qui suscepisti munera abel. . . . Alia. Dominator omnipotens rex gloriose. . . . Dehinc postquam clerici finierint benedictus es domine, episcopus dicat oratio Deus qui tribus pueris. . . .
2. De quo igne accendatur cereus. & quasi ex occulto proferatur in puplico.	2. His dictis, et domno episcopo procedente, diaconus ascendit in ammonem.
3. Tunc episcopus uel presbyter cum ipso cereo accendatur [*sic*] cereum preparatum ad benedicendum.	3. Tunc episcopus aut presbyter accendat cereum preparatum ad benedicendum;
4. Et accensum tangat eum cum chrisma faciens in illum signum crucis.	4.
5. Deinde tangens diaconus cereum ter pronuntiet Lumen xpisti. Respondeant cunctis. Deo gratias.	5. deinde diaconus tangens cereum pronuntiet ter Lumen christi. R. in choro Deo gratias.
6. Deinde dicat diaconus. Exultet . . . [in extenso].	6. Et incipit benedicere his uerbis. Exultet iam angelica turba celorum. Qua completa. . . .

But there are differences, which may represent changes in ceremonial. In the early ordo, a candle lit from the new fire (but not the great candle to be blessed) is brought in (§ 2), and with this candle the bishop (or the priest) lights the Paschal candle. Then the bishop touches the Paschal candle with chrism and makes the sign of the cross (§ 4). By the twelfth century, the deacon goes up into the ambo (§ 2): and although the bishop still lights the Paschal candle (§ 3), it is no longer specified that he uses a candle (which might not reach high enough), and he no longer anoints the candle with chrism.

Benevento remains traditional: the placement, at least of the Exultet, remains unchanged, even when a new text is adopted. The convent of Saint Peter's *extra muros* in Benevento rewrote Vat. lat. 9820 with the Roman text, but we can see from the Macerata pontifical, and in the missal of Saint Peter's convent *intra muros,* that in those churches at least the shape of the rite remains Beneventan.[21] Elsewhere in Benevento, the twelfth-century ordinals of the monastery of Santa Sofia (Naples VI E 43, Vat. lat. 4928: see Appendix 3) make it clear that the Exultet comes after the lections; this is particularly interesting, since the ordinals otherwise use exactly the language of Montecassino but stop short of full revision by retaining the Beneventan placement. Unfortunately, we do not know how the Exultet was sung at Santa Sofia at that time: we have no surviving text of the Exultet from the monastery.

Montecassino Adopts Franco-Roman Practice

The abbey of Montecassino, producer of so many beautiful Exultets, did not always sing the Exultet in the same way. The Desiderian and Oderisian Exultet rolls are part of the liturgical renewal of the abbey that saw a revision in the fabric, the books, and the liturgical practice.[22] Older materials were destroyed or reused: there is no complete chant book of Montecassino from before the time of Abbot Desiderius (1058–87). It is thus not easy to reconstruct the practices of Montecassino before the middle of the eleventh century.

We can be sure, though, that Montecassino at one time practiced the Beneventan chant and its liturgy. Survivals from the abbey include the palimpsest pages of a Beneventan gradual reused by the Cassinese librarian Peter the Deacon in the twelfth century. These pages include material of Beneventan origin: the Mass for the Holy Twelve Brothers of Benevento. In earlier centuries, then, the liturgy of Montecassino was similar to that of Benevento.[23]

EARLY MONTECASSINO FOLLOWED THE BENEVENTAN ORDO

For the rites of Holy Saturday, two documents, from the eighth or ninth and the tenth centuries, give orders for Holy Saturday at Montecassino. The information is sketchy, but it is clear at least that the order is Beneventan: the vigil begins with lessons, with prayers and chants (tracts), including the Canticle of the Three Children (*Benedictus es, Domine,* or *Benedictiones,* so called from the beginning word of each verse), and continues with the blessing of fire, the blessing of the candle, and the blessing of water for baptism.

21. A rubric in the missal indicates that no lections follow the Exultet: "Tunc [after the Exultet] incipiant letanie, et cum dixerint Kyrieleyson Xpisteleyson Kyrieleyson procedant de secretario sacerdos cum ministris [uestibus?] sollempnis. Deinde *Gloria in excelsis* . . ." (London, BL Eg. 3511, fol. 162v).

22. On the renewal of the arts at Montecassino under Desiderius, see Bloch, *MMA,* 1:40–110; on musical questions, Kelly, *TBC,* 39–40; see especially Francis Newton's forthcoming work on the scriptorium of Montecassino under Desiderius and Oderisius.

23. See Kelly, "Montecassino and the Old Beneventan Chant."

On Saturday after the ninth hour when the bells are rung let all go into the oratory. After a prayer, twelve lections are begun, with nine prayers and as many graduals. And then follow the "Benedictiones" and the blessing of the candle and of the water. Then, exiting with a litany, they proceed to the church of Saint Peter. The litany finishing there, and likewise a prayer being said, they proceed to the church of Saint Benedict with another litany, which finishes there, and another prayer being said, they begin another (litany) and with this they proceed to the principal Mass.

Sabbato uero post horam Nonam pulsato signo intrent in oratorio. Dicta oratione incipiunt lectiones duodecim cum nouem orationibus totidemque Gradalibus. Et sequuntur benedictiones et benedictio cerei et aquae. Exeuntes uero cum laetania procedunt ad sanctum Petrum. Finita ibidem ipsa letania, dicta oratione procedunt inde ad sanctum Benedictum cum alia letania et illa ibidem finita, similiter dicta oratione incipient aliam et cum ipsa procedunt ad missam maiorem. (from the "Ordo officii in domo Sancti Benedicti," from a lost manuscript of s8/9, as edited in Hallinger, *Initia consuetudinis Benedictinae*, 118, and Albers, *Consuetudines*, 21).

Essentially the same ceremonies are used in the tenth century, to judge from the ordo contained in Montecassino 175:

Likewise, on Holy Saturday at Matins, as to the extinguishing of the candles, it is to be done just as on Maundy Thursday. After the ninth hour they begin the lections, with prayers and tract and *Benedicite*. Then follows the blessing of the fire and of the candle and of water. And then they begin the litany, and they go to the church of blessed Peter the apostle, and when a prayer has been said there they proceed to [the church of] Saint Benedict; and when the litany has finished they begin the principal Mass.

Item in Sabbato Sancto ad Matutinum de candelis extinguendis sic faciant quomodo et in Cena Domini. Post horam Nonam incipiunt lectiones cum orationibus et tracto et *Benedicite*. Inde sequitur benedictio ignis et cerei et aquae. Et tunc incipiunt laetaniam et ibunt in eclesiam beati Petri apostoli, et dicta ibi oratione pergunt ad sanctum Benedictum. Et finita letania incipiunt missam maiorem. (Montecassino 175, fol. 265v; ed. in Hallinger, *Initia consuetudinis Benedictinae*, 118, and Albers, *Consuetudines*, 21 n.)

We are not told whether the Exultet is the text used to bless the candle or what text of the Exultet it might be. Probably the candle was blessed with the Beneventan text of the Exultet; at all events, the blessing comes in the Beneventan position, after the lections.

ARRIVAL OF THE FRANCO-ROMAN ORDO

In the course of the eleventh century, Montecassino adopted aspects of the Franco-Roman rites introduced by the reform papacy. We can see the process of importation by careful attention to one Montecassino manuscript, which borrows from a Frankish ordo some language that would remain permanently embedded in Montecassino ritual.

Montecassino 318, a manuscript of the second half of the eleventh century containing mostly musical treatises, contains an "ordo secundum Romanum" for Holy Saturday; much of it has the same language as Ordo Romanus 28 (the numbering is that of Andrieu, *Les ordines*); Ordo 28 does not specify the Exultet, as Montecassino does, but both agree on placing the blessing of the candle at the beginning, whereas at Montecassino it is preceded by the *Lumen Christi,* not specified in Ordo 28. (These texts are compared in Appendix 2.)

This Montecassino ordo derives from a Frankish ordo related to Ordo 28 but otherwise unattested; it has been imported for study, but not for unquestioning adoption. It is not the ordo of Montecassino. We can see this imported ordo adjusted for local usage in a Montecassino pontifical of the later eleventh century. The scribe of this manuscript (Vat. Barb. lat. 631) begins with the ordo as found in Montecassino 318; but having copied the ordo as far as the Exultet, he realizes that this is not the local practice, and he stops and shows the difference: "Apud nos autem" (Among us, however), he writes, and he goes on to describe the same rite as practiced at Montecassino. And he uses precisely the wording of all surviving later documents from Montecassino. This local text, translated below, is found in a variety of sources and influences churches for centuries. Its development and adoption at Montecassino may be related to the liturgical changes brought about by Desiderius, in particular the construction of a new basilica, successive new ambos, and a candlestick six cubits in height.[24] We have no source for this ordo older than the late eleventh century.

THE DESIDERIAN TRADITION OF THE EXULTET

The Holy Saturday ordo of Montecassino, as found in a number of documents from the eleventh through the thirteenth centuries, is remarkably uniform. In translation it reads as follows:

> At the ninth hour let the priests and ministers go into the sacristy and put on their solemn vestments and, preceded by an acolyte with a lit candle in a candlestick, let them proceed in silence in the usual way into the church, and having bowed to the altar, go and be seated.
>
> All those, however, who are to read the lections and sing the tracts, dressed in chasubles, should stand in order at the head of each choir.
>
> Then let the deacon, having asked a blessing from the priest, take the *benedictio cerei* from off the altar; and passing through the middle of the choir say silently to the brothers while bowing his head, "Pray for me." In front of him should go two subdeacons and the aforementioned acolyte carrying a candle in a candlestick.
>
> The deacon then going up into the ambo should say three times in a loud voice, "Lumen Christi," and all respond, "Deo gratias," likewise three times.

24. On the ambo and candlestick of Desiderius, see Appendix 3.

Meanwhile let the acolyte light the great candle which is to be blessed, and after this the deacon should begin the blessing of it: "Exultet iam angelica"; when it is finished let him return to the altar.

Then at the altar two candles are to be lit in two candelabra, and from that flame fire is to be lit in every house, for every fire should have been extinguished beforehand.

When the blessing of the candle is finished, the priest should not say a prayer, but immediately let the first lector going up to the *gradus* begin to read, "In the beginning God created the heaven and the earth."

Hora nona ingrediantur secretarium sacerdotes et ministri et induant se vestimentis sollempnibus et antecedente acolito cum accensa candela in arundine procedant de more in ecclesiam cum silentio, et inclinati ad altare, vadant sedere.

Qui autem lectiones legere et tractus debent cantare omnes induti pluvialibus stent in capite utriusque chori per ordinem.

Tunc diaconus postulata benedictione a sacerdote tollat benedictionem cerei desuper altare. Et egrediens per medium chori inclinato capite dicat secrete fratribus: "Orate pro me." Quem precedant duo subdiaconi et predictus acolitus ferens cereum in arundine.

Diaconus vero ascendens in ammonem, dicat tribus vicibus alta voce: "Lumen Christi." Et respondeant omnes: "Deo gratias," similiter tribus vicibus.

Interim acolitus illuminet cereum magnum qui benedicendus est, et post hec diaconus incipiat benedictionem ipsius: "Exultet iam angelica." Qua expleta revertatur ad altare.

Tunc accendantur ad altare in duobus candelabris duo cerei. Et de ipso igne accendatur in omni domo, quia omnis ignis anterior extingui debet.

Finita vero benedictione cerei non dicat sacerdos orationem, sed mox primus lector ascendens in gradum incipiat legere: "In principio creavit Deus celum et terram." (Leutermann, *Ordo Casinensis*, 114–15; from Vat. Barb. lat. 631 ed. Andrieu, *Le pontifical* 1:292–93)

This ordo, influential in many ways, is the ordo for which the Exultet rolls made at Montecassino were designed. It is related to Franco-Roman practices but is not a simple adaptation of an ordo known elsewhere.[25] It places the Exultet at the beginning of the rite. Particular features are the fact that a small lit candle is brought into the church by an acolyte (note the similarity with the early Benevento practice of bringing in a candle); the "benedictio cerei," the Exultet roll, is laid on the altar and is removed by the deacon (it has not, therefore, been displayed before the singing); the deacon sings *Lumen Christi* from up on the ambo (and not in procession with a candle, as is done almost everywhere except for southern Italy); the Paschal candle is lit by the acolyte while the deacon is singing *Lumen Christi* (or perhaps while he is still on his way to the ambo):

25. The Montecassino ordo does retain language used in Ordo Romanus 28 and elsewhere. See Appendix 3.

it is not lit by a priest or bishop (this is, of course, a monastic ordo, though the monastery was well supplied with priests and even an abbot with episcopal prerogatives). After the Exultet, two further candles are lit at the altar,[26] and from these new light is passed to all.

These two forms of ceremonial, Beneventan and later Cassinese, warrant further discussion and comparison. This is best done in the context of individual elements of the ceremonial of the Exultet.

The Ceremony of the Exultet: Some Details

Some details of the ceremony contribute to what we know about the use of the Exultet rolls. And, conversely, the Exultet rolls themselves contribute to our knowledge of the ceremony through the illustrations that sometimes depict specific moments in the liturgy.

Lighting the Candle

BENEVENTAN STYLE: THE BISHOP LIGHTS THE CANDLE

According to the old Beneventan ordo found in Benevento 33 and Vat. lat. 10673, the Paschal candle is lit by the bishop or the priest, using the smaller candle lit elsewhere from new fire ("Tunc episcopus aut presbyter cum eodem cereo accendat cerei preparatum ad benedicendum"); the bishop or priest touches it with chrism; then the deacon begins *Lumen Christi.* This older system involving the bishop survives in later ceremonial orders. Montevergine retains much of the old system in its fifteenth-century ordo (p. 143); the priest (no bishop would be available) carries in the small candle and lights the large one; and (then?) the deacon sings *Lumen Christi* from the ambo; from the large candle are lit candles and lamps. Likewise at Naples, as we have seen (p. 141), the archbishop carries the candle into church; he then gives the deacon the rest of the chrism consecrated on Maundy Thursday.

This is not, however, the scene shown in the earliest Exultet illustrations. The oldest Beneventan-text Exultets, if they preserve this scene, show the deacon on the ambo and the bishop lighting a very large candle with an object that is more akin to a pole than a processional candle.[27] In

---

26. This is probably a reminiscence of the practice of the papal rites of Rome, which for a long time used no Paschal candle, but provided two lights at the corners of the altar; cf. Ordo Romanus 24: "Sabbato Sancto, veniunt omnes in ecclesiam et tunc inluminantur duo cerei . . ." (Andrieu, *Les ordines,* 3:295).

27. Is this the "arundo" mentioned in later ordines of Montecassino, Santa Sofia of Benevento, Capua, and Montevergine (Appendix 3, texts 14, 17, 21, and 23)? Probably not, since the arundo in those cases seems to be a processional candlestick that has a candle placed in it ("candela in arundine," "ferens cereum in arundine"); here the bishop's apparatus does not contain a candle and is more a practical than a processional object.

Vat. lat. 9820, the bishop lights the candle and an assistant holds a vessel doubtless containing the chrism; the deacon, without a roll, holds one hand in the air and with the other touches the candle (he is singing *Lumen Christi*, which is not on the roll as it survives). In Mirabella 1 the candle is lit from below by the bishop, while the deacon touches the candle and lifts his other hand. In Troia 1, the deacon in the ambo, having finished the *Lumen Christi*, which precedes the illustration, sings *Exultet* from his scroll while the Paschal candle is lit with a long taper from below by a figure wearing a stole or a pallium (the bishop?); an assistant stands by with chrism. According to the old Beneventan ordo, the deacon ought to sing *Lumen Christi* after the lighting of the candle: perhaps the arrangement of text and illustration on the scroll is approximate.

Another sort of scene, however, which sometimes appears in these same early rolls, shows a much smaller candle, either held by an assistant or placed on a low base, with the deacon on a very low platform, which may not be an ambo. It appears, as we will see, that the early Beneventan ordo did not use the ambo as the place for singing the Exultet.

We have, in short, no illustration that depicts accurately the early ordo of Benevento, where the bishop either lights the Paschal candle with a candle he has carried in or touches the candle with chrism. What we do have are scenes in which the smaller candle is replaced by a very long taper and in which the ambo is a regular feature of the principal illustration. This represents a later stage in the development of the ceremonial, as exemplified by the rubrics in the Macerata pontifical (which no longer mentions a candle for the bishop and does specify the ambo). The earlier stage may not have used the ambo and may be represented by the illustration in Vat. lat. 10673 (Plate 9) and others mentioned below.

The touching of the candle with chrism by the bishop, described in the old Benevento ordo, is perhaps depicted in Vat. lat. 9820; the deacon sings "ut superne benedictionis munus accommodes" (it is written on the scroll in the picture) as the bishop touches the candle; an assistant stands by with the vial of chrism, and the hand of supernal benediction appears from the heavens. This is not the moment in the Beneventan ordo when the bishop should touch the candle, but it would have been difficult to show him lighting the candle and touching it with chrism in the same picture; the former scene stands at the head of the text, and perhaps this later one represents the chrismation. This practice soon drops out of use, probably as a result of the adoption of a high ambo and a tall candle. At Salerno, the bishop places incense into the candle before it is blessed by the deacon.[28] This practice of using five grains of incense perhaps replaces the chrism, but it is a relatively late phenomenon, adopted no doubt

28. See Appendix 3, text 20.

because of its presence in Franco-Roman practice, where, however, the incense grains are pressed into the candle during the Exultet itself.[29]

MONTECASSINO STYLE: THE ACOLYTE LIGHTS THE CANDLE

The Montecassino ordo, as established at the end of the eleventh century, is very clear: the deacon asks and receives a blessing from the priest (the abbot celebrant?), takes the roll off the altar, passes through the middle of the choir (hence out into the nave of the monastic church?), preceded by two subdeacons and the acolyte carrying a lit candle in a candlestick; he goes up to the ambo and sings "Lumen Christi" three times while the acolyte lights the Paschal candle. After the Exultet, two candles are lit on the altar (see text pp. 148–49).

Does this description match the depictions in the many Exultet rolls manufactured at Montecassino in the same period? Essentially, the answer is affirmative: a more or less standard scene, in which the deacon appears on the ambo holding out his hand (a gesture of singing), while the candle is lit by an acolyte with a long instrument, fits this ceremony well. However, there is nothing in such scenes to specify that this is the Montecassino ordo: there is no picture of the deacon taking the scroll from the altar, which would localize the practice to the influence of Montecassino; nor are there pictures of the bishop lighting the candle, which would indicate the older Beneventan tradition. At Montecassino, the acolyte lights the Paschal candle while the deacon sings *Lumen Christi*, while at Benevento the *Lumen Christi* is sung after the bishop (or priest) lights the candle. But this is a very difficult determination to make from the illustrations, which do not intend to show us the specific isolating detail, but to portray the ceremony in a larger sense.

Nevertheless, some Montecassino rolls seem to make a real effort to portray the moment: the lost frontispiece of the Barberini roll shows the candle being lit while the deacon unrolls a scroll, and around his head and the candle are written three times the words of *Lumen Christi*, possibly an attempt at showing the simultaneity of the *Lumen Christi* and the lighting of the candle. A similar scene appears in the related British Library roll, but this scene appears at "fratres karissimi," so that the simultaneity of *Lumen Christi* is not demonstrated; just such a generic scene appears (at "fratres karissimi") in Vat. lat. 3784. The Pisa roll, also a Montecassino product, shows the deacon touching the candle as he sings *Lumen Christi* (the words appear on either side of his head), but the candle is already lit.

---

29. They are called for, for example, in the eleventh-century Roman manuscript Florence, Riccardiana 299, during the course of the Exultet; typical is the Roman pontifical of the twelfth century: "Ubi vero ventum fuerit ad illum versum qui sic incipit: *Suscipe, sancte pater, incensi huius sacrificium vespertinum,* infigat firmiter in ipso cereo quinque grana incensi in modum crucis" (Andrieu, *Le pontifical,* 1:238–41, from London, BL add. 57528).

The Lumen Christi

The singing of *Lumen Christi* before the Exultet is specified by the earliest Beneventan ordo and retains its place in the ceremony throughout the Middle Ages. The deacon, either touching (Vat. lat. 10673) or holding (Benevento 33) the candle, sings "Lumen Christi" three times and is answered each time with "Deo gratias."

The *Lumen Christi* is not a part of the Exultet itself, though it is usually part of the ceremony: the same manuscripts that transmit the old Beneventan ordo each have a full Exultet, and in neither case is the *Lumen Christi* presented as a part of the Exultet's text: it is mentioned only in the rubrics. So the absence of this little text in a given source does not mean that the *Lumen Christi* is not sung: it seems evident that the transmission of the ceremony is separate from that of the text, and thus it means little whether the text includes this moment or not. Table 11 shows the use of *Lumen Christi* in the sources related to southern Italy.

The *Lumen Christi* is already in regular use in the Beneventan Exultet, so that by the time the Franco-Roman text arrives in the south the *Lumen Christi* has a familiar melody, and that melody is retained to precede the Franco-Roman Exultet. The *Lumen Christi* may have been imported along with the Roman text and had its melody altered, or it may have been grafted onto the Franco-Roman text if the latter arrived without *Lumen Christi*.[30]

The triple performance of "Lumen Christi" is documented from the earliest ordo and is repeated in Montecassino ordines and elsewhere.[31] What is not always specified, but is a frequent feature of this moment, is the practice of altering each of the repetitions, either by raising the voice or by singing a more elaborate melody each time. The practice of singing at a higher pitch each time is not easy to notate, but something of the sort is evidently intended by the notation of London, Br. Lib. add. 30337, which shows an increasingly large opening interval (see Plate 15).

Writing a single "Lumen Christi" is no sure sign of a single, rather than a triple, performance. Both the Benevento and Montecassino ordines specify a triple performance, though many manuscripts write the text only once. The Beneventan missal London, Br. Lib. Eg. 3511, in so many ways similar to Vat. lat. 6082,[32] has *Lumen Christi* written out only once, with no directions, but surely it is sung three times; one could also raise the pitch each time, without needing to notate it. Many of the manuscripts that write only a single *Lumen Christi* (e.g., the rolls of Avezzano, Pisa,

---

30. The *Lumen Christi* was not always a part of the Exultet ceremony elsewhere. It was added at a later stage in Rome, for instance; see Kelly, "The Exultet in Rome." Gamber, *Sacrificium vespertinum*, 82, believes that Rome borrowed the practice of the *Lumen Christi* and the Exultet from the liturgy of Benevento.

31. See Appendix 3.

32. In Vat. lat. 6082 the *Lumen Christi* is written three times.

TABLE 11. The *Lumen Christi* in south Italian sources of the Exultet

Date	Deposit	Text	Type	Lumen Christi?
South Italian sources with Beneventan text				
10ex	Vat. lat. 9820	Ben	Exultet roll	no
10/11	Benevento 33	Ben	missal	(3×, *sn in rubrics*)
10/11	Vat. lat. 10673	Ben	gradual	(3×, *sn in rubrics*)
10/11	Manchester, Rylands 2	Ben	Exultet roll	no (lacuna?)
11½	Bari, Exultet 1	Ben	Exultet roll	no
11	Farfa-Trento A	Ben	gradual	lacuna
11	Mirabella Eclano Exultet 1	Ben	Exultet roll	1× "tribus uicibus"
11	Gaeta, Exultet 1 (LS)	Ben	Exultet roll	lacuna
11	Montecassino 1	Ben	Exultet roll	lacuna
11⅔	Vat. lat. 3784	Ben	Exultet roll	no
11⅔	Troia, Exultet 1	Ben	Exultet roll	1×
11ex	Bari, Exultet 2 (LS)	Ben	Exultet roll	no
15	Salerno 3	Ben	missal	3×
15	Salerno 4	Ben	missal	3×
South Italian sources with Roman text				
11	Farfa-Trento B	Rom	gradual	lacuna
11med	Avezzano, Curia vescovile	Rom	Exultet roll	1×
11½	Capua, Bibl. Arcivescovile	Rom	Exultet roll	lacuna
11	Gaeta, Exultet 2	Rom	Exultet roll	lacuna
11	Pisa, Exultet 2	Rom	Exultet roll	1×
11⅔	Rome, Vall. C 32	Rom	ritual	1× "iij uicibus"
11ex	Velletri, Museo Capitolare	Rom	Exultet roll	lacuna
11ex	London, BL add. 30337	Rom	Exultet roll	3× (Lumen Chr. only)
11ex	Vat. Barb. lat. 592	Rom	Exultet roll	lacuna
11ex?	Montecassino 451	Rom	pontifical	no
11ex?	Rome, Vall. D 5	Rom	pontifical	no
12in	Gaeta, Exultet 3	Rom	Exultet roll	lacuna
12½	Paris, B. N., n.a. lat. 710	Rom	Exultet roll	lacuna
12½	Troia, Exultet 2	Ben	Exultet roll	lacuna
1106–20	Montecassino 2	Rom	Exultet roll	no
12½	Mirabella Eclano Exultet 2	Rom	Exultet roll	lacuna
12	London, BL Eg 3511	Rom	missal	1×
12	Troia, Exultet 3 (LS)	Rom	Exultet roll	1×
12	Rome, Casanat. 724	Rom	Exultet roll	no
12	Vat. lat. 6082	Rom	missal	3×
12ex	Naples VI G 34	Rom	processional	no
12ex	Vat. Barb. lat. 699	Rom	missal	1× (added)
12/13	Salerno, Exultet	Rom	Exultet roll	lacuna
12/13	Vat. Ottob. lat. 576	Rom	missal	1× "iij uicibus" (added)
12/13	Vat. Barb. lat. 603	Rom	missal	1× "iij"
13	Bari, Exultet 3	Rom	Exultet roll	1× "iij"
13	Bari 2 (US melody 1)	Rom	Exultet roll	no
13⅔	Bari 2 (US melody 2)	Rom	Exultet roll	no

13?	Naples VI G 38	Rom	missal	3×
14	Vat. lat. 3784A	Rom	Exultet roll	no
15	Rome, Casanat. 1103	Rom	missal	1× sn "iij uicibus"

Dalmatian sources

11ex	Oxford, Bod. Can. Bibl. lat. 61	Rom	evangelistary	1× "iij uicibus"
1082	Vat. Borg. lat. 339	Rom	evangelistary	1× "iij uicibus"
12	Berlin, Staatsb. Lat. fol. 920	Rom	missal	1× Lumen "iij uicibus"
13	Oxford, Bod. Can. liturg. 342	Rom	missal	1× "ter dicat"

Central Italian sources

11med	Vat. lat. 4770	Rom	missal	3×
11½	Vat. Barb. lat. 560	Rom	missal	no (*or erased?*)
11/12	New York, Morgan M 379	Rom	missal	3×
12in	Rome, Vall. F 29	Rom	ritual	3×
12	Rome, Vall. B 23	Rom	missal	3×
12ex	Rome, Vall. B 43	Rom	missal	1× "tribus uicibus"
13	Subiaco XVIII	Rom	missal	3×

Abbreviations: 3× = 3 times; sn = without musical notation; LS = lower script; US = upper script.

Troia 1, and Troia 3) probably intend that it will be sung three times, perhaps raising the voice. A special ornamented version of the melody would require notation, particularly when it is more elaborate each time: this is the case in the series of central Italian manuscripts beginning with Vat. lat. 4770 and continuing with Morgan M 379, Vall. F 29 and B 23, and Subiaco XVIII. These central Italian manuscripts preserve a single written tradition. A similar but unrelated tradition involves the fifteenth-century missals Salerno 3 and 4, which detail an increasingly elaborate *Lumen Christi* (see Example 13) in the extravagant style that characterizes the Exultet in these sources.

The *Lumen Christi* is not sung in procession in southern Italy.[33] All the ceremonial rubrics of the south indicate that the *Lumen Christi* is sung, usually in the ambo, by a deacon who is touching or holding the candle to be blessed. At Salerno, it is sung by the deacon just after ascending the ambo. (Surviving rubrical indications may be examined in Appendix 3.)

33. Despite Cavallo, *Rotoli*, 3, and many others.

Ambo and Candelabrum

THE EXULTET WAS NOT ORIGINALLY SUNG FROM THE AMBO

The question of the early use of the ambo is a delicate one, and it turns
on the use of a single word: *puplicum.* The old Beneventan ordo, surviving
in Benevento 33 and in Vat. lat. 10673, prescribe that light "proferatur in
puplicum" (or "puplico"). Does this mean "in public" or "into the pulpit"? The light is brought "as though out of the obscure" ("quasi ex
occulto"), and the public place is a natural antithesis. The word *puplice* is
used in the Montecassino *ordo officiorum* Vatican, Bibl. Apostolica Urb.
lat. 585, describing the offices of Holy Week: "et in fine non dicatur *Kyrie*
neque preces puplice sed unusquisque apud se cum silentio finiat" (fol.
209). Other versions of this ordo spell the word "publice." Surviving
ordines for the Exultet in the south almost always refer to an "ammo" and
very rarely to a "pulpitum": the pulpitum is mentioned in the texts of
Appendix 3 only in the fifteenth-century missals of Salerno and in Leo of
Ostia's description of the new Desiderian "pulpitum" for Montecassino
(no doubt the same object as the "ammo" mentioned in so many Montecassino documents for the Exultet). The old Beneventan ordo may not
be referring to a pulpit, but to a public place.

The Exultet was not sung from an ambo in Rome in the earlier stages
of its adoption. The Gelasian ordo, and a long series of ordines Romani,
as well as the Roman-German Pontifical of the tenth century, specify the
placement and the blessing of the candle in front of the altar.[34] Only at a
later date, in Rome probably in the late eleventh and the twelfth century,
did the ambo come to be used regularly for this function. A similar transition took place in the Beneventan zone.

At Bari, as at Benevento, the bishop must touch the candle with
chrism, according to the Bari benedictional (see the rubrics above): he
must thus be able to reach it, which is not feasible if the candle is large
enough for the deacon to touch it from the ambo. The Bari benedictional
also indicates that the candle is lowered into the font for blessing (as is true
for many such ceremonies, though not always the Paschal candle). Is the
candle shown in the benedictional's illustration of this moment the Paschal
candle? It is carried by an assistant and looks very like the Paschal candle
held by an assistant in the illustration of Bari 1 at "fratres karissimi." In

---

34. We know that the ambo was not used at Rome in the early stages of the adoption
of the Exultet. The Gelasian sacramentary describes the candle blessing in front of the altar:
"Deinde ueniens archidiaconus ante altare, accipiens de lumine quod VI feria absconsum
fuit, faciens crucem super cereum et inluminans eum, et completur ab ipso benedictio caerei" (Vatican City, BAV Reg. lat. 316, fols. 67v–69, edition in Mohlberg, Eizenhöfer, and
Siffrin, *Liber sacramentorum,* 68–70. See also ordines 27, 28, 30A, 31, 32, 50, and the Roman-
German Pontifical, from the seventh through the ninth and tenth centuries (see the texts in
Andrieu, *Les ordines,* 3), and Vogel and Elze, *Le pontifical,* Ordo 99 (= Ordo Romanus 50);
see also the discussion in Kelly, "The Exultet in Rome."

this latter picture, the deacon is on a low platform, the candle in the hands of an assistant, and the bishop on a high throne. Bari 2 shows a similar scene with the deacon's feet at the bottom of the picture, but panels sketched behind him (perhaps a later addition, as ceremony changed) may represent an ambo; here the assistant is on a little platform, touching the candle, which is either decorated itself or is on a small base. Other assistants hold a cross and a three-pronged candlestick like a trident.[35]

Now if the Paschal candle is so large that the deacon on the ambo can touch it while he sings *Lumen Christi,* as he does in the old Beneventan ordo, then it is unlikely that the bishop could either light it with his processional candle or touch it with chrism, since it would doubtless be on a base so high that its bottom would be out of convenient reach. So either the deacon is not in the ambo or the bishop must go up into the ambo also. I think we must conclude that in the early practice of Benevento and Bari the Paschal candle is of moderate size and blessed from the floor.

There is no mention of an ambo at Naples. The new fire is brought *before the altar,* then the lections are read, and then the deacon blesses the candle: perhaps he does so in front of altar (see text p. 141 and Appendix 3).

Some further illustrations, in addition to that of Bari 1, may show this practice of blessing the candle without the ambo. In the illustration that precedes the Exultet in Vat. lat. 10673 (Plate 9), the deacon is shown in a void with nothing under his feet; the candle, nearby, is taller than a man, but it is one with its base, so that we cannot judge the size of the candle itself; and a figure, drawn smaller than the deacon, and not obviously a bishop, touches the candle, while a third figure holds the roll open for the deacon. They are in an open field, at more or less the same level: there is no ambo. Gaeta 1 shows no ambo: its only liturgical illustration shows a deacon on a small step, the bishop nearby, and an assistant holding a large candle on a small base. The little Dalmatian deacon in Vat. Borg. lat. 339 fol. 38 (Plate 12), standing in a void and blessing a candle whose base is one line higher in the void than he is, may not be a representation of the absence of an ambo: the candle is raised, and perhaps he too is raised to reach it.

Other rolls give both versions of the scene, with and without the ambo. The illustration in Troia 1 (and Troia 2) at "Saluum fac" has deacon and candle on the ground in a void: but the same roll (Troia 2 is lacunary at the beginning) had earlier shown an elaborate ambo. This "Saluum fac" illustration, like perhaps other similar scenes, may be a stylized illustration

---

35. Such a triple candlestick is known from usage in Rome and elsewhere: a triple candelabrum is mentioned, for example, in the Roman pontifical of the twelfth century ("triplicem candelam coniunctam": see Andrieu, *Le pontifical,* 1:238–41, MS "L"); in the ordinal of Innocent III ("arundinem trium cubitorum et dimidii cubiti triplicem candelam": van Dijk, *The Ordinal,* 262), and in the Franciscan Regula missal (ibid., 276). For other evidence of this triple candle, see Kelly, "The Exultet at Rome."

showing only the desired details.[36] The later Pisa 2, made at Montecassino and featuring a large ambo in an early scene, later ("oramus te domine ut cereus iste") shows the deacon in a void, touching the candle placed on a little platform.

If the ambo was not the original site of the singing of the Exultet, its transfer to the ambo must have taken place already in the tenth century, since the ambo is depicted in our earliest illustrated sources. Vat. lat. 9820, the earliest of a series of illustrated Exultets reflecting Benevento usage, shows an ambo at its beginning (Plate 10); the Macerata pontifical confirms the adoption of the ambo at Benevento. Likewise, the early Beneventan text Troia 1 shows an ambo with two ramps and an eagle lectern.

PICTURES OFTEN DO NOT REPRESENT CEREMONY

Illustrations in later rolls may sometimes show an archaic or imported scene that does not correspond to the ceremonial in which the roll is actually used. The Salerno roll, whose illustration is modeled on those in Vat. lat. 9820, retains the arrangement of the earlier roll, even though Salerno practice as we later understand it from the twelfth-century ordinal (see p. 140) and the fifteenth-century missals (see Appendix 3) is not reflected in the illustration.[37] The roll illustrates Beneventan practice and the Roman text, even though at Salerno, where the roll was used, both ceremony and text (remember the Beneventan text in two fifteenth-century missals) were different.

In the Paris roll, from Fondi, a generic scene is present: the candle is lit by an acolyte as the bishop stands by (the roll is for a cathedral church); but there is no evidence of *Lumen Christi*. The lighting by an acolyte and not by the bishop himself is not in the earlier Benevento tradition, especially when the bishop is present.[38] This may be a picture of Montecassino practice, but it is not sufficiently detailed to identify a moment from a specific ordo.

36. Ladner, "The 'Portraits,' " 181f., says the Exultet roll arises from the fact of singing from the ambo. This is not possible if the ambo is not always demonstrably a part of the ceremony. As Cavallo (*Rotoli*, 43n91) points out, singing from the ambo might give rise to the inversion of pictures.

37. The Salerno Exultet shows the same scene as Vat. lat. 9820, but the figure lighting the candle is not obviously a bishop (he has no miter, and his pallium would not be visible under his outer cloak); the assistant is standing by with chrism as in 9820. But the Salerno ordo as we have it in the ordinal and the missals specifies that the candle is lit, along with seven lamps and other candelabra, before the deacon ascends the ambo; the bishop puts incense into the candle, but there is no mention of chrism.

38. In some rolls, there are additions in later hands indicating the lighting either of the candle or of additional lights at a later point in the Exultet; see pp. 164–67. The beginning of the Manchester roll is missing, but another (but early) hand writes "Hic accendat" at the words "Unde nox ipsa sidereo": Is this for the lighting of further lights? London, BL Eg. 3511 also has later indication of lighting. See the editions presented in Appendix 2.

The illustrations of the ceremony, useful as they are, are clearly not sufficient to determine the provenance of a roll or the ceremonial family to which it belongs. The illustrations are often not depictions of specific moments of the ceremony, but of a grouping of its physical, spatial, or temporal elements in a composition based perhaps as much on tradition and composition—or indeed on innovation and *varietas?*—as on a desire to provide prescriptive detail.[39] This is especially evident in rolls in which one picture provides a scene that is inconsistent with the information provided elsewhere in the same roll, such as the liturgical illustrations in Pisa 2, Troia 1, and Troia 2, where the deacon is seen sometimes in the ambo and sometimes apparently at ground level.

FURNITURE

These illustrations raise the question of church furnishings, in particular ambos and candlesticks. The Exultet ceremony from the eleventh century onward requires, at least, an ambo or pulpit and a candle with its candlestick. Many of these are depicted in the liturgical scenes painted on Exultet rolls. Some of these pictures are so detailed, like those of Pisa 2, Mirabella 1, and others, that we can be sure the artist had a very good idea of how ambos ought to look—or, perhaps, how his own local ambo did look.

There are of course many famous sets of such church furnishings surviving in southern Italy.[40] Many readers can recall the paired ambos of Ravello, including wonderful representations of Jonah; or the two ambos of Salerno; or the series of twelfth-century pulpits carved by Nicodemus in Abruzzo. Much research remains to be done about the liturgical use of these pulpits: they were used for things other than the Exultet, of course, and this has to be taken into account.

39. Illustrations of liturgical ceremonies are not unprecedented in the early Middle Ages: but they are fairly rare. Liturgical illustrations are infrequent in pre-iconoclastic Byzantine manuscripts (so are the manuscripts themselves, of course); there are many more in eleventh-century (and later) menologia. In the West, the few precedents are Carolingian and Ottonian. Examples include the famous covers of the Drogo sacramentary (Pais, B. N. lat. 9428, s9), showing detailed liturgical scenes that cannot be seen when the book is in use (on the liturgical significance of these scenes, see Reynolds, "Image and Text"). Nearer the Exultet rolls in date, if not in place, are Ottonian manuscripts such as the famous group of Fulda sacramentaries (Palazzo, *Les sacramentaires de Fulda*, esp. chap. 4). Some Anglo-Saxon manuscripts also contain illustrations of liturgical performance.

This is not the place for a history of the depiction of liturgical rites. But it might make an interesting study to consider the circumstances in which a patron, or an artist, undertook to include such uncommon illustration, and to consider their purpose. Perhaps such a study would find important parallels with the liturgical scenes in the Exultet rolls.

40. The literature on the subject is considerable, though it is not comprehensive and takes little account of the liturgical use of these furnishings. Cf. Rohault de Fleury, *La messe*, 3:1–72; 6:47; Bertaux, *L'art; Aggiornamento;* Glass, *Romanesque Sculpture;* Schneider-Flagmeyer, *Der mittelalterliche Osterleuchter;* Lehmann-Brockhaus, "Die Kanzeln der Abruzzen"; Claussen, *Magistri doctissimi.*

It is difficult to match any Exultet roll to specific contemporaneous furniture: for some reason, surviving ambos from churches that also are connected with Exultet rolls are usually later in date than the Exultet. New ambos were made in the thirteenth and fourteenth centuries; Exultet rolls seldom were. Many elements of older ambos survive in museums, set into walls, or reused in later furniture;[41] and there were perhaps many ambos of decorated wood, like Desiderius's pulpits at Montecassino, which have not survived. But the vogue for new, highly decorated ambos, character-istic of the late twelfth through the thirteenth and fourteenth centuries, has removed almost all the ambos from which the surviving Exultet rolls were sung.

In particular, one regrets that the ambos and candlesticks used with the rolls of Benevento and Bari have not survived. In the cathedral of Benevento, the two ambos that existed until the bombardment of World War II dated probably from the thirteenth century.[42] A piece of a con-temporaneous Paschal candle is in the Museo del Sannio, Benevento.[43] Also in the Museo del Sannio is a piece from an earlier cathedral ambo, probably from the eleventh century, showing part of the monster that is surely swallowing or disgorging Jonah.

At Bari we have even less. Fragments survive of an ambo, perhaps of the first half of the thirteenth century; there survive a decorated sculp-tural ball (like those on the ambo rail at nearby Bitonto cathedral) and pieces of the lectern: an eagle and a human figure.[44] The second and third Exultets of Bari may have been sung from this ambo. The second Exultet was rewritten in the thirteenth century, and perhaps at this point the illustration ("Vt qui me non meis meritis") that shows the deacon at a lectern had the rectangular and angled panels added to it to simulate an ambo. Probably some earlier ambo existed, but we have suggested that the first Exultet of Bari was not sung from an ambo; perhaps the second roll also began its career at pavement level.

Of the other candelabra and ambos surviving from churches where extant Exultet rolls may have been used, almost none of the furniture seems to predate its Exultet. The cathedral of Capua (where the Exultet now kept there may have been used) had a pulpit given by the Norman Archbishop Hervey (1073–87); this is early, but the Exultet is earlier. The cathedral evidently had two pulpits or ambos, of which columns survive in the crypt; the beautiful Paschal candelabrum, perhaps dating from the late twelfth century, was reconstructed from fragments only in the early

41. Pieces of an ambo are mounted into the campanile of the cathedral of Gaeta, in the Museo del Sannio at Benevento, and elsewhere. See the notes below and the general literature cited in n. 40.

42. Bertaux, *L'art*, 786; *Aggiornamento*, 836, 985.

43. Bertaux, *L'art*, 786; *Aggiornamento*, 836, 985; however, Schneider-Flagmeyer, *Der mittelalterliche Osterleuchter*, 348, dates this fragment to the fourteenth century.

44. Bertaux, *L'art*, 659, 674, fig. 312; Carabellese, *Bari*, 144.

years of this century.[45] Particularly noteworthy is a relief on the candelabrum that depicts a procession, including the bishop supported by two
assistants, in which an acolyte carries a candle in procession. This might
be seen as a representation of the bringing of the new fire into the church
on the vigil of Easter; however, another acolyte carries an object now
broken off, probably a matching candle, so this is probably a more normal
liturgical procession. Another relief shows the Paschal candle being lit
(apparently by an acolyte).[46]

The ambo, perhaps of the twelfth century, in the cathedral of Fondi
is unfortunately not the place where the Fondi roll now in Paris was sung,
since the ambo was moved to the cathedral only in the sixteenth century,
from the church of San Giovanni Gerosolimitano at nearby Ponte Selce.[47]
The Fondi roll in Paris, although it appears to be a monastic roll (the
commemorations include "cum omni congregatione sancti Petri"), may
well have been used at the cathedral, since Bishop Benedictus is named in
the roll.

Gaeta preserves portions of two ambos. Set into the campanile of the
cathedral are two polygonal panels with representations of Jonah, from an
ambo of the thirteenth century;[48] in the Museo Diocesano are fragments
of an earlier ambo (if that is what it is) consisting of sculptural fragments
of two lions and an eagle.[49] Perhaps the Exultet rolls of Gaeta were used
on these ambos; however, the ambo depicted in Gaeta 2 and repeated in
Gaeta 3 (Gaeta 1 does not show an ambo) has unusual high arches on
twisted columns, with an arch under the ambo. This is not consistent with
the remains of either ambo. The magnificent Gothic Paschal candelabrum
of Gaeta, doubtless inspired from the importance of the ceremony in the
region, is later than the surviving rolls and does not seem to have a direct
iconographical connection with the Exultet rolls of the city.[50]

At Troia cathedral the ambo was sculpted in 1169, during the reign
of William, son of William "King of Sicily and Italy."[51] It was made,
evidently, after the manufacture of the first two Exultet rolls of Troia
and possibly after the third Exultet; and it did not at first stand in the

45. In Natale's day (1776) the candelabrum stood in the atrium of the cathedral
arranged as a decorative column (*Lettera:* see the full title). On surviving fragments, see
Glass, *Romanesque Sculpture*, 111–15; Bertaux, *L'art*, 606–7; *Aggiornamento*, 758–59;
Schneider-Flagmeyer, 350–51. Natale, *Lettera*, 8, says that two lions used in 1776 for the
font were originally part of an ambo.

46. Natale, *Lettera*, in 1776 printed a plate (before p. 5) showing clearly the two
torchbearers, as well as the lighting of the candle. For the present state of the sculptures,
see Glass, *Romanesque Sculpture*, fig. 128; Rotili, "L' 'Exultet' della cattedrale." Glass points
out (115) that the scene of the three Marys at the tomb may have been inspired from the
illustrations in the Capua roll.

47. Bertaux, *L'art*, 609–10; *Aggiornamento*, 643, 764–65.

48. Glass, *Romanesque Sculpture*, figs. 230, 231.

49. Glass, *Romanesque Sculpture*, 208–9; Bertaux, *L'art*, 775; *Aggiornamento*, 979–80.

50. On the Gaeta candelabrum, see Pippal, "Der Osterleuchter."

51. Bertaux, *L'art*, 444; *Aggiornamento*, 646, pl. 178.

cathedral, but in the church of San Basilio.[52] Troia 1 shows an ambo with double staircases and a central sculpted eagle; this does not match the twelfth-century ambo, although it could represent an earlier furnishing, perhaps of wood, later replaced. Troia 2 shows no ambo. The third Exultet of Troia, highly original in so many ways, is roughly contemporaneous with the ambo now standing in the cathedral. The roll shows two views of an ambo resembling a three-sided stone folding screen and two views of ambos supported on double arches (one of them with an eagle lectern); none of these resembles the existing ambo enough to assure us that there is any attempt at representation of it (or of any particular ambo). What seems certain is that an ambo was used at Troia and that the depiction of the ceremonial in the rolls, here and probably elsewhere, is not meant to describe a particular ceremonial object in prescriptive detail.

The larger ambo of Salerno might have been used in conjunction with a surviving Exultet. The ambo, like the Exultet roll, was made in the thirteenth century. There are, of course, two ambos at Salerno, of which the larger has the Paschal candle attached to it by what is perhaps an original iron clamp.[53] This is the same "maior pulpitum" to which the ordo of Salerno refers on Good Friday for the reading of a prophecy. This larger pulpit is ascribed to the pontificate of Niccolò d'Aiello, archbishop 1181–1221, to whom Carucci assigns also the commissioning of the Exultet.[54] This is the pulpit from which the Exultet was sung in the fifteenth century (though it did not then stand where it stands now) and from which, according to Rohault de Fleury, the Salerno Exultet roll was displayed in his day.[55]

MONTECASSINO AMBOS

Of the medieval ambos from which the Exultet was sung, none is of more interest to us than the ambo that Abbot Desiderius caused to be made for his new basilica at Montecassino, dedicated in 1071.[56] Two successive ambos are described by Leo of Ostia in the chronicle of Montecassino: Desiderius's wooden pulpit replaced an earlier lower one (there was evidently only one such item of furniture in the basilica at the time, not two). The new pulpit, for reading and singing, was reached by six steps: it was decorated with color and with gold leaf. In front of it was the Paschal candlestick, a partially gilded silver column on a porphyry base, six cubits high, on which was mounted the great candle to be blessed on Holy Saturday.[57]

52. Bambacegno, *Troia*, 182.

53. On these pulpits and other furnishings of Salerno cathedral, see Glass, *Romanesque Sculpture*, 65–90.

54. Carucci, *Il rotolo*, 55–59.

55. *La messe*, 6:92 (1888).

56. On the Desiderian basilica, see Carbonara, *Iussu Desiderii*, 33–97, with many illustrations; Cowdrey, *The Age of Abbot Desiderius*, 12–17; Bloch, *MMA*, 1:40–71.

57. *Chron. mon. Cas.*, 3:32; for the text, see Appendix 3.

Janine Wettstein[58] has pointed out the relationship of the illustration in the Pisa roll to the Desiderian ambo, and more recently Bianca Zanardi has made similar observations for the Barberini and London rolls from Montecassino.[59] The illustrators of these rolls, all probably working shortly after the construction of the new pulpitum, are not making reproductions of a single object with a view to accuracy of detail. Nevertheless, we can see elements in common that may give some idea of the Desiderian pulpit.[60]

London 30337 has three views of the ambo and the candle: (1) a carefully drawn side view (?) with arches below, panels, and a ramp; the candle is tall, with what appear to be metalwork ornaments (Plate 16); (2: "incensi huius sacrificium") the same type of ambo but smaller, the relation of ramp to lectern is not the same, and the candle shows only a little base; (3: "oramus te domine ut cereus iste") the third is very like (1), but less attention is given to the decoration on the ambo (or perhaps the picture is overpainted). The arcade behind the ambo may be an iconostasis, not a church.

The opening drawing of the related Barberini Exultet reproduced from the lost original by Gerbert may not be accurate as to its decoration, but its shape matches that of the ambo further along in the same roll ("sacrificium uespertinum"): two ramps, a semicircular ambo, panels with rosette decorations;[61] one corner of one ramp may be attached to a column (of the church? of the iconostasis?). The candle has the same sort of metalwork floral decorations as that in the London roll.

The Pisa roll, also of Montecassino, shows the same ambo three times, but with decreasing detail. The first illustration shows arches on the side, figures of the Evangelists, carved panels, an eagle between Jonah panels, a "Testa barbuta,"[62] and a candlestick attached to the ambo, made of such small pieces that it might be metalwork. The next picture ("Fratres karissimi") shows the triangular shape, the sea monsters (without Jonah), but no eagle holding the lectern, and the same attached candle. A third picture ("Incensi huius sacrificium") shows the bishop at the altar with two deacons holding thuribles and two acolytes with incense boats while the deacon on the ambo touches the lit candle: only the top of the ambo and the top of the candelabrum are shown. A fourth picture ("Oramus te domine ut cereus iste") shows the deacon in a void, touching the

58. Wettstein, "Un rouleau campanien."

59. Zanardi, "Gli Exultet cassinesi."

60. If Brenk ("Bischöfliche und monastiche 'Commitenza,' " 297) is correct in dating Vat. lat. 3784 before 1071, then that fragment may give us a view of the situation at Montecassino before the new ambo was made: it shows a plain ambo, with a single arch under it, and a single ramp of stairs. The ambo, however, appears to be made of the same material as the sides of the church, apparently plain masonry, whereas we know from the chronicle of Montecassino that the earlier ambo, like the later, was made of wood.

61. Brenk, ibid., points out the similarity of these rosettes to those in a surviving fragment of the main portal of the Desiderian basilica: see his figs. 25 and 26.

62. On this bearded head, its appearance in southern Italian art, and its significance, see Glass, *Romanesque Sculpture*, 80–82, 157, 205, 217; figs. 58, 76, 77, 184.

candle which is on a little platform. There is evidently a variety of ways to represent an ambo, even in the same document.

Reconstructing the Desiderian ambo is impossible from these documents. Pisa seems to include all the decorative elements ever found on a south Italian ambo; the architectural shape varies from one roll to another; and within a single document the drawing seems more often to be of "an" ambo rather than of "the" ambo. Nevertheless, the drawings in the London manuscript are so carefully executed, and so consistent with each other, appearing to describe a single piece of furniture including the sort of arch, screen, and panel that would be characteristic of a wooden structure, that it seems plusible that they are modeled on the Desiderian ambo.[63]

The representations of the liturgy in the Exultet rolls are not specific portrayals of individual elements, visual sets of ceremonial directions, but instead they portray the ceremony by joining together important, characteristic, or easily understood elements of this moment in the liturgy. Evidently the representation of the furniture seen in these pictures is undertaken in the same spirit: it is important that the deacon be seen on the ambo; and it is important that the object be seen to be an ambo; but it is not evident that the picture must be that of a particular ambo, let alone of the ambo where the roll is made or intended to be used.

Later Changes in Ceremonial

The thirteenth-century ritual adopted as the papal-curial rite of Rome, possibly through Franciscan books,[64] spread ultimately also to southern Italy. For Holy Saturday, this reform involved fixing five grains of incense into the candle at a certain point in the Exultet; lighting the Paschal candle at the words "ignis accendit"; and lighting further lamps (usually seven) at "qui licet sit diuisus in partes."

Two versions of rubrics for this ceremony seem to have influenced south Italian manuscripts and ceremonial: the Franciscan missal of the early thirteenth century (an adaptation of papal rites for broader use) and the ordo of the Mass as revised by Haymo of Faversham in the 1240s. We present the relevant rubrics from each, in van Dijk's editions.

Franciscan Regula missal

> *Exultet . . . et curvat imperia.*
> (A) Hic ponat incensum in modum crucis in facula.
> *In huius igitur noctis . . . rutilans ignis accendit.*

---

63. Zanardi's drawings ("Gli Exultet cassinesi," 49) seem a reasonable schematic reconstruction reconciling all the illustrations in the London roll.

64. On this question, and on the debate between Andrieu and van Dijk on the influence of the Franciscans on the papal office, see Gy, "L'unification liturgique."

(B) Hic accendatur facula.
  Qui licet sit . . . apis mater eduxit.
(C) Hic accendantur lampades ante altare.[65]

Ordo missalis of Haymo of Faversham

  Pervento autem ad *In huius igitur noctis gratia*
(A) quinque grana incensi predicti a diacono infiguntur cereo in modum crucis.
  In loco autem *Qui licet sit divisus in partes*
(B) accenditur cereus a predicto subdiacono;
  et cum dicitur *O vere beata nox*
(C) accenduntur lampades.[66]

Table 12 shows the related rubrics added later to older Exultets in southern Italy and the rubrics incorporated into newer ones.

Naples VI G 38 has the rubrics built in, and they are those of the Regula missal, of which this is in fact an early witness. The Haymonian ordo was adopted at Gaeta sometime after 1200 and added to Gaeta 3 and used also in the text substituted in Gaeta 1 (1335–42). That ordo seems also to be the source of the integrated rubrics of the fourteenth-century Vat. lat. 3784A. Perhaps Haymo provides some of the language also for the much later rubrics added to London, Br. Lib. Eg. 3511, doubtless for use at Benevento. Naples VI G 34 has three marginal additions, using words that are not directly derived from either of these sources. The Barberini Exultet apparently was adapted to later ceremonial, to judge from the late thirteenth-century Italian "ystoria" attached to one of its pictures, which describes the use of a thurible and the fixing of five grains of incense in the shape of a cross and gives a translation of the prayer used to bless the incense.[67]

The later practice of lighting the candle in the course of the Exultet is seen in rubrics added to the original text at Troia and Bari. In the fifteenth-century Montevergine missal, which retains some old elements, an unusual ceremonial is included in the main text; during the Exultet, the priest blesses the incense and places it in the candle; and at a later point he says another prayer and censes the candle and sprinkles it with holy water. Such a practice might remind us of the old Beneventan usage that involved the bishop in the lighting of the candle and in touching it with chrism. Apparently the candle is lit before the Exultet, and further lamps are not mentioned.

65. Edited in van Dijk, *The Ordinal*, 277.
66. Edited in van Dijk and Walker, *The Origins*, 2:246.
67. "In parte ista se figura che lu levita, lu quale benedice lu ciiriu, vole recepire lu turribulu una cum granis quinque de incensu, et lo dittu incensu pune ad modum crucis nellu ciriu dicendo: sengiore dyo, pregamote che questo incensu, lo quale en . . . sacrifitiu offerimu nella sanctificatione de questa nocte, placciave de recepirelo et averello acceptu, perche la sancta sacrata ecclesia sci ve lu dona."

TABLE 12. Rubrics indicating later ceremonial

Naples VI G 38 (southern Italy, Franciscan 13th century)
    (A) "Hic ponat incensum in modum crucis in facula"
    (B) "Hic accenditur facula"
    (C) "Hic accendantur lampades ante altare"

Gaeta, Exultet 3 (additions, 13th century)
    (A) "hic quinque grana incensi predicti a diacono infiguntur cereo in modo
        crucis"
    (B) "Hic accenditur cereus a predicto subdiacono"
    (C) "Hic accenduntur lampades" (*before* "Apis mater eduxit")

Gaeta, Exultet 1, upper script (1335–42)
    (A) "Hic ponatur incensum" (*before* "in huius");
    (B) "hic accendatur cereus a subdyacono" (*after* "ignis accendit")
    (C) "hic accendantur lampades" (*after* "apis mater eduxit")

Vat. lat. 3784A (Naples, 14th century)
    (A) "Hic quinque grana incenci predicti adiatur [*sic* for *a diacono*] infi-
        guntur
        cereo in modo crucis"
    (B) "Hic accendatur cereus a subdyacono"
    (C) "Hic accendantur lampades"

London, BL Eg. 3511, later hand (13th century?)
    (A) "+ quinque grana incensi ponit in cereo in modum crucis" (*before*
        "In huius igitur")
    (B) "accendatur cereum" (*before* "Sed iam columne")

Naples VI G 34 (Troia, late 12th century), later hand (13th century?)
    (A) "Hic ponatur incensi" (*sic; before* "In huius")
    (B) "hic accenditur cereum" (*before* "Qui licet")
    (C) "Hic accenduntur lampada" (*before* "O vere beata nox")

Troia 3, later hand of uncertain date
    (B) *a now-illegible rubric added at* "ignis accendit"

Bari, Exultet 2 (13th-century revision); Bari Exultet 3 (13th century)
    (B) "hic accendatur" (*after* "ignis accendit")

Rome, Casanatense 1103 (Montevergine, 15th century)
    (A) "Hic dicat sacerdos secrete *Dominus vobiscum. R. Et cum spiritu tuo.*
        Oratio. *Deus qui israeliticam plebem in columpna.* . . . Fingat .v. grana
        incensi in cereo" (*before* "Huius igitur sanctificatio")
    (B) "Alia oracio: *Deus qui inicias* [*sic* for *divitias*] *misericordie tue.* . . . hic
        incensetur et aspergatur aqua" (*before* "In huius igitur noctis")

Rome, Vallicelliana B 43 (central Italy, late 12th century)
    (A) "Hic ponatur incensum in modum crucis"
    (B) "hic accendatur facula"

Subiaco XVIII (Subiaco, 13th century)
    (A) "Hic incensetur"
    (B) "hic accendatur"
    (C) "hic diuidatur"

Rome, Vallicelliana B 23 (Norcia, 12th century)
  (A) "hic ponatur incensum"
  (B) "hic accenditur cereum"
  (C) "Hic mutatur cereus," *perhaps a corruption confused with the following rubric,* "Hic mutat sensum quasi legens"

New York, Pierpont Morgan Library M 379 (11th/12th century)
  (A) "Benedictione incensi plana locutione. *Oremus. Veniat . . . (before* "in huius") "hic ponat diaconus incensum in modum crucis" (*before* "quod tibi in hac cerei")
  (B) (after "Ignis accendit") "Tunc cantor dicat alta uoce *Accendite* [musical notation]. Diaconus autem extendat manum et accendat cereum; deinde cantor dicat excelsa uoce *Lumen Christi accensus est in nomine domini* [musical notation]. Omnes fratres respondeant *Deo gratias* [musical notation]. Item diaconus [the Exultet continues].

The monastic manuscripts of central Italy that are related to the Beneventan rite also use these practices of inserting incense and of lighting the candle during the course of the Exultet. Vallicelliana B 43 already in the twelfth century uses two rubrics of the Regula missal, though it does not mention the lighting of further lamps; the lighting of the church takes place after the baptisms, as later rubrics make clear. The missals Subiaco XVIII and Vallicelliana B 23 have rubrics at all three places, and Vall. B 23 has a special melody on "accendit" to accompany the lighting of the candle.

The unusual ceremony in Morgan M 379 reminds us both of Montevergine, with its simultaneous prayers, and of the special music in Vall. B 23 for lighting the candle. Here there are interruptions of the Exultet for blessing incense and loud singing for the lighting of the candle.[68]

MAKING THE SIGN OF THE CROSS

The presence, or addition, of signs of the cross in the texts of some Exultets (when they are not cues to marginal notes) gives a glimpse of the deacon making a sign: they usually occur in relation to words related to the candle and suggest that the deacon indicates the candle, or touches it, or, most likely, makes the sign of the cross on or over it. Possibly original crosses, in red, are found in the Fondi Exultet in Paris, over the words "cerei huius," "quod tibi in hac cerei," "Oramus te domine ut cereus iste." Such signs do not occur in the earliest south Italian sources, and they do not occur with the Beneventan text. They may be later

68. I find it difficult to agree with Lucinia Speciale's speculation (in *Exultet,* 446) about the ceremonial origin of the illustration cycle. If I understand her correctly, the Beneventan cycle may have originated from three liturgical scenes, corresponding to the three points of incense, lighting the candle, and lighting of further lamps; from this, with the addition of biblical and allegorical scenes, a full illustrative cycle might have developed. The difficulty here is that there is much evidence that these actions are not part of the ceremonial until well after the full illustrative cycle of Benevento—and others—were developed.

importations, like the lighting of the candle during the Exultet, from ceremonies first practiced elsewhere.[69]

USING THE SCROLL: WHO KEEPS THE ROLL OPEN?

If the scroll has lain on the altar and then is taken up into the ambo and unrolled, it will not behave the way it is seen to behave in many of the miniatures: limply hanging toward the ground. A parchment roll will not stay unrolled unless it has a weight on the lower end, or unless somebody holds it down. Perhaps the most accurate surviving representation of how an Exultet roll really works is the illustration in Troia 3 (Plate 14) that shows an assistant on the floor with the lower end of the roll: his real job is to keep the roll open for the deacon;[70] an illustration from Vat. lat. 10673 (Plate 9) shows an assistant keeping the scroll from snapping shut like a window shade.

There are other indications of scrolls being held by an assistant. A roll is shown held by an assistant in the Casanatense *benedictio fontis;* this is because the bishop is doing something else: lowering a candle into the water. At Milan, it was the usual practice for an assistant to hold the scroll during the Exultet.[71] Arturo Carucci suggests that at Salerno the Exultet was sung from the ambo while another deacon unrolled the roll from a lower level:[72] the evidence for this conclusion would be welcome, as the practice is otherwise not known in the area.

The display of the roll, from the pulpit or elsewhere, at a time other than the singing of the Exultet, is occasionally done, evidently to allow the roll and its pictures to be inspected at leisure: a museum function rather than a liturgical one. The Pisa roll was evidently displayed in this fashion, but perhaps in pieces, in the sixteenth century;[73] Rohault de Fleury reports the Salerno Exultet still in use as a display item at the end of the nineteenth century.[74] These late phenomena, however, may result from the presence in the rolls of a long series of uninterrupted pictures; the Pisa frontispiece is only generally connected to the Exultet to follow; and the Salerno roll is all pictures: it could have no other use than to be looked at. I know of no other evidence of the display of Exultet rolls as decoration, for a more or less extended period, allowing them to be inspected at will, until their later display—usually upside down—in modern museums.

69. Signs of the cross in the text of the Exultet are reported in the edition in Appendix 2.

70. And not, evidently, for the viewers, at least in this case, since the Troia 3 pictures are not inverted.

71. See p. 209 n.50.

72. "Si stabilì, quindi, che un diacono cantasse il preconio sull'ambone da un messale e un altro svolgesse davanti al popolo il rotolo da un piano inferiore" (Carucci, *Il rotolo,* 58).

73. The rapid inventory made after the fire of 1595 cites "Quattro pezzi di carte pecore lunghe antiche, in un cassetta, che si metteano per le Pasque al Pulpito grande del Duomo" (Masetti, Fonseca, and Cavallo, *L'Exultet,* 73).

74. Rohault de Fleury, *La messe,* 6:92, reports it still in use (1888); this is echoed by Bertaux, *L'art,* 231–32.

7

MAKING AND USING
EXULTET ROLLS

We have discussed the text and the music of the Exultet and the ceremonial context in which it was sung; we now turn to a consideration of the Exultet rolls themselves — their manufacture and their use. It is no easy matter to make a manuscript, and illustrated luxury documents require particular skill. The roll-form, and the turning of illustrations upside down, add further complexities, making the construction of an Exultet roll a very difficult matter. We will consider the problems in manufacturing such rolls, with a view to understanding their nature and purpose.

The Scribes

It is notoriously difficult to know precisely who the scribe of a particular document is. In a roll probably from Sorrento, now Montecassino 2, a small figure presents the roll to Christ: he is labeled *Bonifacius diaconus*. There is nothing to say that the presenter is also the scribe of the roll, and indeed Myrtilla Avery considered the figure of Boniface to be a later addition: but other manuscripts have such pictures in which the presenting figure is the scribe. (There is also another Exultet where a presenting figure is a priest: the Exultet of Saint Peter's, Benevento, Vat. lat. 9820).[1]

   Is it possible that Exultet rolls, or at least some of them, were made by deacons, for the use of deacons? Even when an Exultet roll belonged to a bishop, it was not the bishop who would sing from it, but the deacon.

---

1. On Bonifacius, see Avery, *The Exultet Rolls*, 22; Bonifacius is seen in *Exultet*, 392; Avery, *The Exultet Rolls*, pl. 71; "Johannes presyter et praepositus" is the presenting figure in Vat. lat. 9820: *Exultet*, 118; Avery, *The Exultet Rolls*, pl. 146; *Exultet—Codex Vaticanus.*

Many medieval monks were deacons. Whereas now we may be accustomed to the diaconate as a short stage on the way to the priesthood, in the period of the Exultet rolls there were many permanent deacons. Monastic necrologies confirm this, with the number of deacons roughly half that of priests in the eleventh and twelfth centuries.[2]

Many of these deacons, surely, were scribes. Certainly, some were authors. Paul the Deacon, monk of Montecassino, was the author of the history of the Lombards and was actively engaged in liturgical matters;[3] Peter the Deacon, librarian of Montecassino, was the author of a variety of works, some of which survive in his hand.[4] Professor Newton's classic survey of the known scribes in Beneventan script lists four scribes who are called *subdiaconus,* five who are priests (*sacerdos* or *presbyter*), but eight deacons: a very high percentage of deacon-scribes.[5] We will probably never know how many of the Exultet scribes were deacons, but we do know that all the Exultet singers were deacons, and it is easy to imagine a deacon taking special pains over the pictures in a document meant for himself or only for members of his own ecclesiastical rank, whether or not the pictures are reversed with respect to the viewers.

Scribe, Illustrator, and Notator: Practical Considerations in the Manufacture of a Roll

The business of making an Exultet roll is a complicated one; there are many jobs to be done; these tasks, in the great medieval scriptoria, were often done by specialist workers, so that a manuscript is the result of several successive operations: ruling, writing, drawing, notating, painting: four or more jobs, done sucessively, though not necessarily by different persons.

It is generally understood that in most illuminated manuscripts the text is written first and the pictures added later;[6] this is true of many, but not all, of the Exultet rolls. The problems in making an Exultet arise partly from the roll-form, partly from the presence of music, partly from the presence of pictures, and partly from the problem of presenting the pictures upside down.

2. Charles Hilken, FSC, has kindly provided me with figures from his forthcoming study of the necrology of the monastery of San Nicola di Cicogna (Montecassino, Archivio della Badia 179), begun about 1031–37. The monastery was closed in the fourteenth century, but most of the names in the necrology were entered before the end of the thirteenth century. There are 829 monks, of whom 382 were ordained: 300 priests (sacerdotes), 41 deacons (diaconi, levitae), 21 subdeacons, and 16 bishops or archbishops. One presumes that the relative number of priests increased with time; in any event, significant numbers of monks did not go beyond the diaconate.

3. The history is edited in *MGH SS Lang.;* on his activities in the south, see Kelly, *TBC,* 22–24.

4. See Kelly, *TBC,* 30–31.

5. Newton, "Beneventan Scribes."

6. Alexander, *Mediaeval Illuminators,* 50.

The specific problems that need to be solved are these:

1. Laying out the text so that it reflects the prosodic and musical structure that is inherent in its performance.
2. Arranging text and pictures in the individual membranes so that when the membranes are joined there will be no necessity for text or pictures to be written over the joints.
3. Planning the layout so that illustrations are placed appropriately with respect to the text.

In what follows we will consider the process of making an Exultet roll, so far as it can be determined from the documents. A few general remarks can serve as an introduction to what follows:

1. The Exultet rolls in general are written rather large: indeed, some of them include some of the largest surviving examples of Beneventan script. This is a matter of practicality in part, making it easy for the deacon to see his text; but there are many other manuscripts designed to be read (lectionaries, gospel books, epistolaries, and the like) whose writing is much smaller. Like the large lectionary of Desiderius, Vat. lat. 1202, which contains readings for the three most important festivals of Montecassino, the Exultets are for a special occasion and deserve a special grandeur.
2. Many of the Exultets seem to have had at least some preliminary drawing done in the relatively early stages of production, the color being laid on at a later stage. In such cases the maker of the drawings might well also be the text scribe.
3. Musical notation seems to come at a late stage: after writing and illustration, as a last addition, perhaps saved as a sort of check of the text (it is well known that texts in musical manuscripts contain many fewer errors than the same texts without notation).
4. Hardly anybody gets everything right in a cycle of illuminations: that is, each picture in the same relationship to the text it illustrates and all the pictures turned the same way. This suggests that making an Exultet is difficult, often a new undertaking.

All of the Exultet rolls are described with respect to their manufacture in Appendix 1; the discussion below is intended to present an overview of aspects of manufacture.

Laying Out the Text

Exultet rolls are unusual in the very fact that they are rolls; but the space required in laying out an essentially syllabic recitation tone with musical notation is a further remarkable indication that they are luxurious artifacts. Usually, texts that are sung to a recitation tone are not arranged for musical notation. Gospels, epistles, prayers, are all sung, but they are normally written as prose, with the understanding that the reader or the celebrant will make the necessary adjustments as he or she proceeds; sometimes a system of puctuation is used to show half and full closes. Model prefaces, and occasionally the canon, are sometimes notated in missals, and particularly complex or unusual passages are sometimes notated (Lamentations, Genealogies, Sybilline Prophecies, the Solemn Prayers of Good Friday, dramatic moments of the Passions, and so on). But the norm, even in musical books, is to allow lection tones and prayer tones to take care of themselves, thereby sparing the very large amount of parchment that musical notation requires even when the melody is simple.

And so it is a matter of some luxury to provide the Exultet with complete musical notation. Versions of the text without notation were written in southern Italy, but not on rolls; and the Exultet is found with notation in other documents also: missals, pontificals, and the like.

Texts written to be sung, and for which musical notation is anticipated, must normally be written by an expert. In most musical documents, the melody affects how the text must be written; a relatively elaborate melody requires leaving more space among the syllables where there are many notes in the melody: thus, except when copying from a writen examplar, the scribe must know the music in order to be able to space the words to allow for musical notation. Even though its melody is relatively simple, the scribe of a well-made Exultet must also be able to sing the melody in order to write it.

A Well-Made Exultet: The Avezzano Roll

With respect to the arrangement of its text, the best-made Exultet is the Avezzano roll (Plate 2). An understanding of the Exultet as a sung text is clear in its layout on the page, from the largest element of the structure to the smallest. The scribe knows how the Exultet is sung.

The two parts of the Exultet—the prologue and the preface—are indicated with enormous initial letters for each. Within these two parts, the individual periods are arranged in ways that make their textual and musical structure clear.

Each period begins with a decorated capital letter. In the prologue there is a very large centered letter for the beginning of each period; the letter occupies the space of four normal text lines; a short line of text remaining from the previous period is written as an incomplete line ending at the right, and the remaining space to the right of the initial is occupied with the initial words of the new period, written in capital letters on a gold band. For the preface, after the *Sursum corda,* periods begin not with a centered letter, but with a two-line initial followed by a band of capital letters. As the preface proceeds, two-line and one-line capitals begin to alternate ("O" is usually given one line, and short periods are often given one-line initials), and by the end all the initials occupy a single line.

Within the periods, each of the internal beginnings after an intermediate musical cadence has a colored initial: these can only have been placed correctly by a scribe who understood how the musical divisions were to be made. Further close attention is given in a second pass through the text: accented syllables are marked on most words of three or more syllables, and divisions between words are marked where they might have been unclear. This is remarkably well understood and laid out as to the relation of text to music.

Writing the Text

In the best rolls, the text is written with rhetorical, and thus musical, periods beginning on new lines, as just described for the Avezzano roll. A number of rolls, however, especially early ones, write their periods in run-on fashion, a new period, even when it begins with a colored letter, using the rest of an incomplete line. This is true, for example, for the Manchester roll (though it changes later to periods beginning with a new line), Montecassino 1, Mirabella 1, and Troia 2 and 3. In the Casanatense roll, the periods are regularly made, but not particularly well planned; new periods start at the left, but they have only one-line initials, so that not much planning is required. In the second part of the same roll, space is more at a premium: there are long stretches of text where paragraphs run on without new starts at the left.

Planning and Ruling

Writing a scroll requires planning like any written document: arranging for the writing to fit conveniently in the space provided. To this end, rulings are made to align the writing and the musical notation; the layout must be designed to accommodate illustrations, and the arrangement of writing, notation, and illustration has to be planned membrane by membrane, so as to avoid awkward moments when the end of one membrane and the beginning of another might interrupt a unit of writing or of illustration.

Ruling in the Exultet rolls is in most cases normal as regards the text: a single or double line is ruled at the sides of the membrane to serve as margins, and individual lines are scored across the short dimension to serve as baselines for the writing. Prickings used to guide these rules are sometimes visible in the margins. The text rules of Exultet rolls are generally very far apart compared to most documents, to provide for the exceptionally large writing. The space between these lines is shown in Table 11.

For musical notation, a number of systems may be used. In musical books such as graduals, sometimes the page is ruled with lines spaced widely apart, the text being aligned on the rules, leaving space above for musical notation *in campo aperto* (Vat. lat. 10673; Farfa). In missals and other books that contain both notated and nonnotated texts, those texts that are to receive musical notation are written on alternate lines, leaving a blank line between lines of text that can serve as a guideline for the notation (Vat. lat. 6082; Vat. Ottob. lat. 576; London, Br. Lib. Eg. 3511; Berlin 920; Vat. Barb. lat. 603; Oxford Canon. bibl. lit. 61). Sometimes two, or even more, dry-point lines are left blank to serve as a musical staff; one or more of these lines may be colored or marked with a clef-letter (Naples VI G 34; Oxford, Canon. liturg. 342; Troia 3). Only in much later sources is there a fully formed musical staff (Gaeta 3 upper script; Subiaco XVIII; Salerno 3, 4; Vat. lat. 3784A; upper script of Bari 2; Bari 3).

In Exultet rolls, the usual practice is to rule the membrane for lines of text, leaving ample space, but no separate line, for the musical notation. This is the usual manner of ruling books for music and is employed from the time of the earliest Exultet rolls.[7] The real questions, the real difficulties in ruling a membrane for an Exultet roll are two: how to plan ahead for the joints between membranes, and whether to leave unruled spaces in which the artist may make illustrations.

Planning for Joints between Membranes

Like the pages of a codex, the membranes of a roll pose a physical barrier to the regular line-by-line continuation of a text, and they make a joint, when sewn together with thongs, that is generally avoided when planning the placement of pictures. The size and content of individual membranes is thus taken into consideration when planning an Exultet roll.

The average size of membranes in the south Italian Exultets is indicated in Table 13. Membranes vary in width (excluding late and non-Beneventan rolls) from about 200 mm for the first two rolls of Troia to the 475 mm of the Salerno roll. Most illustrated rolls of south Italy, though, are between 270 and 330 mm wide. Narrower rolls include those of Troia and Mirabella and the Casanatense roll; of larger formats only Bari 2 and Salerno exceed this range. Lengths vary considerably, but they average about 700 mm.

In most rolls, some effort is made to see that text periods end on the membrane on which they began. But there are many exceptions: Bari 1 has one period that extends over two membranes; in Bari 2, a new membrane usually begins with a new period, except for membrane 5, which starts with the last line of the period "Apis siquidem." In Troia 2, one period goes from one membrane to another and is split by a decorative border that hides the joint. In the Capua roll, planning ahead for the end of the membrane (or even the end of the line) does not always work well: at the end of the first membrane, the scribe chooses to have a line that contains only the last two syllables of "pruinosa" rather than split a word between

---

7. They include Manchester; Troia 1; Capua; Troia 2; Bari 1; Pisa; Velletri; Avezzano; BL Add. 30337; Montecassino 2; Paris; Gaeta 2; Gaeta 3.

TABLE 13. Dimensions of south Italian Exultet rolls

Roll	Width	Length	Module
Avezzano	270	771	33
Bari 1	270	707.5	24
Bari 2	390	680	20
Bari 3	125	711	25
Capua	230	711	23
Gaeta 1	330	578	28
Gaeta 2	325	791	22
Gaeta 3	275	707	27
London	280	609	25
Manchester	310	603	21
Mirabella 1	230	502.5	19
Mirabella 2	231	688	26
Montecassino 1	273	690	32
Montecassino 2	260	708	20
Paris 710	240	765	25
Pisa 1	225	470	18
Pisa 2	280	692	28
Pisa 3	450	1080(?)	?
Rome, Casanatense	230	753	36
Salerno	475	805	
Troia 1	200	650	15
Troia 2	200	795[a]	max 25
Troia 3	250	852	max 33
Vat. Barb. lat. 592	280	840[b]	26
Vat. lat. 3784	275	631	22
Vat. lat. 3784A	265	791	22
Vat. lat. 9820	275	655	max 22
Velletri	305	unknown	30
Average[c]	278.5	703.6	25.7

Note: Measurements are in millimeters. Dimensions are average widths and lengths of membranes. Average lengths are established by averaging only membranes that appear to be full length, generally judged by their continuity with membranes at both ends or by the presence of slits at both ends. Details of the measurements of these rolls can be found in Appendix 2. The term *module* refers to the average space between ruled lines for text; this is not an absolutely accurate measure of the size of the writing, but generally the larger the module, the larger the script.

[a]Average of two pieces 630 + 960.

[b]Judging from the one surviving full membrane.

[c]Average of Beneventan illustrated rolls, excluding the rolls not in the Beneventan tradition (Pisa 1, Pisa 3, Vat. lat. 3784A) or not illustrated (Bari 3).

membranes; elsewhere, the same problem causes him to use a whole line for the last three letters of "castitatem": this, however, allows him to finish the period at the end of the membrane; and despite his best efforts, one period ("Hec explorata") carries over two membranes.

In some cases, however, there seems to be no particular effort to keep a period from continuing onto a new membrane. In Mirabella 1, several periods carry over. Even in the splendid Avezzano roll, there is no attempt to make a period end before the end of the membrane: the word "Exultet" has its second letter on a new membrane; the period beginning "Flammas eius" (among others) continues onto a second membrane. In this roll, a problem would occur when a period begins on the last line of the membrane, for its two-line capital would normally extend down a second line, thus onto the next membrane: but in the only place where this problem arises, "Hec nox est de qua scriptum est," there is a one-line capital, which follows on several other one-line capitals. The next membrane goes back to two-line capitals.

The placement of pictures on membranes occasionally causes difficulties. In the second Exultet roll at Montecassino, one picture (a Resurrection scene of the Marys at the tomb) is delayed because it would not fit in the space remaining on the membrane even if its relevant text were postponed to the next membrane. Instead, the text period is placed at the end of the membrane and the picture begins on the next: the result is that the picture is out of the usual order for reasons of space.

Sometimes a picture is allowed to extend over two membranes; this is the case for a picture of bees in Troia 1; and in Bari 2, one of the joints is covered with a horizontal border, the thong joining the membranes skillfully painted in a pattern matching the border through which it passes.

Sometimes there is too much room at the end of a membrane. In the Capua roll, the last membrane, where the text finishes before the end, has the border painted only alongside the text, leaving the rest blank to wrap around the umbilicus. In the Paris roll, occasional sheets (cf. membrane 4, after "deliciis meis") have room for several more lines of text: one wonders why this extra parchment was not cut off before assembling the roll: was it already assembled? This seems an awkward way to work. Elsewhere in the Paris roll, periods unfortunately have to carry over to the start of the next membrane ("redimi/profuisset").

Planning Ahead for Illustration: Ruling

The physical preparation of an illustrated membrane might proceed in either of two ways. Simplest is to rule the whole membrane for writing; lines can then be left blank to provide space for pictures. This procedure is only rarely used throughout an Exultet roll—although it is true in some portions of Capua, Gaeta 3, and a substantial portion of Troia 1 and of the Manchester roll.

More careful preparation requires that spaces be left blank to accommodate pictures, so that they can be drawn on unlined parchment. This means that the ruling has either to be accomplished with a very clear estimate of how much room is needed by each portion of text or ruled line by line as the writing proceeds, pausing before each new period to consider whether it needs illustration—and if it does, skipping over enough space to accommodate an illustration and beginning the ruling again. Difficulties arise when the estimate of the number of lines required by each section of text is miscalculated: in such a case, either one or more text lines will not be used for writing (illustrations may expand to cover them) or the text will need to invade the space set aside in advance for illustration. Cases where problems arise are relatively few; this suggests that careful planning was the rule, but there is further evidence that the difficulties that would arise from a two- or three-stage process—ruling, writing, painting—often are avoided by the fact that the whole process happens at once: scribe and artist working together or being the same person.

In many Exultets, it appears that preliminary drawings are made for the pictures, often before the text is written; this allows for the composition of the picture within the space provided and alerts the maker to difficulties that may arise when the picture expands to take more space than was planned in the original ruling. Coloring is often left until a later stage.[8] Examples where this process is clear include Bari 2 (whose coloring was never completed), Gaeta 2 (Plate 13), and Montecassino 2.[9]

A few exceptional arrangements in the relationship of ruling to space are worth noting.

In Gaeta 1, some illustrations were not ruled (that is, they were anticipated when the membrane was prepared): most of these are at one end of a membrane, and space is left for them in the preparation. Those not at the end of the membrane are sometimes painted over regular rules: the scene combining bees with the nativity is ruled through, and the rules serve the artist to align beehives and manger. The procession of offerings, though space was prepared for it, actually begins earlier in the membrane and covers one text rule (which is used to align the bottom of a tabernacle). Evidently, the estimate of space needed for the text was wrong by one line when the membrane was prepared. If rulings were made as periods were written, this would not have happened.

The Casanatense Exultet follows a changing system depending on the content of the membrane: ruling generally skips over the illustrations, except for the bees, which is painted over regular rules. The first two membranes, consisting only of pictures and decorative letters, are not ruled across at all; the third, which has two pictures, is also not ruled, and its text as a result is not well aligned. At the fourth membrane begin the

---

8. On preparatory drawings, and on the process of illumination in general, see Alexander, *Mediaeval Illuminators*, 40–47, 54–56.

9. See the discussion of manufacture of these manuscripts in Appendix 1.

text rules, which skip space for pictures. But the fifth membrane, consisting mostly of pictures with the elaborate "Vere dignum," is again not ruled.

Planning Ahead for Illustration: Placement

The basic plan in most Exultets is to place an illustration just before the period containing the text it refers to. The related text then becomes a caption, a subscription: this is the same procedure normally followed in illustrating codices. It requires some, but not very much, planning.[10]

And it requires not very much more planning to paint the picture upside down in the same space. The effect of reversing the picture is not that it appears at a different time from before: even when pictures are oriented like the text, they come off the roll before their subscription text. The effect of reversing the pictures is that viewers looking at the roll the other way can see the pictures. (But they will still not appear simultaneously in the context of the Exultet's performance: the ambo prevents the picture from being seen until long after its text is sung).

Particular questions arise when, as happens surprisingly often, a picture is not at the place we expect: not preceding its period; or attached immediately after another picture; or exchanging places with another picture. In such cases, one has to posit either a considerable inattention on the part of the illustrator—not noticing that the picture does not match the text—or a process in which membranes were prepared for pictures by leaving space for them and the pictures drawn in right away, before the text is written, so that the artist has no textual control for the placement of the picture. Examples of both will be seen below.

The basic plan just described for placing pictures is followed in most of the Exultet rolls. Each of the rolls is discussed at its place in Appendix 1, but here we will select some illustrative examples of the challenges and problems of illustration in these rolls.

SOME EXAMPLES

Bari 1 solves most of the problems just presented. The large letters E and V, of course, must precede their text immediately, just as pictures normally do. Five of the seven illustrations are painted immediately before

---

10. Here I must disagree with Lucinia Speciale, whose admirable work on the rolls of Montecassino has added much to our knowledge. Speciale suggests (in *Exultet,* 250) that a Beneventan tradition of illustration, accompanying the Beneventan text, tended to place the pictures after the texts they illustrate; while a Montecassino tradition of the Roman text, begun with the British Library roll, places the pictures, inverted, before the text so that they will appear while the text is read. There are two difficulties here (besides the central question of the real purpose of the pictures); first, the early Beneventan rolls in fact tend to place their pictures before the text in question, just as later rolls do (cf. Vat. lat. 9820, Bari 1, Mirabella, 1, etc.); second, the pictures in the British Library roll, which will be examined presently, tend to be placed after, not before, the related text period.

their text periods: a scribe could just glance ahead a line or two and skip space if a picture-subject is in his next period. This is easy, but the result will not allow simultaneous seeing and singing. The last two pictures, of ecclesiastical and secular rulers, are placed, both in the next-to-last membrane, far from their text, and each a different distance ahead of its text. They are probably arranged in this way to provide a harmonious look to the membrane as a whole.

Reversing the pictures is not always easy. When Troia 2 was made, the process got confused: this confusion probably results from a first attempt to reverse pictures based on those in Troia 1, which are not reversed.[11] The last three pictures in Troia 2 are very likely based on Troia 1, but their order is confused: it must be that the spaces for the illustrations were left to be filled in and that the illustrations were put in the wrong holes. Such placement raises questions about the importance of seeing the illustrations while the text is being sung.

Making additions or alterations to a received cycle may be risky. In the Casanatense Exultet the pictures are inverted and generally come before the relevant period, in the normal manner. But this roll, on account of its Franco-Roman text, includes two pictures (the Red Sea and a Crucifixion) that are not in the series it shares with Vat. lat. 9820. The Red Sea, however, is attached to the Crucifixion, and thus at the wrong place;[12] this makes a rather long series of pictures—the letter V of "Vere," the Crucifixion, the Red Sea—without much text (only "Vere quia dignum et iustum est," in decorative capitals). A Harrowing of Hell in an earlier series of frontispiece pictures in the Casanatense roll is also not at the place where it might illustrate the text. Does the maker have a long series of pictures without text? Is the Salerno Exultet, which apart from the opening ten words has pictures and no text, a descendant of an illustration-cycle that traveled without its text?[13]

The arrangement of pictures in Gaeta 2 (Plate 13) shows most of the problems that can arise when coordinating pictures with text. In this roll, where further errors are not found, the general principle is for the scribe to stop after he has written something that ought to be illustrated (not before, as is more usual), and leave a space. These spaces evidently get filled in considerably later. The letter V, one of two Harrowings of Hell, and the Red Sea appear after the periods to which they are related; the

11. We ignore for the moment the very odd pictures that do not correspond between the two rolls. See Appendix 1.

12. It is true, even if it was not the scribe's intent, that this is one of the few places where at least one picture would be seen in relation to its text. The sequence V–Crucifixion–Red Sea precedes a long section of text and would be visible over the ambo for some time; the Red Sea picture in particular would have been perfectly placed when its text arrived, and the whole illustrative group would have been visible together during the longish textual passage.

13. For fuller discussions, see the discussions of Casanatense, Salerno, and Vat. lat. 9820 in Appendix 1; see also pp. 129–31.

illustration "Fratres karissimi" comes just after those words, in the middle of a period. But the two pictures on the third membrane are in each other's place, and each is seen after the (ir)relevant period is read: the period including the text "sacrificium uespertinum" is followed by the illustration "Curuat imperia," and vice versa. These inversions and their placement suggest that pictures were put into holes without rereading the text; or perhaps, reading from the top, the illustrator saw the space before "sacrificium uespertinum," inserted the picture (not realizing that it ought to come *after* the period), and then put the other picture in the remaining place, without checking its appropriateness. The collaboration of scribe and artist is not close here.

When pictures are evidently painted in the wrong place, or painted the wrong way round, we can see that they have been produced by illustrators who are not aware of the relationship of picture to text: either because they do not read it or because it is not yet there. This may have been true of the illustrator in Gaeta 2: but it is perhaps more surprising to find the same apparent negligence in the beautiful twin Exultets from Montecassino, now in London and in the Barberini collection.

ILLUSTRATIONS IN MONTECASSINO ROLLS

In the London roll (Plates 15–17), the pictures are generally in the wrong place if they are intended to precede their text periods. The illustrations "Angelica turba" and "Mater ecclesia" are painted after their periods; "Tellus," attached after "Ecclesia," is not just on the wrong side of its period, it is on the wrong side of the wrong period: Is it perhaps included as an afterthought? Other pictures ("Fratres karissimi," the Red Sea, Adam and Eve) all appear after the relevant periods.

But the idea that a picture is placed after its period is not pursued systematically. A number of pictures precede their periods, in the fashion more normal in other rolls: the Crucifixion is correct (if it is meant to illustrate the period "Hec sunt enim festa paschalia in cuius uere ille agnus occiditur"), as is "sacrificium uespertinum"; the illustration of bees is appropriate, and the illustration of the Virgin Mary and of "cereus iste" precede their periods.

Some other pictures in the London roll are puzzling: a "Noli me tangere" scene precedes the period "Huius igitur sanctificatio noctis, fugat scelera, culpas lauat, reddit innocentiam lapsis, mestis letitiam, fugat odia, concordiam parat, et curuat imperia"; if it illustrates that text it is in the right place: but it has no real relation to it.[14] A Harrowing of Hell scene precedes the period including the text "ut seruum redimeres filium tra- didisti": but surely the scene illustrates "Hec nox est in qua destructis

---

14. Some rolls have other pictures about here: a Visitatio sepulcri in Capua; the Kiss of Judas in the Paris roll.

uinculis mortis christus ab inferis uictor ascendit," in which case it appears two periods late.

Why is a luxurious roll so inconsistent as to its illustrations? If the general principle is to place pictures before their periods, then only the last three (of seven) membranes are correctly made—and the last has no pictures. How does this happen? Did an artist start at one end of an already-written roll and make either a correction or a slip that confused the placement of all the rest of the pictures? It is difficult to discover an error or a train of errors that would produce the roll as we have it. It may be important to note, however, that the roll was produced, and that no evident attempt was made to correct inconsistencies in the placement of illustrations. Perhaps their placement was not so important as we might think. Narrative consistency is secondary to the gesture, the idea, the pleasing result.

In the Barberini Exultet, all the surviving pictures that are not lost, and that have analogous pictures in the London roll, are in the same place as they are in London, with one exception: in the Barberini roll, "Tellus" follows its period (as it does not in London). Two additional Barberini pictures, Pope and Emperor, are not used in the London roll: here they too come after their text periods.

The Barberini roll is thus relatively consistent in its placement of pictures: all of them are wrong for simultaneous viewing except for "Sacrificium uespertinum."[15]

Despite the closeness of their texts and their use of the same illustration cycle, these two rolls are evidently not copies of a model whose text and illustrations were fully and systematically integrated. The London roll seems an inexpert and unsystematic attempt to integrate pictures, switching from one way to another of relating picture to period, now placing the picture first, now the text.

This is not, however, the first attempt at Montecassino to write and illustrate the Roman text. The handsome Avezzano roll may be the first Exultet made at Montecassino with Franco-Roman text,[16] but the elegant roll now at Pisa, made at Montecassino, has an entirely successful picture cycle, with each illustration preceding its text period.[17] By the time the London roll was made, the Pisa roll had long been absent and its systematic approach evidently forgotten.

The Barberini roll, more systematic, places almost all its pictures after the relevant period: this may be a methodical reworking of the disorder in the London roll. Although the Barberini pictures are reversed, they are not calculated to appear to a viewer as the deacon sings.

15. The Barberini roll lacks the portion that would have contained the picture of the Virgin, which in the London roll is correctly placed for viewing.

16. Vat. lat. 3784, an earlier roll of Montecassino, survives only in part and probably did not have the Franco-Roman text; Brenk, however, believes it did: in *Exultet*, 211–12.

17. Even though the initial V is turned upside down with respect to the script, so that it cannot be read by the deacon.

The Barberini and London rolls achieve a handsome balance of illustration with text, but only when they are viewed as visual compositions
and not as practical documents. The Barberini roll especially, judging
from what survives, is a handsome compilation of words and images,
pleasingly laid out as to space. The London roll, beautiful too in its aspect,
has one unbalanced juxtaposition of two pictures. But they are as successful, in their own way, as the Pisa roll. The issue becomes what success
meant at the time.

Collaborations of Scribe and Painter

When space is left for pictures in the laying out of a membrane, it is clear
that some integration of pictures and text is planned at the outset. The
relationship of pictures to text and music, the amount of cooperation
among the makers of the roll, varies from one document to another: but
in the best cases there appears to be a close collaboration.

In many rolls there is a first stage in the illustration: a drawing in
which the picture is composed, arranged in the space, and the details
established: this is done with a fine pen. A second stage is the addition of
gold and of color. In the best rolls, the overlay of color does not obliterate
the drawing, but serves to heighten it: the drawing remains the backbone,
as it were, of the picture. The later overpainting in some rolls, like Salerno, covers this original drawing. In many cases, perhaps almost all, the
drawing is done, in the context of the text and the notation, before the
coloring takes place. This seems clear from Gaeta 2 (Plate 13), where some
of the later pictures are lacking some colors, and Bari 2 evidently was
colored from the beginning after all the drawing was done, but the work
was not finished, so that the colors gradually drop out one by one as the
end of the roll is approached. Mirabella 1 perhaps was meant to have more
color, but was never finished.

On the other hand, when pictures are put in the wrong place, or
oriented in the wrong direction, the painter is not directly conforming to
the writing that appears on the same membrane. In Troia 2, for example,
the pictures seem to be a subsequent addition. Red clef-lines are added,
freehand, after the musical notation; the pictures avoid these red lines, or
have the figures almost stand on them (secular rulers; "Saluum fac"). This
order of working may explain the confusion in the last three pictures (see
Appendix 1), which seem to have been placed in the wrong spaces: one
is no longer thinking about the relationship of the pictures to the text and
its music.

In other cases, however, it appears that the scribe and artist collabo-
rate closely—indeed, that they may be the same person. Some examples
will suggest that writing and illustration may alternate in production, so
that the writing continues only after the drawing is done: in this method
either scribe and painter are progressing together, or a single person does

both tasks (for our purposes, there is no available distinction between the two).

In Mirabella 1, the illustrations (inverted) were done by, or in collaboration with, the scribe, unless they were all painted before the text. Unruled space is provided for the V of "uere," after which the text continues, not where the ruling resumes, but after skipping two lines, because the illustration went too far. The same situation is true after the angel illustration: one wing causes the next text to begin later than it would have had the illustration not already been there. A similar situation is seen in Mirabella 2, probably made as a Franco-Roman continuation of the older roll. In this later roll the illustrations, not inverted, are simultaneous with or anterior to the writing: the text and notation after the second picture skip around the picture, dividing the word "debi-tum" to accommodate the decoration.

A similar case is Troia 3. In its last membrane, there is ruling at the top, and then a space is left, and then ruling begins again. But the Emperor takes up too much space, and the writing resumes one line lower than planned. Does this mean, as in Mirabella, that writing was continued only after the illustration was at least drawn? Or is it possible that the pictures were painted before the writing was begun?[18] The last membrane is unusual in its preparation. It appears to be ruled at the top (where there is no writing), and then a space is left, and then ruling begins again. Apparently it was intended to have one text period or a portion of one ("Precamur ergo": the period includes clergy, people, pope, bishop, and king, a lot to illustrate), followed by an illustration and a continuation of text. Instead, the membrane begins directly with the illustration (clergy, people, pope, bishop, king); but the picture takes up too much space, and the writing begins one line lower than planned. The writing had to have been imagined, or sketched in, because illustrations often use the space left at the top by incomplete lines of text; the annunciation fits into one such line, and the top of the Paschal candle extends into the space after the line ending "terrenis celestia iunguntur" (Plate 14). There is careful planning of the layout, probably by a single scribe/painter.

Writing and drawing are related, picture and text are related, in all the illustrated rolls. But the handsome results are usually not entirely consistent, and in no Exultet are all the pictures arranged so that they can be viewed while their text is sung. This relationship of word to image was evidently not uppermost in the concerns of scribes and artists. We will return to this question in the next chapter.

---

18. Guglielmo Cavallo has pointed out (*Rotoli,* 177) that many of the pictures here precede the text: a halo is erased in part; text splits to accommodate a cross; "in deliciis meis" is split between two groups of figures, rather than starting a new line at left; in the first writing of the line "Fugat odia . . ." (later erased to put in under its illustration), the "curuat imperia" was divided because of the crowned head.

New Rolls for Old

Exultet rolls continued to be made and used for a long time. A new church (or new bishop) might wish to have a new Exultet; or an older institution might want to have a new roll corresponding to modern needs. The reasons for creating new Exultets, and for recycling old ones, are various, and they tell us much about the functions of the rolls themselves.

Reasons for Creating a New Roll

We may have lost many documents, but those that survive tell us much about the persistence of tradition even in the face of mandated change. In cities that preserve more than one Exultet roll—Bari, Troia, Gaeta, and Mirabella Eclano—the successive documents reflect altered needs, and successive changes reveal a regular pattern:

1. The oldest roll in each city has the Beneventan text. This is, of course, a reason for the existence of multiple rolls, since the newer Franco-Roman version soon arrives to replace or alternate with the older text.
2. Sometimes, as at Bari and Troia, a second roll is manufactured probably to clarify the musical notation of the older Beneventan Exultet.[19]
3. At some point in the late eleventh or early twelfth century, each center creates a new Exultet roll using the Franco-Roman text (these are Bari 3, Troia 3, Gaeta 2, Mirabella 2); but usually—and here the musicologist can help the art historian in detecting Lombard conservatism—the new text retains the old Beneventan melody.
4. At a still later stage, an older roll is sometimes reused to fill the desire for a "Roman" melody, a Roman text, or both. This accounts for many of the mutilations and alterations in surviving rolls.

Changes in Older Rolls

Exultet rolls are precious on account of their illustrations, and they are not readily discarded, like many other manuscripts, when needs change. Often they are altered, more or less drastically, to preserve their pictures while their text or their music changes.

Some rolls are erased and rewritten, to substitute the Franco-Roman text. Bari 2 was altered in the thirteenth century in two stages to convert a Beneventan Exultet into a Roman one (Plate 3). The preface portion of the text was erased and substituted with the Franco-Roman text written

---

19. It might be, of course, that the second roll is for the use of a different church: but the clear development of notation, and the similar level of luxury, suggests that the second roll is designed as a replacement.

in a Gothic hand. The opening portion, however, was left in the original Beneventan script, since this prologue is common to both versions. The decorated initials from the Beneventan text, which organized the text into musical periods, were left intact in the margin, though they no longer correspond to the visible text; instead, the Roman text is written in run-on fashion, each new period now following immediately after the preceding, without the original scribe's concern for beginning new periods on new lines. The entire original melody was also erased and substituted with a more elaborate version of the Beneventan melody, written in an awkward square notation on a staff of from three to five red lines provided with a clef. The original underlying Beneventan melody can be recognized from the shape of the erasures.

Gaeta 1 was altered in the fourteenth century,[20] leaving almost nothing of its original Beneventan text.[21] The pictures are reversed, as they were in the original; however, the pictorial cycle does not work equally well for both texts: the scene with bees and the virginity of Mary have no place here, since the praise of the bees is omitted in this version of the Roman text. The Gothic script and square notation on a four-line staff obscure essentially all of the original text; a few original initials are preserved.

Vat. lat. 9820, the oldest Exultet of Benevento and the oldest exemplar of an important iconographic series, was also altered—or perhaps mutilated is a better term, for in the twelfth century the roll was erased and reordered to become a Franco-Roman text. By reversing the scroll the original pictures were now presented upside down with respect to the text, and in fact the initial letters of the older text survive upside down in the present right margin.

A brutal way to change the text was simply to chop off the parts of an old roll that do not correspond to the Franco-Roman text and to append new text and music. This was the fate of a number of rolls, and it may account for the fragmentary state of some others.

Vat. lat. 3784 is a handsome roll of Montecassino of which only the preface survives (through the initial V of "Vere"). Until recently, it had a late Gothic roll with the full Franco-Roman text glued to it as a continuation (Vat. lat. 3784A). It is presumed (but not proven) that the missing portion was amputated because it contained the Beneventan text, no longer useful. But it must have been beautiful, and perhaps one or more of its illuminations survive unrecognized.

Capua preserves an incomplete Exultet roll that begins only partway into the Franco-Roman preface. It may be that this roll never was complete, that it was made as a Roman continuation for an Exultet whose beginning was retained but is now lost.

---

20. Between 1335 and 1341; see the description in Appendix 1.

21. A few words in capitals ("Vere quia dignum et iustum est per Christum dominum nostrum") survive around the decorated letter V; the last four words, commonly used in Beneventan versions of the text, are not used in the Roman text.

Mirabella 2 is an Exultet roll of three pieces, beginning with "Vere quia dignum"; it is evidently a continuation of Mirabella 1, which must once have been complete and contained the Beneventan text. The scribe of Mirabella 2 can be seen to copy the notation of "Vere dignum" from Mirabella 1, though he misinterprets its meaning.

Velletri preserves four pieces of a Montecassino Exultet roll. These pieces retain only enough text for us to see that the Beneventan text was being written at Montecassino relatively late (while Franco-Roman texts were also being written). But these pieces survive undoubtedly for their pictures, the rest having been rejected because of the inappropriate text. Perhaps the opening of this roll, now lost, was saved to serve with a Roman preface.

Montecassino 1 is a single membrane from a Beneventan Exultet. It contains almost exclusively the praise of the bees: it might have been excised from a longer roll, on the analogy of the omission of the praise of the bees from some versions of the Franco-Roman text. However, we have no other evidence that the Beneventan text, or the praise of the bees, was ever treated in this way.

The Rolls of Montecassino

The six Exultet rolls known to have been produced at Montecassino far exceed the number required for liturgical services there. Some are apparently for use at Montecassino, but the abbey's scriptorium also produced rolls for use elsewhere. In this group of Exultets we can see the confluence of a variety of traditions.

Several Montecassino Exultets are produced for external use. The Avezzano roll was made for Bishop Pandulf of the Marsi near the beginning of Desiderius's abbacy.[22] Likewise, the roll now at Pisa is in the hand of a Montecassino scribe,[23] perhaps manufactured at Montecassino before the disastrous expedition of the 1060s when Abbot Desiderius sent twelve monks under Aldemarius (who had been Leo Marsicanus' novice-master) to found a new monastic cell at the invitation of King Bareso I of Sardinia. At the Isola di Gigli, the Pisans, "maxima Sardorum inuidia ducti," attacked the monks and stole everything they had, probably including the roll that the Pisans still hold.[24] And the roll at Velletri, now only a few fragmentary illustrations, may have been made for the use of Leo Marsicanus when he was made cardinal bishop of Ostia (the bishops of Ostia were also bishops of Velletri), and so he left it where it lies today.

---

22. It is perhaps in the same hand as Montecassino 453. See Newton, "Due tipi," 470.

23. I am grateful to Professor Newton for his opinion on this; his full description will appear in *The Scriptorium,* forthcoming.

24. *Chron. mon. Cas.,* 387–88 (bk. III, 21).

But other rolls of Montecassino were made for the use of the abbey itself. Vat. lat. 3784, clearly the product of Montecassino, may have been intended for the use of the abbey. This is Brenk's opinion: the roll was written and decorated by the same artists who later worked on the famous lectionary Vat. lat. 1202, made in 1071.[25] The roll is now so incomplete that we cannot compare it textually with other rolls, and we cannot tell whether it contained names of ecclesiastical or secular authorities. It has been assumed that the roll contained the Beneventan text and that this is the reason for its mutilation and the substitution of a much later roll using the Franco-Roman text. This seems a reasonable conjecture and also provides a reason for the fabrication of further rolls for the use of the same abbey, since the substitution of the Franco-Roman text in the liturgy is everywhere to be seen in the eleventh century, and as champion of the universal Roman church Montecassino would surely make the same addition.[26]

The famous pair of Exultets from Montecassino, now in London and in the Barberini collection at the Vatican Library, are the chief witnesses to the Franco-Roman text for use at Montecassino. At least one of these rolls (that now in London) was at Montecassino until the early years of the nineteenth century.[27] According to Brenk, the London roll was made shortly after Vat. lat. 3874, to provide a Franco-Roman text for use at Montecassino; and the Barberini roll is a second version of this, based on the London roll, made at the moment of Desiderius' elevation to the papacy as Victor III in 1087.[28] A similar precedence is supported by Lucinia Speciale, who sees the transition from Beneventan to Franco-Roman text as part of the Gregorian reform of which Desiderius and Montecassino were such strong supporters.[29]

And this may well be. But there are two problems. First, there is not much to show that the change to the Franco-Roman text is evidence of a new adherence to the Roman liturgy and therefore an element of "reform"; we have seen that the Beneventan *melody* at least persists for a

---

25. Brenk, *Das Lektionar*, iiif.; "Bischöfliche und monastiche 'Committenza,' " 297.

26. On Montecassino's championing of the Roman liturgy, see Kelly, *TBC*, 38–40; see also Speciale, *Montecassino e la riforma;* Cowdrey, *The Age of Abbot Desiderius*, 71–106.

27. The roll was acquired by the British Museum in 1877; it was "believed to have remained at Monte Cassino until the beginning of the 19th century" (Gilson, *An Exultet Roll*, 5).

28. Brenk, "Bischöfliche und monastiche 'Committenza,' " 298–99; see also Speciale in *Exultet*, 235; this latter roll, then, is perhaps the only one that gives a clear view of the Desiderian ambo made for the new basilica. See Zanardi, "Gli Exultet cassinesi," and the discussion on pp. 162–64.

29. The creation of the Barberini roll as a special symbolic celebration of the elevation of Desiderius to the papacy is at least plausible, if not demonstrable. Speciale sees signs of haste in its preparations and supposes it was rushed for use at Easter 1087, when Desiderius had been chosen for the papacy (Speciale, *Montecassino e la riforma*, 136).

long time after the visit of Stephen IX in 1058. Second, it is not clear that Montecassino did in fact change definitively to the Franco-Roman text.

Montecassino's slowness to reject the Beneventan text of the Exultet is curious. Pope Stephen IX's forbidding of "ambrosianus cantus" at Montecassino in 1058 is often cited as the moment of Montecassino's definitive rejection of the old Beneventan chant.[30] But if this is true, then it must follow that the Beneventan text of the Exultet, with its Beneventan melody, was not considered necessarily a part of the liturgy to be replaced, for this text continued to appear: probably in Vat. lat. 3784 in the 1060s, in the quotations from the Beneventan text found in the Pisa roll, and certainly in the Velletri roll, written much later still.

Of the Montecassino rolls, perhaps Vat. lat. 3784 and London were intended for use at Montecassino, to provide two versions of the Exultet: after all, there seems to have been some survival of alternative practices at Montecassino, to judge from other places where alternatives are presented, Roman and Beneventan.[31] Why might one roll not have been used in one church, or year, and the other in another?

Nothing in the surviving ordinals of Montecassino (see Appendix 3) indicates which text of the Exultet is meant to be sung. Montecassino changed its ceremonies at some time between the tenth and the end of the eleventh century. Formerly the Paschal candle was blessed after the lessons, but in Desiderian times it was blessed, with considerable ceremony, at the beginning of the vigil: the candle was lit by an acolyte, and a show was made of taking the Exultet roll off the altar. We cannot be certain that this change of ceremony accompanied the change from Beneventan to Franco-Roman text; it may have been the result of the differences that naturally arise between monastic and episcopal ceremonies, or indeed of the tendency of liturgy to become more elaborate.

The presence of alternatives, in the Farfa-Trento fragments, and perhaps at Montecassino, makes a considerable contrast with places where the Beneventan Exultet is physically rejected in order to write a Franco-Roman text. Cities like Bari and Troia may have used the older Beneventan roll as an alternative; but the physical alteration of Vat. lat. 9820, Gaeta 1, and others suggests that in most places the change from Beneventan to Franco-Roman was not a gradual one.

---

30. See pp. 62–63.

31. A leaf in the Montecassino *Compactiones* gives an alternative communion in Beneventan chant for a Mass of Saint Benedict; see Boe, "Old Beneventan Chant"; Kelly, *TBC*, 308. A rubric in a manuscript certainly derived from Montecassino practice, and possibly from the abbey, provides two sets of antiphons for the monastic Maundy service and provides a rubric indicating alternative practice: "likewise, when we do not sing these antiphons according to the Roman rite, as they are written here, we sing them according to the Ambrosian [i.e., the Beneventan], in this way" (Vat. Ottob. lat. 145, fol. 124: "Item quando non canimus ipse a[ntiphone] secundum romano, quo modo supra scripte sunt, canimus secundum ambro[sianum] hoc modo"). Although the fragment appears to date from the late eleventh century, it cannot be shown to have been written before the visit of Stephen IX; see Boe, "A New Source"; Kelly, *TBC*, 25.

Persistence of the Roll: Layers of Influence

There are a great many later alterations in Exultet rolls, which show that many of them were used for centuries, presumably on an annual basis. A fifteenth-century missal of Molfetta shows a deacon using a roll for the Exultet.[32] Pisa evidently displayed a scroll—perhaps the south Italian one—in the sixteenth century;[33] Vat. lat. 3784 remained in use, with its late continuation, in the fifteenth century; and the substantial repainting of many rolls indicates their long use. Indeed, Bertaux wrote in 1904 that the Salerno Exultet was still displayed from the pulpit.[34] The Barberini Exultet, before its eighteenth-century dismemberment, was used, indeed probably "restored," in the late thirteenth century, and the Italian "ystorie" makes clear that the ceremonial used then was not that represented by the original state of the roll.[35] Benevento cathedral used an Exultet roll in the fifteenth century, to judge from the cathedral's inventory of 1447.[36]

A particularly interesting example is Gaeta 3, a roll that was in use from its manufacture in the early twelfth century until at least the fourteenth century and probably the sixteenth. The various states of its additions have been sorted out by Valentine Pace[37] and are detailed in Appendix 1. This is a roll to which a succession of names have been added, whose ending has been altered at least four times, in which the Norman finale has been substituted, whose text has been altered to remove the praise of the bees, to which rubrics have been added to change the liturgical placement of the lighting and censing of the candle, and in which additional small corrections have been made in the course of the text. The roll seems still to have been in use in 1508.[38]

Many Exultets were made for special recipients, and some provide proper names at the suitable places; Paris 710, Montecassino 2, and Avezzano are examples of such rolls. But most Exultets were made with the understanding that they would be used for a long time; as a result, the places where the ecclesiastical authorities (pope, bishop, abbot) and secular rulers are named were generally left with a generic sign (*.N.* or *.il.*) where the deacon filled in the appropriate names each year. But many deacons might have wished to have the names available to a faulty memory or might have feared having to adjust on the spot the music provided in the roll to the number of syllables in the name. Many deacons surely wrote

---

32. A facsimile of the picture is reproduced by Cavallo in *Exultet*, 55.

33. See p. 235.

34. *L'art*, 231–32.

35. See the description in Appendix 2 and on p. 165.

36. "Item carta ubi est *exultet iam angelica*" appears among the list of books not in Beneventan script in the inventory of 1430–35. See p. 29.

37. *Civiltà*, 54–56.

38. An inventory cited in Ferraro, *Memorie*, 180, lists "Item una carta di coyro grande scripta notata et figurata dove si cantha Exultet jam angelica; circha palmi venti longa."

these details down, but only where someone had been thoughtless enough to write them on the roll itself do they survive.

Bari 1 has many names added, on front and back,[39] including names of archbishops, popes, Byzantine emperors, local authorities, and Norman lords. The roll was altered, or portions added in margins or on the back, at least ten times between the making of the roll, sometime in the early years of the eleventh century, through the time of Archbishop Urso (1080–89).[40]

Avezzano, which provided the name of Bishop Pandulfus in the original text, had generic names for emperor and prince, which were later altered more than once. Vat. lat. 9820 provides, on the back of its final membrane, additional text for insertion on particular dates, one of which is of the thirteenth century. The Capua roll has many names added, evidently over a long time, though many are now illegible. A number of other rolls and manuscripts give evidence of repeated use by the addition of names: Mirabella 2, Naples VI G 38, Vat. Barb. lat. 699.

We have seen that Exultets, in order to retain their usefulness, may have had to have their texts adjusted to meet changing needs. Thus in particular the praise of the bees needed to be adjusted (usually eliminated) in order to correspond with the usual practices of the thirteenth century and later.[41] Likewise, the changing ceremonial was sometimes indicated by additions to rolls, in which the original liturgical events depicted on the roll (such as the candle being lit at the start of the ceremony) were negated by later rubrics. After such changes in text and ceremonial practice, an illustrated Exultet roll as it was used in later centuries was no longer a visual record, or prescription, of how the ceremony was to proceed; probably it never was intended to be exactly that. What was wanted in such cases, evidently, was to preserve the history and beauty that belong to the church, without being out of step with current liturgical trends and requirements.

---

39. The best description of these is Cavallo, *Rotoli*, 49–50. See also Antonucci, "Le aggiunte all' 'Exultet,' " and "Le aggiunte interlineari."
    40. See the list of these additions in Appendix 1.
    41. See pp. 65–69.

8

CONCLUSION: THE PURPOSE OF MAKING EXULTET ROLLS

❦

The remarkable phenomenon of the Exultet roll results, as we see, from the work of many contributors and the confluence of many traditions, textual, musical, and visual. And yet some central questions remain to be addressed, which can best be posed—if not always answered—after the foregoing consideration of the constituent elements.

Why Write Down the Music of the Exultet?

The reason for writing the Exultet with musical notation might seem self-evident: an unusual and unfamiliar piece is a good candidate for writing. The deacon sings the Exultet only once a year; adjusting the musical formula on the spot would make its extemporaneous performance inconvenient.

But the situation in southern Italy is not like that elsewhere: no part of the Exultet is sung to the preface tone as it is elsewhere, and the tone of the Exultet is one that is sung on other occasions. As we have seen, the Beneventan Exultet tone is sung during Holy Week as part of lections sung from the ambo: the prayer of Jonah on Maundy Thursday, the Canticle of the Three Children on Good Friday, the prayer of Jeremiah on Holy Saturday, all were sung to a version of the same tone. This is a special melody, used in reading only when the text turns to the quotation of a prayer; and whereas it provides an impressive liturgical succession leading up to the Exultet, it does not suggest that the Exultet was unfamiliar to the deacon, at least as regards the workings of its melody. It is not the unfamiliarity of the music that causes it to be written out for the Exultet.

The reason is probably more related to the importance of the occasion. This tone was solemn enough, or unusual enough, that it was notated in full when it appears for the other readings where it is used, even when the rest of the lection in which it appears is not given musical notation. Evidently it is a special case.

Equally important is that the deacon in some sense acts as the bishop's deputy in the matter of the Exultet, and the roll is in some sense an episcopal possession, even though the deacon will use it in performance.

Why the Deacon?

One of the most difficult problems about the Exultet is the question of why it is sung by a deacon. Whereas deacons have specific roles in the liturgy, assisting in the celebration of the eucharist and reading the Gospel, they do not normally perform acts that involve a benediction, a blessing of objects or persons. And yet, in this very important and dramatic moment of the liturgical year, the deacon takes a central role in a ceremony that has much symbolic meaning and does indeed appear to be a blessing.[1] In the Old Spanish, Milanese, Beneventan, and Roman liturgies, the deacon sings a prayer of the eucharistic type, including a beginning like that of the eucharistic preface ("Vere dignum"); this is especially unusual in the many cases where the bishop is present. Perhaps the Exultet descends from an *admonitio diaconalis* of the evening lucernarium, the exuberance of such texts being desirable on such an occasion, but inappropriate for the senior members of the clergy, as Pinell has suggested.[2]

Since the Gospel is normally read from the ambo, and the Exultet is also read from there, the deacon, as the usual reader from the ambo, might have assumed this function because of its physical location. But there are two objections to this. First, the deacon is not alone in using the ambo: bishops and priests when they preach, subdeacons when they read the epistle, may also use the ambo,[3] and any of these might have as much justification for performing the Exultet as the deacon. Second, the ambo

1. Juglar, "À propos de la vigile pascale," argues strongly that the Exultet does constitute a blessing; the title "benedictio cerei" dates at least from the fifth century.

2. Pinell, "La benedicció," 10.

3. The question of double ambos, used for Epistle and Gospel, and common in major churches from at least the twelfth century, is not the issue here: only the practice of going up into a pulpit.

is probably not the original site of the Exultet. We know that in Rome the candle was at first blessed in front of the altar and only later moved to the ambo. We have seen that in the Beneventan rite the Exultet was not at first sung from the ambo.[4]

It may be that the blessing of the candle was originally the function of the bishop, later delegated to deacons. If, as Juglar suggests, the ceremony descends from the early lucernarium, then it originally was the province of the bishop; the lucernarium, known in the West as early as the Apostolic Constitutions of Hippolytus, is a thanksgiving, in the form of a preface, sung by the bishop, giving thanks for the gift of light.[5]

In Ravenna, it was the bishop who sang the praeconium, to judge from Pope Gregory the Great's letter of 601, in which he encourages the ailing Bishop Marinianus to avoid the exertions of the approaching Easter season, which for him would include the "prayers which are to be said over the candle in the church of Ravenna."[6]

But as early as 384, Saint Jerome, in his caustic letter to Praesidius of Piacenza, notes that it is the deacon who blesses the candle, and he disapproves of the practice: "Esto haec iucunda sint . . . quid ad diaconum, quid ad Ecclesiae sacramenta, quid ad tempus Paschae . . . , cum, tacente episcopo, et presbyteris in plebeium quodammodo cultum redactis, leuita loquitur, docetque quod pene non didicit?"[7] This is the one time in the year in most rites that the deacon sings the tone normally reserved for the preface at the altar.[8]

Pinell, too, wonders how it happens that the deacon sings the Exultet and sings the preface tone only once in the year. He supposes that the deacon may be delegated by the bishop, who has, after all, a long night ahead of him, with many prayers to say, water to bless, baptisms and confirmations, Mass, and so on.[9]

In southern Italy, at least, there seems to be a clear connection of the Exultet with the bishop, and the connection is through the Exultet roll. Many of these rolls are evidently made for bishops: the bishop is the owner of the roll; he consigns it for use to the deacon, who is in some sense singing the Exultet in the presence of, in the stead of, and almost directed toward the bishop. Many of the liturgical illustrations in the rolls make this clear.

---

4. See pp. 156–58.

5. Botte, "La 'Tradition,' " 60–61.

6. "A vigiliis quoque temperandum est; sed et preces illae quae super cereum in Ravennati civitate dici solent vel expositiones evangelii, quae circa paschalem sollemnitatem a sacerdotibus fiunt, per alium dicantur" (*MGH Epistolae* 2, 282–83).

7. On this letter, see chapter 3, n. 9.

8. "C'est la seule occasion où il soit permis au lévite de prendre le ton de la prédication liturgique ou préface": Morin, "Un écrit méconnu," 26.

9. Pinell, "La benedicció," 10.

Why Write the Exultet on a Scroll?

Solemnity may be the reason for writing the Exultet on a roll for use in the ambo on Holy Saturday. But there are other kinds of documents in which the Exultet appears, and it might be well to consider the reason for the Exultet's appearance in its various transmissions before returning to the phenomenon of the roll.

The Exultet in Other Books

The Exultet in sources related to southern Italy, in addition to its transmission in twenty-six rolls, is found in twenty-seven other manuscripts: eighteen missals, two evangelistaries, two pontificals, two rituals, two graduals, and one processional. These have been listed in Table 1 and are described in Appendix 1.

In the Franco-Roman rite, the Exultet is often found in sacramentaries (books of prayers for use by the celebrant at Mass), but in southern Italy sacramentaries are rare and missals seem to occupy their place. These latter are books that contain all the necessary materials for the celebration of the Mass: celebrant's prayers, lectors' texts, singers' chants (though not always with musical notation). They thus would be expected to contain the materials needed also for the special rites of Holy Week, which, while they are unusual, still are days of the greatest solemnity and engage the activity of these same participants. For Holy Saturday, missals customarily contain the lections, the prayers, and the canticles of the vigil, as well as materials for the Mass and sometimes also the pontifical rites of baptism. It thus seems perfectly appropriate that eighteen missals related to the Beneventan practice of the Exultet contain the Exultet along with so much other material: the missal in many ways serves as a standard book of reference, and perhaps as the priest's book. But this is not, except in small parishes and priories, the book from which the Exultet will normally be performed, any more than it is regularly used by the singers, or the readers.

The evangelistary is the book containing gospel pericopes in liturgical order, from which the deacon sings the Gospel at Mass. This is in many ways an appropriate book to contain the Exultet: it is the deacon's book, and the Exultet is a deacon's chant. The Exultet appears in two Dalmatian evangelistaries,[10] but not elsewhere in the Beneventan zone, so far as we know. Eight other evangelistaries[11] of the Beneventan region

---

10. Oxford, Bodl. Canon. bibl. lat. 61, Zadar s11ex; Vat. Borg. lat. 339, written 1082.

11. Vat. Ottob. lat. 296 (s11); Berlin Th. lat. Quart. 278 (s11ex); Bisceglie Duomo SN (s11ex); Rimini, Bibl. Civica Gambalunga SC-MS. 24 (s11ex); Vat. lat. 3741 (s11ex); Bitonto, Bibl. Comunale A. 45 (s11/12); Benevento, Bibl. cap. 31 (s11/12, ends incomplete before Holy Saturday); Vat. lat. 5100 (s13).

from the mid-eleventh to the mid-thirteenth century that survive more or less complete, and fragments of four others,[12] preserve no further evidence of the Exultet. Perhaps the fact that the Exultet is written into Dalmatian gospel books explains the absence of Exultet rolls from that region.

Pontificals are books that contain ceremonies performed by the bishop: baptisms, confirmation, ordinations, and the like. They often, but not always, contain materials for the rites in which the bishop participated during Holy Week: the special Masses and ceremonies of Maundy Thursday, Good Friday, and Holy Saturday, in which the bishop has a special role. Interestingly, the only south Italian pontificals in which the Exultet is written are the twin copies of the Roman-German Pontifical made at Montecassino in the late eleventh century.[13] They transmit their particular version of the text and its ceremonies, but without notation and without much obvious effect on the practice of the Exultet in the south.[14] Other pontificals give us much useful information about the ceremony, but since they are essentially intended for the bishop, they often omit the text of the Exultet.[15] A particularly significant element of the pontifical in southern Italy is the presence of certain pontifical rites on rolls; two rolls from Benevento in the Biblioteca Casanatense[16] and the benedictional at Bari[17] are illustrated rolls that the bishop used for ordinations, the blessing of water, and baptisms. They have clear connections with the practice of using Exultet rolls and with the question of the use of illustration in liturgical scrolls.

Two rituals (which normally include rites performed by priests), contain the Exultet: Rome, Vall. C 32, and the central Italian manuscript Rome, Vall. F 29. The first includes the Exultet as part of the priest's ritual of Holy Saturday; the latter, a composite volume including a number of monastic rites, provides the Exultet as a separate element. Although the Exultet is not normally a part of rituals elsewhere, we cannot be certain about southern Italy, for the only other ritual besides Vall. C 32 that

12. Rab, Nadzupski Ured SN (s12); Zagreb, Nacionalna i Sv. Bibl. R 4106 (s12); Trogir, Riznica Katedrale, Chapter Library SN, SN(1), s12; SN(2), 1259. For notices on all these, see Lowe, *TBS* and Brown, "A Second New List."

13. Montecassino 451 and Rome, Vall. D 5, perhaps its model.

14. See p. 000.

15. Of these, the first two listed here provide important information about ceremonial (they are edited in Appendix 3); Vat. Barb. lat 631 (s11ex); Macerata, Bibl. Com. 378 (s12in); Leningrad, Academy of Sciences F. No. 200 (s12); Rome, Casanatense 614 (s12/13); Dubrovnik, Franjevački Samostan 5310/230/7 (fragment s12); also related to the periphery of the Beneventan zone are Vat. lat. 7818 (Chieti, not in Beneventan script, s12); Vat. Burgh. 49 (Sora, not in Beneventan script, s13); Vat. lat. 7701, s10/11, of unknown provenance, not in Beneventan script.

16. Rome, Biblioteca Casanatense 724(i), s10ex (pontifical roll); 724(ii) s10/11 (blessing of fonts); the bibliography on these is very large: see Lowe, *TBS*, and the bibliography there; commentary by Beat Brenk, and complete facsimiles, in *Exultet*, 75–100.

17. Complete facsimile and commentary in Cavallo, *Rotoli;* commentary by Magistrale and facsimile in *Exultet*, 143–50.

survives is the handsome Oderisian ritual from Montecassino, Vat. Borg. lat. 211, though ritual elements appear in some missals and pontificals.

Two graduals contain the Exultet: the early Vat. lat. 10673 (where the Exultet is unfortunately incomplete) and the Farfa-Trento fragments. The latter is a very unusual document, because it is the only place in which the Beneventan and the Roman texts appear together. It consists of two fragmentary bifolia from what appears to be a gradual, since it contains only musical items, but it may have been an exceptional book in other ways as well; we cannot tell.

Processionals are often catch-all volumes: not only do they contain music for use in procession, but they often provide a variety of other special, occasional, or unusual musical items for which no convenient place is found elsewhere. Naples VI G 34 is such a volume; processional chants, tropes, and sequences take their place with a group of specialized readings: "farced" epistles, two special genealogical readings, and the Exultet. The only other complete south Italian processional, Vat. Reg. lat. 334 (s12), limits itself to processional music.

The Exultet on Scrolls

Why is the Exultet written on a scroll? It is probably not, in the first instance, because the Exultet will be sung from the ambo or because it will be sung by the deacon. The reason, as is so often true of the rotulus in the Middle Ages, is to lend importance, solemnity, and splendor to the occasion. But the importance is not only that of the occasion: there are many other liturgical events that might warrant the use of a rotulus, even when used by the deacon: the Easter or Christmas Gospels, for instance, or the readings on patronal feast-days: but the Exultet is the only such moment regularly recorded on rolls in the south, with one important exception: the pontifical scrolls of Bari and Benevento just mentioned.[18] In these, the bishop's prayers are written on scrolls that can be carried to the place where he is to perform his episcopal functions of baptism, benedictions, ordinations. All of these pontifical scrolls are illustrated with liturgical scenes, pictures of the ceremony whose texts, pronounced by the bishop, are contained on the scroll.

Like the pontifical rolls, the Exultet rolls are designed for their possessors, and in most cases the possessor is a bishop or his institution, even if the roll was used in the ceremony by the deacon.

Scrolls for the Bishop

It is no coincidence that among the sources of the earliest Exultet scrolls are cities where the bishop also uses a pontifical roll: Benevento and Bari.

18. There is a fragmentary scroll at Montecassino carrying solemn prayers of Good Friday: see Gyug, "A Fragment"; commentary by Magistrale and facsimile in *Exultet*, 477–79.

At Benevento, the elevation of the see to an archbishopric in 969 may be the occasion for the creation of the Casanatense pontifical roll at the order of Bishop Landolf. This has been plausibly argued by Brenk, who suggests that the "benedictio fontis" of the Casanatense is also a commission of Landolf.[19] The Exultet Vat. lat. 9820, made for the convent of Saint Peter, is a copy, as Belting has shown, of a roll originally commissioned by the same Landolf.[20] It also contains pictures of the liturgy, pictures of the bishop, and other illustrations related to subjects figuring in the text of the Exultet.

Exultet rolls were, in fact, used by bishops. The three rolls now in the Biblioteca Casanatense were attached one to another as a single continuous roll when they arrived at the library, and it is possible that they were used in this way, as a single roll, for a long time. In such a situation, the bishop and the deacon would use the same roll: first the deacon for the Exultet, and then the bishop for the blessing of the water of baptism. The Benevento roll Vat. lat. 9820 must also have been used by both celebrant and deacon, at least at a later stage of its existence. The erased and rewritten roll contains the prayers "Deus qui per filium tuum angularem scilicet lapidem" and "Veniat"; these formed part of the revised roll (although they are now separate pieces, as are all the surviving membranes of the roll). The roll would thus be used first by the celebrant: that is, he would read these prayers for blessing new fire (and incense) from the scroll before the deacon used the same scroll for the Exultet. The frontispiece (Plate 11) might be a depiction of the moment when the bishop, having finished his use of the roll for the moment, hands it to the deacon for the Exultet. Perhaps the episcopal roll whose pictures served as a model for Vat. lat. 9820 and two later rolls contained more than the Exultet. This was certainly true for other rolls.

The bishop of Bari also blessed the new fire from a roll (he used only the first of the two prayers in Vat. lat. 9820), but a different one: the benedictional, also an illustrated document, which he used later in the vigil for other purposes. This benedictional was once attached to the first Exultet of Bari;[21] it is not easy to estimate when they were joined, but they may have funtioned for a time as a single roll, used first by the bishop for the blessing of new fire, then by the deacon for the Exultet, and by the bishop again for the blessing of baptismal water.

That the same roll is used by two persons is not unique to Benevento and Bari: the tenth-century roll given by Duke Gregory of Gaeta to the church of Saint Michael in Planciano, described in 964 as "unum rotulo

19. Brenk, "Bischöfliche und monastiche 'Committenza.' "

20. Belting, *Studien*, 168f.

21. It is possible that the first Exultet roll of Bari contained an illustration at its head that is now lost: the opening membrane would surely not be other than standard size; and if so, there is room for one or two more pictures. At the orresponding place in Vat. lat. 9820 comes first a picture of the bishop handing the roll to the deacon. Brenk, "Bischöfliche und monastiche 'Committenza,' " 289–91, sees the consignment of the roll as a depiction of episcopal authority and permission to copy the roll.

ad benedicendum cereum et fontes,"[22] must have been used first by the
deacon for the candle and then by the celebrant (the bishop?) for the
baptismal water. Similarly, the roll given around 1000 to Sancta Maria de
Fontanella in Amalfi by its founder Giovanni da Fontanella was evidently
used for multiple purposes: penitential rites, the blessing of water, and the
blessing of either wax or the great candle itself. The document is described
in Giovanni's 1007 testament as "rotulum unum de penitentia cum benedictione da fonti et alia benedictione de ipso cirio."[23]

A great many of the surviving Exultet rolls are made for bishops or
are preserved in cathedrals for which they were most likely executed. Of
rolls found at cathedrals, the list is long (Bari 1, 2, 3; Mirabella 1, 2; Gaeta
1, 2, 3; Capua; Troia 1, 2, 3; Velletri; Salerno), and there are others that
ought to be added as formerly belonging to cathedrals (Avezzano, from the
diocese of the Marsi; Paris, from Fondi).

The importance of bishops in many of these rolls is obvious from
their prominence in illustrations. Where Christ appears in glory at the
beginning of the first Bari Exultet and the Bari benedictional, the bishop
appears at the beginning of Vat. lat. 9820 (Plate 11) and the rolls whose
iconography is related to it: the Casanatense and Salerno rolls. In addition,
cathedral rolls or ones based on them (Vat. lat. 9820, Casanatense, Salerno, Bari, Troia, Mirabella, others) naturally feature the bishop in illustrations of some portions of the ceremonial, since he is the chief pastor of
the cathedral and the celebrant at the rites of Holy Saturday.

Bishops participated in other aspects of the Exultet ceremonial. In
the early Beneventan ordo, followed also at Bari, it is the bishop who
brings new fire into the church, who lights the great candle, and who
touches it with chrism. He is the chief celebrant, and the deacon is in some
sense his assistant, a narrator.

In many later Exultet rolls the bishop is not apparently a participant
in the ceremonial of the Exultet, but he features prominently nevertheless;
the reason is surely that the intended recipients of the roll are episcopal
churches or the bishops themselves. In the Fondi roll now in Paris, for
instance, the bishop in his bicorn miter stands by while the candle is lit
by an acolyte; in two other illustrations he sits enthroned while the deacon
sings. Note that the opening sheet of this roll, which might have had a
grand episcopal frontispiece, is missing.

The Exultet roll at its origin, then, is a pontifical roll. It is the bishop's roll, for use in the ceremonies where he presides. Just as an assistant
holds the roll for the bishop when he blesses water, so the deacon holds
the roll (and sings) while the bishop lights the candle and touches it with
chrism. The illustrated Exultet roll is nothing more than a continuation
of the tradition of pontifical rolls known in the south from the tenth-
century pontifical rolls of Benevento now in the Biblioteca Casanatense.

22. See Appendix 3, text 2.
23. Camera, *Memorie*, 1:221–22. See Appendix 3.

Once launched, the idea spread to other places where a bishop might not be present, but where the Exultet was sung. Indeed, Vat. lat. 9820, the oldest surviving Exultet roll, was made for a monastic house, even though it faithfully reproduces a grand archiepiscopal roll. Montecassino 2 was probably originally intended for a monastic house in the diocese of Sorrento. Clearly, the later practice was not limited to episcopal churches, though most Exultet rolls do continue to be pontifical documents.

The Montecassino ordo, where the deacon gets the scroll from the altar,[24] has no place for the bishop. Deacon, subdeacons, and acolyte are the participants in the ritual of the Exultet. Yet bishops are present in the illustrations.[25] In the British Library roll, the bishop is present as an observer in one scene ("cereus iste") and in the Barberini roll he is standing beside the pope (a scene not present in the London roll). Bishops are natural subjects for pictures of "Mater ecclesia" or the commemoration of ecclesiastical authorities, but the presence of bishops in illustrated Exultet rolls is far larger than might be expected unless one remembers that they originated as bishops' rolls.

Why Put Pictures on an Exultet Roll?

Almost all the Exultet rolls that survive from southern Italy are designed to represent a solemn moment in splendid form and to be in the possession of a bishop, a pope, or an abbot, for whom the roll is, as Brenk calls it, a sort of status symbol, a sign, not only by its form as a roll, but by the care and luxury of its preparation and illustration, of the high standing of its possessor.

The fact that these are magnificent productions is a sign of the standing of their owners, not their users. The elements that make a manuscript a luxury item—space, quality of parchment, care of preparation, use of gold, presence of illustrations—all these are in some sense for the owner, *whether or not the owner is the user.* This is an important consideration when we consider the pictures on the rolls.

A deacon will not be the owner of an Exultet roll, though he will certainly be the user. In many cases, though, an Exultet roll might be considered the possession of an institution: a cathedral, an abbey, a church. In this sense the magnificence of the roll gives dignity at once to the institution, to the person (bishop, abbot, provost) who leads it, and to the liturgy performed there.

24. It is possible, of course, that the scroll has lain upon the altar only for the interval between its use for the blessing of new fire and the Exultet. This is unlikely, however, for two reasons: first, the fire coming directly into the church would make it difficult to get the roll onto the altar without unseemly haste; and second, the very name of the document, *benedictio cerei*, suggests its use for a single function.

25. The principal celebrant in the Montecassino ordo is described as a priest; but Montecassino had an abbot with episcopal prerogatives (including dress?), so some of the "bishops" in Montecassino pictures may be abbots.

Every figural work implies, as Valentino Pace says when discussing Exultets, the transmission of a message.[26] This message, if only because of its medium, is in some sense different from the message conveyed by the text that it accompanies in the same documents; but it is designed to bear some more or less close relation to the text, either as a whole or to some specific passage that a picture accompanies. And the message of the picture has something to do not only with its content, but with its context.

What Is the Purpose of the Pictures?

The pictures on an Exultet roll have several purposes, but most important is that they are designed to be seen. A complexity arises, for many, from the fact that in many of the Exultet rolls the pictures are reversed with respect to the text, so that they are upside down to the deacon who is singing the Exultet. Clearly, then, these pictures are not designed for the singer of the Exultet at the moment of performance. For a long time it has been assumed that the pictures are for viewing by those to whom, or before whom, the deacon sings: the assisting clergy, the congregation, the people.

This view has been held for so long, and by so many scholars, that to tell its history would be tedious. But it captivates the imagination, and has made the Exultet rolls a source of continuing interest. "Might we acknowledge," ask Grabar and Nordenfalk, "in this rather special use of illustrated roll a noble ancestor of our cinema?"[27] A series of pictures, of course, is the ancestor of the cinema, and it goes much farther back than the Exultet rolls; but it is the *talking* pictures, the sound and pictures together, that are the ancestor of the modern cinema, and only if the pictures are meant to be seen while the Exultet is sung is the cinematic analogy useful.

Are They Reversed in Order to Instruct the "People"?

It is usually assumed that the pictures, being reversed, are designed for instructing and edifying the bystanders: those who can learn from pictures perhaps better than from words, much like one of the traditional views of the use of stained glass windows as a visual repertory of literary material. Such views can be carried to an extent that takes us beyond the proprieties of scholarship, but the persistence and pervasiveness of this view ought to be understood. Emilio Lavagnino, to take an admittedly egregious example, informs us in his history of medieval Italian art that "exultets" (his lower-case spelling suggests that he misunderstands the first word of the text to be a generic noun) are recited by priests; they contained prayers and tales of miracles worked by saints; they needed to be clear and popular

26. Pace in *Civiltà*, 9.
27. Grabar and Nordenfalk, *La peinture romaine*, 146, translated by the author.

and hence in their pictures had "accenti deliberatamente popolareschi."[28] Much recent scholarship has dealt with the question of images as the bible of the illiterate, often expressing skepticism about the general applicability of the idea.[29] At any rate, we shall argue that the images in Exultet rolls are not designed for the instruction of the congregation.

Pictures Are Not for Use While the Exultet Is Sung

Reversing the pictures in the Exultet roll is a wonderful idea. Its origin is unknown; it might have arisen from the observation of frontispiece paintings, headpieces turned the other way from the script. Such frontispieces as that in the British Library roll, and the christological cycle in the Pisa roll, show the currency of the idea of pictures oriented differently from the rest of the roll. But we have no roll that has only a headpiece turned the other way from the script. Such a roll, or such an idea, could give the idea of reversing pictures also in the course of the text. Though the practice of illustrated headpieces is common in Byzantine rolls, it is not common practice to turn the picture with its bottom toward the outside of the roll. Indeed, the Byzantine headpiece is often ornamental, and the question of orientation does not arise; but where figures are present as the headpiece of a Byzantine roll, they are generally oriented the same way as the script. The important point here—if it is of any significance at all—is the idea of the headpiece, the picture, as a separate element from the roll to follow. Occupying the same membrane, perhaps, but not meant to be part of the text immediately adjacent, it serves as a decoration for the roll or, more often in Byzantine rolls, as a representation of the author of the liturgy to follow. Whatever its origin, it must be admitted that the idea of reversing the pictures has fascinated all observers of Exultet rolls ever since. And it must also be true that the purpose of reversing the pictures is so that they can be seen by someone who is not oriented so as to be able to read the text. It also follows that the pictures can be seen while the deacon sings, provided that (1) the roll hangs down from an ambo, (2) there is sufficient light to see, and (3) the observer is near enough to the picture. Surely this must have been thought about whenever someone painted a picture on a scroll upside down.

But it is not the central reason for these pictures, or for their placement. The idea of reversing the pictures is a fascinating one, and one that was much imitated, but it confuses us about the nature of these documents.

Although the notion of the pictures as visual elements to be perceived during the Exultet has found such wide acceptance, a few scholars have expressed concern: Niels Krogh Rasmussen warns against Moneti's

---

28. Lavagnino, *Storia dell'arte medioevale italiana*, 442.

29. See, for example, Gougaud, "Muta praedicatio"; Duggan, "Was Art Really 'the Book of the Illiterate?' "; Chazelle, "Pictures, Books, and the Illiterate"; Camille, "Seeing and Reading"; Kessler, "Pictorial Narrative"; Curschmann, "Pictura laicorum litteratura?"

idea of the roll as being for "la moltetudine ignorante": as Rasmussen points out, the multitude, ignorant or not, can't see the roll.[30] Penelope Mayo also questions the perception of these rolls as "a rather endearing medieval experiement in *cinéma vérité*."[31]

There are, I think, several reasons to believe that the pictures in Exultet rolls, even those with pictures reversed, are not principally designed to be viewed *while the Exultet is being sung.*

1. *The viewer can't see the pictures,* whichever way they are turned: they are too small, and it is too dark. Although the ceremonies of Holy Saturday may sometimes have taken place in the late afternoon, the light available in church was never bright.[32] Anyone placed more than a few feet from the roll will see that it is decorated, but the detail will be lost. The width of Exultet rolls is that of a fair-sized manuscript, and pictures are full-width: they are thus very generally a foot across and usually rather square or wider than they are tall. They are roughly the size of a small computer or television screen; they cannot be seen at a distance, even illuminated with gold, as anything other than decoration. The illumination of churches, especially where the Exultet comes at the beginning of the ceremony (as it most likely does with most Exultets using the Franco-Roman text), is very dim on purpose, since the single light of the new fire and the Paschal candle has special symbolic significance. In the Beneventan rite, the Exultet comes after the lections, and it might be argued that the church would be illuminated by this time in the ceremony; but it is also true that the rolls with Beneventan text, especially the early ones where this idea might have begun, do not have reversed pictures: it is mostly at a later stage that the Exultets with reversed pictures are made.

2. *The pictures will not appear at the right time.* If pictures may be placed at a variety of locations in the course of a column of text, and if these pictures are intended to explicate the text in some sense, and if these pictures are meant to be seen at the same moment that the text being explicated is being said, would it not be best to place the pictures where they will be seen at the right time? This is the assumption behind the notion of simultaneous words and pictures, and it is erroneous. The pictures are not placed in such a way that they will appear with their text. A placement designed at its origin for the viewer of the ceremony would locate the pictures at a greater distance in front of their texts, so that text and picture might be almost a meter apart.

        30. Rasmussen, "Les pontificaux," 428; Moneti, "Considerazioni e ricerche," 247–48.
        31. Mayo, *Vasa sacra,* 375.
        32. The vigil was anticipated in the afternoon at Montecassino from the twelfth century; the ordinal indicated that the rites begin at the ninth hour, that is, around three o'clock in the afternoon; see Leutermann, *Ordo casinensis,* p. 114, and Appendix 3 in this volume. This ordo was used also at Santa Sofia in Benevento from the twelfth century. Unfortunately, we know little about the time of day for these ceremonies in other churches, or for Montecassino and Benevento before the adoption of this ordo.

The discussion in chapter 7 of the manufacture of Exultets goes into this question in more detail, which we can summarize by saying that the process of inserting picture into text is a simple one: find the textual period in which the reference is made to which the picture applies, and leave a space before it into which the picture is painted, so that the text appears underneath like a caption. When the picture in this space is reversed, it does indeed come over the top of the ambo before the text, and thus appears first: but it is never far enough ahead of the text really to be seen: generally the picture will not have appeared, or only its border will be visible, while the relevant text is sung. By the time the picture is visible (if it is visible at all), the reader will have passed on to other subjects. It might be argued that the deacon could have memorized the text and music so as to show the right picture at the right time; but then one wonders why the illustrated rolls have any text at all and why, if the text were present but not needed, the pictures should be reversed: why not reverse the whole roll?

In view of the care with which such luxury manuscripts are made, it seems inconceivable that the placement of pictures could not have been better aligned if simultaneous reading and viewing had been of primary importance.

3. *Pictures of the ceremony being performed are not for use during the ceremony.* If the ideal moment of viewing is really that of the ceremony, while the deacon is singing from the ambo, it seems hardly necessary that there should be pictures of a deacon on an ambo singing the Exultet. To bring into the present scenes that are not and cannot be present—the Red Sea, the heavenly choir of angels—is a laudable aim, but the liturgical scenes in such an event are unnecessary and redundant.

Hans Belting has suggested that the liturgical scenes in the tenth-century Casanatense pontifical are demonstration and teaching models for the liturgy;[33] these are the only pictures in that early and handsome document, and their type may be that of the liturgical pictures in the Exultets: pictures of the bishop (or, in the Exultet, his delegate) performing his function and using this roll. But in the Casanatense pontifical, the pictures are not reversed, and, although they will be seen by the bishop when he says the prayers, there is no evidence that they are intended to be seen by bystanders *during* the pontifical rites. They will certainly be looked at when the bishop shows his treasure and when he or someone else wants to consider details of how the liturgy might look, but neither of these events will take place *during* the liturgy.

4. *Why are there no representations of reversed pictures?* If the illustrator of the Pisa roll takes the trouble to represent the colored sculptures and carvings on the ambo he illustrates, why does the roll illustrated in the same document not have pictures? Here is an artist who has a taste for detail, and if viewing the reversed illustrations is a central part of the

---

33. "Schau- und Lehrbilder für die liturgische Praxis"; Belting, *Studien,* 146.

practice of the roll, he might well, it seems to me, have indicated this in his drawing of the Exultet being unrolled from the top of the ambo. Instead he places the words *Lumen Christi* on the roll, no doubt to indicate what the deacon is singing at the moment being illustrated. But if seeing the pictures were important, he might have found a way to represent the act of seeing the pictures.

Many other rolls with reversed pictures have representations of the surface of the roll. Some write text on the picture of the roll,[34] some simulate writing with horizontal or wavy lines or with rows of little strokes;[35] and others leave the roll blank;[36] but no artist shows pictures on the roll. If seeing the pictures were an important part of the ceremony itself, one imagines that an effort might have been made.

5. *Exultet rolls with illustrations not reversed suggest a more fundamental purpose for the pictures.* Making illustrated rolls for singing the Exultet is a happy innovation. The rolls continue to be functional, but they achieve a level of decoration, of solemnity, of luxury, that sets apart this liturgical moment and the possessors of such documents—their churches, their commissioners, their possessors—in an extraordinary way.

But the reversing of the pictures comes at a second stage. The original function of the pictures is that of any set of pictures associated with a text, in a codex or a roll: the illustration and beautification of the document, of its function and of its text. This continues to be their purpose even when they are reversed in later rolls. Reversing the pictures makes one thing clear: the pictures are not designed for the edification of the deacon as he sings.

In the earliest rolls the pictures are not reversed. Mirabella Eclano 1 and the Manchester roll, both fragmentary, and the more complete Vat. lat. 9820 and Troia 1 all have illustrative cycles produced at the time of manufacture and oriented in the same direction as the script. They are, in essence, illustrated documents made in the same way as a codex: illustrations are placed in the course of the text, generally arranged so that the related text will be a subscription for the picture. It is at a second stage, around the beginning of the eleventh century, that the reversing of illustrations takes place. It is not, by the way, the moment of liturgical change to the Franco-Roman text that brings the reversal of pictures: two early Beneventan Exultets already have reversed pictures: the first rolls of Bari and Gaeta. It was just a good idea.

This reversal, when it happens, is simple. There is no further rethinking of how pictures are situated in the text: they are still placed before the text to which they are related, but now they are painted upside

34. Gaeta 1, Troia 1, Pisa (and Vat. lat. 9820, whose pictures are not reversed).
35. The Casanatense and Capua artists use zigzag lines; Montecassino 2 has broad lines drawn across the roll; Troia 1, Gaeta 2 (pl. 13), and Gaeta 3 have simulated writing with little vertical strokes.
36. Bari 1, Troia 2, Paris, Vat. lat. 3784, London (pl. 16), Barberini (the picture of the scroll in the Barberini Exultet has text written in a much later hand).

down in the space provided for them. The result is fascinating, but it is a second-stage innovation, and nowhere do makers of rolls depart from the older practice of placement. The idea, once launched, had a prosperous voyage. Most later Exultets continue the practice of reversing the pictures, even where, as with Vat. lat. 9820, it involved a disastrous restructuring of the entire manuscript.

The Bari benedictional, made for use by the bishop, and not used in the ambo, has its pictures reversed. This roll is inspired by the beautiful first Exultet of Bari made only a short time before, but here there are no biblical scenes, only liturgical ones, like those of the Casanatense pontifical, along with a frontispiece of Christ enthroned. These reversed pictures will not be helpful to the bishop during the blessing of fire or of water, and any bystanders who see them during the ceremony will see a representation of the ceremony being performed. The nature of these episcopal functions, performed outside the choir, in the sacristy, the atrium, or the baptistry, suggests that the pictures are not directed at the "people."

Two relatively late rolls, however, Troia 3 and Mirabella 2, each made in a place where reversed rolls were known, and each made in an idiosyncratic way, repeal this idea and place their illustrations in the same direction as the text. This may not be a return to a known older practice, since the only known earlier rolls of Troia and Mirabella have reversed pictures: the artists may have made active decisions to make a normal illustrated document, perhaps with the scribe executing the illustration as the work proceeds. These later rolls, surely, do not have the intention of displaying the pictures for the edification of the faithful during the ceremony. I think we can conclude that such liturgical display was never the principal intention of the pictures, even though the fact of reversing them does produce a happy consequence.[37]

Why Are the Pictures Reversed?

The pictures on Exultet rolls are for the bishop; that is, their origin is as decorations for pontifical documents. The liturgical illustrations in the pontifical and benedictional rolls for the bishop of Benevento, showing the ceremony whose text is provided in the document, are paralleled by the liturgical pictures in his Exultet roll. Additional illustrations enrich the roll further, to make it suitably splendid for episcopal use and ownership.

The Exultet, however, is one pontifical that the bishop himself does not use. The pictures are for the bishop to look at, and reversing them is an idea probably arising from the fact that the bishop does not himself sing from the scroll. We have just argued that the pictures are not designed to

---

37. Cavallo (*Rotoli*, 177) and Magistrale (in *Exultet*, 424) have suggested that Troia 3, because of its unreversed pictures, is not intended for liturgical use, but for the enrichment of the cathedral treasury. I cannot see any impediment to the use of this roll in the liturgy, since it has everything that the liturgy requires: text and music accurately presented for use by the deacon.

be seen while the Exultet is being sung, but everybody who can see the roll can see that it is richly illustrated. Those who are nearest can see it best. And even though the simultaneity of picture and text seldom works, and even though the liturgical scenes are not really needed in the ceremony itself, yet there is the idea of showing them to the bishop. This is probably why so many illustrations, especially in earlier rolls, feature the bishop not only prominently, but placed very near the Exultet roll itself. The bishop must be near the candle in the Beneventan ordo, of course, in order to light it, and he is shown doing so in Vat. lat. 9820 and the other versions of this picture (Mirabella 1, Casanatense, Salerno). But there are many liturgical pictures where the bishop is shown very close to the ambo, either seated on a throne (Bari 1, Paris, Gaeta 2, Gaeta 3) or standing nearby (all of these plus Vat. lat. 9820, Casanatense, Salerno, Gaeta 1, Montecassino 2). In the Paris roll, it almost looks as though the episcopal throne is part way up the steps to the ambo.

Not only do these pictures show the bishop (not surprising in a cathedral document), but they also, I think, show him looking at the pictures. He will not really be able to see them very well, and he does not need visual instruction from the deacon; but they are his pictures, and the artists are showing this in their illustrations.

Whether it was the artist of Bari 1 or of Mirabella 1, or some scribe whose roll has perished, who first turned the illustrations the other way cannot now be determined. But I think his intention was to make a gesture of showing the pictures to the owner of this pontifical roll, and not to its singer or the bystanders at the Exultet.

Such a tradition was rapidly adopted almost everywhere in the south. It becomes a token of a continuing stylistic tradition (rather like a gentleman's breast-pocket handkerchief), acknowledging a practice of long standing, not necessary but desirable.

Origins and Purposes

Questions of the origin of the Exultet rolls will never be entirely resolved, and they must not distract us from the dynamic fact of the existence and the use of these rolls. Many scholars have given specific attention to the origins of the Exultet roll.[38] The best and most carefully considered discussion of this matter is by Guglielmo Cavallo, especially in his article "La genesi dei rotoli liturgici beneventani alla luce del fenomeno storico-librario in Occidente ed Oriente." Cavallo writes a careful survey of liturgical rotulus, East and West, including notice of their use at Milan. His conclusion after surveying all the evidence is to doubt whether the Exultet came from an existing Western liturgical tradition. He strongly rejects

---

38. For surveys of the literature, see *Aggiornamento*, 461–63; and the bibliography in *Exultet*.

Baldass's notion of a lost tradition of Exultets descending from Augustine or Ambrose, of antique "Gründtypen" passed on as a patrimony of southern Italy.[39] Surveying Byzantine rolls, Cavallo demonstrates Greek influence in southern Italy; he concludes that the Exultet roll is a phenomenon related to Byzantine practice. "It is probable, that is to say, that hymns or consecration-formulae of the 'Beneventan' liturgy then in use were extracted from the Sacramentary and transcribed on rotuli in imitation of a practice far from unknown to Greek ritual."[40] Cavallo sees it as unlikely that Exultet rolls were used before the tenth century, and he proposes a Beneventan origin for the Exultet rolls, perhaps under Landolf I (952–82).

I do not wish here to enter into detailed discussions of previous scholarship or to propose new theories of the origins of the south Italian Exultet rolls. Cavallo's survey is measured and well considered, and I would only add some observations that may broaden the view of this remarkable phenomenon arising from the cultural crossroads of medieval southern Italy.

Rolls and Books

First, it is not obvious that the Exultet roll should be considered an extract of the sacramentary.[41] The Exultet is not a normal part of a sacramentary in the sense that the sacramentary is an altar book for priests, providing the variable prayers for the Mass. Many sacramentaries, it is true, include other material, often additional material for special ceremonies; but this does not change the central purpose of the collection. That many early sacramentaries do contain the text of the Exultet is also true, but this does not indicate that the Exultet originates there. The sacramentary is itself a collection of elements earlier maintained separately. The Exultet is, after

39. Baldass, "Die Miniaturen," 205–19, esp. 215–19; see also Cavallo, *Rotoli*, 43 n.86.

40. Cavallo, "La genesi," 224; my translation.

41. We have seen here that the placement of the Exultet has always been problematical. Whereas the earliest sources of the Exultet in the Frankish traditions are indeed sacramentaries, there are many sacramentaries in which the Exultet is not present, probably as being not appropriate in a book consisting essentially of prayers said by a priest. In other Latin liturgies, the Exultet is not a normal component of the sacramentary. In the Old Spanish liturgy, the Mozarabic sacramentary (ed. Férotin) has no blessing for the Paschal candle; it is found instead in the antiphoner of Léon and elsewhere. In the Ambrosian rite, whose importance for the development of Exultet rolls will be discussed later, the Exultet is not an invariable feature of sacramentaries. Some of the earliest Milanese sacramentaries do not have the Exultet: the sacramentary of Biasca (edition in Heiming, *Das ambrosianische Sakramentar*) does not include it, nor does the sacramentary D 3-3 in the Biblioteca Capitolare of Milan cathedral (edition in Frei, *Das ambrosianische*). It is found, however, in the sacramentary of Bergamo (edition in Cagin, *Codex sacramentorum*), in the unusual reference book known as the Sacramentarium Triplex (edition in Heiming, *Corpus Ambrosiano liturgicum*, vol. 1), and the eleventh-century *manuale* (edition in Magistretti, *Manuale*). On the early sacramentaries of the Milanese rite, see Frei, *Das ambrosianische*, 4–6. At Milan, the Exultet is normally sung from a roll, as we shall see.

all, a deacon's text, and might more reasonably be expected in a book of liturgical readings used by the deacon.

The Exultet is a single text for a unique occasion, not suitable for collection in larger groups. And thus, when collections came to be made (from *libelli* or other individual sources) and gathered into sacramentaries, lectionaries, pontificals, rituals, and the like, there is no specifically evident place for the Exultet.

And so, the Exultet as a single document is really its most logical form. The single Exultet (rolled or not) is surely the original form of this prayer; it is not an extract from a larger volume, but comes to be included, in some versions of some later volumes, at a second stage.

We lack evidence of a continuous tradition of the Exultet as a single document, just as we lack almost any evidence of individual Mass libelli, from the several centuries before the tenth. At the same time, however, we do have the existence of the Exultet rolls of southern Italy; and since their earliest exemplars are as old as other musical documents of the area, we can at least suggest that there is no evidence that the Exultet roll results from an extract made from another and older kind of source. Indeed, the earlier tradition of the Exultet can be posited by extrapolation from other evidence.

Benevento and Milan

In this connection, I should first like to underline the importance of the link between Milan and Benevento, between the liturgy of the Lombard north and south.

The relation between the old Beneventan liturgy and the rites of Milan has been shown to be a close one, based on musical and textual connections.[42] As we have seen, this connection was well known to the scribes and liturgists of the tenth and eleventh centuries, for when they referred to their regional liturgy (that which we call Beneventan) they called it "Ambrosian"; Pope Stephen IX called it by that name in 1058;[43] and there are many more references, in chant books and elsewhere, to the "Ambrosian" rite as practiced in southern Italy. One of them refers to the Beneventan practice of the Exultet.[44]

Unfortunately, we do not have complete books of texts and ceremonies for the Beneventan rite, so we cannot compare differences in ceremonial and usage between it and the Ambrosian practice of Milan. But the closeness of musical and textual practice, and the awareness in southern

---

42. Kelly, *TBC*, 181–203; Bailey, "Ambrosian Chant in Southern Italy."

43. *Chron. mon. Cas.*, 353 (II, 94); see pp. 62–63.

44. "Lectio hec est hereditas que quinta est ordinata secundum romanum legatur hic; secundum ambrosianum legatur post benedictionem cerei" (Vat. lat. 10673, fols. 34–34v), an explanation of the divergence in lessons for Holy Saturday and the placement of the Exultet between the Roman and the local rites. Kelly, *TBC*, 181–82, cites all known references in the south to "Ambrosian" practice.

Italy of the link with Milan,[45] gives special importance to what we can learn about the use of the rotulus in the rites of Milan.

We have seen in chapter 3 that the Exultet may have been an addition to the Beneventan rite and that the adoption of the Paschal candle at Benevento may have derived from the rites of Milan or from a common northern Lombard ancestor.[46] What is more, we have seen that the rotulus is used extensively in the Milanese rite.[47] It is used often and preeminently by the archbishop;[48] it is laid on the altar before being used;[49] and the Exultet itself is sung from a rotulus.[50]

The documents describing the Milanese use of the rotulus date only from the twelfth century and later: but they are the oldest surviving ceremonial descriptions from a very much older liturgy; although they may represent a rearrangement of an older ordo (accounting in part for differences between Milan and Benevento), it seems unlikely that the archaizing rotulus should be adopted at Milan only in the twelfth century. Much more likely is that it had been in regular use for a long time. One use of the roll, for litanies,[51] might have a long ancestry; the litanies of Pentecost can be traced back to the time of Bishop Lazarus (438–49),[52] and perhaps the litany rolls were used continuously ever since. They were certainly in use from the thirteenth to the fifteenth centuries, as surviving rolls attest.[53]

The use of the rotulus in southern Italy has many similarities to its use at Milan:

1. *Rolls have a regular place in the liturgy.* The Milanese documents make clear that the liturgy regularly requires the use of a rotulus for Vespers, for litanies, for prayers said by the archbishop, for the Exultet. Although there are occasional witnesses to the use of rolls in the liturgy

---

45. See chapter 2, n. 88.

46. See pp. 56–57.

47. See pp. 26–28.

48. ". . . Sed si archiepiscopus adfuerit, rotularius ejus porrigit ei," (Magistretti, *Beroldus*, 57); "Sed si archiepiscopus aderit, idem custos porrigit rotulario, et rotularius archiepiscopo"; (*ibid.*, 59).

49. "Et notandum, quia antequam vesperum incipiatur, minor custos ebdomadarius ponit rotulum orationum super altare . . ." (*ibid.*, 55); "Sed praesciendum quia minor custos ebdomadarius ponit rotulum letaniarum super altare uniuscujusque diei . . ." (*ibid.*, 57).

50. "Et unus subdiaconus ebdomadarius debet portare rotulum similiter indutus alba, et debet tenere ipsum rotulum ante diaconum, donec legerit, et benedixerit ceram et ignem [here "Beroldus novus" clarifies by adding] dicendo sic: *Exultet iam*, etc." (*ibid.*, 109–10); the passage from "Beroldus novus" is cited in Magistretti, *Manuale*, 2:198n1.

51. There are references to a *rotulus letaniarum* in Magistretti, *Beroldus*, 57, 89, 91; the *rotulus letaniarum* is also referred to as a *rotulus letaniarum et vespertinum* both in the Beroldus ordinal (*ibid.*, 101) and in the Codex Metropolitanus (*ibid.*, 84); according to one passage, there seem to be at least three separate litany rolls, for use on three separate occasions (*ibid.*, 89).

52. Gamber, *CLLA*, 281.

53. See pp. 27–28.

elsewhere in Latin Europe, the largest surviving collection is from southern Italy: several pontifical rolls (two from Benevento, one from Bari), a
roll of prayers for Good Friday (at Montecassino), and twenty-six Exultet
rolls. In addition to these, the twelve liturgical rolls inventoried at Benevento in the fifteenth century (of which three were for use in litanies),
suggest the frequent and continuous use of rolls in the liturgy there.[54]

2. *The use of the roll is focused on the (arch)bishop.* The liturgical rolls
of southern Italy are also closely related to the bishop or archbishop. Not
only are there specifically pontifical rolls from Benevento and Bari, but the
Exultet rolls themselves, as we have seen, often have a very close relation
with the bishop and seem in some sense to be his property.

3. *A roll is used for the singing of the Exultet.* Nowhere else in Europe
is the Exultet regularly sung from a roll, so far as we know, except for
Milan and southern Italy: that is to say, in the two related liturgies of the
Lombards. We have no surviving Milanese Exultet roll, but we know that
the Exultet was sung from a roll. We have many Beneventan rolls, which
survive doubtless because of their beautiful illustrations: we can surmise
that the Milanese rolls were not items of such luxurious production — but
they *were* rolls.

4. *The roll is laid upon the altar before being used.* At Milan, it is the
custom to place the roll on the altar, whence it is taken by the priest or
the rotularius.[55] The similar practice of laying the Exultet on the altar at
Montecassino and related churches[56] may well be more than coincidence.

In view of these facts, it seems hardly necessary to posit a Byzantine
influence to explain the existence of rolls bearing the text of the Exultet
in southern Italy in the tenth century. Byzantine influence there undoubtedly was, and scrolls were indeed used in the Byzantine liturgy — though
not usually for the same functions as in the West, and probably not at so
early a date.[57]

The Exultet was certainly written on rolls in tenth-century southern
Italy. Archival evidence shows the donation of Exultet rolls in 945 ("rutu-
lum de cereum benedicere .i." given by Leo, presbyter and abbot, to Saint
Benedict in Larinum) and 964 ("unum rotulo ad benedicendum cereum
et fontes" given by Petrus presbyter to the church of Saint Michael "in
loco Planciano" near Gaeta).[58] The Exultet roll depicted on folio 35v of
the missal Vat. lat. 10673, apparently not illuminated, is an early witness
to the existence of tenth-century Exultet rolls, especially if Cavallo's dating
of the manuscript in the mid-tenth century is accepted.[59] The Exultet on
which Vat. lat. 9820 was modeled, an original likely made for Bishop

54. On these rolls of Benevento, see pp. 28–29.
55. See n. 49.
56. For texts related to this practice, see Appendix 3; see also pp. 143, 148.
57. See Gerstel, *Liturgical Scrolls.*
58. See Appendix 3.
59. Cavallo, *Rotoli,* 42n80.

Landolf I, perhaps for his elevation to archbishop in 969,[60] might well have been the first illustrated Exultet roll. But if so, it was neither the first Exultet roll (earlier ones have just been mentioned), nor the first illustrated roll in the area, since the Casanatense pontifical roll, also made for Landolf, preceded it by some years.[61]

The creative moments in the development of the Exultet rolls are several, not one: the use of the roll-form for the Exultet (already traditional, perhaps, in the Lombard liturgies); the use of illustration in rolls (used already in pontifical rolls); the brilliant idea of reversing the pictures (not originally part of the conception at Benevento), perhaps imagined by an inventive scribe of Bari.

The varying character of the Exultet rolls reflects a mixture of tradition and innovation. The scribes—perhaps they were deacons—who made these rolls were aware of what an Exultet roll was like, but their creations are seldom versions of an older roll. The deacons, or whoever produced the rolls, deliberately sought distinction and *uarietas,* perhaps to match local conditions, but probably above all to accord with the artistic and liturgical sensibilities of deacon and (especially) bishop. The individual for whom a roll is made may have a substantial influence on its formulation.

The personal connection of a roll with its user, its patron, its bishop, has significant implications for the variety of artistic solutions found in the rolls and also perhaps for the apparent discontinuities in a center like Montecassino. How could Montecassino produce the variety in the rolls of Pisa, Velletri, London, and the Barberini collection? Against a background of tradition such as the Benevento picture series, they reflect a combination of two factors, the experimenting artist and the personality of the recipient. The roll in Velletri, with its Beneventan text, its Beneventan-style border and illustration, its small initials that point to the past, may well reflect the personal preference of Leo Ostiensis. In this roll, the decoration is characterized by restraint, but (on the other hand) the blue ground is costly, and so there is a combination of luxury and sobriety.

The Exultet rolls are a complex cultural phenomenon. They are the result of the collaboration of artist, musician, liturgist, scribe, patron. In their use, they combine the sounds of a singer with the rolling classical cursus of a poetic prayer, the sights, the sounds, indeed the fragrance of an elaborate ceremonial performed in a context in which Byzantine, Roman, Lombard, and Norman arts meet at a unique cultural crossroad.

60. Cavallo, "La genesi," 228; Belting, "Studien," 180–83; Brenk, "Bischöfliche und monastiche 'Committenza,' " 287–92.

61. The first Exultet roll was certainly, therefore, not made for purposes of "divulgazione populare," as is suggested by Moneti ("Considerazioni e ricerche," 243–44) and so many others.

APPENDIX I
THE SOURCES

The Rolls

Sources for the Exultet in southern Italy are described here in alphabetical order according to the city in which they now lie; rolls are presented first, followed by codices, the latter divided into codices from southern Italy and those from central Italy. The descriptions of the Exultet rolls give brief physical descriptions, dates, history, and provenance, and a discussion of the process of making the roll, so far as this can be determined, along with a brief bibliography of each. Average lengths are calculated by omitting incomplete membranes. Brief mentions in general studies of the Exultet are not listed for individual documents. There are no extensive discussions of illustrative content, or of textual tradition. Textual details can be found in Appendix 2, and further discussions about each can be found by consulting the index of manuscripts. Bracketed references in the descriptions refer to the brief bibliography on each manuscript.

Avezzano, Archivio Diocesano, Exultet SN

Exultet roll, s11med, made at Montecassino for Pandolf, bishop of the Marsians, ca. 1057; Franco-Roman text, Beneventan melody; elaborate initials but no (surviving) pictures.

DESCRIPTION   Exultet roll, eight membranes, 270 × 5660 mm (423 + 746 + 757 + 778 + 860 + 812 + 737 + 709) [Brenk], average 771; beginning of first membrane missing. Rolled on a replacement umbilicus. Franco-Roman text, Beneventan script, and type 3 notation, module of 33 mm. Pricking for horizontal ruling is visible at the sides. The dark brown ink of the text is darker than that of the notation; the initials, finely drawn, might be in the same ink as the text. Writing very like Grimoald (Wettstein); no illustrations. The illuminated letters have been likened to early Desiderian work (Orofino, "La prima fase," 57).

DATE   s11med (Lowe); ca. 1057 (Avery).

HISTORY   Manufactured at Montecassino for Pandolf, bishop of the Marsians from 1056, whose substantial gifts to the abbey in 1057 are enumerated in part in *Chron. mon. Cas,* 354 (were these countergifts after receiving the Exultet roll?), who was present at the dedication of the basilica in 1071, and who was a regular visitor to Montecassino. The diocese of Marsi was transferred from Pescina to Avezzano after the earthquake of 1915. The roll was brought from the prepositura of Celano in 1932 by Mons. Giovanni de Medicis (Chiappini, "Profilo," 438). The reference in the end to "barbaras nationes," unique in the rolls, is likened by Hans Hirsch ("Der mittelalterliche Kaisergedanke," 8 n32) to a passage from Pope Hadrian to Charlemagne, in which the pope prays that God "victorem te super omnes barbaras nationes faciat . . ." (*MGH Epistolae 3,* 589, no. 62).

The roll provides the name of Bishop Pandolf in the original text, but has generic names for emperor and prince; these were later altered: (1) "Memento etiam domine famulorum tuorum imperatorum . . ." is altered first to "Memento domine famuli tui regis nostri W" and then to "famuli nostri gloriosissimi et excellentissimi regis nostri W"; (2) for the prince, "famuli tui principibus . . ." is changed to "famuli tui domni nostri berardi." "W" may be William the Bad (1154–56) or William the Good (1166–89); Gabbrielli suggests that Berardus is one of the counts of Celano.

Brenk suggests that the absence of pictures in this roll must be at the request of Pandolf, since Montecassino was certainly in a position to provide illustrated rolls, which were by then the standard for Exultet rolls; instead, it may have been Pandolf who requested such large initial letters (the E is the largest initial in all the surviving Exultet rolls). Brenk notes also that the making of a large initial at Montecassino would have taken more time and trouble than a picture of similar size, with the result that the Avezzano roll is in a sense more luxurious than the illustrated roll Vat. lat. 3784. (It remains a possibility, however, that there was an illustrated frontispiece preceding the letter E: the opening membrane, shorter than all the others, could have accommodated one or more pictures.)

MANUFACTURE Single vertical lines are ruled down each side. The decoration consists of decorated initials of three sizes; the opening E and the VD of the preface occupy the full width; initials in the prologue are centered on the scroll; and initials in the preface, usually of two lines or, toward the end, of one, are set at left. After each initial, one or more gold bands contain, in capitals, the first few words of the text period. The prologue is made with huge central letters for the beginning of each period, previous paragraphs ending to the right. This involves skipping down four lines from the last full line, allowing any remaining syllables after the last full line to fill in unused space. Each of the internal beginnings after an intermediate cadence has a colored initial; accented syllables are marked regularly in the text, and strokes are used where needed to clarify word division.

There is no attempt to make a period end before the end of the membrane: *Exultet* has its second letter on a new membrane; the period beginning "Flammas eius" goes over a membrane, etc. A problem would occur when a period begins on the last line of the membrane, for its two-line initial would normally extend down a second line, thus onto the next membrane. At the only place where this occurs, "Hec nox est de qua scriptum est," there is a one-line capital, which follows on several other one-line capitals. The next membrane goes back to two-line capitals.

After *Sursum corda,* periods do not start with a centered letter, but with a two-line initial followed by a band of capitals. Internal divisions are still marked with capitals. As this second part proceeds, two-line and one-line initials begin to alternate (O is usually given one line, and short periods are often given one line), and by the end all initials are of one line.

The initials plus bands are also written in another, non-Beneventan hand: these would appear to provide help for a later singer who found it difficult to resolve the initials and the letters in gold bands. However, the presence of what appears to be original notation over "equum et salutare" suggests that these texts may have been part of the manufacture, giving the words that the artist was to provide with initials and gold. Since the "equum et salutare" was not provided by the illuminator, there was nowhere else to put the notation. A contemporaneous Beneventan hand provided the gap of "et nox [ut dies illuminabitur; et nox] illuminatio mea." Perhaps the order of manufacture is: text, words for illuminator and corrections, illumination, notation (last).

BIBLIOGRAPHY   *Aggiornamento*, 423; Avery, *The Exultet Rolls*, 11, pl. 1–3; Beat Brenk in *Exultet*, 221–34 with facsimile; Brenk, "Bischöfliche"; Gabbrielli, "Un 'Exultet' cassinese"; Gamber, *CLLA*, no. 495e; *Inventario degli oggetti*, 4:91–96 and complete facsimile; Kelly, *TBC*, 298; Lowe, *TBS*, 2:13; Newton, "Due tipi," 469–73; Righetti Tosti-Croce, "Abruzzo"; Wettstein, *Sant'Angelo*, 144.

Bari, Archivio del Capitolo Metropolitano, Exultet 1

Exultet roll, s11½, Bari; Beneventan text and melody; pictures reversed.

DESCRIPTION   ca. 395 × ca. 5300 mm, eight membranes (Magistrale: 506 × 382, 770 × 397, 688 × 394, 703 × 398, 719 × 398, 685 × 395, 685 × 397, 605 × 390), average ca. 680; pieces attached with thongs through slits. Bari-type Beneventan script, Beneventan notation type 1, module of 24. Text, notation, and drawing are in a blackish-brown ink. Beneventan text and melody, illustrations reversed. A border includes a series of forty-eight portrait-medallions of bishops, apostles, saints, labeled in Greek and including many saints especially revered in the Byzantine church (see Mayo, "Borders in Bari").

DATE   s11¾ (Cavallo, *Rotoli*, 51; Magistrale in *Exultet*, 129: beginning of second quarter); Belting dates it with Constantine IX ("Byzantine Art," 15 and n51, 16n55), 1042–55; ca. 1000 (Weitzmann, in *L'art byzantin*, 351); ante 1028 (Bertaux, 219); ante 1056 (Lowe, Ladner); 1024–25 (Mayo, "*Vasa Sacra*," 387); for a summary of questions regarding dating, see *Aggiornamento*, 437–40.

Mayo's date of 1024–25 is the date of the elevation of the see of Bari to an archbishopric. It might be added that the Bari benedictional, older than this roll, has labels over two figures, now erased: one was an "archipresbiter," the other an "episcopus." Unfortunately, the names are not legible. The bishop's headgear is altered to add a conical miter in the accompanying picture. If the labels are original (Magistrale thinks they are not), it suggests that the benedictional, at least, was made before 1024–25.

HISTORY   Bari, perhaps the monastery of Saint Benedict (founded 978), for use at the cathedral. Magistrale says that the large initials are based on Cassinese decorative models (*Exultet*, 131). Cavallo and Magistrale note the similarities of writing in this roll and in two archiepiscopal documents of Bari written in 1024 and 1028. Natale (*Lettera*, 51) indicates that in 1776 this roll and two others of Bari were owned by Canon Allessandro Maria Calefat, whose edition of them was then imminent.

ADDITIONS

1025–28 or 1042–55: "Memorare domine famuli tui imperatoris nostri Constantini et cunctorum exercituum eius" (Constantine IX Monomachus [1042–55] or Constantine VIII, sole emperor of Byzantium, 1025–28).

1035–61: a name read by Lowe as "Nicolao" (Avery, *The Exultet Rolls*, 13n6; see Cavallo, *Rotoli*, 127n8) has been erased above "antistite"; this would be Nicholas, archbishop 1035–61.

1055–56: On the back of the roll: "Memorare domine famule tue imperatricis nostre Theodore et cunctorum exercituum eius quam et senioris nostri Argiro benignissimi magistri et omnium circumastantium" (empress Theodora, 1055–56; Argirus, son of the Melo who led a rebellion against Byzantium, d. 1068).

1059–67: in the main text, "imperatorum nostrorum *Constantini et Ebdokie*" (Constantine X Dukas, 1059–67, and empress Eudoxia, 1067–68).

1061–73: to the main text is added "Alexandro" for Pope Alexander II (1061–73).

1071 or shortly after?: "Memorare domine famulorum tuorum imperatorum nostrorum domni Michahil et domni Constantini atque domne Olimpiade, Simulque lucidissimi ducis nostri domni Rubberti et domne Sikelgaite ac domni Ruggerii et cunctum exercitum eorum et omnium circumastantium" (Michael VII, emperor 1071–78 and his brother Constantine; Robert Guiscard, who took Bari from the empire in 1071, his consort Sikelgaita and their son Roger Borsa, duke of Apulia in 1075); Cavallo (*Rotoli*, 127n9) notes that Michael VII was deposed before Easter 1078, so the addition must date not later than Easter 1077. Magistrale, noting that the Norman portion of this text is in a second hand, observes that negotiations between Robert Guiscard and Michael VII with respect to the marriage of their children took place 1074–76, providing a date for the second part of this text (*Exultet*, 130).

well after 1071? second item on the back: "Memorare domine famulorum tuorum ducum nostrorum domni Robberti et domne Sikelgaite ac domni Roggerii cunctorumque exercituum eorum et omnium circumastantium."

before 1078: "Memorare domine famul . . ." First noticed by Cavallo (*Rotoli*, 49, and 127n14), this unfinished addition precedes the one that follows.

1078–80? "una cum beatissimo papa nostro domno Gregorio et antistite nostro quem deus prouiderit sed et omnibus . . ." (Gregory VII, 1073–85, and perhaps the archiepiscopal seat vacant from 1078 filled by Urso 1080–89).

1080–89: the name "Ursone" is added in the text as archbishop.

MANUFACTURE   Ruling is done carefully and lightly, and space is left unruled for the pictures; these do not, however, interrupt the regular spacing of lines. The regularity of the spacing, resulting from regular prickings in the margins, means that each picture occupies a specific number of lines, the succeeding text beginning on a regularly spaced rule. (The same system is used in the Bari benedictional roll, although in this latter all the pictures come at the extremities of membranes.)

Each period begins with a decorated initial; only once does a period extend over two membranes. It appears as though the order of production involves writing, text initials, notation, and pictures last. The bee illumination avoids an initial; the notes for very large letters (*Sursum*) cannot be written until the letters themselves are made or at least drawn; and the way the trees in the "Tellus" picture flirt with the neumes is surely no accident. A similar case, however, does not work so well: the haloes of the ecclesiastical rulers actually touch the neumes. The border is painted on each piece before it is attached to adjacent membranes. (Note that the Bari benedictional, whose decoration is based on this, is more sophisticated: the border is painted after assembly, and one picture goes over a joint—the hand of God blessing the font.) The decorative border contains portrait medallions of saints and bishops (some appear to have been altered from angels); the Greek labeling of the medallions, according to Belting ("Byzantine Art," 5), is used intentionally to match the Byzantine style, but is produced by Latin scribes.

There are two large decorated letters, a substantial frontispiece, and seven further pictures placed within the text. Pictures are inverted, including the medallions in the borders, and the figure of Christ in the omega-shaped letter V is also inverted. Individual text periods have colored initials of two or three lines, with interlace and zoomorphic figures.

The large letters E and V, of course, must precede their text immediately. They are placed, that is, like most of the pictures. Five of the seven illustrations are painted immediately before their text periods. The last two pictures, of ecclesiastical and secular rulers, are placed, both in the next-to-last membrane, far from their text, and each a different distance ahead of its text. It would have been possible, but awkward, to place them in the same way as the other paintings. There are eighteen lines after the bee picture before the place where the ecclesiastical rulers would be needed to precede their period: in an average-sized membrane, this might split the picture between two membranes, but a shorter membrane, containing just these eighteen lines, would have accommodated both sets of rulers, placed like the other pictures, on the next membrane, without needing another membrane to finish the roll.

It is possible that the roll contained an illustration at its head that is now lost: the opening membrane would surely not be other than standard size; and if so, there is room for one or two more pictures.

BIBLIOGRAPHY *Aggiornamento,* 437–40; Avery, *The Exultet Rolls,* 11–13, plates 4–11; Babudri, *L'Exultet;* Belting, *Studien,* 185n9; Bertaux, *L'art,* 217–21; Cavallo, *Rotoli,* 47–55, tav. 1–11; idem, "Struttura," 357–61; Kelly, *TBC,* 299; Ladner, "The 'Portraits,' " 185–86; Lowe, *Scriptura,* tav. 65; Lowe, *TBS,* 2:16; Magistrale, in *Exultet,* 129–41, with facsimile; Mayo, "Borders in Bari"; "*Vasa sacra*"; Natale, *Lettera,* 51; Schlumberger, "Les rouleaux."

Bari, Archivio del Capitolo Metropolitano, Exultet 2

Exultet roll, s11¾, Bari; Beneventan text and melody, later altered to Franco-Roman text; pictures reversed.

DESCRIPTION   Five membranes, ca. 325 × ca. 3980 mm (265 + 810 + 830 + 782 + 840 + 570), average 815. Bari-type Beneventan script, Beneventan notation (type 2?), now erased, module of 20 mm. Drawing is done in a blackish-brown ink similar to that of the text (the original notation is not visible). Prickings for original ruling are visible in side margins. Quadruple lines are scored for each side border. Beneventan text, later accommodated to Franco-Roman; after the beginning of the preface, the text is erased and rewritten in Gothic script, with square notation on a staff of three to five lines, with clef and custos. The older initials are preserved, but no longer serve as part of the text. Borders on the sides are interrupted by medallions of what appear to be bishops and perhaps saints; they are not labeled like those in Bari 1.

Horizontal decorated borders are used occasionally: once in the surviving frontispiece pictures, once between the decorated V and its following text "Vere"; once at the joint between the last two membranes: thus the illustrations are not normally enclosed in a frame. In one case, however (illustrating the bees), simple red lines at top and bottom combine with the side borders to frame the picture; and horizontal lines are used in two pictures (Mater ecclesia; Fratres karissimi) as a sort of groundline.

In addition to the two decorated initials, there are seven illustrations; three of these, illustrating the life of Christ (Baptism, Transfiguration, Pentecost), are the conclusion of a now-incomplete frontispiece; the remaining illustrations (Mater ecclesia; Fratres karissimi; Christ in mandorla; Bees) are placed in the course of the text. Illustrations are reversed.

DATE   s11¾ (Cavallo, *Rotoli*, 100; Magistrale), rewritten s13¾ (Cavallo), s13½ (Magistrale).

HISTORY   Bari, perhaps the monastery of Saint Benedict.

MANUFACTURE   The roll is ruled for text throughout, even through the pictures. Each textual period begins with a large colored two-line initial at left. A new membrane usually begins with a new period, except for membrane 5, which begins with the last line of the period "Apis siquidem." The joints are uniformly not well made; the running side border never matches that of the next membrane and has not been carried up to the end. On two occasions a rough border has been made to cross at the joint.

Space was left for illustrations as the text was entered, and the large initials at least may have been sketched: the large E of "Exultet" must have had its larger shape indicated before the following text was entered. However, the text and initials seem to have preceded the pictures, to judge from the initial of "Vt qui me," which the picture avoids.

Pictures are not regularly arranged to come before their periods as in Bari 1. It appears that they are drawn in after the relevant text period. This is certainly true of "Mater ecclesia" and probably also of "Fratres karissimi," which actually comes after the opening line of the next period. The picture of Christ in a mandorla borne by two angels, originally preceding "Apis siquidem," occurs at a place where Bari 1 has a more typical illustration of bees. The picture here seems adapted from the similar picture that serves as the frontispiece to Bari 1 and is perhaps intended to illustrate the preceding period ("Totus ac plena in te es"). The placement of the last picture (Bees) comes between two periods in praise of the bees.

The decoration was never finished: the last two membranes have progressively fewer colors, until at the end there is only drawing of initials, borders, medallions, with a very little red.

Bari 2 reproduces, in a less imaginative way, the layout, the borders, and certain illustrations of Bari 1. But the artist is not very skilled, and his purpose is different; he included a headpiece with scenes from the life of Christ, which was not like Bari 1; he skipped most of the elaborate paintings in Bari 1; he changed the arrangement of the liturgical scenes; and he produced a document with much less illustrative content and much less luxurious quality. Nevertheless, he knew the existing models.

BIBLIOGRAPHY   Avery, *The Exultet Rolls*, 14–15, pl. 17–23; Cavallo, *Rotoli*, 99–102, tav.18–27; Kelly, *TBC*, 299; Lowe, *TBS*, 2:16; Magistrale, in *Exultet*, 201–10, with facsimile.

Bari, Archivio del Capitolo Metropolitano, Exultet 3

Exultet roll, s13, made from an erased Byzantine roll, Bari. Franco-Roman text and an elaborated version of the Beneventan melody; no illuminations.

DATE   s12 (Lowe); s12ex (Cavallo, *Rotoli*, 131n.104), s13½ (Magistrale)

DESCRIPTION   Four membranes, 120–30 × 2845 mm (637 + 794 + 740 + 733), average 711. The membranes are held together by (new) parchment strips. Not an elegant product, the roll itself is made from an erased Byzantine roll. Its original headpiece, not erased, is visible at the end of the roll, and traces of lower script—writing and illustrations in the form of a series of busts—can still be seen (Plate 4). The Exultet does not occupy the full length of the original roll. A blackish-brown ink is used for text and notation. Beneventan script and square notation on a staff of three dry-point lines. Franco-Roman text, and an elaborated Beneventan melody that is a development from that of Bari 2.

MANUFACTURE   The membranes are ruled throughout (including the portion left unused), irregularly, maximum module of 25 mm for four lines, three of which are used for musical notation. There are no illustrations or borders; initials are touched with red; a space was left for the initial V, but it was never executed. New periods do not begin a new line, unless they also begin a new membrane.

BIBLIOGRAPHY   Avery, *The Exultet Rolls*, 15–16, pl. 24; Kelly, *TBC*, 299; Kelly, "Structure and Ornament"; Lowe, *TBS*, 2:16; Magistrale, in *Exultet*, 409–21, with facsimile.

Capua, Tesoro della Cattedrale, Exultet Roll

Exultet roll, incomplete, s11½; provenance uncertain: Montecassino? Capua? Franco-Roman text, Beneventan melody; pictures inverted.

DESCRIPTION Incomplete; five membranes (of seven?), now separated. 230 × 3285 mm (710 + 715 + 710 + 710 + 417), average 711 (Orofino). Beneventan script and early type 2 notation, module of 23 mm. A dark brown ink, faded in places, is used for text and notation; this is perhaps the same ink as that used for drawing, but with a finer pen. It is possible that the roll was never complete: it may be a Franco-Roman continuation of another roll, now lost. Painted borders and six surviving illustrations (four of six are reversed). Unusual in this roll is the picture of the women at the sepulcher. There are no pictures of ecclesiastical and secular authorities.

DATE s11 (Lowe); before 1022 (when Henry II was recognized as emperor by the Capuans; Rotili, "La miniatura," 320); s11½ (Avery; Orofino); s11med (Wettstein); Avery later (according to unpublished material consulted by Mayo); Garrison (*Studies*, 34n5) and Mayo date it s11⅔.

HISTORY The roll has been thought to have originated at Montecassino; Rotili ("L' 'Exultet,' " 205) is not certain whether Montecassino or San Benedetto at Capua. Don Mauro Inguanez commented to Avery that the commemoration speaks of an abbot with a congregation of Saint Benedict. But San Benedetto di Capua depended on Montecassino and had a provost (*praepositus*), not an abbot (Avery, 16n2; on the abbey see Bloch, *MMA*, 1:234–37). The textual tradition here is not that of most Montecassino rolls. Speciale ("Spigolature") excludes it from Montecassino on the basis of size and impagination. The Beneventan text was used at Capua in the eleventh century, according to a fragment of a missal reported by Natale, *Lettera*, 65–66.

The emperor "enrici" added in Beneventan might be Henry II, whose expedition of 1022 resulted in his recognition by the Capuans (Rotili, "L' 'Exultet' "); Speciale (*Montecassino*, 120n183) thinks the correction should be dated with the conquest of Capua by Guaimar V (1038–47); Mayo ("Borders in Bari") suggests Henry III (1039–56). The correction of princes to the singular, with the name Robertus, can be assigned to 1107–20, when Capua was conquered by the Normans and ruled by Robert I.

Additions of names in fourteenth-century cursive script suggest that the roll was then at Montecassino: Benedicto (Benedict XII, 1334–42); episcopo Raymondo (abbot of Montecassino, 1326–40; but not apparently archbishop of Capua, according to the list in Granata, *Storia sacra*, 2:165–76); Robert, king of Naples (1309–43).

MANUFACTURE The membranes are ruled regularly throughout, the pictures painted over rules. The last membrane, where the text finishes before the end, has a border painted only alongside text, leaving the rest blank to wrap around the umbilicus.

Text periods start at left margin with a one-line colored initial; final short lines are aligned to left. The initials must have been entered, or sketched, at or before the time of writing, since subsequent lines of text avoid the long descenders of initial letters of "In huius igitur" and "Partim ore legere." On four occasions, the last few words are set at right so a new period may begin on the same line. Internal divisions are marked with punctuation, but not with capitals. Planning ahead for the end of the membrane (or even the end of the line) does not always succeed: one period ("Hec explorata") carries over two membranes; at the end of one membrane the scribe chooses to have a line that contains only the last two syllables of "Pruinosa" rather than split a word between membranes. Elsewhere, the same problem causes him to use a whole line for the last three letters of "castitatem": this, however, allows him to finish the period at the end of the membrane.

The pictures are painted after the text is entered: two of them (Harrowing of Hell, Annunciation) take advantage of the space left by a shorter line. This does not agree with Speciale ("Spigolature"), who suggests that the pictures precede the text, judging from what she sees as awkwardnesses in the layout of the text. According to Speciale the pictures are the work of two artists alternating by membrane. The border is evidently made before assembling the roll, since the borders never quite extend to the end of the membrane, but are tapered like ribbons. In membrane 1, the border of interlace also forms frames around the two pictures, and the interlace is unbroken. Other pictures are not bounded by horizontal borders; for all of them except the bees, the relation of text to pictures makes such a border unworkable. It appears that the borders were added where possible after the pictures; the (not reversed) Harrowing of Hell on membrane 2 has Adam's foot in front of the border, which is not painted under the foot: this is possible only if the border is painted later.

Four pictures are inverted before their periods, but two others are problematical: a picture of the bees is not inverted; and the Harrowing of Hell is not inverted, and it comes after the period "Huius igitur," with "reddit innocentiam lapsis." This is not an obvious place for this picture. It might have gone better where a Crucifixion now stands, before "Hec nox est in qua destructis uinculis mortis, christus ab inferis uictor ascendit." And in its place, inverted, a "sacrificium uespertinum" would have been correct. A scene of the deacon on the ambo, apparently related to "Oramus te domine ut cereus iste," has no candle in it. The Annunciation actually comes a period too soon: but it would appear simultaneously with its text; this must be an accident, given the placement of the other pictures, and it may be related to a desire to give the picture enough space before the membrane runs out.

BIBLIOGRAPHY   *Aggiornamento*, 446–47; Avery, *The Exultet Rolls*, 16, pl. 25–29; Di Resta, "Exultet di Capua"; Kelly, *TBC*, 304; Lowe, *TBS*, 2:29–30; Orofino in *Exultet*, 291–302, with facsimile; Rotili, "L' 'Exultet' della cattedrale di Capua"; Wettstein, *Sant'Angelo*, 145–56.

Gaeta, Tesoro della Cattedrale, Exultet 1

Exultet roll, s11, Gaeta (?). Beneventan text and melody, pictures inverted; later altered to Franco-Roman text.

DESCRIPTION   Seven (of the original eight) membranes, width varies 325–32 × 3656 mm (total length separated = 185 [incomplete] + 556 + 592 + 570 + 587 + 552 + 614, average 578). Original ruling is visible under the picture of the Nativity, module of 28 mm. The drawing is in a medium brown ink. Presumably Beneventan text and notation; the text "per christum dominum nostrum" after "Vere dignum" is usual in the Beneventan text and survives here from the original; several lines in capitals beginning with "Dominus uobiscum" survive from the original; a few original initials can be seen, e.g. "Vna cum"; text and music were erased and rewritten in Gothic rotunda script with Franco-Roman text and melody in square notation dated 1335–42 by letters B and R in the commemorations, Benedict XII (1335–42) and Robert of Naples (1309–43); (Dom Latil first pointed this out to Avery; *The Exultet Rolls,* 17n2). The surviving pictures (five and a portion of a sixth, "Mater ecclesia") are reversed. An initial VD and a stelliform D ("Dominus uobiscum") also form part of the original decoration.

DATE   Ante 964 (?) (Pace in *Civiltà*); s11 (Lowe; Pace in *Exultet*); s11½ (Avery; Lavagnino and Salerno, *Il museo,* 11; Wettstein); s11 (*Aggiornamento*).

HISTORY   From Gaeta (?); Pace (in *Civiltà*) thought this might be the roll given by the priest Pietro to the church of San Michele in Planciano in 964 (see Appendix 3 for the text). Cavallo (*Exultet di Salerno*) thinks not, since the pictures would not have been inverted until after the "discovery" of this idea, which surely postdated the making of Vat. lat. 9820. Pace later (in *Exultet,* 343) agreed; he suggests that the size of the roll, its extensive use of gold, and the importance given in the illustrations to a bishop (not an archbishop) suggest a commission by a bishop of Gaeta; he suggests Bishop Bernard, in office by 997, a personage of particular religious and political importance (on Bernard, see Delogu, "Patroni," 205–12). It was likely at the cathedral of Gaeta that the reworking took place. Note that the bishop of Gaeta was a suffragan of the archbishop of Capua.

MANUFACTURE   There are no borders. The original preparation is practically undecipherable, since the layout has been erased and rewritten. Evidently, some illustrations were not ruled (that is, they were anticipated when the membrane was prepared): most are at one end of a membrane, and space is left for them in the preparation. Those not at the end of a membrane are sometimes painted over regular rules: the scene combining bees with the Nativity is ruled through, and the rules serve the artist to align beehives and manger; the procession of offerings, though space was prepared for it, actually begins earlier in the membrane and covers one text rule (which is used to align the bottom of a tabernacle). Evidently the estimate of space needed for the text was wrong by one line when the membrane was prepared. If rulings were made as periods were written, this would not have happened. But if illustrations had been drawn before the writing this picture would not have used space prepared for text; evidently, the writing and illustration took place simultaneously.

 The pictures are reversed and remain so in the revised text. The scene combining the bees and the nativity has no place in the revised roll, since the praise of the bees is omitted in the upper script.

BIBLIOGRAPHY   *Aggiornamento,* 447–48; Avery, *The Exultet Rolls,* 17, pl. 30–33; Ferraro, *Memorie,* 171–75; Kelly, *TBC,* 304; Lowe, *TBS,* 2:45; Pace in *Civiltà,* 15–35; Pace in *Exultet,* 341–51, with facsimile; *Trésors d'art;* Wettstein, *Sant'Angelo,* 144–45.

Gaeta, Tesoro della Cattedrale, Exultet 2

Exultet roll, s11, Gaeta(?), Franco-Roman text, Beneventan melody, pictures inverted.

DESCRIPTION   Incomplete, four membranes, ca. 199–203 × 2683 mm (= 807 + 779 + 787 + 198inc), average 791 (Pace's measurements in *Exultet,* which do not quite match those of Avery or of Inguanez [?] in *Libraries Guests of the Vatican,* 44, or those of his own earlier measurements in *Civiltà*). A brown ink is used for text and notation; the drawing is in another, grayer ink. Beneventan script and type 3 notation, though without lines or clefs. Franco-Roman text. The opening membrane is missing; it contained the beginning up to "Quapropter"; the roll now ends "sicut sancta concepit uirgo Maria." The roll has been "ruthlessly repainted" (Avery, 17); it does not appear so now.

DATE   s11med (Pace, *Civiltà,* 26); s11½ (Pace, *Exultet*); s11/12 (Lavagnino and Salerno, *Il museo,* 12); s11 (Lowe); s11ex (Avery).

HISTORY   Gaeta (?).

MANUFACTURE   It appears that the illustrations are not ruled through; there are hints of vertical rules at the present (trimmed) border. Text periods are made simply: they begin with a one-line initial; and short final lines are not treated specially: they begin at left like the others. It does not look as though the illustrations are ruled. Illustrations are drawn in before color is applied and before the notation is written. "Sacrificium uespertinum," for example, takes advantage of the incomplete line written before (beneath) it; but it extends a little too far into the text (or at least notation) area to come: the notation was added last, the illustration drawn taking account of the writing, but not of the notation to come. Coloring, here incomplete (red, yellow, and blue have been added), is evidently done at a later stage, after writing, drawing, and notation.

The placement of illustrations is not always good: "Fratres karissimi" comes just after the words "fratres karissimi," in the middle of a period. The letter V, really a circle with a crucifixion, is in the wrong place: it follows the prologue and it precedes "Dominus uobiscum." Its appearance, however, would be close to simultaneous with the singing of "Vere." There are two Harrowing of Hell pictures: the first precedes "Qui pro nobis tibi eterno patri ade debitum soluit," which is possible; there is a Red Sea, which is placed (incorrectly) after its period; the second Harrowing is also placed after its period ("Hec nox est que destructis uinculis mortis Christus ab inferis uictor surrexit"). The next two pictures are in each other's place, and each is seen after the (ir)relevant period is read. The "sacrificium uespertinum" period is followed by the "Curuat imperia" picture, and vice versa. Generally, where further errors are not found, the principle here is for the scribe to stop when he has written something that ought to be illustrated and leave a space. These spaces evidently get filled in considerably later: the inversions on membrane 3 suggest that the illustrator put pictures into spaces without re-reading the text or, while reading from the top and, seeing the hole before "sacrificium uespertinum," inserted the picture (in the wrong place) and then put the other one in the remaining place, without checking to see whether the fit was correct.

As Avery points out, a Harrowing of Hell here and the "Regis uictoria" (Christ in mandorla or circle) are drawn from the iconography of Vat. lat. 9820, where each suits the Beneventan text. Here they are placed somewhat awkwardly; the Harrowing (right-facing Christ leading souls out) is placed after the V of "Vere," as in 9820, where here it really ought to follow the Red Sea.

BIBLIOGRAPHY *Aggiornamento*, 448; Avery, *The Exultet Rolls*, 17–18, pl. 34–47; Ferraro, *Memorie*, 171–75; Kelly, *TBC*, 304; Lowe, *TBS*, 2:46; Pace in *Exultet*, 353–62, with facsimile; Pace in *Civiltà*, 36–53; Trésors d'art.

Gaeta, Tesoro della Cattedrale, Exultet 3

Exultet roll, s12 (before 1130), Gaeta(?). Franco-Roman text, Beneventan melody, inverted illustrations; based on Gaeta 2.

DESCRIPTION Eight (of nine) membranes, of which the first is incomplete: ca. 270 × 5316 mm (= 362 + 638 + 697 + 723 + 741 + 700 + 721 + 730), average 707 (Pace, in *Exultet*). Now separated, the joints were attached with double thongs in all cases but one, where there is a single row of slits for a thong. A faded brown ink, used for writing and drawing, has been rewritten here and there in a black ink. The membranes are ruled at the sides and are ruled throughout for text, module of 27 mm. Beneventan script and type 3 notation, but without clef or any additional line for alignment. Franco-Roman text, Beneventan melody. Ten illustrations (inverted) and the large initial VD survive.

DATE s12 (ante 1130) (Pace in *Exultet*), based on "imperatoris" being changed to "regis," coronation of Roger II in 1130; s12 (Lavagnino and Salerno, *Il museo*, 12).

HISTORY Gaeta (?). This roll is based, some seventy years later, on the same illustrative model as Gaeta 2, but its text is not copied from the earlier roll (variants bear this out).

This roll has many, many textual corrections, witnesses of long use. The original ending of Gaeta 3, as well as it can be reconstructed, is as follows:

> Precamur ergo te domine ut nos famulos tuos omnem clerum et deuotissimum populum. Una cum beatissimo papa nostro .ill. Et antistite nostro .ill. [cum omni congregatione beati xxx presentis uite quiete concessa gaudiis facias perfrui sempiternas. (The portion in brackets, whose text is illegible, is suggested by the surviving neumes. Curiously, the notes for "omni congregatione" do not match exactly: there is one punctum too many; and there is exactly the same phenomenon for this text in Paris 710.)] Memento etiam domine famuli tui imperatoris nostri .ill. [1⅓ lines erased] . . . et celestem ei concede uictoriam cum omni exercitu eius. Et his qui offerunt hoc sacrificium laudis premia eterna largiaris. R[espice? 2½ lines of this have now been erased] . . . Ciuitatemque istam et populum eius custodire digneris. Per dominum nostrum iesum christum filium tuum, Qui tecum et cum spiritu sancto uiuit et regnat deus, Per omnia secula seculorum. Amen.

The many subsequent changes may be chronicled as follows:

1. Sometime after 1130, "imperatoris nostri .ill." is changed to "regis nostri Guilielmus" in a Beneventan hand.
2. Late twelfth century (?): the erasures above and additions were made, so that the ending reads:

Precamur ergo te domine ut nos famulos tuos omnes cleros et deuo-tissimum populum. Vna cum beatissimo papa nostro .ill. Et antistite nostro .ill. *quiete temporum concessa in his paschalibus gaudiis conseruare digneris.*

Memento etiam domine famuli tui *regis nostri Guilielmus* Ciuitatemque istam et populum eius custodire digneris. Per dominum nostrum iesum christum filium tuum, Qui tecum et cum spiritu sancto uiuit et regnat deus, Per omnia secula seculorum. Amen.

3. Thirteenth century, textual and rubrical changes made in the text (see Appendix 2).
4. Between 1316 and 1334, names of pope, bishop, and king added, adjustments made in text, and the Norman finale added, rejecting all the rest of the ending:

> Precamur ergo te domine ut nos famulos tuos omnes cleros et devotissimum populum. Vna cum beatissimo papa nostro *Johanne* Et *episcopo* [this word is above the line: it is not clear whether it is intended to replace the following word or to follow the name added in the margin] antistite nostro *Francisco* quiete temporum concessa in his paschalibus gaudiis *assidua protectione* conseruare digneris.
>
> *Qui uiuis regnas imperas necnon et gloriaris solus dominus solus altissimus ihesu christe cum sancto spiritu in gloria dei patris. Amen.*

Pace's dates (1322–34) for these final revisions (in *Civiltà*, 56) are based on the dates of Pope John XXII (1316–34), Robert of Anjou (1309–43), and Bishop Francesco Gattola (Aug. 1321–Oct. 1340), elected to succeed another Francesco, the former a Franciscan. It is not clear that the second Franciscus is being referred to here rather than the first (which would allow these last revisions to have been made 1316–21). It is likely that a Franciscan would have urged the liturgical changes in the text and ceremonial operated in stage 3 above, since they correspond to the practices in the Franciscan books adopted by Innocent III. These alterations are written in a different hand from those made on the last membrane and might well date from the time of the earlier Bishop Francesco (on these two bishops, see Ferraro, *Memorie*, 211).

   It is probably this roll that was still in use in 1508, according to an inventory cited in Ferraro, *Memorie*, 180: "Item una carta di coyro grande scripta notata et figurata dove si cantha Exultet jam angelica; circha palmi venti longa."

MANUFACTURE Double vertical lines are ruled for margins; the membranes are ruled for text throughout, so that illustrations are painted over text rules. Text paragraphs begin at left, with a one-line colored initial; interior cola are occasionally begun with a capital touched with color. Pictures are surrounded by a painted frame, which is sometimes, but not always, aligned at one end (rarely both) on a text rule. In this roll, the pictures are correctly placed: that is, they come before the deacon reads the relevant period. They are essentially the same illustrations as in Gaeta 2. The remarkable procession of offerings with the church as a crowned female figure might have figured also in Gaeta 2, since it would have come after its period, and the space after that period is now lost.

BIBLIOGRAPHY   *Aggiornamento,* 448; Avery, *The Exultet Rolls,* 18–19, pl. 38–42; Ferraro, *Memorie,* 171–75; Pace in Civiltà, 54–77; Pace in *Exultet,* 363–75, with facsimile; Kelly, *TBC,* 304–5; Klauser, "Eine rätselhafte"; Lowe, *TBS,* 2:46; *Trésors d'art.*

London, British Library, add. MS 30337

Exultet roll, Montecassino, ca. 1075; Franco-Roman text, Beneventan melody, inverted pictures.

DESCRIPTION   Twelve membranes, 280 × 6850 mm (Avery), 585 + 619 + 619 + 618 + 407 + 617 + 614 + 610 + 585 + 592 + 657 + 583 (Speciale), average 609 (omitting membrane 5). The roll is complete, the membranes joined with parchment thongs. There are double vertical rules at the sides, for which prickings are visible; the black ink used for text is not that of the drawings. Beneventan script, module of 25 mm; the type 3 neumes are written in red. Franco-Roman text, illustrations inverted. There are two initials and fourteen illustrations, the latter inverted. One of the illustrations (Virgin enthroned) has been mutilated by the removal of two flanking figures, almost certainly angels. Smaller initials are gold with touches of color. The "Lumen Christi," and the entire first period, are written in capitals on bands of gold (similar to the gold bands that begin each of the periods in the Avezzano and Barberini rolls).

"The most beautiful of all existing Exultet rolls, because of its sure line and pure tones" (Avery, 19).

DATE   1070–80 (Toubert, 241–44); ca. 1072 (Baldass, "Die Miniaturen"); 1060–70 (Belting, "Byzantine Art," 17 and n56); after 1071 (Brenk, "Bischöfliche"); s11, third/last quarter (Speciale).

HISTORY   The notation of names is written four times differently, with liquescents, as though they corresponded to actual names; the roll was at Montecassino until the nineteenth century (Bertaux, 226); it was acquired by the British Museum in 1877; "believed to have remained at Monte Cassino until the beginning of the 19th century" (Gilson, 5); Don Faustino Avagliano, archivist of Montecassino, reports in a private communication that the roll was removed from the abbey during the time of the Napoleonic occupation and was acquired by the British Museum from a French source.

This roll is closely related to the roll in the Barberini collection, though neither is a copy of the other; the London roll is thought by many (Baldass, Speciale, Brenk) to precede the Barberini roll. This roll, whose pictures were executed by perhaps three artists (Baldass, Speciale), is associated with the monuments of manuscript illumination of the time of Abbot Desiderius of Montecassino. There is no depiction here of ecclesiastical and secular authorities.

MANUFACTURE   The membranes are ruled, leaving blank space for pictures. The text periods are carefully made; all match the musical paragraphs. The initials are one-line, except where they are extended a little. Neither first nor second lines are indented to make space for initials: the whole period is indented a little, and the first line begins at the same left margin as successive lines, omitting the opening letter to be added in color. Interior articulations are not marked with capitals or color. Ending lines are sometimes centered when short.

I see no reason to think that illustration precedes the writing of the text; many illustrations fit very well between the existing lines of text (though of course an adept scribe putting illustrations onto blank parchment might have used the existing ruled lines to estimate placement); but the notation, at least, was not present when the illustrations were made. Speciale points out the awkwardness of the notation near the illustration of the Crucifixion. There is, however, no alteration in the placement of the notation at this place: there could not be for the notation to have any meaning. But it is true that the top of the cross comes perilously close to the neumes: the illustrator did not need to extend the cross so close to the written portion; and indeed before the notation was added, the illustration fit the space well.

The pictures preceded the initials, to judge from the initial H that obscures faces crossing the Red Sea; and the text preceded the initials, to judge from the wrong-sized P added for the final "Per omnia secula" at the end of the preface.

Though it seems an awkward order in which to proceed, an order of manufacture beginning with the text, followed by illustration, and finishing with initials and notation gives the best account of the state of the roll.

Membrane 5, containing only the large initial V and its following text ("quia dignum et iustum est aequum et salutare") is unusually short; this may have been designed to allow the Crucifixion picture to appear in the middle of the next membrane. But the point at which the membrane stops is exactly the point of divergence between the Beneventan and the Roman text. Was another continuation begun and rejected? Was the prologue conceived (and made) as a separate, all-purpose item?

The pictures are generally in the wrong place if they are intended to precede their text periods. "Angelica turba" and "Mater ecclesia" are painted after their periods; "Tellus," attached after "ecclesia," is not only on the wrong side of its period, it is on the wrong side of the wrong period: is it perhaps included as an afterthought? "Fratres karissimi," the Red Sea, and Adam and Eve all appear after the relevant periods. But the placement of a picture after its period is not systematic. A number of pictures precede their periods, in the fashion more normal in other rolls: the Crucifixion is correct (if it is meant to illustrate the period "Hec sunt enim festa paschalia in cuius uere ille agnus occiditur"), as is Sacrificium uespertinum; the illustration of bees is appropriate, and the pictures of the Virgin Mary and of "cereus iste" precede their periods. Some other pictures here are puzzling: a "Noli me tangere" scene precedes the period "Huius igitur sanctificatio noctis, fugat scelera, culpas lauat, reddit innocentiam lapsis, mestis letitiam, fugat odia, concordiam parat, et curuat imperia"; if it illustrates that text it is in the right place, but it has no real relation to it. A Harrowing of Hell scene precedes the period including the text "ut seruum redimeres filium tradidisti"; but surely the scene illustrates "Hec nox est in qua destructis uinculis mortis christus ab inferis uictor ascendit," in which case it appears two periods late.

If the general principle is to place pictures before their periods, then only the last three (of seven) membranes are correctly made—and the last has no pictures. How does this happen? Did an artist start at one end of an already-written roll and make either a correction or a slip that confused all the rest of the placement? It is difficult to discover an error or a train of errors that would produce the roll as we have it.

The threefold "Lumen Christi" precedes an illustrated headpiece of Christ in majesty; this text is turned the other way from the rest: it is oriented with the pictures.

BIBLIOGRAPHY *Aggiornamento*, 450–51; Avery, *The Exultet Rolls*, 19–20, pl. 43–51; Baldass, "Disegni," 107, 111–12; Baldass, "Die Miniaturen"; Bertaux, *L'art*, 226–27; Brenk, *Das Lektionar*, 100–101, 111; Brenk, "Bischöfliche," 295–99; Gilson, *An Exultet Roll;* Kelly, *TBC*, 305; Lowe, *TBS*, 2:52; Newton, "Due tipi," 469; Speciale in *Exultet*, 249–64, with facsimile; Toubert, "Le bréviaire," 239–61; Wettstein, *Sant'Angelo*, 148–49; Zanardi, "Gli Exultet."

Manchester, John Rylands University Library, MS Lat. 2

Exultet roll, incomplete; s10/11, provenance unknown; Beneventan text and melody, pictures not inverted.

DESCRIPTION Incomplete, three pieces, 310 × 1810 mm (Avery), 691 × 212, 723 × 212, 423 × 212 (Speciale); module of 21 mm. Only the middle section is clearly full-length; text and notation are in a brown ink; the drawing is in a lighter brown ink. Beneventan text and type 1 notation; pictures are not inverted.

DATE s10/11 (Avery; Speciale); s11in (Lowe); s10, probably Montecassino (Diringer, *The Illuminated Book*, 299).

HISTORY The manuscript is first mentioned by Wattenbach in 1877 as being in the possession of the antiquary S. Pickert in Nuremberg ("Ein 'Exultet' "); it came to the Rylands Library in 1901 as part of the collection of Lord Crawford.

MANUFACTURE The first and third membranes are ruled throughout, including the opening E (which is set to left with text to right). In the opening membrane, new text periods do not begin at left, but run on from the previous period, beginning with a decorated one-line letter. In the third membrane, the new periods do begin at left, and the spaces remaining are sometimes filled in with pictures. The second membrane has two lines of text followed by three text rules, over which are painted the upper part of the Crucifixion; the rest of the membrane is unruled.

The manner of illustration is puzzling: it would be highly interesting to see the rest of the roll. Initial letters, E and V, are normal. In the central membrane, a series of full-width scenes (Crucifixion; descent to limbo 1 and 2) appears after the words "resurrectio mortuorum" and concludes the membrane; the next membrane begins with "Solutis quippe nexibus." The pictures thus come between, and illustrate, words from two successive periods. In the third membrane, decoration is made in the space left blank by incomplete lines in the text; decorations consist of representations of bees and hives. In one place, however, the scribe—probably also the artist—has skipped a line to allow for a little more elaboration of the little scene; this Nativity scene is on a line and a half left empty: Joseph sits on the line, wittily.

Was there perhaps a series of pictures as a frontispiece? The first membrane is now not full-length.

Speciale points out that the arrangement of the opening letter and the illustration right-side up (I would add the ruling of entire membranes) point to an early stage in the develoment of illustrated rolls.

The style of the initial E, as well as that of the pictures, does not seem to bear a close relationship with other Exultets or indeed other illustrated manuscripts of the south.

BIBLIOGRAPHY   *Aggiornamento*, 434; Avery, *The Exultet Rolls*, 21, pl. 52–55; Diringer, *The Illuminated Book*, 229; James, *A Descriptive Catalogue*, 1:4–6, 2: pl. 2–7; Kelly, *TBC*, 306; Lowe, *TBS*, 2:56; Speciale in *Exultet*, 119–27, with facsimile.

Mirabella Eclano, Archivio della Chiesa Collegiata, Exultet 1
(on Deposit in the Biblioteca Nazionale, Naples)

Exultet roll, s11½, Beneventan text and melody, reversed pictures. From Benevento?

DESCRIPTION   Incomplete at end (ends "commendas"), four membranes, 223–30 × 2010 mm (455 + 585 + 600 + 370), average 502.5. Brown ink, rubbed and faded, is used for writing and, with a smaller pen, for notation; the same ink may have been used for drawing. Beneventan script and type 1 notation, Beneventan text. Two large initials and three illustrations (inverted) remain, along with fragments of a fourth picture. The parchment is much darkened, disguising the elegance of the pictures. The three sections of Mirabella 2 were once attached to these as a single roll. They have been separated at least since their restoration at the Vatican Library in 1910. The four membranes, with those of Mirabella 2, are numbered on paper labels pasted to their backs.

DATE   Campania, s11in (Lowe); s11½ (Avery; Wettstein, *L'art roman*, 10); s11med (Orofino).

HISTORY   The provenance is uncertain: Mirabella (Lowe; Avery); San Vincenzo (Wettstein); Bari (Garrison); Benevento? (Orofino). The see of Quintodecimo (site of ancient Aeclanum, modern Mirabella, at the fifteenth mile from Benevento), a suffragan diocese of Benevento, was ruined by an earthquake in 986; the town and the diocese were revived near Frigento, the first known bishop named in 1061 (Kehr, IP, 9:134–35), and Orofino suggests that this might have been the occasion of the creation of the roll. There was a monastic church of Saint Peter at Quintodecimo dependent on Saint Peter's *extra muros*, Benevento (Kehr, IP, 9:136). The quality of the roll makes an otherwise unattested scriptorium an unlikely source; though historians of art have seen connections with Cassinese and Puglian styles, Orofino's suggestion of Beneventan manufacture seems possible. The text is close to that of Benevento 33 (which was probably not made at Benevento).

MANUFACTURE   There is a single vertical rule on each side; text rules, module of 19 mm (on membrane 3), do not go through the illustrations. Beside the initial letter E there are text rules only to the right where text appears. Text periods run on, and there is no effort to finish a period before the end of a membrane: several periods carry over.

The illustrations are essentially drawings with a brown wash, with the addition of orange-red and another color that has now eaten through the parchment in many places. It may be that further colors were intended. The pictures were done by, or in collaboration with, the scribe. The V of "Vere" has unruled space provided for it, but the following text begins not at the ruling, but after skipping two lines, doubtless because the illustration went too far. The same situation is true after the angel illustration: one wing causes the next text to begin later than it would have had the illustration not already been present.

The planners of the roll may have been working from a model like Vat. lat. 9820: many of the pictures are derived from that series (a picture in which the bishop lights the candle; the layout of the initial E on the left side of the membrane; the "Angelica turba"; the Bees). Placement of the pictures suggests that this is an early attempt at reversing pictures using a model with pictures not reversed. The VD initial has a figure of Christ in a mandorla; this initial is reversed, with the result that the letters are upside down to the reader, but the figure of Christ is oriented the same way as the other pictures (cf. the later solutions in the Casanatense and Salerno Exultets). An "Angelica turba" is placed reversed in the space provided, but well after its text. The following text, "Letetur et mater ecclesia," would suggest that this space might better have contained a picture related to that and that the angels might better have appeared in the frontispiece (thus before the words "angelica turba"); here the frontispiece is very incomplete, but it included a fragment showing the top of an ecclesiastical building with a cross-topped tower: perhaps the angels and the "Mater ecclesia" have been switched in error.

BIBLIOGRAPHY   *Aggiornamento*, 441; *L'art roman*, 10–11; Avery, *The Exultet Rolls*, 21, pl. 52–55; Bertaux, *L'art*, 221; Garrison, *Studies*, 2:35; Guarini, "Osservazioni"; Kelly, *TBC*, 306; Lowe, *TBS*, 2:57; Orofino in *Exultet*, 303–13, with facsimile; Wettstein, in *L'art roman*, 10–11; "Les Exultet."

Mirabella Eclano, Archivio della Chiesa Collegiata, Exultet 2 (on Deposit in the Biblioteca Nazionale, Naples)

Exultet, s12½, made as a Franco-Roman continuation of Mirabella 1, Beneventan melody. Campania (Benevento?).

DESCRIPTION   Incomplete, three membranes, 230 × 1580 mm (680 + 695 + 205), average 688. A blackish-brown ink is used for text and notation. Beneventan script and type 3 notation with one red line (added after notation: cf. "tenebras") and another line pitched a third higher. Franco-Roman text, beginning with "Vere." There is one initial (VD) and two pictures, not reversed (Harrowing of Hell, Red Sea). The membranes are numbered 5–7 on paper labels pasted to their backs and were once attached to Mirabella 1 (they were made as a continuation).

DATE   s11½ (Lowe); s11/12 (Avery); Campania, s12 (Wettstein, in *L'art roman*, 12); after 1131 (Bertaux, *L'art*, 234n.1, derived from reference to "rex," who must be Roger, king of Sicily, crowned 1131); s12½ (Wettstein; Orofino, who suggests Beneventan origin).

HISTORY   The roll has a number of names added in much later hands; legible are "domni nostri malfridi principis tarantini" (Manfred, prince of Taranto, who assumed the title of king in 1258), "regis choradi secundi" (Conradino, king from 1254); in addition, the original king has been altered to emperor.

MANUFACTURE   Text rules are spaced on a module of 26 mm. The text gives the appearance of being crowded: there are no margins, and new periods do not start a new line; they have small capitals touched with red and yellow. There is no effort to finish a period on a membrane.

   Illustrations, not reversed, are drawn and decorated with red and yellow only. The pictures may have been painted first, or else text and illustration are simultaneous: the text and notation after the second picture skip around the picture, dividing the word "debi-tum" to accommodate the decoration. The appearance is generally sloppy and inartistic. The pictures feature "quelques bonshomme tous maculés de rouge" (Bertaux, *L'art*, 234).

   This roll was made as a Franco-Roman continuation of Mirabella 1. Its first membrane (now labeled Mirabella 5) was once attached to Mirabella 4; the scribe seems to have copied its opening notes from Mirabella 1. The new roll uses the quilisma and the melodic patterns of Mirabella 1 for the "Vere dignum" section, but these features are then abandoned.

BIBLIOGRAPHY   *Aggiornamento*, 441–42; Avery, *The Exultet Rolls*, 21, pl. 60; Guarini, "Osservazioni"; Kelly, *TBC*, 306–7; Lowe, *TBS*, 2:57–58; Orofino in *Exultet*, 313–18, with facsimile; Wettstein, in *L'art roman*, 12; "Les Exultet."

Montecassino, Biblioteca dell'Abbazia, Exultet 1

Exultet roll, incomplete, s11; Amalfi (?). Beneventan text and melody, illustration inverted.

DESCRIPTION   Fragmentary, one membrane ("inops potentie . . . gratiam predicemus"), 273 × 690 mm; slits are visible at one end only. Beneventan script and type 1 notation. A brown ink, much faded, is used for text and notation; the drawing is in a darker ink. Beneventan text, one surviving illustration (reversed).

DATE   s11 (Lowe; Bertaux; Orofino in *Exultet*); s11med (Wettstein; Belting, *Studien*, 185; Mayo, "Borders in Bari," 63).

HISTORY   Written in pencil on the back, probably in the hand of Montecassino librarian Piscicelli-Taeggi: "cav. Camera. Frammento d'exultet di S. Lorenzo del Piano" (*not* nel Piceno as in Bertaux or in Venturi, *Storia*). On the monastery, see Camera, *Memorie*, 1:184–85; Camera gives a partial report on a fifteenth-century inventory of the monastery of San Lorenzo, incuding several old liturgical books "de lictera longobarda," but there is no mention of an Exultet. Bertaux (225n4) reports: "Dom Latil a publié un fragment d'*Exultet* figurant, en une seule miniature, *Les Abeilles* et la scène de *la Nativité*. Ce fragment, qui remonte au XIe siècle, a été donné a Mgr Piscicelli-Taeggi par un grand collectionneur de parche-mins, Matteo Camera, l'historien d'Amalfi." The Amalfi provenance, proposed by Mayo and suggested in any case by the acquisition of the piece from an Amalfi historian, remains to be demonstrated. Avery, on Lowe's advice, proposes "Southeast Italy."

The membrane contains almost exclusively the praise of the bees. It might almost have been excised from a longer roll; however, we have no other evidence that the Beneventan text was ever treated in this way, though we do know that the related passage was often removed from the Franco-Roman text.

MANUFACTURE   The membrane is ruled (module of 32 mm) skipping the picture. Text periods are not started at the left of a new line: the whole text is written continuously. Initial letters for periods are infilled with red, green, yellow.

The picture is not well placed: a Nativity, coming after the period "Totus ac plenus in te es qui dum per uirginea uiscera" and inverted, is seen too late (it does have some bees, most added later, which are suitable for the text that follows). The picture is made (or at least colored) after the notation, judging from how the blue surrounding the star avoids the neumes.

BIBLIOGRAPHY   *Aggiornamento*, 449; Avery, *The Exultet Rolls*, 21, pl. 52–55; Bertaux, *L'art;* Orofino in *Exultet*, 175–78, with facsimile; Kelly, *TBC*, 308; Lowe, *TBS*, 2:93; Wettstein, *Sant'Angelo*, 146.

Montecassino, Biblioteca dell'Abbazia, Exultet 2

Exultet roll, Sorrento, 1105–18 (?). Franco-Roman text, Beneventan melody, illustrations inverted.

DESCRIPTION   Seven membranes, 260 × 4900 mm (735 + 780 + 720 + 620 + 620 + 655 + 825), average 708, glued and attached with parchment thongs that pass through slits in the membranes; rolled on a replacement umbilicus. A blackish ink, much rubbed, is used for text and notation; the drawing is in (the same?) black, and sometimes red. Beneventan script and type 2 notation. Franco-Roman text, with additions from the Beneventan version. Illustrations (a composite frontispiece of three scenes and sixteen pictures in the text) and the large monogram VD use gold, much of which has disappeared; illustrations are reversed. Much sets its text apart from Montecassino rolls; it does have some textual similarities to the Casanatense roll, but also many differences. Orofino (in *Exultet*) notes the similarity of many scenes, and of the illustrative plan in general, to the Montecassino series accompanying the Franco-Roman text (what Speciale (*Montecassino e la Riforma*, 85 and passim) calls the "reformed" series). Speciale is right to point out also the many unusual pictures, and unusual versions of usual scenes, in this roll.

DATE   ca. 1110 (Bertaux, 229); 1105–18: the roll names Bishop Barbatus (archbishop of Sorrento, 1105–after 1130) and Pope Paschal II (1099–1118).

HISTORY   The roll contains many proper names: Bishop Barbatus (archbishop of Sorrento, 1105–after 1130, according to Capasso, *Memorie storiche*, 58), Pope Paschal II (1099–1118), and Abbot Petrus of Saint Benedict's monastery; and there is a labeled picture of Bonifacius Diaconus presenting the roll to Christ and another indicating that a figure is "Iohannes [presbiter?]." Avery notes that the figure of Bonifacius could be a later addition, since Christ is not shown receiving a roll.

The bishop is not featured in the pictures of this roll: he is not present at the beginning, although he does stand by at "Dominus uobiscum." This document no doubt has a monastic, not a cathedral, destination. Bonifacius himself, however, is probably not a monk, since he is not so labeled ("diaconus [et monachus]").

There are several possible monasteries of Sorrento: Badia Sorrentina, San Salvatore; Santa Agrippina; San Giovanni Crisostomo (female); San Renato fuori città. Nobody knows how the roll came to Montecassino (if indeed it ever left). Sorrento, along with a long stretch of coast on that side of the peninsula, at least until 1083 was in the effective control of the prince of Capua (Tirelli, *Osservazioni*, cited in Masetti, *L'Exultet*, 125n.127).

MANUFACTURE   Membranes are ruled for text (module of 21 mm) with space left for pictures. The illustrations are drawn in before the text is written, to judge from the occasional overlapping, usually resulting from the use of a text rule as the bottom of a drawing. Text periods start at left and have colored one-line initials. Interior cola are marked with capitals in regular ink color. Occasional initials are linked (there is a witty set of Os).

Pictures are generally placed reversed preceding the text period to which they refer. Exceptions are the Nativity and the first picture of the Bees, which are right-side up; the VD monogram, which is preceded by the text it begins ("Vere quia dignum et iustum est per Christum dominum nostrum"); and a Resurrection (Marys at the Tomb), which comes after its period because it would not have fit on its membrane, even if the period were delayed to the next membrane. Instead, the text is placed at the end of the membrane and the picture begins the next.

A frontispiece includes the deacon on the ambo, Christ in Glory with turba of angels, then the beginning of the text. Perhaps there was something more: the beginning is mutilated; but the opening membrane is approximately full-length, so any additional scenes in this frontispiece series would have been on a further membrane, unlikely given the state of the present opening membrane.

BIBLIOGRAPHY   Avery, *The Exultet Rolls*, 22, pl. 62–71; Bertaux, *L'art*, 229–30; Caravita, *I codici*, 1:303–8; Kelly, *TBC*, 308; Lowe, *TBS*, 2:94; Orofino in *Exultet*, 377–92, with facsimile.

Paris, Bibliothèque Nationale, MS n. a. lat. 710

Exultet roll, s12½, Fondi. Franco-Roman text, Beneventan melody, pictures inverted.

DESCRIPTION   Eight (of nine?) membranes, 235–45 × 6120 mm (800 + 690 + 865 + 890 + 760 + 805 + 833 + 510), average 765. Begins incomplete with "Quapropter astantibus." Rolled on a (replacement) umbilicus. Brown ink, somewhat faded, is used for text and notation and may be the same ink used for drawing. Beneventan script and type 3 notation; Franco-Roman text. One initial (V) and thirteen pictures, reversed with respect to the text, survive. Like the roll in the

British Library, this Exultet does not include pictures of ecclesiastical and secular authorities. Some paintings are much retouched.

DATE   S12¼ (Załuska); ca. 1100 (Lowe); s12in (Avery); ca. 1136 (Speciale).

HISTORY   The text is clearly Montecassino, almost identical with the London and Barberini rolls. The melody is essentially that of Montecassino (it matches London, Barberini, Avezzano, Pisa at "Curuat imperia"). Though its melodic formula is not exactly that of Avezzano, it is applied to the text as in Avezzano in some solutions (see examples in chapter 4). Lowe says "written at Fondi but closely allied to Montecassino" (Avery, 23). The style of the initials is Desiderian, and the pictorial cycle is similar in many ways to the Cassinese roll in the British Library. The roll is made for a church dedicated to San Pietro, Fondi. Bishop Benedictus (1100–30) is named (Ferraro, *Memorie*, 231); cf. *Chron. mon. Cas.*, 4:518 (he was a monk of Montecassino). Consul Leo (1113–36) is also named. There was another Bishop Benedictus, 1193–99 (Ferraro, *Memorie*). Speciale notes that the cathedral of Fondi was given a new dedication to Saint Peter in 1136. The see of Fondi was a suffragan of Capua. The roll was among the possessions of the cathedral of Fondi in the fifteenth century (Fedele, "L' 'Exultet' ").

The roll was bought in Paris in 1900 (Załuska, 2); Parente ("Le miniature," 43) wrote in 1917 that the roll of the Badia di Fondi was sold, "pochi anni or sono," for more than 8,000 lire to the Bibiliothèque Nationale. The situation was described in more detail by Giovanni Conte-Colino:

> E a nostra conoscenza che i detti Padri Cassinesi nel restituirla dissero essere quella un tesoro. Bastò questo quei reverendi canonici allo scopo di tenerla maggiormente conservata l'avessero ceduta all'Abbadia di Monte Cassino, dopo averne ottenuta facoltà dal Santo Padre con rescritto della sacra congregazione del concilio in data 6 aprile 1900, erogandone il ricavato di L. 8500, in una artistica balaustrata in marmo, col relativo pavimento al presbitero ed alla chiesa. Di questa pergamena i Padri di quell'Abbadia ne riprodussero copia con litografia, ed illustrata la mandarono nell'ultima esposizione di Parigi, dove ottennero la medaglia d'oro. Ora su quel Cenobio la detta pergamena si sta pubblicando a dispensa, e noi ne abbiamo già viste le prime tre, in grande formato ed il costo di ogni dispenso è di Lire dieci. (*Storia di Fondi*, 176–77).

MANUFACTURE   A double rule runs down both sides of each membrane; text ruling is not very regular: the distance between lines is variable, average 25 mm. Space is left in the ruling for the pictures; the planning is not perfect, however, and occasional unused text lines appear in the spaces for illustrations; and occasional sheets (cf. membrane 4, after "deliciis meis") have room for several more lines of text. One wonders why this extra parchment was not cut off before assembling the roll: was it already assembled? This seems an awkward way to work. Elsewhere, some periods unfortunately have to carry over to the start of the next membrane ("redimi/profuisset"). Periods often begin, with a small letter, in the middle of a line: initials are guaranteed only when starting again after pictures. Interior cola are marked with colored letters, as in Avezzano. The initials are painted after the notation is entered: cf. the notation of "A vitiis," which is avoided by an initial H.

Pictures are placed very regularly, inverted before their period. Załuska believes they are the work of at least two artists; Speciale ("Spigolature") says that two artists alternate by membrane. The pictures may have been painted, or at least sketched, before the writing was done; this might explain the situation for the membrane in which two text periods are crowded between the Red Sea and the Crucifixion and the situation elsewhere where empty parchment results from leaving text lines blank.

BIBLIOGRAPHY   *Aggiornamento*, 453–54; Avery, *The Exultet Rolls* 29–30, pl. 82–97; Bertaux, *L'art*, 228–29; Kelly, *TBC*, 310; Lowe, *TBS*, 2:116; Speciale in *Exultet*, 273–89, with facsimile; Załuska in Avril, *Dix siècles*, 20.

Pisa, Capitolo del Duomo, Exultet 1

Exultet roll, s11, Pisa. Ordinary minuscule script, Franco-Roman text, melody unrelated to Beneventan; two drawings at top, not reversed.

DESCRIPTION   Six membranes, 210–226 × 2820 mm (395 + 523 + 447 + 550 + 460 + 445), average 470. Membranes are ruled throughout and written in an ordinary minuscule with central Italian notation without lines or clefs. A brown ink is used for text and with a smaller pen for notation. Franco-Roman text; the melody for the opening portion is not related to that of southern Italy; the second portion is sung to a preface tone. The text, close to that of the Roman-German Pontifical, especially with its omission of the praise of the bees, is not derived from that of the Beneventan Exultet roll of Pisa. Two drawings (Crucifixion and Deposition) on the much-worn opening membrane are now almost invisible; this opening membrane, whose pictures have the remains of gold leaf, but no further evidence of color, might be an addition to the roll.

DATE   s10 (Bertaux, *L'art*, 237); s11 (Lowe, as reported by Avery); s11med (Avery); s12 at latest (Garzelli, citing others; Masetti, "L'Exultet"); s12½ (Masetti in *Exultet*).

HISTORY   The roll seems to have been always in Pisa; it has belonged to the cathedral *ab antiquo* (Masetti in *Exultet*). It is likely a practical version, for use by the deacon, of the luxury version known in Pisa through the roll Pisa 2, whose Beneventan script, interruptions from pictures, and inappropriate text (praise of the bees; additions from the Beneventan Exultet) made it arguably theologically unsuitable and difficult to use. Masetti points out that the two drawings on this roll would complete a christological cycle when combined with the frontispiece of Pisa 2.

MANUFACTURE   Membranes are regularly ruled (module of 18 mm), with double vertical rules for the margins. Initials for E and V are red; initials beginning text periods are touched with green. The same green was used to color the parchment strips that passed through slits to attach the membranes.

BIBLIOGRAPHY   *Aggiornamento*, 460; *Catalogo del Museo* (1906), 52; Avery, *The Exultet Rolls*, pl. 81; Garzelli, "La deposizione"; Masetti in *Exultet*, 457–64, with facsimile; Masetti, *L'Exultet*, 21 and 27n.28.

Pisa, Capitolo del Duomo, Exultet 2

Exultet roll, s11, made at Montecassino. Franco-Roman text, Beneventan melody, pictures inverted.

DESCRIPTION   Twelve (of original thirteen) membranes, c280 × 9000 mm, average 692; Avery's measurements of lengths: 745 + 720 + 810 + 900 + 730 + 710 + 790 + 820 + 730 + 740 + 720 + 540 (Masetti's lengths are slightly different: 750 + 730 + 815 + 890 + 725 + 690 + 780 + 840 + 730 + 750 + 720 + 560), average 765, omitting the last membrane. A light brown ink, much faded, is used for text and notation and may be the same ink as that of the drawings. Franco-Roman text with additions from Beneventan and Gelasian texts (see Appendix 2 and p. 000), Beneventan script, and type 2 notation. At least one membrane, containing the text "Hec sunt enim" through "sociat sanctitati," is missing; much use of gold. Illustrations are reversed; there is a series of twelve frontispiece paintings (a Christ in Glory preceding eleven chronologically arranged scenes from the life of Christ); then follow a painting of the deacon on the ambo, the first of fifteen illustrations (of varying sizes) that decorate the text, along with two large initial letters and forty-seven smaller initials. There might have been further material at the head of the roll, to judge from the incomplete state of preservation.

DATE   s11med; 1059–71 (Masetti, *L'Exultet*); Masetii's dating centers on the "il." provided for the bishop's name, which she proposes may have been Ildebrandus of Capua; however, the "il." is almost certainly an abbreviation for "ille," an invitation to supply the name, as is done in this roll also for the pope and in many other rolls.

HISTORY   No abbot is mentioned in the commemorations: an episcopal destination seems clear. Masetti points out that the pallium is archiepiscopal. The text mentions a duke. In the eighteenth century, the roll was displayed on the anniversary of the dedication of the cathedral (Martini, *Appendix ad Theatrum*, cited Masetti, in "L'Exultet," 217–18n.1).

The roll is in the hand of a Montecassino scribe (I am grateful to Francis Newton for his opinion on this; his full description will appear in his forthcoming study of the scriptorium of Montecassino); Cavallo and Masetti have detected Puglian influences in the large initials and in the writing. The roll was doubtless manufactured at Montecassino before the disastrous expedition of the 1160s during which the Pisans attacked the twelve monks under Aldemarius (who had been Leo Marsicanus's novice-master). The monks had been sent by Desiderius to Corsica; the Pisans stole everything they had, doubtless including the roll that the Pisans still hold. *Chron. mon. Cas.*, III, 21, 387–88, describes the expedition of c1063: the roll was for an abbot of a new cell of Montecassino, or possibly for the bishop, or for Bareso I, king of Sardinia. Masetti sees it as a princely or episcopal commission, for the cathedral (of Capua), perhaps by the new Norman conqueror Richard Quarrel (*L'Exultet*, 117–18). Masetti (*L'Exultet*, 115) says it may have been made for Ildebrandus, archbishop of Capua (ca. 1059–71). Her argument from "il." in the text is not convincing, particularly as the notator does not give the notation for "Ildebrandus," but for "ille" (or some other two-syllable word using a liquescent on the first syllable). There is no close textual relation to the roll now in Capua.

MANUFACTURE   Groups of four prickings arranged in a lozenge are visible in both side margins; they may have served to hold the membranes flat, for manufacture or display. The ruling (module of 28 mm) leaves space for pictures. The text and notation are evidently entered first. The paintings take advantage of incomplete lines of text to use floors of different heights, and the column surmounted by an eagle does not use all the space allotted to it. The notation must have come before the paintings: the way the notes of "Deo gratias" are on either side of the deacon's head cannot be fortuitous; and surely the V of "Vere quia dignum" would have gone higher had the notation not been there.

The "Sacrificium uespertinum" picture, however, looks as though it is oriented to the ruled line, not the text. The coloring avoids the text, but the drawing appears related to the line, forgetting that the descenders of the text will cause trouble with stoles and garments at the bottom of the picture; in this case it looks as though ruling was followed by drawing as part of the original layout.

The borders were decorated after the text was written, and each border was painted separately: they are different on each membrane and make no attempt to join patterns from one membrane to the next. The membranes were assembled into a roll as a last step. But at least one initial overlaps the border ("Cum sit," see also the L of "Letetur et mater"), so perhaps these initals were made after the border. The pictures in the frontispiece are separated by gold horizontal borders, which together with the vertical borders make frames for each picture; they also disguise the joints between membranes. But beginning with the text of the Exultet on membrane 4, there are no more horizontal borders, the pictures being placed on blank spaces left between lines of text.

This roll has a long frontispiece, with scenes from the life of Christ; they likely have a liturgical inspiration, since among other subjects they portray the scenes described in the Lenten Gospels. This series, whose pictures are reversed with respect to the text to follow, is nevertheless intended to be read with the outermost picture last; that is, unrolled like a frontispiece and read from the top down (or from the center of the roll toward the outside: the opposite way from the direction of the Exultet to follow). The other pictures go in the order of the text, with the outermost first.

All the illuminations in the text are placed, reversed, after their relevant periods, except for the column that goes alongside the period it illustrates and thus is revealed mostly after the word "columne" has been said.

BIBLIOGRAPHY   Avery, *The Exultet Rolls*, 24–26, pl. 82–97; *Catalogo del Museo* (1906), 43–44; Kelly, *TBC*, 310; Lowe, *TBS*, 2:119; Masetti, *L'Exultet;* Masetti in *Exultet*, 151–74, with facsimile; Wettstein, "Un rouleau campanien."

Pisa, Capitolo del Duomo, Exultet 3

Exultet roll, Pisa, s13; Franco-Roman text, Gothic script, pictures reversed.

DATE   ca. 1300 (Bertaux, *L'art,* 238); s13 (*Catalogo del Museo;* Masetti, "L'Exultet"); s13ex (Avery); 1240–60 (Masetti in *Exultet*).

DESCRIPTION   Six membranes, 450 × 6200 mm (1000 + 610 + 740 + 770 + 870 + 700 + 750 + 790), average 779, now separated. Gothic script, central Italian musical notation on four lines, using colored clef lines. Franco-Roman text and a non-Beneventan melody, like that of Pisa 1, concluding with the Roman preface tone. The text is very close to that of Pisa 1. A decorative border, drawn with the same ink as the script, begins on the short dimension of the first membrane and continues down both sides, meeting again at the end of the roll. There are ten pictures, inverted.

HISTORY   Made for and used at the Cathedral of Pisa (Masetti), the pictorial series does not depend directly on either of the other two rolls at Pisa. The textual tradition is nearer to that of the Exultet 1, and to other Tuscan texts, than to the Beneventan Exultet roll at Pisa.

MANUFACTURE   Membranes are ruled leaving space for pictures; regularly spaced rules close together are used in groups of six, two for text and four for notation. The pictures, inverted, generally come before their periods. The roll was evidently assembled before being illustrated, given that certain illustrations overlap joints.

BIBLIOGRAPHY   *Aggiornamento*, 460–61; Avery, *The Exultet Rolls*, 26–27, plates 98–103; *Catalogo del Museo* (1906), 51; Bertaux, *L'art*, 237–38; Masetti in *Exultet*, 465–75, with facsimile; Masetti, "L'Exultet."

Rome, Biblioteca Casanatense, MS 724 (B I 13) III

Exultet roll, s12, Benevento. Franco-Roman text, Beneventan melody, pictures inverted.

DESCRIPTION   Ten membranes, 230 × 6855 mm (900 + 600 + 700 + 680 + 690 + 600 + 960 + 890 + 495 + 340; the last section has a trapeziodal form), average 753. A brown ink, much rubbed, is used for text; the notation is written in a lighter ink. The drawing, with a fine pen, is made with a brown ink similar to that of the text. Beneventan script and type 2 notation. The notation of "Dominus uobiscum . . . Vere quia dignum et iustum est" is in a different hand and an earlier style of notation using the quilisma. Franco-Roman text. There is much wear on the outer portion of the roll. There are fifteen pictures (reversed) and two large initials. The illustrative cycle is derived from that in Vat. lat. 9820 and is used also in the Salerno Exultet: however, the textual tradition here is not that of Vat. lat. 9820 (which originally had Beneventan text) or that of its upper script (Salerno has essentially no text). Many details of decoration, especially in the large initials, reflect the post-1071 style of Montecassino, combining the golden interlaces of Regensburg with the traditional Cassinese initials.

DATE   s12 (authorities generally agree).

HISTORY   Benevento? The facts that the roll was attached to two early rolls of Benevento and that the roll stands in the iconographical tradition of Benevento suggest the origin; Brenk (in *Exultet*, 324) suggests that the attention to details of the archbishop's vesture makes sense in the context of a commission from such a figure, probably an archbishop of Benevento. The roll was in the collection of Cardinal Casanate (d. 1700), who left it to the Dominicans of Santa Maria sopra

Minerva, and it has always been in that collection, now housed in the Biblioteca Casanatense. The roll was seen there by Mabillon and Ciampini; it was still rolled in 1770 or 1775 when Gerbert saw it, but was displayed flat in 1814 to Seroux D'Agincourt. The roll was formerly attached to two other important rolls of Benevento: Casanatense 724 I (pontifical, 957–69) and Casanatense 724 II (benedictional of Archbishop Landolphus, written 969–82). On these, see especially Belting (*Malerei*, 144–66).

MANUFACTURE   Double vertical rules on each side define the border. The text ruling (module of 36 mm) skips over the illustrations, except for the bees, which is ruled under. The first two membranes, consisting only of pictures and decorative letters, are not ruled across at all; the third, which has two pictures, is also not ruled, and its text is as a result not well aligned. At the fourth membrane begin the text rules, which skip space for pictures. But the fifth membrane, consisting mostly of pictures with the elaborate "Vere dignum," is also not ruled at all.

The roll is assembled, after the borders are painted, by sewing with thread or string, to judge from the small surviving holes.

Borders and text lines are ruled, and the borders painted, before writing: compare "in quibus uerus ille agnus occiditur," where the writing extends into the border; writing and notation are produced before the illustrations, to judge from the "Tellus," which expands into space ruled for the scribe but left unused. (Writing and illustration may have proceeded in a single campaign.)

Text periods are correct, but not particularly well planned. Initials are one-line, so not much planning is required. In the second part, space is more at a premium: there are long stretches of text in which paragraphs run on without starting new at left.

Horizontal borders, at the tops of pictures only, divide pictures from text. Pictures are inverted and generally come before the relevant period, in the normal manner. The Red Sea, however, is attached to the Crucifixion and is at the wrong place in the text; this makes another long series of pictures: Vere; Crucifixion; Red Sea, without much text (two of these pictures—the Crucifixion and the Red Sea—are not part of the cycle transmitted by Vat. lat. 9820). The Harrowing of Hell in the first series is also not at the place where it might illustrate the text.

The pictures are essentially the series of Vat. lat. 9820, with a few exceptions; the same series of pictures appears also in the Salerno roll. It must be remembered, however, that the process of inverting the pictures makes for a considerable difference in appearance. Though the picture may come in the same order, the process of inverting each picture at its place means that the bottom, for example, of each picture is not adjacent to the same picture as in a series not inverted. The process of inverting this series of pictures requires planning and skill, particularly since it involves the addition of new pictures for the Roman text. The scribe is solving these problems as the roll is manufactured (cf. Mirabella 1, whose scribe faces similar problems).

The "Mater ecclesia" here is a different composition from that found in 9820 and Salerno; this roll, like Salerno, includes an illustration of the Virgin and child, appropriate for the Franco-Roman text ("sicut sancta concepit"), but not for the Beneventan. Two subjects that appear in all three rolls have different compositions in each: (1) the liturgical subject involving the deacon that appears at "Oramus te domine ut cereus iste" (for the Roman text) or "Vt superne benedictione"; (2) the commemoration of secular rulers.

The Casanatense roll has a series of frontispiece paintings, derived from the same illustrative cycle whose oldest (but not original) exemplar is Vat. lat. 9820. The series, beginning with the outside end of the roll: (1) a picture of the bishop handing the roll to the deacon; there follow a series of scenes related increasingly to the Exultet itself: (2) first a frontispiece painting of the Agnus Dei amid Evangelist symbols; (3) the "Angelica turba celorum"; (4) a Harrowing of Hell (not much related to the Exultet as a whole, or to any nearby text, but suitable in general to the period between Good Friday and Easter); (5) a depiction of the lighting of the candle; and, finally, (6) the initial E, which begins the text. The Salerno roll has essentially the same series, but with some additional complexities discussed there.

Apparently the scribe worked from a text that omitted the praise of the bees: he writes "Apis mater eduxit. O uere beata nox que expoliauit Egyptios ditauit Hebreos." This last sentence, which skips over the passage in question, is canceled with "uacat," followed by an illustration and the full text of the praise of the bees. The continuation, "O uere beata," is repeated at its place; the second time it has different music, because it does not end the period. This must mean that the notator is not copying a model at least for the music, but is adjusting the music to the text as he sees it laid out.

BIBLIOGRAPHY *Aggiornamento*, 454–55; Avery, *The Exultet Rolls*, 29–30, pl. 118–129; Brenk in *Exultet*, 319–39, with facsimile; Kelly, *TBC*, 310; Langlois, "Le rouleau"; Lowe, *TBS*, 2:123; Wettstein, *Sant'Angelo*, 141–42.

Salerno, Museo Diocesano, Exultet

Exultet roll, s13, Salerno; contains almost exclusively pictures, based on the Benevento series.

DESCRIPTION Eleven folios, now separated, 464–78 × 8395 mm (345 + 762 + 818 + 815 + 832 + 840 + 739 + 824 + 803 + 813 + 804), average 80.5 (Carucci's measurements; they differ somewhat from Avery's and d'Aniello's). One piece, incomplete, contains the opening portion of the text, in capital letters, and the initial E. All the other membranes, evidently complete, have only illustrations (of which there are eighteen, along with the monogram VD), each within a painted border. This compass-drawn border, of rhomboids inscribed within circles, is a simplified version of the border of the Casanatense Exultet. Membranes generally contain two illustrations, except for the scene of the Crucifixion, double-sized, which occupies an entire membrane. The restoration of 1989 has removed a portion of the substantial later overpainting.

These pictures are the same cycle as that which appears in Vat. lat. 9820 and the Casanatense Exultet, consisting of a series of frontispiece paintings and illustrations placed throughout the text of the Exultet. Within their decorative borders, pictures are painted, probably by a single artist, in a rich blue ground, usually surrounded by a border of a green now faded.

Was this roll originally texted and later abbreviated to remove the full text? Carucci believes the roll never bore more than the opening text it now contains; d'Aniello thinks the texted portions have been removed (*Exultet*, 395), based on what she sees as a reorganization of the joints between membranes. I cannot agree:

if the roll had originally been texted, the placement of pictures would be highly unusual and would bear little relationship to the text. The pictures, being painted two to a membrane, cannot have had text between members of those pairs ("Mater ecclesia" and "Fratres karissimi," spiritual and temporal authorities, for example); the fact that pairs of pictures that illustrate different places in the text are painted adjacent on the same membrane suggests at least that the pictures are not intended for placement within the sequence of the text as they are placed in the Vatican and Casanatense rolls.

DATE   s13ex (Avery; Ladner; Carucci) s13½ (Toesca); s12 (Capone); s13med (d'Aniello).

HISTORY   Painted at Benevento, says Carrucci; perhaps commissioned by Archbishop Nicola d'Aiello of Salerno. D'Aniello points out the similarity of the border to that used in an eleventh-century series of frescoes recently recovered in the lower church of Santa Maria della Lama, Salerno. The similarity of the illustrations here with the cycle from Benevento is unquestioned.

Rohault de Fleury (*La messe*, 6:92) reports the roll still in use (1888). It was restored in 1918 by Nestore Leoni, at which time the membranes, held together with threads, were separated. A 1917 photograph on display in the Museo Diocesano and reproduced in Cavallo and d'Aniello (*L'Exultet di Salerno*, 31–35) shows the roll in its state before restoration. The pictures are arranged so as to appear in essentially the same order as in the Casanatense roll.

The Exultet is preserved in two fifteenth-century missals of Salerno, in which the Beneventan text is provided with a melody of considerable exuberance. The melody has been discussed in chapter 4, and the missals are described below. It is not easy to explain how a roll produced in the thirteenth century and illustrating the Franco-Roman text (this roll includes scenes, including that of the Red Sea, not related to the Beneventan text) should be succeeded by missals of the fifteenth century that revert to the Beneventan text, long superseded everywhere else. Perhaps there was a brief change to the Franco-Roman text and a return to the Beneventan. Carucci (58 and n1) reports that the Beneventan text is indicated also in a Salerno pontifical of the end of the thirteenth century. It is possible that the roll was meant for possession, even for display, but was made elsewhere, and the particular practices of Salerno were not kept clearly in mind. More likely is that the two texts were viewed as alternatives.

MANUFACTURE   Pictures are based on the cycle that appears also in Vat. lat. 9820 and Casanatense. However, in both 9820 and Casanatense, there is an extensive headpiece, including bishop; Lamb with evangelists; "Turba celorum"; a Harrowing scene ("Regis victoria"); and the lighting of the candle, before the initial E that begins the text. In Salerno, however, the letter E, on a separate membrane, cannot have come where it does in the other rolls, since the lighting of the candle and the "Tellus" picture are painted on the same membrane with no separation: between these comes the E in the other two rolls.

Is this roll inverted? Mayo ("Borders in Bari," 35n11) says not, that inversion was rejected in making this roll; but in fact the pictures read from the bottom upward, successive pictures placed above those that precede: this is true only of rolls with pictures inverted.

The V of "Vere dignum" is turned the other way with respect to the illustrations themselves—it is oriented, that is, for a reader of a roll with pictures reversed, in which the letters must nevertheless retain their reading orientation. The figure of Christ, however, is also oriented for the reader (even though there is no text). These pictures, therefore, even without their text, represent a roll with the pictures reversed. The Casanatense roll is not the model, for in the Casanatense roll the figure of Christ is reversed also, to be seen the other way. There would be no reason for the Salerno artist, if he were working from a document like the Casanatense roll, to invert the figure again. His model must have been a cycle with reversed pictures, but with the figure in the letter V retaining its textwise orientation: a model like the reordered series in 9820 (though the model cannot be 9820 itself, in either of its forms). This is a summary of the pictorial cycle, as it is applied in rolls with pictures reversed (as in Casanatense). Perhaps it is an attempt to work out the problems that arise when reversing the illustrations in a non-inverted model such as Vat. lat. 9820. Was this roll really intended for liturgical use? If an "illustrative cycle" exists by itself, this is it.

Various problems and divergences in the placement of pictures arise when this roll is compared to the others to which its illustrations are related. One membrane, which now contains a "maiestas domini" and a portrait of a ruler (Carucci: "magnis populorum vocibus"), interrupts the series as found in the other two documents (assuming its position in the 1917 state of the roll is original—but there is no less awkward place for this membrane). The Christ in majesty, in fact, is the upper part of the "Terra" illustration as found in the other two rolls, but here it is separated and made into a distinct illustration: this may have caused the artist to relate it to the picture with a crowned figure, which is not derived from any of the surviving illustrations in this cycle. It is not evidently a misplaced commemoration of rulers, since such a picture appears at its place later in the Salerno roll.

Like the Casanatense roll, Salerno includes two pictures (Red Sea and Crucifixion) that are not in Vat. lat. 9820. However, the Salerno order is not that of Casanatense, which is Vere, Crucifixion, Red Sea. In Salerno, the Vere is followed by the Red Sea on the same membrane, which is preceded by the Crucifixion. Even if the Crucifixion in the 1917 Salerno arrangement is not original, it is still not possible for the Crucifixion to have come at its Casanatense (and Mass book) place after the "Vere dignum."

BIBLIOGRAPHY *Aggiornamento*, 455–56; Avery, *The Exultet Rolls*, 36–37, pl. 153–163; Bertaux, *L'art*, 230–31; Capone, *Il duomo*, 1:165–76; Cavallo and d'Aniello, *L'Exultet di Salerno*; Carucci, *Il rotolo*; d'Aniello in *Exultet*, 393–407, with facsimile; Schlumberger, "Les rouleaux"; Rohault de Fleury (*La messe*, 6: pl. 474) published a series of drawings by Aubin Louis Millin of the pictures in this roll as being an Exultet roll from Policastro. See Avery, 44.

Troia, Archivio Capitolare, Exultet 1

Exultet roll, s11med, Troia; Beneventan text and melody, illustrations not inverted.

DESCRIPTION   Five membranes, ca. 200 × 2640 mm (659 + 678 + 610 + 651 + 145) (Magistrale), average 650; rolled on a replacement umbilicus. The parchment strips joining membranes are modern. A brownish-black ink is used for text and notation and seems also to be used for highlights and outlines in the drawings, which, however, are drawn in a lighter brown ink. Beneventan script, type 1 notation. Beneventan text; illustrations are oriented in the same direction as the text. When Avery examined it, the roll was attached to the end of Troia 2; see her plate 164. The membranes are signed on the back by Raffaele Petrilli and Antonio Maria Falcone, archivist and canon theologian, respectively, of Troia in 1902.

DATE   s11med (Cavallo, 136; Magistrale); s11½ (Lowe); Magistrale points out that Troia acknowledged the rule as *comes* of Robert Guiscard in 1066 and suggests that the *imperator* invoked in the roll is the emperor of Byzantium, the roll antedating 1066.

HISTORY   Apparently the roll never left Troia. All the bishops of late eleventh-century Troia were Benedictines, according to Bambacegno (*Troia*). The bishops of Troia were suffragans of Benevento in 1058; by 1066 the diocese was subject directly to the Holy See (Pratesi, "Note di diplomatica," 28 and n3). The cathedral was built in the late eleventh century; this roll may thus antedate the present cathedral and its magnificent ambo.

MANUFACTURE   Ruling (module of 15 mm) is generally made leaving spaces for pictures. Text is written in periods, each period beginning a new line with a one-line initial infilled with red. No particular care is taken to finish a period on a single membrane. The notation is added last, and the space provided for it is not entirely adequate. A neume overlaps, and is on top of, the "Vere quia dignum" initial.
    The first membrane is ruled only where needed: space is left for illustrations; however, the picture preceding the text of Exultet overlaps two rules that must have been intended for the start of the text. The illustration was evidently made, or at least drawn, before the text continued, when it was seen that the picture would descend farther down the page than planned when the membrane was ruled. Then "Exultet" was written, not where it was planned, but where it could now start. (This is not in agreement with Magistrale, in *Exultet*, 180, who says the illustration is made after the writing.) The letter V, however, is painted over regular rules, as is the picture of the bees (which, in fact, goes over a joint). "Saluum fac," Pope, and Emperor, all on one membrane, are all in unruled spaces, so planning for pictures had to take the length of text and size of picture into account. All of these pictures come immediately before the text that describes them. This is standard for books: the text becomes a caption under the picture.

BIBLIOGRAPHY   *Aggiornamento*, 434; Avery, "A Manuscript from Troia"; Avery, *The Exultet Rolls*, 37, pl. 164–167; Cavallo, *Rotoli*, 135–38, tav. 28–35; Kelly, *TBC*, 312; Lowe, *TBS*, 2:141; Magistrale in *Exultet*, 179–89, with facsimile.

Troia, Archivio Capitolare, Exultet 2

Exultet roll, incomplete, s12½, Troia. Beneventan text and melody, pictures reversed.

DESCRIPTION   Badly preserved, incomplete, three membranes, ca. 200 × ca. 1905 mm (616 + 965 + 327) (Magistrale). Beneventan script and type 3 notation with one red line. Beneventan text (incomplete), illustrations inverted. There are six surviving illustrations, of which one ("Mater ecclesia"?) is very incomplete and one (a horseman) is probably a later addition to the end. The three surviving pieces of the roll were attached to Troia 1 until its recent restoration. The pieces are now glued together and attached to a (probably original) umbilicus of wood. The first membrane is signed on the back by Raffaele Petrilli and Antonio Maria Falcone, archivist and canon theologian, respectively, of Troia in 1902.

DATE   s12¼ (Cavallo, 158); after 1130 (coronation of Roger II of Sicily: Ladner, "The 'Portraits,' " 188); perhaps after 1066, coronation of Robert Guiscard (*Aggiornamento*); s12in (Lowe; Avery); s12½ (Magistrale).

HISTORY   This roll may have been made at Troia to improve on the first roll in the matter of musical notation or out of a desire for inverted pictures. The melody, somewhat more elaborated than that of Troia 1, might also create a desire for a new roll. It is possible that this is a portion of a roll discarded when a change was made to a Franco-Roman text. If so, the lost opening may have been used elsewhere. Magistrale (*Exultet*, 192) mentions the time of Bishop Guglielmo II (1106–41), who added the splendid bronze doors to the cathedral and who from 1108 to 1137 made an annual gift of books to the cathedral.

MANUFACTURE   The membranes are ruled (irregularly, maximum module of 25 mm), leaving space for illustrations. There do not appear to be rules guiding the ornamental borders. Text periods do not begin a new line and are not particularly well planned. One period goes from one membrane to another and is split by a decorative border that hides the joint. The membranes were painted, at least their borders, before being joined.

The red line orienting the notation is added, freehand, after the notation itself (the line can be seen making adjustments), but it crosses the initials often, but not always (so they must have been present when the line was added). The pictures were put in after the notation (they avoid red lines or have the figures almost stand on them). This may explain the confusion in the last three pictures: the illustrator is no longer thinking about the text and its music.

Two pictures are placed immediately before their period: bees (before "Apis ceteris"), people (before "Saluum fac"). But most are oddly placed. Both ruler pictures are in puzzling places: the picture of Christ crowning secular rulers comes long after its place in the text, two other pictures that should precede it actually coming later. A picture of the bishop comes after the period referring to the clergy (there is no pope in the picture), at the place where secular rulers ought perhaps to appear. And there is the misplaced Ecclesia (or whatever it was) at the beginning of the roll, and the very odd hanged man preceding "O ammirandus apum feruor" (Cavallo, 159, followed by Magistrale, says it is the "Castigo di Giuda"; Avery, 38, had said it originally "doubtless represented a man working around a tree or shrub," later reworked). The final picture, of a horseman, must be a later addition; it occupies the remaining space at the end of the roll and is turned the other way from the other illustrations.

Does this unusual roll result from a first attempt to reverse pictures, based on Troia 1, which is not reversed? The last three pictures, and indeed the bees, are very likely based on Troia 1. But the last three have their order confused: it must be that the spaces for the illustrations were left to be filled in, and that they were put in the wrong holes. The result was not corrected so that pictures correspond to text; one wonders whether such correspondence was of great importance.

BIBLIOGRAPHY   *Aggiornamento,* 434–45; Avery, *The Exultet Rolls,* 37–38, pl. 168–170; Cavallo, *Rotoli,* 157–59, tav. 36–41; Kelly, *TBC,* 313; Lowe, *TBS,* 2:141; Magistrale in *Exultet,* 191–99, with facsimile.

Troia, Archivio Capitolare, Exultet 3

Exultet roll, s12, Troia. Franco-Roman text; Beneventan melody for the prologue, the Roman preface tone for the preface. The highly original illustrative cycle is not inverted.

DESCRIPTION   Incomplete at beginning, eight membranes, ca. 250 × 6510 mm (692 + 865 + 865 + 812 + 874 + 822 + 875 + 848) (Cavallo), average 852. The roll is wound around, but not attached to, an umbilicus probably not original; the membranes are glued together and have holes suggesting that they were once also attached with string. Joints have a simple painted border disguising the overlap. The membranes are numbered and signed on their backs by Raffaele Petrilli and Antonio Maria Falcone, archivist and canon theologian, respectively, of Troia in 1902. Beneventan script and type 4 Beneventan notation (s13?), on three dry-point staff lines; colored clef lines added. Franco-Roman text. The Beneventan melody is used for the prologue and the Roman preface tone for the preface. Two later alterations were made in the music: (1) the prologue was replaced with the "Roman" Exultet tone; (2) some beginnings of periods in the second portions were rewritten to be more musically elaborate. Illustrations, including many unusual scenes, are not inverted; there is a substantial frontispiece of at least nine pictures with scenes of the appearances of Christ after the Resurrection; twenty-five pictures appear in the course of the text, and there are two large decorated initials.

DATE   s12²⁄₂ (Cavallo; Magistrale); s12 (Lowe)

HISTORY   The text has a number of unique variants; like the illustration cycle here, this is a product of local inspiration. This is the only Exultet roll with the "Norman finale" of the text (used also in Naples VI G 34: see chap. 3). Provenance: Troia (the text and music are closely related to Naples VI G 34, also from Troia; this roll is probably earlier). The writing looks Cassinese, as do some decoration and the illuminated letters. But the roll is mostly notable for its originality. Drawings of the illustrations are Naples I B 49.

MANUFACTURE   The roll seems to be the work of a single scribe/artist, who generally draws in the pictures before writing the text, but not without careful estimate of the length of text lines. Membranes are generally ruled (irregularly, module varying between 20 and 33 mm), leaving space for pictures. Text periods begin a new line only when they follow an illustration. Periods begin with one-line capitals generally alternating red and blue, sometimes placed on a gold ground. Some periods are interrupted for illustration, for example after "mestis letitiam," where a portion of text was erased so that it could be placed after the illustration.

The last membrane is unusual in its preparation. It appears to be ruled at the top (where there is no writing), and then a space is left, and then ruling begins again. Apparently, it was intended to have one text period or a portion of one ("Precamur ergo . . .": the period includes clergy, people, pope, bishop, and king: a lot to illustrate), followed by an illustration and a continuation of text. Instead, the membrane begins directly with the illustration (clergy, people, pope, bishop, king); but the picture takes up too much space, and the writing begins one line lower than planned. Cavallo (*Rotoli*, 177) points out further evidence that the pictures are drawn before the text is written. And yet the writing had to have been imagined, or sketched in, because illustrations often use the space left at the top by incomplete lines of text.

Troia 3 has a series of frontispiece paintings, unfortunately incomplete, including several Resurrection scenes. Cavallo (*Rotoli*, 231–32 and 236nn.51–52) points out certain similarity in these scenes with "peregrinus" plays in which many of these scenes are enacted. These scenes are right-side up, not intended for display from the ambo. The series is incomplete at its beginning and might have had a whole life of Christ. But probably only a little is missing (15 cm) unless a whole membrane now lost was used; this is unlikely, however, given the wear on the present first membrane. There are really two frontispieces in Troia 3, for, after the series of six (or more) Resurrection scenes, there follows a group of three frontispiece paintings related to the Exultet itself, preceding the initial E. Perhaps the first membrane is a sort of prelude to the frontispiece and perhaps had a separate purpose. See p. 000.

BIBLIOGRAPHY *Aggiornamento*, 435–36; Avery, *The Exultet Rolls*, 38–40, pl. 171–180; Cavallo, *Rotoli*, 175–85, tav. 42–61; Kelly, *TBC*, 313; Lowe, *TBS*, 2:141; Magistrale in *Exultet*, 423–43, with facsimile; Whitehill, "A Twelfth-Century Exultet Roll."

Vatican City, Biblioteca Apostolica Vaticana, MS Barb. lat. 592

Exultet roll, incomplete; s11ex, Montecassino; Franco-Roman text, Beneventan melody, pictures inverted.

DESCRIPTION Incomplete, five membranes (of original eight?), numbered on labels pasted to the backs, 280 × 3780 mm (750 + 830 + 820 + 640 + 745), average 835–40, judging from the one full membrane (no. 2) remaining. The missing first membrane, now lost, was published in facsimile by Gerbert, *De cantu* (table 4), whose plate is reproduced by Avery (in *Exultet*), Speciale (*Montecassino e la riforma*, fig. 1), and others. The ink of the text and music, dark brown and faded where the stroke is wide, is the same color as the ink of the drawing (which, however, is not faded). Franco-Roman text, Beneventan script, and type 3 notation. Illustrations are inverted.

There are several later alterations in the roll, which conceivably were undertaken simultaneously as a sort of renewal. These alterations include (1) Latin labels, in red ink, of major subjects in the pictures ("Tellus"; "Turba angelorum"; "Populus"; etc.); (2) commentaries in old Italian (late thirteenth century), describing the subjects of the pictures (these are transcribed by Speciale in *Exultet*, 236–38; see also Baldelli, "Le 'ystorie' "); (3) the repainting of almost all of the pictures; (4) the addition of tiny neumes above certain portions of the text, usually the beginnings of periods. Where they can be read, they seem to represent a more elaborate melody than that provided by the original notator. For transcriptions of some of these, see Example 15. Added music appears over the following passages: Membrane 1: *Gaudeat . . . totius/Letetur.* Membrane 2: *Huius . . ./Sed iam . . ./Alitur.* Membrane 3: *Hec igitur . . ./Hec nox est . . ./Hec nox est. . ./Nichil . . ./O uere . . ./O certe . . ./O beata . . ./Hec nox est de qua . . .* Membrane 4: *O uere mirabilis . . .* Membrane 5: *. . . filium tuum . . .*

The ten surviving pictures are reversed with respect to the text. The two major initials are lost (though the first appears in Gerbert's plate). The ends of membranes with slits allowing binding-thongs to pass have been cut away.

DATE   ca. 1100 (Seroux d'Agincourt; Bannister); 1070–1110 (Lowe); s11ex (Bloch, *MMA*, 1:201–2; Wettstein); 1191 (Pieralisi, Bertaux); s12ex (Ladner); s11¼ (Baldass); 1087 (Brenk); 1081–1105 (Speciale).

HISTORY   The roll, judging from its script and decoration, and its close relationship to other documents, was evidently made at Montecassino. Since the explications in Italian appear also on the headpiece, the roll must have been complete at least until the fourteenth century. Pieralisi surmises that it might have formed part of the collection assembled in southern Italy by Cardinal Antonio Santorio (d. 1602); this is repeated by Bertaux, p. 227. The roll was first mentioned as being in the Barberini collection by Gerbert, who published a partial facsimile (1774). It was Bertaux who first recognized that a plate of Gerbert's *De cantu* reproduced the missing headpiece.

This roll is closely related by its text and its pictures to the London roll, British Library Add. 30337. See the discussion, pp. 180–82. They are the most closely related of any two surviving Exultet rolls. Scholars have not agreed on whether one was copied from the other or, if they descend from a common model, which is older than the other. Ladner thought the London roll was "probably" the model for this one. Speciale and Baldass agree that the London roll precedes this one. Avery thought that the Barberini roll was the elder. Brenk ("Bischöfliche") says that this roll was made when Abbot Desiderius became Pope Victor III in 1087, on the model of the London roll: he suggests that it shows the new ambo and candlestick of the Desiderian basilica. Speciale (in *Exultet*, 238) points out that the tiara and the bicorn miter, as well as the pope's purple robe, make their first appearance here and are signs of the reform papacy. Desiderius, as Victor III, may have been the first pope crowned with the tiara.

MANUFACTURE   The membranes have a single vertical rule to define the outer margins of text; the present first membrane is ruled horizontally throughout; the remaining membranes are ruled (module of 26 mm) for text, leaving space for pictures. Text periods are begun on a new line and begin with a two-line initial with gold and a band of gold that contains the first word or two in capitals. The initials occupy the left margin, so space does not need to be planned for them within the writing area. Final punctuation is placed at the right margin regardless of where the text of the line ends. Speciale ("Spigolature") says the pictures were painted by two artists in collaboration. The musical notation may have been added after the illustrations: the neume that overlaps the tree from which Eve takes fruit from the serpent could not have been placed elsewhere than at a specific height above its specific syllable; but the tree, if painted in a space already containing the neume, could well have avoided it. The colored initials, however, may precede the illustrations, to judge from a tree in the "Noli me tangere" scene, which avoids an initial. The order of work, then, might be: initials, text, illustrations, notation (though the text might also come after the illustrations). Speciale (in *Exultet*, 235) indicates, without giving reasons, that in this roll, as well as in the British Library roll and in Vat. lat. 3784, the pictures and the initials are made before the text and notation.

The placement of pictures here, and in the London roll, is problematical (see pp. 180–82). The general system here is to place pictures, inverted, after the period that refers to them: a system unusual in Exultet rolls and in illustrated manuscripts in general.

All the pictures here that are not lost are in the same place as they are in the British Library roll, except that "Tellus" here follows its period, as do the other pictures, and it seems misplaced in the London roll. Two additional pictures, Pope and Emperor, are not used in BL Add. 30337 but here are consistent in their placement after their paragraphs.

The arrangement of frontispiece illustrations differs from that in the London roll. If Gerbert's reproduction is accurate, the disposition is puzzling. Either the E is at the very beginning of the roll, without further text, and followed by several pictures; or the headpiece of Christ with angels is preceded by a candle-lighting scene with "Lumen Christi" written three times in the opposite orientation from the letter E of "Exultet."

BIBLIOGRAPHY *Aggiornamento*, 451–53; Avery, *The Exultet Rolls*, 34–35, pl. 147–153; Avery, "The Barberini Exultet Roll"; Baldass, "Die Miniaturen"; Bannister, *Monumenti*, no. 366 (p. 128), pl. 74; Bertaux, *L'art*, 227–28; *Die Exultetrolle Codex Barberini*, including Cavallo, "Die Bedeutung," Speciale, "Die Exultetrolle," complete facsimile; Gerbert, *De cantu*, 447, 534, tables 3–4; Kelly, *TBC*, 313; Ladner, "The Commemoration Pictures"; Lowe, *TBS*, 2:161–62; Pieralisi, "Il preconio"; Speciale in *Exultet*, 235–48, with facsimile; Speciale, *Montecassino e la riforma;* Wettstein, *Sant'Angelo*, 147–48; Wilpert, "Die Darstellung."

Vatican City, Biblioteca Apostolica Vaticana, MS Vat. lat. 3784

Exultet roll, incomplete, s11¾, Montecassino; text uncertain (Beneventan?), Beneventan melody, pictures reversed.

DESCRIPTION Incomplete, now in four pieces ca. 275 × 2405 mm, allowing for overlap (275–80 × 620, 275–87 × 620, 280 × 650, 275–85 × 635), average 275 × 631.25. Amputated after the prologue, the roll is usually thought to have contained the Beneventan text. The dark brown ink used for text and notation is darker than that of the drawing. Beneventan notation of an early type 2. Much of the text has been erased or rewritten, so that only the first two periods on the third membrane ("Quapropter . . ." and "Vt qui me . . .") show the original hand and notation. At the end of membrane 4, the text (in hand 1) "quia dignum et iustum est" has been erased. Slits with thongs are present at both ends of all membranes except the beginning of membrane 1 (which would not have had slits unless there had been a frontispiece) and the end of membrane 4 (which must have been altered, since it also contains erased writing), perhaps at the time the Naples roll Vat. lat. 3784A was attached.

DATE "vers la fin du XIe siècle" (Bertaux, 226); ca. 1060 (Avery); after 1071 (Baldass); 1060–1070 (Brenk); 1058–87 (Lowe).

HISTORY Made at Montecassino. Very closely related to the style of initials ("parfaitement identiques": Bertaux, 226) of the famous Desiderian lectionary Vat. lat. 1202. Brenk says the painter is the same as 1202, but earlier: the V of this roll is old fashioned and does not have Regensburg-style infill as does the V in the lectionary (on the new Germanic style of illumination at Desiderian Montecassino, see Bloch, MMA, 1:71–82). Speciale attributes the illustrations to two distinct artists. Bertaux, 225n5: "Conservé [at the Vatican] dans une boîte de cuir gaufré aux armes du pape Grégoire XVI (1831–1846) et du cardinal Albani." Speciale suggests that this roll, along with Vat. lat. 3784A, may have come to the Vatican Library in the later sixteenth century along with the Desiderian lectionary Vat. lat. 1202, known to have remained at Montecassino at least until the pontificate of Paul III.

MANUFACTURE The membranes have a double rule down each side and are ruled for text (module of 21 mm), leaving space for pictures. The estimates are not always ideal: too much space is left on the third membrane, resulting in much blank parchment. The first membrane has gold capitals for the opening period, written within the letter E, with no text rules. Two text rules following this text may suggest that the next period was intended to come immediately (though three rules are actually needed for it). Instead, the "Turba celorum" occupies the rest of the membrane, ignoring and covering the text rules. Membrane 2 also begins with two text rules, covered by seraphs.

Text periods begin with a new line; the initials are one line, with no indentation of the second line. The final line of a period may be centered when short. The opening period is in gold capitals, the other periods beginning with a word or two in gold, and in the final surviving period the following portions are in gold: "Per dominum nostrum ihesum christum filium suum; Amen; Dominus vobiscum; Sursum corda; Gratias agamus domino deo nostro."

In addition to the two large initials, there are five surviving pictures ("Angelica turba"; "Tellus"; "Magnis populorum vocibus(?)"; "Mater ecclesia"; "Fratres karissimi"). Pictures are appropriately placed, inverted before their periods; in one case a single period is preceded by two pictures ("Magnis populorum uocibus[?]"; "Mater ecclesia"), which would not appear in the order of their mention in the period ("populus," at the end of membrane 2, precedes "ecclesia" at the beginning of membrane 3, and both precede the text period "Letetur et mater ecclesia . . ."). The pictures are beautifully made, apparently based on no earlier models from Exultets.

The pictures seem to be put in after the notation: "Tellus" is almost playful in the way angel halos and wings come close to the notes. Elsewhere, the space left blank is larger than needed, as on the same membrane, where the figures of the populus float in a void (not at all like the way the angels of the Exultet membrane use the initial to reflect their various levels). Another picture in a void is the "Fratres karissimi." In this I disagree with Speciale, who writes (in *Exultet,* 235) that this roll, like the Barberini roll and that in the British Library, was created by making the pictures and the initials first, the text and notation later.

BIBLIOGRAPHY   *Aggiornamento,* 449–50; Avery, *The Exultet Rolls,* 30–31, pl. 130–134; Baldass, "Disegni," 102, 105–9; Bannister, *Monumenti,* no. 346 (pp. 119–20), pl. 69; Bertaux, *L'art,* 225–26; Brenk in *Exultet,* 211–19, with facsimile; Brenk, "Bischöfliche"; Brenk, *Das Lektionar,* 97–121; Kelly, *TBC,* 313; Lowe, *TBS,* 2:148; Newton, "Due tipi," 471–73; Speciale, "Spigolatura"; Wettstein, *Sant'Angelo,* 146–47.

Vatican City, Biblioteca Apostolica Vaticana, MS Vat. lat. 3784A

Exultet roll, Naples, 1334–42. Gothic script and square notation, no illustration. Franco-Roman text and melody.

DESCRIPTION   Five pieces, ca. 265 × 3780 mm (313 + 816 + 768 + 768 + 813), average 791; a complete Exultet, in Gothic script and square notation, formerly attached to the incomplete Vat. lat. 3784. Franco-Roman text (but including a quotation of the Beneventan text), Franco-Roman melody. No illustrations. The manuscript is usually cited as Vat. lat. 3784A, the result of its separation from Vat. lat. 3784. The number 5 is added by hand to the printed signature on the container, from which Speciale (in *Exultet*) cites the manuscript as 3784 (5).

DATE   s15 (Salmon); Naples, 1334–42 (Avery; Speciale)

HISTORY   The date is that of Pope Benedict VI, the first letter of whose name appears in the roll; this has been corrected several times, the last time to "Paulo" [Paul III, 1534–49]. The original bishop IO[hannes, 1327–58] has been changed to Ior[dano Orsini], 1400–1405, and to Alessan[dro Caraffa, 1484–92]; King R[obert the Good, King of Naples, 1309–43] has been changed to F[erdinand, 1510–16] and Carolum [1516–56]; see Avery, p. 31. Speciale suggests that this roll, along with Vat. lat. 3784, may have come to the Vatican Library in the later sixteenth century along with the Desiderian lectionary Vat. lat. 1202, known to have remained at Montecassino at least until the pontificate of Paul III.

There is an inscription on a piece added to the beginning in the eighteenth century that reads "Agglutinanda fortè superiori, dudum dignanter accepte à Tua Illustrissima Amplitudine."

MANUFACTURE   This is a complete roll, made without elaboration, and not apparently intended as a continuation of another roll, since it is complete in itself. Membranes are glued together and were apparently assembled before the parchment was ruled for text and music. Prickings are visible in the outer margins. Text periods do not start with a new line and begin with alternating red and blue capitals with filigree.

There is now no physical evidence of this roll having been attached to Vat. lat. 3784, though they share the same signature.

BIBLIOGRAPHY   Avery, *The Exultet Rolls,* 31, pl. 134; Salmon, *Les manuscrits,* 2:89; Speciale in *Exultet,* 445–55, with facsimile.

Vatican City, Biblioteca Apostolica Vaticana, MS Vat. lat. 9820

Exultet roll, mutilated, s10⁴⁄₄, Benevento; Beneventan text and melody, pictures not inverted; now reversed and rewritten (s12ex) to contain Franco-Roman text with Beneventan melody.

DESCRIPTION   This is a very beautiful roll: delicate colors, touches of gold throughout, elegance provided by the border. The roll is now badly mutilated. Now in twenty pieces, owing to subsequent rearrangement, it measures ca. 270 mm wide, and its membranes averaged 655 mm in length, to judge from the three surviving full-length pieces (pieces 2, 7, 11). The brown ink used for the text and notation (of which a little is visible at the end) may be the same ink used in the drawings. The original roll contained the Beneventan text (a roll in a picture has "Vt superne benedictione munus accommodes") and pictures oriented with the text. In the late twelfth century the roll was dismembered, its text erased, and the membranes reversed and reordered to receive the Franco-Roman text (in black ink) with new type 2 notation (in a lighter ink) of the Beneventan melody; the later melody has slight elaborations, particularly at the beginnings of periods (cf. "Hec nox est"; "Alitur"; "Sed iam"). The neumes were rewritten s13 (Bannister), s12–13 (Pace), but there is no indication that there were two subsequent sets of neumes; the upper script neumes must have been written at the same time as the upper script itself.

Although the beginning and the end are present, one membrane is missing from the middle, not necessary for the length of the upper script. (It might have had pictures of the Crucifixion, or of the passage of the Red Sea, both of which appear in the two later rolls—Casanatense and Salerno—modeled on this one; the scene of the Red Sea, however, does not figure in the original Beneventan text.) Little of the lower script is visible except the opening period and a few lines at the end. Bannister's manuscript diagrams of the original ordering and the reordering of the roll, kept at the Vatican Library with the roll, are reproduced in Avery, *The Exultet Rolls.*

The twenty separate pieces are numbered on labels pasted on their backs. The early separation of the headpiece (piece 1a) from the rest of the roll accounts for the dual numbering of the first piece.

Dimensions of each piece follow (they differ only slightly from Pace's measurements, in *Exultet,* 101), with indications of how complete the surviving piece appears. Unfortunately, Pace's descriptions in *Exultet* refer to numbers that are not quite the same as those on the pasted labels (the latter are used here).

1a. [headpiece with Bishop] 271 at widest × 331
1b. [Lamb] 277 × 213, slits at original bottom which were painted after the (now-missing) thong was inserted
2. [Turba] 276 × 648, full length, slits top and bottom
3. [Bishop lights candle] 273 × 320, slits at old top

The Sources

4. [Exultet] 265 × 322, slits at old bottom. Two old text rules are visible, 20–22 mm apart, which the original scribe follows only approximately. The old notation has been replaced on this piece.
5. [Tellus] 250 × 295, both dimensions incomplete
6. [Ecclesia] 250 × 202, both dimensions incompete; painted thong in slits
7. [Populus; Fratres] 254 × 615, full length, slits both ends
8. [VD] 271 × 604, almost full length; slits at old top
9. [Limbo] 273 × 331, full width
10. ["Celestia iunguntur"] 276 × 246, full width, slits at old bottom, painted after assembly
11. [Bees] 267 × 182, full width
12. ["Veniat"] 270 × 95, full width
13. ["Deus qui per filium"] 272 × 84, full width
14. ["Ecclesia. Sed iam"] 269 × 376 full width, slits at old bottom
15. [Deacon and bishop, scroll says "Vt superne . . ."] 273 × 440; the joint in the middle of this piece is painted over, suggesting that painting comes after the assembly of the roll, at least for joints over membranes
16. [Bishop with two saints] 272 × 469, full width
17. [Bishop enthroned] 272 × 343 full width, slits at old top
18. [Emperor(?)] 262–72 × 370, full width, slits at old bottom: pieces 17–18 form one full-length piece, 700 + mm?
19. [Army; Presentation of roll] 269 × 605 not quite full width

DATE Benevento, 981–987, based on a note added on the back of the roll with the names of Prince Pandolf of Benevento, and of a second mention over the first of Pandolf together with Landolf (Pandolf II ruled 981–1014, with his son Landolf V from 987; see Cavallo, *Rotoli*, 42n78; Lowe, *Scriptura*, pl. 54; Pace, in *Exultet*, 101). Belting (179) dates it 985–87, for Alfanus, the first legal successor to Archbishop Landolf; not Pandolf III, who ruled alone 1035–38 and 1038–39 with his son Landolf IV, on account of the script and painting, so near the style of the Casanatense pontifical (Belting, 168n6); Seroux d'Agincourt proposed, and some have accepted, 1038–59, for Pandolf III and Landolf VI. For paleographical reasons, Francis Newton inclines to this later date (private communication). For a summary of dating questions, see *Aggiornamento*, 442–46. The upper script is s12ex (Lowe; Avery, 31; Pace in *Exultet*, 101).

HISTORY This roll, perhaps the most important of all surviving Exultets, was presented by a certain "Iohannes presbiter et praepositus" to the abbey of San Pietro *extra muros*, Benevento. An illustration with a legend shows Iohannes presenting the roll to Saint Peter; and in the text of the original roll, the concluding invocations include prayers for the abbess and her congregation ("necnon et famulam tuam abbatissam nostram cum universa congregacione beatissimi petri sibi commissa").

Generally thought to be from Benevento, though Avery (followed by Moneti; Garrison; Caleca) asserted its origin at San Vincenzo al Volturno. There is a dedication: "Hoc paruum munus dignanter suscipe, sancte Petre apostole, quod deuote tibi con[didit] Johannes presbyter atque semper precibus tuis confidentem. Gaudia cum sanctis illi ut concedat ha[bere?] Amen. Deo gratias" (Bertaux, 222). This might be John III, abbot of San Vincenzo, 981–84 (Lowe), the roll being writen for San Pietro *extra muros*, Benevento, a Volturno dependency, but it seems unlikely that the abbot of San Vincenzo would be called "praepositus." Additions on back of part 18: "famuli tui roffridi comestabuli consuliumque nostrorum, et totius militie beneventane" (s13, according to Lowe); "et principe nostro paldolfo" (almost illegible, type 1 notation); "et principibus nostris paldolfo et landolfo" (type 1 notation) (datable only 987 and 1028, says Lowe). The text of the upper script is very closely akin to that of the Exultet in London, B. L. Egerton 3511, a missal of Saint Peter's *intra muros*.

The roll is generally understood to be a copy, executed for Saint Peter's, of a roll originally made for Archbishop Landolf of Benevento (969–82). The existence of other liturgical rolls evidently made for Landolf (those at the Biblioteca Casanatense) and the extraordinary attention given to the archibishop in the illustrations make a strong case for the present roll being a copy of an archiepiscopal original. The part of the text that differs from the original is written after the presentation scene, suggesting that a final presentation scene, but different from this one, may have been present in the archiepiscopal original, on the model of the "LANDOLFI EPISCOPI SUM" found at the end of the Casanatense benedictional Biblioteca Casanatense 724 (B I 13) I.

This roll, together with the benedictional rolls at the Casanatense, is presumably of Beneventan manufacture. There is little evidence that either the cathedral or the convent of Saint Peter had scriptoria capable of executing such extraordinary documents. Perhaps they were all commissioned from the scriptorium of the monastery of Santa Sofia.

The history of the roll is unknown between its origin and 1776 when, as Lucinia Speciale has discovered, it was in the possession of the Theatine fathers at Capua. Perhaps it is the "carta una ubi est exultet iam angelica" inventoried at the cathedral of Benevento in 1447. The abbey of Saint Peter's was closed in 1294; perhaps, as Francescantonio Natale suggests, the roll came first to the cathedral and then, in 1300, to Capua, when Archbishop Iohannes was translated to the metropolitan see of Capua, bringing with him "molti sacri arredi" (Natale, *Lettera*, 49). At any rate, the roll came to Capua by 1776, where it was attested by Natale (*Lettera*, 49–66), who gives a complete transcription—of the upper script—and descriptions of the pictures: there can be no doubt that this is the same roll. The roll came into the possession of Cardinal Stefano Borgia when he passed from Capua to Benevento to take up his position as papal legate. Seroux d'Agincourt acquired the roll from his friend Stefano Borgia, and from him it passed to the Vatican Library. The headpiece must have remained in the possession of Cardinal Borgia, whence it would have passed to the Museo Borgiano of the Propaganda Fidei and thence to the Borgia collection at the Vatican, where it was recognized in 1927 by Avery as belonging to this roll and reunited with it (see Avery, 231).

MANUFACTURE   The original planning is difficult to determine, owing to the later serious mutilation. The little evidence of ruling suggests a varying module of 17–22 mm. The somewhat irregular lines at the end are apparently made without rules. The side borders do not have straight sides. The lines of the upper script, much straighter than the lower, do not use old lines for alignment, but they do not seem to be ruled. There may be bits of ruling on piece 9, about 17 mm apart. The original roll had one-line gold capitals that are still visible; it thus appears that each new period began at the left margin with a new gold letter. With the exception of the group of five illustrations that form a frontispiece before the text, the pictures were originally placed before the relevant text periods, at least in most cases.

But on piece 18, the picture of temporal authority (a prince or emperor crowned by angels) is painted after its text period ("Memorare domine famulum tuum imperatorem nostrum *il.*, et principem nostrum *il.*," etc.). The membrane is incomplete, although no text is missing before this. Perhaps there was once another picture preceding this paragraph: an emperor preceding the text would make the surviving picture a (Lombard) prince and make further sense of the following scene ("et eorum exercitum universum"), which shows two groups of soldiers: perhaps the armies of the emperor and the prince.

Apparently the painting was accomplished after the roll was assembled, at least for those borders that cover joints between membranes.

The roll was separated, its text erased, and its membranes reversed and reordered to provide space for writing and reversed illustrations for a roll with Franco-Roman text. This later text is accommodated into the erased space, with little regard for calligraphic arrangements of musical-textual periods.

Two prayers ("Deus qui per filium tuum angularem scilicet lapidem" and "Veniat quesumus omnipotens deus super hunc incensum"), normally used in the Roman rite for the blessing of new fire and the blessing of incense, are written on erased pieces of the original roll.

An addition to the original text, piece 19: "necnon et famulam tuam abbatissa nostra ill. cum uniuersa congregatione [in a smaller, later hand, over erasure of next three words: beatissimi petri apostoli sibi commissa ac] beati petri apostoli temporum uite quiete concessa gaudiis facias perfrui sempiternis. Qui uiuis" [apparently intended to continue with the 'cum patre' written above on the same piece].

There are seventeen illustrations, all except for the opening Bishop enthroned framed at top and bottom by decorative borders that separate pictures from text, and on the sides by the interlace border that runs down both sides of each membrane. The initials E and VD are highly decorated.

The illustrative cycle present in this roll is that used for the rolls now in the Biblioteca Casanatense and at Salerno. The considerable series of frontispiece paintings, including an enthroned bishop consigning the roll to the deacon, must have been derived from an earlier roll, probably for the use of the cathedral.

BIBLIOGRAPHY *Aggiornamento*, 442–46; Avery, *The Exultet Rolls*, 31–34, 46–49, pl. 135–146; Bannister, *Monumenti*, no. 345 (pp. 118–19), pl. 68; Belting, *Studien*, 167–80, 234–36; Bertaux, *L'art*, 221–24; Brenk, "Bischöfliche"; *Exultetrolle* (complete facsimile); Kelly, *TBC*, 316; Lowe, *Scriptura*, pl. 54; Lowe, *TBS*, 2:153; Pace in *Exultet*, 101–18, with facsimile; Wettstein, *Sant'Angelo*, 142–44.

Velletri, Archivio Diocesano, Exultet

Exultet roll, fragmentary, s12in (?), Montecassino; Beneventan text and melody, pictures reversed.

DESCRIPTION Four fragments, varying between 300 and 310 mm wide; lengths are 500, 380, 320, 850, but all are cut down. Beneventan text, Beneventan script, and type 3 notation; surviving decoration consists of the initial V and three illustrations (reversed).

DATE   s11ex (Avery; Lowe); s13? (Pace); s13¼ (Garrison, *Studies*, 2:33n2).

HISTORY   From Montecassino. Fedele, judging from the script, proposed that it arrived with Leo Marsicanus, monk of Montecassino, author of the chronicle of Montecassino, and Cardinal Bishop of Ostia, 1101–6; Speciale (*Montecassino e la riforma*, 42–43n77) thinks not. Paleographers generally incline to the early twelfth-century date, while art historians have grave doubts that the painting style and that of the initials on membrane 4 could have been made so early. The surviving inventory of 1708 records "antiquissimae pergamenae pictae repertae in archivio veteris Rev.mi Capituli" (Mortari, 35); evidently it was already dismembered. It must have been at the moment of finding the fragments that Canon Giovanni Battista De Pauli transcribed (in 1708) the surviving Beneventan text onto the roll.

The nature of the surviving pictures—especially the Ecclesia as a figure seated on a church building—and the decorative borders suggests that this roll is in the tradition of rolls from Benevento (Vat. lat. 9820, Casanatense, Salerno). The small initials also have an archaizing quality. The roll may record the personal preferences of Leo Marsicanus himself.

MANUFACTURE   The membranes apparently are ruled (module of 30 mm) for text, leaving space for pictures. Text periods begin at left with a two-line (three cases; or one-line: one case) initial, for which indentation needs to be provided. Initial letters (three large and one smaller) are drawn, but not colored, on membrane 4; perhaps they are incomplete. These were sketched in before the notation was written (neumes are required to overlap the initial V) and conceivably before the writing. In any case, it is clear that notation is done at a very late stage.

The joints between membranes are carefully made and borders painted after joining. The three paintings that survive (in addition, there is an illuminated V) are fully filled in, like full-page miniatures in a book.

The relation of pictures to text seems to be normal, so far as can be determined; that is, pictures are painted upside down before the text period they illustrate. However, the "ecclesia" picture, elsewhere used to illustrate the period "Gaudeat et mater ecclesia . . ." (Vat. lat. 9820, Casanatense, cf. Salerno), is here used for "Vnde nox sidereo pro ecclesiarum ornatu. . . ."

BIBLIOGRAPHY   *Aggiornamento*, 436; Avery, *The Exultet Rolls*, 40, pl. 186–189; Fedele, "L' 'Exultet' "; Kelly, *TBC*, 318; Lowe, *TBS*, 2:170; Mortari, *Il Museo*; Pace in *Exultet*, 265–72, with facsimile.

South Italian and Dalmatian Codices

Benevento, Biblioteca Capitolare, MS 33

A plenary missal, in Beneventan script and notation, s10/11, of unknown provenance, but probably not from Benevento. Incomplete at beginning and end (extends from the vigil of Christmas to 11 November). One of the oldest witnesses of Gregorian chant in southern Italy and of Beneventan notation. The absence of any materials for the Holy Twelve Brothers or for the Translation of Saint Bartholomew suggests a non-Beneventan origin. On a possible connection with Salerno, see Mallet and Thibaut, *Les manuscrits*, 1:90. 139 fols., 330 × 227 mm, writing area 310 × 200, two columns of twenty-eight to twenty-nine lines.

BIBLIOGRAPHY Lowe, *TBS*, 2:21; Gamber, *CLLA*, no. 430; Kelly, *TBC*, 300; *PM*, 13:96–99 and fig. 12; *PM*, 14:216, see table, p. 469, pl. I–VII (fols. 45–46v, 130–31); *PM* 15: no. 10 (p. 53); *PM* 20 (complete facsimile, with introduction and tables); *PM* 21:79–90, 342–45; Rehle, "Missale Beneventanum" (edition).

Berlin, Staatsbibliothek Preussischer Kulturbesitz, MS Lat. fol. 920

A notated missal from Kotor, in Beneventan script of the "Bari type" and type 3 notation without clef, s12. 169 fols., 190 × 30 cm, thirty lines.

BIBLIOGRAPHY Rehle, "Missale Beneventanum in Berlin," (edition); Lowe, *TBS*, 2:24; Huglo, "L'ancien chant," with a facsimile of the Exultet, p. 290; Gamber, *CLLA*, no. 477.

Farfa, Biblioteca dell'Abbazia, MS AF. 338 Musica XI
(formerly AB.F. Musica XI)

Gradual, s11, perhaps from Veroli. A mutilated bifolium (275 × 173 mm, writing area 260 × 150, at least eleven lines) next to innermost in its quire; the innermost bifolium survives as Trento, Museo Provinciale d'Arte FC 135. The two bifolia were folios 91–94 of the original manuscript. Beneventan script and notation without lines or clefs. The four leaves contain part of the ceremonies of Holy Saturday; they preserve parts of two versions of the Exultet (the end of the Franco-Roman Exultet and most of the Beneventan version) and conclude with the neumes of the old Beneventan Alleluia *Laudate pueri*. The Franco-Roman Exultet mentions the congregation of Saint Paul. The two bifolia were still together and known as the Palmieri fragments, when their Exultets were edited in *PM*, 14:385–86, 390–99 (1931). The Veroli provenance of these fragments has been suggested by Virginia Brown on paleographical grounds.

BIBLIOGRAPHY Lowe, *TBS*, 2:41; Gamber, *CLLA*, no. 484a; Kelly, *TBC*, 304; *PM* 2: pl. 20; *PM* 14: pl. XXVI–XXVII (in the original printing labeled "Cava"), see table, p. 470; *PM* 21:227–30, 373–74.

London, British Library, MS Egerton 3511

Missal, s12, from Saint Peter's *intra muros*, Benevento (315 × 210 mm, writing area 270 × 170, two columns of twenty-five to twenty-six lines); the manuscript was formerly Benevento, Biblioteca Capitolare MS VI 29. Beneventan script with occasional type 3 notation without clef but using a vacant text line for heightening; it contains the Exultet with Franco-Roman text and Beneventan melody, as well as notated lection tones for the canticles of Jonah and Azarias.

BIBLIOGRAPHY Lowe, *TBS*, 2:53; Gamber, *CLLA*, no. 452; Kelly, *TBC*, 305; *PM* 14: see table, p. 469 (under Benevento VI 29); *British Library: Catalogue of Additions 1946–1950*, 330–33.

Macerata, Biblioteca Comunale "Mozzi-Borgetti," MS 378

Pontifical of Benevento s12in. This pontifical, containing very little notation, provides an ordo for Holy Saturday that reflects the old Beneventan usage. It cues the Beneventan melody of the canticle *Benedictus es, Domine* for Holy Saturday, and it places the Exultet in Beneventan position. The Exultet itself is cued without notation, so we cannot determine either the melody or the textual version. 216 fols., 283 × 190 mm, writing area 213 × 130, seventeen to nineteen lines.

BIBLIOGRAPHY   Adversi, *Inventari*, 1:92; Garbelotto, "Catalogo," 110–14; Gyug, "A Pontifical"; Kelly, *TBC*, 306; Lowe, *TBS*, 2:55; Paci, *Inventario*, pp. 142–43.

Montecassino, Archivio dell Badia, MS 451

Pontifical, s11in (436 pages, 305 × 175 mm), copied at Montecassino on the model of the Roman-German Pontifical of the tenth century. A companion volume, perhaps a copy of this one, is Rome, Vall. D 5.

BIBLIOGRAPHY   Andrieu, *Les ordines*, 2:176; 5:14–18; Gyug, "The Pontificals"; Vogel, *Le pontifical*, 1:xiii and *passim*, and 2:95–99, where the Exultet is edited; Gamber, *CLLA*, 566.

Naples, Biblioteca Nazionale, MS VI G 34

A processional from Troia, s12ex or (Hiley) s13in (139 fols., 200 × 135 mm), including tropes for Kyrie and Gloria, farced epistles, hymns, in Beneventan script and type 3 notation with lines and clefs. The Exultet, fols. 77–83, has the Franco-Roman text (with Norman finale) and Roman melody. The text of the Exultet is closely related to that of the third Exultet roll of Troia.

BIBLIOGRAPHY   Arnese, *I codici*, 146–49 and pl. 10; Hiley, "The Liturgical Music," 51; Hiley, *Western Plainchant*, 591–93; Kelly, *TBC*, 308–9; Lowe, *TBS*, 2:102; *PM* 21: 265–66, 383.

Naples, Biblioteca Nazionale, MS VI G 38

A Franciscan notated missal, s13, in Gothic script (297 fols., 180 × 178 mm), made before the institution of Corpus Christi, which appears in an appendix. The Exultet, fols. 129v–132v, has the Franco-Roman text and melody. The square notation of the Exultet is later than the Beneventan-style notation of the rest of the manuscript. A now-illegible name is written above the line (a bishop?). A portion of the praise of the bees, all of which is omitted in the main text, is added in a bottom margin, from "O uere beata et mirabilis . . . uirgo permansit." Marginal additions to the Exultet include "hic ponatur incensi" (before "In huius"), "hic accenditur cereus" (before "Qui licet"), and "hic accenduntur lampada" (before "O uere beata nox").

BIBLIOGRAPHY   Arnese, *I codici*, 151–58, pl. 16; van Dijk and Walker, *Origins*, 241–44 (see also index, p. 547).

Oxford, Bodleian Library, MS Canon. Bibl. lat. 61

A decorated gospel lectionary (197 fols., 286 × 195), s11ex (Novak), in Beneventan script with occasional type 2 notation, using a vacant text line for alignment, and using the quilisma; made at the monastery of Saint Chrysogonus, Zadar, at the behest of Princess Večenega, second abbess of the Benedictine convent of Saint Mary. The Exultet (fols. 116v–123) has the Franco-Roman text with additions from the Beneventan.

BIBLIOGRAPHY Gamber, *CLLA*, no. 1,170; Kelly, *TBC*, 309; Lowe, *Scriptura beneventana*, pl. 74; Lowe, *TBS*, 2:109–10; Nicholson, *Early Bodleian Music*, xiii, lxxiii–lxxiv, and plates 37 (fols. 115v–116) and 38 (fols. 122v–23); Novak and Telebaković-Pacarski, *Večenegin*, including facsimiles of fols. 121, 122v, 115v (color), 117 (color): the text of the Exultet is edited on pp. 38–44.

Oxford, Bodleian Library, MS Canon. liturg. 342

A Dalmatian missal, s13, probably from Dubrovnik (122 fols., c250 × 165 mm); Beneventan script and type 3 notation; the manuscript has been mutilated and rearranged. The Exultet (fols. 52v–53v, incomplete Franco-Roman text) has a highly elaborated melody (see *PM* 14:399–416).

BIBLIOGRAPHY Gyug, *Missale ragusinum* (complete edition); Kelly, *TBC*, 309–10; Lowe, *TBS*, 2:111; *PM* 14: see table, p. 471.

Rome, Biblioteca Casanatense, MS 1103

Missal of Montevergine (300 fols.), s15, in Gothic script without notation. The ordo of Holy Saturday preserves some Beneventan elements; the Exultet, fols. 118v–120v, is written without notation.

Rome, Biblioteca Vallicelliana, MS C 32

Ritual, s11½, of unknown provenance, possibly Montecassino (105 fols., 252 × 175 mm, twenty-one lines); two opening flyleaves (Apocalypse) are s11ex; fols. 97–105 (palimpsest, lower script ca. s11, upper script s12/13). Beneventan script and occasional early type 3 notation, using a clefline for alignment, and omitting the quilisma. The ordo for Holy Saturday contains rubrics derived from Montecassino use; the Franco-Roman Exultet is notated, the melodic version being that of Montecassino.

BIBLIOGRAPHY Avitabile, Censimento 2, 1,040–41; Gamber, *CLLA*, no. 1,593; Kelly, *TBC*, 312; Lowe, *TBS*, 2:128; *PM* 14: see table, p. 471; *PM* 21:276–77, 387–88; Odermatt, *Ein Rituale*, edition.

Rome, Biblioteca Vallicelliana, MS D 5

Pontifical, s11, from Montecassino (150 fols., 360 × 240 mm); a copy of the Roman-German Pontifical of the tenth century, perhaps a copy of Montecassino 451. Beneventan script and notation in two columns. The Exultet is without musical notation.

BIBLIOGRAPHY Andrieu, *Les ordines*, 5:14–18; Avitabile, Censimento 2, 1,053–54; Lowe, *TBS*, 2:128; Vogel and Elze, *Le pontifical*, 28 and passim.

Salerno, Archivio Capitolare, MS without shelf number (Capone 3)

Missal, dated 1431, for Salerno Cathedral, according to the explicit (324 fols., 340 × 250 mm). Gothic script in two columns of thirty lines; occasional musical notation on a staff of four lines. The Exultet, with Beneventan text, is notated with an elaborate melody. Cf. Salerno 4.

BIBLIOGRAPHY Capone, *Il duomo*, 1:261–63; *PM*, 21:279–84, 388–89.

Salerno Archivio Capitolare, MS without shelf number (Capone 4)

Missal, s15, for Salerno Cathedral (265 fols., 310 × 222 mm). Gothic script in two columns of thirty lines; occasional musical notation on a staff of four lines. The Exultet, with Beneventan text, is notated with an elaborated melody; it reproduces Salerno 3.

BIBLIOGRAPHY Capone, *Il duomo*, 1:265–66; *PM* 21:285–99 (reproduces the entire Exultet), 390.

Trento, Museo Provinciale d'Arte (Castel del Buonconsiglio), MS FC 135 (formerly Lawrence Feininger Collection)

Gradual, s11, perhaps from Veroli. A mutilated bifolium (275 × 173 mm, at least eleven lines) innermost in its quire; the next outer bifolium survives as Farfa, Biblioteca dell'Abbazia, Ms. AF. 338 Musica XI. The two bifolia were folios 91–94 of the original manuscript. Beneventan script and notation without lines or clefs. The four leaves contain parts of the ceremonies of Holy Saturday; they preserve parts of two versions of the Exultet (the end of the Franco-Roman Exultet and most of the Beneventan version) and conclude with the neumes of the old Beneventan Alleluia *Laudate pueri*. The Franco-Roman Exultet mentions the congregation of Saint Paul. The two bifolia were still together and known as the Palmieri fragments, when their Exultets were edited in *PM*, 14:385–86, 390–99 (1931). The Veroli provenance of these fragments has been suggested by Virginia Brown on paleographical grounds.

BIBLIOGRAPHY Kelly, *TBC*, 312; Lowe, *TBS*, 2:139; *PM* 21:303–6, 392–93.

Vatican City, Biblioteca Apostolica Vaticana, MS Barb. lat. 603

A noted missal, from Caiazzo (near Caserta), s12/13 (90 fols., 377 × 267 mm in two columns) extending from the Ember Days of Advent to the Fourth Sunday after Pentecost, with lacunae. Beneventan script and notation using the dry-point text line, without clefs. The Exultet (fols. 57–58) is in a somewhat later hand; its Franco-Roman text uses the Beneventan melody at its beginning and end, but the preface tone for most of its length.

BIBLIOGRAPHY Bannister, *Monumenti*, no. 371 (p. 130), no. 889 (p. 192); Gamber, *CLLA*, no. 458; Kelly, *TBC*, 313–14; Lowe, *TBS*, 2:162; *PM*, 14 (see index, p. 471); Salmon, *Les manuscrits*, 2: no. 256.

Vatican City, Biblioteca Apostolica Vaticana, MS Barb. lat. 699

A missal, s12ex, perhaps from Veroli or Sulmona (198 fols., 310 × 190 mm), Beneventan script and type 3 notation without clefs. The Exultet, Franco-Roman text, is transmitted without melody. A later hand after "rege nostro" adds "magno nostro heremano."

BIBLIOGRAPHY Lowe, *TBS*, 2:162; Salmon, *Les manuscrits*, 2: no. 268.

Vatican City, Biblioteca Apostolica Vaticana, MS Borg. lat. 339

A decorated evangelistary, 1081–82, from San Nicola, Osor (Dalmatia) (59 fols., ca. 560 × 390 mm, nineteen lines). Beneventan script of the "Bari type," Beneventan type 2 notation, aligned on a dry-point line, using quilisma and episemata. The Exultet (fols. 53–58v) contains the Franco-Roman text with an extended praise of the bees (this latter edited in *PM*, 14:383, col. 1), using the Beneventan melody.

BIBLIOGRAPHY Bannister, *Monumenti*, no. 365 (pp. 127–28) and pl. 73b (Exultet, fol. 58); Lowe, *TBS*, 2:163–164; Novak, "Praeconium paschale"; *PM* 14:382, 383; Salmon, *Les manuscrits*, 2: no. 73.

Vatican City, Biblioteca Apostolica Vaticana, MS Ottob. lat. 576

A plenary monastic missal, s12 (fols. 2–220), s13 (fols. 221–337) in two volumes (377 fols., 270 × 175 mm, twenty-four to twenty-eight lines); the provenance is unknown. Beneventan script and type 3 notation on lines with clefs (fols. 123–95 are in "Bari type" script); notation is not continued after the second Sunday after the Octave of Easter. Parts of two missals are the lower script of palimpsest folios (fols. 341–77; see Gamber, *CLLA*, no. 437; Dold, "Ein Palimpsestblatt"). The manuscript contains the Exultet with Franco-Roman text and Beneventan melody and notated Beneventan lection tones for Holy Saturday.

Despite some textual similarities, the Exultet is not closely related to versions from Montecassino. The melody is close to that of Benevento. A certain amount of nonstandard grammar and case endings, usually leaving off a consonant (collectu, sexu, inqua) suggest aural transcription: ("ac mentis affectu" = augmentis effectu; "fugat odia" = fuga hodie; "homini" = omni[a]); but the copying of the line "ille inquam" twice is really a visual error: so perhaps the Exultet at least is made by an illiterate scribe copying an aurally transcribed document.

BIBLIOGRAPHY Bannister, *Monumenti*, no. 368 (pp. 128–29) and pl. 75a (fol. 171); Gamber, *CLLA*, no. 454; Kelly, *TBC*, 314–15; *PM* 14: see table, p. 471; Lowe, *TBS*, 2:166; Salmon, *Les manuscrits*, 2: no. 305.

Vatican City, Biblioteca Apostolica Vaticana, MS Vat. lat. 6082

A noted missal, s12, from Montecassino, perhaps for the use of San Vincenzo al Volturno (319 fols., 294 × 200 mm, thirty-one lines); Beneventan script and type 3 notation; the Franco-Roman Exultet has the Beneventan melody (fols. 120v–22v), and the Holy Saturday rite contains notated lections from Jonah and Daniel for Holy Saturday using Beneventan recitation tones. A number of variants in the Exultet are shared with other Cassinese manuscripts, though the praise of the bees omits an unusual amount. The melody is not obviously Cassinese.

BIBLIOGRAPHY Bannister, *Monumenti*, no. 369 (pp. 129–30) and pl. 75b (fol. 251); Dold, "Die vom Missale"; Duval-Arnould, "Un missel"; Fiala, "Der Ordo missae"; Gamber, *CLLA*, no. 455; Kelly, *TBC*, 316; Lowe, *TBS*, 2:152; *PM* 14 (see table, p. 471); Salmon, *Les manuscrits*, 2: no. 413; 3: nos. 103, 278.

Vatican City, Biblioteca Apostolica Vaticana, MS Vat. lat. 10673

An incomplete gradual, s11in (Lowe), s10med (Cavallo), of unknown provenance: probably not Benevento, perhaps Capua (Cavallo). Contents extend from Septuagesima to Holy Saturday Exultet (35 fols., 260 × 175 mm, fifteen to sixteen lines). Beneventan script and notation without lines or clefs. Only the beginning of the Exultet survives; it undoubtedly had the Beneventan text, in view of the substantial Beneventan contents of the rest of the manuscript.

BIBLIOGRAPHY Bannister, *Monumenti*, no. 347 (pp. 120–22) and pl. 70a (fol. 10v); Gamber, *CLLA*, no. 470; Kelly, *TBC*, 317–18; Lowe, *TBS*, 2:155; *PM* 13:99–106 and fig. 13; *PM* 14: pl. 1–71 (complete facsimile), table, pp. 474–76 (see index, p. 471); *PM* 21:326, 402; Salmon, *Les manuscrits*, 2: no. 202; Vatasso, *Codices*, 641–2.

Central Italian Codices

New York, Pierpont Morgan Library, MS M 379

An almost complete missal, s11/12, Foligno (273 fols., 387 × 222 mm, two columns of twenty-six lines); Romanesca writing; the sparse musical notation is derived from the Beneventan. The Franco-Roman text of the Exultet (fols. 108v–10v) is preceded by an elaborate *Lumen Christi* similar to those of Vat. lat. 4770, Rome, Vall. B 23 and Subiaco XVIII. The Beneventan melody, slightly elaborated, is used up to *Vere dignum;* the Roman preface tone is used thereafter, but it is interrupted twice, for the blessing of incense and the lighting of the candle.

BIBLIOGRAPHY Ricci, *Census*, 2:1,437; Kelly, *TBC*, 309; Supino Martini, *Roma*, 225.

Rome, Biblioteca Vallicelliana, MS B 23

An almost complete missal, s12½, from Norcia (monastery of Saint Bartholomew?); Romanesca writing with occasional peripheral Beneventan notation. On fols. 124v–26v, the Franco-Roman Exultet (preceded by an elaborate *Lumen*

Christi like that of New York, Morgan M 79, and Subiaco XVIII) has the Beneventan melody up to *Vere dignum*, the Roman preface tone thereafter. The praise of the bees (from *Apis ceteris*), without notation, is marked "hic mutat sensum quasi legens," notation resuming with "O uere beata nox que expoliauit."

BIBLIOGRAPHY Avitabile, Censimento 2, 1,024; Kelly, *TBC*, 311; Supino Martini, *Roma*, 223–24.

Rome, Biblioteca Vallicelliana, MS B 43

A complete sacramentary, with calendar and *ordo missae;* s12ex, of undetermined provenance, but not from Subiaco (Supino Martini, 334); it was used at Santa Maria de Ninfa, Rome (131 fols., 290 × 195 mm, twenty-six lines). Ordinary minuscule writing with sparse Beneventan notation. On fols. 49–53v, the Franco-Roman Exultet is provided with the Beneventan melody. Four spaces provided during the Exultet for pictures have not been filled.

BIBLIOGRAPHY Avitabile, Censimento 2, 1,028–29; Kelly, *TBC*, 311; Supino Martini, *Roma*, 334.

Rome, Biblioteca Vallicelliana, MS F 29

A monastic volume including collectar, capitular, breviary, rituale, s12in, from Farfa (128 fols., 200 × 120 mm). The Franco-Roman Exultet, preceded by *Lumen Christi* with the increasingly ornate melody characteristic of Subiaco XVIII, New York, Morgan M 379, and Vat. lat. 4770, begins on fol. 36v and continues on fols. 7–8, now out of order. The Beneventan melody is written for the beginning of the Exultet up through "salutaris."

BIBLIOGRAPHY Avitabile, Censimento 2, 1,069; Supino Martini, *Roma*, 264–65.

Subiaco, Biblioteca del Protocenobio di Santa Scolastica, MS XVIII (19)

A missal of Subiaco, s13, in Gothic script, only partially notated, with notation derived from the Beneventan using colored lines (171 fols., 790 × 400 mm, two columns of thirty-two lines). The Franco-Roman Exultet (preceded by an elaborate *Lumen Christi* like that of New York, Morgan M 79, and Rome, Vall. B 23) has the Beneventan melody up to *Vere dignum*, the Roman preface tone thereafter.

BIBLIOGRAPHY Allodi, *Inventario*, 9 (no. 19); Kelly, *TBC*, 312; *PM* 21:302, 392.

Vatican City, Biblioteca Apostolica Vaticana, MS Barb. lat. 560

Missal without notation, s11½, from the area around Rome, perhaps Subiaco (Supino Martini). The contents extend from Lent to Saint Paul (106 fols., 320 × 262 mm, in two columns); in Romanesca script, with no musical notation in the original hand. One line in Beneventan writing and notation (s12) is added in upper margin of fol. 16v. The manuscript is related to Vat. lat. 4770 by its script and its liturgy; the rites of Holy Week have been altered in this missal by the erasure of almost all the rubrics indicating chants, ceremonies, and the like. The order of the Holy Saturday vigil is Beneventan, the Exultet following the lections: all the rubrics have been erased and new ones substituted to bring the manuscript into line with Roman usage. Original rubrics indicate the chanting of the canticles of Jonah and of the three children on Holy Saturday. The Franco-Roman Exultet is without musical notation.

BIBLIOGRAPHY Bannister, *Monumenti*, no. 311 (p. 118), no. 361 (p. 125); Frénaud, "Les témoins," 67–68; Gamber, *CLLA*, no. 1,414; Kelly, *TBC*, 313; Lowe, *TBS*, 2:161; Salmon, *Les manuscrits*, 2: no. 250; *PM* 15: no. 155 (p. 81); Supino Martini, *Roma*, 163–65.

Vatican City, Biblioteca Apostolica Vaticana, MS Vat. lat. 4770

A monastic missal-gradual, s10ex (Lowe), s11med (Supino Martini), temporal and sanctoral mixed, beginning incomplete in the second mass of Christmas (254 fols., 345 × 270 mm, twenty-nine to thirty-five lines), written in ordinary minuscule, central Italian notation. Its provenance is uncertain: Teramo? (Supino Martini); monastery of Saint Bartholomew, Musiano, near Bologna (Salmon); Abruzzo (Gamber); Subiaco (*PM*, 1:243 n.5). A connection with south Italy is seen in the use of Beneventan script to continue the main text on fols. 216–16v. The Beneventan liturgy is represented by pieces for the Good Friday adoration and chants for the Easter vigil Mass, without notation. The Franco-Roman Exultet is provided without musical notation, but the *Lumen Christi* is notated and has the same increasingly elaborated melody as is found in Rome, Vall. B 23, Subiaco XVIII, and New York, Morgan M 379.

BIBLIOGRAPHY Bannister, *Monumenti*, no. 162 (pp. 47–49) and pl. 21 (fol. 13v); Gamber, *CLLA*, no. 1,413; Kelly, *TBC*, 315–16; Lowe, *TBS*, 2:149; *PM* 14 (see table, p. 471); *PM* 21:319–21, 398–99; Salmon, *Les manuscrits*, 2: no. 401; Supino Martini, *Roma*, 153–59.

APPENDIX 2

EDITIONS OF THE
SOUTH ITALIAN
EXULTET

T hese editions of the Beneventan and the Franco-Roman texts of the Exultet are based on examination of manuscript sources from southern Italy and a few related manuscripts from central Italy. There is also an edition of the earliest texts of the Franco-Roman Exultet, for use in comparison with the southern Italian versions. The text is presented as it might be sung, arranged by larger and smaller textual divisions—cola and commata—and punctuated to reflect the musical formulas that were regularly applied to the text. Variants are presented along with the text, since the relation among manuscripts is here at least as important as the base text itself.

Rules of the Edition

The texts are arranged and punctuated according to the musical setting of particular manuscripts: Bari Exultet 1 for the Beneventan text, and the Avezzano Exultet for the Franco-Roman.

Punctuation of individual manuscripts has not been retained.

The diphthongs *oe* and *ae*, and the letter *e* with cedilla, have been regularized to *e*.

Orthographic variants have generally not been retained. These include variants in the *Nomina sacra* (*hiesus, iesus; christus, xpistus*), the use of *c* for *t* (*tocius, totius; uitiis, uiciis*); *b* for *v* (*hiberna, hiuerna*), and *set* for *sed*, and many others (*irradiata, yrradiata; paschalia, paskalia; nihil, nichil*).

263

Words in capital letters indicate places where many, most, or all sources vary from the text presented.

Signs Used in the Edition

//// indicate the beginning or end of a lacuna

< > enclose portions of text with musical notation

] separates a portion of the main text from its variants to follow

| separates variants of one portion of the text from the next portion of text with its variants

: separates variants of a single passage

add. added to the text

corr. corrected, apparently by the principal scribe or a corrector

illeg. now illegible

l. h. in a hand later than that of the principal scribe

lac. not present in the source owing to a physical lacuna

om. omitted

s. n. without musical notation

above l. above the text line

sign + a cross is written over the text

The Beneventan Text of the Exultet

The Beneventan text survives in only a few sources, most of which are fragmentary. This edition collates all those sources, and it presents all significant variants in the known sources of the text.

The Beneventan text has been printed many times. They include the following: Andoyer, "L'ancienne liturgie," 22:41–42 (1913–14; the version of Benevento 33, beginning with *Vere quia*); *Aggiornamento*, 430–31 (from *PM*, 14); Bannister, "The *Vetus Itala* Text"; Bertaux, in the tableau "Iconographie comparée des rouleaux de l'exultet," in *L'art;* Duchesne, *Origines*, 557–60 (from Nitto de Rossi); *Exultet*, 485–86 (from *PM*, 14); Hesbert, "L' 'antiphonale missarum,'" 185–87; Kruft, "Exsultetrolle," cols. 723–24; Nitto de Rossi and Nitti di Vito, *Codice diplomatico* (the text from Bari 1, with errors, 205–7); *PM*, 14:385–86; Pinell, "La benedicció," 96–97 (from *PM*, 14). With the exception of Bannister, which contains errors, and *PM*, 14, which did not take all sources into account, none of these is a critical edition.

The text is arranged by cola and commata, as it might be sung; the arrangement here is that of Bari 1. A capital letter indicates the beginning of a textual period, to which a special musical formula is sung; and the closing formula of the period is indicated by a full stop. The intermediate cadential formula (B) is indicated with a semicolon, and the intermediate pause (M) is indicated by a comma. For a full explanation of these musical formulas, see chapter 4. Not all Exultets arrange the text identically, and the variants in this, interesting as they are, cannot be accommodated here. Many of these questions have been addressed in chapter 4.

The prologue ("Exultet iam . . .") is edited here from these manuscripts only; other south Italian versions of the prologue are edited with the Franco-Roman text.

Some of these manuscripts (especially Bari 1) contain many later additions to the commemorations of ecclesiastical and secular authorities. These are not generally reported here but may be seen in the descriptions of manuscripts in Appendix 1.

Variants are reported here from the passages of the Beneventan text quoted in Franco-Roman versions of the Exultet in southern Italy. These incude Pisa 2 and Montecassino 2, which cite two passages: "Flore utuntur coniuge . . ." and "Cuius odor suauis" (the former passage quoted also in Oxford, Canon. bibl. lat. 61). Vat. lat. 3784A quotes "Apis siquidem"; Bari 2 and Bari 3 use the commemoration beginning "Saluum fac." For details on these passages, see the edition of the Franco-Roman text and chapter 3, pp. 57–59.

The Manuscripts

Fuller descriptions of these manuscripts are seen in Appendix 1.

Bari, Archivio del Capitolo Metropolitano, Exultet 1; s11½ Bari. = B1

Bari, Archivio del Capitolo Metropolitano, Exultet 2, s11¾ Bari. The prologue and the first words of the preface ("Vere quia dignum et iustum est per Christum dominum nostrum") are all that survive of the text; the rest has been erased and substituted with the Franco-Roman text (edited elsewhere). = B2

Benevento, Biblioteca Capitolare 33, fols. 76v–77v; missal, s10/11 of unknown provenance. = Bb

Farfa, Biblioteca dell'Abbazia, Ms. AF. 338 Musica XI (formerly AB.F. Musica XI) and Trento, Museo Provinciale d'Arte (Castel del Buonconsiglio) FC 135 (formerly Lawrence Feininger Collection); fragments of a gradual of unknown provenance, s11. The fragments present both the Franco-Roman and the Beneventan texts; the Beneventan text begins with the preface. = Fb

Manchester, Rylands Library lat. 2. Exultet, s10/11, provenance unknown. The text is incomplete. = Ma

Mirabella Eclano, Archivio della Chiesa Collegiata, Exultet 1 (on deposit in the Biblioteca Nazionale, Naples), Exultet 1; s11½, provenance unknown; Benevento? = M1

Montecassino, Biblioteca dell'Abbazia, Exultet 1, a fragment s11, Amalfi? = Mc

Salerno 3, fols. 141v–47; missal of Salerno, s15. = Sa

Troia, Archivio Capitolare, Exultet 1, Troia, s11²⁄₂. = T1

Troia, Archivio Capitolare, Exultet 2, Troia, s12½. The roll is incomplete at the beginning, starting with "apes siquidem." = T2

Vatican City, Biblioteca Apostolica Vaticana Vat. lat. 3784; Exultet roll, s11²⁄₂, Montecassino. Only the prologue of this roll survives, and it cannot be proven that the text was originally Beneventan; but the amputation suggests it. = Ve

Vatican City, Biblioteca Apostolica Vaticana Vat. lat. 10673; missal of unknown provenance, s10/11. Only the first seven lines of text survive. = Vg

Vatican City, Biblioteca Apostolica Vaticana Vat. lat. 9820; Exultet, s10ex, Benevento. Only lines 1–4 and a passage at the end survive of the lower script. The initials of the erased text periods can be seen in the margins but have not been reported here; the Franco-Roman text of the upper script is edited below. = Vm

Velletri, Archivio diocesano, Exultet; s11ex(?), Montecassino; only fragmentary text survives. = Vl

The Manuscripts Arranged by Sigla

B1 = Bari, Exultet 1
B2 = Bari, Exultet 2
Bb = Benevento 33
Fb = Farfa-Trento fragments
M1 = Mirabella, Exultet 1
Ma = Manchester, Rylands Lat. 2
Mc = Montecassino, Exultet 1
Sa = Salerno 4
T1 = Troia, Exultet 1
T2 = Troia, Exultet 2
Ve = Vatican lat. 3784
Vg = Vatican lat. 10673
Vl = Velletri Exultet
Vm = Vatican lat. 9820, lower script

Exultet iam angelica turba celorum;
> Exultet . . . celorum *om.* Fb : *lac.* Mc T2 Vl

exultent diuina misteria;
> exultent] exultet T1 | exultent . . . misteria *om.* Fb : *lac.* Mc T2 Vl

et pro tanti regis uictoria, tuba intonet salutaris.
> tanti] tantis Vg T1 : tantis *corr. to* tanti B2 | et . . . salutaris *om.* Fb : *lac.* Mc T2 Vl

Gaudeat se tantis tellus, irradiata fulgoribus;
> irradiata] inradiata B1 Bb T1 | gaudeat . . . fulgoribus *om.* Fb : *lac.* Mc T2 Vl Vm

et eterni regis splendore lustrata;
> et . . . lustrata *om.* Fb : *lac.* Mc T2 Vl Vm

totius orbis se sentiat, amisisse caliginem.
> caliginem] caligine *corr. l. h. to* caliginem B2 | sentiat . . . caliginem *lac.* Vg : totius . . . caliginem *om.* Fb : *lac.* Mc T2 Vl Vm

Letetur et mater ecclesia; tanti luminis, adornata FULGORIBUS;
> fulgoribus] fulgore B2 Bb M1 Ma Sa | letetur . . . fulgoribus *om.* Fb : *lac.* Mc T2 Vg Vl Vm

et magnis populorum uocibus, hec aula resultet.

> *lac.* Mc T2 Vg Vl Vm : *om.* Fb

Quapropter astantibus uobis, fratres karissimi;

> quap. . . . karissimi *om.* Fb : *lac.* Mc T2 Vg Vl Vm

ad tam miram sancti huius, luminis claritatem;

> ad . . . claritatem *om.* Fb : *lac.* Mc T2 Vg Vl Vm

una mecum queso dei, omnipotentis, misericordiam inuocate.

> una . . . inuocate *om.* Fb : *lac.* Mc T2 Vg Vl Vm

Vt qui me non meis meritis,

> me] *added above line* B2 Bb | ut . . . meritis *om.* Fb : *lac.* Mc T2 Vg Vl Vm

INTRA leuitarum numerum, dignatus est aggregare;

> intra] in B1 B2 Bb M1 T1 : infra Sa | numerum] numero Bb M1 T1 : numerum *corr. to* numero B2 | intra . . . aggregare *om.* Fb : *lac.* Mc T2 Vg Vm Vl

luminis sui, gratiam INFUNDENTE;

> gratiam] gratia T1 Ve | infundente] infundens B1 B2 Bb M1 Ma Sa T1 | luminis . . . infundente *om.* Fb : *lac.* Mc T2 Vg Vl Vm

cerei huius, laudem implere precipiat.

> cerei] *sign* + T1 | precipiat] *rewritten* M1 | cerei . . . precipiat *om.* Fb : *lac.* Mc T2 Vg Vl Vm

Per dominum nostrum, iesum christum, filium suum;

> per . . . suum *om.* Fb : *lac.* Mc T2 Vg Vl Vm

uiuentem secum, atque regnantem;

> secum atque regnantem] atque regnantem secum B2 | atque] adque M1 | uiu . . . regnantem *om.* Fb : *lac.* Mc T2 Vg Vl Vm

in unitate spiritus SANCTI;

> sancti] sancti deus B1 B2 Sa T1 Ve : sancti deum Bb M1 | in . . . sancti *om.* Fb : *lac.* Mc T2 Vg Vl Vm

per omnia secula seculorum. Amen.

> per . . . Amen *om.* Fb : *lac.* Mc T2 Vg Vl Vm

Dominus uobiscum

> Dominus uobiscum *om.* Fb : *lac.* Mc T2 Vg Vl Vm

Et cum spiritu tuo

> Et . . . tuo *added l. h.* B2 : *om.* Fb : *lac.* Mc T2 Vg Vl Vm

Sursum corda

> Sursum corda *om.* Fb : *lac.* Mc T2 Vg Vl Vm

Habemus ad dominum

> habemus ad dominum *add. l. h.* B2 : *om.* Fb : *lac.* Mc T2 Vg Vl Vm

Gratias agamus domino deo nostro

> gratias . . . nostro *om.* Fb : *lac.* Mc T2 Vg Vl Vm

Dignum et iustum est

> dignum . . . est *om.* B1 Fb : *add. l. h.* B2 : *lac.* Mc T2 Vg Vl Vm

Vere quia dignum et iustum est

> | quia . . . est] *erased* Ve; *the manuscript breaks off at this point* | uere . . . est *rewritten* M1 : *lac.* Mc T2 Vg Vm

per Christum dominum nostrum.

> nostrum] B2 *is erased after this word, although the initial letters of the text periods remain in the margin* | per . . . nostrum *rewritten* M1 : *lac.* Mc T2 Ve Vg Vm

Qui nos ad noctem istam, non tenebrarum,

> noctem] nocte Fb | qui . . . tenebrarum *rewritten* M1 : *lac.* B2 Mc T2 Ve Vg Vl Vm

sed luminis matrem, perducere dignatus est;

> est] es Fb | sed . . . est *rewritten* M1 : *lac.* B2 Mc T2 Ve Vg Vl Vm

in qua exorta est ab inferis, in eterna die, resurrectio mortuorum.

> exorta] exhorta B1 | eterna die] eternam diem Ma | in qua . . . mortuorum *rewritten* M1 : *lac.* B2 Mc T2 Ve Vg Vl Vm

Solutis quippe nexibus, et calcato, mortis aculeo;

> nexibus] nescibus Vl | aculeo] eculeo Bb Fb M1 T1 | solutis . . . aculeo *lac.* B2 Mc T2 Ve Vg Vm

resurrexit a mortuis, qui fuerat inter mortuos liber.

> resurrexit . . . liber *lac.* B2 Mc T2 Ve Vg Vm

Unde et nox ipsa sidereo, pro ecclesiarum ornatu;

> unde] *add. s. n.* hic accendat Ma | et] *om.* Bb Ma Sa Vl | sidereo] sideria Bb | -natu *lacking owing to lacuna of one line* Fb | unde . . . ornatu *lac.* B2 Mc T2 Ve Vg Vm

cereorum splendore, tamquam dies, illuminata collucet;

> cereorum . . . collucet *lac.* B2 Fb Mc T2 Ve Vg Vm

quia in eius matutino, resurgente Christo;

> quia] *lac.* Fb | quia . . . Christo *lac.* B2 Mc T2 Ve Vg Vm

mors occidit redemptorum; et emersit uita credentium.

> redemptorum] redemptorem Sa T1 | mors . . . credentium *lac.* B2 Mc T2 Ve Vg Vm

Vere tu pretiosus es opifex; formator es omnium;

> vere . . . omnium *lac.* B2 Mc T2 Ve Vg Vm

cui qualitas in agendi, non fuit officio; sed in sermonis imperio.

> qualitas] equalitas Fb | agendi] agendis Vl | cui . . . imperio *lac.* B2 Mc T2 Ve Vg Vm

Qui ornatum, atque habitum mundo;

> qui] qui*corr. to* quia T1 | ornatum] natum *corr. to* ornatum M1 : ornatu Sa | atque] *om.* Bb | habitum] abitum B1 Fb abitu Sa | mundo] mundi B1 Fb M1 Ma Sa T1 Vl | qui . . . mundo *lac.* B2 Mc T2 Ve Vg Vm

nec ad ampliandum quasi inops potentie;

> ampliandum] amplicandum Fb | nec . . . quasi *lac.* Mc | nec . . . potentie *lac.* B2 T2 Ve Vg Vm

nec ad ditandum quasi egenus, glorie condidisti.

> ad ditandum] addiutandum (?) *corr. to* ad ditandum Ma | egenus] egenis Sa | nec . . . condidisti *lac.* B2 T2 Ve Vg Vm

Totus ac plenus in te es; qui dum per uirginea uiscera, mundo illaberis;
> te] se *corr. to* te Fb | es] est Bb | illaberis] illaueris Bb Fb M1 Ma Mc T1 |
> totus . . . illaberis *lac.* B2 T2 Ve Vg Vl Vm

uirginitatem etiam, creature commendas.
> creature] creatura Bb Fb M1 T1 | commendas] *corr. l. h. to* -ans Fb : *add.*
> *s. n.* Cum autem uentum fuent ad hunc uersum Sa | uirg. . . . commendas
> *lac.* B2 T2 Ve Vg Vl Vm

Apes siquidem, dum ore concipiunt; ore parturiunt;
> dum] *add. l. h.* Ma | apes . . . parturiunt *lac.* B2 M1 Ve Vg Vl Vm

casto corpore; non fedo desiderio copulantur.
> fedo] de fedo (*the syllable de lacks a note*) Fb : fetido Vat. lat. 3784A | copu-
> lantur] *add. s. n.* Tunc uadant septem presbiteri cum duobus subdiaconibus
> totidemque acolitis ad fontes; et dicant ibi septenas letanias, et redeant ad loca
> sua. Sa | casto . . . copulantur *lac.* B2 M1 Ve Vg Vl Vm

Denique uirginitatem seruantes; posteritatem generant;
> | uirginitatem] *over erasure* T1 | generant] generans Bb | denique . . . generant
> *lac.* B2 M1 Ve Vg Vl Vm

sobole gaudent; matres dicuntur; intacte perdurant;
> intacte] intacta Fb T2 | sobole . . . perdurant *lac.* B2 M1 Ve Vg Vl Vm

filios generant; et uiros non norunt.
> uiros] -os *over erasure* T1 | filios . . . norunt *lac.* B2 M1 Ve Vg Vl Vm

Flore utuntur coniuge;
> flore] flores Fb | flore . . . coniuge *lac.* B2 M1 Ma Ve Vg Vl Vm

flore funguntur genere;
> flore] flores Fb | genere] genera Fb | flore . . . genere *lac.* B2 M1 Ma Ve Vg
> Vl Vm

flore domos instruunt;
> flore domos] flores domum Fb | flore . . . instruunt *lac.* B2 M1 Ma Ve Vg
> Vl Vm

flore diuitias conuehunt;
> flore] flores Fb | conuehunt] conueunt B1 Bb Fb Mc Sa T1 T2 | flore . . .
> conuehunt *lac.* B2 M1 Ma Ve Vg Vl Vm

flore ceram conficiunt.
> ceram] cera *corr. to* -am Mc | flore . . . conficiunt *lac.* B2 Fb M1 Ma Ve Vg
> Vl Vm

O admirandus apium feruor;
> admirandus] ammirandum Bb | apium] apum T2 Sa | o . . . feruor *lac.* B2
> Fb M1 Ma Ve Vg Vl Vm

ad commune opus, pacifica turba concurrunt;
> ad commu- *lac.* Fb | concurrunt] concurrit T2 | ad . . . concurrunt *lac.* B2
> M1 Ma Ve Vg Vl Vm

et operantibus plurimis, una augetur substantia.
> augetur] augeatur Bb T1 | et . . . substantia *lac.* B2 M1 Ma Ve Vg Vl Vm

O inuisibile artificium;
> inuisibile] inuisibilis Fb | o . . . artificium *lac.* B2 M1 Ma Ve Vg Vl Vm

primo culmina pro fundamentis edificant;
> culmina] culmine T1 | primo . . . edificant *lac.* B2 M1 Ma Ve Vg Vl Vm

et tam ponderosam mellis sarcinam;

> ponderosam] ponderosa Bb T1 | mellis sarcinam] mellisarcinam Fb | et . . . sarcinam *lac.* B2 M1 Ma Ve Vg Vl Vm

pendentibus domiciliis, imponere non uerentur.

> pend . . . uerentur *lac.* B2 M1 Ma Ve Vg Vl Vm

O uirginitatis insignia;

> uirginitatis] uirginitas *corr. to* uirginitatis Bb | o . . . insignia *lac.* B2 M1 Ma Ve Vg Vl Vm

que non possessori damna, sed sibi lucra conuectant;

> possesori] possessoris T1 T2 | sed] *om.* T2 | conuectant] connectant T1 : (*or* connectunt?) T2 | que . . . conuectant *lac.* B2 M1 Ma Ve Vg Vl Vm

auferunt quidem predam, et cum preda, minime tollunt peccatum.

> auferunt] auferetur Fb | preda] predam Fb Mc T1 | tollunt] tolunt T2 | peccatum] peccata Fb | auferunt . . . peccatum lac. B2 M1 Ma Ve Vg Vl Vm

Spoliant quidem florum cutem; et morsuum non annotant cicatricem.

> spoliant . . . cicatricem *lac.* B2 M1 Ma Ve Vg Vl Vm

Sed inter hec que CREDIMUS; huius cerei, gratiam predicemus.

> credimus] dinumeravimus B1 Fb Mc Sa T1 T2 | cerei] *sign* + T1 | sed . . . que] *rewritten* (over erasure?) Mc | sed . . . predicemus lac. B2 M1 Ma Ve Vg Vl Vm

Cuius odor suauis est; et flamma hilaris;

> flamma] flammam Fb | cuius . . . hilaris *lac.* B2 M1 Ma Mc Ve Vg Vl Vm

non tetro odore, aruina desudat; sed iocundissima suauitate;

> desudat] resudet Sa | non . . . suauitate *lac.* B2 M1 Ma Mc Ve Vg Vl Vm

qui peregrinis non inficitur pigmentis; ILLUMINATUR spiritu sancto.

> illuminatur] sed illuminatur B1 Bb Fb Sa T1 T2 | spiritu] spiritum T2 spiritus *corr. to* spiritu Fb | qui . . . sancto *lac.* B2 M1 Ma Mc Ve Vg Vl Vm

Qui ut accensus, proprias corporis, compages depascit;

> proprias] propria Fb | compages] compagos Sa | qui . . . depascit *lac.* B2 M1 Ma Mc Ve Vg Vl Vm

ita coagolatas lacrimas; in riuulos fundit guttarum.

> fundit] infundit Bb | fundit guttarum *lac.* Fb | ita . . . guttarum *lac.* B2 M1 Ma Mc Ve Vg Vl Vm

Quique semiusta membra; ambroseo sanguine, flauea uena distollit;

> quique] qui cum T2 | flauea] flammea T2 | flauea uena] flabea bena Fb | quique . . . sanguine *lac.* Fb | quique . . . distollit *lac.* B2 M1 Ma Mc Ve Vg Vl Vm

habitum bibit ignis humorem.

> habitum] abitum B1 : auidus T2 | bibit] uiuit B1 | habitum . . . humorem *lac.* B2 M1 Ma Mc Ve Vg Vl Vm

In huius autem, cerei luminis corpore; te omnipotens postulamus;

> in . . . postulamus *lac.* B2 M1 Ma Mc Ve Vg Vl Vm

ut superne benedictionis munus accommodes.

> benedictionis] *add. sign* + Bb B1 Sa T1 T2 | ut . . . accommodes *lac.* B2 M1 Ma Mc Ve Vg Vl Vm

Ut si quis hunc sumpserit, aduersus flabra uentorum;
> | ut] et Bb Sa | hunc] hinc B1 Bb T1 | flabra] flaura Bb : fabra Sa | ut . . .
> uentorum *lac.* B2 M1 Ma Mc Ve Vg Vl Vm

aduersus spiritus procellarum; sit ei domine, singulare perfugium;
> ei] eis Fb | aduersus . . . perfugium *lac.* B2 M1 Ma Mc Ve Vg Vl Vm

sit murus ab hoste fidelibus.
> murus] *second letter was originally* e, *clarified first syllable added above line* Bb
> | sit . . . fidelibus *lac.* B2 M1 Ma Mc Ve Vg Vl Vm

Saluum fac populum tuum domine, et benedic hereditatem tuam;
> benedic] *add. sign* + B1 Sa T1 T2 | saluum . . . tuam *lac.* B2 M1 Ma Mc
> Ve Vg Vl Vm

ut redeuntes ad festiuitatem pasche;
> ut . . . pasche *lac.* B2 M1 Ma Mc Ve Vg Vl Vm

per hec uisibilibus, et inuisibilibus, tuis INHIANTES;
> hec] *om.* Fb | uisibilibus] uisibilia Sa | et] *om.* Sa | tuis] tu (*possibly corrected
> by erasing a longer word*) T1 : *om.* T2 | inhiantes] inhians Bb Fb : inhiantes
> *over erasure* T1 : inhyantes Sa | per . . . inhiantes *lac.* B2 M1 Ma Mc Ve Vg
> Vl Vm

dum presentium usufruuntur; futurorum desideria accendantur.
> futurorum] futurarum Fb | desideria] desiderio Sa T2 (*last letter over erasure*
> T1) | accendantur] accendatur Sa : *add.* Precamur ergo te domine ut nos
> famulos tuos omnem clerum et deuotissimum populum, una cum beatissimo
> uiro papa nostro ill. et antistite nostro il. et his qui tibi offerunt hoc sacri-
> ficium laudis. Memento etiam domine famulorum tuorum principum nos-
> trorum il. et il. et omni exercitum (*an additional line is trimmed of its text*) Fb
> | dum . . . accendantur *lac.* B2 M1 Ma Mc Ve Vg Vl Vm

Una cum beatissimo, papa nostro il.;
> il.] N. Sa: illo T1 | una . . . il. *lac.* B2 Fb M1 Ma Mc Ve Vg Vl Vm

et famulo tuo pontifice nostro il.;
> et famulo tuo pontifice *lac.* Fb | famulo . . . il.] antistite nostro ill. B1 (illo)
> T1 T2: archiepiscopo nostro N. Sa: *add.* necnon et famulam tuam abbatissam
> nostram cum uniuersa congregatione [*l. h. over erasure:* beatissimi Petri apos-
> toli sibi commissa ac] temporum uite quiete concessa gaudiis [*add.* ea] facias
> perfrui sempiternis Vm | et . . . il. *lac.* B2 Fb M1 Ma Mc Ve Vg Vl Vm

sed et omnibus presbiteris; diaconibus; subdiaconibus;
> subdiaconibus] *om.* Bb | sed . . . subd. *lac.* B2 Fb M1 Ma Mc Ve Vg Vl Vm

cunctoque clero uel plebe.
> cunctoque . . . plebe *lac.* B2 M1 Ma Mc Ve Vg Vl Vm

Memorare domine, famulum tuum, imperatorem nostrum il.;
> memorare] memora Fb | famulum . . . il.] famulorum tuorum imperatorum
> nostrorum il. et il. B1 : famulo tuo imperatore nostro ill. T1 : imperatorum
> nostrorum il. et il. Fb | imperatorem] imperatore Bb : regem T2 | nostrum]
> -o Bb | Memorare . . . il.] Respice quesumus domine super deuotissimum
> famulum tuum regem nostrum N. cuius tu deus desiderii uota prenoscens
> ineffabilis pietatis et misericordie tue munere iocundum perpetue pacis ac-
> comoda et in his pascalibus gaudiis regere gubernare et conseruare digneris
> Sa | mem . . . il. *lac.* B2 Fb M1 Ma Mc Ve Vg Vl Vm

et principem nostrum il.;

> | et . . . il.] et principum nostrorum il. et il. Fb : *om.* B1 Sa T1 T2 : *lac.* B2
> Fb M1 Ma Mc Ve Vg Vl Vm

et eorum exercitum uniuersum;

> eorum] eius T2 | exercitum universum] exercitus (*but final syllable also has*
> *-um abbreviation*) universus Bb | et . . . uniuersum] et cunctum exercitum
> eorum et omnium circumadstantium B1 : et eius exercitu (*originally had a*
> *further letter*) universu (*originally had a further letter*) T1 : *om.* Sa : *lac.* B2 Fb
> M1 Ma Mc Ve Vg Vl Vm

Qui uiuis cum patre, et spiritu sancto;

> qui uiuis] qui uiuis et regnas Fb : *lac.* Vm | et spiritu Sancto] in unitate
> spiritus sancti Fb Sa | qui . . . sancto *lac.* B2 Fb M1 Ma Mc Ve Vg Vl

et regnas deus, in secula seculorum. Amen.

> et regnas] et regnans B1 : *lac.* Vm : *om.* Fb | in] per omnia Fb Sa T2 | et . . .
> amen *lac.* B2 Fb M1 Ma Mc Ve Vg Vl

The Franco-Roman Text of the Exultet in South Italy

This edition presents the versions of the Franco-Roman text as it is found in manuscripts of southern Italy. It does not attempt to establish an original text or to suggest that a single version of the text was everywhere in use in southern Italy. The variants here are as interesting as the text.

The base text given here is based on editions of the earliest sources and is derived from the texts edited as the early texts of the Franco-Roman Exultet. Words and passages in capital letters indicate places where many, most, or all south Italian manuscripts diverge from this tradition.

The text is arranged by cola and commata, as it might be sung; the arrangement here is that of the Avezzano roll. A capital letter indicates the beginning of a textual period, to which a special musical formula is sung; and the closing formula of the period is indicated by a full stop. The intermediate cadential formula (B) is indicated with a semicolon, and the intermediate pause (M) is indicated by a comma. For a full explanation of these musical formulas, see chapter 4. Not all Exultets arrange the text identically, and the variants in this, interesting as they are, cannot be accommodated here. Many of these questions have been addressed in chapter 4.

Below each line where appropriate, a summary is given of variants from early sources of the Roman text: the "Gallican" missals (GALL), Gelasian sacramentaries of the eighth century (GEL8), the supplement to the Gregorian sacramentary (GREG), and the Roman-German Pontifical (PRG). These are summaries only and do not reflect all the details of the variants in these sources, which can be seen in a separate summary edition.

Manuscripts Used in the Edition

Fuller descriptions of these manuscripts are in Appendix 1.

Avezzano, Archivio diocesano, Exultet SN = Av

Bari, Archivio del Capitolo Metropolitano, Exultet 2, upper script (lower script
  has been included in this edition where not erased from earlier Beneventan
  usage). = B2

Bari, Archivio del Capitolo Metropolitano, Exultet 3 = B3

Berlin, Staatsbibliothek Preussischer Kulturbesitz, MS Lat. fol. 920, fols. 123–25 = D4

Capua, Tesoro della cattedrale, Exultet roll = Cp

Farfa, Biblioteca dell'Abbazia, MS AF. 338 Musica XI, with Trento = Fr

Gaeta, Tesoro della Cattedrale, Exultet 1, upper script = G4

Gaeta, Tesoro della Cattedrale, Exultet 2 = G2

Gaeta, Tesoro della Cattedrale, Exultet 3 = G3

London, British Library, MS Egerton 3511, fols. 159v–62v = Lb

London, British Library, Add. MS 30337 = Lo

Mirabella Eclano, Archivio della Chiesa Collegiata, Exultet 2 (on deposit in the Biblioteca Nazionale, Naples) = M2

Montecassino, Biblioteca dell'Abbazia, Exultet 2 = Mb

Montecassino, Archivio dell Badia 451: reported as PRG; see the edition, p. 289 f.

Naples, Biblioteca nazionale, MS VI G 34, fols. 77–83 = Na

Naples, Biblioteca nazionale, MS VI G 38, fols. 129v–32v = Nb

New York, Pierpont Morgan Library, MS M 379, fols. 108v–11 = S1

Oxford, Bodleian Library, MS Canon. Bibl. lat. 61, fols. 115v–23v = D1

Oxford, Bodleian Library, MS Canon. liturg. 342, fols. 52v–54v = D2

Paris, Bibliothèque nationale, MS n. a. lat. 710 = Pa

Pisa, Capitolo del Duomo, Exultet 2 = Pi

Rome, Biblioteca Casanatense, MS 724 (B I 13) III = Cs

Rome, Biblioteca Casanatense, MS 1103, fols. 118v–20v = Mv

Rome, Biblioteca Vallicelliana, MS B 23, fols. 124v–26v = S3

Rome, Biblioteca Vallicelliana, MS B 43, fols. 49–153 = S4

Rome, Biblioteca Vallicelliana, MS C 32, fols. 24v–30 = Rv

Rome, Biblioteca Vallicelliana, MS D 5: reported as PRG; see the edition, p. 289f.

Rome, Biblioteca Vallicelliana, MS F 29, fols. 36v–38v = S2

Subiaco, Biblioteca del Protocenobio di Santa Scolastica, MS XVIII (19), fols. 77v–79 = S5

Trento, Museo Provinciale d'Arte (Castel del Buonconsiglio), MS FC 135 (formerly Lawrence Feininger collection), with Farfa = Fr

Troia, Archivio capitolare, Exultet 3 = T3

Vatican City, Biblioteca Apostolica Vaticana, MS Barb. lat. 592 = Bb

Vatican City, Biblioteca Apostolica Vaticana, MS Barb. lat. 560, fols. 68v–69v = C2

Vatican City, Biblioteca Apostolica Vaticana, MS Barb. lat. 603, fols. 57–58 = Vd

Vatican City, Biblioteca Apostolica Vaticana, MS Barb. lat. 699, fols. 104–104v = Vc

Vatican City, Biblioteca Apostolica Vaticana, MS Borg. lat. 339, fols. 53–58v = D3

Vatican City, Biblioteca Apostolica Vaticana, MS Ottob. lat. 576, fols. 167–71 = Ot

Vatican City, Biblioteca Apostolica Vaticana, MS Vat. lat. 3784A = Vf

Vatican City, Biblioteca Apostolica Vaticana, MS Vat. lat. 4770, fols. 99v–100v = C1

Vatican City, Biblioteca Apostolica Vaticana, MS Vat. lat. 6082, fols. 120v–122v = Va

Vatican City, Biblioteca Apostolica Vaticana, MS Vat. lat. 9820, upper script = Vb

Manuscripts Arranged by Sigla

Av = Avezzano
B2 = Bari, Exultet 2, upper script
B3 = Bari, Exultet 3
Bb = Vatican, Barberini lat. 592, plus lost piece published by Gerbert
C1 = Vatican lat. 4770
C2 = Vatican, Barb. lat. 560
Cp = Capua, Exultet
Cs = Rome, Bibl. Casanatense 724 (B I 13)
D1 = Oxford, Bodl. Canon. Bibl. lat. 61
D2 = Oxford, Bodl. Canon. liturg. 342
D3 = Vatican Borg. lat. 339
D4 = Berlin 920
Fr = Farfa-Trento, Roman text
G2 = Gaeta, Exultet 2
G3 = Gaeta, Exultet 3
G4 = Gaeta, Exultet 1, upper script
Lb = London, BL Eg. 3511
Lo = London, Br. Lib. Add. MS 30337
M2 = Mirabella, Exultet 2
Mb = Montecassino, Exultet 2
Mv = Rome, Casanatense 1103
Na = Naples VI G 34
Nb = Napes VI G 38
Ot = Vatican, Ottoboni lat. 576
Pa = Paris, BN n. a. lat. 710
Pi = Pisa, Exultet 2
Rv = Rome, Vall. C 32
S1 = New York, Morgan M 379
S2 = Rome, Vall F 29
S3 = Rome, Vall B 23
S4 = Rome, Vall B 43
S5 = Subiaco XVIII
T3 = Troia, Exultet 3
Va = Vatican lat. 6082
Vb = Vatican lat. 9820, upper script
Vc = Vatican, Barb. lat. 699
Vd = Vatican, Barb. lat. 603
Vf = Vatican lat. 3784A

Exultet iam angelica turba celorum;
          ex . . . celorum *lac.* Bb Cp Fr G2 G3 G4 M2 Pa

exultent diuina misteria;
          PRG mysteria
          | exultent] exultet S1 | exultent . . . misteria *lac.* Bb Cp Fr G2 G3 G4 M2 Pa

et pro tanti regis uictoria, tuba intonet salutaris.
          GALL victuria PRG insonet
          tanti] tantis C2 D3 D4 Nb Ot T3 : tantis *corr. to* tanti B2 | regis] *corr. to* regi
          T3 | et pro tan] *lac.* Bb | et . . . salutaris *lac.* Cp Fr G2 G3 G4 M2 Pa

Gaudeat se TANTIS TELLVS, irradiata fulgoribus;

> GALL, GEL8 gaudeat se tantis illius inradiata GREG gaudeat se tellus inradi]ata PRG gaudeat tellus tantis
> gaudeat] gaudeatque Vc | tantis tellus] tellus tantis Na S1 S2 S4 S5 T3 Vc Vd Vf : tellus tantis luminis S3 | irradiata] irradiatam Bb C1 Lo S2 Vc | fulgoribus] fulforibus Vc | gaudeat . . . fulgoribus *lac.* Cp Fr G2 G3 G4 M2 Pa

et eterni regis, splendore lustrata;

> PRG illustrata
> regis] regi *corr. to* regis C2 | splendore] plendore Vc | lustrata] lustrata *corr. to* illustrata S5 : illustrata D2 D4 Nb S2 S4 Va Vf : inluxtrata Ot : illustratam S2 | et . . . lustrata *lac.* Cp Fr G2 G3 G4 M2 Pa

totius orbis, se sentiat, amisisse caliginem.

> se] *added l. h.* Vf | amisisse] aminisisse T3 : amisise C1 D4 | caliginem] caligine D2 D4 Nb S3 | totius . . . caliginem *lac.* Cp Fr G2 G3 G4 M2 Pa

Letetur et mater ecclesia, tanti luminis, adornata FULGORIBUS;

> GALL, GEL8, fulgore
> luminis] lumini Na | fulgoribus] fulgore B2 B3 D2 Ot | tanti . . . fulgoribus] *illeg.* G4 | letetur . . . fulgoribus *lac.* Cp Fr G2 G3 M2 Pa

et magnis populorum uocibus, hec aula resultet.

> magnis] magnus Na | aula] *added l. h.* Na | resultet] resultent Ot | et . . . resultet *lac.* Cp Fr G2 G3 M2 Pa

Quapropter astantibus uobis, fratres karissimi;

> GALL, GEL8, GREG adstantibus PRG astantes uos
> astantibus uobis] uos astantes Lo : astantes uos Vc | fratres k. *illeg.* G4 | quap . . . karissimi *lac.* Bb Cp Fr G3 M2

ad tam miram sancti huius, luminis claritatem;

> miram] mira Av C1 C2 D3 D4 S1 S2 S3 S5 | sancti huius] huius sancti C2 G4 S4 Vf | ad . . . claritatem *lac.* Bb Cp Fr G3 M2

una mecum queso, dei omnipotentis, misericordiam inuocate.

> misericordiam] misericordia Ot | inuocate] inuocante *corr. to* -ate Cs : inuo-camus D3 | misericordiam inuocate *lac.* Mb | una . . . inuocate *lac.* Bb Cp Fr G3 M2

Vt qui me non meis meritis,

> ut] et (*erroneous initial?*) D4 | me] *add. above l.* B2 : om. Ot S1 S5 | ut . . . meritis *lac.* Bb Cp Fr G3 M2

intra leuitarum numerum, dignatus est aggregare;

> GALL, GEL8, GREG adgregare
> | -tra leuitarum *l. h. over erasure* D1 | intra] infra Av G2 Mb Mv S5 : in B2 B3 D3 | leuitarum numerum] numerum leuitarum S4 | numerum] numerum *corr. to* numero B2 : numero D3 | est] es Mb S3 | aggregare] aggregari S3 (agre-) D2 | intra . . . aggregare *lac.* Bb Cp Fr G3 M2

luminis sui, gratiam INFVNDENTE;

> GREG gratia PRG infundendo
> sui] suis D3 | gratiam] gratia D3 D4 Na Pa Rv S1 S2 T3 : gratias S3 : claritatem G4 Nb : *add. sign* + D1 S1 | infundente] infundente *corr. to* in-fundens Cs : infundentem Av : infundendo C1 Lo S4 Vc Vd Vf : infundens B2 B3 C2 D1 D2 D3 G4 Lb Mb Mv Nb Pi S1 S3 S5 Vb | luminis . . . infundente *lac.* Bb Cp Fr G3 M2

cerei huius, laudem implere precipiat.

GREG perficiat

cerei] *add. sign* + B2 C2 Mb Na Pa S5 | laudem]lampadem S4 | implere] impleri S4 | precipiat] perficiat *corr. l.h.* to precipiat Cs : perficiat D4 G4 Na Nb S4 Vc Vd : perficiant T3 : precipias S3 | cerei . . . precipiat *lac.* Bb Cp Fr G3 M2

Per dominum nostrum, iesum christum, filium suum;

GALL, GEL8 Per.

per . . . nostrum] *illeg.* G3 | Per . . . suum] iesus christus dominus noster *corr. to* per dominum nostrum iesum christum filium suum Cs : iesus christus dominus noster S1 S2 S3 S5 | suum] eius C2 T3 : tuum G4 Ot | per . . . suum *lac.* Bb Cp Fr M2

uiuentem secum atque regnantem,

GREG CVM QVO uiuit et regnat PRG QVI CVM EO uiuit et regnat DEVS

uiuentem] uiuente Pa | secum] *om.* S4 | uiu . . . regnantem] *illeg.* G3 : *l. h. over erasure* D1 : uiuentem atque regnantem secum B2 : qui uiuit et regnat cum deo patre *corr. to* uiuentem secum atque regnantem Cs : qui cum eo uiuit et regnat C2 Na : qui cum eo uiuit et regnat deus (deus *erased* T3) D4 Pi T3 : qui uiuit et regnat S2 : qui uiuit et regnat cum patre S1 S3 S5 : cum quo uiuit et regnat G4 Nb Vf : qui tecum uiuit et regnat deus Ot : qui cum eo et sancto spiritu uiuit et regnat C1 : *lac.* Bb Cp Fr M2

in unitate, spiritus SANCTI;

unitate] unitatem *corr. to* unitate B2 | spiritus] spiritu D2 D3 S3 | sancti] sancti deus Av B2 B3 Cs D2 D3 G3 G4 Na Nb Pa Rv S1 S2 S3 S4 S5 T3 Va Vb Vc Vd Vf : sancti deum Lb Lo Mb | in . . . sancti *om.* C1 : *lac.* Bb Cp Fr M2

per omnia secula seculorum. Amen.

per . . . amen *lac.* Bb Cp Fr M2

Dominus uobiscum

dominus uobiscum *lac.* Bb Cp Fr M2

Et cum spiritu tuo

spiritu tuo *om.* Lb | et . . . tuo *lac.* Bb Cp Fr M2

Sursum corda

sursum corda *lac.* Bb Cp Fr M2

Habemus ad dominum

habemus] Aabemus G2 | ad dominum *om.* Lb | habemus ad dominum *lac.* Bb Cp Fr M2

Gratias agamus domino deo nostro

gratias . . . nostro *lac.* Bb Cp Fr M2

Dignum et iustum est

et iustum est] *om.* Lb | dignum . . . est *lac.* Bb Cp Fr M2

Vere quia dignum et iustum EST,

quia] *om.* Mv | est] est equum et salutare D1 D3 D4 Lo Ot Pa Rv Va (*over erasure* Pi) (*add.* Av G3) : est per christum dominum nostrum B2 B3 G2 D2 Mb (*add. l. h.*) Cs : est *followed by four to five erased syllables* Vd | uere . . . est *lac.* Bb Cp Fr

INVISIBILEM deum, OMNIPOTENTEM PATREM;

GEL8, GREG ut invisibilem

inuisibilem] te inuisibilem Av D3 D4 G2 G3 Lo Ot Pa Rv : te inuisilem Va : ut inuisibilem C1 C2 D2 M2 : (*illeg.*)-uisibilem Vd | omn. patrem] patrem onipotentem S4 : patrem omnipotem Na : patrem omnipotentem Av B2 B3 C1 Cs D1 D2 D3 D4 G2 G3 G4 Lb Lo M2 Mb Mv Nb Ot Pa Pi Rv S4 T3 Va Vb Vf : | inu . . . patrem *lac.* Bb Cp Fr

FILIVMQVE VNIGENITVM, dominum nostrum iesum christum;
> PRG filiumque eius
> filiumque] filium tuum que *corr. to* filiumque Ot : filiumque tuum Av D4 Lo Pa Rv Va : filiumque tuum *corr. to* filiumque eius G3 : filiumque eius B2 B3 C1 C2 Cs D1 D2 D3 G2 G4 Lb Mb Mv Na Nb Pi S1 S2 S3 S4 S5 Vb Vc Vf : filiumque eius (*over erasure*) T3 : filium eius M2 | unigenitum *om.* D4 | nostrum *om.* D1 | iesum christum *om.* M2 | christum] christum cum spiritu sancto Cs : christum sanctum quoque spiritum Av Lb Mv S1 S2 S3 S5 Vb Vf : christum cum sancto spiritu D4 | filiumque . . . christum *lac.* Bb Cp Fr

toto cordis, ac mentis affectu;
> ac] hac S3 | ac mentis] *om.* M2 : augmentum Ot | affectu] affectum C2 Pi : effectum Ot : affectur *corr. to* affectu Vf : (*over erasure*) Na | toto . . . affectu *lac.* Bb Cp Fr

et uocis MINISTERIO personare.
> ministerio] misterio *corr. to* ministerio Cs : misterio C1 D2 D3 M2 Mb Na Ot S4 T3 (mysterio C2 S1 S3) | personare] personemus D2 | et . . . personare *lac.* Bb Cp Fr

Qui pro NOBIS ETERNO patri, ade debitum soluit;
> nobis] nobis tibi *corr. to* nobis G3 : nobis tibi Av D1 D3 D4 Lo Pa Rv Va | patri] patris *corr. to* patri B3 : patris S3 | qui . . . soluit *lac.* Bb Cp Fr

et ueteris piaculi cautionem; pio cruore detersit.
> ueteris] ueteri D3 S3 S5 T3: eternis S1 | piaculi] piaculis B2 C2 Pi : piaculo S3 | cautionem] cautione C2 S3 : cautionum *over erasure* Pi | pio *om.* Ot | cruore detersit] detersit cruore Mb | et . . . detersit *lac.* Bb Cp Fr

Hec sunt enim, festa paschalia;
> GALL (GEL8) paschalium
> sunt] est C2 | enim] *add.* D1 : et enim Na | paschalia] paschalium G3 : *add. l. h.* gaudiorum D1 : paschalia gaudiorum D2 : paschalium gaudiorum D3 | hec . . . paschalia *lac.* Bb Cp Fr Pi

in quibus uerus ille, agnus occiditur;
> uerus ille] ille uerus M2 | ille *om.* Mv | in . . . occiditur *lac.* Bb Cp Fr Pi

eiusque SANGVIS, POSTIBVS CONSECRATVR.
> GALL sanguis] sanguenis Bo | consecratur] consegratur Ga GEL8 postibus] postebus Ph | consecratur] consegratur Ge Sg (GREG), PRG sanguine postes consecrantur
> postibus] postes Rv | consecratur] consecrantur *corr. to* consecratur M2 : consecrantur Av Rv | sanguis postibus consecratur] sanguine postibus consecrantur G2 *add. l. h.* Av : sanguine postes consecrantur B2 C1 D4 G3 Lb Lo Mv Na Nb Pa S1 S2 S3 S4 T3 Va Vb Vc Vd : sanguine postes consecratur S5 (*corr. to* consecratur) B3 : sanguine postes fidelium consecrantur G4 Vf : sanguine (fidelium *add. l. h.*) postes consecrantur Cs | eiusque . . . consecratur *lac.* Bb Cp Fr Pi

IN QVA primum patres nostros,
> GREG in quo PRG hec nox est in qua
> in] hec nox est in Av B2 B3 C1 Cs D1 D4 G4 Lb Lo M2 Na Nb Pa Rv S1 S2 S3 S4 S5 Va Vc Vd Vf : hec nox est *add. l. h.* T3 : hec nos est in Vb |

qua] quo T3 : quibus D2 D3 G2 Mb Mv Ot | primum] primus Ot : primos
C2 | patres] parentes Mv | in . . . nostros *lac.* Bb Cp Fr Pi

filios israhel, eductos DE egypto;
>   PRG eduxisti domine
> eductos] deductos *corr. to* eductos D1 : eductos domine (domine *erased*) Nb
> : educens domine Lb (*almost illeg?*) Vb : eduxisti domine B3 C1 S1 S2 S3 S4
> S5 | de] ex Av D4 G3 Lo Pa Rv Va : dei Na | filios . . . egypto *lac.* Bb Cp
> Fr Pi

rubrum mare, sicco uestigio, transire fecisti.
>   PRG quos postea rubrum
> rubrum] quos postea rubrum S4 quos postestea rubrum C1 | rubrum mare]
> mare rubrum Ot | uestigio] uestigia T3 : uestitio B3 | transire] transsire Vd
> | fecisti] fecit *corr. to* fecisti Vd : fecisti *corr. l. h. to* fecit G3 : fecit *over erasure*
> (fecisti?) T3 : fecit B2 Na Vc | rubrum . . . fecisti *lac.* Bb Cp Fr Pi

Hec igitur nox est, que peccatorum tenebras;
>   hec . . . tenebras *om.* S3 : *lac.* Cp Fr Pi

columne illuminatione purgauit.
>   GALL, GEL8, GREG inluminatione
> illuminatine] illustratione G4 : illunatione *corr. to* illuminatione S1 | columne
> . . . purgauit *om.* S3 : *lac.* Cp Fr Pi

Hec nox est, que hodie per uniuersum mundum, in christo credentes;
>   hodie] *om.* C2 Mv Ot | mundum] mundum omnes C2 | christo] christum B2
>   C1 Na Vc Vd | hec . . . credentes *lac.* Fr Pi

a uitiis seculi, SEGREGATOS, ET CALIGINE PECCATORVM;
>   PRG et caligine peccatorum segregatos
> a uitiis seculi] *written twice, the second erased* S3 | uitiis] uiciis Vf : uitius Cs
> Mb Vb | seculi] *add. l. h.* S5 : huius seculi Vf | segregatos . . . peccatorum]
> et caligine peccatorum segregatos C1 D4 G4 Na Nb S1 S4 T3 | segregatos *om.*
> S3 | et caligine peccatorum *om.* S2 S5 | caligine] caliginem C2 D1 D2 M2 S3
> Vf | a . . . peccatorum *lac.* Fr Pi

reddit gratie; SOCIAT sanctitati.
>   PRG sociatque
> reddit] redit S5 : reddidit D4 : redditet C2 | gratie] *add. sign* + B2 : gratia
> Ot | sociat] et sociat B3 : socia B2 : sociatque *corr. to* sociat Av S4 : sociatque
> C1 C2 Cs D4 Lb M2 S1 S2 S3 S5 Vb Vd Vf | sanctitati] sanctitate S3 Vb :
> sanctitatem D2 | reddit . . . sanctitati *lac.* Fr Pi

Hec nox est, in qua destructis, uinculis mortis;
>   GALL, GEL8, GREG distructis
> destr.] distructis *corr. to* des- C1 | est in] *over erasure* T3 | in] de Mv | hec . . .
> mortis *lac.* Fr

christus ab inferis uictor ascendit.
> | christus] *add. sign* + B2 | ascendit] surrexit Nb | christus . . . ascendit
>   *lac.* Fr

Nihil enim, nobis nasci profuit; nisi redimi profuisset.
>   GEL8 redemi
> enim nobis] enim S4 : enim *corr. to* enim nobis B3 | nasci] nascit Ot | profuit]
> profuerat D3 Mb Mv : profuerat *corr. to* profuit Cs : *corr. to* profuerat D1 |
> redimi] redemi G2 : reddimi Vd | profuisset] profuisse S1 | nihil . . . pro-
> fuisset *lac.* Fr

O mira circa nos, tue pietatis dignatio;

       mira] uere Bb | nos] nox *corr. to* nos Cs | o . . . dignatio *lac.* Fr

o inestimabilis, dilectio caritatis;

       inestimabilis] inextimabilis D3 Mv Vf : inestabilis Ot | o . . . caritatis *lac.* Fr

ut seruum redimeres, filium tradidisti.

       GEL8 redemeres tradedisti

       ut] qui ut G2 Ot | redimeres] redimeret G2 Ot | tradidisti] tradisti B2 : tra-
didisum C1 | ut . . . tradidisti *lac.* Fr

O certe necessarium, ade peccatum;

       GREG peccatum nostrum PRG *om.*

       peccatum] peccatum nostrum C2 D4 Vd : peccatum nostrum (nostrum
marked for omission) S4 : nostrum *add. l. h.* Nb : peccatum nostrumque D1
M2 Mb Pi (nostrumque *marked for omission* Cs) | o . . . peccatum *om.* C1 S1
S2 S3 Vc : *om. notation* Vd : *lac.* Fr

quod christi morte deletum est.

       PRG *om.*

       deletum est *lac.* Vb | quod . . . est *om.* C1 S1 S2 S3 Vc : *om. notation* Vd :
lac. Fr

O felix culpa; que talem ac tantum, meruit habere redemptorem.

       GALL (GEL8) filex PRG *om.*

       O felix] felix (*with space for initial*) Va | felix] felis B2 | talem] tale C2 | talem
ac tantum] tantum ac talem Ot | ac] hac B2 Vd | habere] hare *corr. to* habere
Cp Ot : abere C2 | o . . . redemptorem *om.* C1 S1 S2 S3 Vc : *om. notation*
Vd : *lac.* Fr Vb

O beata nox, que sola meruit scire, tempus et HORAM;

       (GALL, GEL8 hora)

       O] *om.* C1 | beata] uere beata D1 G4 Mb Mv Nb S4 : beata *corr. to* uere beata
Cs | scire] exire C1 | tempus] tempis *corr. to* tempus Cp | horam] oram Na :
hora C2 D4 Mv Ot Pi S1 S3 S5 : ora *corr. to* hora Cp : hora *corr. to* horam
T3 : horum Nb | o . . . horam *lac.* Fr Vb

in qua christus ab inferis resurrexit.

       christus] *add. sign* + B2 | ab] hab C1 | in . . . resurrexit *lac.* Fr Vb

Hec nox est de qua scriptum est;

       hec] ec C1 | nox est] est nox S4 | hec . . . scriptum est *lac.* Fr Vb

et nox UT dies, illuminabitur;

       GALL, GEL8, GREG inluminabitur

       et] *om.* B3 | et nox ut dies] *lac.* Vb : et nox illuminatio *skipped to next line by
error, corrected by the addition, l. h. of* ut dies illuminabitur et nox Av | ut] sicut
B2 G2 G4 Na Nb S5 T3 Vc : sicut *over erasure* Vd : *om.* Rv | et . . . illu-
minabitur *lac.* Fr

et nox illuminatio mea, in deliciis meis.

       GALL, GEL8, GREG inluminatio GALL (GEL8) diliciis

       meis] meis. hic dicat sacerdos secrete. Dominus uobiscum. R. Et cum [spiritu
tuo]. Oratio. Deus qui israeliticam plebem in columpna nubis et ignis ex
egypto progredientem ad pastum manne perducere misericorditer uoluisti,
concede nobis famulis tuis per columpne huius sacrificium spiritus sancti
illuminacionem; et uultus tui dilectacionem sine fine percipere; per. fingat .u.
grana incensi in cereo. Mv | et . . . meis *lac.* Fr

Huius igitur, sanctificatio noctis;

       sanctificatio] *add. sign* + B2 D1 | noctis] *om.* S1 | sanctificatio noctis] noctis
sanctificatio S4 | huius . . . noctis *lac.* Fr

fugat scelera; culpas lauat;

| fugat] fuga Ot : purgat Vf | lauat] labat G2 | fugat . . . lauat *lac.* Fr

ET REDDIT innocentiam lapsis; mestis letitiam;

et] *om.* Av Bb Cp G3 Lo Pa Rv Va Vc | reddit] reddet C2 : redit T3 : reddidit Vd : redimit Mb | innocentiam] innocentia B2 S1 S3 | mestis] et mestis Cs G4 Vf | letitiam] letitia B2 S3 S5 | et . . . letitiam *lac.* Fr

fugat odia; concordiam parat; et curuat imperia.

GALL (GEL8) concordia

fugat] fuga Ot | odia] hodie Ot | concordiam] concordia *corr. to* concordiam T3 : concordia C2 G2 Ot | curuat] curat Vd | imperia] *add. s. n.* Benedictio incensi plana locutione. OR Veniat . . . S1 : *add. s. n.* Hic quinque grana incensi predicti a diatur [*sic*] infiguntur cereo in modo crucis ponatur Vf : *add. l. h. s. n.* Hic quinque grana incensi predicti a diacono infinguntur [*sic*] cereo in modo crucis G3 : *add. s. n.* Hic ponat incensum in modum crucis in facula. Nb : *add. s. n.* : Hic ponatur incensum G4 : *add.* Alia oracio. Deus qui diuicias . . . Hic incensetur et aspergatur aqua. Mv : *add. s. n. l. h.* quinque grana incensi ponit in cereo in modum crucis Lb: *add. s. n.* Hic ponantur quinque grana incensi in modum crucis D2 | fugat . . . imperia *lac.* Fr

In huius igitur noctis gratia,

PRG huius ergo

noctis] nocte Ot | gratia] *corr. l. h. to* gratiam Av : gratiam Mb S3 S5 : *om.* Ot | in . . . gratia *lac.* D2 Fr

suscipe sancte pater, incensi huius sacrificium uespertinum;

suscipe] *add. sign +* G2 : sucipe *corr. to* suscipe Cp | pater] pater omnipotens (*add. above line* deus) Ot | incensi] *add. sign +*, *add. in margin* ad incensum Vc : incesi B3 | huius] *add. sign +* G2 Vd : huius igitur noctis gratia suscipe sancte pater incensi huius C2 | pater] *add. (l. h.* Na) *s. n.* hic ponatur incensum Na S3 : *add. s. n.* hic incensetur S5 | uespertinum] *add. s. n.* Hic ponat diaconus incensum in cereum in modum crucis S1 : *add. s. n.* Hic ponatur incensum in modum crucis S4 : *add.* hic ponat incensum (*illeg.*) D1 | suscipe . . . uespertinum *lac.* D2 Fr

quod tibi in hac cerei oblatione sollemni, per ministrorum manus;

(GEL8 munus)

quod] quod quod C1 | hac] hac *corr. to* hanc Ot | hac cerei] *add. sign +* B3 G2 G3 Mb Nb Pa | oblatione] oblationem B2 Ot S3 : oblationes C2 | sollemni] sollemne Pi : sollempnem B2 Ot | ministrorum] ministrorum tuorum Lb Vb | quod . . . manus *lac.* D2 Fr

de operibus apum, sacrosancta reddit ecclesia.

apum] apium *corr. to* apum B3 : apium B2 : apis G4 | reddit] reddidit D4 Vd | ecclesia] ecclesiam Ot | de . . . ecclesia *lac.* D2 Fr

Sed iam columne huius, preconia nouimus;

columne] columbe S3 Vb | huius] ipsius S3 : om. Ot : ignis S1 | preconia] preconiam C2 | sed . . . nouimus *om.* Va *lac.* D2 Fr

quam in honore dei, rutilans ignis accendit.

(GEL8) GREG, PRG honorem

quam] quamn S5 | in] *add. l. h.* D1 | honore] honorem Av B3 C2 Cp Cs Mb Pi T3 Vc Vd Vf : horem *corr. to* honorem M2 | dei] tuo D3 | ignis] *add. sign +*, *add. in margin* ad ignem Vc | accendit] *add. sign +* Vd : accendat, *add. above line* hic accendatur B2 : *add. s. n.* Hic accendatur B3 S5 : accende Fr

: ascendit D4 : *add.* Cuius odor suauis est et flama hilaris, non tetro odore
aruina desudat sed iocundissima suauitate. Qui peregrinus non inficitur pic-
mentis sed illuminatur spiritu sancto. Mb : *add. s. n.* Tunc cantor dicat alta
uoce <Accendite>. Diaconus autem extendat manum, et accendat cereum.
deinde cantor dicat excelsa uoce <Lumen christi accensus est in nomine
domine>. Omnes respondeant <Deo gratias>. Item diaconus. S1 : *add. l.
h. s. n.* Hic accenditur cereus a predicto subdiacono G3 : *add. s. n.* Hic
accendatur cereus a subdyacono (G4 : subdiacono) G4 Vf : *add. s. n.* Hic
accenditur facula Nb : *an illeg. rubric add.* T3 : *add. s.n.* hic accenditur S3
: *add. s. n.* Hic accendatur facula S4 : *add. s. n.* Hic accenditur cereus D1
Na : *add. l. h. s. n.* Accendatur cereus Lb | quam . . . rutilans *lac.* Fr | quam
. . . accendit *om.* Va *lac.* D2

Qui LICET DIVISVS in partes;

  licet] licet sit B2 B3 Bb Cs G4 Lo Na Nb S5 T3 Vc Vd Vf : *add. l. h.* sit G3
  | diuisus] diuisum Ot : *add. s. n.* hic diuidatur S5 | partes] parte S1 S3 | qui
  . . . partes *om.* Va : *lac.* D2

MVTVATI luminis, detrimenta non nouit.

  mutuati] mutuati tamen B3 Bb Cp D4 Fr G2 G3 G4 Lb Lo Na Nb Pa Rv
  T3 Vb Vc Vd : (tamen *marked for omission*) Av : mutuati tamen *corr. l. h. to*
  mutuatim tamen D3 : mutuati tam *corr. to* mutuati tamen Vf : mutati Ot :
  mutuati sui D1 : *add. s. n.* Hic mittatur cereus S3 | luminis] luminis clari-
  tatem T3 | mutuati . . . nouit *om.* Va : *lac.* D2

Alitur liquantibus ceris;

  (GALL: liquantibus) GEL8, GREG, PRG liquentibus
  alitur] alitur enim B2 B3 Lb Vb : *add.* enim Cs T3 : aliter C2 Ot | liquantibus]
  liquentibus C1 Nb S1 Vc Vd (*corr. l. h. to* liquantibus Cs) | ceris] cereis B2
  Mv Ot S1 S3 Vf (*corr. l. h. to* ceris) Cs : ceris *corr. to* cereis S5 | alitur . . .
  ceris *om.* S4 Va *lac.* D2

QVAM in substantiam pretiose huius lampadis, apis mater eduxit.

  GALL substantia GREG, PRG quas
  quam] quas B2 B3 C1 Cp Cs D1 D3 G4 M2 Mb Na Nb Pi T3 Vc Vd Vf :
  quam *corr. l. h. to* quas Av G3 | substantiam] substantia Av B2 D1 G2 Ot S3
  S5 T3 : substantiam beatam *corr. to* substantia beatam Nb | pretiose] pretiosa
  Ot | apis] apes Bb C1 D3 Lo : *add.* S1 | eduxit] exultat. Flore utuntur coniuge,
  Flore funguntur genere, Flore domos instruunt, Flore diuitias conueunt,
  Flore ceram conficiunt Mb : eduxit. O uere beata nox que expoliauit egyptios
  ditauit ebreos (O . . . ebreos *l. h. marked.* ua . . . cat) Cs : *add. s. n.* Hic mutat
  sensum quasi legens S3 : Hic accendantur lampades G3 G4 : eduxit. Apes
  siquidem dum ore concipiunt ore parturiunt casto corpore non fetido desiderio copulantur. (*the following rubric s. n.*) Hic accendantur lampades. Vf
  | quam . . . eduxit *om.* S4 Va : *lac.* D2

Apis ceteris, que subiecta sunt homini; animantibus antecellit.

  PRG *omits*
  apis] apes D3 Mb: *in margin, l. h.* : non Cs G3 | homini] hominis Pi : omni
  corr. to omnia Ot : humanis S3 | apis . . . antecellit *om.* B2 B3 C1 D4 G4 Lb
  Na Nb S1 S2 S4 S5 T3 Va Vb Vc Vd Vf : *lac.* D2

Cum sit minima corporis, paruitate;

  PRG *omits*
  sit] sit enim Av Bb Fr G2 G3 Lo Pa Rv | minima] nimia M2 | parvitate] par
  over erasure Cs | cum . . . paruitate *om.* B2 B3 C1 D4 G4 Lb Na Nb S1 S2
  S4 S5 T3 Va Vb Vc Vd Vf : *lac.* D2

ingentes animos, angusto uersat in pectore;

        PRG *omits*

        ingentes animos] ingens animo C2 : ingentis animus Ot | angusto] angusto *corr. to* angustos Fr | angusto . . . uiribus] *illeg.* G2 | uersat] seruat D3 | ingentes . . . pectore *om.* B2 B3 C1 D4 G4 Lb Na Nb S1 S2 S4 S5 T3 Va Vb Vc Vd Vf : *lac.* D2

uiribus inbecillis; sed fortis ingenio.

        PRG *omits*

        uiribus . . . ingenio *om.* B2 B3 C1 D4 G4 Lb Na Nb S1 S2 S4 S5 T3 Va Vb Vc Vd Vf : *lac.* D2

Hec explorata, temporum VICE;

        PRG *omits*

        hec] his Pa Rv : hec *corr l. h. to* hunc Cs : et Ot : huic Mv | expl. temporum *illeg.* G2 | vice] vices Av Bb D1 G2 G3 Lo M2 Mb Pa Pi Rv : uicem S3 | hec . . . uice *om.* B2 B3 C1 D4 G4 Lb Na Nb S1 S2 S4 S5 T3 Va Vb Vc Vd Vf : *lac.* D2

cum canitiem PRUINOSA, hiberna posuerint;

        GALL proinosa PRG *omits*

        canitiem] canitie C2 D1 Fr G2 (-icie Ot) Mv : canities Mb | pruinosa] pruinosam Av Bb Fr G3 Lo Mv Pa Pi Rv | hiberna] ybernam Mv | posuerint] deposuerit D3 : posuerit S3 | cum . . . posuerint *om.* B2 B3 C1 D4 G4 Lb Na Nb S1 S2 S4 S5 T3 Va Vb Vc Vd Vf : *lac.* D2

et glaciale SENIO, uerni temporis moderata deterserint;

        GALL deterserit (GEL8) GREG glatiali PRG *omits*

        glatiale] glatiali Cs : glaciali Av C2 Cp D1 Fr G2 G3 M2 Mb Ot Pi S3 : glacie Pa : glacialem Mv | senio] senium Bb D3 Lo Mv Ot Pa Rv S3 | uerni temporis] *corr. l. h. to* uerno tempore Cs : uerno tempore Mv | moderata] immoderata D1 M2 Mb Pi : moderata *corr. to* moderato Cs | deterserint] deterserit D3 : detersit Ot | et . . . deterserint *om.* B2 B3 C1 D4 G4 Lb Na Nb S1 S2 S4 S5 T3 Va Vb Vc Vd Vf : *lac.* D2

statim prodeundi, ad laborem cura succedit.

        PRG *omits*

        statim] statimque C2 | prodeundi] prodeundo Mb | laborem] labore Ot | cura] curam *corr. to* cura Fr G2 : curam C2 | succedit] succendit Cs | statim . . . succedit *om.* B2 B3 C1 D4 G4 Lb Na Nb S1 S2 S4 S5 T3 Va Vb Vc Vd Vf : *lac.* D2

Disperseque per agros, libratis paululum pennis; cruribus suspensis insidunt.

        GALL libratim paulolum pinnibus (GEL8 pinnibus) PRG *omits*

        libratis] librati G2 Ot | paululum] paulum Fr | paululum pennis] *over erasure* Bb | pennis] pinnis S3 | -ribus . . . insi- *illeg.* G2 | suspensis] supensis D1 | insidunt] insidiunt Ot : *add.* Legunt pedibus flores et nullum damnum in flores inuenitur Pi | disp . . . insidunt *om.* B2 B3 C1 D4 G4 Lb Na Nb S1 S2 S4 S5 T3 Va Vb Vc Vd Vf : *lac.* D2

PARTE ore, legere flosculos;

        PRG *omits*

        parte] partim Av Bb Cp Cs D1 D3 Fr G2 G3 Lo M2 Mb Mv Ot Pa Pi Rv | legere] legentes Bb Lo Pa Rv : ligere G2 : om. Ot : elegere S3 : eligere Mv | legere flosculus] *lac.* Fr | parte . . . flosculos *om.* B2 B3 C1 D4 G4 Lb Na Nb S1 S2 S4 S5 T3 Va Vb Vc Vd Vf : *lac.* D2

ONERATIS uictualibus suis ad castra remeant.

> PRG *omits*
>
> oneratis] onerate Av Bb D1 Lo Mv Pa Rv : honerate Ot : honeratis C2 Cp Cs S3 : oneratisque D3 : colligentes G2 | -tualibus . . . -tra *illeg.* G2 | suis] sic S3 | remeant] remeat Mb : remeantur C2 | oneratis . . . remeant *lac.* Fr : *om.* B2 B3 C1 D4 G4 Lb Na Nb S1 S2 S4 S5 T3 Va Vb Vc Vd Vf : *lac.* D2

Ibique alie inestimabili arte, cellulas tenaci glutino instruunt;

> GALL in(e)stimabile; cellolas GEL8 cellolas PRG *omits*
>
> ibique] ubique Cs | inestimabili arte] inestimabilis arte C2 : inestimabilis artem Ot | cellulas] cellula Ot | glutino] gluttino C2 G3 M2 Pa S3 : gluttino *corr. l. h. to* glutino Cs : glugtino Ot : gluctino Mv | -truunt *illeg.* G2 | ibique . . . instruunt *lac.* Fr : *om.* B2 B3 C1 D4 G4 Lb Na Nb S1 S2 S4 S5 T3 Va Vb Vc Vd Vf : *lac.* D2

alie liquantia mella stipant;

> PRG *omits*
>
> liquantia] liquentia Cs : quantia *corr. to* liquantia Cp : liquantie Ot S3 | mella] melle S3 | alia . . . stipant *om.* B2 B3 C1 D4 G4 Lb Na Nb S2 S4 S5 T3 Va Vb Vc Vd Vf : *lac.* D2 Fr

alie uertunt flores in ceram;

> PRG *omits*
>
> ceram] cera C2 Ot S1 : ceream S3 : *illeg.* G2 | alie . . . ceram *om.* B2 B3 C1 D4 G4 Lb Na Nb S2 S4 S5 T3 Va Vb Vc Vd Vf : *lac.* D2 Fr

alie ore natos fingunt;

> GALL (GEL8) natus PRG *omits*
>
> alie] *lac.* Fr | ore natos] honeratis *corr. l. h. to* hore natos Cs | alie ore natos *illeg.* G2 | alie . . . fingunt *om.* B2 B3 C1 D4 G4 Lb Na Nb S2 S4 S5 T3 Va Vb Vc Vd Vf : *lac.* D2 Fr

alie COLLECTIS e foliis, nectar includunt.

> PRG *omits*
>
> | alie . . . foli-] *illeg.* G2 | collectis] collectum Av Bb Cp D1 D3 Fr G3 Lo M2 Mb Mv Pa Pi Rv S3 : collectu Ot | e foliis] effoliis Cs : se foliis S1 | includunt] indudunt S3 : *add.* Flore utuntur coniuge, flore funguntur genere, flore domos instruunt, flores divitias conveunt, flore cera (D1 : ceram) conficiunt Pi, D1 : *add.* o ammirandus apium ferbor, ad commune opus pacifica turba concurrit et operantibus plurimis una augetur substantia. Pi | alie . . . includunt *om.* B2 B3 C1 D4 G4 Lb Na Nb S2 S4 S5 T3 Va Vb Vc Vd Vf : *lac.* D2

O uere BEATA ET mirabilis apis;

> PRG *omits*
>
> beata et] *om.* Av Bb D1 D3 Fr G2 G3 Lb Lo M2 Mb Mv Ot Pa Pi Rv S3 Va Vb Vf : et S5 : beata erant *over erasure* Cs | mirabilis] amiralis *corr. to* amirabilis B3 : ammirabilis T3 : et mirabilis S5 : *add.* et laudabilis D3 (*add. l.h.* D1) | apis] apes D3 Nb : apex Vf | o . . . apis *om.* C1 D4 G4 S4 Vc : *l. h.* Nb : *lac.* D2

cuius nec sexum masculi uiolant;

> PRG *omits*
>
> nec *om.* B3 | sexum] sexu B2 Mv Ot Pi T3 : sexus C2 Cs *corr. to* sexum D3 : sexum ne B3 | masculi] *add. above line* M2 : masculini B2 D1 S1 S5 : masculus C2 | uiolant] uiolat C2 Pa Rv S1 : *illeg.* G2 | cuius . . . uiolant *om.* C1 D4 G4 S4 Vc : *l. h.* Nb : *lac.* D2

fetus non QVASSANT;
>> GEL8 quassat PRG *omits*
>> fetus] fetus *corr. to* nec fetus Cp | quassant] quassat Av B2 Bb Cp D1 Fr Lo
>> M2 Mb Pa Rv S1 S3 Va | fetus non quassant *om.* B3 C1 D4 G4 S4 Vc *l. h.*
>> Nb *lac.* D2 G2

nec filii destruunt castitatem.
>> GALL distruunt PRG *omits*
>> nec filii *lac.* G2 | destruunt] dextruunt Cp S3: dextrunt *corr. to* dextruunt M2
>> | castitatem] *add.* cuius odor suavis est et flamma hilaris *later pasted over by*
>> *next piece* Pi | nec . . . castitatem *om.* C1 D4 G4 S4 Vc : *l. h.* Nb : *lac.* D2

Sicut sancta concepit uirgo maria;
>> PRG *omits*
>> sicut] sed sicut Na T3 : *add. l. h.* sed Vd | sicut . . . maria *om.* C1 D4 G4
>> S4 Vc : *l. h.* Nb : *lac.* Bb D2 : *illeg.* G2

uirgo peperit; et uirgo permansit.
>> PRG *omits*
>> permansit] *add. s. n.* Hic accendantur lampades ante altare Nb : *add. s.n.* Hic
>> accenduntur lampa//// Na | uirgo pep . . . permansit *om.* C1 D4 G4 S4 Vc :
>> *l. h.* Nb *lac.* : Bb D2 G2

O uere beata nox, que expoliauit egyptios; ditauit hebreos;
>> uere] *add. l. h.* Na : *om.* T3 | que *add. l. h.* Cs | expoliauit] expoliabit C2:
>> spoliauit D1 M2 Nb Pi | egyptios] egiptio *corr. to* egiptios Ot | ditauit] ditabit
>> C2 | o . . . hebreos *om.* S4 : *lac.* Bb D2 G2

nox in qua terrenis, celestia iunguntur.
>> nox] nos S3 | qua] quam Vd | celestia] celestia humanis diuina G4 Nb : celestia
>> divina humanis Vf | iunguntur] coniunguntur B3 D3 Mv : conguntur Pa:
>> iunguntur *corr. l. h. to* coniunguntur D1 | nox . . . iunguntur *om.* S4 : *lac.*
>> Bb D2 G2

Oramus te domine, ut cereus iste, in HONOREM nominis tui consecratus;
>> oramus] oramus ergo B3 D4 G4 S2 Vf : oramus *corr. l. h. to* oramus ergo B2
>> Cs G3 Na Nb | te] namque *l. h. over erasure* T3 | ut] itaque ut D4 | cereus
>> iste] *add. sign* + Av B2 B3 Cs D1 D4 G3 G4 M2 Mb Nb Pa Rv S5 | honorem]
>> honore B2 C2 D4 Fr G4 Mv Ot S1 S5 Va : ononorem *corr. to* onorem B3 |
>> nominis tui] tui nominis B3 Mv | tui] tuis S3 | consecratus] consecratum Ot
>> : dicatus Vf : *add. sign* + D1 Fr S1 S4 Vd | oramus . . . consecratus *lac.* Bb
>> D2 G2

ad noctis huius, caliginem destruendam; indeficiens perseueret.
>> GALL (GEL8) distruendam
>> noctis] nocti Ot | caliginem] calligine M2 | destruendam] dextruendam B2 :
>> dextruendas S3 | ad . . . perseueret *lac.* Bb D2 G2

IN ODOREM suauitatis acceptus;
>> PRG atque in
>> in] et in Cs D3 G4 Lo Mv Pa Va : *add. l. h.* et Av : ut in B3 : atque in D4
>> S4 | suauitatis] suatatis *corr. to* suauitatis M2 | acceptus] acceptum S3 : ac-
>> census Fr Nb Vf (*over erasure* Vd) : accensum Ot | in . . . acceptus *lac.* Bb
>> D2 G2

supernis luminaribus misceatur.
>> supernis] superni Fr Rv | luminaribus] luminibus Na T3 | misceatur] *add.*
>> cuius odor suabis est et flamma ylaris non tetro odore aruina desudat sed
>> iocundissima suabitate inficitur Pi | sup . . . misceatur *lac.* Bb D2 G2

Flammas eius lucifer, matutinus inueniat;

> flammas] flammam (-corr. l. h. to -as Av) Mb Pi : flamas B3 : flammas *over erasure* Vd : flamma M2 Ot | matutinus] *first six letters over erasure* Na | flammas . . . inueniat *lac.* Bb D2 G2

ille inquam lucifer, qui nescit occasum;

> inquam] inqua (*both times: see below*) Ot | occasum] occasus S3 | ille . . . occasum *written twice, second canceled by notator* Ot : *lac.* Bb D2 G2

ille qui regressus ab inferis, humano generi serenus illuxit.

> GALL, GEL8, GREG inluxit
> generi] generis Ot T3 : *om.* C1 | generi serenus illuxit *lac.* Fr | serenus] sereno Pi : serenas *corr. to* serenus Vf | ille . . . illuxit *lac.* Bb D2 G2

Precamur ergo te domine,

> ergo te] te ergo Mb | precamur . . . domine *om.* B2 : *lac.* Bb D2 Fr G2

ut nos famulos tuos omnem clerum, et deuotissimum populum;

> nos famulos tuos] nobis famulis tuis B3 | omnem] et omnem *corr. to* omnem Cs : omne C2 S1 S5 T3 : omne *corr. l. h. to* omnes G3 : omnique B3 : omnemque S4 Vc Vd | clerum] clerun Vb : clero B3 : clero *corr. l. h. to* cleros G3 | deu. populum] deuotissimo populo B3 : deuotissimum populum tuam misericordiam largiaris Ot | ut . . . populum *om.* B2 : *lac.* Bb D2 Fr G2

una cum beatissimo, papa nostro il.;

> GALL, GEL8 patre nostro beatissimo uiro ill. GREG patre nostro
> papa ill. PRG beatissimo papa nostro N. et gloriosissimo rege nostro
> N. eiusque nobilissima coniuge N. et antistite nostro N.
> beatissimo papa nostro ill.] papa nostro N. C1 S3 S5 T3 : papa nostro ill. S1
> : papa nostro papa illo. S2 : beatissimo patre nostro papa ill. Pi : patre nostro
> beatissimo viro papa ill. *corr. to* beatissimo papa ill. (ill. *corr. l. h. to* Bene-
> dicto) Cp : papa nostro beatissimo uiro ill. C2 : famulo tuo beatissimo papa
> nostro ill. Ot : uenerabilissimo famulo tuo papa nostro il. S4 | ill.] dompno
> ill. B3 : N. Cs D3 G4 Mv Nb Pa S5 Vc Vd Vf : *space* Lo : paschale Mb |
> una . . . il. *om.* B2 : *lac.* Bb D2 Fr G2

et antistite nostro il.;

> GALL, GEL8, GREG, *om.*
> et] simulque et C2 | antistite] archiepiscopo Mb : abbate Ot Rv Va : abbate
> *corr. l. h. s. 14? to* episcopo nostro Gaymundo Cp | il.] N. Cs D3 T3 Vc Vf
> : dompno. il. B3 : il. *corr. to* domno ill. Ot : Pandulfo Av : Benedicto Pa :
> *space* Lo : domno Barbato Mb | et . . . il. *om.* B2 C1 Fr G4 Mv Nb S1 S2
> S3 S4 S5 : *lac.* Bb D2 G2

INSERT 1

Av, B3: sed et omnibus presbiteris diaconibus subdiaconibus cunctoque clero uel plebe
(Av *adds in lower margin* in his pascalibus conseruare digneris.)

B2: Salvum fac populum tuum domine et benedic hereditate tue ut redeuntes ad fes-
tivitate pasche per hec visibilibus et in//// dum presencium usufruuntur//// papa
nostro domno ill. //// *the end missing*

B3: *see* Av

C1: et gloriosissimo imperatore .N.

Cp, Va, Rv: cum omni congregatione beatissimi benedicti

Cs: et preposito nostro N. presentis uite (et . . . uite *over erasure*)

D3: et abbate nostro N. cum omni congregatione beatissimi nicolai

D4: necnon et abbate nostro il. cum omni congregatione beatissime marie semper uir-
ginis

Fr: ////gatione beati pauli apostoli

G3: *original hand:* cum omni congregatione beati xxxx xxxx X x; *another hand:* Et
    gloriosissimo rege nostro xx (*later:* Robberto) quiete temporum concessa in hiis
    paschalibus gaudiis (*later still:* assidua protectione conseruare) digneris. *Later
    still:* Qui uiuis regnas necnon et gloriaris solus dominus solus altissimus ihesu
    christe cum sancto spiritu in gloria dei patris Amen

Lb, Vb: et abbatissa nostra il. cum omni congregatione sanctissimi petri

Mb: et abbati nostro domno petro et [omnem?] hanc sanctam nostram congregationem
    tuo ineffabili nomini atque beati benedicti ascriptam

Mv: simulque cum patre nostro ill. huius uidelicet congregacionis beate marie

Na: necnon et gloriosissimo rege nostro il.

Ot: cum omni congregatione beatissimi benedicti misericordiam sempiternam largiaris

Pa: cum omni congregatione beatissimi PETRI apostolorum principis

Rv: *see Cp*

S1: et gloriosissimo imperatore nostro il. cum cuncta congregatione sibi commissa [*sic:
    cf. S3*]

S2: et patre nostro illo cum cuncta congregatione sibi commissa

S3: et imperatore nostro N. et abbate nostro N. cum cuncta congregatione sibi com-
    missa

S5: et gloriosissimo imperatore nostro N. et patre nostro N. cum cuncta congregatione
    sibi commissa

T3: necnon et rege nostro (*plus blank space*)

Va: *see Cp*

Vb: *see Lb*

Vc: et rege nostro (*corr. l. h. to* mag° nro heremano) N.

Vd: et rege nostro N.

QVIETE TEMPORVM concessa,

> quiete temp. concessa] presentis uite quiete concessa D1 D3 Fr (G3 *specu-
> lative, based on neumes*) Lb Lo Pa Rv Va Vb : presentis uite concessa D4 |
> temporum] tempora C1 | quiet t. concessa *om.* Av B2 B3 Cp M2 Mb Ot Pi
> S4 Vf : *lac.* Bb D2 G2

in his PASCHALIBVS conseruare digneris.

> GREG paschalibus gaudiis PRG paschalibus festis
> his] hiis G4 Mv Nb | paschalibus] paschalibus gaudiis C1 Cp Cs G4 M2 Mb
> Mv Na Nb Pi S1 S2 S3 S5 T3 Vc Vd Vf : paschalibus festis C2 D4 S4 |
> conseruare] conseruare et custodire Mb : assidua protectione regere gu-
> bernare et conseruare G4 S4 Vf : assidua protectione regere gubernare con-
> seruare *the first four words marked for omission* Nb | in . . . digneris] gaudiis
> facias perfrui sempiternis (Fr: sempiterni) D1 D3 Fr (G3 *speculative, based
> on neumes*) Lb Lo Pa Rv Va Vb : *om.* Av B2 B3 Ot : *lac.* Bb D2 G2

INSERT 2

Av: Memento domine famulorum tuorum imperatorum nostrorum il., et exercitus eo-
    rum uniuersi, atque barbaras nationes illorum dicioni potenter substerne. (*above
    the line, l. h.* famuli tui regi nostri W [regi nostri W *canceled; l. h. adds* glorio-
    sissimi et excellentissimi regis nostri W.]) Memento etiam domine principibus
    nostris il. et il., (*corr. l. h. to* famuli tui dni [*illeg.*] nostri berardi) et celestem
    eis concede uictoriam cum omni exercitu eorum.

B3: Memorare domine famulum tuum regem nostrum il. et cuctum [*sic*] eius exercitum
    et omnium circumstantium. Saluum fac populum tuum domine et benedic
    hereditati *corrected from* hereditatem) tue ut redeuntes ad festiuitatem pasce per

hec uisibilibus et inusibilibus tuis inians dum presentium usu fruuntur futoro-
rum desiderio accendantur. (*cf. insert 1,* B2)

Bb, Fr, Lo, Pa, Rv, Va: Memento etiam domine famuli tui imperatoris (Rv: *corr.* —*s.*
14? —*to* regis) nostri il. (il.] *blank space* Bb Lo : N. Pa) necnon et famuli tui
(famulorum tuorum Fr) consulis (comitis Bb Lo: principum Fr : principis Rv
Va) nostri (nostrorum Fr) il. (*blank space* Bb Lo : il. et il. Fr : LEONI Pa) et
celestem (celesti *corr. to* -em Pa) eis concede uictoriam cum omni exercitu eorum
(cum . . . eorum *om.* Bb) (cum omni exercitu eorum et celestem eis concede
uictoriam Lo)

Cp: Memento etiam domine famulorum tuorum (*corr. l.h. to* famulo tuo) imperatorum
nostrorum ill. et ill. (*corr. l. h. to* rege nostro robberto *other additions as well*) et
celestem eis (*corr. to* ei) concede uictoriam cum omni exercitu eorum (*corr. to*
eius). Protege quoque domine piisimos (*corr. l. h. to* piisimum) principes nostros
ill. et ill. cum omni exercitu eorum (*corr. l. h. to* eius) et concede eis (*corr. l. h.*
to ei) ubique uictoriam ad laudem nominis tui et ad nostram qui tibi sacris
famulamur officiis prope tuam defensionem.

D1: (*cf.* Pi) Memento etiam domine famuli tui imperatoris ill. necnon et famuli tui
prioris nostri ill. et uniuersi populi huius ciuitatis qui tibi offerunt hoc sacrificium laudis. ut his omnibus premia eterna largiaris. Respice quesumus domine
ad deuotionem famule tue abbatisse nostre n. totiusque congregationis sancte
marie sibi commisse. Huius tu deus desiderii uota prenoscens ineffabilis pietatis
et misericordie tue munere tranquilitatem perpetue pacis accommoda. Et eas per
hec paschalia festa assidua protectione regere gubernare et conseruare digneris.

D3: Memento etiam domine famuli tui imperaris [*sic*] nostri N. cum omni exercitu suo,
et famuli tui regi nostri cum omni populo christiano.

D4: (*cf.* Bb) Memento etiam domine famuli tui imperatoris nostri n. et regem nostrum
n. et celestem illi concede uictoriam

Fr: *see* Bb

G3: Memento etiam domine famuli tui imperatoris (*corr. l. h. to* regis) nostri ill. (*blank*
line) et celestem ei concede uictoriam cum omni exercitu eius.

G4: Respice etiam ad deuotissimum regem nostrum N. cuius tu deus desiderii uota pre
. . . (*end wanting*)

Lo: *see* Bb

M2 (*cf.* Pi) Memento etiam (domine *l. h.*) famuli tui (imperatoris *l. h.*) domini nostri
regis il. et celestem illi de tuo throno concede uictoriam cum omni exercitu eius
nobis ipsum redde placatum. Respice quesumus domine super deuotissimum
famulum tuum comitem nostrum [c]uius tu deus (desiderii *add.*) uota prenoscens ineffabili pietatis et misericordie tue munere tranquillum perpetue pacis
accommoda; ut in his paschalibus gaudiis assidua protectione regere gubernare
conseruare digneris. *Later additions:* serenissimi (*changed to* excellentissimi) dni
ni walfridi principis tarantani; serenissimi regis choradi secundi; *others illeg.*

Mb: Memorare domine famulum tuum il. imperatorem nostrum et consules et duces
nostros, ut per hec pascalia gaudia excellentiores eos facias, et semper uictoriam
de celo concedas, gloria multiplices, letitiam muneres, honor[e] exaltes, et eorum exercitum uniuersum.

Mv: quatinus in presenti seculo nos feliciter gubernet, et in futuro ante conspectum
tuum sine macula representet. Memorare domine famuli tui regis nostri N. et
eius exercitus uniuersi. Memento etiam domine famuli tui comitis nostri N. cum
uniuerso exercitu suo, ut celestem eis concedas uictoriam.

Nb: (*cf.* D1, G4, M2, Pi) Respice etiam ad deuotissimum famulum tuum imperium
nostrum cuius tu deus desiderii uota prenoscens ineffabilis pietatis et misericordie tue munere tranquillum perpetue pacis accomoda et celestem uictoriam
cum omni populo suo.

Ot: Memento domine famulo tuo regi nostro ill. et celeste ei concede uictoriam cum
   omni exercitu suo.

Pa: *see* Bb

Pi: Memento etiam domine famulorum tuorum imperatorum nostrorum il. et il. et
   celestem illis de tuo throno concede uictoriam cum omni exercitu eorum. Respice quesumus domine super deuotissimos famulos tuos duces nostros quorum
   tu deus desideria uota prenoscens ineffabilis pietatis et misericordie tue munere
   tranquillos perpetue pacis accomoda; ut in his pascalibus gaudiis assidua protectione regere gubernare et conseruare digneris

Rv: *see* Bb

S4, Vf: Respice etiam et (domine ad Vf) deuotissimum famulum tuum imperatorem
   (regem Vf) nostrum il. (.n., *add.* Carolum Vf) cuius tu deus desiderii uota prenoscens ineffabili pietate (ineffabilis pietatis Vf) et misericordie tue munere tranquillum perpetue pacis accomoda; et celestem illi de throno tuo concede uictoriam cum omni populo suo (eius Vf).

Va: *see* Bb

Vb: *added on back of roll:* (1) et principibus nostris paldolfo et landolfo (2) famuli tui
   roffridi comestabuli. consulisque nostrorum et totius militie beneuentane.

Vf: *see* S4

ET HIS QVI TIBI OFFERVNT, HOC SACRIFICIVM LAVDIS;
   GALL, GEL8, GREG, PRG *om.*
   et his] et in his D4 : *om.* D3 : et hiis Mv | tibi offerunt] offerunt tibi Mb |
   et . . . laudis *om.* B2 B3 C1 C2 Cp Cs (D1: *see Insert 2*) Lb Na Nb S1 S2 S3
   S4 S5 T3 Vb Vc Vd Vf : *lac.* D2 G2 G4

PREMIA ETERNA LARGIARIS.
   GALL, GEL8, GREG, PRG *om.*
   largiaris] largire digneris D3 : largire *corr. to* largiare Fr : *add.* (*two and a half
   lines, incl.* consulem? . . . misteria/misericordia? . . .) ciuitatemque istam et
   populum eius custodire digneris G3 | premia . . . largiaris *om.* B2 B3 C1 C2
   Cp Cs (D1: *see Insert 2*) Lb Na Nb S1 S2 S3 S4 S5 T3 Vb Vc Vd Vf : *lac.*
   D2 G2 G4

Per dominum nostrum, iesum christum filium tuum;
   GALL, GEL8, GREG per PRG per eundem dominum
   per dominum . . . tuum] per dominum. *the rest* (*as here*) *add. l. h.* Cs : Qui
   semper uiuis regnas imperas necnon et gloriaris solus deus solus altissimus
   (altissimus] dominus S3) iesu christe cum sancto spiritu in gloria dei patris.
   Amen. Na S1 S2 S3 S5 T3 | per] per eundem D3 | tuum] *om.* Vc | per . . .
   tuum *lac.* B2 D2 G2 G4 Lo Vb

qui tecum et cum spiritu sancto, uiuit et regnat deus;
   GALL, GEL8, GREG *om.* PRG qui tecum uiuit et regnat deus in
   unitate eiusdem spiritus sancti
   qui . . . deus] qui tecum uiuit et regnat D3 : qui tecum C1 : qui uenturus
   est iudicare uiuos et mortuos et omne seculum per ignem uiuens et regnans
   deus M2 Pi : qui tecum uiuit et regnat in unitate spiritus sancti deus Cp Mb
   Mv Nb Vd (*add. l. h.* Cs) : qui tecum uiuit et regnat deus (deus *l. h.* Ot) in
   unitate spiritus sancti C2 Ot : una cum spiritu sancto uiuentem tecum atque
   regnantem S4 : tecum uiuentem atque regnantem in unitate spiritus sancti
   deus Vf : *om.* Na S1 S2 S3 S5 T3 Vc : *lac.* B2 D2 G2 G4 Lo Vb

per omnia secula seculorum. Amen
> GALL, GEL8, GREG *om.*
> per omnia] in D3 | Amen] *lac.* Bb | per . . . amen *om.* C1 Na S1 S2 S3 S5
> T3 Vc : *l. h.* Cs : *lac.* B2 D2 G2 G4 Lo Vb

Early Versions of the Franco-Roman Text of the Exultet

This edition of early witnesses of the Franco-Roman text of the Exultet is based on modern scholarly editions and is designed as a complement to the edition of Franco-Roman texts in southern Italy. In that edition, versions of early texts are presented for comparison, and usually a single reading is given, even when the sources are not unanimous. This edition is designed to allow the reader to check the situation in those earlier sources.

With that purpose in mind, certain aspects of these early texts have not been reported in this edition.

1. Variants in the spellings of the *Nomina sacra* are not usually recorded.
2. The diphthongs *ae, oe,* as well as *e* with cedilla, are usually reported as *e.*
3. Variants in the spelling of many proper names (*Egyptios, Hebreos*) are not recorded.
4. Many cases where *t* and *c* are interchanged (*senciat, gracia*) are not recorded.
5. Variants with *h* are sometimes omitted (*nichil, huniuersum*).
6. In Pr (see "The Sources," below), corrected words whose original evidently matched a common variant are recorded in their corrected form, the letter or letters written over erasure indicated here by italics.
7. In the Saint Gall sacramentary, I have generally ignored the readings resulting from later correction.
8. In the Roman-German pontifical (PRG), I have omitted from the edition rubrical materials included by Andrieu relating to the end of the prologue and the beginning of the preface.
9. Variants printed in capital letters have been reported as the version of this text in the apparatus to the edition of the Franco-Roman text of southern Italy.

Note that sigla for GALL, GEL8, GREG, and PRG are those used by editors, and thus a single siglum may represent different manuscripts in different categories. The punctuation here is that of Deshusses, *Le sacramentaire grégorien.*

The Sources

GALL = "Gallican" sources
> Bo = Bobbio missal (Paris, B. N. lat. 13246), in Lowe, ed., *The Bobbio Missal,* 69–70
> Ga = Missale Gallicanum uetus (Vatican Pal. lat. 493), in Mohlberg, Eizenhöfer, and Siffrin, eds., *Missale Gallicanum Vetus,* 35–36.
> Go = Missale Gothicum (Vatican Reg. lat. 317), in Mohlberg, ed., *Missale Gothicum,* 59–61

GEL8 = "Gelasian" sacramentaries of the eighth century
   En = Angoulême sacramentary (Paris, Bibl. nat. lat. 816), in Saint-Roch, *Liber sacramentorum Engolismensis*, 108–10 (nos. 733–34)
   Ge = Gellone sacramentary, (Paris, Bibl. nat. lat. 12048), in Dumas and Deshusses, *Liber sacramentorum Gellonensis*, 93–95 (no. 677)
   Ph = Berlin, Deutsche Staatsbibliothek lat. 105 (*olim* Phillipps 1667), in Heiming, ed., *Liber sacramentorum Augustodunensis*, 61–63 (nos. 520–21)
   Pr = Prague, Metropolitni kapitoly 0.83, in Dold and Eizenhöfer, eds., *Das prager Sacramentar*, 55*–57* (no. 95)
   Rh = Zürich, Zentralbibliothek Rheinau 30, in Hänggi and Schönherr, eds., *Sacramentarium Rheinaugense*, 130–32 (nos. 424–25)
   Sg = Saint Gall 348, in Mohlberg, ed., *Das fränkische*, 81–83 (no. 97). In the case of many erasures in the manuscript, I have presumed the earlier reading, no longer visible, with the aid of the other Gelasians of the eighth century. I have not taken account of the many later corrections.

Letters in italics are written over erasures.

GREG = the supplement of Benedict of Aniane to the Gregorian sacramentary of Hadrian, as edited in Deshusses, *Le sacramentaire grégorien* 1:360–63 (nos. 1,021–22) from the following manuscripts:
   A = Cambrai, Bib. mun. 164, anno 811–12
   B1 = Verona, Bibl. cap. XCI, s9½
   B2 = Verona, Bibl. cap. LXXXVI, s9⅔
   C1 = Vienna, Öst. Nationalbibliothek lat. 1815, s9med
   C2 = Donaueschingen, Hofbibliothek 191, s9¾
   D = Oxford, Bodleian Lib. Auct. D. I.20, s9²⁄₂
   E = Oxford, Bodleian Lib. Add. A 173, s9²⁄₂
   F = Mainz, Seminarbibliothek 1, s9ex
   G = Modena, Bibl. cap. O. II. 7, s9med
   H = Autun, Bibl. mun. 19, c845
   J   = Le Mans, Bibl. mun. 77, s9¾
   K = Paris, Bibl. nat. lat. 2812, s9½
   L = Rome, Bibl. Ap. Vaticana Regin. 337, s9½
   N = Paris, Bibl. nat. lat. 2292, s9¾
   O = Paris, Bibl. nat. lat. 9429, s9²⁄₂
   P = Rome, Bibl. Ap. Vaticana Ottob. 313, s9¾
   Pa = Padova, Bibl. cap. D 47, s9¾
   Q = Paris, Bibl. nat. lat. 12050, c853
   R = Paris, Bibl. nat. lat. 2290, s9²⁄₂
   S = Cambrai, Bibl. mun. 162–63, s9²⁄₂
   T1 = New York, Pierpont Morgan Library, G 57, c860
   T2 = Reims, Bibl. mun. 213, c870
   U = London, Br. Lib. Add. 16605, s9²⁄₂
   V1 = Köln, Bibliothek des Metropolitankapitels 88, s9/10
   V2 = Köln, Bibliothek des Metropolitankapitels 137, s9ex
   W = Düsseldorf, Landes- und Staatsbibliothek D1, s9¼
   Ω = Trento, Castel del Buon Consiglio, MS without number, s9½

X = Paris, Bibl. Ste.-Geneviève 111, s9⅔
Y = Firenze, Bibl. Medicea-Laurenziana Edili 121, s9/10
Z4 = Monza, Bibl. cap., Sacramentary of Berengar, s9med
Z5 = fragments from Salzburg, Studienbibliothek; Munich, Bayerische Staatsbibliothek; Vienna, Nationalbibliothek, parts of a sacramentary s9¼

In these sources a superscript "1" indicates the original hand, a superscript "2" that of a later hand.

PRG = The Roman-German Pontifical of the tenth century, as edited by Vogel and Elze in *Le pontifical* 2:97–99, the Exultet no. 347, from Montecassino MS 451, s11½, and, in its form as part of Ordo romanus 50, by Michel Andrieu in *Les ordines romani*, 3:268–71 from the following manuscripts:

A = Rome, Bibl. Alessandrina 173, s11in
B = Milan, Bibl. Ambrosiana Z 52 Sup., s11½
C = Montecassino 451, s11½
D = Bamberg, Staatsbibliothek Lit. 50, s11
E = Eichstätt, Pontifical of Gondekar II, s11¾
F = Vienna, Öst. Nationalbibliothek 1832, s11
G = Vienna, Öst. Nationalbibliothek 701, s11
H = Bamberg, Staatsbibliothek Lit. 53, s11
J = London, British Library Add. 17004, s11
L = Lucca, Bibl. capitolare 607, s10ex (*omits prologue*)
M = Munich, Bayerische Staatsbibliothek 6425, s11½
N = Paris, Bibl. nationale lat. 1231, s11½
P = Paris, Bibl. nationale lat. 820, s11½ (*omits a large portion of the text*)
Q = Wolfenbüttel, Herzog-August-Bibliothek 164, s12½
R = Wolfenbüttel, Herzog-August-Bibliothek 530, s12in
S = Wolfenbüttel, Herzog-August-Bibliothek 4099, s11
T = Wolfenbüttel, Herzog-August-Bibliothek 603, s12½
V = Vendôme, Bibl. mun. 14, s11½
W = Vitry-le-François, Bibl. mun. 36, s11/12
Z = Vienna, Öst. Nationalbibliothek 1817, s12⅔

INTRODUCTORY RUBRICS

GALL
Benedictio caerei (Go, Ga: caerae) beati (B: sancti) augustini episcopi quam (Bo: cum) adhuc diaconus esset (Go: cum esset; Bo: essit) cecinit dicens (Go: edidet et caecinit; Ga: edidit et cecinnit feliciter)
GEL8
En: Item dicta beati augustini episcopi quam adhuc diaconus cum esset edidit et cecinit feliciter.
Ge: Item alia
Ph, Sg: Sabbato sancto postquam (Sg *begins* Postquam) reddunt symbolum (Sg: simbulum) et catecizantur (Sg: catezyzantur) infantes impletur cerei benedictio his orationibus

Pr, Sp: Benedictio cerei
Rh: Ad ceram benedicendum
GREG Benedictio caerei (V2: Incipit benedictio caerei)
PRG Benedictio cerei (*om.* A J P V)

TEXT OF THE EXULTET

Exultet iam angelica turba celorum,
> GALL Exultet] Exultit Bo

exultent diuina misteria,
> GALL misteria] mistiria Bo mysteria Go
> GEL8 misteria] mysteria Ph Pr Rh Sg
> GREG misteria] mysteria
> PRG misteria] MYSTERIA *except* misteria A G J T

et pro tanti regis uictoria tuba intonet salutaris.
> GALL uictoria] VICTVRIA Bo Ga Go | tuba] toba B | intonet] intonat Ga intonit
> Bo | salutaris] saluatores Bo
> GEL8 tanti] tantis Pr | regis] regni En | intonet] INSONET Ge Ph Pr Rh Sg
> GREG intonet] insonet V1 Y
> PRG intonet] INSONET *except* intonet A F P V W insonent Z

Gaudeat se tantis tellus inradiata fulgoribus,
> GALL tellus] ILLIVS Ga Go Bo
> GEL8 gaudeat] gaudiat Ge | tellus] illius En Ge Ph : *tel*lus Sg : *tel*lius Pr :
> stellis Rh
> GREG se tantis tellus] SE TELLVS *except* se tantis tellus P² V1² V2 : tantis tellus
> P¹ V1¹ : tantis *add.* K² X : tantis illius *add.* Y² | inradiata] inradiatam J¹
> K¹ O Q
> PRG Gaudeat se] GAVDEAT *except* gaudeat se tantis A J P Q T V W | se] *add.*
> *corr.* FG | tantis tellus] TELLVS TANTIS *except* tantis tellus D H J: tantis tellis
> illius H N (illius *erased* H) | tantis] illius Q : tantis illius B | inradiata]
> IRRADIATA *except* irradiatam A F G P V W : irradiatam *corr. to* irradiata J

et eterni regis splendore lustrata,
> GALL et] *om.* B | regis] regni Go | lustrata] inlustrata Ga
> GEL8 regis] regni Ph Pr Rh : *add.* Sg | lustrata] inlustrata Pr
> GREG lustrata] inlustrata V² X²
> PRG et] ut S | lustrata] ILLVVSTRATA *except* illustra Z

totius orbis se sentiat amisisse caliginem.
> GALL orbis] urbis Go | sentiat] senciat Bo Go | amisisse] amisse Go amississe
> Ga | caliginem] caligine Bo Ga
> GEL8 amisisse] ammisisse Ge: amisse Rh
> GREG orbis] noctis V2²
> PRG orbis] *om.* S | amisisse] amisisse orbis S

Letetur et mater ecclesia, tanti luminis adornata fulgore,
> GALL et] *om.* Bo | adornata] ornata Bo
> GEL8 et] *om.* Pr | adornata] adurnata Sg Ph
> GREG fulgore] FVLGORIBVS
> PRG et] *superscript corr.* C | fulgore] FVLGORIBVS

et magnis populorum uocibus, hec aula resultet.
> GALL resultet] resultit Bo
> PRG resultet] resultat Q

Quapropter adstantibus uobis fratres karissimi,

> GALL quapropter] qua Bo
> GREG adstantibus uobis] adstantibus V2¹ : adstantes uos O² : a uocibus Y¹
> PRG adstantibus uobis] ASTANTES VOS *except* adstantes uos F R S T : asstantes uos G V W: astantibus uobis JQ

ad tam miram sancti huius luminis claritatem,

> GALL miram] mira Bo | claritatem] claritate Ga
> GEL8 sancti] *add. sign* + Pr | claritatem] claritatis Rh

una mecum queso dei omnipotentis misericordiam inuocate,

> GEL8 una] unum Rh
> PRG dei omn.] omnipotentis dei J

ut qui me non meis meritis

> GALL me . . . meritis] om. Bo | meritis] meretis Ga
> GEL 8 meritis] meretis Ph

intra leuitarum numerum dignatus est adgregare,

> GALL intra . . . est] dignatos est Bo | leuitarum] sacerdotum Go | numerum] numero Go
> GEL8 numerum] numer*um* Pr | adgregare] adgregaret Rh
> PRG est] es MNQ | adgregare] AGGREGARE

luminis sui gratiam infundente

> GALL luminis] *prefixes* ut Ga : lumenis Bo | gratiam] graciam Bo : gratia Ga : gracia Go
> GEL8 gratiam] gratia En Ge Ph
> GREG gratiam] GRATIA except gratiam O¹ V1¹ Y¹ | infundente] infundendo V2²
> PRG gratiam] claritatem Z | infundente] INFVNDENDO *except* infundente A

cerei huius laudem implere precipiat.

> GALL precipiat] percipiat Bo
> GEL8 huius] hius Rh | precipiat] percipiat Ge
> GREG precipiat] PERFICIAT

Per

> GALL per] *om.* Bo Ga : *add.* resurgentem filium suum Go
> GEL8 per] *om.* Sg : *add.* dominum Ge : *add.* dominum nostrum Ph : *add.* dominum nostrum iesum christum En
> GREG per] PER DOMINVM NOSTRVM IESVM CHRISTVM FILIVM SVVM CVM QUO VIVIT ET REGNAT IN VNITATE SPIRITVS SANCTI PER OMNIA SECVLA SECV-LORVM. AMEN. *except* per dominum . . . suum] iesus christus dominus noster O P V1 : *om.* K L | iesum . . . amen] *om.* X Y¹ | suum] tuum J Q | cum quo] qui tecum Q : qui cum eo V2² Y² : *om.* J K L X: qui cum patre V1 | regnat] *add.* deus Q V2² | uiuit . . . amen] *om.* J K L X | spiritus . . . amen] *om.* Q
> PRG per] PER DOMINVM NOSTRVM IESVM CHRISTVM FILIVM SVVM QVI CVM EO VIVIT ET REGNAT DEVS IN VNITATE SPIRITVS SANCTI PER OMNIA SECVLA SECV-LORVM. AMEN. *all except* iesus christus dominus noster qui cum deo patre et spiritu sancto uiuit et regnat per omnia secula seculorum. Amen. Q

Dominus uobiscum.

> GALL *om.* Bo Ga Go
> GEL8 dominus uobiscum] *om.* En Ph Pr Sg : *prefixes* et dicit Ge
> GREG *om.*

Et cum spiritu tuo.

    GALL et . . . tuo] *om.* Bo Ga Go
    GEL8 et . . . tuo] *prefixes* Resp. G : respondetur Rh : *om.* En Ph Pr Sg
    GREG et . . . tuo *om.*

Sursum corda.

    GALL Sursum corda *om.* Go
    GEL8 Sursum] *prefixes* Explicit praefatio consecratio nunc En
    GREG *prefixes* post haec dicit V2

Habemus ad dominum.

    GALL habemus ad dominum *om.* Bo Go Ga
    GEL8 dominum] domino *Ph*

Gratias agamus domino deo nostro.

    GALL gratias . . . nostro *om.* Bo Go | agamus . . . nostro *om.* Ga

Dignum et iustum est.

    GALL Dignum . . . est *om.* Bo : *prefixes* Consecratio caere Go : *prefixes* Con-
    testatio nunc Ga

Vere quia dignum et iustum est

    GALL uere quia] *om.* Bo
    GEL8 uere quia dignum] V+D En Ge: *prefixes* V+D Ph Rh: V+D quia
    dignum Pr
    GREG uere quia dignum] VD quia dignum O^2 V2 : VD J O^1
    PRG quia] *om.* BQ | est] *above the line* aequum et salutare C

inuisibilem deum omnipotentem patrem

    GALL inuisibilem] inuisibile Bo | deum] dominum Bo
    GEL8 inuisibilem] VT INVISIBILEM | omnipotentem] *prefixes* patrem Pr
    GREG inuisibilem] VT INVISIBILEM *except* ut *om.* L P^2 Q^2 V X^2 | patrem *om.*
    O^1
    PRG inuisibilem] te inuisibilem C : in inuisibilem Q | deum] *add. above the*
    line patrem C | omn. patrem] patrem omnipotentem AC'FJZ | patrem]
    canceled C

filiumque unigenitum dominum nostrum iesum christum,

    GALL filiumque] *add.* eius Go
    GREG filiumque] *add.* eius P^2 V1^2 X^2 | christum] *add.* sanctum quoque
    spiritum V1 X
    PRG filiumque] FILIVMQUE EIVS *except* eius] *above the line* tuum C | nostrum]
    om. A | christum] *add.* sanctum quoque spiritum M

toto cordis ac mentis affectu,

    GALL toto] totum Bo | affectu] affecto Bo
    GREG ac mentis] *om.* P

et uocis ministerio personare.

    GALL ministerio] misterio Ga : ministerium Bo
    GEL8 et] ut Ge Ph Rh Sg | uocis] uoces Ph | ministerio] misterio Ge : mysterio
    Ph Sg : ministerium Rh
    GREG ministerio] mysterio V2 | personare] *add.* per christum dominum nos-
    trum V

Qui pro nobis eterno patri ade debitum soluit,

    GEL8 debitum] bitum Pr
    GREG pro] *om.* Y^1
    PRG eterno] *above the line* tibi C

et ueteris piaculi cautionem pio cruore detersit.

> GALL piaculi] peculi Bo : piacoli Go | cautionem] caucionem Bo Go | cruore] cruori Bo
> GREG detersit] debitum H
> PRG ueteris piac.] piaculi ueteris A P V W

Hec sunt enim festa paschalia,

> GALL paschalia] PASCHALIVM Bo Ga Go
> GEL8 paschalia] paschalium Ph Sg : paschaliaum Rh

in quibus uerus ille agnus occiditur,

> GALL ille] illi Ga

eiusque sanguis postibus consecratur.

> GALL sanguis] sanguenis Bo | consecratur] consegratur Ga : conscratur Bo
> GEL8 postibus] postebus Ph | consecratur] consegratur Ge Sg
> GREG sanguis postibus consecratur] sanguis postes consecrantur X^1 : sanguine postes consecrantur J^2 O^2 P V X^2
> PRG] EIVSQVE SANGVINE POSTES CONSECRANTVR

In qua primum patres nostros

> GALL primum . . . nostros] primum scire (*skips the next seventeen lines*) om. Bo
> GEL8 in] *prefixes* hec nox est Rh | qua] quo Ge
> GREG in qua] IN QVO *except* in quibus O^1 : hec nox est in qua O^2 P V
> PRG in qua] HEC NOX EST IN QVA | qua] *superscript corr.* G

filios israhel eductos de egypto,

> GALL eductos] educens Ga Go | filios . . . egypto *om.* Bo
> GEL8 filios] filius Ge | eductos] educens En Pr : eductus Ge Sg
> GREG eductos] eduxisti P^1 : domine eduxisti V^1 | egypto] *add.* quos postea P^2 V1
> PRG eductos] EDVXISTI DOMINE *except* domine] *om.* Q : *erased* J

rubrum mare sicco uestigio transire fecisti.

> GALL rubrum] rubro Ga | rubrum . . . fecisti *om.* Bo
> GEL8 rubrum] rubro Ph Rh Sg
> PRG rubrum] QVOS POSTEA RVBRVM

Hec igitur nox est, que peccatorum tenebras

> GALL hec . . . tenebras *om.* Bo

columne inluminatione purgauit.

> GALL inluminatione] inluminacione Go | columne . . . purgauit *om.* Bo
> PRG inluminatione] ILLVMINATIONE

Hec nox est, que hodie per uniuersum mundum in christo credentes

> GALL hec . . . credentes *om.* Bo
> GEL8 credentes] credentibus Sg
> GREG christo] christum L Y

a uitiis seculi segregatos, et caligine peccatorum

> GALL a . . . peccatorum *om.* Bo
> GEL8 segregatos] segregatus Ge : segregatos Pr | caligine] caliginem Ge Pr
> GREG segregatos . . . peccatorum] et caligine peccatorum segregatos V
> PRG segregatos . . . pecc.] ET CALIGINE PECCATORVM SEGREGATOS *except* segregatos et caligine peccatorum F

reddit gratie sociat sanctitati.

> GALL reddit] reddedit Ga | sanctitati] sanctitate Go | reddit . . . sanctitati *om.* Bo
>
> GEL8 reddit] redit Rh | sociat] socia Ge : sotiat Ph Rh | sanctitati] sanctitati Pr
>
> GREG reddit] reddat Y¹ | sociat] sociatque O P² V | sanctitate] sanctitatem Y¹
>
> PRG sociat] SOCIATQVE

Hec nox est, in qua distructis uinculis mortis,

> GALL distructis] destructis Bo | hec . . . mortis *om.* Bo
>
> GEL8 distructis] destructis Pr | uinculis] uincolis Ge Rh
>
> GREG distructis] DESTRVCTIS
>
> PRG distructis] DESTRVCTIS

christus ab inferis uictor ascendit.

> GALL christus . . . ascendit *om.* Bo

Nihil enim nobis nasci profuit nisi redimi profuisset.

> GALL nobis] *om.* Go | nihil . . . profuisset *om.* Bo
>
> GEL8 redimi] redemi Ge Ph Rh Sg: redimi Pr
>
> PRG nobis nasci] nasci nobis N

O mira circa nos tue pietatis dignatio.

> GALL o . . . dignatio *om.* Bo

o inestimabilis dilectio caritatis,

> GALL inestimabilis] instimabilis Go | dilectio] dileccio Go | o . . . caritatis *om.* Bo
>
> GEL8 inestimabilis] instimabilis Ph Sg : inaestimabilis Pr
>
> PRG caritatis] claritatis *corr. to* caritatis C

ut seruum redimeres filium tradidisti.

> GALL redimeres] redimeris Go : redemeris Ga | tradidisti] tradedisti Ga | ut . . . tradidisti *om.* Bo
>
> GEL8 redimeres] redimeres Pr : redemeris Rh Sg : redémeres Ge Ph | tradidisti] tradedisti Ge Ph Rh Sg : tradidisti Pr

O certe necessarium ade peccatum,

> GALL peccatum] *add.* nostrum Ga | o . . . peccatum *om.* Bo
>
> GEL8 necessarium] nessarium Sg | peccatum] *add.* nostrum En Ge Ph Sg
>
> GREG peccatum] PECCATVM NOSTRVM *except om.* nostrum J P *om.* O certe . . . peccatum V
>
> PRG *omits*

quod christi morte deletum est.

> GALL morte] mortem Ga | quod . . . est *om.* Bo
>
> GREG quod . . . est *om.* V
>
> PRG *omits*

O felix culpa, que talem ac tantum meruit habere redemptorem.

> GALL felix] filex Ga Go | o . . . redemptorem *om.* Bo
>
> GEL8 felix] filex Ge
>
> GREG o . . . redemptorem *om.* V
>
> PRG *omits*

O beata nox, que sola meruit scire tempus et horam
>   GALL O . . . meruit] *om.* Bo | horam] hora Bo Go
>   GEL8 horam] HORA Ge Ph Pr Rh Sg
>   PRG beata] uere beata J

in qua christus ab inferis resurrexit.
>   GEL8 ab] ad En | inferis] inferos Ph
>   PRG resurrexit] uictor ascendit J

Hec nox est, de qua scriptum est,
>   GEL8 qua] qa Ge

et nox ut dies inluminabitur,
>   GEL8 ut] sicut Ph Pr : et Rh
>   PRG inluminabitur] ILLVMINABITVR

et nox inluminatio mea in deliciis meis.
>   GALL illuminatio] inluminacio Bo Go | mea] *om.* Ga | deliciis] DILICIIS Bo
>   Go Ga
>   GEL8 mea] *om.* En | deliciis] diliciis Ge Ph Rh Sg : *deliciis* Pr : delitiis En
>   GREG mea] *om.* X^2
>   PRG inluminatio] ILLVMINATIO

Huius igitur sanctificatio noctis,
>   GALL sanctificatio] sanctificacio Bo Go
>   GEL8 noctis] noct*is* Pr
>   PRG igitur] ergo A P V W

fugat scelera, culpas lauat,
>   GALL lauat] leuat Go
>   GEL8 scelera] scera Sg

et reddit innocentiam lapsis, mestis letitiam,
>   GALL et] *om.* Go | mestis] *prefixes* et Go
>   GEL8 reddit] reddat Rh | letitiam] leticiam Sg

fugat odia, concordiam parat, et curuat imperia.
>   GALL concordiam] CONCORDIA Bo Ga Go
>   GEL8 odia] hodia Pr Sg | concordiam] concordia En Ph Pr Rh
>   PRG curuat] curbat *corr. to* curuat C

In huius igitur noctis gratia
>   GALL gratia] graciam Bo
>   GEL8 igitur] *om.* Sg | gratia] gratiam Rh
>   PRG huius igitur] HVIVS ERGO *except* huius igitur B C F G M Z | gratia]
>   gratiam C

suscipe sancte pater incensi huius sacrificium uespertinum,
>   PRG incensi] *add. sign* + A C Z *add. in margin* pone incensum A

quod tibi in hac cerei oblatione sollemni, per ministrorum manus
>   GALL tibi] *om.* Bo | oblatione] oblacionem Bo | sollemni] sollempni Go :
>   sollempne Ga : sollemniter Bo | per] *om.* Bo | ministrorum] *add.* tuorum
>   Ga Go
>   GEL8 hac] hanc Rh | sollemni] solemni En Sg : solempni Pr : solemnii Rh
> | ministrorum] ministeriorum Pr : *add.* tuorum En Pr | manus] munus Ge
>   Ph Rh Sg
>   GREG oblatione] oblationem Y
>   PRG sollemni] sollempni C G J T

de operibus apum, sacrosancta reddit ecclesia.
> GALL sacrosancta] sacrumsancta Ga | ecclesia] aecclesiae Ga
> GEL8 apum] apium Pr Sg | ecclesia] eclesia Ge Sg
> GREG apum] apium K L O¹ Y
> PRG apum] apium B

Sed iam columne huius preconia nouimus,
> GALL preconia] praconia Go
> GEL8 nouimus] nou*i*mus Pr
> GREG iam] etiam Y

quam in honore dei rutilans ignis accendit.
> GEL8 honore] honorem En Ge Rh
> GREG honore] HONOREM *except* honore V1
> PRG honore] HONOREM *except* honore C D E J N Q R | accendit] ascendit B

Qui licet diuisus in partes,
> GALL licet] licit Bo | *add.* sit Ga | partes] partis Bo Ga
> GEL8 qui] quia En | diuisus] diuis*u*s Pr
> PRG licet] *add.* sit A

mutuati luminis detrimenta non nouit.
> GALL mutuati] mutati Bo : mutuatim Ga | luminis] lumenis Bo
> GEL8 mutuati] mutati Rh Sg mutua*t*i Pr
> GREG mutuati] *add.* tamen P²

Alitur liquentibus ceris
> GALL alitur] aliter Bo : halitur Ga | liquentibus] liquantibus Bo Go | ceris] caereis Ga
> GEL8 alitur] aletur Ph : alit*u*r Pr | liquentibus] liquantibus Ge | ceris] caereis En Rh Pr
> GREG alitur] aliter Z5 | liquentibus] liquantibus V1¹ Y Z5 | ceris] CEREIS *except* ceris H
> PRG alitur] *add.* enim A Z : *add.* igitur N : aliter enim V W | liquentibus] liquantibus C

quam in substantiam pretiose huius lampadis apis mater eduxit.
> GALL substantiam] substancia Go Bo : SUBSTANTIA Ga | pretiose] praeciosi Ga | lampadis] lampades Ga | apis] *om.* Ga
> GEL8 quam] quas En Rh | substantiam] substantia Sg | pretiose] preciose En Sg | lampadis] lampades Ph
> GREG quam] QVAS *except* quam V2 | apis] apes P Q V1
> PRG quam] QVAS *except* quam A E G V W | huius lamp.] lampadis huius Z apis] apes C G H J M

Apis ceteris que subiecta sunt homini, animantibus antecellit.
> GALL apis] apes Ga | ceteris] citeris Bo Ga | homini] homeni Bo
> GEL8 apis] apes En | homini] humani Ph : humanis Rh Sg : hominibus Pr | antecellit] antecellet En Ph
> GREG Apis . . . permansit *om.* V X | apis] apes P Q V1
> PRG *omits*

Cum sit minima corporis paruitate,
> GALL minima] nimia Ga | corporis] corpores Bo : corpore Ga
> GREG paruitate] prauitate Y
> PRG *omits*

ingentes animos angusto uersat in pectore.

> GALL ingentes] ingentis Ga Go | animos] animus Ga
> GEL8 ingentes] ingentis Ge Ph Sg | ingentes animos] animos ingentes Pr | animos] animus Ge
> PRG *omits*

Viribus inbecillis, sed fortis ingenio.

> GALL inbecillis] inbicella Ga : inbecilla Go | fortis] fortes Bo
> GEL8 inbecillis] inbicillis Ge : inbicilis Ph Sg : inbecilla Pr
> GREG uiribus] uirilibus Y
> PRG *omits*

Hec explorata temporum uice,

> GALL explorata] exflorata Go : inplorata Ga | uice] uicem Go
> GEL8 uice] uicem Ge Ph *om.* Pr
> GREG uice] uicem Y[1]
> PRG *omits*

cum canitiem pruinosa hiberna posuerint,

> GALL pruinosa] PROINOSA Bo Ga Go | posuerint] posuerunt Bo
> GEL8 canitiem] canicie Pr : caniciem En Ge Ph Sg | pruinosa] pruinosa Rh
>   : pruinos ad En : proinosa Sg | hiberna] hiuerna Rh | posuerint] posuerent
>   Ge
> GREG canitiem] canitie Z5
> PRG *omits*

et glaciale senio uerni temporis moderata deterserint,

> GALL glaciale] glatiale Ga : glacialem Go : glaciales Bo | deterserint] DE-
>   TERSERIT Bo Ga Go
> GEL8 glaciale] glatiali Ge En Rh : glaciali Sg | senio] seni*um* Pr | deterserint]
>   detersit Rh
> GREG glaciale] GLACIALI except glatiale P Q | senio] senium P Q Z5
> PRG *omits*

statim prodeundi ad laborem cura succedit.

> GALL prodeundi] prodiundi Bo | cura] curam Ga | succedit] succendit Bo
> PRG *omits*

Disperseque per agros libratis paululum pennis cruribus suspensis insidunt.

> GALL disperseque] dispersique Ga | libratis] LIBRATIM Bo Ga Go | paululum]
>   PAVLOLVM Bo Ga Go | pennis] PINNIBUS Bo Ga Go | cruribus] cruoribus
>   Go | insidunt] insedunt Ga Go
> GEL8 disperseque] dispersaque Ge : dispers*e*que Pr | libratis] liberatis Pr
>   : liberatim Ph Sg | paululum] paulolum Ge Ph Rh Sg | pennis] pinnis Ge
>   Rh : pinnibus Ph Pr Sg | suspensis] suspensus Rh
> GREG libratis] libratim Z5 | pennis] pinnis L : perennis Y | insidunt] in-
>   sidiunt O
> PRG *omits*

Parte ore legere flosculos,

> GALL parte] partem Go | flosculos] floscolus Ga
> GEL8 partim] *prati* Pr | ore] hore Rh | flosculos] flosculis Pr
> GREG parte] partim Q : partem Z5
> PRG *omits*

oneratis uictualibus suis, ad castra remeant.

> GALL suis] *om.* Bo
> GEL8 remeant] remaneant Rh
> GREG oneratis] partim oneratis Q
> PRG *omits*

Ibique alie inestimabili arte, cellulas tenaci glutino instruunt,

> GALL inestimabili] inaestimabile Go: instimabile Bo Ga | cellulas] cellolas Bo
> Ga cellosas Go | glutino] glotino Bo
> GEL8 inestimabili] inaestimabil*i* Pr : inestimabile Ph | cellulas] cellolas En
> Ph Rh Sg | glutino] gluttino Pr
> GREG inaestimabili arte] inaestimabile O¹
> PRG *omits*

alie liquantia mella stipant,

> GALL liquantia] liquancia Bo : liquencia Go : liquentia Ga
> GEL8 liquantia] liquentiae En Pr : liquanti Rh
> GREG liquantia] liquentia Q
> PRG *omits*

alie uertunt flores in ceram,

> GALL ceram] caeram Ga : cera Bo : caera Go
> GEL8 ceram] cera Ph : caera Rh
> GREG ceram] cera Z5
> PRG *omits*

alie ore natos fingunt,

> GALL natos] NATVS Bo Ga Go
> GEL8 natos] natus Rh : nat*o*s Pr | fingunt] figunt Rh
> PRG *omits*

alie collectis e foliis nectar includunt.

> GEL8 collectis] collectum En Pr Rh | e foliis] *om.* Pr | includunt] ingludunt
> Rh
> GREG collectis] *prefixes* namque P
> PRG *omits*

O uere beata et mirabilis apis,

> GALL mirabilis] mirabiles Bo
> GEL8 apis] apes Ph
> GREG apis] apes J P Q
> PRG *omits*

cuius nec sexum masculi uiolant,

> GALL masculi] mascoli Bo
> GEL8 sexum] sexsum En : sexus Ph | masculi] masculini Rh
> PRG *omits*

fetus non quassant,

> GALL fetus non quassant] *om.* Bo | fetus] faetus Go
> GEL8 fetus] foetos Ph Sg | quassant] QVASSAT En Ge Ph Pr Rh Sg
> GREG quassant] quassat Z5
> PRG *omits*

nec filii destruunt castitatem.

> GALL destruunt] DISTRVVNT Bo Ga Go
> GEL8 destruunt] distruunt Ge Sg Rh : d*e*struunt Pr
> PRG *omits*

Sicut sancta concepit uirgo maria,
>
> GALL uirgo] *om.* Bo
> PRG *omits*

uirgo peperit, et uirgo permansit.
>
> PRG *omits*

O uere beata nox, que expoliauit egyptios, ditauit hebreos.
>
> GALL egyptios] aegypcius Bo
> GEL8 egyptios] egyptius Ge | hebreos] hebreus Ge

nox in qua terrenis celestia iunguntur.
>
> GEL8 iunguntur] *add.* humanis diuina Rh
> GREG celestia] *add.* humanis diuina V1²

Oramus te domine, ut cereus iste in honorem nominis tui consecratus
>
> GALL cereus] cerei Bo | honorem] honore Ga Go | consecratus] consecrati Bo
>   : consegratus Ga
> GEL 8 domine] *add. sign* + Ge Pr Sg | cereus] cereos En : *add. sign* + Pr
> | iste] ite Sg | honorem] honore Ph Sg
> GREG tui] *add. sign* + *all except* L O X
> PRG oramus] *add.* ergo J M Q Z : ergo *above the line* C | honorem] honore
>   B C D H J M N S | consecratus] *add. sign* + A

ad noctis huius caliginem destruendam indeficiens perseueret,
>
> GALL noctis] noctem Ga | caliginem] caligines Bo | destruendam] DISTRV-
>   ENDAM Ga Go : distruenda Bo | indeficiens] indificiens Bo | perseueret]
>   perseuerit Ga : *om.* Bo
> GEL8 destruendam] distruendam En Ge Rh : destruendam Pr | indeficiens]
>   *prefixes* sit et Pr | perseueret] perseuerit Sg : perseueret Pr : sit et perse-
>   ueret Pr
> PRG noctis huius] huius noctis N

in odorem suauitatis acceptus,
>
> GALL acceptus] acceptis Bo
> GEL8 in] *prefixes* et En | acceptus] acceptus Pr
> GREG in] *prefixes* atque V2² | acceptus] acceptis Z5 accensus W²
> PRG in] ATQVE IN *except om.* atque B D M N

supernis luminaribus misceatur.
>
> GALL misceatur] misceantur Bo
> GEL8 misceatur] misciatur Ge

Flammas eius, lucifer matutinus inueniat.
>
> GALL flammas] *add.* que Bo
> PRG matutinus] matutinis *corr. to* matutinus C

Ille inquam lucifer, qui nescit occasum.
>
> PRG nescit . . . ille] *om.* S

Ille qui regressus ab inferis, humano generi serenus inluxit.
>
> GALL generi] genere Bo Ga
> GEL8 regressus] regessus Pr | humano] humanu Ge | generi] generi Pr
> GREG serenus inluxit] *om.* O¹
> PRG inluxit] ILLVXIT

Precamur ergo te domine,
>
> GALL te] *om.* Bo Go

ut nos famulos tuos omnem clerum et deuotissimum populum,

>GALL tuos] et famulas tuas Go | omnem] omnemque Go | clerum] clero Ga
>GEL8 tuos] tuus Ge

una cum patre nostro beatissimo uiro ill.,

>GALL una . . . ill] *om.* Bo Ga
>GEL8 nostro] *om.* Ge | uiro] *add* papa Sg : *add.* papa nostro Ge Pr | beatissimo
>uiro] *om.* Ph | ill] *add.* necnon et clementissimo rege nostro illo coniugeque
>eius ac filiis cunctuque exercitu fraucorum Rh
>GREG patre nostro beatissimo uiro] PATRE NOSTRO PAPA *except* patre papa
>nostro O² : papa nostro P² V | ill.] Gregorio (?) O¹
>PRG patre nostro beatissimo uiro] BEATISSIMO PAPA NOSTRO N. ET GLORIO-
>SISSIMO REGE NOSTRO N. EIVSQVE NOBILISSIMA CONIVGE N. ET ANTISTITE
>NOSTRO N. *except* beatissimo] *om.* B F | papa nostro N.] papa nostro ill.
>B E H M Q : papa nostro N. et antistite (uenerabili antistite Q) nostro
>N. C F Q : papa nostro N. et uenerabili antistite nostro HERIMANNO J :
>papa nostro N. *in marg., cursive script* : et abbate nostro cum omni con-
>gregatione beatissimi patris nostri Benedicti praesentis uitae quiete con-
>cessa C | rege nostro N.] imperatore nostro N. C Q : imperatore N. A V
>W : imperatore Heinrico N | eiusque . . . antistite nostro N.] cum omni
>congregatione et familia sanctae Mariae F. | nobilissima] *add.* prole siue
>J Q | coniuge N.] *om.* M : coniuge J : *add.* pariter cum prole S | coniuge
>. . . nostro N.] prole C | et antistite nostro N.] *om.* J | et antistite . . .
>concessa] *om.* B E Q : *add. in marg.* H | antistite] reuerentissimo antistite
>N. | antistite nostro N.] antistite nostro A : antistite nostro Ottone N :
>antistite nostro Egilberto cum omni congregatione sanctae Mariae M

quiete temporum concessa,

>GALL quiete] quietem Ga
>PRG quiete t. concessa] *om.* GRSTZ

in his paschalibus conseruare digneris.

>GALL paschalibus] *add.* gaudiis Go
>GEL8 digneris] dignetur Rh
>GREG paschalibus] PASCHALIBVS GAVDIIS *except* festis paschalibus P
>PRG paschalibus] PASCHALIBVS FESTIS | digneris] dignetur A V W : dignetur
>*with the following added in the margin* Memento etiam, domine, famuli tui
>imperatoris nostri N. et celestem illi concede uictoriam et his qui tibi
>offerunt hoc sacrificium laudis praemia aeterna largiaris. Per dominum. C

Per.

>GALL per] *om.* Bo *add.* resurgentem a mortuis dominum nostrum filium
>tuum Go
>GEL8 per] *om.* Pr : *add.* dominum Rh : *add.* dominum nostrum En Ge Ph
>Sg
>GREG per] per eundem . . . Amen V2
>PRG per] PER EVNDEM DOMINVM NOSTRVM IESVM CHRISTVM FILIVM TVVM QVI
>TECVM VIVIT ET REGNAT DEVS IN VNITATE EIVSDEM SPIRITVS SANCTI PER
>OMNIA SAECVLA SAECVLORVM. AMEN. *except* eundem . . . Amen] *om.* AFV
>| filium . . . Amen *om.* W | eiusdem] *om.* BEHJ | Amen] *om.* EJT

TEXTS RELATED TO
THE SOUTH ITALIAN
EXULTET

References to Exultet Rolls

1. (945 C.E.) Among the donations of Leo, presbyter and abbot, to Saint Benedict in Larinum.

> rutulum de cereum benedicere .i.
>
> Inguanez, Catalogi codicum, 62

2. (964 C.E.) A document recording gift of land by "Gregorius consul et dux" to Petrus presbyter of the church of Saint Michael "in loco Planciano" and naming Petrus' gifts to the church includes:

> modum de terra bobis [= uobis] dedimus pro eo quod tu suprascriptus petrus veneravilis presbyter dedisti in ista suprascripta unum liber comite. et unum antiphonarium et unum codice da leiere in nocte. et unum codice de sancta trinitate. et unum rotulo ad benedicendum cereum et fontes. et unum pannum de sericu. . . .
>
> Montecassino, Archivio, caps. LXX fasc. XII no. 140, printed in Codex Diplomaticus Cajetanus, 1:123

3. (1007 C.E.) In the testament outlining his gifts to the Benedictine monastery of Sancta Maria di Fontanella, Amalfi, its founder Giovanni da Fontanella includes:

> rotulum unum de penitentia cum benedictione da fonti et alia benedictione de ipso cirio.
>
> Camera, Memorie, 1:221–22.

4. (Thirteenth century) An eighteenth-century description of a thirteenth-century Exultet roll in Capua:

> Un rotolo in pergamena del XIII. secolo, sotto il nostro Arcivescovo Marino Filamarino, sfornito di miniature, che contiene il cantico Exultet, adorno di note espresse maravigliosamente in otto righe, non ordinarie in quel Secolo. . . . La lezione del medesimo niente varia dalla nostra [i. e., the Franco-Roman text], se non nella sola preghiera, che la persona del Papa, del Vescovo, e del Re in cotal guisa commemora: *Precamur ergo te, Domine,*

ut beatissimum papam nostrum Nicolaum, una cum devoto Marino, Regem nostrum Karolum, nos etiam famulos tuos, subditum clerum et devotissimum populum capuanum, quiete temporum concessa in his paschalibus gaudiis conservare digneris. Per dominum nostrum, etc.

Natale, Lettera, 65

5. (1373 c.e.) From an inventory of the goods of the monastery of Saint Mary, Lucus Marsorum, made by Frater Ludovicus, provost, in 1372, but not listed in the inventory of 1405:

Item carta benedictionis cerei .I. isturiata.

Inguanez, Catalogi codicum, 63

6. (1430–35 c.e.) From the inventory of the Biblioteca capitolare, Benevento, of 1430–35, reviewed by the librarian Theuli in 1447; there seem to be at least twelve rolls (if we can assume that a *carta* in this context is a roll). They include the following among the items in non-Beneventan script:

Item carta ubi est *exultet iam angelica.*

Zazo, "L'Inventario" (with errors). For a larger extract from this list, see p. 29.

7. (1508 c.e.) A Gaeta inventory of 1508, perhaps referring to Gaeta, Exultet 3:

Item una carta di coyro grande scripta notata et figurata dove si cantha Exultet jam angelica; circha palmi venti longa.

Ferraro, Memorie, 180

References to the Ceremonial of the Exultet

Sources from Benevento

8. Location unknown, late tenth century (Vatican lat. 10673)

9. Location unknown (Salerno?), tenth or eleventh century (Benevento 33)

(fols. 34–34v)
Lectio *Hec est hereditas.* que quinta est ordinata secundum romanum
  legatur hic.
Secundum ambrosianum legatur post benedictionem cerei.

(fols. 35–35v)
Post hec [lessons and canticles]
accendatur ignis nouus ex ignario
uel alio quoliuet modo
dicaturque super eum oratio hec.

Deus qui per filium tuum angularem

  . . .
de quo igne benedicto accendatur
  cereus
& quasi ex occulto
proferatur in puplicum.
Tunc episcopus aut prebyter
cum eodem cereo
accendat cerei preparatum ad benedicendum.

Et accensum tangat cum crisma
faciendo in illum signaculum sancte
  crucis.
Deinde diaconus sumens cereum
ter pronuntiet. *Lumen xpisti.*
Respondit in choro *Deo gratias.*
et incipit benedicere benedictio
que hic notata est.
Deinde incipit benedictionem cereis.
  Exultet . . . [incomplete, owing to lacuna].

(fols. 76v–77)
Post hec [lessons and canticles]
accendatur ignis nouum ex ignario
uel alio quolibet modo.
dicaturque super eum oratio superscripta.

De quo igne accendatur cereus.

& quasi ex occulto
proferatur in puplico.
Tunc episcopus uel presbyter
cum ipso cereo
accendatur [*sic*] cereum preparatum
  ad benedicendum.

Et accensum tangat eum cum chrisma
faciens in illum signum crucis.

Deinde tangens diaconus cereum
ter pronuntiet *Lumen xpisti.*
Respondeant cunctis. *Deo gratias.*

Deinde dicat diaconus.
Exultet . . . (in extenso).

10. Benevento Pontifical, twelfth century (Macerata, Biblioteca comunale "Mozzi-Borgetti" MS 378, pontifical of Saint Peter's *extra muros*, Benevento, fols. 125–31.

> Incipit ordo de sabbato sancto. Expleto matutino cum prima, diuidantur clerici in quattuor partes; et unaqueque pars faciat letanias per singulas basilicas eius ecclesie, ut insimul fiant quattuor paria.

In hora uero officii, stante episcopo ad sedem sacerdotalibus pannis induto cum tot ministrorum altaris, iterum incipiantur a cleris in choro hec letania:

Kyrieleyson. Xpisteleyson . . . [in extenso, with notation]. Qua expleta dicat presul Or. *Deus qui diuitias.* . . .

Tunc legatur lectio libri genesis *In principio creauit deus celum et terram.* Tractus *Domine audiui.* [Or.] *Deus qui mirabiliter creasti.* . . . Sequitur lectio libri exodi *Factum est in uigilia matutina.* Tractus *Cantemus domino.* Deinde or. *Deus cuius antiqua miracula.* . . . Lectio libri deuteronomii *In diebus illis, Scripsit moyses canticum.* Tractus *Adtende celum.* Oratio *Deus celsitudo humilum.* . . . Lectio *In diebus illis, Apprehendent septem mulieres uirum unum.* Tractus *Vinea facta est.* Or. *Deus qui nos ad celebrandum.* . . . Lectio *In diebus illis, Angelus domini. Benedictus es domine* [with musical notation].

Dum hoc canitur, interim episcopus benedicat ignem incenden[dum]. Benedictio. *Deus qui per filium tuum angularem scilicet lapidem.* . . . Alia. *Domine deus pater omnipotens exaudi nos lumen indeficiens.* . . . Benedictio incensi noui. *Omnipotens sempiterne deus mundi conditor.* . . . Alia. *Domine deus noster qui suscepisti munera abel.* . . . Alia. *Dominator omnipotens rex gloriose.* . . .

Dehinc postquam clerici finierint *Benedictus es domine,* episcopus dicat oratio *Deus qui tribus pueris.* . . .

His dictis, et domno episcopo procedente, diaconus ascendit in ammonem. Tunc episcopus aut presbyter accendat cereum preparatum ad benedicendum; deinde diaconus tangens cereum pronuntiet ter *Lumen christi.* R. in choro *Deo gratias.* Et incipit benedicere his uerbis. *Exultet iam angelica turba celorum.* Qua completa legatur lectio *Hec est hereditas seruorum domini.* Tractus *Sicut ceruus.* Oratio *Omnipotens sempiterne deus, respice propitius ad deuotionem.* . . .

Post hec cum processione clerus et populus procedant ad fontem cantando hos uersus, *Rex sanctorum angelorum.* . . .

Sources from Bari

11. Bari, Archivio della Cattedrale from the benedictional, eleventh century (facsimiles in Cavallo, *Rotoli;* Avery, *The Exultet Rolls; Exultet; PM,* 21). Prayers and chant pieces given complete in the document are given with cues only here.

Benedictio ignis nouo in sancto sabbato. Quando uult diaconus ire ad cereum benedicere. [Or.] *Deus qui per filium tuum angularem.* . . . Post completa[m] benedictionem cerei dicatur hec oratio: *Domine deus pater omnipotens exaudi nos lumen indeficiens.* . . . Hac oratione data, intingat pollicem episcopus in chrisma, et faciat crucem in ipso cereo. Tunc procedit pontifex ad fontem cantante clero antiphonam hanc: *Omnes sitientes.* . . . Venientes ad fontem, incipit episcopus letanias: *Christe audi nos.* . . . Deinde legitur lectio *Hec est hereditas.* Tractus *Sicut cervus.* . . .

Sources from Montecassino

12. Montecassino, eighth century

Sabbato vero post horam Nonam pulsato signo intrent in oratorio. Dicta oratione incipiunt lectiones duodecim cum novem orationibus totidemque Gradalibus. Et sequuntur benedictiones et benedictio cerei et aquae. Exeuntes vero cum laetania procedunt ad sanctum Petrum. Finita ibidem ipsa letania, dicta oratione procedunt inde ad sanctum Benedictum cum alia letania et illa ibidem finita, similiter dicta oratione incipient aliam et cum ipsa procedunt ad missam maiorem.

> From "Ordo officii in domo Sancti Benedicti," from a lost manuscript of s8/9, in Hallinger et al., eds., *Initia Consuetudinis*, 118, and Albers, *Consuetudines*, 3:21. On the Cassinese provenance, see Berlière, "Les coûtumiers."

13. Montecassino, tenth century

Item in Sabbato Sancto ad Matutinum de candelis extinguendis sic faciant quomodo et in Cena Domini. Pos horam Nonam incipiunt lectiones cum orationibus et tracto et *Benedicite*. Inde sequitur benedictio ignis et cerei et aquae. Et tunc incipiunt laetaniam et ibunt in eclesiam beati Petri apostoli, et dicta ibi oratione pergunt ad sanctum Benedictum. Et finita letania incipiunt missam maiorem.

> From Montecassino 175, fol. 265v, in Hallinger et al., eds., *Initia Consuetudinis*, 118, and Albers, *Consuetudines*, 21 n.

14. Montecassino, ca. 1100

Paris, Bibl. Mazarine MS 364, 1099–1105 (A); Vatican MS Urb. lat. 585, fols. 213–14, 1099–1105 (B); Montecassino MS 198, s12/13 (C); Vat. Barb. lat. 631, fols. 75–76: Pontifical, s11ex (D); Montecassino 127, pp. 190–91: Missale, s11ex (E); Montecassino 198, pp. 63–65: ordo officii s12/13 (F); Montecassino 562, p. 65: Breviarium sive ordo officiorum, s13 (G); Benevento 66, fols. 62–62v: San Pietro, Benevento, s12 (H); Malibu, J. Paul Getty Museum IX. 1, ordo officii, a. 1153, fols. 4v–5 (I).

1. Hora[1] nona ingrediantur[2] secretarium sacerdotes[3] et ministri[4] et induant[5] se vestimentis sollempnibus[6] et antecedente acolito cum accensa candela in arundine[7] procedant de more in ecclesiam[8] cum silentio, et inclinati ad altare, vadant sedere.

2. Qui[9] autem lectiones[10] legere et tractus debent cantare omnes induti pluvialibus stent in capite utriusque[11] chori per ordinem.

---

1. For ¶1, D uses text from Ordo Romanus 28: see edition there. 2. ingrediantur] ingrediuntur D 3. sacerdotes] pontifex sacerdotes D 4. ministri] leuite D 5. induant] induunt D 6. sollempnibus] sollemnibus E F G H I *om.* D 7. arundine] harundine E 8. ecclesiam] ecclesia F I 9. Qui . . . ordinem (¶2) appears later, D E 10. lectiones] *om.* E 11. utriusque] *om.* D

3. Tunc[12] diaconus postulata benedictione a sacerdote[13] tollat benedictionem cerei desuper altare. Et egrediens per medium chori inclinato capite dicat secrete[14] fratribus: *Orate pro me.* Quem precedant duo subdiaconi et predictus[15] acolitus ferens cereum in arundine.[16]

4. Diaconus vero ascendens in ammonem, dicat tribus vicibus[17] alta voce: *Lumen Christi.* Et respondeant omnes: *Deo gratias,* similiter[18] tribus vicibus.

5. Interim acolitus illuminet cereum magnum qui benedicendus est,[19] et post hec diaconus incipiat[20] benedictionem ipsius:[21] *Exultet iam angelica.* Qua expleta revertatur ad altare.[22]

6. Tunc accendantur ad altare in duobus candelabris duo cerei. Et de ipso igne accendatur[23] in omni domo, quia omnis ignis anterior extingui debet.[24]

7. Finita vero benedictione cerei non dicat sacerdos orationem, sed mox primus lector[25] ascendens in gradum incipiat[26] legere: *In principio creavit Deus celum et terram.* . . .

> in Leutermann, ed., *Ordo casinensis,* 114–15; the portion from Vat.
> Barb. lat. 631 in Andrieu, ed., *Le pontifical,* 1:292–93

12. Tunc] Apund nos autem, postquam sacerdos cum omnibus ministris ordine quo supra ad altare processert, tune D   13. postulata . . . sacerdote] *om.* D   14. secrete] *om.* DE
15. predictus] unus D   16. arundine] harundine E F G   17. tribus vicibus] *om.* D
18. similiter] *om.* DE   19. magnum qui ben. est] *om.* D   20. incipiat] *om.* E F
21. ipsius] cerei D ipsius incipiat EFG   22. altare quo venerat E altare ordine quo venerat D   23. accendatur] *om.* G   24. ¶ 2 appears here, DE   25. primum lectorum D
26. incipiat] incipit E

15. Montecassino 318, p. 296; Vat. Barb. lat. 631, fols. 75–76

1. Sabbato sancto ordo secundum romanum [318]; Incipit ordo qualiter agendum sit in sabbato sancto [631]

2. Hora nona ingrediuntur [318: in] secretarium sacerdos [631: pontifex sacerdotes] et leuite et induunt se uestimentis cum quibus uigilias sanctas celebrare debent.

3. Et accenso cereo, procedunt simul omnes de sacrario cum ipso cereo in ecclesia cum silentio.

4. Et posito in candelabro cereo portante acolito procedunt ad altare.

5. Acolitus uero portat cereum ad ammonem et dicat tribus uicibus *Lumen Christi* plane, et respondeant omnes *Deo gratias* similiter plane.

6. Tunc dicat diaconus [631: diaconus dicat] *Orate pro me* et [631: et uadens] ascendit in ammonem et dicat *Exultet*

[631: Apud nos autem . . . see text 14, n.12]

7. [318 only:] qua finita dicit *Dominus uobiscum* R. *Et cum spiritu. Sursum corda*. R. *Habemus. Gratias agamus*. R. *Dignum et iustum*. Inde uero accedat in consecrationem cerei decantando quasi canonem.

8. Postea uero accenduntur [631: Postea acc. ad altare] in duobus candelabris duo cerei, et de ipso igne accendunt [631: accendatur] in omni domo, quia omnis ignis anterior extingui debet.

16. Ordo Romanus 28

Hora nona ingrediuntur in sacrarium sacerdos et levitae et induunt se vestimentis cum quibus vigilias celebrare debent.

et, accenso cereo, procedunt simul omnes de sacrario cum ipso cereo in ecclesia cum silentio, nichil cantantes.

et ponitur in candelabro ante altare.

Et unus diaconus rogat unum de sacerdotibus vel levitis, qui ibidem revestiti adstant, pro se orare. Et, ut surrexerit, dicit ipse diaconus *Dominus vobiscum*. Resp: *Et cum spiritu tuo*. Et dicit orationem, sicut in Sacramentorum continetur.

Postea sedent sacerdotes in sedilia sua; diaconi permanent stantes.

Ipsa expleta, dicit: *Dominus vobiscum*. Resp.: *Et cum spiritu tuo*. Inde: *Sursum corda*. Resp.: *Habemus ad dominum*. Inde: *Gratias agamus domino Deo nostro*. Resp.: *Dignum et iustum est*. Inde vero accedit in consecrationem cerei, decantando quasi canonem.

Inde vero accenduntur in duobus candelabris duo cerei et de ipso igne accendunt in omni domo, quia omnis anterior extingui debet.

Andrieu, *Les ordines*, 3:403–4

17. Benevento, Santa Sofia, twelfth century

Hora nona ingrediantur secretarium sacerdos et ministris et induant se uestimentis sollempnibus et procedant de more in ecclesiam cum silentio, et inclinati ad altare uadant sedere.

Mox primum lectorum ascendens in gradum incipit legere *In principio creauit Deus celum et terram*. . . . [twelve lections, with four tracts]

Quibus expletis sacerdos cum ministris reuertantur in secretarium et accenso cereo de igne in cena Domini benedicto, ponit(ur) in arundine quam gestans acolitus procedant in ecclesiam antecedendo accolito cum accensa candela in arundine.

Tunc diaconus postulata benedictione a sacerdote tollat benedictionem cerei desuper altare.

Et egrediens per medium chori inclinato capite silenter dicat fratribus: *Orate pro me*. Quem precedant duo subdiaconi.

Diaconus vero ascendens in ammonem, dicat tribus uicibus alta voce: *Lumen Christi*. Et respondeant omnes: *Deo gratias*, similiter tribus uicibus.

Interim acolitus illuminet cereum magnum qui benedicendus est, et post hec diaconum sucipiat benedictionem ipsius: *Exultet iam angelica*. Qua expleta reuertatur ad altare.

Tunc accendantur ad altare in duobus candelabris duo cerea. Et de ipso igne accendatur in omni domo, quia omnis ignis anterior extingui debet.

Finita benedictione cerei reuertatur sacerdos cum ministris in secretario. dehinc benedicatur aqua a sacerdote priuatim, at aspergatur in omni domo. Deinde illuminentur candele et pergant tres clerici ante altare et incipiant canere letanias. . . .

Naples, Biblioteca nazionale, MS VI E 43, fol. 51
Vatican, Vat. lat. 4928, fols. 57–58

18. Leo of Ostia's description of the ambo and the Paschal candlestick in the basilica of Desiderius, consecrated 1071.

Fecit quoque et pulpitum ligneum ad legendum sive cantandum longe priori prestantius et eminentius, in ascensu scilicet graduum sex, idque diversis colorum fucis et auri petalis de pulchro pulcherrimum reddidit. Ante quod columnam argenteam viginti et quinque librarum partim deauratam ad modum magni candelabri sex cubitorum in altitudine habens supra basem porfireticam statuit, super quam videlicet cereus magnus, qui sabbato paschali benedicendus est, sollemniter debeat exaltari.

Chr. mon. Cas., 404

19. Naples, twelfth (?) century

In die Sabbati sancti Dominus Archiepiscopus induere se consuevit in cappella palatii sui, ad quam convenire debent et se pluvialibus induere Diaconi et presbyteri Cardinales. Comitus autem pluviali indutus et quattuor diaconi acoliti camisis, cum Cruce cannulis candelabris thuribulo aliisque necessariis, ad eandam cappellam convenire debent. Dictus Archiepiscopus cum omnibus supradictis processionaliter ad ecclesiam pergit, modo et ordine servatis ut in festo Nativitatis Domini, addito quod in principio Officii Dominus Archiepiscopus, indutus pluviali de colore violato, accedit ad ignem benedictum per Cimilarcha ante fores ecclesiae, et accendit cereum et portat in manu usque ad altare, quem dare cumsuevit Sacristae ecclesiae Neapolitanae; et sic indutus Dominus Archiepiscopus stare consuevit in sede iuxta altare, et eo sedente legi debent duodecim lectiones, quibus lectis, statim Diaconus qui legit evangelium accedit et benedicit cereum, indutus dalmatica alba. Dominus Archiepiscopus supradictus Diacono qui cereum benedicit dare consuevit residuum balsami, quod reservavit in ampulla die Iovis sancto. Cereo vero benedicto, dictus Dominus Archiepiscopus cum toto Capitulo cum processione accedit ad benedicendum fontem, et in eundo et redeundo magister scholarum chori Primicerii vadit cantando litanias cum uno socio, et habere consuevit a Domino Archiepiscopo tarenum unum de Amalphia.

> From the constitutions drawn up in 1337 by Archbishop Giovanni Orsini, "cum in hac nostra Neapolitana ecclesia certi ritus modi et consuetudines ab antiquo fuerint et debeant observari . . . ," transcribed from the now-lost original in the seventeenth century by Camillo Tutini (Naples, Biblioteca Nazionale, Bibl Brancacciana I.F.2), as transcribed in Mallardo, "La Pasqua," 33

20. Salerno, thirteenth century

Sciendum est quod in ecclesia Salernitana de antiquo more leguntur duodecim lectiones, octo latine et quattuor grece; et si greci non fuerint, leguntur latine. et post duodecimam lectionem dicto tractu et dicta oratione, benedicitur cereus . . . [lections and prayers named; blessing of new fire]

Qua [the blessing of fire after the lections] finita aspergatur aqua benedicta et adoleatur incenso. De hinc accendatur cereus de nouo igne similiter septem lampada et cerei qui sunt in candelabris illuminentur. Post hec episcopus infigat in cereo in modum crucis quinque frusta incensi benedicti. Deinde diaconus postulet benedictionem, qua recepta uadat ad benedicendum cereum. Postque uero ascenderit pulpitum, primo media uoce dicat cum notis *Lumen xpisti,* secundo alciori, tercio excelsa uoce clero et populo uice qualibet respondente *Deo gratias. Exultet* . . . [in extenso, Beneventan text]

> Thirteenth-century copy of twelfth-century ordinal, Salerno, Archivio capitolare, MS Capone 7; fifteenth-century missals, Salerno, Archivio capitolare, MS Capone 3 and Capone 4

21. Capua, thirteenth (?) century

Hora septima, post signum tabule, pontifice seu sacerdote cum ministris vestimentis solemnibus indutis ad altare accedentibus lectiones sine pronunciatione absolute incipiunt legi sic *In principio creavit.* et orationes dicuntur sine salutatione cum *Oremus* absque *Flectamus genua.* Et dum legitur XI. lectio *Naducodonosor* pontifex cum ministris processionaliter euntes ad fores ecclesie benedicant [sic] ignem incensum et cereum parvum, deinde accendentes candelas tres imponentesque in arundine revertant ad chorum, et pontifex flexis genibus ter incipiat hymnus *Veni Creator Spiritus.* parum procedendo qualibet vice chorus finiat at sequitur alternatim usque ad V. *Accende lumen.* cum fuerit prope pulpitum magnum pontifex ter incipiens choro prosequente: *Accende lumen sensibus,* predictis tribus candelis accendat cereum majorem quo a diacono benedicto ac finita XII. lectio *Hec est hereditas* cum tractu et Oratio omnes cum processione cantantes Letaniam accedant ad benedicendos fontes, etc.

> From the "antico Breviario Capuano," now apparently lost, quoted in Natale, *Lettera,* 33–34.

22. Capua, fourteenth century

> Deinde leguntur lectiones. Sed in aliquibus locis primo benedicitur cereus et postea leguntur lectiones [fol. 28]
>
> Completo baptismo, in aliquibis ecclesiis legitur lectio *Hec est hereditas* [fol. 21]
>
> Paris, Bibl. nat. MS lat. 829; missal, in Gothic script

23. Montevergine, fifteenth century

> Quibus expletis [lessons and collects], Sacerdos cum ministris redeant in sacrario. Tunc accipiat arundinem de manu sacriste cum cereo paruulo accenso, antecedentibus ministris ritu sollempni uidelicet ceroferarii cum candelabris extinctis et duobus diaconibus et subdiaconus cum thuribulo fumigante, medius pergant ad ammonem. diaconus qui benedicendus est cereum tollat benedictionem cerei desuper altare faciatque suam orationem ante abbatem cedat et uersus ad conuentus dicat: *Orate pro me fratres.* Cui omnes assurgant et ascendant [*sic*] ad ammonem. Sacerdos accendat cereum; et diaconus incensato testa euangelii dicat festiue .iij. uicibus *Lumen xpisti.* Respondeant omnes *Deo gratias.* et dicat in modo precis. *Exultet.* Accenso cereo accendantur candele et omnes lampades. et stent omnes erecti. *Exultet* . . . [in extenso]
>
> Rome, Biblioteca Casanatense MS 1103, fol. 118v; missal, in Gothic script

BIBLIOGRAPHY

Ackerman, Robert W., and Roger Dahood. *Ancrene riwle. Introduction and Part I.* Medieval and Renaissance Texts and Studies, no. 31. Binghamton: Center for Medieval and Early Renaissance Studies, 1984.

Adacher, Sabina and Giulia Orofino, *L'età dell'abate Desiderio I. Manoscritti cassinesi del secolo XI. Catalogo della mostra*, with introduction by Francis Newton. Miscellanea cassinese, 59. Montecassino: Pubblicazioni Cassinesi, 1989.

Adversi, Aldo. *Inventari dei manoscritti delle biblioteche d'Italia.* Vol. 100, *Macerata: Biblioteca Comunale "Mozzi-Borgetti."* 2 vols. Florence: Olschki, 1981, 1987.

Albers, Bruno. *Consuetudines monasticae*, vol. 3. Montecassino: Typis Montis Casini, 1907.

Alexander, Jonathan James Graham. *Mediaeval Illuminators and Their Methods of Work.* New Haven: Yale University Press, 1992.

Allodi, Leone. *Inventario dei manoscritti della biblioteca di Subiaco.* Forli: Casa Editrice Luigi Bordandini, 1891.

Altsalos, Basile [Vasileios]. *La terminologie du livre-manuscrit à l'époque byzantine.* Vol. 1, *Termes désignant le livre-manuscrit et l'écriture.* Hellenika: Periodikon syngramma hetaireias Makedonikon Spoudon, no. 21. Thessalonika: Hetairea Makedonikon Spoudon, 1971.

Amato, Pietro, ed. *Tesori d'arte dei Musei Diocesani (Mostra, Roma, Castel Sant'Angelo 18 dicembre 1986–31 gennaio 1987)* [Turin:] Umberto Allemandi, [1986].

Analecta hymnica medii aevi, ed. Guido Marie Dreves, Clemens Blume, and Henry Marriott Bannister. 55 vols. Leipzig: O. R. Reisland, 1886–1922. [Analecta hymnica].

Andoyer, Raphaël. "L'ancienne liturgie de Bénévent," *Revue du chant grégorien* 20 (1911–12): 176–83; 21 (1912–13): 14–20, 44–51, 81–85, 112–15, 144–48, 169–74; 22 (1913–14): 8–11, 41–44, 80–83, 106–11, 141–45, 170–72; 23 (1919–20): 42–44, 116–18, 151–53, 182–83; 24 (1920–21): 48–50, 87–89, 146–48, 182–85.

Andrieu, Michel. *Le pontifical romain au moyen-âge.* 4 vols. Studi e testi 86–88, 99. Vatican City: Biblioteca Apostolica Vaticana, 1938–41.

Andrieu, Michel. "Le sacre épiscopal d'après Hincmar de Reims," *Revue d'histoire ecclésiastique* 48 (1953): 22–73.

Andrieu, Michel. *Les ordines romani du haut moyen âge.* 5 vols. Spicilegium Sacrum Lovaniense. Études et documents nos. 11, 23, 24, 28, 29. Louvain: Spicilegium Sacrum Lovaniense, 1931, 1948, 1951, 1956, 1961.

Antonucci, Giovanni. "Le aggiunte all' 'Exultet' della cattedrale di Bari," *Japigia* 14 (1943): 166–73.

Antonucci, Giovanni. "Le aggiunte interlineari all'*Exultet* del duomo di Bari," *Japigia* 9 (1938): 273–80.

Arnese, Raffaele. *I codici notati della Biblioteca Nazionale di Napoli.* Biblioteca di bibliografia italiana, 47. Florence: Olschki, 1967.

Arns, Evaristo. *La technique du livre d'après Saint Jérôme.* Paris: E. de Boccard, 1953.

L'art byzantin: Art européen. Neuvième exposition sous l'égide du Conseil de l'Europe; Palais du Zappeion. Athens: Ministère de la Présidence du Conseil, 1964.

L'art roman. Exposition organisée par le gouvernement espagnol sous les auspices du Conseil de l'Europe. Barcelone et Santiago de Compostela, 1961. Pp. 9–12 (by Janine Wettstein) on Exultets: Capua, Mirabella.

Auf der Maur, Hansjörg. "Die osterliche Lichtdanksagung: Zum liturgischen Ort und zur Textgestalt des Exsultet," *Liturgiewissenschaftliches Jahrbuch* 21 (1971): 38–52.

Auf der Maur, Hansjörg. "Eine Vorform des Exsultet in der griechischen Patristik," *Trierer theologische Zeitschrift* 75 (1966): 65–88.

Augustinus, Aurelius. *De civitate dei,* ed. Emanuel Hoffmann. 2 vols. Corpus scriptorum ecclesiasticorum latinorum, 40.V.1–2). Prague: Tempsky, Freytag, 1899–1900.

Avery, Myrtilla. "The Barberini Exultet Roll in the Vatican Library," in *Casinensia* (Monte Cassino, 1929), 243–46, 2 pl.

Avery, Myrtilla. "The Beneventan Lections for the Vigil of Easter and the Ambrosian Chant Banned by Pope Stephen IX at Montecassino," *Studi gregoriani* 1 (1947): 433–58, with table after p. 456.

Avery, Myrtilla. *The Exultet Rolls of South Italy.* Vol. 2. Princeton: Princeton University Press, 1936.

Avery, Myrtilla. "A Manuscript from Troia: Naples VI B 2," in Wilhelm R. W. Koehler, ed., *Medieval Studies in Memory of A. Kingsley Porter.* 2 vols. Cambridge: Harvard University Press, 1939, 1:153–64.

Avery, Myrtilla. "The Relation in St. Ambrose to the 'Exultet' Hymn," in Dorothy Miner, ed., *Studies in Art and Literature for Belle da Costa Greene.* Princeton: Princeton University Press, 1954, 374–78.

Avery, Myrtilla. "The Relation of the Casanatense Pontifical (MS. Casanat. 724 B I 13) to Tenth-Century Changes in the Ordination Rites at Rome," *Miscellanea Giovanni Mercati,* Vol. 6. Studi e Testi no. 126. Vatican City: Biblioteca Apostolica Vaticana, 1946, 258–71 with 8 charts.

Avitabile, Lidia, Maria Clara Di Franco, Viviana Jemolo, and Armando Petrucci. "Censimento dei codici dei secoli 10–12," *Studi medievali,* ser. 3, 9/2 (1968): 1,115–94. [Avitabile, Censimento 1].

Avitabile, Lidia, Franca De Marco, Maria Clara Di Franco, and Viviana Jemolo. "Censimento dei codici dei secoli 10–12," *Studi medievali,* ser. 3, 11/2 (1970): 1,013–133. [Avitabile, Censimento 2].

Babudri, Francesco. "L'Exultet di Bari del sec. XI," *Archivio storico pugliese* 10 (1957): 8–167.

Bailey, Terence. "Ambrosian Chant in Southern Italy," *Journal of the Plainsong and Mediaeval Music Society* 6 (1983): 1–7.

Baini, Giuseppe. *Memorie storico-critiche della vita e delle opere di Giovanni Pierluigi da Palestrina.* 2 vols. Rome: Società tipografica, 1828.

Balboni, Dante. "Uso napoletano del cero pasquale nel sec. VIII," *Asprenas* 8 (1961): 96–99.

Baldass, Fred von. "Zur Initialornamentik der süditalienischen Nationalschrift," *Anzeiger der Kaiserlichen Akademie der Wissenschaften [Wien], philosophische-historische Klasse* 48 (1911): 290–97.

Baldass, Peter. "Die Miniaturen zweier Exultet-Rollen. London add. 30336; Vat. Barb. lat. 592," *Scriptorium* 8 (1954): 75–88, 205–19, pl. 2–7.

Baldass, Peter. "Disegni della scuola cassinese del tempo di Desiderio," *Bollettino d'arte* 37 (1952): 102–14.

Baldelli, Ignazio. "Le 'ystorie' dell' 'Exultet' Barberiniano," *Studi di filologia italiana* 17 (1959): 97–125. Repr. in idem, *Medioevo volgare da Montecassino all'Umbria.* 2d. ed. Bari: Adriatica, 1983, 97–125.

Bambacegno, Vincenzo. *Troia in Capitanata.* Troia: Collana dell'Abside, [1988].

Bannister, Enrico [Henry] Marriott. *Monumenti vaticani di paleografia musicale latina.* 2 vols. Leipzig: Harrassowitz, 1913.

Bannister, Henry Marriott. "The *Vetus Itala* Text of the *Exultet*," *Journal of Theological Studies* 11 (1909): 43–54.

Banting, H. M. J. *Two Anglo-Saxon Pontificals: The Egbert and Sidney Sussex Pontificals.* Henry Bradshaw Society no. 104. London: Boydell Press, 1989.

Die Barberini-Exultetrolle Barb. lat. 592. Codices e vaticani selecti no. 76. Zurich: Belser, 1988.

Barracane, Gaetano. "Gli Exultet di Bari: Confronti e Ipotesi." Tesi di Laurea, Bari: Istituto di Teologia Ecumenica "San Nicola," 1989.

Belli D'Elia, Pina, ed. *Alle sorgenti del Romanico: Puglia XI secolo. Bari, Pinacoteca Provinciale, Giugno–Dicembre 1975.* Bari: Dedalo, [1975].

Belting, Hans. "Byzantine Art among Greeks and Latins in Southern Italy," *Dumbarton Oaks Papers* 28 (1974): 1–29 and 29 plates.

Belting, Hans. *Die Basilica dei SS. Martiri in Cimitile und ihr frühmittelalterlicher Freskenzyklus.* Forschungen zur Kunstgeschichte und christlichen Archäologie no. 5. Wiesbaden: Franz Steiner, 1962.

Belting, Hans. "Studien zum beneventanischen Hof im 8. Jahrhundert," *Dumbarton Oaks Papers,* 16 (1962), 141–93 plus 6 plates.

Belting, Hans. *Studien zum beneventanischen Malerei.* Wiesbaden: Franz Steiner, 1968.

Benoît-Castelli, Georges. "Le 'praeconium paschale,' " *Ephemerides liturgicae* 67 (1953): 309–34.

Benz, Suitbert. *Der Rotulus von Ravenna nach seiner Herkunft und seiner Bedeutung für die Liturgiegeschichte kritisch untersucht.* Liturgiewissenschaftliche Quellen und Forschungen no. 45. Münster: Aschendorff, 1967.

Bergman, Johann. *Aurelii Prudentii Clementis carmina.* Corpus scriptorum ecclesiasticorum latinorum no. 61. Vienna and Leipzig: Hoelder-Pilcher-Tempsky, 1926.

Berlière, Ursmer. "Les coutumiers monastiques des VIIIe et IXe siècles," *Revue bénédictine* 25 (1908): 95–107.

Bernal, J. "La 'laus cerei' de la liturgia hispana: Estudio crítico del texto," *Angelicum* 41 (1964): 317–47.

Bernard, Philippe. "Le cantique des trois enfants (*Dan.* III, 52–90): Les répertoires liturgiques occidentaux dans l'antiquité tardive et le haut moyen âge," *Musica e storia* 1 (1993): 231–72.

Bertaux, Émile. *L'art dans l'Italie méridionale.* Vol. 1. *De la fin de l'Empire Romain à la conquête de Charles d'Anjou.* Paris: Albert Fontemoing, 1904.

Bertolini, G. Lod. "Della rosa dei venti dell'*Exultet* di Bari, e di una figurazione geografica degli Atti degli Apostoli," *Bollettino della Società Geografica Italiana,* ser. 4, 12 (1911): 85–97.

Bethmann, Ludwig Konrad, ed. *Chronicon novalicense.* MGH Scriptores VII. Hannover: Hahn, 1846, pp. 73–133.

Biehl, Ludwig. *Das liturgische Gebet für Kaiser und Reich: Ein Beitrag zur Geschichte des Verhältnisses von Kirche und Statt.* Görres-Gesellschaft, Veröffentlichungen der Sektion für Rechts- und Staatswissenschaft no. 75. Paderborn: Ferdinand Schöningh, 1937.

Birt, Theodor. *Die Buchrolle in der Kunst: Archäologisch-antiquarisch Untersuchungen zum antiken Buchwesen.* Leipzig: B. G. Teubner, 1907.

Bischoff, Bernhard. *Latin Paleography: Antiquity and the Middle Ages* (translation of *Paläographie des römischen Altertums und des abendländischer Mittelalters,* 2d ed., with rev. refs.), trans. Dáibhí Ó. Cróinín and David Ganz. Cambridge: Cambridge University Press, 1990.

Bischoff, Bernhard. *Lorsch im Spiegel seiner Handschriften.* Münchener Beiträge zur Mediävistik und Renaissance-Forschung, Beiheft. Munich: Arbeo-Gesellschaft, 1974.

Bischoff, Bernhard. *Paläographie des römischen Altertums und des abendländischer Mittelalters.* 2d ed. Berlin: Erich Schmidt, 1986.

Blanchard, Alain. *Les débuts du codex* (*Actes de la journée d'étude organisée à Paris les 3 et 4 juillet 1985 par l'Institut de Papyrologie de la Sorbonne et l'Institut de Recherche et d'Histoire des Textes*). Bibliologia: Elementa ad librorum studia pertinentia no. 9. Turnhout: Brepols, 1989.

Bland, David. *A History of Book Illustration.* 2d ed. London: Faber and Faber, 1969.

Blatt, Franz. "Ministerium—Mysterium," *Archivum Latinitatis medii aevi* 4 (1928): 80–81.

Bloch, Herbert. "Der Autor der 'Graphia aureae urbis Romae,' " *Deutsches Archiv für Erforschung des Mittelalters,* 40 (1984): 55–175, plus pl. 1–4.

Bloch, Herbert. *Monte Cassino in the Middle Ages.* 3 vols. Cambridge: Harvard University Press, 1986. [*MMA*].

Boe, John. "A New Source for Old Beneventan Chant: The Santa Sophia Maundy in MS Ottoboni lat. 145," *Acta Musicologica* 52 (1980): 122–33.

Boe, John. "Old Beneventan Chant at Monte Cassino: Gloriosus Confessor Domini Benedictus," *Acta Musicologica* 55 (1983): 69–73.

Boeckler, Albert. *Abendländische Miniaturen bus zum Ausgang der romanischen Zeit.* Tabulae in usu scholarum no. 10. Berlin: W. de Gruyter, 1930.

Bömer, Aloys, "Die Schrift und ihre Entwicklung," in Fritz Milkau, ed., *Handbuch der Bibliothekswesen.* 3 vols. Leipzig: O. Harrassowitz, 1931–40, 1:27–149.

Bond, E. A., and E. M. Thompson, eds. *The Palaeographical Society: Facsimiles of Manuscripts and Inscriptions.* Series 1, vol. 3. London: printed by William Clowes and Sons, 1873–83.

Bosio, Luciano. *La tabula peutingeriana.* Rimini: Maggioni, [1983].

Botte, Bernard. *Hippolyte de Rome: La "Tradition apostolique" de S. Hippolyte—essai de reconstitution.* Liturgiewissenschaftlichen Quellen und Forschungen no. 39. Münster: Aschendorff, 1963.

Bréhier, Louis. "Les peintures du rouleau liturgique no 2 du monastère de Lavra," *Annales de l'Institut Kondakov (Seminarium Kondakovianum)* 11 (1940): 1–20, 4 pl.

Brenk, Beat. "Bischöfliche und monastische 'Committenza' in Süditalien am Beispiel der Exultetrollen," in *Committenti e produzione artistico-letteraria nell'alto medioevo occidentale (4–10 aprile 1991).* Settimane di studio no. 39. Spoleto: Centro Italiano di Studi Sull'alto Medioevo, 1992, 275–302.

Brenk, Beat. *Das Lektionar des Desiderius von Montecassino. Cod. Vat. lat. 1202: Ein Meisterwerk italienischer Buchmalerei des 11. Jahrhunderts.* Zurich: Belser, 1987.

The British Library. Catalogue of Additions to the Manuscripts 1946–1950. Part I: Descriptions. London: The Library, 1975.

Brown, Carleton, and Russell Hope Robbins. *The Index of Middle English Verse.* New York: Printed for the Index Society by Columbia University Press, 1943.

Brown, Virginia. "A Second New List of Beneventan Manuscripts (II)," *Mediaeval Studies* 50 (1988): 584–625.

Brückmann, J. "Latin Manuscript Pontificals and Benedictionals in England and Wales," *Traditio* 29 (1973): 391–458.

Buchwald, R. "Osterkerze und Exsultet," *Theologisch-praktische Quartalschrift* 8 (1927): 240–49.

Bühler, Curt F. "Prayers and Charms in Certain Middle English Scrolls," *Speculum* 39 (1964): 270–87.

Bünger, Fritz. *Admonter Totenroteln (1442–1496).* Beiträge zur Geschichte des alten Mönchtums und des Benediktinerordens no. 19. Münster: Aschendorff, 1935.

Büttner-Wobst, Teodor. *Ioannes Zonarae epitomae historiarum.* 3 vols. Corpus scriptorum historiae Byzantinae. Bonn: Weber, 1891–97.

C., A. J. (article signed A. J. C.), "A Book of Hours in Roll Form," *British Museum Quarterly* 4 (1929–30): 111 and pl. 63.

[Cagin, Paul], ed. *Codex sacramentorum Bergomensis.* Auctuarium Solesmense, Series liturgica, no. 1. Solesmes: St. Pierre, 1900.

Cahn, Walter. "Représentations de la parole," *Connaissance des arts* (1982): 82–89.

Camera, Matteo. *Memorie storico-diplomatiche dell'antica città e ducato di Amalfi.* 2 vols. Salerno, 1876. repr. Salerno: W. Casari-Testaferrata, 1972.

Camille, Michael. "Seeing and Reading: Some Visual Implications of Medieval Literacy and Illiteracy," *Art History* 8 (1985): 26–49.

Capasso, Bartolommeo. *Memorie storiche della chiesa sorrentina.* Naples: Antologia Legale, 1854.

Capelle, Bernard. "La procession du Lumen Christi au Samedi-Saint," *Revue bénédictine* 44 (1932): 105–119.

Capelle, "L' 'Exultet' pascal oeuvre de Saint Ambroise," in *Miscellanea Giovanni Mercati,* vol. 1 (Studi e Testi, no. 121). Vatican City: Biblioteca Apostolica Vaticana, 1946, 219–46.

Capone, Arturo. *Il duomo di Salerno.* 2 vols. Salerno: F.lli Di Giacomo di Giov., 1927, and Spadafora, 1929.

Carabellese, Francesco. *Bari*. Italia artistica no. 51. Bergamo: Istituto Italiano d'Arti Grafiche, 1909.

Caravita, Andrea. *I codici e le arti a Monte Cassino*. 3 vols. Montecassino: Tipi della Badia, 1869–71.

Carbonara, Giuseppe. *Iussu Desiderii: Montecassino e l'architettura campano-abruzzese nell'undicesimo secolo*. Saggi di storia dell'architettura diretti da Renato Bonelli no. 2. Rome: Università degli Studi di Roma, Istituto di Fondamenti dell'Architettura, 1979.

Carotti, Anna. *Gli affreschi della Grotta della Fornelle a Calvi Vacchia*. Studi sulla pittura medioevale campana no. 1. Rome: De Luca, 1974.

Carucci, Arturo. *Il rotolo salernitano dell'Exultet*. Salerno: n.p., 1971.

Caspar, Erich. *Petrus diaconus und die Monte Cassineser Fälschungen*. Berlin: Springer, 1909.

Catalogo del Museo Civico di Pisa. Pisa: T. Nistri, 1894.

Catalogo del Museo Civico di Pisa. Pisa: Tipografia Municipale, 1906.

Cavallo, Guglielmo. "Die Bedeutung des Exultetrolle Barb. lat. 592 der Biblioteca Apostolica Vaticana," in *Die Barberini-Exultetrolle Barb. lat. 592*. Codices e vaticani selecti no. 76. Zurich: Belser, 1988, 11–16.

Cavallo, Guglielmo. "La genesi dei rotoli liturgici beneventani alla luce del fenomeno storico-librario in Occidente ed Oriente," in *Miscellanea in memoria di Giorgio Cencetti*. Milan: Bottega d'Erasmo, 1973, 213–29, and 4 plates.

Cavallo, Guglielmo, and Antonia d'Aniello. *L'Exultet di Salerno*. Rome: Istituto Poligrafico e Zecca dello Stato, 1993.

Cavallo, Guglielmo, Giulia Orofino, and Oronzo Pecere, eds. *Exultet: Rotoli liturgici del medioevo meridionale*. Rome: Istituto Poligrafico e Zecca dello Stato, 1994. *[Exultet]*.

Cavallo, Guglielmo. *Rotoli di Exultet dell'Italia meridionale*. Bari: Adriatica, 1973.

Chavasse, Antoine. *Le sacramentaire gélasien (Vaticanus Reginensis 316): Sacramentaire presbytéral en usage dans les titres romains au 7e siècle*. Bibliothèque de théologie, série 4. Histoire de la théologie no. 1. Tournai: Desclée, 1958.

Chazelle, Celia M. "Pictures, Books, and the Illiterate: Pope Gregory's Letters to Serenus of Marseilles," *Word and Image* 6 (1990): 138–53.

Chronica monasterii Casinensis [Die Chronik von Montecassino], ed. Hartmut Hoffmann. Monumenta Germaniae Historica Scriptores 34. Hannover: Hahn, 1980.

Cipolla, Carlo. *Monumenta novaliciensia vetustiora*. 2 vols. Fonti per la storia d'Italia nos. 31–32. Rome: Tipografia del Senato, 1898, 1901.

Civiltà del manoscritto a Gaeta: Exultet e Corali dal X al XVII secolo. Catalogue edited by Rita Cosma, Valentino Pace, and Alessandro Pratesi. Gaeta: Centro Storico Culturale "Gaeta," 1982.

Clanchy, M. T. *From Memory to Written Record*. 2d ed. Oxford: Blackwell, 1993.

Clausberg, Karl. "Spruchbandaussagen zum Stilcharacter," *Städel-Jahrbuch*, n. s., 13 (1991): 81–110.

Claussen, Peter Cornelius. *Magistri doctissimi romani: Die römischen Marmorkünstler des Mittelalters*. Corpus cosmatorum no. 1. Forschungen zur Kunstgeschichte und christlichen Archäologie, no. 14. Stuttgart: Franz Steiner, 1987.

Clercq, Charles de. *Concilia Galliae A. 511–A. 695*. Corpus Christianorum, Series Latina, no. 148A. Turnhout: Brepols, 1963.

Codex diplomaticus Cajetanus. 3 vols. (1, 3/1, 3/2). Tabularium casinese nos. 1–4. Montecassino: Typis arcicenobiis, 1887–1960.

Coebergh, C. "Sacramentaire léonien et liturgie mozarabe," *Miscellanea liturgica in honorem L. Cuniberti Mohlberg.* 2 vols. Bibliotheca "Ephemerides liturgicae" nos. 22–23. Rome: Edizioni liturgiche, 1948–49, 2:295–304.

Connolly, Thomas. "The *Graduale* of S. Cecilia in Trastevere and the Old Roman Tradition," *Journal of the American Musicological Society* 28 (1975): 413–58.

Conte-Colino, Giovanni. *Storia di Fondi.* Naples: Francesco Giannini e figli, 1901.

Conybeare, Frederick Cornwallis. *Rituale Armenorum, Being the Administration of the Sacraments and the Breviary Rites of the Armenian Church Together with the Greek Rites of Baptism and Epiphany, Edited from the Oldest Manuscripts.* Oxford: Clarendon, 1905.

Cowdrey, H. E. J. *The Age of Abbot Desiderius: Montecassino, the Papacy, and the Normans in the Eleventh and Early Twelfth Century.* Oxford: Clarendon, 1986.

Curran, Michael. *The Antiphonary of Bangor and the Early Irish Monastic Liturgy.* [Dublin?]: Irish Academic Press, 1984.

Curschmann, Michael. "Pictura laicorum litteratura? Überlegungen zum Verhältnis von Bild und volksprachlicher Schriftlichkeit im Hoch- und Spätmittelalter bis zum Codex Manesse," in H. Keller-Grubmüller and N. Staubach, eds., *Pragmatische Schriftlichkeit im Mittelalter: Erscheinungsformen und Entwicklungsstufen.* Münstersche Mittelalter-Schriften no. 65. Munich: Fink, 1990, 211–22.

Damiani, Paola. "Il canto beneventano dei rotoli dell'Exultet." Tesi di Laurea. Rome: Facoltà delle Lettere, 1986.

D'Ancona, Paolo. *La miniature italienne du Xe au XVIe siècle.* Paris: G. Van Oest, 1925.

Davis, Norman, ed. *Non-Cycle Plays and Fragments.* Early English Text Society, supplementary text no. 1. London: Oxford University Press, 1970.

Davis, Ralph Henry Carless. *The Normans and Their Myth.* London: Thames and Hudson, 1976.

Decreta authentica congregationis sacrorum rituum . . . sub auspiciis . . . Leonis Papae XIII. 7 vols. in 6, Rome: ex Typographia Polyglotta, 1898–1912.

Deér, Josef. "Ein Doppelbildnis Karls der Grossen," in *Wandlungen christlicher Kunst im Mittelalter.* Forschungen zur Kunstgeschichte im christlichen Archäologie no. 2. Baden-Baden: Verlag für Kunst und Wissenschaft, 1953, 103–56.

Dekkers, Eligius. *Clavis patrum latinorum: Qua in novum corpus christianorum edendum optimas quasque scriptorum recensiones a Tertulliano ad Bedam.* 2d ed. Steenbrugis: In Abbatia Sancti Petri, 1961.

De la Fage, Adrien. *Essais de diphthérographie musicale.* Paris: O. Legouix, 1864.

de la Mare, Albinia. *Catalogue of the Collection of Medieval Manuscripts Bequeathed to the Bodleian Library Oxford by James P. R. Lyell.* Oxford: Clarendon, 1971.

Delisle, Léopold. *Rouleaux des morts du IXe au XVe siècle.* Paris: Renouard, 1866.

Delisle, Léopold. *Rouleau mortuaire du B. Vital, abbé de Savigni.* Paris: Berthaud, 1909.

Dell'Oro, Ferdinando. "Frammento di rotolo pontificale del secolo XI (Asti, Bibl. Capit., Cod. XIII)," *Studia anselmiana* 95 (1988): 177–204.

Dell'Oro, Ferdinando. "Il Sacramentario di Trento," in Ferdinando Dell'Oro et al., eds., *Fontes liturgici: Libri sacramentorum*. Monumenta liturgica ecclesiae tridentinae saeculo XIII antiquiora no. 2/a. Trent: Società Studi Trentini di Scienze Storiche, 1985, 1–416.

Delogu, Paolo. "Patroni, donatori, commitenti nell'Italia meridionale longobarda," in *Committenti e produzione artistico-letteraria nell'alto medioevo occidentale (4–10 aprile 1991)*. Settimane di studio no. 39. Spoleto: Centro Italiano di Studi Sull'alto Medioevo, 1992, 303–34.

de'Maffei, Fernanda. "Roma, Benevento, San Vincenzo al Volturno e l'Italia settentrionale," *Commentari* 24 (1973): 255–84.

Demus, Otto. *Byzantine Art and the West*. London: Weidenfeld and Nicolson, 1970.

de Santis, Mario. *L'anima eroica della cattedrale di Troia*. Foggia: Ente Provinciale per il Turismo, [1958].

Deshusses, Jean. *Le sacramentaire grégorien: Ses principales formes d'après les plus anciens manuscrits*. 3 vols. Spicilegium Friburgense nos. 16, 24, 28. Fribourg: Presses Universitaires, 1971 (2d ed. 1979), 1979, 1982.

di Capua, F. "Il ritmo nella prosa liturgica e il praeconium paschale," *Didaskaleion* n. s. 5 (1907): 1–23 (fasc. 2).

Di Resta, Isabella. "Exultet di Capua," in Giuseppe Galasso and Rosario Romero. *Storia del mezzogiorno*. 15 vols. Vol II, tomo I. *Il medioevo*. Naples: Edizioni del sole, 1988, pp. 208–09 plus seven unnumbered color plates.

Dictionnaire d'archéologie chrétienne et de liturgie, ed. Fernand Cabrol, Henri Leclercq, and Henri Marrou. 15 vols. Paris: Letouzey et Ané, 1903–53.

Diringer, David. *The Illuminated Book: Its history and production*. New ed. London: Faber and Faber, [1967], 107; 196–97; pls. VI-6, VI-7.

Dold, Alban. "Colligere fragmenta, ne pereant!" *Scriptorium* 4 (1950): 92–96, pl. 3.

Dold, Alban. "Die vom Missale Romanum abweichenden Lesetexte für die Messfeiern nach den Notierung des aus Monte Cassino stammenden Codex Vat. Lat. 6082," in *Zeugnis des Geistes: Gabe zum Benedictus-Jubilaeum 547–1947*. Beiheft zum 23. Jahrgang der Benediktinischen Monatschrift. Beuron: Beuroner Kunstverlag, 1947, 293–332.

Dold, Alban. "Ein Palimpsestblatt mit zwei verschiedenen Messliturgien (Fol. I im Sammelcodex Ottob. lat. 576 P I)," *Ephemerides liturgicae* 52 (1938): 187–88.

Dold, Alban, and Leo Eizenhöfer. *Das prager Sacramentar [Cod. O. 83 (fols. 1–12) der Bibliothek des Metropolitakapitels]*. 2 vols. Vol. 1, *Lichtbildausgabe*. Vol. 2, *Prologomena und Textausgabe*. Beuron: Beuroner Kunstverlag, 1944, 1949.

Dölger, Franz. *Antike und Christentum*. 6 vols. Münster: Aschendorff, 1929–50.

Duchesne, Louis Marie Olivier. "Lettre à M. L. Delisle au sujet de la découverte de chartes byzantines à Bari, par M. l'abbé Duchesne," *Académie des inscriptions et belles-lettres: Comptes rendus* 14 (1886): 276–80.

Duchesne, Louis Marie Olivier. *Le liber pontificalis*. 2d ed. 3 vols. [Vol. 3, ed. Cyrille Vogel]. Paris: E. de Boccard, 1955–57.

Duchesne, Louis Marie Olivier. *Origines du culte chrétien*. 5th ed. Paris: E. de Boccard, 1925.

Dufour, Jean. "Les rouleaux des morts," *Codicologia* 3 [Litterae textuales] (1980): 96–102, plates.

Duggan, Lawrence G. "Was Art Really the 'Book of the Illiterate?' " *Word and Image* 5 (1989): 227–51.

Dumas, Antoine, and Jean Deshusses. *Liber sacramentorum Gellonensis.* 2 vols. Corpus Christianorum series Latina nos. 159–159A. Turnhout: Brepols, 1981.

Dümmler, Ernst. "Die handschriftliche Überlieferung der lateinischen Dichtungen aus der Zeit der Karolinger," *Neues Archiv* 4 (1878): 239–322.

Durandus, Gulielmus. *Rationale divinorum officiorum.* Venice: Gratiosus Perchianus, 1568. Many further editions.

Duval-Arnould, Louis. "Un missel du Mont-Cassin chez les chanoines du Saint-Sauveur de Bologne (Vat. lat. 6082)," *Rivista di storia della chiesa in Italia* 35 (1981): 450–55.

Ebner, Adalbert. "Handschriftliche Studien über das Praeconium paschale," *Kirchenmusikalisches Jahrbuch* 8 (1893): 73–83.

Ebner, Adalbert. *Quellen und Forschungen zur Geschichte und Kunstgeschichte des Missale Romanum im Mittelalter: Iter italicum.* Freiburg: Herder, 1896.

Eisenhofer, Ludwig. *Handbuch der katholischen Liturgik.* 2 vols. Freiburg: Herder, 1932–33.

Ercolano, Fausto. *La cattedrale di San Clemente I P. M. e il Museo capitolare in Velletri.* Itinerari d'arte e di cultura: Basiliche. Rome: Palombi, [1988].

Exultet Codex Vaticanus lat. 9820: Vollständige Facsimile-Ausgabe in Originalformat des Codex Vaticanus lat. 9820 der Biblioteca Apostolica Vaticana. Graz: Akademische Druck- und Verlagsanstalt, 1974.

Fabre, Paul, and Louis Marie Olivier Duchesne. *Le liber censuum de l'église romaine.* 3 vols. [Vol. 3 of indices, by Duchesne with Pierre Fabre and G. Mollat]. Bibliothèque des Écoles françaises d'Athènes et de Rome, 2d series, no. 6. Paris: Fontemoing, 1905 (vols 1–2), E. de Boccard, 1952 (vol. 3).

Farmakovskii, B. V. "Vizantijskii pergamennyi rukopisnyi svitok s miniatiurami," *Izvestiia Russkago arkheologicheskago instituta v Konstantinopole (Bulletin de l'Institut Archéologique Russe à Constantinople)* 6 (1901): 253–359.

Fedele, Pietro. "L' 'Exultet' di Velletri," *Mélanges d'archéologie et d'histoire* 30 (1910): 313–20, and pl. 7–11.

Férotin, Marius. *Le Liber Mozarabicus sacramentorum et les manuscrits mozarabes.* Monumenta ecclesiae liturgica no. 6. Paris: Firmin-Didot, 1913.

Ferraro, Salvatore. *Memorie religiose e civili della città di Gaeta.* Naples: Francesco Grannini e Figli, 1903.

Ferretti, Paolo M. *Il cursus metrico e il ritmo delle melodie gregoriane.* Rome: Tipografia del Senato, 1913.

Ferretti, Paolo M. "I manoscritti musicali gregoriani dell'archivio di Montecassino," in *Casinensia.* Montecassino: [Montecassino Monastery], 1929, 187–203, 3 plates.

Fiala, Virgil. "Der Ordo missae im Vollmissale des Cod. Vat. lat. 6082 aus dem Ende des 11. Jahrhunderts," in *Zeugnis des Geistes: Gabe zum Benedictus-Jubilaeum 547–1947.* Beiheft zum 23. Jahrgang der Benediktinischen Monatschrift. Beuron: Beuroner Kunstverlag, 1947, 180–224.

Fischer, Bonifatius. "Ambrosius der Verfasser des österlichen Exultet?" *Archiv für Liturgiewissenschaft* 2 (1952): 61–74.

Fischer, Bonifatius. "Exsultent divina mysteria!" *Zeugnis des Geistes: Gabe zum Benedictus-Jubilaeum 547–1947.* Beiheft zum 23. Jahrgang der Benediktinischen Monatschrift. Beuron: Beuroner Kunstverlag, 1947, 234–35.

Flett, Alison. R. "The Significance of Text Scrolls: Towards a Descriptive Terminology," in Margaret M. Manion and Bernard J. Muir, eds., *Medieval Texts and Images: Studies of Manuscripts from the Middle Ages*. Chur, Switzerland: Harwood Academic Publishers, 1991, 43–56.

Franz, Adolph. *Die kirchlichen Benediktionen im Mittelalter*. 2 vols. Freiburg: Herder, 1909.

Frei, Judit. *Das ambrosianische Sakramentar D 3–3 aus dem mailändischen Metropolitankapitel*. Liturgiewissenschaftliche Quellen und Forschungen no. 56. Münster: Aschendorff, 1974.

Frénaud, Georges. "Les témoins indirects du chant liturgique en usage à Rome aux IXe et Xe siècles," *Études grégoriennes* 3 (1959), 41–74.

Fuchs, Guido, and Hans Martin Weikmann. *Das Exultet: Geschichte, Theologie, und Gestaltung der österlichen Lichtdanksagung*. Regensburg: Pustet, 1992.

Gabbrielli, Mariarosa. "Un 'Exultet' cassinese dell XI secolo," *Bollettino d'arte* 26 (1933): 306–13.

Gajard, Joseph. "Le chant de l' 'Exsultet,' " *Revue grégorienne* 29 (1950): 50–69.

Galasso, Giuseppe, and Rosario Romero. *Storia del mezzogiorno*. 15 vols. Vol. 2, pt. 1, *Il medioevo*. Naples: Edizioni del Sole, 1988.

Galbraith, Vivian Hunter. *Studies in the Public Records*. London, New York: T. Nelson, 1948.

Gamber, Klaus. "Eine ältere Schwesterhandschrift des Tassilo-Sakramentars in Prag," *Revue bénédictine* 80 (1970): 156–62.

Gamber, Klaus. "Älteste Eucharistiegebete der lateinischen Osterliturgie," in Balthasar Fischer and J. Wagner, eds., *Paschatis sollemnia*. Freiburg: Herder, 1959, 159–78.

Gamber, Klaus. *Codices liturgici latini antiquiores*. 2 vols. in 3 parts. Spicilegii Friburgensis subsidia no. 1. Fribourg: University Press, 1963. Vols. 1, pt. 1 and 1, pt. 2, 2d ed. 1968; vol. 1A (supplement), 1988. [*CLLA*].

Gamber, Klaus. *Sacramentartypen*. Texte und Arbeiten I. Abteilung, 49/50. Beuron: Beuroner Kunstverlag, 1958.

Gamber, Klaus. *Sacrificium vespertinum: Lucernarium und eucharistisches Opfer am Abend und ihre Abhängigkeit von den Riten der Juden*. Studia patristica et liturgica no. 12. Regenburg: Pustet, 1983.

Gandolfo, Francesco. "La cattedra 'Gregoriana' di Salerno," *Bollettino storico di Salerno e Principato Citra* 2 (1984): 5–29.

Gandolfo, Francesco. "Simbolismo antiquario e potere papale," *Studi romani* 29 (1981): 9–28, with 12 plates.

Garbelotto, Antonio. "Catalogo del fondo musicale fino all'anno 1800 della Biblioteca Comunale di Macerata." In Aldo Adversi, ed., *Studi sulla Biblioteca Comunale e sui tipografi di Macerata*. Macerata: Cassa di Risparmio della Provincia di Macerata, 1966.

Gardthausen, Viktor. *Catalogus codicum Graecorum Sinaiticorum*. Oxford: Clarendon, 1886.

Garrison, Edward B. *Studies in the History of Mediaeval Italian Painting*. 4 vols. Florence: L'impronta, 1953–62.

Garzelli, Annarosa. "La deposizione dell'exultet nel duomo di Pisa: un problema della cultura figurativa pisana del secolo XIII," in Giorgia Vailati Schoenberg Waldenburg, ed., *Le miniature italiane in età romanica e gotica: Atti del I convegno di Storia della miniatura italiana (Cortona 26–28 maggio 1978)*. Florence: Olschki, 1979, 51–62.

Gay, Jules. *L'Italie méridionale et l'empire byzantin depuis l'avènement de Basile Ier jusqu'à la prise de Bari par les Normands (867–1071)*. Bibliothèque des Écoles françaises d'Athènes et de Rome no. 90. Paris: A. Fontemoing, 1904; repr. New York: B. Franklin [1960].

Gennadius, *Liber de viris inlustribus*, ed. Ernest Cushing Richardson, *Hieronymus Liber de viris inlustribus. Gennadius Liber de viris inlustribus* (Texte und Untersuchungen zur Geschichte der altchristlichen Literatur, XIV.1). Leipzig: Hinrichs, 1896.

Gerbert, Martin. *De cantu et musica sacra a prima ecclesiae aetate usque ad praesens tempus*. 2 vols. Sankt Blasien: Typis San-Blasianus, 1774.

Gerstel, Sharon E. J. "Liturgical Scrolls in the Byzantine Sanctuary," *Greek, Roman, and Byzantine Studies* 35 (1994): 195–204.

Gilson, Julius Parnell, ed. *An Exultet Roll Illuminated in the 11th Century at the Abbey of Monte Cassino. Reproduced from Add. Ms. 30337*. London: Trustees of the British Museum, 1929.

Glass, Dorothy. *Romanesque Sculpture in Campania*. University Park: Pennsylvania State University Press, 1991.

Gottlieb, Theodor. *Mittelalterliche Bibliothekskatologe Österreichs*. Vol. 1, *Niederösterreich*. Vienna: Adolf Holzhausen, 1915.

Gougaud, Louis. "Muta predicatio," *Revue bénédictine* 4 (1930): 168–71.

Grabar, André, "Les illustrations de la chronique de Jean Skylitzès à la Bibliothèque Nationale de Madrid," *Cahiers archéologiques* 21 (1971): 191–211.

Grabar, André. *Les manuscrits grecs enluminés de provenance italienne*. Bibliothèque des Cahiers Archéologiques no. 8. Paris: Klincksieck, 1972.

Grabar, André, "Un rouleau liturgique constantinopolitain et ses peintures," *Dumbarton Oaks Papers* 8 (1954): 161–99, 23 pl. and 2 facs.

Grabar, André, and Carl Nordenfalk. *La peinture romaine*. Geneva: Albert Skira, 1958.

Granata, Francesco. *Storia sacra della chiesa metropolitana di Capua*. 2 vols. Naples: Simoni, 1766.

Guarini, Raimondo. "Osservazioni sopra un rotolo eclanese ecclesiastico," *Atti dell'Accademia Pontaniana di Napoli* 1 (1832): 75–107.

Gy, Pierre-Marie. "L'unification liturgique de l'occident et la liturgie de la curie romaine," *Revue des sciences philosophiques et théologiques* 59 (1975): 601–12.

Gyug, Richard Francis. "A Fragment of a Liturgical Roll at Montecassino (Compactiones XVI)," *Mediaeval Studies* 52 (1990): 268–77, 2 plates.

Gyug, Richard Francis. *Missale Ragusinum: The Missal of Dubrovnik (Oxford, Bodleian Library, Canon. Liturg. 342)*. Texts and Studies no. 103; Monumenta Liturgica Beneventana, 1. Toronto: Pontifical Institute of Mediaeval Studies, 1990.

Gyug, Richard Francis. "A Pontifical of Benevento (Macerata, Biblioteca Comunale 'Mozzi-Borgetti' 378)," *Mediaeval Studies* 51 (1989): 355–423.

Gyug, Richard Francis. "The Pontificals of Montecassino," in *L'età dell'abate Desiderio* vol. III, 1, *Storia arte e cultura. Atti del IV convegno di studi sul medioevo meridionale (Montecassino–Cassino, 4–8 ottobre 1987)*, ed. Faustino Avagliano and Oronzo Pecere. Miscallanea cassinese, no. 67. Montecassino: Pubblicazioni Cassinesi, 1992, pp. 413–39.

Hallinger, Kassius, et al. *Initia consuetudinis Benedictinae*. Corpus consuetudinum monasticarum no. 1. Siegburg: Franciscum Schmitt, 1963.

Hänggi, Anton, and Alfons Schönherr. *Sacramentarium Rheinaugense: Handschrift Rh 30 der Zentralbibliothek Zürich.* Spicilegium Friburgense no. 15. Fribourg, Switzerland: Universitätsverlag, 1970.

Hanssens, Jean Michel. *Amalarii episcopi opera liturgica omnia.* 3 vols. Studi e Testi nos. 138–40. Vatican City: Biblioteca Apostolica Vaticana, 1948–50.

Hartel, Guilelmus [Wilhelm]. *Magni Felicis Ennodii opera omnia.* Corpus scriptorum ecclesiasticorum Latinorum no. 6. Vienna: Carl Gerold's Sohn, 1882.

Heiming, Odilo. *Das ambrosianische Sakramentar von Biasca.* Liturgiewissenschaftliche Quellen und Forschungen no. 51. Münster: Aschendorff, 1969.

Heiming, Odilo. *Corpus ambrosiano liturgicum 1. Das Sacramentarium triplex — die Handschrift C 43 der Zentralbibliothek Zürich.* Liturgiewissenschaftliche Quellen und Forschungen no. 49. Münster: Aschendorff, 1968.

Heiming, Odilo. *Liber sacramentorum Augustodunensis.* Corpus Christianorum series Latina no. 159B. Turnhout: Brepols, 1984.

Herklotz, Ingo. *"Sepulcra" e "monumenta" del medioevo: Studi sull'arte sepolcrale in Italia.* 2d ed. Collana di studi di storia dell'arte no. 5. Rome: Edizioni Rari Nantes, 1990.

Hesbert, René-Jean. "L' 'Antiphonale missarum' de l'ancien rit bénéventain: Le Samedi-Saint," *Ephemerides liturgicae* 61 (1947): 153–210.

Hiley, David. "The Liturgical Music of Norman Sicily." Ph.D. diss. London: King's College, University of London, 1981.

Hiley, David. *Western Plainchant: A Handbook.* Oxford: Clarendon, 1993.

Hirsch, Hans, "Der mittelalterliche Kaisergedanke in den liturgischen Gebeten," *Mitteilungen des Österreichischen Instituts für Geschichtsforschung* 44 (1930): 1–20.

Holder-Egger, Otto. "Agnelli qui et Andreas Liber pontificalis ecclesiae Ravennatis," in *Monumenta Germaniae Historica. Scriptores rerum langobardicarum et italicarum saec. VI–IX.* Hannover: Hahn, 1878; repr. 1964, 265–391.

Huglo, Michel. "L'ancien chant bénéventain," *Ecclesia orans* 2 (1985): 265–93.

Huglo, Michel. "L'auteur de l'*Exultet* pascal," *Vigiliae Christianae* 7 (1953): 79–88.

Huglo, Michel. "Codicologie et musicologie," in Pierre Cockshaw, Monique-Cécile Garand, and Pierre Jodogne, eds., *Miscellanea codicologica F. Masai dicata 1979.* 2 vols. Les publications de *Scriptorium* no. 8. Ghent: E. Story-Scientia, 1979, 1:71–82 and plates 9–10.

Huglo, Michel. "Exultet," in *The New Grove Dictionary of Music and Musicians,* ed. Stanley Sadie. 20 vols. London: Macmillan, 1980, 6:334–36.

Huglo, Michel, Luigi Agustoni, Eugène Cardine, and Ernesto Moneta Caglio. *Fonti e paleografia del canto ambrosiano.* Archivio ambrosiano no. 7. Milan: n.p., 1956.

Hunger, Herbert. "Antikes mittelalterliches Buch- und Schriftwesen," *Geschichte der Textüberlieferung,* vol. 1 (Zurich: Atlantis-Verlag, 1961), 25–147.

Hunt, Arthur S., ed. *The Oxyrhynchus Papyri.* vol. 17, London: Egypt Exploration Society, 1927.

Huyghebaert, Nicolas. *Les documents nécrologiques.* Typologie des sources du moyen âge occidental no. 4. Turnhout: Brepols, 1972.

Inguanez, Mauro. *Catalogi codicum casinensium antiqui (saec. 8–15).* Miscellanea cassinese no. 21. Montecassino, 1941.

Inguanez, Mauro. *Un dramma della passione del secolo 12.* Miscellanea cassinese no. 18; Montecassino, 1939.

Inouye, Susana. "[Gaeta 1]," in Pierre Amato, ed. *Tesori d'arte dei Musei Diocesani (Mostra, Roma, Castel Sant'Angelo 18 dicembre 1986–31 gennaio 1987).* [Turin]: Umberto Allemandi, [1986], 130–34 plus 3 b/w plates.

Inouye, Susana. "[Salerno Exultet]," in Amato, *Tesori d'arte dei Musei Diocesani (Mostra, Roma, Castel Sant'Angelo 18 dicembre 1986–31 gennaio 1987).* [Turin]: Umberto Allemandi, [1986], 218–22 plus 3 b/w plates.

Inventario degli oggetti d'arte d'Italia. Vol. 4, *Provincia di Aquila.* Rome: La Libreria dello Stato, 1934.

James, Montague Rhodes. *A Descriptive Catalogue of the Latin MSS. in the John Rylands Library at Manchester.* 2 vols. London: Quaritch, 1921.

Janson, Tore. *Prose Rhythm in Medieval Latin from the Ninth to the Thirteenth Century.* Studia Latina Stockholmiensia no. 20. Stockholm: Almqvist and Wiksell International, 1975.

Jerphanion, G. de. "Le 'Thorakion' caractéristique iconographique du 11ᵉ siècle," in *Mélanges Charles Diehl* 2 vols. Paris: Ernest Leroux, 1930, 71–79.

Josua-Rolle: Vollständige Faksimile-Ausgabe des Codex Vaticanus Ms. Pal. graec. 431 der Biblioteca Apostolica Vaticana. Codices selecti no. 77; Codices e Vaticanis selecti, no. 43. Graz: Akademische Druck- und Verlaganstalt, 1983.

Jounel, Pierre. *Le culte des saints dans les basiliques du Latran et du Vatican au douzième siècle.* Collection de l'École française de Rome no. 26. [Rome:] École Française de Rome, 1977.

Juglar, Jean. "À propos de la vigile pascale: La 'benedictio cerei,' " *Ephemerides liturgicae* 65 (1951): 182–87.

Junyent, Esuardo. "Le rouleau funéraire d'Oliba, abbé de Notre-Dame de Ripoll et de Saint-Michel de Cuixa, Évêque de Vich," *Annales du Midi* 63 (1951): 249–63.

Kantorowicz, Ernst H. *Laudes regiae: A Study in Liturgical Acclamations and Mediaeval Ruler Worship.* University of California Publications in History no. 32. Berkeley: University of California Press, 1946.

Kantorowicz, Ernst H. "A Norman Finale of the Exultet and the Rite of Sarum," *Harvard Theological Review* 34 (1941): 129–43.

Kartsonis, Anna D. *Anastasis: The Making of an Image.* Princeton: Princeton University Press, 1986.

Kehr, Paul Fridolin. *Regesta pontificum Romanorum: Italia pontificia.* 10 vols. Berlin: Weidmann, 1906–77. Esp. vol. 2, *Latium,* 1907, and vol. 9, *Samnium—Apulia—Lucania,* ed. Walther Holtzmann, 1962. [Kehr, *IP*].

Kelly, John Norman Davidson. *Jerome: His Life, Writings, and Controversies.* London: Duckworth, 1975.

Kelly, Thomas Forrest. "Abbot Desiderius and the Two Liturgical Chants of Montecassino," in *L'età dell'abate Desiderio* vol. III, 1, *Storia arte e cultura. Atti del IV convegno di studi sul medioevo meridionale (Montecassino–Cassino, 4–8 ottobre 1987),* ed. Faustino Avagliano and Oronzo Pecere. Miscellanea cassinese, no. 67. Montecassino: Pubblicazioni Cassinesi, 1992, pp. 389–411.

Kelly, Thomas Forrest. *The Beneventan Chant.* Cambridge: Cambridge University Press, 1989. [*TBC*].

Kelly, Thomas Forrest. "Beneventan and Milanese Chant," *Journal of the Royal Musical Association* 112 (1987): 173–95.

Kelly, Thomas Forrest. "The Exultet in Rome," in *Le chant romain* (Fondation Royaumont, in press).

Kelly, Thomas Forrest. "Montecassino and the Old Beneventan Chant," *Early Music History* 5 (1985): 53–83.

Kelly, Thomas Forrest. "The Oldest Musical Notation of Montecassino," *Miscellanea Cassinese*. In press.

Kelly, Thomas Forrest. "Structure and Ornament in Chant: The Case of the Beneventan Exultet," in Graeme Boone, ed., *Essays on Medieval Music in Honor of David G. Hughes*. Cambridge, Mass.: Harvard University Department of Music, 1995, 249–76.

Ker, N. R. *Medieval Manuscripts in British Libraries*. Vol. 1, *London*. Oxford: Clarendon, 1969.

Kessler, Herbert L. "Pictorial Narrative and Church Mission in Sixth-Century Gaul," in Herbert L. Kessler and Marianna Shreve Simpson, eds., *Pictorial Narrative in Antiquity and the Middle Ages*. Studies in the History of Art no. 16. Washington, D.C.: National Gallery of Art, 1985, 75–91.

Klauser, Theodor. "Eine rätselhafte Exultetillustration aus Gaeta," *Corolla Ludwig Curtius* (Stuttgart, 1937), 168–76, repr. in Ernst Dassman, ed., *Theodor Klauser: Gesammelte Arbeiten zur liturgiegeschichtliche Kirchengeschichte und christlichen Archäologie*. Jahrbuch für Antike und Christentum, Ergänzungsband 3. Münster: Aschendorff, 1974, 255–63 and Pl. 1a.

Kruft, Hanno-Walter. "Exsultetrolle," in *Reallexikon zur deutschen Kunstgeschichte*, 8 vols. to date. Stuttgart: Metzler, 1937– . Vol. 6, Munich: Alfred Druckenmuller, 1973, cols. 719–39 with 7 figures.

Ladner, Gerhart Burian. "The Commemoration Pictures of the Exultet Roll Barberinianus Latinus 592," in *Paradosis: Studies in Memory of Edwin A. Quain*. New York: Fordham University Press, 1976, 61–69; repr. in *Images and Ideas*, 1:337–46 plus 3 plates.

Ladner, Gerhart Burian. *Images and Ideas in the Middle Ages*. 2 vols. Storia e letteratura; Raccolta di studi e testi nos. 155–56. Rome: Edizioni di Storia e Letteratura, 1983.

Ladner, Gerhard Burian. "Die italienische Malerei im 11. Jahrhundert," *Jahrbuch der kunsthistorischen Sammlung in Wien*, n.s. 5 (1931): 33–160.

Ladner, Gerard Burian. "The 'Portraits' of Emperors in Southern Italian *Exultet* Rolls and the Liturgical Commemoration of the Emperor," *Speculum* 17 (1942): 181–200; repr. in *Images and Ideas*, 1:309–36.

Ladner, Gerhart Burian. "The So-called Square Nimbus," *Mediaeval Studies* 3 (1941): 15–44, with 11 figures; repr. in *Images and Ideas*, 1:115–66.

Lambert, Bernard. *Bibliotheca Hieronymiana manuscripta: La tradition manuscrite des oeuvres de Saint Jérôme*. 4 vols. Steenbrugis: in abbatia S. Petri ['s-Gravenhage, Martinus Nijhoff], 1969–72. Instrumenta patristica; 4

Langlois, Ernest. "Le rouleau d'Exultet de la Bibliothèque Casanatense," *Mélanges d'archéologie et d'histoire* 6 (1886): 466–82.

Latil, Agostino Maria. "De praeconio paschali," *Ephemerides liturgicae* 16 (1902): 123–32.

Latil, Agostino Maria. "Un 'Exultet' inedito," *Rassegna gregoriana* 7 (1908): cols. 125–34.

Latil, Agostino Maria. *Les miniatures des rouleaux d'Exultet.* Documents pour l'histoire de la miniature, 3d series. Montecassino, 1899. (Same plates as Latil, *Le miniature*).

Latil, Agostino Maria. *Le miniature nei rotoli dell'Exultet: Documenti per la storia della miniatura in Italia.* Montecassino: Litografia di Montecassino, 1899.

Lavagnino, Emilio, and Luigi Salerno. *Il Museo Diocesano di Gaeta.* Gaeta: Ente Provinciale per il Turismo di Latina, 1956.

Lazareff, Viktor. *Storia della pittura bizantina.* Biblioteca di sturia dell'arte no. 7. Turin: Einaudi, [1967].

Leclercq, Henri. "Pâques: §7. Le *praeconium paschae*," *DACL* 13.2: cols. 1,521–74.

Leclercq, Henri. "Cursus," *DACL* 3: cols. 3,193–3,205.

Leclercq, Jean. "Un nouveau manuscrit d'Hautmont," *Scriptorium* 9 (1955): 107–9.

Lehmann-Brockhaus, Otto. "Die Kanzeln der Abruzzen im 12. und 13. Jahrhundert," *Römisches Jahrbuch für Kunstgeschichte* 6 (1942–44): 257–428.

Le Roux de Lincy, Antoine Jean Victor. "La bibliothèque de Charles d'Orléans à son château de Blois," *Bibliothèque de l'École des chartes,* 5 (1843–44): 59–82.

Leutermann, Teodoro. *Ordo Casinensis hebdomadae maioris.* Miscellanea cassinese no. 20. Montecassino: Badia di Montecassino, 1941.

Levy, Kenneth. "*Lux de Luce:* The Origin of an Italian Sequence," *The Musical Quarterly,* 57 (1971), 40–61.

Lewis, Naphtali. *Papyrus in Classical Antiquity.* Oxford: Clarendon, 1974.

Libraries Guests of the Vatican during the Second World War: With the Catalogue of the Exhibition. Vatican City: Biblioteca Apostolica Vaticana, 1945.

Der Lorscher Rotulus: Stadt- und Universitätsbibliothek Frankfurt am Main MS. Barth. 179: Interimskommentar. Graz, 1994.

Lowden, J. *The Octateuchs.* University Park: Pennsylvania State University Press, 1990.

Lowe, Elias Avery. *Scriptura Beneventana.* 2 vols. Oxford: Clarendon, 1929.

Lowe, Elias Avery. *The Beneventan Script: A History of the South Italian Minuscule.* 2 vols. 2d. ed. prep. and enl. by Virginia Brown. Sussidi eruditi nos. 33–34. Rome: Edizioni di Storia e Letteratura, 1980. [Lowe, *TBS*]. An expanded version of the first edition, Oxford, 1914.

Lowe, Elias Avery. *The Bobbio Missal: A Gallican Mass-Book (MS. Paris Lat. 13246).* 3 vols. Henry Bradshaw Society nos. 53, 58, and 61. London: Harrison, 1917–24.

Magistretti, Marcus. *Beroldus sive ecclesiae Ambrosianae mediolanensis kalendarium et ordines saec. 12.* Milan: Josephi Giovanola, 1894.

Magistretti, Marcus. *Manuale Ambrosianum ex codice saec. 11 olim in usum canonicae vallis travaliae.* 2 vols. Monumenta veteris liturgiae ambrosianae nos. 2–3. Milan: Hoepli, 1904–5.

Maitilasso, Francesco Antonio. *La città di Troia e la sua storica cattedrale.* Troia: Comune di Troia, 1935.

Malherbe, G. "Le chandelier pascal," *Bulletin paroissal et liturgique* 12 (1930): 108–16.

Mallardo, Domenico. "La Pasqua e la settimana maggiore a Napoli dal secolo 5 al 14," *Ephemerides liturgicae* 66 (1952): 3–36.

Mallet, Jean, and André Thibaut. *Les manuscrits en écriture bénéventaine de la Bibliothèque Capitulaire de Bénévent.* Vol. 1. *Manuscrits 1–18.* Paris: Éditions du CNRS, 1984.

Mansi, Johannes Dominicus [Giovanni Domenico]. *Sacrorum concilium nova, et amplissima collectio.* 31 vols. Florence: Antonio Zatta, 1759–98.

Marle, Raimond van. *The Development of the Italian Schools of Painting.* 18 vols. The Hague: Nijhoff, 1923–36.

Martène, Edmundus. *De antiquis ecclesiae ritibus.* 4 vols. Antwerp: Johannes Baptista de la Bry, 1736–38.

Martini, Aldo. *Il cosiddetto pontificale di Poitiers.* Rerum ecclesiasticarum documenta, Series maior, fontes 14. Rome: Herder, 1979.

Martini, Giuseppe [Josephus Martinus]. *Appendix ad Theatrum Basilicae Pisanae.* Rome: Antonius de Rubeis, 1723.

Masetti, Anna Rosa Calderoni. "L'Exultet duecentesco del Museo Nazionale di Pisa," in *Studi di storia dell'arte in memoria de Mario Rotili.* Naples: Banca Sannitica, 1984, 211–20, pl. 71–75.

Masetti, Anna Rosa Calderoni, Cosimo Damiano Fonseca, and Guglielmo Cavallo. *L'Exultet "beneventano" del duomo di Pisa.* [Galatina]: Congedo, 1989.

Mather, Frank Jewett, and Chalfant Robinson. "Two Manuscript Rolls," *Record of the Museum of Historic Art, Princeton University* 5 (1946): 6–9.

Maunde Thompson, Edward. *An Introduction to Greek and Latin Palaeograpy.* Oxford: Clarendon, 1912.

Mayo, Penelope. "Borders in Bari: The decorative program of Bari I and Montecassino under Desiderius," in *Monastica IV. Scritta raccolti in memoria del XV centenario della nascita di S. Benedetto (480–1980).* Miscellanea Cassinese no. 48. Montecassino: Pubblicazioni cassinesi, 1984, 31–67 and figs. 1–13.

Mayo, Penelope C. "*Vasa sacra:* Apostolic Authority and Episcopal Prestige in the Eleventh-Century Bari Benedictional," *Dumbarton Oaks Papers* 41 (1987): 375–89.

Mazzucchelli, Pietro. *Osservazioni . . . intorno al saggio storico-critico sopra il rito ambrosiano.* Milan: Giovanni Pirrota, 1828.

Mercati, Giovanni. *Antiche reliquie liturgiche ambrosiane e romane.* Studi e testi no. 7. Rome: Tipografia Vaticana, 1902.

Mercati, Giovanni. *I. Un frammento delle ipotiposi. . . . II. Paralipomena ambrosiana con alcuni appunti sulle benedizioni del cereo pasquale.* Studi e testi no. 12. Rome: Tipografia Vaticana, 1904.

Meyvaert, Paul. "The Autographs of Peter the Deacon." *Bulletin of the John Rylands Library* no. 38 (1955–56): 114–38, plus 4 plates.

Migne, Jacques-Paul. *Patrologiae cursus completus: Series latina.* 221 vols. Paris: Migne, 1878–90. [*PL*].

Mocquereau, André. "Le cursus et la psalmodie," *PM* 4: 27–40.

Mohlberg, Leo Kunibert [Cunibert]. *Das fränkische Sacramentarium Gelasianum in allamanischer Überlieferung (Codex Sangall. No. 348).* Liturgiegeschichtliche [later Liturgiewissenschaftliche] Quellen und Forschungen nos. 1–2. Münster: Aschendorff, 1918. 3d ed., St. Galler Sakramentar-Forschungen 1, 1971.

Mohlberg, Leo Cunibert. *Missale Gothicum. (Vat. Reg. lat. 317).* Rerum ecclesiasticarum documenta, Series maior, no. 5. Rome: Herder, 1961.

Mohlberg, Leo Cunibert, Leo Eizenhöfer, and Petrus Siffrin. *Liber sacramentorum Romanae aeclesiae ordinis anni circuli (Cod. Vat. Reg. lat. 316/Paris Bibl. Nat. 7193, 41/56)*. Rerum ecclesiasticarum documenta, Series maior, no. 4. Rome: Herder, 1960.

Mohlberg, Leo Cunibert, Leo Eizenhöfer, and Petrus Siffrin. *Missale Gallicanum vetus (Vat. Palat. lat. 493)*. Rerum ecclesiasticarum documenta, Series maior no. 3. Rome: Herder, 1958.

Mohlberg, Leo Cunibert, Leo Eizenhöfer, and Petrus Siffrin. *Sacramentarium Veronense*. Rerum ecclesiasticarum documenta, Series maior no. 1. Rome: Herder, 1956.

Mohrmann, Christine. "Exultent divina mysteria," *Ephemerides liturgicae* 66 (1952): 274–83.

Monasticon italiae. Vol. 1, *Roma e Lazio*, ed. Filippo Caraffa. Cesena: Badia di Santa Maria del Monte, 1981.

Moneti, Elena. "Considerazioni e ricerche sui rotoli liturgici miniati dell'Italia meridionale," in *Scritti di paleografia e diplomatica in onore di V. Federici*. Florence: Olschki, 1944, 243–53.

Monroe, William H. "A Roll Manuscript of Peter of Poitiers' Compendium," *Bulletin of the Cleveland Museum of Art* 65 (1978): 92–107.

Monumenta germaniae historica. [*MGH*].

MGH Epistolarum tomus 1: Gregorii I papae registrum epistolarum Tomus 1, ed. Paul Ewald and Ludwig M. Hartmann. Berlin: Weidmann, 1887–91. [*MGH Epistolae 1*].

MGH Epistolarum tomus 2: Gregorii papae registrum epistolarum Tomus 2, ed. Ludwig M. Hartmann. Berlin: Weidmann, 1893–99. [*MGH Epistolae 2*].

MGH Epistolarum tomus 3. Epistolae merowingici et karolini aevi, 1. Berlin: Weidmann, 1892. [*MGH Epistolae 3*].

MGH Scriptorum tomus 7. Hannover: Hahn, 1986. [*MGH Scriptores 7*].

MGH Scriptores rerum Langobardicarum et Italicarum saec. 6–9. Hannover: Hahn, 1878; repr. 1964. [*MGH SS Lang.*].

Moorat, S. A. J. *Catalogue of Western Manuscripts on Medicine and Science in the Wellcome Historical Medical Library*. Vol. 1, *MSS. Written before 1650 A.D.* London: Wellcome Historical Medical Library, 1962.

Mordek, Hubert. "Karolingische Kapitularien," in Hubert Mordek, ed., *Überlieferung und Geltung normativer Texte des frühen und höhen Mittelalters*, Quellen und Forschungen zum Recht im Mittelalter no. 4. Sigmarinen: Thorbecke, 1986, 25–50.

Morgan, Nigel. *Early Gothic Manuscripts*. Vol. 1, *1190–1250*. Vol. 2, *1250–1285*. A Survey of Manuscripts Illuminated in the British Isles no. 4, ed. J. J. G. Alexander. London: Harvey Miller, 1982, 1988.

Morin, Germain. "Le catalogue des manuscrits de l'abbaye de Gorze au 11e siècle," *Revue bénédictine* 22 (1905): 1–14.

Morin, Germain. "Un écrit méconnu de Saint Jérôme," *Revue bénédictine* 8 (1891): 20–27.

Morin, Germain. *Études, textes, découvertes*. Anecdota maredsolana, 2d series, no. 1. Paris: A. Picard, 1913.

Morin, Germain. "La lettre de Saint Jérôme sur le cierge pascal: Réponse à quelques difficultés de M. l'abbé L. Duchesne," *Revue bénédictine* 9 (1892): 392–97.

Morin, Germain. "Pour l'authenticité de la lettre de S. Jérôme à Présidius," *Bulletin d'ancienne littérature et d'archéologie chrétiennes* 3 (1913): 52–58.

Morin, Germain. "Un rouleau mortuaire des moniales de Sainte-Marie d'Helfta," *Revue bénédictine* 37 (1925): 100–103.

Morisani, Ottavio. "L'icongrafia della discesa al limbo nella pittura dell'area di Montecassino," *Siculorum gymnasium*, n. s. 14 (1961): 84–97, and plates (2 pp.) after p. 88 and (4 pp.) after p. 96.

Morrison, Karl F. *History as a Visual Art in the Twelfth-Century Renaissance*. Princeton: Princeton University Press, 1990.

Mortari, Luisa. *Il Museo Capitolare della cattedrale di Velletri*. Rome: De Luca, 1959.

Mostra storica nazionale della miniatura: Palazzo di Venezia—Roma, ed. Giovanni Muzzioli. Florence: Sansoni, 1954.

Mütherich, Florentine, "Handschriften im Umkreis Friedrichs II," in Josef Fleckenstein, ed., *Probleme um Friedrich II*. Vorträge und Forschungen no. 16. Sigmarinen: Jan Thorbecke, 1974, 9–21, plus 8 plates.

Natale, Francescantonio. *Lettera dell'abate Francescantonio Natale intorno ad una sacra colonna de' bassi tempi eretta al presente dinanzi all'atrio del duomo de Capua*. Naples: Vincenzio Mazzola-Vocola, 1776.

Newton, Francis, "Beneventan Scribes and Subscriptions with a List of Those Known at the Present Time," *The Bookmark: Friends of the University of North Carolina Library* 43 (1973): 1–35.

Newton, Francis. "Due tipi di manoscritti ed il rinnovamento culturale nell'epoca di Desiderio," in *L'età dell'abate Desiderio*. Vol. III, 1, *Storia arte e cultura. Atti del IV convegno di studi sul medioevo meridionale (Montecassino–Cassino, 4–8 ottobre 1987)*, ed. Faustino Avagliano and Oronzo Pecere. Miscallanea cassinese, no. 67. Montecassino: Pubblicazioni Cassinesi, 1992, pp. 467–80 and pls. 1–9.

Newton, Francis. *The Scriptorium of Montecassino under Abbots Desiderius and Oderisius*. Cambridge: Cambridge University Press, in press.

Newton, Francis. "A Third and Older Cassinese Lectionary for the Feasts of Saints Benedict, Maur, and Scholastica," *Miscellanea Cassinese* 47. Montecassino: Abbazia di Montecassino, 1983, 45–75.

Nicholson, Edward Williams Byron. *Early Bodleian Music. Introduction to the Study of Some of The Oldest Latin Musical Manuscripts in the Bodleian Library, Oxford*. London: Novello, 1913.

Nicolau, Mathieu G. *L'origine du "cursus" rythmique et les débuts de l'accent d'intensité en latin*. Collection d'études publiées par la Société d'études latines no. 5. Paris: Société d'édition "Les belles lettres," 1930.

Nilgen, Ursula, "Maria Regina—ein politischer Kultbildtypus?" *Römisches Jahrbuch für Kunstgeschichte* 19 (1981): 1–33.

Nitto de Rossi, G. B., and Francesco Nitti di Vito. *Codice diplomatico barese 1: Le pergamene del duomo di Bari (952–1264)*. Bari: Commissione provinciale di archeologia e storia patria 1897.

Norberg, Dag, ed. *S. Gregorii magni registrum epistolarum*. 2 vols. Corpus Christianorum Series Latina no. 140–40A. Turnhout: Brepols, 1982.

Novak, Viktor, "Praeconium paschale u Osorskom Evanđelistaru" [The Praeconium paschale in the Evangeliarium of Osor], *GLAS CCL* (Classe des Sciences Sociales de l'Académie Serbe des Sciences et des Arts), Vol. 10. Belgrade: Naucno delo, 1961, 131–40 and 5 facs.

Novak, Viktor, and B. Telebaković-Pacarski. *Većenegin Evanđelistar (Evangelium Većenegae)*. Zagreb: Izdavački zavod Jugoslavenske akademije, 1962.

Odermatt, Ambros. *Ein Rituale in beneventanischer Schrift, Roma, Biblioteca Vallicelliana, Cod. C 32: Ende des 11. Jahrhunderts*. Spicilegium Friburgense no. 26. Fribourg, Switzerland: Universitätsverlag, 1980.

Orofino, Giulia. "La prima fase della miniatura desideriana (1058–1071)," in Guglielmo Cavallo, ed., *L'età dell'abate Desiderio II—la decorazione libraria: Atti della tavola rotonda (Montecassino, 17–18 maggio 1987)*. Miscellanea cassinese no. 60. Montecassino: Pubblicazioni cassinesi, 1989, 47–63 plus 4 pages of plates.

Ortolani, Sergio. "Inediti meridionali del duecento," *Bullettino d'arte* 33 (1948): 291–319.

Das Osterspiel von Muri: Faksimiledruck der Fragmente mit Rekonstruktion der Pergamentrolle. Basel: Alkuin-Verlag, 1967.

Pace, Valentino. "La decorazione dei manoscritti pre-desideriani nei fondi della Biblioteca Vaticana," in Giovanni Vitolo and Francesco Mottola, eds., *Scrittura e produzione documentaria nel mezzogiorno longobardo: Atti del convegno internazionale di studio (Badia di Cava, 3–5 ottobre 1990)*. [Cava dei Tirreni]: Badia di Cava, 1991, 405–56.

Pace, Valentino. "I rotoli miniati dell'Exultet nell'Italia meridionale medievale," *Lecturas de historia del arte*, 4 (1994): 15–33.

Paci, Libero. *Inventario dei manoscritti musicali della Biblioteca Comunale "Mozzi-Borgetti,"* ed. Aldo Adversi. Macerata, 1974.

Palazzo, Eric. "Iconographie et liturgie: La mosaïque du baptistère de Kélibia (Tunisie)," *Archiv für Liturgiewissenschaft* 34 (1992): 102–20.

Palazzo, Eric. *Les sacramentaires de Fulda: Étude sur l'iconographie et la liturgie à l'époque ottonienne*. Liturgiewissenschaftliche Quellen und Forschungen no. 77. Münster: Aschendorff, 1994.

Paléographie musicale: Les principaux manuscrits de chant grégorien, ambrosien, mozarabe, gallican, publiés en facsimilés phototypiques par les moines de Solesmes. Sucessively edited by André Mocquereau, Joseph Gajard, and Jean Claire. Solesmes and elsewhere: 1899– . [*PM*]. Vol. 4, *Le codex 121 de la Bibliotheque d'Einsiedeln*. Solesmes, 1894; repr. Bern: Lang, 1974. See "Praeconium paschale du midi de l'Italie," 171–85. Vol. 13, *Le codex 903 de la Bibliothèque Nationale de Paris (11e siècle): Graduel de Saint-Yrieix*. Tournai: Desclée, 1925; repr. Bern: Lang, 1971. Vol. 14, *Le codex 10 673 de la Bibliothèque Vaticane, fonds latin (11e siècle): Graduel bénéventain*. Tournai: Desclée, 1931; repr. Bern: Lang, 1971. Vol. 15, *Le codex VI.34 de la Bibliothèque Capitulaire de Bénévent*. Tournai: Desclée, 1937. Vol. 20, *Le missel de Bénévent VI-33*. Introduction by Jacques Hourlier, tables by Jacques Froger. Bern and Frankfurt: Lang, 1983. Vol. 21, *Les témoins manuscrits du chant bénéventain*, ed. Thomas Forrest Kelly. Solesmes: Abbaye Saint-Pierre, 1992.

Pantoni, Angelo, "Opinioni, valutazioni critiche e dati di fatto sull'arte benedettina in Italia," *Benedictina* 13 (1959): 111–58.

Pantoni, Angelo. "Il codice 3 di Montecassino e le sue relazioni con l'area e l'arte beneventana," *Benedictina* 24 (1977): 27–45, and plates.

Parente, Pasquale. "Le miniature nei rotoli dell' 'Exultet,' " *Arte e storia* 36 (1917): 41–44.

Parkes, Malcolm Beckwith. *The Medieval Manuscripts of Keble College Oxford.* London: Scolar Press, 1979.

Pieralisi, Sante. *Il preconio pasquale conforme all'insigne frammento del codice barberiniano.* Rome: Tipografia Poliglotta, 1883.

Pierpont Morgan Library. *Review of the Activities and Acquisitions of the Library* ` *from 1930 through 1935.* New York: Pierpont Morgan Library, 1937.

Pinell, Jordi. "La benedicció del ciri pasqual i els seus textos," in *Liturgica 2: Cardinali I. A. Schuster in memoriam.* Scripta et documenta no. 10. Montserrat: Abbatia Montserrat, 1958, 1–119.

Pinell, Jordi. "Vestigis del lucernari a Occident," in *Liturgica 1: Cardinali I. A. Schuster in memoriam.* Scripta et documenta no. 7. Montserrat: Abbatia Montserrat, 1956, 91–149.

Pippal, Martina. "Der Osterleuchter des Doms S. Erasmo zu Gaeta," *Arte medievale* 2 (1984): 195–244.

Powitz, Gerhard. *Die datierten Handschriften der Stadt- und Universitätsbibliothek Frankfurt am Main.* Datierte Handschriften in Bibliotheken des Bundesrepublik Deutschland, ed. Johann Autenrieth, no. 1. Stuttgart: Anton Hiersmann, 1984.

Prandi, Adriano, ed. *L'art dans l'Italie méridionale: Aggiornamento dell'opera di Émile Bertaux.* 4 vols. (numbered 4–6 plus Indici). Rome: École Française de Rome, Palais Farnèse, 1978. [Aggiornamento]. Various authors contributed materials related to page numbers in Bertaux's volume. The portions of particular importance here are: Rosalba Zuccaro, 4:423–66 (Exultet rolls); on aspects of sculpture and church furniture, Letizia Pani Ermini, 4:177–82; Vittoria Kienerk, 4:251–57; Antonio Thiery, 5:639–67, 681–85; Valentino Pace, 5:723–42; Anna Carotti, 5:751–68, 5:975–85; Sabine Schwedhelm, 5:799–809; Maria Stella Calò Mariani, 5:843–901, 957–66.

Pratesi, Alessandro. "Note di diplomatica vescovile beneventana," *Bulettino dell'Archivio paleografico italiano,* n. s. 1 (1955): 19–91.

Quindicesimo centenario della nascita di S. Benedetto 480–1980. Catalogo dell mostra. Vatican City: Biblioteca Apostolica Vaticana, 1980.

Rasmussen, Niels Krogh. "Les pontificaux du haut moyen âge: Genèse du livre de l'évêque." 3 vols. Diss. Paris: Institut Catholique de Paris, 1977. Copy at Biblioteca Apostolica Vaticana.

Rasmussen, Niels Krogh. "Unité et diversité des pontificaux latins au 8e, 9e, et 10e siècles," in *Liturgies de l'église particulière et liturgie de l'église universelle: Conférences Saint-Serge, 22e semaine d'études liturgiques, (Paris, 30 juin–3 juillet 1975).* Biblioteca "Ephemerides liturgicae, subsidia" no. 7. Rome: Edizioni Liturgiche, 1976, 393–410.

Rebenich, Stefan. *Hieronymus und sein Kreis: Prosopographische und sozialgeschichtliche Untersuchungen.* Historia Einzelschriften no. 72. Stuttgart: F. Steiner, 1992.

Rehle, Sieghild. "Missale Beneventanum (Codex VI 33 des Erzbishöflichen Archiv von Benevent)," *Sacris erudiri* 21 (1972–73): 323–405.

Rehle, Sieghild. "Missale Beneventanum in Berlin," *Sacris erudiri* 28 (1985): 469–510.

Reynolds, Roger E. "Image and Text: A Carolingian Illustration of Modifications in the Early Roman Eucharistic Ordines," *Viator* 14 (1983): 59–74.

Reynolds, Roger E. "Rites and Signs of Conciliar Decisions in the Early Middle Ages," in *Segni e riti nella chiesa altomedievale occidentale, 11–17 aprile 1985.* Settimane di studio del Centro italiano di studi sull'alto medioevo no. 33. Spoleto: Presso la Sede del Centro, 1987, 207–49, 22 pl.

Ricci, Seymour de. *Census of Medieval and Renaissance Manuscripts in the United States and Canada.* 3 vols. New York: H. W. Wilson, 1935–40.

Richter, Gregor, and Albert Schönfelder. *Sacramentarium Fuldense saeculi 10: Cod. Theol. 231 der K. Universitätsbibliothek zu Göttingen.* Quellen und Abhandlungen zur Geschichte der Abtei und der Diözese Fulda no. 9. Fulda: Fuldaer Aktiendruckerei, 1912. 2d ed., Henry Bradshaw Society no. 101. Farnborough: Saint Michael's Abbey Press, [1977].

Righetti Tosti-Croce, Marina. "Abruzzo," in *Enciclopedia dell'arte medievale.* Rome: Istituto della Enciclopedia Italiana, 1991, 1:60–75.

Roberts, Colin Henderson. "The Codex," *Proceedings of the British Academy* 40 (1954): 169–204, 1 pl.

Roberts, Colin Henderson, and T. C. Skeat. *The Birth of the Codex.* London: Published for the British Academy by Oxford University Press, 1987.

Roberts, Eileen. "The *Exultet* Hymn in Twelfth-Century Sicily as an Indicator of Manuscript Provenance," *Ecclesia orans* 5 (1988): 157–64.

Roberts, Jane, "An Inventory of Early Guthlac Materials," *Mediaeval Studies* 32 (1970): 193–233.

Rodgers, Robert H. *Petri diaconi ortus et vita iustorum cenobii Casinensis.* Berkeley: University of California Press, 1972.

Rohault de Fleury, Charles. *La messe: Études archéologiques sur ses monuments.* 6 vols. Paris: Veuve A. Morel, and later Librairie des Imprimeries Réunies, 1883–88.

Rossi, Paola, "Ambone," in *Enciclopedia dell'arte medievale.* Rome: Istituto della Enciclopedia Italiana, 1991, 1:491–94.

Rotili, Mario. *Corpus della scultura altomedioevale 5: La diocesi di Benevento.* Spoleto: Centro di Studi Sull'alto Medioevo, 1966.

Rotili, Mario. "L' 'Exultet' della cattedrale di Capua e la miniatura 'beneventana,' " in *Il contributo dell'archidiocesi di Capua alla vita religiosa e culturale del Meridione: Atti del Convegno Nazionale di studi storici promosso dalla Società di Storia Patria di Terra di Lavoro (26–31 ottobre 1966).* Rome: De Luca, 1967, 197–210 and plates 26–38.

Rotili, Mario. "La miniatura 'beneventana' dell'alto medioevo," *Corsi di cultura sull'arte ravennate e bizantina* 14 (1967): 309–22.

Rouse, Richard H. "Roll and Codex: The Transmission of the Works of Reinmar von Zweter," in Gabriel Silagi, ed., *Paläographie 1981; Colloquium du Comité International de Paléographie (München, 15.–18. September 1981).* Münchener Beiträge zur Mediävistik und Renaissance-Forschung no. 32. Munich: Arbeo-Gesellschaft, 1982, 107–23 and pl. 11–15.

Rudt de Collenberg, Wipertus H. "Le 'thorakion' recherches iconographiques," *Mélanges de l'École française de Rome: Moyen age—temps moderne* 83 (1971): 263–361, plus table.

Rule, Martin. *The Missal of St. Augustine's Abbey Canterbury.* Cambridge: Cambridge University Press, 1896.

Sacra congregatio rituum. "Decretum de solemni vigilia paschali instauranda (cum commentario)," *Ephemerides liturgicae* 65, supp. (1951): 1–48.

Saint-Roch, Patrick. *Liber sacramentorum Engolismensis (Manuscrit B. N. Lat. 816. Le Sacramentaire Gélasien d'Angoulême)*. Corpus Christianorum, Series Latina, no. 159C. Turnhout: Brepols, 1987.

Salazaro, Demetrio. *Studi sui monumenti della Italia meridionale*. 2 vols. Naples: A. Morelli, 1871–77.

Salmon, Pierre. *Les manuscrits liturgiques latins de la Bibliothèque Vaticane*. 5 vols. Studi e testi nos. 251, 253, 260, 267, 270. Vatican City: Biblioteca Apostolica Vaticana, 1968–72.

Salvati, Catello, and Rosaria Pilone. *Gli archivi dei monasteri di Amalfi (S. Maria di Fontanella, S. Maria Dominarum, SS. Trinita)*. Centro di cultura e storia amalfitana, Fonti, no. 2. Amalfi: Presso la Sede del Centro, 1986.

Salvoni Savorini, Grazia. "Monumenti della miniatura negli Abruzzi," in *Convegno storico Abruzzese-Molisano 25–29 marzo 1931: Atti e memorie*. 3 vols. Casalbordo: Nicola de Arcangelis, 1935–40, 2:495–519.

Santifaller, Leo. *Beiträge zur Geschichte der Beschreibstoff im Mittelalter, mit besonderer Berücksichtigung der päpstlichen Kanzlei*. Vol. 1, *Untersuchungen*. Mitteilung des Instituts für Österreichische Geschichtsforschung, Ergänzungsband 16, Heft 1. Graz-Cologne: Hermann Bohlaus, 1953.

Santifaller, Leo. "Über Papierrollen als Beschreibstoff," in *Mélanges Eugène Tisserant*. 7 vols. Studi e testi nos. 231–37. Vatican City: Biblioteca Apostolica Vaticana, 1964, 7:361–71.

Santifaller, Leo. "Über späte Papyrusrollen und frühe Pergamentrollen," in Clemens Bauer, Laetitia Boehm, and Max Müller, eds., *Speculum historiale: Geschichte im Spiegel von Geschichtsschreibung und Geschichtsdeutung*. Freiburg/Munich: Karl Alber, 1965, 117–33.

Schlumberger, Gustave. "Les rouleaux d'*Exultet* de Bari et de Salerne," *Académie des inscriptions et belles-lettres: Comptes rendus* 25 (1897): 96–101, and unnumbered plate after p. 58.

Schmid, Otto. "Die St. Lambrechter Todtenrotel von 1501–1502," *Studien und Mittheilungen aus dem Benediktiner- und dem Cistercienser-Orden* 7 (1886): 176–83, 424–34; 9 (1888): 130–38, 272–76, 650–57; 10 (1889): 106–18.

Schmidt, Hermanus [Hermann] A. P. *Hebdomada sancta*. 2 vols. Rome: Herder, 1956, 1957.

Schneider-Flagmeyer, Michael. *Der mittelalterliche Osterleuchter in Süditalien: Ein Beitrag zur Bildgeschichte des Auferstehungsglaubens*. Europäische Hochschulschriften Ser. 28, Kunstgeschichte no. 51. Frankfurt: Peter Lang, 1986.

Schröbler, Ingeborg. "Zur Überlieferung des mittelateinischen Gedichts von 'Ganymed und Helena,' " in Klaus Lazarowicz and Wolfgang Kron, eds., *Unterscheidung und Bewahrung: Festschrift für Hermann Kunisch zum 60. Geburtstag 27. Oktober 1961*. Berlin: W. De Gruyter, 1961, 321–30.

Schubart, Wilhelm. *Papyri Graecae Berolinenses*. Bonn: A. Marcus and E. Weber, 1911.

Seroux d'Agincourt, Jean-Baptiste Louis Georges. *Histoire de l'art par les monuments*. 6 vols. Paris: Treuttel et Würtz, 1810–23.

Sieben, Hermann Josef. *Konzilsdarstellungen, Konzilsvorstellungen: 1000 Jahre Konzilsikonographie aus Handschriften und Druckwerken*. Würzburg: Echter, 1990.

Skubiszewski, Piotr. "*Ecclesia, Christianitas, Regnum*, et *Sacerdotium* dans l'art des 10e–11e s.: Idées et structures des images," *Cahiers de civilisation médiévale* 28 (1985): 133–79.

Speciale, Lucinia. "Die Exultetrolle Barb. lat. 592: Ein Beitrag Montecassinos zur gregorianischen Reform," in *Die Barberini-Exultetrolle Barb. lat. 582.* Codices e vaticani selecti, no. 76. Zurich: Belser, 1988, 17–27.

Speciale, Lucinia. *Montecassino e la riforma gregoriana: L'Exultet Vat. Barb. lat. 592.* Studi di arte medievale no. 3. Rome: Viella, 1991.

Speciale, Lucinia. "Spigolatura per la manifattura dei manoscritti cassinesi in età desideriana," *Miscellanea cassinese.* In press.

Stäblein, Bruno. *Schriftbild der einstimmigen Musik.* Musikgeschichte in Bildern, ed. Werner Bachmann, v. 3: Musik des Mittelalters und der Renaissance, Lieferung 4. Leipzig: Deutscher Verlag für Musik, 1975.

Steinen, Wolfram von den. *Notker der Dichter und seine geistige Welt.* 2 vols. Bern: A. Francke, 1948.

Stiennon, Jacques. "Routes et courants de culture: Le rouleau mortuaire de Guifred, comte de Cerdagne, moine de Saint-Martin du Canigou (+ 1049)," *Annales du Midi* 76 (1964): 305–14.

Stones, Alison. Review of Morgan, *Early Gothic Manuscripts* vol. 1, *Speculum* 68 (1993): 213–16.

Strittmatter, Anselm. "The Pentecost Exultet of Reims and Besançon," in Dorothy Miner, ed., *Studies in Art and Literature for Belle da Costa Greene.* Princeton: Princeton University Press, 1954, 383–400, and pl. 332–33.

Stroll, Mary. *Symbols as Power: The Papacy following the Investiture Contest.* Leiden: E. J. Brill, 1991.

Suñol, Gregorio M. "Versione critica del canto del 'praeconium paschale' ambrosiano," *Ambrosius* 10 (1934): 77–95, pl. 3–4.

Supino Martini, Paola. *Roma e l'area grafica romanesca (secoli 10–11).* Alessandria: Edizioni dell'Orso, 1987.

Tamassia, Nino. "Libri di monasteri e di chiese nell'Italia meridionale," *Atti del Reale Istituto Veneto di Scienze, Lettere ed Arti* 64 (1904–5): 273–86.

Testi Rasponi, Alessandro, ed. *Codex pontificalis ecclesiae Ravennatis.* Vol. 1, *Agnelli liber pontificalis.* Rerum italicarum scriptores no. 2,3. Bologna: Zanichelli, 1924.

Thiele, Franz W. "Die Feier des Osternacht: Aufbau und Elemente im Vergleich," in Ildebrando Scicolone, ed., *La celebrazione del triduo pasquale — anamnesis e mimesis: Atti del 3 Congresso Internazionale di Liturgia, Roma, Pontificio Istituto Liturgico, 9–13 maggio 1988.* Rome: Pontificio Ateneo S. Anselmo, 1990, 227–58.

Toubert, Hélène, "Le bréviaire d'Oderisius (Paris, Bibliothèque Mazarine, MS 364) et les influences byzantines au Mont-Cassin," *Mélanges de l'École Française de Rome: Moyen age — temps moderne* 83 (1971): 187–261.

Toubert, Hélène, "Les représentations de l' 'Ecclesia' dans l'art des 10, 11, et 12 siècles," in *Musica e arte figuratica dei secoli 10–12.* Convegni del Centro di Studi Sull Spiritualità Medievale no. 13. Todi: Accademia Tudertina, 1973, 67–101, plus 16 plates.

Tredanari, Alfonso. *Inventario del tesoro della cattedrale di Troia.* Lucca: Frattarolo, 1911.

Trésors d'art du moyen âge en Italie: Petit palais mai–juillet 1952. Paris: Les presses artistiques, [1952], no. 81, three Gaeta rolls.

Trésors des bibliothèques d'Italie, 4e–16e siècles. 2d ed. Paris: Bibliothèque Nationale, 1950, nos. 38–39, plates 2–3.

Tsuji, Sahoko G. "Analyse iconographique de quelques miniatures des rouleaux d'Exultet dans leurs rapports avec le texte," in Shigenobu Kimura, ed. *Problems in the relation between text and illustration.* Studia artium orientalis et occidentalis, no. 1 [Osaka, Japan?]: SAOO, 1982.

van Dijk, Stephen J. P. *The Ordinal of the Papal Court from Innocent III to Boniface VIII and Related Documents,* completed by Joan Hazelden Walker. Spicilegium Friburgense no. 22. Fribourg: University Press, 1975.

van Dijk, Stephen J. P., and Joan Hazelden Walker. *The Origins of the Modern Roman Liturgy.* Westminster, Md.: Newman Press, 1960.

Vatasso, Marco and H. [Enrico] Carusi. *Bibliothecae Apostolicae Vaticanae codices manu scripti recensiti. Codices Vaticani latini, Codices 10301–10700.* Rome: Typis Vaticanis, 1920.

Verbraken, Patrick. "Une 'laus cerei' africaine," *Revue bénédictine* 70 (1960): 301–6.

Vives, José. *Concilios visigóticos e hispano-romanos.* España cristiana: Testo; v.1 Barcelona: Consejo Superior de Investigaciones Cientificas, Instituto Enrique Florez, 1963.

Vogel, Cyrille. *Medieval Liturgy: An Introduction to the Sources.* Rev. and trans. William G. Story and Niels Krogh Rasmussen with the assistance of John K. Brooks-Leonard. Washington, D.C.: Pastoral Press, 1986.

Vogel, Cyrille, and Reinhard Elze. *Le pontifical romano-germanique du dixième siècle.* 3 vols. Studi e testi nos. 226–27, 229. Vatican City: Biblioteca Apostolica Vaticana, 1963–72.

Vogel, Fredericus [Friedrich]. *Magni Felicis Ennodii opera.* MGH Auctores antiquissimi no. 7. Berlin: Weidmann, 1885.

Vogüé, Adalbert de. *Histoire littéraire du mouvement monastique dans l'antiquité.* Part 1, 2 vols. Paris: Editions du Cerf, 1991–93.

Volbach, Wolfgang Fritz, "Ein antikisierendes Bruchstück von einer kampanischen Kanzel in Berlin," *Jahrbuch der preussischen Kunstsammlung* 53 (1932): 183–97.

Walker, Christopher. *L'iconographie des conciles dans la tradition byzantine.* Archives de l'orient chrétien no. 13. Paris: Institut Français d'Études Byzantines, 1970.

Walpole, Arthur Sumner. *Early Latin Hymns, with Introduction and Notes.* Cambridge: Cambridge University Press, 1922; repr. Hildesheim: Olms, 1966.

Warner, George. *The Guthlac Roll: Scenes from the Life of St. Guthlac of Crowland by a Twelfth-Century Artist, Reproduced from Harley Roll Y. 6 in the British Museum.* Oxford: n.p., 1928.

Warren, Frederick Edward. *The Antiphonary of Bangor.* 2 vols. Henry Bradshaw Society nos. 4, 10. London: Harrison and Son, 1893–95.

Wattenbach, Wilhelm. *Das Schriftwesen im Mittelalter.* 3d ed. Leipzig: S. Hirzel, 1896.

Wattenbach. Wilhelm, "Ein 'Exultet,' " *Anzeiger für Kunder der deutschen Vorzeit,* n. s. 24 (1877): cols. 266–67 plus b/w facs.

Weber, Robert, ed. *Biblia sacra iuxta Vulgatam versionem.* 2d ed. 2 vols. Stuttgart: Württembergische Bibelanstalt, 1975.

Weber, Robert. *Le psautier romain et les autres anciens psautiers latins.* Vatican City: Tipografia Poliglotta Vaticana, 1953.

Weitzmann, Kurt. *Illustration in Roll and Codex: A Study of the Origin and Method of Text Illustration.* 2d ed. Princeton: Princeton University Press, 1970.

Weitzmann, Kurt. *The Joshua Roll: A Work of the Macedonian Renaissance.* Studies in Manuscript Illumination no. 3. Princeton: Princeton University Press, 1948.

Wessely, Karl. "Eine Pergamentrolle des 6. Jahrhunderts," *Wiener Studien* 4 (1882): 214–23.

West, Martin Litchfield. *Textual Criticism and Editorial Technique Applicable to Greek and Latin Texts.* Stuttgart: B. G. Teubner, 1973.

Wettstein, Janine. "Les Exultet de Mirabella Eclano," *Scriptorium* 17 (1963): 3–9, pl. 1–5.

Wettstein, Janine. *Sant'Angelo in Formis et la peinture médiévale en campanie.* Travaux d'humanisme et renaissance no. 42. Geneva: E. Droz, 1960.

Wettstein, Janine. "Un rouleau campanien du 11e siècle conservé au Musée San Matteo à Pise," *Scriptorium* 15 (1961): 234–39, pl. 23–32.

Whitehill, Walter Muir. "A Twelfth-Century Exultet Roll at Troja," *Speculum* 2 (1927): 80–84.

Wichner, Jacob. "Eine Admonter Totenrotel des 15. Jahrhunderts," *Studien und Mittheilungen aus dem Benediktiner- und dem Cistercienser-Orden* 5 (1884): 61–82, 314–40.

Willcock, Christopher. "La bénédiction du cierge pascal: Étude littéraire et théologique de ce rite." Thèse de doctorat de IIIe Cycle. Paris: Université de Paris—Sorbonne, 1987.

Wilpert. Josef. "Die Darstellung der Mater ecclesia in der barberinischen Exultetrolle," *Römische Quartalschrift für christliche Alterthumskunde und für Kirchengeschichte* 13 (1899): 23–24, and pl. 1–2.

Wurfbain, M. L. "The Liturgical Rolls of South Italy and Their Possible Origin," *Essays Presented to G. I. Lieftinck.* 4 vols. Litterae textuales, ed. J. P. Gumbert and M. J. M. de Haan. Amsterdam: A. L. van Gendt, 1972–76. Vol. 4, *Miniatures, Scripts, Collection,* 9–15.

Wüstefeld, W[ilhelmina] C. M. *Middeleeuwse Boeken van het Catharilneconvent.* Zwolle: Waanders, 1993.

Young, Karl. *The Drama of the Medieval Church.* 2 vols. Oxford: Clarendon, 1933.

Załuska, Yolanda. Catalogue entry on MS lat. 710, in François Avril et al., eds., *Dix siècles d'enluminure italienne.* Paris: Bibliothèque Nationale, 1984, 20–21, and plate 6, color plate 1.

Zanardi, Bianca. "Gli exultet cassinesi della Biblioteca Vaticana e della British Library," in Anna Rosa Calderoni Masetii, ed., *Studi di miniatura. Ricerche di storia dell'arte* 49 (1993): 37–49.

Zazo, Alfred. "L' 'Inventario dei libri antichi' della Biblioteca Capitolare di Benevento (sec. 15)," *Samnium* 8 (1935): 5–25.

Works Containing References to Exultets

Ancona, Paolo d'. "L'allegoria di *sapientia domini* in due pulpiti dell'Italia meridionale e in un codice della Mediceo-laurenziana," *Rivista delle bibliotheche e degli archivi* 19 (1908): 17–21. Mention of Gaeta.

Avril, François, and Yolanda Załuska. *Manuscrits enluminés d'origine italienne.* Vol. 1, *6e–12e siècles.* Paris: Bibliothèque Nationale, 1980, 18, pl. A (color), 7 (Paris 710).

Baltrusaitis, Jurgis. "Rose des vents et roses de personnages à l'époque romane," *Gazette des beaux-arts* 80/2 (1938): 265–76. One sentence on Bari 1 rose, p. 266.

Bologna, Ferdinando. *Opere d'arte nel salernitano dal 12 al 18 secolo.* [Catalogue]. Naples: Soprintendenza alle gallerie della Campania, 1955, 74–75 and pl. 6, Salerno Exultet.

Bologna, Ferdinando. *La pittura italiana delle origini.* [Rome:] Editori Riuniti, [1962], 27–28.

Bonicatti, Maurizio. "Considerazioni su alcuni affreschi medioevali della Campania," *Bollettino d'arte* 43 (1958): 12–25. Mentions similarity of columns in church of Rongolise (Sessa) to "Fratres karissimi" in British Library Exultet.

Caleca, Antonio. "La miniatura," in Carlo Ludovico Ragghianti, ed., *L'arte in Italia.* Vol. 2, *Dal secolo 5 al secolo 11.* Rome: Gherardo Casini, 1968. Cols. 583–88, 864, and figs. 591–97 (color, Bari 1).

Carta, Francesco, C. Cipolla, and C. Frati, eds. *Monumenta paleografica sacra: Atlante paleografico-artistico compilato sui manuscritti exposti in Torino . . . 1898.* Turin: Fratelli Bocca, 1899, 28 and pl. 32 on Capua Exultet.

Cecchelli, Carlo. *La vita di Roma nel medio evo.* 2 vols. Rome: Fratelli Palombini, 1951–60, 584–95 with 9 photos, most from Avery, on Exultets.

Chiappini, Aniceto. "Profilo di codicografia abruzzese," *Accademie e biblioteche d'Italia* 26 (1958): 433–58. Brief notice on Avezzano Exultet, p. 438.

Cochetti Pratesi, Lorenza. "Il candelabro pasquale della capella palatina," in *Scritti di storia dell'arte in onore di Mario Salmi.* 2 vols. Rome: De Luca, 1961–62, 1:291–304.

Colette, Marie-Noël. "De l'image du chant au moyen âge," in Joël-Marie Fauquet, ed., *Musique signes images: Liber amicorum François Lesure.* Geneva: Minkoff, 1988, 75–82. One plate of Fondi Exultet is labeled as B. N. lat. 1087, and vice versa.

Crisci, Generoso, and Angelo Campagno. *Salerno sacra.* Salerno: Curia Arcivescovile, 1962, 129–30. A poor notice of Salerno Exultet.

Dalli Regoli, Gigetta. "La miniatura: Gli 'exultet' e i libri corali," in Guglielmo De Angelis d'Ossat, ed., *Il Museo dell'Opera del Duomo a Pisa.* Pisa: Silvana, [1986], 145–55, figs. 160–64.

De Francovich, Géza. "Problemi della pittura e della scultura preromanica," *Settimane di studio* 1954 (Spoleto 1955): 355–519 plus plates (notice of Exultets).

Degenhart, Bernhard. "Autonome Zeichnungen bei mittelalterlichen Künstlern," *Münchner Jahrbuch der bildenden Kunst,* ser. 3, 1 (1950): 93–158. Mention of Exultet in general on p. 132n88.

D'Elia, Michele, ed. *Mostra dell'arte in Puglia.* Rome: De Luca, 1964, 7–9, pls. 6–9. Bari 1 and benedictional.

Diehl, Charles. *Manuel d'art byzantin.* 2 vols. Paris: Picard, 1925–26. Mention, 2:631, 716.

Dodwell, C. R. *Painting in Europe, 800 to 1200.* The Pelican History of Art, vol. 34. Harmondsworth: Penguin, 1971, 126–29, w. 4 b/w plates, on Exultets.

Fillitz, Hermann. *Das Mittelalter 1*. Propyläen Kunstgeschichte no. 5. Berlin: Propyläen, 1969. Illustrations of Vat. 9820 (fig. 62), Barberini (fig. 376), and Troia 3 (fig. 377), with commentary by Florentine Mütherich.

Fornari, Ave. "Le scene miniate dell'Exultet di Bari," *Arte cristiana* 59 (1971): 81–92 plus 8 plates, 4 in color. A weak article; all plates reversed.

Freeman, Margaret B. "Lighting the Easter Candle," *Metropolitan Museum of Art Bulletin*, n. s. 3 (1944–45): 194–200. Illustration of Troia, Mirabella.

Gabrielli, Attilio. *Velletri artistica*. Rome: E. Calzone, 1924, 25 mentions Exultet; 1 plate.

Herbert, John Alexander. *Illuminated Manuscripts*. London: Methuen, 1911. Mention, 164–67; pl. 20.

Kraus, Franz Xaver. *Geschichte der christlichen Kunst*. 2 vols. Freiburg: Herder, 1896, 1897, 1900. 2:59–62, general on Exultets. Barberini Ecclesia after Pieralesi, p. 59, fig. 37.

Lavagnino, Emilio. *Storia dell'arte medioevale italiana*. Storia dell'arte classica e italiana no. 2. Turin: UTET, 1936, 439–42 and figs. 509–10 on Exultet; very inadequate.

Luciani, S. A. "L' 'Exultet' del duomo di Bari," *Japigia* 3 (1932): 293–98. A weak article; includes transcriptions furnishing Roman melody!

Moneti, Elena. "L'arte nei manoscritti medievali dell'Italia meridionale," *Accademie e biblioteche d'Italia* 13 (1939): 348–57 plus 6 plates (no Exultets). Mention of Exultet, 352–53.

Morisani, Ottavio. *Bisanzio e la pittura cassinese*. Palermo: Istituto di Storia dell'Arte della Università, [1955], 62–63. On Vat. lat. 9820.

Oppenheim, Filippo. "Exultet," *Enciclopedia cattolica*. Vatican City: Ente per l'Enciclopedia Cattolica e per il Libro Cattolico, [1950], 5:921–22.

Robb, David M. *The Art of the Illuminated Manuscript*. South Brunswick, N.J., and New York: A. S. Barnes, [1973], 166–69 and fig. 107.

Rosini, Giovanni. *Storia della pittura italiana esposta coi monumenti*. 7 vols. Pisa: Presso Niccolò Capurro, 1839–47.

Rotili, Mario, "La cultura artistica," in Mario Brozzi et al., eds., *Longobardi*. Milan: Jaca Book, 1980, 231–72. On Exultets at 268–69.

Rotili, Mario. "La miniatura 'beneventana' dell'alto medioevo," *Corsi di cultura sull'arte ravennate e bizantina* 14 (1967): 309–22. Mentions of Vat. lat. 9820, Casanatense pontifical and benedictional, Capua Exultet.

Rotili, Mario. *Origini della pittura italiana*. Bergamo: Istituto Italiano d'Arti Grafiche, 1963, 46–48 and pl. 30 (Bari) on Exultet.

Salmi, Mario. *La miniatura italiana*. Milan: Electa (for Banca Nazionale del Lavoro), 1955.

Schlumberger, Gustave. *L'épopée byzantine*. 3 vols. Paris: Hachette, 1896–1905, 1:215 and 217, illustration of Casanatense Exultet.

Toesca, Pietro. *Storia dell'arte italiana*. Vol. 1, *Il medioevo*. Turin: Unione Tipografica Editrice Torinese, 1927.

Toubert, Hélène. "L'illustration des rouleaux médiévaux: Les *Exultet* d'Italie méridionale," in Henri-Jean Martin and Jean Vezin, eds., *Mise en page et mise en texte du livre manuscrit*. [Paris?], Editions du Cercle de la Librairie-Promodis, 1990, 412–15.

Toubert, Hélène. "Le renouveau paléochrétien à Rome au début du 12e siècle," *Cahiers archéologiques* 20 (1970): 99–154.

Vacandard, Elphège. "Le cursus: Son origine, son histoire, son emploi dans la liturgie," *Revue des questions historiques* 78 (1905): 59–102.

Venturi, Adolfo. *Storia dell'arte italiana.* Vol. 3, *L'arte romanica.* Milan: Hoepli, 1904.

Volbach, Fritz. "Exultet I," "Exultet II," and "Benedizionario," in Pina Belli D'Elia, ed., *Alle sorgenti del Romanico.* Bari: Amministrazione provinciale, [1975], 113–17.

INDEX OF
MANUSCRIPTS

Manuscripts are listed by city, depository, and shelf/catalog number (e.g., Paris, Bibliothèque Nationale, MS lat. 13246); the original provenance will be found in the general index (e.g., Bobbio). Page numbers are separated from the manuscript number by a colon. Full descriptions in Appendix 1 are indicated by page numbers in boldface; otherwise, the appendixes have not been indexed.

GENERAL INDEX

Notes belonging to text referred to by page numbers are not indexed separately, but when the information is only in the note, both page and note number are given (e.g., 88 n.15). Individual manuscripts are listed by current depository in a separate Manuscript Index, but original provenances (when cited in the text) are indexed here.